MAXIMIZING TREATMENT GAINS

Transfer Enhancement in Psychotherapy

D1521410

DATE DUE

MAR 1 2 '82			
APR 2 0 '82			
MAY 8 '86			

DEMCO 38-297

MAXIMIZING TREATMENT GAINS

Transfer Enhancement in Psychotherapy

Edited by

ARNOLD P. GOLDSTEIN
Department of Psychology
Syracuse University
Syracuse, New York

FREDERICK H. KANFER
Department of Psychology
University of Illinois
Champaign, Illinois

ACADEMIC PRESS   New York   San Francisco   London

A Subsidiary of Harcourt Brace Jovanovich, Publishers

ACADEMIC PRESS, INC.
111 Fifth Avenue, New York, New York 10003

United Kingdom Edition published by
ACADEMIC PRESS, INC. (LONDON) LTD.
24/28 Oval Road, London NW1 7DX

Library of Congress Cataloging in Publication Data
Main entry under title:

Maximizing treatment gains.

    Includes bibliographies.
    1. Psychotherapy. 2. Transfer of training.
I. Goldstein, Arnold P. II. Kanfer, Frederick H.,
Date
RC480.5.M352   616.8'914   78–31265
ISBN 0–12–288050–1

PRINTED IN THE UNITED STATES OF AMERICA

79 80 81 82   9 8 7 6 5 4 3 2 1

To Lenore, for backing me up, helping me move on, and always being there when I need her most

APG

To Ruby, Ruth, and Larry, for their enduring support, affection, and inspiration

FHK

Contents

Contents

List of Contributors

Numbers in parentheses indicate the pages on which the authors' contributions begin.

ROBERT R. FREEDMAN (445), Biofeedback Laboratory, Lafayette Clinic, Detroit, Michigan 48226.

ARNOLD P. GOLDSTEIN (1), Psychology Department, Syracuse University, Syracuse, New York 13210.

DAVID O. GREENLEAF (1), Psychology Department, Syracuse University Syracuse, New York 13210.

KENNETH HELLER (353), Psychology Department, Indiana University, Bloomington, Indiana 47401.

FREDERICK H. KANFER (185), Psychology Department, University of Illinois, Champaign, Illinois 61820.

JEFFREY M. KERN (429), Psychology Department, SUNY at Stony Brook, Stony Brook, New York 11790.

MICHAEL P. LEVINE (87), Psychology Department, University of California, Santa Barbara, Santa Barbara, California 93106.

T. I. LIDSKY (429), Psychology Department, SUNY at Stony Brook, Stony Brook, New York 11790.

MARTITA LOPEZ (1), Psychology Department, Virginia Polytechnic Institute and State University, Blacksburg, Virginia 24060.

STEVEN JAY LYNN (445), Psychology Department, Ohio University, Athens, Ohio 45701.

MARIAN L. MacDONALD * (429), Psychology Department, SUNY at Stony Brook, Stony Brook, New York 11790.

DAVID MARHOLIN II ** (303), Department of Special Education, Boston University, Boston, Massachusetts 02215.

WILLIAM R. McPEAK (155), School of Social Work, Syracuse University, Syracuse, New York 13210.

W. ROBERT NAY (249), Psychology Department, University of Illinois, Champaign, Illinois 61820.

RICHARD H. PRICE (383), Community Psychology, University of Michigan, Ann Arbor, Michigan 48109.

JOHN L. SHELTON (225), Department of Rehabilitation Medicine, School of Medicine, University of Washington, Seattle, Washington 98195.

A. ROBERT SHERMAN (25, 87), Psychology Department, University of California, Santa Barbara, Santa Barbara, California 93106.

PAUL E. TOUCHETTE (303), Eunice Kennedy Shriver Center, 200 Trapelo Road, Boston, Massachusetts 02215.

* PRESENT ADDRESS: Department of Psychology, University of Massachusetts, Amherst, Massachusetts 01003.

** Deceased.

1

Introduction

ARNOLD P. GOLDSTEIN, MARTITA LOPEZ,
DAVID O. GREENLEAF

Approximately two-thirds of the patients who participate in psychotherapy appear to derive some appreciable benefit therefrom (Bergin,
1971) an outcome which apparently occurs almost independent of the
type of psychotherapy involved.[1] This often cited "two-thirds improved"
figure, however, almost always indicates "benefit" as measured **at the
termination** of treatment. While the potential importance of such enhanced self-attitudes or newly learned behavioral competencies are not
to be minimized, the truly significant questions of psychotherapy outcome concern, not change at the time of termination, but change at later
points in time and in other, real-life settings. Psychotherapy is valuable
if, and only if, therapeutic gains both endure and are available to the

---

[1] This generalization must be viewed as an **average** outcome in the light of
differential treatment results which indicate considerable variability in treatment
gains as a function of the adequacy of the given patient-therapist-treatment match
(Goldstein, 1978, Goldstein & Stein, 1976).

MAXIMIZING TREATMENT GAINS:
Transfer Enhancement in Psychotherapy

patient when needed in his real-life settings and with his real-life significant others. That is, in our view, psychotherapy can be said to have
been successful only when end-of-treatment therapeutic gains show both
response maintenance and transfer to contexts other than the therapy
setting per se. Response maintenance concerns the durability of change,
especially during the later absence of reward for such changed behavior.
A behavior learned in treatment is said to have been maintained when it
(the **same** behavior) is used by the (ex-) patient in the absence of any
immediate or planned reward for performing it. Response maintenance is
equivalent to resistance to extinction.

Transfer of training, which concerns the spread or permeability of
change, is of two types. In the case of stimulus generalization, behavior
learned in treatment is said to have transferred when it (the **same** behavior) is used by the (ex-) patient in settings and contexts other than
that in which he originally learned the behavior. Transfer in the form
of response generalization occurs when real-life stimuli elicit behaviors
from the (ex-) patient which are similar to, but different from, those
behavioral or other treatment gains demonstrated by the (ex-) patient
during psychotherapy per se. We agree with Kazdin (1975) who comments:

> Response maintenance and transfer of training usually are not separate
> problems. In most instances, both of them are at issue simultaneously. For
> example, if a psychiatric patient leaves the hospital and returns home, both
> resistance to extinction and transfer of training are important. Reinforce-
> ment is no longer forthcoming (i.e., extinction) and the setting is different
> from the hospital where the program was conducted (i.e., transfer) [p. 76].

When an intervention results in transfer of behavior change to nontreatment settings, and/or when these changed behaviors persist in the
absence of reward, treatment gains may be said to have been maximized.
Both components of this broad goal of maximizing treatment gains—
response maintenance and transfer of training—will be the joint focus
of this book.

NONTRANSFERABILITY OF THERAPEUTIC GAINS

Examination of both relevant clinical reports and therapy outcome research findings reveals that maintenance and transfer of gain is not a
common outcome and, in fact, is much more the exception than the rule
in treatment results. In the large majority of psychotherapeutic encounters—be they psychodynamic, behavioral, existential, or other-

wise—patient improvement neither persists nor generalizes to new settings (Ford & Urban, 1963; Goldstein, Heller, & Sechrest, 1966; Kazdin, 1975; Marholin, Siegel, & Phillips, 1976). This contention is readily supported by the results of an extensive number of therapy outcome studies which are summarized in Table 1.1. Though the number of studies in Table 1.1 reporting positive therapeutic outcomes at the termination of treatment is high (85%), only 14% of the studies conducted report maintenance or transfer of therapeutic gains. The total sample of studies, furthermore, was selected on criteria reflecting high levels of methodological soundness, thus adding further to the tenability of the conclusion that transfer is a relatively uncommon psychotherapeutic outcome. It is true, of course, that follow-up evaluation of therapeutic outcome was absent in many of these studies. Thus, the 14% rate of response maintenance and positive transfer **may**, in fact, be artificially low and a truer rate **may** be somewhat higher. We think this to be unlikely, however.

TABLE 1.1

Therapy Outcome Study Results on Termination and Transfer [a]

Diagnosis	Number of studies	Number with positive results on termination	Number with positive results on transfer
Psychoneuroses			
Phobic reaction	55	45	11
Obsessive–Compulsive	6	3	0
Hysteria	3	3	1
Depression	7	6	1
Psychophysiological disorders			
Bronchial asthma	8	6	1
Ulcerative colitis	5	4	1
Hypertension and hypertensive headaches	4	4	1
Sexual deviations			
Sexual orientation disturbance	14	8	0
Orgasmic dysfunctioning	7	5	0
Fetishism and transvestism	5	4	2
Exhibitionism	2	1	0
Antisocial behavior	15	11	1
Obesity	12	9	3
Insomnia	4	4	2
Schizophrenia	45	28	4
Totals	192	163	28

[a] Adapted from Goldstein and Stein, 1976.

Keeley, Shemberg, and Carbonell (1976) examined an essentially different series of therapy outcome studies and came to the same conclusion as we have. They focused on the 146 investigations of operant interventions reported in a series of behaviorally oriented journals during 1972–1973. Even moderately long-term concern with transfer was rare. For the total number of investigations examined, follow-up (response maintenance), stimulus generalization, and response generalization each appear to occur in approximately 3% of the studies surveyed. They comment: "It seems clear that workers are not seriously researching operant interventions beyond prosthesis. Only 8 of the 146 studies analyzed present hard data collected at least 6 months past termination, and short term generalization data are conspicuously absent [p. 302]." Based on surveys of outcome investigations such as these, it appears appropriate to maintain that positive maintenance and transfer of therapeutic gain is much more often the exception than the rule, a conclusion also emerging in the therapeutic writings of many, many other investigators and theorists (Ayllon & Azrin, 1968; Bandura, 1969; Bijou & Redd, 1975; Burchard, 1971; Davidson & Seidman, 1974; DeMeyer & Ferster, 1962; Grindee, 1964, 1965; Hington, Sanders, & DeMeyer, 1965; Isaacs, Thomas, & Goldiamond, 1960; Kazdin, 1975; Marholin, Siegel, & Phillips, 1976; Meichenbaum, Bowers, & Ross, 1968; Meyer & Crisp, 1964; O'Leary, Becker, Evans, & Saudargas, 1969; Reiss, 1973).

Nonmaintenance and nontransferability of therapeutic gains appears to occur as frequently as it does because psychotherapy theorists and practitioners either assume it will occur automatically or, if aware that transfer-enhancing procedures must be purposefully built into ongoing treatment, do not yet know how to do so adequately enough. Ford and Urban (1963) examined the attention paid to maintenance and transfer, if any, in a number of traditional therapy systems, and generally found such concern to be minimal or lacking entirely. In classical psychoanalysis, for example, they note that:

> If the patient's behavior toward the therapist is modified, the changes are expected to transfer automatically to other situations. The conflicts involved in the neurosis all became directed toward the therapist during the "transference neurosis." They are not situation–specific. They are response looking for an object to happen to. Thus, if they are changed while they are occurring in relation to the therapist, they will be permanently changed, and can no longer attach themselves to any object in their old form. No special procedures are necessary to facilitate the transfer from the therapist to other situations if the therapist has successfully resolved the transference pattern of behavior [p. 173].

Such purported automaticity of maintenance and transfer, diversely explained, also characterizes the therapeutic position of Adler (1924),

Horney (1939), Rank (1945), Rogers (1951), and Sullivan (1953). In each instance, the view put forth is that when the given therapy process results in positive intrapsychic changes in the patient, the patient is assumed to be able to "take these changes with him" and apply them where and when needed in his real-life environment. For example, in a manner analogous to Freud, Rogers

> assumes that changes in behaviors outside of the therapy interview will follow automatically upon changes in the self-evaluative thoughts and associated emotions during the therapy hour. Changes in the self-evaluative thoughts and their emotional concomitants result in reduced anxiety, improved discrimination among situational events and responses, more accurate symbolization of them, and greater confidence in one's own decisions. These provide the conditions from which more appropriate instrumental and interpersonal responses will naturally grow [Ford & Urban, 1963, p. 435].

Thus, we would hold, a major basis for the failure of maintenance and transfer following most traditional psychotherapies is this pervasive assumption of its automaticity. Empirical evidence, as we have noted earlier, quite clearly refutes this assumption.

A different assumption regarding response maintenance and transfer of therapeutic gains has in recent years begun to emerge in the psychotherapy research literature, especially that devoted to the outcome of behavior modification interventions. This assumption also rests on the belief that maintenance and transfer of therapeutic gain are not common events but, instead of positing that they should occur via an automatic process whose instigation lies within the procedures of the therapy itself, the position taken is that new maintenance-enhancing and transfer-enhancing techniques must be developed and purposefully and systematically incorporated into the ongoing treatment process. Thus, not satisfied that "behaviors usually extinguish when a program is withdrawn [Kazdin, 1975, p. 213]" or that "removal of the contingencies usually results in a decline of performance to or near baseline levels [Kazdin, 1975, p. 215]," a number of therapy practitioners and researchers, as the chapters which follow make clear, are actively seeking to identify, evaluate, and incorporate into ongoing treatment a series of procedures explicitly designed to enhance the level of transfer which ensues. As we have stated elsewhere, the starting point in this search for effective gain maintenance and transfer-enhancers is clear:

> We need specific knowledge of the conditions under which learning or other changes that take place in therapy will be carried over into extra-therapy situations. . . . We cannot assume that a behavior acquired in the therapy situation, however well learned, will carry over into other situa-

tions. Unquestionably the phenomena of therapy are orderly and lawful; they follow definite rules. We must, then, understand the rules that determine what responses will be generalized, or transferred, to other situations and what responses will not. As a first approximation to the rules obtaining in psychotherapy, we suggest the knowledge gained from study of transfer of other habits [Goldstein, Heller, & Sechrest, 1966, p. 224].

There are numerous techniques to enhance the transfer of therapeutic effects. Their description forms the substance of this book. All of them share a change in emphasis of the therapeutic orientation as contrasted with classical psychotherapy. When enhancement procedures are systematically planned, therapists shift from a retrospective to a prospective view. That is, their concern is not only with removal of sources of past difficulties or the unlearning of ineffective behaviors, but with preparing the patient for handling future situations and events outside those that form the complaint that has brought the client into therapy. Secondly, this approach challenges therapists to pay greater attention to ecological factors. It requires an examination of the environmental influences that could support or threaten the changes that have been accomplished in therapy. It also leads the clinician and client to examine future sources of problems and consider changes both in the patient's behavior and in his selection of appropriate environments in which the beneficial results of treatment could flourish.

This, then, is the intent of the present book—to identify lawful, predictable, useful means by which the likelihood that therapeutic gains will maintain and transfer may be increased, to encourage further investigation and elaboration of such maintenance and transfer enhancers and, where appropriate, to encourage their incorporation into clinical practice. It will assist our understanding of response maintenance and transfer of gain, as well as the search for effective enhancement procedures, if we schematically examine possible sources and types of maintenance- and transfer-enhancement.

As Table 1.2 indicates, maintenance and transfer-enhancers differ in source; some derive from procedures inherent in the therapy itself (intherapy events), while others stem from procedures and events which are external to the treatment proper (extratherapy events) and which usually, but not always, follow it in time. The mode of presentation for both types of events may be unplanned (usually labeled "automatic," "spontaneous," or "fortuitous") or planned (usually described as programmed or purposeful). The **planned** intherapy and extratherapy enhancement procedures listed in cells II and IV of Table 1.2 are the subject matter for all other chapters in this book. We have already applauded their appearance on the psychotherapeutic scene and will not have much

TABLE 1.2

Maintenance and Transfer Enhancement Procedures

	Mode of presentation	
	Unplanned	Planned
From in-therapy events	**I** 1. Provision of general principles 2. Maximizing identical elements 3. Maximizing stimulus variability 4. Maximizing response availability	**II** 1. *In vivo* therapies 2. Family therapies 3. Teaching problem-solving strategies 4. Teaching self-management skills 5. Stimulus control techniques
	Source	
From extra-therapy events	**III** 1. Behaviors developed through a reinforcement program came under control of other reinforcers in the setting.[a] 2. Reinforcers which result directly from the activities themselves maintain behavior.[b] 3. Agents administering the original program change in some permanent manner.[c]	**IV** 1. Use of therapeutic homework assignments 2. Training real-life figures (parents, peers, etc.) as contingency managers 3. Building community support networks 4. Building ecological climates 5. Building work environments 6. Use of gain-maintaining drugs 7. Changing environmental contingencies

[a] For example, as Kazdin (1975) observes, "... behaviors may be maintained in a classroom in which token reinforcers were previously used because the teacher has been consistently associated with token reinforcement [p. 214]."

[b] Kazdin (1975) comments, "... reading, social, or eating skills may be maintained because once they are developed, they are reinforced by their normal consequences [p. 214]."

[c] Parents, teachers, or others may continue as effective behavior modifiers even though the original treatment program is completed.

more to say about them in this chapter save to introduce them briefly and to indicate that they represent a decidedly healthy beginning in the absolutely essential psychotherapeutic tasks of isolating, developing, evaluating, and clinically implementing transfer-enhancement procedures. Our focus here will be devoted more to currently unplanned maintenance and transfer-enhancers, especially cell I of Table 1.2. We will concentrate in this discussion on unplanned enhancers deriving from intherapy events in order to illustrate an overriding assumption of this book, one which we feel bears crucially upon the success of efforts to find, develop, and use **all** maintenance and transfer-enhancers, of whatever type. This assumption concerns the potential value of laboratory research on response maintenance and transfer of training as source material for enhancer identification and development in psychotherapy. The editors have developed and illustrated this philosophy extensively elsewhere (Goldstein *et al.*, 1966; Kanfer & Phillips, 1970) and will not do so here. Suffice it to indicate that considerable empirical evidence now exists to support such an extrapolatory research strategy vis-à-vis other aspects of the psychotherapy enterprise. Much of this book is an expression of an extension of this philosophy to the topic of maintenance and transfer of therapeutic gain.

This chapter's focus on unplanned maintenance and transfer enhancement stemming from intherapy events logically may begin by our proposing that many of the classical and newer therapy systems which show little or no explicit concern with such enhancement procedures, nevertheless are implicitly incorporating these techniques in a partial, often unsystematic and incomplete manner in many of their actual therapeutic operations. We now wish to explicate these procedures and broadly illustrate their unplanned and implicit reflection in both traditional and contemporary therapies.

LABORATORY EXTRAPOLATIONS TO THERAPEUTIC MAINTENANCE AND TRANSFER—A SAMPLING

We held earlier in this chapter that maintenance and transfer of therapeutic gains is not a frequent therapeutic outcome. Now we wish to suggest that when such maintenance and transfer **does** occur, it is not because of some "automatic," "natural," or "fortuitous" process. Instead, we would propose that such enhancement occurs as a function of identifiable processes currently operating in an unplanned and implicit manner in many psychotherapeutic approaches. As we have elaborated elsewhere (Goldstein & Stein, 1976), the effectiveness of psychotherapy will advance in direct proportion to our ability to identify and maximize the potency of active therapeutic ingredients. To the extent that we can isolate which therapist behaviors, therapeutic procedures, or patient characteristics are causally related to subsequent maximization of gain, to that extent can the likelihood of such maximization be enhanced. To the degree that maintenance and transfer-enhancing events remain implicit, unplanned, unclear, or unidentified, to that extent will the likelihood of maximization of therapeutic gain remain diminished. The sections which follow represent an attempt at such explication of potentially active, but unplanned, maintenance and transfer ingredients.

Provision of General Principles

In laboratory settings, especially in research concerned with skill acquisition, transfer of training has been shown to be facilitated by providing the learner, experimental subject, or trainee with the general mediating principles which govern satisfactory performance on both the original and transfer tasks. He is given the rules, strategies, or organizing principles that can lead to successful performance. In the earliest research dealing with transfer-enhancement by means of general principles, Judd (1902) sought to teach boys to shoot darts at a target submerged in water. Boys thus instructed about the principle of refraction did better at the task than boys not so instructed. This finding was later replicated on a related task by Hendrickson and Schroeder (1941). In both studies, positive transfer was attributed to the acquisition of the general principles governing successful task performance. A number of other experiments have further confirmed this conclusion. Woodrow (1927) was able to produce improved performance in memorization on transfer tasks requiring memorizing poetry, prose, and factual material by instructing subjects in specific principles and techniques of memorization. Ulmer (1939) found that a special geometry curriculum designed to arouse critical thinking both connected and unconnected with geometry resulted in better performance on later transfer tasks. Duncan (1959), Goldbeck, Bernstein, Hellix, and Marx (1957) and Miller, Heise, and Lichten (1951) are others reporting similar results. Recent interest in the "New Math" is a more current example of anticipated transfer of training mediated by general principles.

This general finding, that mediating principles for successful performance can enhance transfer to new tasks and contexts has, furthermore, been reported in a number of other domains of psychological research. These include studies of labeling, rules, mediated generalization, advance organizers, learning sets, and deutero-learning. It is a robust finding indeed. But, surprisingly, one rarely finds use of general principles explicitly implemented in psychotherapy.

As will become obvious to the reader of this book, the developers of various operant, social learning, or cognitive approaches to behavior modification have each in their own ways been increasingly concerned with maintenance and transfer-enhancement (e.g., see cells II and IV of Table 1.2). And, with particular reference to transfer mediated by explicit provision of general principles, presentations offered later in this book dealing with training in problem-solving strategies are prime examples of such attention and concern. Not so, however, for the vast majority of traditional, nonbehavioral, individual, and group psychotherapies. As noted at the beginning of this chapter, very few seek to enhance maintenance and transfer of treatment gains in any systematic, planned manner. Yet there are at least a handful of traditional therapy approaches whose procedures do seem to reflect at least partial, if implicit, unplanned attention to maintenance and transfer-enhancement via provision of general principles. We now wish to focus briefly on this aspect of these therapy approaches in the spirit noted earlier of seeking to make the implicit explicit and the unsystematic more planful, in the hope that such systematization can lead to enhanced maintenance and transfer of treatment gains.

The **fixed-role therapy** approach described by George Kelly (1955) is a good example of a psychotherapy in which a good beginning, but only a beginning, was made toward use of general principles to enhance transfer. In this approach, a "script" or "fixed-role sketch" is worked out for each patient. The sketch is a description of a general role or set of constructs which the patient is instructed to seek to enact in his or her real world. The content of the sketch is not specific behavioral descriptions but, instead, more general and higher level principles or constructs. The constructs constituting the sketch are, obviously, concerned with prosocial, pro-mental health, pro-satisfaction themes. It was Kelly's intent that the client use his fixed role as one would a scientific theory, that is, to both dictate specific real-life behaviors, and to check the consistency of these behaviors with the theory from which they grew. Kelly comments:

> In the early stage of therapy the client may not play his new role consistently. Of course he lapses into his old role the greater part of the time. But even when he plays his new role he may play it quite differently on different occasions. We have not considered this a matter to be alarmed about; but the clinician, being interested in organized behavior, does keep seeking a comprehensive constructive base upon which all behaviors can be developed, and not merely collective evidence of a set of isolated,

though successful behaviors. The therapist is looking for much more than
an item-by-item reinforcement of behavior trials; he is seeking to establish
a generalization.... He seeks to establish a breath-taking comprehensive
generalization in the form of a fixed role and, from it, help the client
deduce hypotheses for every time and occasion [pp. 409–410].

Kelly's statement, while not a full operational explication of the notion of transfer-enhancement via use of general principles, is an obvious
and important step in such a direction. Unfortunately, fixed role therapy
and its potential transfer-enhancing characteristics have never "caught
on" as either a therapeutic movement or experimental target. Thus
Kelly's fixed role notion—his idea of man as scientist, testing out the behavioral implications of more general guiding principles or constructs
and perhaps even using these constructs to guide overt behavior in ever-
new contexts—has never been adequately developed and tested. His notions as they bear upon our present theme, therefore, must be considered
as a beginning that unfortunately never gathered enough interest. It
remains an undeveloped, unsystematized, and largely implicit application
of the use of general principles for enhancement of treatment gains.

Other statements relevant to the potential usefulness of general principles for maintenance and transfer-enhancement, in the context of traditional, nonbehavioral therapies, are considerably less planned, less explicit, and less developed than even Kelly's. Haley's (1976) problem-
solving therapy makes use of "directives"; Phillips (1956), in his as-
sertion-structured therapy, helps patients develop useful, real-life "strategies"; MacGregor, Ritchie, Serrano, and Schuster (1964) examine with
their clients' family management "principles" in their multiple impact
therapy; Steiner, Wyckoff, and Marcus (1975) give prominence to teaching "problem-solving skills" in their presentation of radical therapy;
Loveless and Brody (1974) in their sketch of "cognitive psychotherapy"
and Watkins (1972) in his therapeutic use of "cognitive maps" also
touch upon the potential protherapeutic utilization of general principles.
Thus, the implicit seeds are present. As we will see later in this book,
other more behaviorally oriented clinicians have championed a rather
different view of psychotherapy and have sought to develop and sys-
tematize the use of general principles for maintenance and transfer-
enhancement in a much more planful and complete manner.

Maximizing Identical Elements

In perhaps the earliest experimental concern with transfer-enhancement, Thorndike and Woodworth (1901) concluded that when there was
a facilitative effect of one habit on another, it was to the extent that and

because they shared identical elements. Ellis (1965) and Osgood (1953) have more recently emphasized the importance for transfer of similarity between characteristics of the training and application tasks. As Osgood (1953) notes, "the greater the similarity between practice and test stimuli, the greater the amount of positive transfer [p. 213]." This conclusion rests on a particularly solid base of experimental support, involving studies of both motor (Crafts, 1935; Duncan, 1953; Gagné, Baker, & Foster, 1950) and verbal (Osgood, 1949, 1953; Underwood, 1951; Young & Underwood, 1954) behaviors.

In the context of psychotherapy, the principle of identical elements could be implemented by procedures which function to increase the "real-lifeness" of the stimuli (people, behaviors, places, events, etc.) to which the therapist is helping the patient learn to respond with effective, satisfying responses. There exists two broad strategies for attaining such high levels of veridicality between intherapy and extratherapy stimuli. The first is to move the therapy out of the typical office setting and into the very interpersonal and physical context in which the patient's real-life difficulties are being experienced. Such *in vivo* therapies are in fact a growing reality, as the locus of at least some treatments shifts to homes, planes, bars, elevators, and other problem sites, and will be the primary focus of Chapters 2 and 3 in this book. In the present chapter, we wish to focus upon a second, and thus far much more unplanned and unsystematically implemented strategy for the implementation of transfer-enhancement via identical elements. This strategy seeks to enhance the real-lifeness of the therapeutic office setting.

As noted above, with the one very major exception of family therapy (see Chapter 4), transfer-enhancement via identical elements in the form of increasing the degree of similarity between office and real world is an uncommon event. In fact, paradoxically, most traditional therapies consist of qualities and events which actually minimize identical elements. As we have observed elsewhere, "the psychotherapy situation is markedly different as a stimulus situation from every other situation in which the individual may be expected to perform. Moreover, the psychotherapist is, himself, unusual if not unique as a stimulus person [Goldstein et al., 1966, p. 224]." Nevertheless, there are a few traditional psychotherapies which reflect at least minimal attempts at this means of increasing identical elements. For example, Phillips and Wiener (1966) comment:

> One might think first of attempting to bring elements from the macrocosm to the clinic. . . . The behavior change sought in the situation, once it reached an acceptable or workable level in the clinic, could be "complicated" by the introduction of typical elements from the environment outside. . . . The patient might be taught actual routines useful for meeting

people under novel circumstances, meeting new people, and introducing people. In a behavioral approach, once these topics were introduced in the clinic, not only would the therapist and patient discuss them, but the patient would be led through steps in the clinic intended to better his skills in these problem areas. After an acceptable level of performance had been reached, satisfactory to both patient and therapist, the "outside" world could be brought into the clinical situation via the introduction of individuals or groups whose presence was intended to test out the patient's improved behavior [p. 76].

Partial and unsystematic utilization of procedures reflecting identical elements is also evident in the therapeutic involvement of friends and associates in Greenwald's (1967) active psychotherapy, in Rosen's (1961) attempt to create a homelike therapeutic environment by means of both physical furnishings as well as the parentlike and siblinglike roles assumed by Rosen and his assistants; and in the real-life-like interpersonal qualities of milieu therapy and therapeutic community approaches.

Maximizing Response Availability

Transfer of training has been shown to be enhanced by procedures which maximize response availability. The likelihood that a response will be available is very clearly a function of its prior usage. We repeat and repeat foreign language phrases we are trying to learn, insist that our child spend an hour per day in piano practice, and devote considerable time in practice seeking to make a golf swing smooth and "automatic." These are simply expressions of the response availability notion, that is, the more we have practiced (especially **correct**) responses, the easier it will be to call them forth in later contexts or at later times. We need not rely solely on every day experience here. It has been well established empirically that, other things being equal, the response that has been emitted most frequently in the past is quite likely to be emitted on subsequent occasions. This finding derives from studies of the frequency of evocation hypothesis (Underwood & Schulz, 1960), the spew hypothesis (Underwood & Schulz, 1960), preliminary response pretraining (Atwater, 1953; Cantor, 1955; Gagné & Foster, 1949) and overlearning (Mandler, 1954; Mandler & Heinemann, 1956). In all of these related research domains, real-life or laboratory-induced prior familiarization with given responses increased the likelihood of their occurrence on later trials. Mandler (1954) summarizes much of this research as it bears upon transfer by noting that "learning to make an old response to a new stimulus showed increasing positive transfer as degree of original training was increased [p. 412]." Mandler's own studies in this domain, that is, studies of overlearning, are especially relevant to our present theme, for it is not sheer practice of attempts at effective behaviors which we feel is of most benefit to the transfer needs of the psychotherapy patient. As will be seen, it is practice of **successful** attempts.

Overlearning is a procedure whereby learning is extended over more trials than are necessary merely to produce **initial** changes in the individual's behavior. In all too many instances of near-successful therapy, one or two successes at a given task are taken as evidence to move on to the next task, or the next level of the original task. To maximize maintenance and transfer via response availability, and in particular from the perspective of research on overlearning, the foregoing is a therapeutic technique error. Mandler's (1954) subjects were trained on the study task until they were able to perform it **without error** (either 0, 10, 30, 50, or 100 consecutive times. As noted earlier, transfer varied with the degree of original learning. To maximize transfer in psychotherapy via this principle, the guiding rule should not be, practice makes perfect (implying simply practice until one gets it right, and then move on), but practice **of** perfect (implying numerous overlearning trials of correct responses **after** the initial success).

As was true for the other maintenance and transfer-enhancers we have considered earlier, concern with response availability for such purposes is already evident in the behavior modification literature (e.g., the several approaches concerned with skill training, behavioral rehearsal, or other psychoeducational techniques which require repetition of effective behaviors), but finds only scant and typically implicit mention in presentations of more psychodynamically oriented psychotherapies. The psychoanalytic technique of "working through," in which interpretive materials are repeatedly dealt with in conjunction with an ever-widening configuration of real-life data, is perhaps the closest approach to overlearning made by psychodynamic therapists. Weiner (1975) comments in this regard:

> Concurrently with the process of working through an interpretation the patient gradually becomes capable of using it to alter his behavior.... Over time the lag between his behaving in a neurotic fashion and his recognizing the neurotic determinants of his behavior will continue to shrink and finally, when the new understanding of himself provided by an interpretation has been fully worked through, he will realize its implication for situations in which he has been behaving neurotically as he encounters them, and *before* he responds, and he will than have achieved fully capacity to control his behavior in those situations [p. 158].

Greenwald's (1973) requirement in his decision therapy that patients engage in continued practice of the decision-making process, Rosen's

(1961) use in his direct analysis of test situations, and the encouragement to practice new behavior described by Beier (1966) are typical of the hints in the traditional therapy literature of essentially unplanned and unsystematic attempts to enhance maintenance and transfer by means of maximizing response availability.

Maximizing Stimulus Variability

In our last section, we addressed ourselves to enhancement of main-tenance and transfer by means of practice and repetition, that is, the sheer **number** of effective responses to a given stimuli which the patient makes. Turning now to the stimulus member of the event, maintenance and transfer are also enhanced by the **variability** or range of stimuli to which the patient responds. For example, Duncan (1958) has shown that on a paired associates task transfer is markedly enhanced by varied training. Training on even only two stimuli is better than training on a single stimulus. Other investigators have obtained similar results in concept attainment tasks, showing more rapid attainment when a variety of ex-amples is presented (Callantine & Warren, 1955; Shore & Sechrest, 1961). As we have noted elsewhere in response to studies such as these: "The implication is clear that in order to maximize positive transfer, training should provide for some sampling of the population of stimuli to which the response must ultimately be given [Goldstein *et al.*, 1966, p. 220]."

As before, awareness of the therapeutic implications of this means of transfer enhancement seems largely confined to behaviorally oriented approaches. For example, Kazdin (1975) comments:

> One way to program response maintenance and transfer of training is to develop the target behavior in a variety of situations and in the presence of several individuals. If the response is associated with a range of settings, individuals, and other cues, it is less likely to be lost when the situations change [p. 211].

But the corresponding picture in more traditional psychotherapies is rather different. In fact, with certain exceptions to be noted later, verbal, insight-oriented, psychodynamic psychotherapies typically consist of pro-cedures which serve to **minimize** stimulus variability! In a satirical pas-sage speaking to this very point, a passage titled "Some Suggestions for Minimizing Transfer in Psychotherapy," we stated:

> If we wish to minimize the transfer of psychotherapy learning to extra-therapy situations, a number of things may be done. First, a single therapist

should provide some rather distinctive personal cues, such as appearance, dress, and manner, that would mark him as a rather special person, differ- ent from others. Second, an unvarying and powerful stimulus pattern should provide a context for the therapy, thus ensuring that whatever responses may be developed would become very strongly attached to the unique therapy stimuli. For example, the therapist would use one office for every situation. The furniture in the office would be distinctive and it would not vary from session to session. There should be some stimuli which would identify the office as such and mark it off from other places; for example, diplomas on the wall, bookshelves, and filing cabinets. And, not to belabor the point unduly, the therapy would be conducted on the same day of every week, at the same time of day, and for some standard length of time, say fifty minutes [Goldstein et al., 1966, p. 226].

As we noted earlier, however, there are traditional therapies less starkly devoid of stimulus variability. Group psychotherapy, particularly that involving heterogeneous groups, is one prime example (Slavson, 1964; Wolf & Schwartz, 1962). A measure of stimulus variability is also present in multiple impact therapy by MacGregor et al. (1964); in the use of multiple therapists by Dreikurs, Schulman, and Mosak (1952), Hayward, Peters, and Taylor (1952), and Whitaker, Malone, and War- kentin (1966); in round robin therapy (Holmes, 1971); in rotational therapy (Slavin, 1967); and in rotational group therapy (Frank, 1973). To reiterate, we mention here the implicit, essentially unplanned use of a transfer-enhancer not to criticize and bemoan but, instead, to praise the clinical wisdom of various psychodynamic therapists and to propose that giant strides forward in the art and science of therapeutic transfer- enhancement will likely be forthcoming when the hints at effective use of transfer-enhancing procedures are more planned, developed, eval- uated, and systematically implemented.

OUTLINE OF THIS BOOK

In the remaining chapters of this book, we present in considerable de- tail the existing maintenance and transfer-enhancing techniques that have, to some appreciable extent, already been evaluated experimentally, and that, at least in certain therapeutic contexts, have begun to find systematic clinical implementation.

Part I of this book is a discussion of systematically investigated and implemented maintenance and transfer-enhancement techniques whose roots lie in the transfer principle of identical elements. As we noted in our earlier discussion of this principle, maintenance and transfer may be enhanced by conducting treatment out of office settings and in locations strongly associated with the client's presenting problems. Such "park bench" (Goldstein *et al.*, 1966) or *in vivo* treatments, as presented by Sherman in Chapters 2 and 3, include *in vivo* desensitization, *in vivo* flooding, reality orientation therapy, use of transitional living centers, and direct analysis. But the client not only experiences his difficulties in certain places, his difficulties are also often tied to certain people. In Chapter 4, McPeak deals with family therapies. He shares with us a description of the history of these approaches, their procedures, their goals, and their associated problems. In particular, he emphasizes the mediating role of family communication patterns and dynamics. Clearly, to the degree that a family therapy intervention is successful, to that degree have we enhanced the likelihood of office–to–real-life transfer of therapeutic gains based on identical elements principles.

Transfer may also be enhanced not only by **where** and **with whom** we treat a given patient, but also by in-depth attention to training the patient in self-management techniques. A great deal of research has been conducted in accord with such a self-generated maintenance and transfer strategy, and a number of clinically useful techniques of this type exist. These techniques are the main focus of Chapter 5. In this chapter, Kanfer describes the instigation therapy roots of self-management strategies and, in particular, describes for us procedures for training clients in problem-solving skills, in self-regulatory methods, in developing coping skills, and in the use of behavioral rehearsal. One additional self-management procedure, also deriving largely from an instigation therapy perspective, is use of therapeutic homework. Shelton (Chapter 6) shares with us the history of this technique, and provides a detailed and concrete picture of the components, specific procedures and materials optimally involved when using therapeutic homework.

The Kanfer and Shelton chapters constitute Part II of this book. The aim of Part III is to describe the nature of transfer-enhancing environments, broadly defined. One very salient characteristic of the real-life, extratherapy environment in which the client must function effectively is the people in it. Nay, in Chapter 7, describes means by which parents may serve as maintenance and transfer-enhancing agents for their children. How such parent training is optimally conducted is his first concern. What they should be taught—about target selection reinforcement, generalization, and the like—are then examined. Throughout this presentation, and in a manner importantly related to the earlier focus on family therapy, Nay maintains a perspective on the family as a consequation system. But it is not just parents who may function as significant figures in a transfer-enhancing environment. So too may peers, spouses, friends, and hired others. Just such persons are the concern of Marholin and

Touchette, as they examine, in Chapter 8, a variety of stimulus control techniques—peer control, rehearsal in the natural environment, use of multiple control settings, and so forth. The authors are also concerned in this chapter with the functional utility of behavior change as it relates to maintenance and transfer, and thus also provide us with examination of techniques of use in selecting real-life behaviors likely to be reinforced and means for strengthening incompatible acceptable behaviors.

Person components of transfer-enhancing environments may also be profitably examined from a less behavioral and more macroscopic perspective. Heller (Chapter 9) does just this in his comprehensive discussion of social support systems. He shares with us what is, in many ways, a new research and application domain. Social support systems, and their likely influence upon gain maintenance and transfer are explored. The nature of support, consequences of its loss, person variables influencing openness to support, and factors maintaining social support systems are among Heller's concerns.

At a similar level of analysis, Price (Chapter 10) also takes us to a realm relatively new to contemporary psychology. His concern is the social ecology of treatment gain. Rather than the person focus of the other chapters in Part III, Price explores the environments themselves. If overt behaviors, such as gain maintenance and transfer, are a joint function in part of the client **and** his environment, how best can we identify, create or change environments to foster such behaviors. This is the question which Price perceptively explores as he draws upon research and technique in environmental psychology and social ecology.

The maintenance and transfer of therapeutic gain also has physiological antecedents. In Part IV of this book, McDonald, Lidsky, and Kern (Chapter 11) explore drug therapy considerations as they relate to maintenance and transfer. They recommend that all schizophrenics undergo drug withdrawal, that there be no routine use of medication, and that drug use be replaced by community-relevant skill training or other alternatives to drug therapy. In these as well as their other clinical recommendations, they explicitly provide the reader with both rationale and specific procedural reasons for continued concern with drug therapy as it relates to maintenance and transfer.

Lynn and Freedman (Chapter 12) focus on the array of physiological variables responsive to biofeedback procedures. The authors concern themselves with what these procedures are, their demonstrated strengths and weaknesses, and their relevance to gain acquisition, maintenance, and transfer. Lynn and Freedman examine a number of especially innovative procedures and types of change-relevant instrumentation. As is a recurrent theme throughout this book, they too invite the reader to view their conclusions as tentative and as stimuli for further experimentation and clinical trial. We second such recommendations, and reiterate that the clinical goals of gain maintenance and transfer are the ultimate goals of any psychotherapy. As such, they are especially deserving of our experimental energies and clinical scrutiny. It is in this spirit that the chapters that follow are offered.

REFERENCES

Adler, A. *The practice and theory of individual psychology.* New York: Harcourt, Brace, 1924.

Atwater, S. K. Proactive inhibition and associative facilitation as affected by degree of prior learning. *Journal of Experimental Psychology,* 1953, *46,* 400–404.

Ayllon, T., & Azrin, N. H. Reinforcer sampling: A technique for increasing the behavior of mental patients. *Journal of Applied Analysis,* 1968, *1,* 13–20.

Bandura, A. *Principles of behavior modification.* New York: Holt, 1969.

Bergin, A. E. The evaluation of therapeutic outcomes. In A. E. Bergin, & S. L. Garfield (Eds.), *Handbook of psychotherapy and behavior change: An empirical analysis.* New York: Wiley, 1971.

Bijou, S. W., & Redd, W. H. Child behavior therapy. In S. Arieti (Ed.), *American handbook of psychiatry* (Vol. 7). New York: Basic Books, 1975.

Burchard, J. D. *Behavior modification with delinquents: Some unforeseen contingencies.* Paper presented at the meeting of the American Orthopsychiatric Association, New York, April 1971.

Callantine, M. F., & Warren, J. M. Learning sets in human concept formation. *Psychological Reports,* 1955, *1,* 363–367.

Cantor, J. H. Amount of pretraining as a factor in stimulus pre-differentiation and performance set. *Journal of Experimental Psychology,* 1955, *50,* 180–184.

Crafts, L. W. Transfer as related to number of common elements. *Journal of General Psychology,* 1935, *13,* 147–158.

Davidson, W. S., II, & Seidman, E. Studies of behavior modification and juvenile delinquency: A review, methodological critique, and social perspective. *Psychological Bulletin,* 1974, *8,* 998–1011.

DeMeyer, M. K., & Ferster, C. B. Teaching new social behaviors to schizophrenic children. *Journal of Psychiatry,* 1962, *1,* 443–461.

Dreikurs, R., Schulman, B. H., & Mosak, H. Patient–therapist in multiple psychotherapy: Its advantages to the therapist. *Psychiatric Quarterly,* 1952, *26,* 219–227.

Duncan, C. P. Transfer in motor learning as a function of degree of first-task learning and inner-task similarity. *Journal of Experimental Psychology,* 1953, *45,* 1–11.

Duncan, C. P. Transfer after training with single versus multiple tasks. *Journal of Experimental Psychology,* 1958, *55,* 63–72.

Duncan, C. P. Recent research on human problem solving. *Psychological Bulletin,* 1959, *56,* 397–429.

Ellis, H. *The transfer of learning.* New York: Macmillan, 1965.

Ford, D. H., & Urban, H. B. *Systems of psychotherapy.* New York: Wiley, 1963.

Frank, R. Rotating leadership in a group therapy setting. *Psychotherapy: Theory, Research and Practice*, 1973, *10*, 337–338.

Gagné, R. M., Baker, K. E., & Foster, H. On the relation between similarity and transfer of training in the learning of discriminative motor tasks. *Psychological review*, 1950, *57*, 67–79.

Gagné, R. M., & Foster, H. Transfer to a motor skill from practice on a pictured representation. *Journal of Experimental Psychology*, 1949, *39*, 342–354.

Goldbeck, R. A., Bernstein, B. B.; Hellix, W. A., & Marx, M. H. Application of the half-split technique to problem-solving tasks. *Journal of Experimental Psychology*, 1957, *53*, 330–338.

Goldstein, A. P. (Ed.). *Prescriptions for child mental health and education*. New York: Pergamon, 1978.

Goldstein, A. P., Heller, K., & Sechrest, L. B. *Psychotherapy and the psychology of behavior change*. New York: Wiley, 1966.

Goldstein, A. P., & Stein, N. *Prescriptive psychotherapies*. New York: Pergamon, 1976.

Greenwald, H. *Active psychotherapy*. New York: Atherton, 1967.

Greenwald, H. *Decision therapy*. New York: Wyden, 1973.

Grindee, K. T. *Operant conditioning of "attending behaviors" in the classroom for two hyperactive Negro children*. Unpublished manuscript, Reed College, Portland, Oregon, September, 1964.

Grindee, K. T. *Operant conditioning of attending behaviors in the classroom; a case study*. Unpublished bachelor's thesis, Reed College, Portland, Oregon, 1965.

Haley, J. *Problem solving therapy*. San Francisco: Jossey-Bass, 1976.

Hayward, M. L., Peters, J. J., & Taylor, J. E. Some values of the use of multiple therapists in the treatment of psychoses. *Psychiatric Quarterly*, 1952, *26*, 244–249.

Hendrickson, G., & Schroeder, W. H. Transfer of training in learning to hit a submerged target. *Journal of Educational Psychology*, 1941, *32*, 205–213.

Hington, J. N., Sanders, B. J., & DeMeyer, M. K. Shaping cooperative responses in early childhood schizophrenics. In L. Ullman, L. Krasner (Eds.), *Case studies in behavior modification*. New York: Holt, 1965.

Holmes, D. S. Round robin therapy: A technique for implementing the effects of psychotherapy. *Journal of Consulting and Clinical Psychology*, 1971, *37*, 324–331.

Horney, K. *New ways in psychoanalyses*. New York: Norton, 1939.

Isaacs, W., Thomas, J., & Goldiamond, I. Application of operant conditioning to reinstate verbal behavior in psychotics. *Journal of Speech and Hearing Disorders*, 1960, *25*, 8–12.

Judd, C. H. Practice and its effects on the perception of illusions. *Psychological review*, 1902, *9*, 27–39.

Kanfer, F. H., & Phillips, J. S. *Learning foundations of behavior therapy*. New York: Wiley, 1970.

Kazdin, A. E. *Behavior modification in applied settings*. Homewood, Illinois: Dorsey Press, 1975.

Keeley, S. M., Shemberg, K. M., & Carbonell, J. Operant clinical intervention: Behavior management or beyond? Where are the data? *Behavior Therapy*, 1976, *7*, 292–305.

Kelly, G. A. *The psychology of personal constructs*. New York: Norton, 1955.

Loveless, A., & Brody, C. The cognitive base of psychotherapy. *Psychotherapy. Theory, Research and Practice*, 1974, *11*, 133–137.

MacGregor, R., Ritchie, A. M., Serrano, A. C., & Schuster, F. P. *Multiple impact therapy with families.* New York: McGraw-Hill, 1964.

Mandler, G. Transfer of training as a function of degree of response overlearning. *Journal of Experimental Psychology,* 1954, 47, 411–417.

Mandler, G., & Heinemann, S. H. Effect of overlearning of a verbal response on transfer of training. *Journal of Experimental Psychology,* 1956, 52, 39–46.

Marholin, II, D., Siegel, L. J., & Phillips, D. Treatment and transfer: A search for empirical procedures. In M. Hersen, R. M. Eisler, & P. M. Miller (Eds.), *Progress in behavior modification* (Vol. 3). New York: Academic Press, 1976.

Meichenbaum, D. H., Bowers, K., & Ross, R. R. Modification of classroom behavior of institutionalized female adolescent offenders. *Behaviour Research and Therapy,* 1968, 6, 343–353.

Meyer, V., & Crisp, A. H. Aversion therapy in two cases of obesity. *Behavior Research and Therapy,* 1964, 2, 143–147.

Miller, G. A., Heise, G. A., & Lichten, W. The intelligibility of speech as a function of the test materials. *Journal of Experimental Psychology,* 1951, 41, 329–335.

O'Leary, K. D., Becker, W. C., Evans, M. B., & Saudargas, R. A. A token reinforcement program in a public school: A replication and systematic analysis. *Journal of Applied Behavior Analysis,* 1969, 2, 3–13.

Osgood, C. E. The similarity paradox in human learning: A resolution. *Psychological Review,* 1949, 56, 132–143.

Osgood, C. E. *Method and theory in experimental psychology.* New York: Oxford University Press, 1953.

Phillips, E. L. *Psychotherapy: A modern theory and practice.* Englewood Cliffs, New Jersey: Prentice-Hall, 1956.

Phillips, E. L., & Wiener, D. N. *Short-term psychotherapy and structured behavior change.* New York: McGraw-Hill, 1966.

Rank, O. *Will therapy and truth and reality.* New York: Knopf, 1945.

Reiss, S. Transfer effects of success and failure training from one reinforcing agent to another. *Journal of Abnormal Psychology,* 1973, 82, 435–445.

Rogers, C. R. *Client-centered therapy.* Boston: Houghton Mifflin, 1951.

Rosen, J. Direct analysis. In A. E. Scheflin & O. Spurgeon English (Eds.), *A psychotherapy of schizophrenia.* Springfield, Illinois: Thomas, 1961.

Shore, E., & Sechrest, L. Concept attainment as a function of number of positive instances presented. *Journal of Educational Psychology,* 1961, 52, 303–307.

Slavin, D. R. *Response transfer of conditioned affective responses as a function of an experimental analogue of rotational psychotherapy.* Unpublished doctoral dissertation, Northwestern University, 1967.

Slavson, S. R. *A textbook in analytic group psychotherapy.* New York: International Universities Press, 1964.

Steiner, C., Wyckoff, H., Marcus, J., Lariviere, P., Goldstine, D., & Schwebel, R. *Readings in radical psychiatry.* New York: Grove Press, 1975.

Sullivan, H. S. *Conceptions of modern psychiatry.* New York: Norton, 1953.

Thorndike, E. L., & Woodworth, R. S. The influence of improvement in one mental function upon the efficiency of other functions. *Psychological Review,* 1901, 8, 247–261.

Ulmer, G. Teaching geometry to cultivate reflective thinking: An experimental study with 1239 high school pupils. *Journal of Experimental Education,* 1939, 8, 18–25.

Underwood, B. J. Associative transfer in verbal learning as a function of response similarity and degree of first-list learning. *Journal of Experimental Psychology,* 1951, *42,* 44–53.

Underwood, B. J., & Schulz, R. W. *Meaningfulness and verbal behavior.* New York: Lippincott, 1960.

Watkins, B. R. The development and evolution of a transductive learning technique for the treatment of social incompetence. *Dissertation Abstracts International,* 1972, *33,* 2361.

Weiner, I. B. *Principles of psychotherapy.* New York: Wiley, 1975.

Whitaker, C. A., Malone, T. P., & Warkentin, J. Multiple therapy and psychotherapy. In F. Fromm-Reichman & M. Moreno (Eds.), *Progress in psychotherapy.* New York: Grune & Stratton, 1966.

Wolf, A., & Schwartz, E. K. *Psychoanalysis in groups.* New York: Grune & Stratton, 1962.

Woodrow, H. The effect of type of training upon transference. *Journal of Educational Psychology,* 1927, *18,* 159–172.

Young, R. K., & Underwood, B. J. Transfer in verbal materials with dissimilar stimuli and response similarity varied. *Journal of Experimental Psychology,* 1954, *47,* 153–159.

I

TRANSFER-ENHANCEMENT BASED ON IDENTICAL ELEMENTS

2

In Vivo Therapies
for Phobic Reactions,
Instrumental Behavior
Problems, and Interpersonal
and Communication Problems[1]

A. ROBERT SHERMAN

INTRODUCTION

Interest in improving the efficacy, efficiency, and durability of therapy for psychological problems has prompted the development of an expanding array of innovative treatment procedures. Some of these are conducted primarily in the client's natural problem settings, while others simulate the central problem features within an office setting. These approaches are generically referred to as *"in vivo* therapies" because they attempt to deal directly with the actual situations, behaviors, and feelings which together constitute the client's difficulties in real life.

---

[1] Some of the information presented in this chapter was assembled during a special seminar on *in vivo* therapies conducted by the author. The contributions of the following students are gratefully acknowledged: Bonnie Gutterman, Laura Hamlin, Janice Jackson, Linda Johnston, Howard Lunche, Lorence Miller, Debbie Mohr, Charles Nasser, Sheri Rego, and Tim Worden.

MAXIMIZING TREATMENT GAINS:
Transfer Enhancement in Psychotherapy

Some of these *in vivo* therapies are reviewed in the present chapter, and others are described in the following companion chapter.

While most psychological interventions traditionally have been conducted in formal treatment settings, the usual goal is to promote enduring improvement in the client which transfers to the natural environment. The alleviation of psychological distress and the development of improved skills must be evident in the client's daily life, not just in the treatment setting. The child who has learned to fondle a puppy in the therapist's office still has a problem if his fear of dogs continues to prevent him from playing outside the house. The woman who is now able to complete chores within her hospital setting following treatment for a "nervous breakdown" still has a problem if she remains unable to return to her family and resume her adult responsibilities. The man who is now able to role-play assertive responses with his therapist in the office still has a problem if he remains intimidated by work associates who continue to take advantage of him. In each of these examples, the client's improvement in the treatment setting did not transfer entirely to the natural environment. This incomplete transfer of improvement, which is rather common for office psychotherapy, is sometimes referred to as *transfer decrement*.

While multiple factors may contribute to transfer decrement, the phenomenon appears predictable from a psychological model of behavior. Put in simple terms, most behaviors and the emotions accompanying them are viewed as being connected in part with the surrounding situations. In other words, there is a *situational specificity* to the behaviors: The probability of particular responses and feelings varies with the setting and the circumstances. The more **dis**similar two situations are, the less likely they are to evoke similar psychological reactions. This is true for psychological **problems** as well, the manifestation of which often varies with the circumstances.

For example, the "dog-phobic" child may exhibit distress outside the house when a dog is in view, but probably will appear content at home watching television cartoons in which doglike characters are present. Likewise, the "unassertive" man may be easily intimidated by his associates at work, but may still be interpersonally effective with his spouse and friends at home. This situational specificity of many psychological problems appears to limit the efficiency and effectiveness of therapy conducted under dissimilar circumstances in an office setting, as well as limiting the transfer of improvement from the office to the problem setting.

Regardless of the theoretical orientation underlying the therapist's approach, most treatments require an accurate understanding of the client's behavioral and emotional problems, and the circumstances surrounding them. For many psychological problems, it may not be possible for these features to be adequately represented by the client in a formal office setting that differs substantially from the client's stressful natural environment. Recognition of these limitations of office psychotherapy has provided much of the impetus for the development of *in vivo* treatment procedures.

The emerging emphasis on the *in vivo* treatment of psychological problems is probably better characterized as evolutionary than as revolutionary. This becomes apparent when one contrasts the trends in mental health care with the trends in physical health care. Many people can still remember when it was common for physicians to make house calls for acute physical illnesses. While that practice was convenient for the patient, it ordinarily did not represent an integral part of any treatment strategy. Unlike many psychological problems, physical problems usually are not situationally specific, and would not be any easier to diagnose or treat in the home than in the office. In fact, quite the opposite is becoming more and more true: Technological advances in physical medicine have equipped the modern physician's office with an array of useful devices and instruments that cannot be packed into the "little black bag" of the physician's house-calling predecessor. We have become accustomed to a high level of physical health care which requires the sophisticated laboratory, diagnostic, and treatment procedures available only in the medical setting, not in the home. The *in vivo* care of acute physical problems is now limited largely to paramedical services provided in emergencies. The transition away from treatment in the home was not the consequence of a sudden revolution in medical theory; instead, it evolved gradually from advances in medical technology which have made the well-equipped medical setting increasingly essential to the provision of optimal health care.

In the area of psychotherapy, it appears that the locus for provision of services has also been shifting gradually, but in the opposite direction. Psychotherapeutic house calls were probably quite rare in the days when Sigmund Freud was conducting psychoanalytic sessions with wealthy clients, and severely disturbed people who were not financially independent were institutionalized in asylums for the "insane." The nature of psychodynamic therapy requires the remote privacy afforded by the therapist's office. Advances in our understanding of the nature and development of certain psychological difficulties have gradually given rise to new approaches to psychological treatment which depart from some of the basic tenets of psychodynamic therapy, and which do not rely entirely on a one-to-one verbal interaction between therapist and client.

Some of these new approaches have been adapted for *in vivo* application. As in the case of physical health care, the trends in mental health care represent an attempt to increase the efficiency and effectiveness of clinical services. In the former case, this is being achieved through an emphasis on the sophisticated resources of the modern medical setting, whereas in the case of mental health care, this is being achieved through an increased emphasis on *in vivo* components of treatment.

There are a variety of features of natural living situations that may be central to understanding and improving psychological problems, depending upon the nature of the client's difficulty. These include family members, friends, or associates that the client has difficulty relating to, essential activities that the client cannot perform skillfully, objects or situations that the client is afraid of, responsibilities that the client is unable to fulfill effectively, and so on. By minimizing the gap between problem and therapy settings through *in vivo* methods, the therapist and client may be better able to focus directly on the situational features, the behaviors, and the feelings which constitute the client's real problems. The therapist can observe the client experiencing psychological difficulty, and any improvement which emerges from the treatment would be manifested by the client in relation to the real situations or their equivalents. There need be little concern about a transfer decrement, because the problem and treatment settings are either identical, or comparable in their relevant features. In essence, the treatment focuses upon the problems as they are manifested in reality, rather than on verbal reports of those problems.

In the pages that follow, a variety of *in vivo* therapies are presented. They are organized according to the kinds of psychological difficulties with which they would be employed: phobic reactions, instrumental behavior problems, and interpersonal and communication problems. The presentation of each treatment strategy includes a summary of the basic procedure and its rationale, a case example illustrating its application, representative findings concerning its effects, and an appraisal of its present status and related issues.

PHOBIC REACTIONS

The present section reviews four categories of *in vivo* approaches to the treatment of phobic reactions. A phobia is an irrational fear reaction to specific objects or situations. The person suffering from a phobia will attempt to avoid the feared situations despite their objective harmlessness, and will experience severe anxiety if such situations are spontaneously encountered. While some stimulus-specific fears are realistic, such as a fear of poisonous snakes, a phobic fear is, by definition, unrealistic or out of proportion to any objective danger in the situation. The specificity of the phobia also distinguishes it from generalized or pervasive anxiety which, although maladaptive, does not appear related to any special circumstances. The clinical severity of a phobic reaction would depend partly on the extent to which the resulting avoidance behavior constrains the person's normal daily-life activities. For example, a child who is afraid of dogs might refrain from going outdoors to play with friends, thereby missing out on the pleasures and stresses of unsupervised peer interaction and their contribution to social and emotional development. In contrast, a fear of harmless snakes in a person residing in a large city paved with concrete is unlikely to have any influence on the person's daily behavior. While the clinical severity of the phobia might influence the person's motivation to pursue therapy, severity as a variable does not generally appear to dictate the therapist's selection of a particular treatment from among the array of alternatives. The various approaches to be reviewed here all involve a central *in vivo* component consisting of exposure to the real objects or situations which the person is afraid of.

Gradual Exposure to Phobic Situations In Vivo

In this approach the fearful client is exposed to the real phobic situations, beginning with mildly threatening situations and gradually progressing to those which are more and more threatening as each is successfully confronted without distress. The basic procedure has been called **gradual exposure therapy** (Sherman, 1972); when accompanied by the systematic use of verbal praise intended to reinforce behavioral progress, it has been variably referred to as *reinforced practice* (e.g., Leitenberg & Callahan, 1973), *shaping* (e.g., Barlow, Agras, Leitenberg, & Wincze, 1970), and *successive approximation* (e.g., Everaerd, Rijken, & Emmelkamp, 1973). In theory, the approach could be applicable to anyone suffering from a phobic fear reaction, regardless of age or other difficulties; in practice, the approach has been used primarily with children and adults who are otherwise basically well-functioning. The setting for treatment would depend largely upon the target of the fear reaction. For certain fears, such as a fear of heights or of elevators, the procedure would be conducted in the natural environment in which the target is ordinarily encountered. For other fears, such as a fear of insects or of taking examinations, which involve small objects or activities which can

be presented in any setting, the procedures could be conducted in an
office or laboratory.

Basic Procedure

Ordinarily, the procedure begins with the formulation of an *anxiety
hierarchy*. This is a list of situations related to the phobic theme which
vary in the degree of anxiety that they evoke in the client, ranging from
situations which would be only mildly threatening to those which would
be extremely threatening. It is sometimes helpful to employ a rating scale
to assist the client in assessing the probable anxiety associated with each
situation (e.g., Wolpe, 1973, p. 120). This enables the situations to be
rank-ordered into a hierarchy, and permits the identification of any large
gaps in the hierarchy which can then be filled by new scenes with intermediate anxiety ratings. When the relevant parameters are few and
straightforward in terms of their probable influence on the anxiety level,
a logical hierarchy may be prepared without extensive effort. For example, in the case of a youngster who is afraid of sleeping in the dark,
the illumination level of the room would probably be the primary variable influencing the child's fear—the darker the room, the greater the
fear. Since the setting (child's bedroom) and activity (going to sleep)
are constant, the hierarchy would consist of a sequence of occasions involving the child going to bed under illumination levels beginning with
several lights on and progressing in small steps to total darkness.

The gradual exposure consists of repeatedly presenting the client with
the real situations from the anxiety hierarchy, beginning with the least
threatening situation and gradually progressing up the hierarchy as each
situation is successfully negotiated without distress. The exposure may
be administered by presenting the client with the feared stimulus objects
in the office (such as insects, small animals, or knives); by showing
photographs or films of the feared objects or situations; by having the
therapist accompany the client outside the office (such as traveling in a
car, entering a swimming pool, or riding in an elevator); or by arranging
for the client to expose himself systematically to the real situations in
his daily life (Sherman, 1973, pp. 74–75). Sometimes the therapist will
attempt to reinforce the client's behavioral progress systematically
through verbal praise or other overtures of social approval.

Rationale

Guthrie (1952) proposed that an associative connection may be eliminated "by increasing the stimulus and keeping it always under the
threshold or within the tolerance of the individual [p. 61]." This implies
that conditioned fear may be extinguished through repeated exposure to
the feared situations in the absence of adverse consequences. In fact,

spontaneous exposure to the feared situations is probably an important factor in the normal reduction of common childhood fears. Provided that a situation is objectively harmless, each exposure is likely to bring about a further decrease in the evoked fear as well as generalizing extinction to related situations. However, reliance on extinction in natural circumstances tends to be inefficient because the phobic individual will try to avoid the feared situations whenever possible. Unless exposure occurs, no extinction will ensue, and with the exception of accidental confrontations, natural exposure will probably be limited to the least threatening situations. Gradual exposure therapy attempts to further this process by systematically arranging conditions of graded exposure and repetition to bring about a reduction in fear and avoidance behavior (Sherman, 1973, pp. 83–84). The client's successful efforts at confronting the feared stimuli may be further reinforced, according to the paradigm of operant conditioning, by the therapist's expressions of approval.

Case Example

Freeman and Kendrick (1964) provided one of the first detailed clinical illustrations of the effectiveness of a gradual exposure approach. They treated a 37-year-old woman who suffered from a longstanding phobic fear of cats.

> The stimuli producing the fear reaction, in descending order of significance, were as follows: (1) the sight of a cat in reality; (2) the thought that a cat might be about to spring out on her while she was walking along the pavement; (3) the thought of going out by herself at night in case she should meet a cat in the dark; (4) pictures of cats, and cats on television; (5) cat-like toys; (6) cat-like fur [p. 56].

The patient would restrict her activities so as to reduce the chances of encountering a cat, and would panic at the sight of a cat. She stated that her fear of cats had existed for as long as she could remember.

According to the report:

> It was considered that the weakest point of the stimulus gradient would be material that had some of the texture of fur without looking like it— for example, velvet.... The psychiatrist began the presentation of stimuli at the day hospital, and told the patient to handle each material in turn, until it caused her no uneasiness.... At the end of three weeks, fur, toys, and pictures had all been fully assimilated and a significant lessening in anxiety had already occurred. She was much less preoccupied with cats in general and her family had noticed that she was altogether more cheerful [pp. 56–57].

About one month after her first attendance, after looking after a kitten at the day hospital for 2 days, she took it home. Eventually she stopped having cat nightmares, and 10 weeks after beginning treatment she was able to touch a full grown cat for the first time. A 3-year follow-up revealed that the patient was "still very well" and "still has her own cat and frequently looks after another one [p. 61]."

Representative Findings

In a classic paper on methods of overcoming fears in children, Jersild and Holmes (1935) described the results of interviews they conducted with parents. Although the parents did not often employ the procedure of graded stimulus presentations, it was reportedly very successful when it was employed. This consisted essentially of "leading the child by degrees into active contact with and participation in the situation that he fears: presenting the stimulus at first in a less intense form, or without some of its most frightening features, or in conjunction with reassuring features, and then gradually introducing all of the conditions that initially evoked fear [p. 102]." Examples were also provided of how the method was used successfully with children who were afraid of alarm clocks, flowing water from faucets, haircuts, masks, and darkness.

Davison (1965) reported a pilot study which evaluated graded exposure in the treatment of college volunteers who were afraid of beetles. After approximately five treatment sessions, all five exposure subjects (two of whom had also been trained to relax) were able to perform the criterion behavior: allowing a beetle to crawl all over their bare hands for 30 sec. No behavioral improvement was evidenced in a posttreatment assessment of two untreated control subjects, while all but one of the exposure subjects had maintained their gains.

Sherman (1972) employed a factorial research design involving six combinations of treatments for 54 female college students who were afraid of the water. For half of the students, the treatment included a series of three 15-min sessions of graded exposure to real water situations in a swimming pool. The results revealed considerable subjective and behavioral improvement associated primarily with the gradual exposure therapy, and a follow-up evaluation revealed the durability of the aquaphobic improvements. This study also provided for comparison with an imaginal systematic desensitization treatment conducted in an office setting. It was found that the reduction of anxiety to the imagined stimuli showed little transfer from the office to the swimming pool unless the treatment had included *in vivo* exposure.

Several studies have investigated the effects of the gradual exposure approach combined with reinforcement, usually consisting of verbal praise, administered contingent on clients' behavioral progress. Barlow et al. (1970) found this "shaping" approach to be more effective than systematic desensitization in reducing behavioral avoidance in snake-phobic college females, and equally effective in reducing anxiety as measured by the galvanic skin response. Crowe, Marks, Agras, and Leitenberg (1972) found a similar procedure to be significantly more effective than systematic desensitization, with imaginal implosion therapy falling between the two and not being significantly different from either. In this study, the subjects were outpatients with a variety of moderately severe phobias. A study by Everaerd et al. (1973) also provided supportive evidence for gradual exposure-plus-praise in the treatment of agoraphobic patients; they called their approach "successive approximation."

Leitenberg and Callahan (1973) described their evaluation of a therapeutic method emphasizing graduated and repeated practice in approaching actual phobic stimuli, and including feedback and reinforcement for performance gains. According to the authors:

> In each of four experiments involving four different fears, namely fear of heights, snakes and electric shock in adults, and fear of darkness in young children, subjects who experienced the "reinforced practice" procedure improved their performance by a significant and substantial margin as compared to untreated control subjects. These results suggest that regardless of different etiologies, regardless of whether or not the fears are "rational" or "irrational," and regardless of whether or not the fears are transitory or long lasting, the same treatment procedure can be equally effective in reducing escape–avoidance behavior [p. 19].

A 2-year follow-up of the acrophobic adults revealed that the behavioral performance was still significantly better than it had been prior to treatment, though there had been some decline.

Several of the above studies provided favorable evidence for the effectiveness of procedures variably referred to as "shaping," "successive approximation," or "reinforced practice," which consist essentially of gradual exposure therapy plus the adjunctive use of verbal praise to further reinforce behavioral progress. Since phobic individuals motivated for treatment are likely to derive satisfaction from their personal progress regardless of external social reinforcement, it is not clear to what extent the addition of systematic verbal praise by the therapist is really necessary. One study addressing this issue (Emmelkamp & Ultee, 1974) found that verbal praise did not add appreciably to the benefits derived from gradual exposure therapy alone; both treatments promoted significant and comparable improvement in agoraphobic patients. Present evidence therefore suggests that the primary therapeutic component of these approaches appears to be the repeated gradual exposure to the feared stimuli in vivo.

Appraisal

Gradual exposure therapy relies primarily upon graded *in vivo* exposure and repetition to bring about a reduction in fear and avoidance behavior. Considerable evidence suggests that this approach, sometimes accompanied by verbal praise to reinforce behavioral progress, can be effective in treating an array of phobic reactions. Once the client has confronted the entire range of feared situations without distress, the treatment is concluded. There is little need for concern about transfer decrement, since the treatment involves the real stimuli (rather than imagined representations) and does not rely upon the use of anxiety-inhibiting responses which may not be present when the feared situations are spontaneously encountered.

In a critical appraisal of behavioral treatments for phobic and obsessive-compulsive disorders, Marks (1975) concluded that "real-life exposure is the most powerful therapeutic factor so far identified [p. 93]." Real-life exposure presented in a graded sequence is the essence of gradual exposure therapy. Further research is required to identify the effective components with a view toward clarifying the mechanisms involved and improving their application. Controlled experiments concerning individual factors and the prediction of response to treatment might assist in selecting the optimal approach for particular persons. In the absence of such information, gradual exposure *in vivo* is sometimes supplemented by other treatment tactics such as exposure in imagery, social reinforcement, anxiety-inhibiting responses, modeling, or skill training (cf. MacDonald, 1975; MacDonald & Bernstein, 1974). For many phobic people, gradual exposure therapy alone may be sufficient.

In Vivo Desensitization with Anxiety-Inhibiting Responses

When anxiety-inhibiting responses are deliberately evoked during the process of gradual exposure to real phobic situations, the approach is called *in vivo desensitization.* A variety of responses or response-evoking techniques have been employed to control the tension and anxiety associated with phobic reactions. These have included relaxation training, feeding responses, sexual responses, emotive imagery, aggressive responses, and drugs. Such responses are thought to be physiologically and/or psychologically incompatible with anxiety. If present in sufficient strength, it is assumed that they will counteract the anxiety ordinarily evoked by the feared stimuli, and that this will reduce the fear-arousing potential of the stimuli in future encounters. The selection of an anxiety-inhibiting response for desensitization purposes would usually depend upon the age, characteristics, and preferences of the client, as well as the nature of the phobic reaction. The latter would also determine whether the therapy should be conducted in the natural environment, or whether the real feared stimuli should be presented within an office treatment setting.

Basic Procedure

In vivo desensitization involves gradual exposure of the client to the real feared situations while the client is experiencing emotional responses incompatible with anxiety. As with other gradual exposure procedures, the treatment ordinarily begins with the formulation of a hierarchy of situations related to the phobic theme which are rank-ordered in terms of their fear-evoking potential. Using any one of a variety of techniques, anxiety-inhibiting responses are aroused in the client prior to exposure to the feared situations. The client is then confronted with the real situations from the anxiety hierarchy, progressing from milder to more threatening items as each is successfully negotiated without distress. Depending upon the nature of the phobic theme, arrangements may be made for the client to approach the feared situations in the natural environment, or the feared stimuli may be presented within an office or laboratory setting. Ordinarily, the procedure would be repeated, and the anxiety-inhibiting responses phased out, until the client can effectively cope with the array of real phobic situations without assistance.

Among the various strategies used to generate anxiety-inhibiting responses in the client are the following:

1. *Relaxation training.* The client may be trained in procedures of self-relaxation, and then instructed to relax prior to the confrontation with phobic stimuli. "Progressive relaxation" (Jacobson, 1938) is an approach to relaxation training often used in desensitization treatment programs (see Wolpe, 1958) and as a self-management skill for controlling tension and anxiety (e.g., Sherman, 1975; Sherman & Plummer, 1973). By alternately tensing and relaxing specific muscle groups, the client learns to discriminate feelings of muscular tension and relaxation, and to relax the muscles more and more deeply. Attending to breathing, and imagining oneself in relaxing situations, are additional techniques which sometimes facilitate relaxation. With sufficient practice, the well-trained client can usually relax deeply in a few minutes. Other procedures, including hypnosis, yoga, transcendental meditation, and autogenic training (Schultz & Luthe, 1959), have also been employed to teach skills of self-relaxation.

2. *Feeding responses.* Responses associated with eating have been

found to counteract feelings of anxiety, which may be why some people tend to snack when under stress. Unlike some of the other anxiety-inhibiting responses, feeding responses are relatively easy to evoke in hungry youngsters. The use of such responses in the treatment of children's fears was described in one of the first published reports involving *in vivo* desensitization procedures (Jones, 1924): "During a period of craving for food, the child is placed in a highchair and given something to eat. . . . While the child is eating, the [feared] object is slowly brought nearer to the table, then placed upon the table, and finally as the tolerance increases it is brought close enough to be touched [p. 388]." It is important that the therapist not proceed so rapidly that the anxiety evoked by the feared object disrupts the eating process.

3. *Sexual responses.* Inadequate responsiveness in, or avoidance of, sexual situations is often the result of anxiety. Since sexual arousal and anxiety about sex are largely incompatible, the situation should be controlled to assure that the strength of the arousal exceeds the strength of the anxiety throughout the desensitization process. The basic strategy is to advise the client to approach the partner and engage in sexual activities only so far as pleasurable feelings of attraction and arousal predominate. According to Wolpe (1958): "It is found that from one love session to the next there is a decrease in anxiety and an increase in sexual excitation and therefore in the extent of the caresses to which the patient feels impelled [p. 131]." While sexual arousal has been used primarily to counteract anxiety related to sexual activities, it would seem that the positive feelings of sexual arousal could also be used systematically to desensitize nonsexual fears as well.

4. *Emotive imagery.* Many people can generate images or fantasies which arouse in them such positive feelings as strength, affection, pride, mirth, excitement, or adventure (see Lazarus & Abramovitz, 1962). By deliberately focusing on such personal images in the presence of real feared situations, the positive responses may counteract the anxiety and facilitate the desensitization process (Horan, 1976).

5. *Aggressive responses.* Several responses or response-producing strategies which have been employed for purposes of desensitization appear to have an aggression-expressing component. These include assertive responses (e.g., Wolpe, 1958), directed muscular activity (Lazarus, 1965), anger (Goldstein, Serber, & Piaget, 1970), and oriental defense exercises (Gershman & Stedman, 1971). The *in vivo* desensitization approach would require that the client engage in the aggressive responses while confronting the graded sequence of feared situations or objects.

6. *Drugs.* Drugs may be employed to induce a state of relaxation in a

person undergoing *in vivo* desensitization (e.g., see Wolpe, 1958). The drug would be administered before the client confronts the feared situations, at a sufficiently strong dosage to assure that a fear reaction and consequent avoidance behavior would not occur. In order to facilitate transfer of improvement to the nondrug state, the drug dosage may be gradually reduced over treatment sessions (cf. Sherman, 1967).

Rationale

There are several different procedural components which together constitute *in vivo* desensitization, and each carries its own rationale. *In vivo* desensitization consists essentially of gradual exposure to real phobic situations while experiencing emotional responses incompatible with anxiety. As noted earlier in the discussion of gradual exposure therapy, repeated exposure to a hierarchy of feared situations in the absence of adverse consequences represents a basic paradigm for the extinction of classically conditioned fear. The use of anxiety-inhibiting responses in *in vivo* desensitization is thought to facilitate this fear-reduction process. Wolpe (1958) employed relaxation as an anxiety-inhibiting response in his imaginal "systematic desensitization" treatment, and referred to the fear-reducing mechanism as *reciprocal inhibition*. The notion of reciprocal inhibition, which was derived from a neurological model, is expressed as follows: "If a response inhibitory to anxiety can be made to occur in the presence of anxiety-evoking stimuli, it will weaken the connection between these stimuli and the anxiety responses [Wolpe, 1962, p. 562]." The same principle has been referred to as *counterconditioning,* whereby "the neutralization of aversive stimuli results from the evocation of incompatible responses which are strong enough to supersede anxiety reactions to these stimuli [Davison, 1968, p. 92]." That cognitive processes may play an important role in desensitization therapy has also been suggested and debated (cf. Davison, 1969; Folkins, Evans, Opton, & Lazarus, 1969; Folkins, Lawson, Opton, & Lazarus, 1968). Finally, to the extent that the treatment includes reinforcement of behavioral progress, according to the operant paradigm, this would be expected to promote and maintain increased approach behaviors toward the feared stimuli (cf. Leitenberg, Agras, Barlow, & Oliveau, 1969).

Case Example

Gershman and Stedman (1971) described the successful treatment of a claustrophobic male through the use of oriental defense exercises as reciprocal inhibitors of anxiety within an *in vivo* desensitization framework. The 31-year-old patient experienced anxiety involving elevators, enclosed places, trains, buses, and locked rooms, with secondary generalization of anxiety to the wearing of tight-fitting clothes and his wedding ring. These maladaptive behaviors reportedly interfered with the patient's occupational adjustment and family life.

Initial interviews revealed that the patient "was a protégé of Kung Fu, liked to engage in this activity, and felt like a 'man' when he did [p. 117]." A trial test revealed that 1 min of Kung Fu reduced the patient's subjective anxiety from a moderate level to zero. It was therefore decided to employ Kung Fu to countercondition the claustrophobic anxiety. "We proposed to lock [the patient] in a room for progressively longer times, starting with 10 sec, and having him engage immediately in Kung Fu exercises as soon as the door was closed [p. 118]." At 10 sec the Kung Fu exercises eliminated his anxiety in one trial, and at 20 sec this was achieved in two trials. The treatment proceeded by gradually increasing the time spent in the locked room, and gradually reducing the time spent on Kung Fu exercises. It was reported that, "As the end of the hierarchy approached [the patient] was able to sit comfortably in the room reading a newspaper [p. 118]." The same method was then employed for the patient's fear of elevators, and "At the end of the second session in an elevator, he was able to go up and down at will [p. 118]."

Generalization of the phobic improvement was evidenced in the patient's ability to again wear tight clothing and his wedding ring. According to a 6-month follow-up, the recovery was maintained.

Representative Findings

Most of the evidence reported on the effects of *in vivo* desensitization treatments has been of a clinical nature. Probably the most widely cited case is that of a 3-year-old child named Peter who suffered from a fear of such things as rabbits, furry objects, feathers, frogs, and mechanical toys. A summary of his treatment by Mary Cover Jones was reported in J. B. Watson (1930). Feeding responses were used to help desensitize the child's phobic fears. He was seated in a highchair and given his midafternoon snack of crackers and milk while a rabbit in a wire cage was introduced into the long room at a sufficient distance not to disturb the child's eating. On successive days the rabbit was brought gradually closer and closer. "Finally the rabbit could be placed upon the table— then in Peter's lap. Next tolerance changed to positive reaction. Finally he would eat with one hand and play with the rabbit with the other . . . [p. 174]." Generalization tests revealed that Peter's fear of white rats was greatly improved, and he was no longer afraid of cotton, feathers, or a fur coat.

Wolpe (1958) reported several clinical examples of the use of assertive responses, sexual responses, or relaxation responses to promote "reciprocal inhibition in the life situation." One case involved a 39-year-old divorcée who was chronically "nervous and hypersensitive and perpetually worried about the future. Many ordinary situations . . . constituted stresses for her, made her anxious and left her fatigued, and sometimes produced epigastric pain [p. 138]." She responded very well to lessons in muscular relaxation which were begun in her seventh interview. The patient "deliberately calmed herself in an increasing range of situations, and their anxiety-evoking power waned and eventually disappeared. The patient had 13 interviews over four months, during which she entirely overcame her neurotic nervousness [p. 138]." A 5-year follow-up revealed no recurrence. Other cases involving *in vivo* desensitization with relaxation responses have also been reported by Wolpe (1969, 1973).

Two small-scale analogue studies were also supportive of the use of relaxation responses for purposes of *in vivo* desensitization. In a study by Cooke (1966), four female college students who were afraid of laboratory rats received four *in vivo* desensitization sessions at 3-day intervals. Performance of hierarchy items was alternated with periods of relaxation. Each item was repeated until there was no report of anxiety and the therapist observed no signs of anxiety. This approach led to a decrease on each of three measures of specific fear. In a pilot study by Garfield, Darwin, Singer, and McBrearty (1967), three undergraduate students who reported extreme fear of snakes showed a reduction in phobic avoidance behavior after eight hours of therapy time. This included relaxation training and four *in vivo* training sessions. While the *in vivo* training was reported to consist of "exposure to the phobic objects at controlled distances not in fantasy or imagination but in the 'real life' situation [p. 517]," the role of relaxation during these *in vivo* sessions was not detailed.

Lazarus (in Wolpe & Lazarus, 1966) described the therapeutic use of sexual responses within an *in vivo* desensitization framework in the treatment of a young married couple having sexual difficulties. The wife suffered severe pain during intercourse and the husband suffered from premature ejaculation. At a joint interview, the couple was instructed to resume lovemaking limited to kissing and caressing. "A week later they were advised to extend their range of physical attentions but never to proceed beyond the point where *both* remained entirely at ease and free from anxiety. They were informed that the act of coitus should not be attempted until both had attained manually induced orgasms [p. 111]."

This general strategy, together with specific instruction in sexual techniques, eventually enabled the couple to attain mutual coital satisfaction which reportedly was maintained through a 5-year follow-up.

The use of *in vivo* emotive imagery to control anxiety related to childbirth, and to minor medical and dental problems, was described by Horan (1976). The report includes the narrative of a relaxation-producing scene which dental patients were asked to imagine while their teeth were being cleaned. In a pilot study, visualizing the scene was found to reduce the heart rates of four subjects during teeth cleaning.

Goldstein *et al.* (1970) described the use of induced anger as a reciprocal inhibitor of fear. Interventions involving at least some *in vivo* desensitization were reported as successful in the treatment of a 34-year-old woman suffering from fear of "losing her balance, falling, or if away from home, being unable to return," and of a 25-year-old woman suffering from "feelings of personal insecurity, fear of rejection, and low self esteem [p. 68]." The authors noted that there appeared to be two factors which were occasionally responsible for the ineffectiveness of using induced anger as a reciprocal inhibitor of fear: "The first was an absence in the patient of felt emotion when acting out the verbal and motor components of anger. . . . The second source of failure was guilt or anxiety attached to the expression of anger [p. 70]."

Another example of the use of aggressive responses was reported by Gershman and Stedman (1971). They described the successful treatment of a 28-year-old man suffering from fears of flying. Six months after the treatment, which included *in vivo* Karate exercises as reciprocal inhibitors of anxiety, "the patient stated that he was flying without anxiety [p. 119]."

There have been several clinical reports of the use of drugs to control anxiety during the *in vivo* desensitization of fear reactions. Wolpe (1958) described the successful treatment by Rachman of a patient suffering from agoraphobia. "Altogether he had 9 treatments in the course of $2\frac{1}{2}$ months, and the range of his excursions progressively increased [p. 203]" while the dosage of demerol (a relaxant) was progressively decreased. Wolpe (1969) also reported the successful use of librium-related drugs in treatments conducted by G. E. Miller, who stated that "The medication was taken only for the purpose of desensitization and never on a routine basis. The patients 'planned' a phobic exposure, took the medication and waited until it began to exert its effect and then exposed themselves to the phobic situation (in real life, not in fantasy) [Wolpe, 1969, pp. 182–183]." Wolpe (1969) also described his own successful use of librium in the treatment of a physician suffering from a severe emotional reaction to noise. The patient was advised to take 30 mg of librium "in every circumstance in which he could anticipate being exposed to any considerable amount of [automobile] honking. This schedule led to very marked improvement without the drug in the course of four months [p. 183]."

Yeung (1968) summarized his successful treatment of two phobic patients with whom diazepam (valium) was administered intravenously prior to *in vivo* exposure to the feared stimuli. The drug was employed on one occasion with the first patient, a 45-year-old man with lifelong claustrophobic symptoms, and on two occasions with the other patient, a 19-year-old woman who suffered from a fear of snakes since childhood. Prior to *in vivo* desensitization with diazepam, each of these patients had made only limited progress with several sessions of imaginal desensitization in which methohexitone sodium (brevital), a short-acting barbiturate, had been administered intravenously. Yeung cited several reasons why diazepam may be more effective than methohexitone for purposes of phobic desensitization, one of which concerned the site of action and its influence on the learning process. There is still disagreement as to which drug should be the preferred agent for desensitization, though, because Munjack (1975) successfully employed intravenous methohexitone for the *in vivo* desensitization of a 32-year-old woman suffering from multiple phobias. Substantial improvement was evidenced within 10 sessions, which included "Gradual withdrawal of the drug during prolonged exposure [which] apparently facilitated transfer of the medication's antianxiety effects to the nondrug state [p. 543]." The durability of improvement was confirmed at an 18-month follow-up.

A comprehensive investigation by Hafner and Marks (1976) provided for, among other things, a comparison of *in vivo* group desensitization with and without oral diazepam. Other factors included group versus individual exposure, and high versus medium anxiety arousal during individual exposure. Fifty-seven chronic agoraphobic patients received 12 hr of *in vivo* exposure to situations involving various travel activities at increasing distances from the hospital. The treatments were carried out on 4 days over 2 weeks. Findings indicated that "patients in all treatment conditions improved significantly in phobias and in related life areas [p. 71]." While diazepam patients experienced less discomfort than placebo patients during the group exposure treatment, improvements of patients in both conditions were comparable and were maintained through a 6-month follow-up. Since diazepam did not facilitate treatment outcome, it was concluded that "the most economical and effective clinical practice is to treat phobics by prolonged exposure in cohesive groups, with emphasis on remaining in the phobic situation, but without undue attempt at anxiety-provocation [p. 87]."

Appraisal

While the literature is replete with case illustrations demonstrating various *in vivo* desensitization treatments, there is a void of experimental evidence concerning *in vivo* desensitization and its effects. Case examples serve a useful purpose in detailing the application of innovative treatments, but lacking adequate controls, such examples cannot establish the role of any particular treatment component in promoting clinical improvement. Furthermore, as "successful" cases are much more likely to appear in the literature than "unsuccessful" cases, it is not possible with case reports alone to estimate the probable effectiveness of any of these *in vivo* desensitization treatments.

Since *in vivo* desensitization consists basically of gradual exposure to real phobic situations while experiencing emotional responses incompatible with anxiety, a basic issue is whether the inclusion of anxiety-inhibiting responses adds anything to the efficacy of gradual exposure alone. In the study by Hafner and Marks (1976), the use of the drug diazepam as an anxiety-inhibiting agent did not appear to enhance the effectiveness of the *in vivo* exposure treatment with agoraphobic patients. This and other strategies used to generate anxiety-inhibiting responses for purposes of *in vivo* desensitization require further investigation under controlled conditions. Since it is unlikely that all phobic problems of all individuals will respond equally well to the array of *in vivo* desensitization approaches, future research should be concerned also with identifying variables which might be predictive of an individual's responsiveness to one or another of the alternative strategies.

Sherman (1973) discussed some specific issues related to the use of anxiety-inhibiting responses for purposes of phobic desensitization. The assumed incompatibility between the anxiety-inhibiting responses and the phobic fear constitutes the rationale for employing the former to counteract the latter. The phobic stimuli are confronted gradually to maintain the evoked fear at a minimal level so it will be neutralized by the anxiety-inhibiting responses. However, suppose that, on a particular occasion, the magnitude of the evoked fear disrupts the relaxation responses, feeding responses, or sexual responses, that had been employed as anxiety-inhibitors. For example, in the case of an animal-phobic youngster receiving *in vivo* desensitization with feeding responses, suppose the presentation of a small animal evokes enough anxiety to disturb the child's eating. From the learning-theory standpoint, it might be predicted that the fear responses would become conditioned inadvertently to the eating situation so that the child might experience fear about eating in the same or similar situations in the future. In other words, the conditioning could backfire. In view of this possibility, and in the absence of definitive evidence to the contrary, the practitioner is advised to exercise caution when using a method of *in vivo* desensitization with incompatible responses. While the use of anxiety-inhibiting responses may at times facilitate the process of fear reduction normally expected with gradual exposure, special vigilance may be required to avoid iatrogenic effects.

In Vivo Therapist Involvement

The two approaches to be considered presently include some of the procedures used in other *in vivo* interventions for phobic reactions, but are distinguished by their deliberate use of the therapist as a central component of the treatment process. **Participant modeling** (Bandura, 1971, 1976), also known as **contact desensitization** (Ritter, 1968), is a well-documented approach emphasizing therapist involvement. Initially, the therapist serves as a model in demonstrating safe interaction with the feared objects or situations, and then guides the client in performing the same sequence of graded activities. As treatment continues, the amount of demonstration, protection, and guidance is gradually decreased until the client can confront the feared situations comfortably and effectively. **Contextual therapy** (Zane, n.d.) also requires active therapist involvement, not just to facilitate the client's gradual exposure to the feared situations but also to help the client attend to the cognitive and affective changes that accompany such exposure. In both approaches, the object of the phobic reaction would determine whether the treatment should be conducted in the natural environment, or whether the feared stimuli should be presented within an office treatment setting. These *in vivo* treatments emphasizing therapist involvement have been used successfully for phobic reactions in children as well as adults.

Basic Procedure

In participant modeling, the therapist structures the environment and uses various techniques to induce the client to perform appropriately:

> The therapist first models threatening activities in easily mastered steps. Clients then enact the modeled conduct with appropriate guidance until they can perform it skillfully and fearlessly.... Joint performance with the therapist, who offers physical assistance if necessary, enables fearful clients to engage in threatening activities which they refuse to do on their own. Graduated subtasks and performances for increasingly longer periods can be used to ensure continuous progress should difficulties arise [Bandura, 1977, pp. 83–84].

The demonstration and guidance are phased out gradually until the situations can be confronted effectively without assistance. Throughout the process, the client's efforts are prompted and socially reinforced by the therapist's encouragement and approval. Bandura (1977) maintains that "Through this form of treatment incapacitated clients lose their fears, become able to engage in activities they formerly inhibited, and develop more favorable attitudes toward the things they abhorred [p. 84]."

According to Zane (n.d.), contextual therapy "derives its mode of treatment and its ideas from direct observation of moment to moment sequential *changes* in human phobic behavior in their contexts [p. 1]." After discussion of the nature and history of the phobic reaction as well as the procedures, rationale, and goals of the contextual approach, the client is given a list of suggestions to make it easier to remain in the phobic situation. These include directives to "Expect fear to arise unexpectedly" and, when it does, "Let it be." The client is advised to "Try to remain focused on things in the present" and to "Label the level of fear from 0 to 10. Watch it go up and down." The client is further instructed to "Find things to do that keep the level of fear manageable. . . . Do *not* try to eliminate fear completely [p. 10]." Whenever possible, the therapist accompanies the patient into the phobic situation "to observe, question, suggest, support, guide, inform and protect [p. 10]." With the therapist's assistance, the client is trained to recognize the external factors influencing changes in his task-directed behavior and to report the feelings, thoughts, imagery, and bodily sensations which accompany such changes. This information about overt and covert reactions, and their degree of task appropriateness, is used to help the patient select and prepare for successive steps of gradual confrontation with the feared situations.

Rationale

The processes involved in behavioral and attitudinal change associated with the participant modeling approach were conceptualized by Bandura (1971) as follows:

> Repeated modeling of approach responses, mainly through its informative function, decreases the arousal potential of aversive stimuli below the threshold for activating avoidance responses, thus enabling persons to engage, albeit somewhat anxiously, in approach behavior. Whenever vicarious extinction alone does not restore desired behavior, physical guidance, through its reassuring and protective functions, serves as an additional means of reducing fear arousal and facilitating performance of previously inhibited responses. Direct contact with threats that are no

longer objectively justified provides a variety of new experiences which, if favorable, further extinguish residual anxiety and avoidance tendencies.... After approach behavior toward formerly avoided objects has been fully restored, the resultant new experiences give rise to substantial reorganization of attitudes [pp. 688–689].

It is noteworthy that, within this formulation, attitudinal improvements are viewed as **following** behavioral improvements. This is somewhat in contrast with the apparent perspective on phobic reactions underlying contextual therapy. Zane, a psychoanalyst who developed this approach, maintains that

Studies of sequential changes in fearful behavior reveal dynamic relationships of cognition and behavior not otherwise observable. Fearful behavior gets worse when conditions cause involvement with fearful, unrealistic cognition which is a product of an unrealistic belief system.... Changing levels of fear . . . [result] from a mixture in varying strengths of derivatives of both coexisting unrealistic belief systems and realistic belief systems.... When running away or avoidance becomes the habitual response, a trusted person's presence may be essential to restore for the panicky person the operations of his realistic belief system in the fearful situation. Then, with the level of fear reduced and with realistic cognitive elements available to react to, new comforting observations and learning can take place [Zane, 1976, pp. 15–16].

In its focus upon cognitive factors influencing behavioral changes in the present environment, contextual therapy represents a departure from the traditional psychoanalytic emphasis upon historic and symbolic factors in the etiology of the phobic reaction.

Case Example

Descriptions of participant modeling are widely dispersed in the literature (e.g., see Ritter, 1969a, for a detailed case study of a street-crossing phobia; also, many of the studies identified under Representative Findings illustrate the approach). Therefore, it will be more informative for present purposes to provide an illustration of contextual therapy because of its greater novelty. The case examples available (Zane, n.d., 1976) consist largely of transcriptions of dialogues taking place during treatment sessions, and serve (with the therapist's commentary) to illustrate the process of therapy rather than the complete treatment.

Zane (1976) presented the case of a 6½-year-old boy who suffered from a phobic fear of walking in grass, an activity which he persistently avoided. The child reportedly could not talk about his fear or his avoidance behavior. On one occasion, while the therapist observed from the edge of a field, the child walked into the grass with his father. Some of the child's apprehensiveness was reflected in his inquiry about "white stuff" which turned out to be dead leaves of grass. As they were leaving the field, the father said, "See this grass isn't bad, is it?" and the child responded "No." In the ensuing discussion with the therapist, the child is quoted as saying, "I'm really not afraid of the grass but all I'm afraid of is the things in it—like mushrooms. And I just feel like when you get in a certain distance from it the stick'll go up and it'll get wide and these walls will come out . . . sort of—like arms—it'll grab me and put it in a box and close up. . . ." When the therapist asked whether the child ever saw that happen, the child said "No . . . I just think that." In response to continued inquiry, the child said "To tell you the truth I really only think that. . . . But—I also believe it! [pp. 10–11]."

In his analysis of the event, Zane discussed the influences of the child's realistic and unrealistic belief systems. In his view, being in the grass with a trusted person enabled the child to act and communicate reasonably, which reflects the dominance of his realistic belief system.

> Afterwards, in our presence, he disclosed how powerfully his unrealistic belief system dominated his cognition and behavior and created terror when he was in the grass alone. . . . He will need many more personal experiences that discriminate imagery from reality before he will be able to construct his realistic belief system about the grass that will be stronger than his unrealistic belief system when he is alone [pp. 11–12].

Parenthetically, Zane noted that ultimately this did happen. The experience in the field represented "the beginning of a process that eventually resulted in an enduring realistic belief system about the grass and a long term realistic change in behavior [p. 12]."

Representative Findings

A number of studies have provided evidence supporting the efficacy of participant modeling or contact desensitization. This approach, consisting of live modeling combined with guided participation, was investigated with snake-phobic subjects by Bandura, Blanchard, and Ritter (1969). It was compared to symbolic modeling, in which subjects observed a film showing models interacting with a snake, and to imaginal systematic desensitization. While subjects in the latter two conditions generally showed more behavioral and attitudinal improvement than no-treatment controls, participant modeling proved to be the most effective approach. It was also the most efficient treatment, requiring only 2 hours and 10 min distributed over several sessions. Behavioral improvements were maintained as of a 1-month follow-up assessment, and many subjects also reported that their fear reductions had generalized to snakes encountered in naturalistic situations.

Several additional studies have also found participant modeling to be more effective than other strategies in improving phobic behavior. While the use of token or money reinforcement for approaching a harmless snake promoted little improvement in subjects participating in a study by Rimm and Mahoney (1969), marked improvement (which generalized to a nontreatment snake) were exhibited after only 40 min of participant modeling. Also working with snake-phobic subjects, Thase and Moss (1976) found guided participant modeling to be more effective than covert modeling procedures in reducing avoidance behavior. Contact desensitization has also been used successfully with a population of mildly retarded subjects in a study by Peck (1977), where it was found more effective and efficient than vicarious symbolic desensitization and systematic desensitization in reducing fears of heights and fears of rats.

According to three studies by Ritter (1968, 1969b, 1969c), physical contact with the therapist in shaping approach responses to feared stimuli or situations appears to be an important component of the contact desensitization treatment. This was true in the group treatment of preadolescent children with fears of snakes (Ritter, 1968), group treatment of acrophobic adults (Ritter, 1969b), and individual treatment of acrophobic adults (Ritter, 1969c).

Increased "response induction aids," in the form of such things as small and large snakes, lightweight and heavyweight gloves, and varying degrees of therapist control of the snake, appear to contribute to the efficacy of participant modeling in the treatment of adult snake-phobic subjects (Bandura, Jeffery, & Wright, 1974). That study also suggested that self-directed practice may help to extinguish residual fears and reinforce personal mastery after the participant modeling has restored inhibited approach behavior. The role of self-directed practice was further explored by Bandura, Jeffery, and Gajdos (1975) in another study with snake-phobic subjects. Following the participant modeling treatment, some subjects spent an additional hour interacting on their own with the same snake used in treatment, while others spent the hour interacting with an unfamiliar snake as well. The self-directed practice was basically unstructured, although the protective aids (e.g., gloves) were available and the therapist was present for the initial part of the practice session. Compared to subjects who received participant modeling alone, subjects who received, in addition, self-directed practice "displayed more generalized behavioral changes, greater fear reduction, higher levels of self-competency, and less fear of threats beyond the one specifically

treated. Self-directed performance with a familiar threat, however, extinguished fears more thoroughly and induced a stronger sense of self-
competency than did coping independently with varied threats [p. 141]."
Further support for the use of self-directed practice was provided in a
study by Smith and Coleman (1977) who worked with females afraid of
rats and mice.

Also relevant to the evaluation of participant modeling is the identification of factors or variables which do not appear to influence the efficacy of the treatment. Rimm and Medeiros (1970), working with snake-
phobic females, found that training in muscular relaxation did not augment the effectiveness of participant modeling, which alone produced "a
very large, generalizable and lasting reduction in snake avoidance behavior [p. 127]." That contact desensitization does not owe its effectiveness to the influence of expectancy and demand characteristics was suggested in a study of female rat-phobics reported by Lick and Bootzin
(1970). The factor of active versus passive participation during contact
desensitization has also been found irrelevant to the overall efficacy of
the treatment in improving children's fears of snakes (Murphy &
Bootzin, 1973). In the active condition, children gradually approached
the snake, whereas in the passive condition, the snake was gradually
brought to the children. It was concluded that "*in vivo* interaction with
feared stimuli is such an effective and efficient technique that the type
of subject participation (active or passive) is of little consequence [p.
210]."

In contrast to participant modeling, contextual therapy is a relatively
new treatment for which only clinical evidence appears to be available.
Zane (1976) attempted to illustrate the process of therapy with transcriptions of dialogue selected from the individual treatments of four
children, three who suffered from fear of the dark and one who was
afraid of walking in grass. Another illustration of the therapy process
was provided in connection with the treatment of a woman with a
longstanding fear of snakes (Zane, n.d.).

In 1971, Zane and his associates established a phobia clinic at White
Plains Hospital in New York. According to his report (Zane, n.d.),
"During the past year two groups totalling 20 patients have been
treated, each for a limited 10 and 12 week period. The first was made up
of people with elevator phobias and the other with varied types of
phobias. Many patients had multiple phobias and previous psychotherapy [p. 11]." Each patient had an individual therapist (a student or
volunteer) who accompanied the patient into the phobic situation once
per week for about 90 min "to help him develop, select and engage in

the steps that he needed to progress towards the therapeutic objective [p. 11]." In addition, 90-min meetings of each group were held weekly with all patients and therapists present; here patients "shared their experiences in trying to cope with their phobic reactions in the phobic situation [p. 11]." These group sessions were found to have a "remarkable therapeutic and motivating effect [p. 11]." According to Zane, even though phobic responses continue to occur at times, all 20 patients "have shown marked improvement objectively and subjectively in their ability to cope with phobic situations of significance to them [p. 11]."

Appraisal

The efficacy of participant modeling has been supported in a number of analogue studies involving the laboratory treatment of recruited subjects with fears of such things as snakes and rats. With these populations, it appears to be a very (and possibly the most) effective and efficient mode of intervention. Whether the approach can be expected to be equally effective with severe phobias in patients seeking clinical treatment still appears to be an open question. From the conceptual standpoint, reason for optimism may reside in the wide array of procedural components which together constitute participant modeling. The treatment includes live modeling by the therapist, prompting, physical guidance, gradual exposure, *in vivo* contact, protective aids, shaping of skills, repeated rehearsal, performance feedback, social reinforcement, and self-directed practice. Some of these elements play a central role in other treatment approaches, including the *in vivo* phobic treatments previously discussed. It remains for future research to isolate the essential components of participant modeling, and to identify its limitations. It is apparent that certain features of the treatment would be more difficult to implement with some fear reactions (e.g., test anxiety; fear of public speaking) than has been the case with fears of snakes or rats. It is also possible that basic research on selected components may permit refinements in those components that will augment their contribution to the efficacy of the treatment. This is especially true for variables which are under the therapist's deliberate control. For example, Goldstein, Martens, Hubben, Van Belle, Schaaf, Wiersma, and Goedhart (1973) examined the effects of several variables in the use of modeling to promote independent behavior in clinical patients. In one study with neurotic outpatients, it was found that, although "trait structuring" of the model as "warm" did not increase the modeling influence, "cold" structuring had a detrimental effect. Since modeling represents a central component of a number of treatment approaches including participant modeling, in-

vestigations such as this which enhance our understanding of the modeling influence can have wide therapeutic impact.

Contextual therapy evolved from a different perspective than participant modeling but, as an *in vivo* approach emphasizing therapist involvement, it shares many of the same procedural features. It is distinguished by its attempt to focus the client's attention on the cognitive
and affective changes that accompany the *in vivo* exposure. Whether this
cognitive focus adds to the therapeutic efficacy of the other basic components, or detracts from them, remains an open question. Controlled
research clearly is needed. It may also be relevant to consider the differential applicability of participant modeling and contextual therapy
from the perspective of the congruence of their underlying theories with
the conceptual orientations of diverse practitioners and clients. Behaviorally oriented people might prefer participant modeling with its
emphasis on extinguishing fear and shaping approach responses; psychodynamically oriented people might instead prefer contextual therapy
with its concern about realistic and unrealistic belief systems. Systematic examination of ideological preferences and their influence on treatment efficacy seems especially warranted here where two procedurally
similar approaches are derived from contrasting conceptual models.

Flooding In Vivo

This approach to phobic treatment differs from other *in vivo* behavioral approaches in the degree of anxiety evoked during the therapy
process. Several treatments have been described which attempt to
minimize the anxiety by providing for brief, graded exposures to mildly
feared stimuli, sometimes accompanied by anxiety-inhibiting responses.
In contrast, the present approach requires direct confrontations with
highly feared situations, usually for prolonged periods in which strong
anxiety is experienced initially and then gradually dissipates. The basic
procedure has been called *flooding in vivo* (e.g., Antman, 1973; Emmelkamp & Wessels, 1975; Naud, Boisvert, & Lamontagne, 1973; Nesbitt, 1973; Rainey, 1972; Wolpe, 1969, p. 191), and has also been referred to as treatment by *prolonged exposure* (e.g., J. P. Watson, Gaind,
& Marks, 1972). While the approach has been employed primarily with
phobic fears, it has also been used occasionally with obsessive–compulsive reactions. The emotional stress that is central to the therapy process
would probably limit the approach to clients who are very highly motivated. Often these will be people for whom other treatments had been
ineffective. Caution is also necessary in conducting the treatment, because there are examples in the literature of clients whose conditions got

worse as a result of the flooding strategy. As with other *in vivo* phobic treatments, the therapy setting would depend largely upon the nature of the fear reaction.

Basic Procedure

The essential feature of the *in vivo* flooding procedure involves keeping the phobic client in contact with the real feared objects or situations for extended periods of time. Since highly feared stimuli are used from the outset, this confrontation will evoke strong anxiety feelings. The client is expected to continue to experience the dysphoric affect without having the option of escaping from the situation. In successful cases, the magnitude of the anxiety gradually decreases with the prolonged exposure. The confrontation process is then repeated using other stimuli which represent variations on the phobic theme. The treatment is continued until the client no longer experiences distress in relation to the previously feared situations.

Sometimes the *in vivo* flooding is preceded by flooding in fantasy (e.g., Boulougouris & Bassiakos, 1973; Everaerd *et al.*, 1973). The degree and nature of therapist involvement has also been manipulated in an attempt to augment the treatment's effectiveness, as with therapist modeling (e.g., Antman, 1973), coaxing (e.g., Nesbitt, 1973), and social reinforcement (e.g., Naud *et al.*, 1973). There has also been considerable variability in the duration of stimulus exposures employed in flooding treatments. Marks (1975) provided a detailed review of these and other variables relevant to exposure treatments, including flooding.

Rationale

It is ordinarily assumed that the process of extinction underlies the effects of the flooding treatment. Phobic reactions involve specific fears which are unrealistic or out of proportion to actual circumstances. The phobic person typically avoids situations in which the feared stimuli are likely to be encountered, so that the essential harmlessness of the stimuli is never experienced. When avoidance or escape is prevented, as in the flooding treatment, the individual is confronted directly with the feared stimuli; in the absence of adverse consequences, it is expected that the fear evoked by the stimuli will gradually extinguish.

It should be noted that not all theorists endorse the extinction explanation. In particular, Wolpe (1973) has argued that it is "unlikely that experimental extinction can be the mechanism of the favorable effects of flooding [p. 196]." Instead, Wolpe suggests that the sustained stimulation in flooding produces an "anxiety-response inhibition" which may account for the apparent reduction in fear.

Case Example

Yule, Sacks, and Hersov (1974) described the successful *in vivo* flooding treatment of an 11-year-old boy with a severe noise phobia. *In vivo* desensitization had previously enabled the child to overcome his fear of cap gun blasts and other loud noises, but he continued to be afraid of balloons bursting. He could not attend children's parties, and was worried that boys at his new school would discover his fear.

The therapist explained at the outset that the treatment would be unpleasant for a short time, but the child still desired to try it. He was placed in a very small room, and about 50 inflated balloons were then brought in. The child "cowered into his chair, started to sweat and shake, and put his fingers into his ears [p. 210]." The therapist then began bursting a few of the balloons, and the child began to cry. The therapist continued bursting balloons until the child no longer flinched.

Next, after much persuasion, the child used his feet to push balloons against a nail that was held by the therapist. Twenty balloons were burst in this manner, by which time the child no longer flinched. Verbal pressure then induced the child to burst balloons with one hand while keeping the other hand over one ear, and finally to burst balloons while both ears were uncovered. In the 90 min of the first session, about 220 balloons were broken. Although "a little shaken" by the experience, the child agreed to return for another session the next day.

About 320 more balloons were burst during the second session, which lasted 45 min. Initially the child was still anxious, but verbal persuasion coupled with actual prompting "soon had him bursting the balloons with occasional signs that he was actually enjoying the experience [p. 210]." By the end of the session "he was bursting balloons next to his uncovered ears, bursting them with his bare hands, and stamping on them in a determined fashion [p. 210]." No signs of the child's former noise phobia were evident in a follow-up 25 months later.

In concluding, the authors noted that "there appears to be a watershed during treatment after which anxiety rapidly diminishes and the subject becomes increasingly confident in his responses to the phobic stimulus. It seems imperative not to terminate the treatment until this stage has been reached [p. 211]." Because the flooding treatment is unpleasant for client and therapist alike, the authors indicated that ordinarily they would still try a desensitization strategy first.

Representative Findings

Several case reports in the literature illustrate the use of *in vivo* flooding with different phobic reactions. Antman (1973) described the treatment of a 29-year-old woman who had a chronic, incapacitating fear of worms and snakes. By the end of six therapy sessions involving 10 hours of *in vivo* flooding combined with some therapist modeling, the patient reportedly showed a marked reduction in her phobic behavior. A 24-year-old female with an intense fear and aversion of escalators was successfully treated with one 29-min session of *in vivo* flooding combined with some coaxing and reassurance by the therapist (Nesbitt, 1973). The patient's freedom from anxiety was maintained through a 6-month follow-up "except on rare occasions when descending [p. 406]." The successful treatment of a firearm phobia in a 43-year-old policeman was described by Naud *et al.* (1973). The phobia originated from a traumatic experience during a robbery 18 months earlier. After one 66-min session of *in vivo* flooding combined with modeling and social reinforcement, avoidance responses toward the phobic object disappeared and the client reported an absence of phobic anxiety. According to a 5-month follow-up the improvement in his firearm phobia had been maintained, but he still suffered from free-floating anxiety.

Agoraphobic patients were the subjects in two experiments comparing flooding with other behavioral approaches to phobic treatment. Flooding sessions were ordinarily 45 min in fantasy followed by 45 min *in vivo*. In the study by Everaerd *et al.* (1973), flooding was compared with a "successive approximation" approach in a crossover research design. Both treatment methods promoted significant improvement on some measures, with few differences between them. In the study by Emmelkamp (1974), flooding was compared with a "self-observation" approach consisting essentially of gradual *in vivo* exposure. Self-observation differs from successive approximation in that, with self-observation, the client monitors his own progress and is not reinforced by the therapist. Results indicated that both flooding and self-observation promoted significant improvement on several measures, with no differences between the treatments. It was also found that a combination of the two treatments tended to be more effective than either alone.

The physiological habituation of ten phobic patients was evaluated during prolonged exposure to phobic situations in fantasy and in reality (Watson *et al.*, 1972). Noteworthy was the finding that, even after habituation to the imagined stimuli, physiological responses were still evoked by exposure to the real situations. With continued exposure, the latter tended to habituate as well. The importance of the *in vivo* component was also demonstrated in a clinical study by Emmelkamp and Wessels (1975) working with agoraphobic patients. They found that "prolonged exposure *in vivo* plainly proved to be superior to flooding in the imagination [p. 7]." Interventions involving an *in vivo* flooding component have also been reported useful in the treatment of certain patients suffering from obsessive–compulsive reactions (e.g., Boulou-

gouris & Bassiakos, 1973; Hackmann & McLean, 1975; Rachman, Hodgson, & Marks, 1971; Rainey, 1972).

It should be emphasized that *in vivo* flooding sessions can be very
stressful for the client, and often for the therapist as well. It is not uncommon for the approach to meet with client resistance, and there are
also reports of patients who have gotten worse as a result of prolonged
exposure to feared situations. For example, Wolpe (1969, p. 192) described the case of a physician whose phobia for insane people became
exacerbated after continuous exposure to the presence of schizophrenic
patients. Emmelkamp (1974) noted difficulties encountered with several
agoraphobic patients who were treated by flooding procedures. A few
clients found it impossible to walk outside alone for 45 min (as required by the *in vivo* flooding procedure); they "came back in panic
after a few minutes and could not be persuaded to go out again immediately [p. 236]." Two of these patients decided to discontinue treatment after this unpleasant experience. Wolpe (1973) summarized his
impressions of the flooding approach as follows: "While I am now convinced of the wide efficacy of the method, and satisfied that the risks are
small, I still advocate a cautious attitude, for little is really known of the
ingredients for success, and prolonged *in vivo* exposure does exacerbate
some neuroses [p. 195]."

Appraisal

There is ample evidence that, under certain conditions and with certain patients, *in vivo* flooding can be a highly efficient and effective treatment for phobic reactions. It is also a stressful treatment, and there is
evidence that the prolonged exposure to feared stimuli may sensitize and
exacerbate the phobias of some people. It would appear that flooding has
little to recommend it over less unpleasant *in vivo* approaches which
keep anxiety at a minimum by employing gradual exposure to the feared
situations. Nevertheless, there are reports of patients who profited from
in vivo flooding after failing to improve with gradual exposure procedures. Unfortunately, there is no definitive information concerning individual variables which are differentially predictive of a person's likely
response to gradual versus flooding approaches. In the absence of prog-
nostic guidelines for practitioners, and considering the stress and occasional risk involved in pursuing the flooding approach, it would appear
that *in vivo* flooding ordinarily should be implemented only after less
stressful interventions have proven ineffective. Research is needed to
identify individual characteristics that are predictive of treatment responsiveness; this, together with further analysis and refinement of the
component features of *in vivo* flooding, could contribute substantially to

maximizing the effective use of this potent but stressful intervention procedure.

INSTRUMENTAL BEHAVIOR PROBLEMS

A great deal of human functioning involves behaviors which, either through their presence or absence, have an impact upon the individual's physical or social environments. Instrumental behavior *problems* sometimes arise when other people are adversely affected by the individual's actions or inactions. For example, a child's noisiness in the classroom may distress the teacher because it disrupts the class' learning activities. As another example, a retarded person's lack of basic self-care skills may represent a continuing burden for institutional staff who must wash, dress, and feed him. Problems involving such excesses or deficits in instrumental behaviors have often been alleviated through behavioral intervention programs administered in the problem environments. These *in vivo* programs typically control reinforcement contingencies and employ related techniques to decrease undesirable responses and to shape and maintain desirable ones. There is a substantial literature describing and illustrating how operant programs may be implemented in educational, clinical, and home settings (e.g., see books by Axelrod, 1977; Becker, 1971; Deibert & Harmon, 1973; Homme, 1970; Kazdin, 1975; Krumboltz & Krumboltz, 1972; Nay, 1976; Patterson & Gullion, 1971; Sulzer-Azaroff & Mayer, 1977; Williams, 1973), sometimes employing token economies to modify the behaviors of groups of people (e.g., see books by Ayllon & Azrin, 1968; Kazdin, 1977). The *Journal of Applied Behavior Analysis* is replete with demonstrations and research evaluations of operant interventions, and investigations in this area also appear in other journals concerned with behavioral treatments (e.g., *Behaviour Research and Therapy; Behavior Therapy; Journal of Behavior Therapy and Experimental Psychiatry; Behavior Modification*). While it is not possible in the present context to examine the entire area, two relatively new innovations are reviewed. "Overcorrection therapy" and the "bug-in-the-ear" technique each have a strong *in vivo* emphasis, as well as favorable evidence to encourage further explorations of their uses in modifying instrumental behavior problems.

Overcorrection Therapy

This *in vivo* treatment has been employed for a variety of instrumental behavior problems, including aggressive behaviors, toilet training, stealing, self-stimulatory behaviors, habitual vomiting, scavenging behavior, and public disrobing. Although the primary population has consisted of both children and adults with mental retardation, **overcorrection therapy** has also been used with autistic children, schizophrenic children, and schizophrenic adults. The intervention consists essentially of requiring the person to correct the environmental effects of the inappropriate act, actually leaving the situation in better condition than before, and then to learn and intensively practice correct behaviors to replace the problem behaviors in the real situations. For certain problems which have no adverse environmental consequences, such as self-stimulatory behaviors, the treatment may focus primarily on requiring intense practice of alternative, adaptive behaviors.

Basic Procedure

Overcorrection therapy has two basic components. The first, referred to as *restitutional overcorrection*, requires the person "to correct the consequences of his misbehavior by having him restore the situation to a state vastly improved from that which existed before the disruption [Foxx & Azrin, 1973, p. 2]." The second component, referred to as *positive practice overcorrection*, requires the person "intensively to practise overly correct forms of relevant behaviors [Foxx & Azrin, 1973, p. 2]." Depending on the nature of the problem behavior, either or both of these features may be emphasized in an overcorrection therapy program.

Foxx and Azrin (1972) described five general classes of disruptive behaviors together with restitution training procedures which were developed to deal with each of them:

1. Household orderliness training. Treatment of misbehavior which causes property disturbance should require that the offender "not only correct the specific disturbance he created in the household but should also improve its overall physical appearance [p. 17]."

2. Social reassurance (apology) training. Therapy for disruptive behavior that annoys or frightens people should require that the offender "reassure all fearful individuals that the misbehavior would not be repeated . . . [and] apologize to all persons present [p. 17]."

3. Oral hygiene training. Treatment of misbehaviors involving unhygienic oral contact, such as biting people or chewing objects, could include washing the offender's mouth with an oral antiseptic.

4. Medical assistance. A person whose inappropriate aggression results in injury to another person should be required "to assist in cleansing and medicating the wound, and in filling out the necessary reports [p. 17]."

5. Quiet training. Behaviors like shrieking or screaming which create a

general commotion "should be corrected and compensated for by a period of exceptional quiet. . . . in which the patient goes to a remote bedroom area where the shouting could not be heard and be required to remain quietly on a bed for a period of time before being allowed to return [p. 18]."

Foxx and Azrin (1972) recommended that positive reinforcement be avoided during the restitution period so that the problem behavior is not inadvertently reinforced. For some individuals, verbal instructions may be sufficient to insure compliance with the restitution requirements. "Another satisfactory alternative is physical guidance in which the educator manually guides the desired movements using as much bodily pressure as necessary but reducing such pressure immediately as the offender begins to perform the movement voluntarily [Foxx & Azrin, 1972, pp. 16–17]." It is expected that, eventually, the graduated guidance should become unnecessary as the behavior becomes more under the control of verbal instructions.

Rationale

According to Foxx and Azrin (1972), "The general rationale of the proposed restitution procedure is to educate the offender to assume individual responsibility for the disruption caused by his misbehaviour by requiring him to restore the disturbed situation to a greatly improved state [p. 16]." It is recommended that the restitution procedure be implemented with attention to certain characteristics, each of which has its own rationale:

1. The restitution should be directly related to the problem behavior so that it does not appear to be arbitrary or punitive, and so that the offender experience the effort normally required by others to correct the effects of the misbehavior.

2. The restitution should take place immediately after the offense so as to prevent the person from experiencing much satisfaction from the results of the offense and to maximize the impact of the punishing aspects of the restitution in discouraging future misbehavior.

3. The restitution should require continuous work and effort on the part of the offender in order to increase its impact as an inhibitory event.

4. The restitution should continue for a while, thereby representing a time out from reinforcement in which the offender is prevented from engaging in other activities that are rewarding (Foxx & Azrin, 1972).

Given the general aversiveness of the restitutional overcorrection, it would not be surprising if difficulties were encountered in getting offenders to perform the required corrective behaviors. As noted above, when verbal instructions alone do not suffice, it may be necessary to apply physical guidance to promote the restitutive performance. According to Foxx and Azrin (1972), the unpleasant aspects of being forced physically to engage in particular responses should motivate the person to initiate the actions voluntarily: "The two procedures of verbal instruction and graduated guidance in combination should constitute a conditioned avoidance situation and lead to the instructions alone being effective, since the instructions would become a signal that the graduated guidance could be avoided by voluntarily initiating the required response at that time [p. 17]."

The positive practice component of overcorrection therapy appears to be at least partly intended to teach the individual appropriate ways of behaving in the situations in which misbehaviors had occurred. Clearly, there is a punitive aspect to this component which, together with the aversiveness of restitutional overcorrection, serves to suppress the undesirable behavior. However, unlike treatments which employ only punishment contingencies, this also has an educational function in teaching the transgressor alternative behaviors which are more appropriate to the problem situations. Some investigators (e.g., Foxx, 1976a) appear to require staff to maintain a neutral posture in relating to the patient during an overcorrection intervention, apparently to avoid inadvertently reinforcing the person for misbehaving in the first place. While positive reinforcement for behavioral improvements may not be a formal feature of the therapy process, it would be expected that behavioral improvements which emerge would eventually encounter social approval from others in the person's daily environment.

Case Example

Foxx (1976a) described the successful use of overcorrection therapy to eliminate public disrobing by two institutionalized retarded women. One of these, Amy, was 52 years old, weighed 190 pounds, was epileptic, partially deaf, and profoundly retarded. A variety of previous attempts to control her stripping behavior had all been unsuccessful. This behavior, which had begun at the age of 12, was found to average about five occurrences per day during a baseline time-out condition.

An overcorrection intervention was then introduced whenever Amy was discovered nude. It included two basic components:

> (1) a Restitutional Overcorrection procedure that consisted of a required dressing in panties, bra, slip, panty hose and tie shoes in addition to the woman's normal ward clothing that consisted solely of a dress and (2) a Positive Practice Overcorrection procedure that required the stripper to

attend to the clothing needs and personal appearance of other ward residents by buttoning or zipping their unfastened clothing, straightening
rumpled or twisted clothing, furnishing footwear to those in bare feet and
combing tousled hair [Foxx, 1976a, p. 53].

Whenever Amy failed to follow the instructions, graduated guidance
was employed in which her hands were manually guided by the trainer,
as needed. While the staff was unable to establish complete verbal control over Amy's behavior during overcorrection, the necessary amount of
graduated guidance decreased over time.

The effects of the overcorrection treatment were evident from the
start. Stripping occurred only once on the first, third, fourth, and eighth
days of the intervention, and not at all on days nine through fourteen.
Reinstatement of the baseline time-out condition then led to a return of
the disrobing behavior, which occurred five times on the twenty-first
day. When overcorrection was reintroduced, disrobing decreased rapidly
and was entirely absent during the final 6 weeks of reported data
(through the eighty-fourth day).

Representative Findings

Overcorrection therapy has been employed successfully with a variety
of behavioral problems according to clinical reports appearing in the
behavioral literature. Foxx and Azrin (1972) described its application to
control aggressive and disruptive behaviors in three institutionalized
women; two of these were profoundly retarded while the third was
severely brain-damaged. The target behaviors included "physical assault,
property destruction, tantrums, continuous screaming, and biting, all of
which had resisted other treatments such as time-out, punishment and
social disapproval [p. 15]." Within one or two weeks, these behaviors
were virtually eliminated and maintained that way with minimal staff
attention. Klinge, Thrasher, and Myers (1975) reported the treatment of
a 34-year-old male, institutionalized with a diagnosis of chronic undifferentiated schizophrenia, whose highly disruptive behaviors included
"swearing, yelling insults at both staff and patients, and threatening to
blow up the clinic [p. 70]." As a result of a "bed-rest" overcorrection
procedure, the average daily frequency of disruptive outbursts was reduced from almost one per day to about one every five days.

Self-stimulatory behaviors represented the treatment targets in reports of the use of overcorrection therapy by Foxx and Azrin (1973) and
by Epstein, Doke, Sajwaj, Sorrell, and Rimmer (1974). According to
Foxx and Azrin (1973), the treatment was successfully applied "in a behavioral day-care program to three retarded children and one autistic

child who exhibited object-mouthing, hand-mouthing, head-weaving and hand-clapping [p. 1]." In the report by Epstein et al. (1974), the side effects of overcorrection in treating two schizophrenic boys at day-care centers were also examined.

> Results for both children indicated the "hand" overcorrection procedure suppressed inappropriate hand movements and inappropriate behaviors [e.g., foot movements] that were topographically dissimilar. In addition, inverse relationships were observed between the second child's inappropriate hand movements and appropriate toy usage [a positive side effect] during free play and between his inappropriate vocalizations and inappropriate foot movements [a negative side effect] during naptime [p. 385].

Harris and Romanczyk (1976) reported that overcorrection procedures produced rapid suppression of self-injurious behavior in an 8-year-old retarded boy who had been head-banging or chin-banging an average of 32 times per day prior to the intervention. It was also noted: "Overcorrection has a marked advantage in terms of staff implementation over other forms of punishment in that it is easily administered in all settings and is not physically dangerous [p. 239]." Overcorrection procedures were also represented in a toilet training program employed by Butler (1976) to enable a neurologically impaired 4½-year-old boy to gain substantial control over bladder functions.

Retarded adults represented the subjects of several other clinical reports in which overcorrection procedures were successfully employed to control problem behaviors. The target problems included habitual vomiting (Azrin & Wesolowski, 1975a), public disrobing (Foxx, 1976a), inattendance at a self-grooming class (Foxx, 1976b), and scavenging behavior consisting of rumaging for and eating such things as paper, cigarette butts, trash, and feces (Foxx & Martin, 1975).

Azrin and Wesolowski (1974, 1975b) described two studies in which overcorrection procedures were employed to change specific behaviors of large groups of retarded adults within the context of their institutional wards. The first study (Azrin & Wesolowski, 1974) focused upon stealing. Under a "simple" correction procedure in which the thief was required merely to return the stolen item, there was an average of 20 thefts per day among the 34 residents. When transgressions occurred under the **over**correction procedure, stealing was entirely eliminated by the fourth day. Here the overcorrection consisted of requiring the thief "to give his victim an item identical to the stolen one in addition to returning the stolen item [p. 577]." It was noted that the overcorrection treatment for stealing "should be especially effective when the victim is disliked by the thief, since the victim emerges from the overcorrection experience in a happier state, rather than the usual bereft condition [p. 580]."

The other group study (Azrin & Wesolowski, 1975b) employed overcorrection procedures to eliminate persistent floor sprawling on a ward with 28 profoundly retarded adults, of which 11 were common transgressors. In this case "the residents were given a period of required practice in seating themselves on several different chairs, this Positive Practice being given whenever the resident had been sprawling on the floor [p. 627]." After 8 days the problem was entirely eliminated, with no evidence of floor sprawling at a 6-month follow-up. As with many of the other reports in this area, it was pointed out that overcorrection had succeeded where other interventions had previously failed. In this case, sprawling on the floor had not been eliminated "by a program of intensive reinforcement for sitting on chairs, by making many more chairs available, nor by continually interrupting instances of floor sprawling [p. 627]."

While most of the reports on overcorrection therapy have been very favorable, there is one study which is less encouraging. Rollings, Baumeister, and Baumeister (1977) systematically evaluated the effects of overcorrection procedures intended to eliminate stereotyped behaviors like body-rocking and head-weaving in two retarded male adults. The basic findings were summarized as follows:

> (a) overcorrection procedures, applied contingently on the occurrence of stereotyped behavior, may produce deceleration in rate of that behavior, but the magnitude of the effect varies considerably between subjects; (b) punishment and non-punishment conditions are well discriminated by the subject, partly on the basis of trainer proximity; (c) increased collateral stereotypic and emotional responding may accompany deceleration of target behaviors; (d) no spontaneous generalization of suppression is observed from training to living areas; and (e) suppression effects obtained under the procedures employed here are not durable [pp. 42–43].

In attempting to account for the relative ineffectiveness of the interventions by Rollings et al. (1977), it is noteworthy that the overcorrection procedures here were conducted not in the in vivo ward living area by multiple staff, but rather in a separate laboratory room by only one "trainer." While this would not explain the emergence of negative side effects noted in (c) above, it could have reduced the generalizability and durability of the suppressive effects of the intervention. In fact, Rollings et al. (1977) concluded with a discussion of possible procedural improvements, including the recommendation that "To maximize generalization of the suppressive effects of overcorrection, training should be conducted by as many different trainers and in as many different situations as possible to prevent the subject from discriminating between 'safe' and 'unsafe' individuals and conditions [p. 45]."

Appraisal

There are many clinical reports on overcorrection therapy which suggest that this approach can be efficient and effective in controlling a variety of problem behaviors. Most of the reported work has focused upon retarded persons in institutional settings, whose deviant or disruptive behaviors can represent a continuing annoyance to staff and other patients. The attempt to "make the punishment fit the crime" is certainly not novel, but in overcorrection therapy it is carefully formulated, systematically applied, and usually provides for training in correct behaviors as well. There is some evidence to suggest that overcorrection therapy may be less effective when it is conducted in a laboratory setting than when it is conducted in the *in vivo* setting, but the latter has always been the more common practice anyway.

In several of the reports it was noted that overcorrection therapy succeeded after other behavioral strategies, such as time-out, punishment, or reinforcement of desirable behavior, had previously failed. It is not clear, however, why these other techniques, whose influence in controlling instrumental behaviors is well documented in the literature, were ineffective. Research is needed to generate guidelines for practitioners in deciding which of the array of alternative procedures, including overcorrection therapy, is likely to be most effective in controlling particular instrumental behaviors in particular individuals. As noted by Rollings *et al.* (1977), "In general, we may conclude that the overcorrection procedure is actually a very complex package of contingencies and that the effects on behavior may also be complex [p. 43]." The wealth of favorable clinical evidence should encourage further research to isolate the effective components of overcorrection therapy, to clarify the learning mechanisms involved, to identify the kinds of people and problems that are most likely to benefit from it, and to establish its limitations.

Bug-in-the-Ear Technique

The *bug-in-the-ear* is a small, wireless audio receiver which rests unobtrusively behind an ear of the person whose behavior is to be modified. It has been used to provide *in vivo* professional guidance and immediate reinforcement to parents who were being trained to improve their methods of encouraging and maintaining adaptive behaviors in their children. It has also been used to teach children to improve their own

behaviors and to shape and reinforce appropriate instrumental behaviors in their peers. While there are few illustrations in the literature
of the application of this technique, the available evidence is encouraging. There are also potential *in vivo* applications which remain to be
systematically explored. The device itself is available for purchase
through a commercial distributor, Farrell Instruments, Inc. (P. O. Box
1037, Grand Island, Nebraska 68801).

Basic Procedure

As described by Clement (1974), the bug-in-the-ear "is an especially
useful device for providing feedback to parents or children in a treatment situation as they attempt new ways of behavior. The bug is worn
by one person at a time, and only he can hear what the psychologist is
saying from behind a one-way mirror." This enables the therapist "to
deliver verbal prompts for what he wants the parent or child to do" and
to praise the person for exhibiting the appropriate behavior. "Thus, the
bug provides for immediate social reinforcement and focused feedback
to the subject who is interacting with other people [p. 88]."

Wimberger and Kogan (1974) reported examples of how the bug-in-
the-ear may be used to improve mother–child interactions by directing
changes in the mother's behavior while she is playing with her child.
The therapist's comments and suggestions to the mother are usually very
brief, and focus on interactional problems which were identified during
initial baseline sessions. The messages fall basically into three categories:
reinforcement, modeling, and teaching. Reinforcing statements are intended to increase appropriate behaviors in the mother. "A typical example here would be the therapist's responding to the mother's being a
good audience to or participant in the child's play, by using statements
like 'that's good,' or 'I like the way you help him with his play' [p.
637]."

With regard to modeling influences, the therapist's acceptance of the
mother plays an important part in promoting the mother's acceptance of
the child and the child's activities. In other words, through observing the
therapist's manner of relating effectively with her, the mother learns to
relate effectively with the child. This includes "taking the other person
seriously, . . . [paying] full attention, and . . . [making] an honest effort
to understand the other's point of view [p. 638]." Wimberger and Kogan
(1974) also provided examples of suggestions for alternative solutions
which might be used when corrective action seems indicated: " 'How
about letting him (the child) figure it out for himself' or 'Maybe Julie
could set the table in the dollhouse' [p. 638]."

The third message category, teaching, is similar in some respects to modeling, but emphasizes providing the mother with specific instructions on how to do something. "As an example, a mother who appears to be ignoring the child's activities may be told by the therapist: 'It's alright for you to work on your own drawing but be sure to pay some attention to what he is doing' [p. 638]." In the Wimberger and Kogan (1974) approach, sessions are sometimes videotape–recorded so that they can later be shown to both parents; with appropriate discussion, this facilitates the training of the parents and helps motivate them "to continue the newly acquired behavior at home in a generalized fashion [p. 638]."

The bug-in-the-ear technique has also been used by supervisors to train beginning therapists in how to conduct psychotherapy (Boylston & Tuma, 1972). This permits "instant communication with the trainee while the latter is working with a patient [p. 92]," in contrast to the more traditional supervisory approach in which the trainee and supervisor base their treatment discussions and strategies upon the trainee's recollection of prior therapy sessions. While Boylston and Tuma (1972) employed the bug-in-the-ear to help trainees learn to conduct traditional psychotherapy, it would seem that the same approach could be readily adapted to teach trainees the application of certain *in vivo* therapies as well.

Rationale

Essentially, the bug-in-the-ear is not itself a treatment but instead represents a technique for facilitating a variety of therapeutic interventions. The most common *in vivo* applications have involved teaching parents or children to improve their own behaviors and the instrumental behaviors of children with whom they interact. The rationale for employing the technique seems to reflect the view that immediate guidance and feedback on actual behavior occurring during the course of spontaneous interaction will be more effective in shaping and maintaining behavioral improvements than delayed feedback on self-reports of previous behaviors. These assumptions about the potential distortions in self-report, and the advantages of immediate feedback, are unlikely to be disputed by most people familiar with the psychological literature. As noted by Wimberger and Kogan (1974):

> Techniques that are based on the patient's reports are affected by his intellectual and emotional limits for this task. The therapist has to consider the factors influencing patient's reports, such as the patient's interactive behaviors with him. In contrast to this, the observation of ongoing behavior offers first-hand knowledge of the patients' behaviors [p. 639].

Additional assumptions appearing in articles concerning the bug-in-the-ear technique, and which seem to be implicit in the rationale for its use, include the following:

1. The therapist's messages to the mother provide her with a model for interacting with the child (Wimberger & Kogan, 1974);

2. Behaviors that are followed by positive social consequences will be strengthened (Clement, Roberts, & Lantz, 1976); and

3. Learning is facilitated by having the learner respond actively and try out new behaviors in the real situations (Clement *et al.*, 1976).

Case Example

Clement (1973) presented in detail the behavioral treatment of a kindergartener named Jeff who, according to reports by his mother and his teacher, was having serious social and academic difficulties. Therapy focused on increasing Jeff's appropriate social play and interactions with his peers, and had two basic components. The first component was a peer-therapy intervention conducted in a clinic; since the bug-in-the-ear technique played a major role in this component, it will be described in some detail. The other intervention component, which was introduced toward the end of the program, was conducted in the child's classroom.

Initially, mothers of some of Jeff's peers from his natural environment were requested to permit their children to participate as therapeutic agents in a special program to help Jeff. Despite considerable resistance, the therapist finally succeeded in recruiting the help of three boys and one girl. In the initial session at the clinic, the five children were placed in a large play therapy room, where they were observed so that certain behaviors could be recorded for baseline purposes. At the conclusion of that 1-hour session, the therapist

> entered the play therapy room and sat down with the children. I showed them the bug-in-the-ear ... and an Indian headdress that said "chief" across the front ... I explained that in the following week we would draw straws, and the winner would get to be chief and wear the secret "walkie-talkie" and get to pass out tokens to the other children. Everyone seemed very interested in the proposed game ... I explained to them that each week when they came, they would win tokens and get to spend them [for small candies and toys] in the "store" at the end of the hour [Clement, 1973, p. 25].

At the beginning of the next session, the children drew straws to establish the sequence of chiefs for that and subsequent sessions. Since Jeff was the winner for that session, the therapist

> placed the bug-in-the-ear on Jeff, keeping it in place with the Indian headdress, and gave him a bag of tokens. Then I left the playroom and entered

the observation room from which I could observe and coach by way of the microphone. I coached Jeff to give tokens to other children when they played cooperatively with each other, and to also verbalize why they were receiving the tokens. At the end of the session, Jeff got the same number of tokens as he had given the child who had received the most tokens for that session. This procedure was followed throughout the remainder of the sessions for each new chief [pp. 25–26].

Later on in the 15-week program, variations were introduced in the clinic intervention, and the classroom intervention was initiated. On a couple of occasions there was a return to baseline conditions. Specific target behaviors were systematically measured throughout the program during 20-min observation periods conducted during peer group therapy sessions in the clinic, and during unstructured play time in the classroom. The multiple repeated measures permitted the investigator to monitor an array of behaviors as a function of the conditions in effect at any time, revealing areas in which changes did and did not take place. For present purposes, the overall effects will be summarized. It was found that Jeff improved considerably in social play, which was the primary target behavior, and (together with his peers) also improved in some related behaviors. Unrelated behaviors which were not focused upon in the program (such as being noisy and disobeying commands) tended not to change. According to Clement (1973), "The data seemed clearly to indicate that peers can be trained to carry out effective interventions by the use of the bug-in-the-ear to provide ongoing coaching, and that when peers are used as therapeutic agents, treatment effects obtained in the clinic transfer to the target child's natural environment [p. 40]."

Representative Findings

Based upon their clinical experience employing the bug-in-the-ear as part of a program to teach mothers to relate more effectively with their children, Wimberger and Kogan (1974) reported that "our observation of change in the majority of our population is highly encouraging [p. 639]." Clement (1973, 1974) also endorsed the utility of the bug-in-the-ear based upon clinical experience employing the technique with parents and peers of child-clients. In addition to the encouraging clinical reports, some supportive evidence was derived from an experimental study conducted to evaluate approaches to the treatment of shy, withdrawn children (Clement et al., 1976). Two of the approaches employed the bug-in-the-ear.

In the "peer-therapist" condition, the bug was used to teach the children to use token and social reinforcers to encourage prosocial behaviors in their peers. The children took turns assuming the role of therapist, which included wearing a feathered headband identifying them as "chief." The group was observed from behind a one-way mirror so that one of the investigators could prompt and reinforce appropriate responses of the chief for the day. In the "mother-therapist" condition, the bug was similarly used to guide and socially reinforce mothers who took turns leading a group of children that included their own child. Twenty-eight socially withdrawn children averaging 8–9 years of age participated in groups of four each, for a total of 16 weekly 1-hour treatment sessions. A variety of behavioral and subjective measures were administered to assess the effects of these and other conditions. In general, it was found that children tended to improve from pretreatment to posttreatment, but not from posttreatment to follow-up 6 months later. Overall, the peer-therapist and mother-therapist approaches, both of which employed the bug-in-the-ear, were basically comparable in their effectiveness and superior to the control conditions. Less encouraging was the finding that behavioral changes evident within the context of therapy showed little generalization to extratherapy situations. In order to enhance generalization from clinical treatment, the investigators suggested in their concluding remarks that the target child be treated in a group consisting of peers from his natural environment (as in the case of Jeff, reported by Clement, 1973), rather than strangers as in the present study.

Appraisal

The bug-in-the-ear device is a clever technological innovation which appears to have a variety of possible applications in facilitating *in vivo* therapies. The major application so far has been in providing guidance and feedback to parents or peers learning to improve their own social behaviors and to shape adaptive instrumental behaviors in targeted children. In addition to the training advantages of dealing directly with ongoing behaviors and providing immediate feedback, the approach reportedly has had some added benefits. For example, the omnipresence of the supervisor tends to reduce the pressure and anxiety experienced by mothers when placed in a therapist role, and the "game" spirit of the "chief-for-the-day" arrangement tends to generate increased enthusiasm in participating children (Clement et al., 1976). Several advantages and disadvantages of the technique have also been reported by Boylston and Tuma (1972) in relation to their use of the bug-in-the-ear to supervise mental health trainees during actual therapy sessions. Advantages include the reduction in the inexperienced therapist's initial anxiety, and the ability to avoid mishandling difficult situations. Potential disadvantages include the increased demand on supervisory observation time, and the possibility that the trainee will not develop his own style but instead merely emulate the supervisor.

Overall, the available reports suggest that the advantages clearly outweigh the disadvantages. The bug-in-the-ear seems especially well-suited for integration into treatment approaches having central *in vivo* components, both for unobtrusively directing and rewarding adaptive behaviors of clients as well as for helping parents, teachers, and paraprofessionals improve their behavioral management skills. The existing clinical reports should provide a model and an impetus for exploring new *in vivo* applications of this promising technique.

INTERPERSONAL AND COMMUNICATION PROBLEMS

Much human activity involves verbal and nonverbal interaction with others. People vary in their abilities to communicate friendliness, verbalize opinions, refuse unreasonable requests, admit fault, and assert displeasure. The ease and effectiveness with which people can express such thoughts and feelings may have considerable impact on their achievement of personal goals and overall sense of well-being. In some cases, problems arise because the person has a particular area of interpersonal difficulty (e.g., relating harmoniously with a spouse); in other cases, problems arise because the person has a general deficiency which has broad effects on social interaction (e.g., an inability to speak fluently). Much has been written concerning the use of modeling, role-playing, rehearsal, and feedback procedures to improve skills of interpersonal expressiveness (e.g., see books by Alberti & Emmons, 1970; Johnson, 1972; and selected chapters or sections in books by Bandura, 1969; Bellack & Hersen, 1977; Craighead, Kazdin, & Mahoney, 1976; Goldfried & Davison, 1976; Kanfer & Goldstein, 1975; Kanfer & Phillips, 1970; Krumboltz & Thoresen, 1976; Lazarus, 1971; Nay, 1976; O'Leary & Wilson, 1975; Rimm & Masters, 1974; Salter, 1949; Sherman, 1973; Wolpe, 1958, 1973). Videotape apparatus has permitted certain refinements and efficiencies in the expressive training area (e.g., Eisler, Hersen, & Agras, 1973; Eisler, Hersen, & Miller, 1973; Hersen, Eisler, Miller, Johnson, & Pinkston, 1973; Rathus, 1973; Sherman, Barone, & Turner, 1977), and methodological innovations such as using the self as a model (Hosford & Brown, 1976; Hosford, Moss, & Morrell, 1976) have also expanded the array of intervention strategies. Most of the work on expressive training has been conducted in office or laboratory settings, often employing "replication" techniques wherein "significant parts of the patient's extratherapeutic environment are replicated or simulated for observation and manipulation in the therapist's presence [Kanfer & Phillips, 1970, p. 232]." In view of the many existing reviews of this general area, the present section focuses instead on two therapeutic innovations which are distinguished by the central roles played by *in vivo* components in the natural environment. The "operant-interpersonal treatment" is designed to improve interpersonal harmony within marriages, and "metronome-conditioned speech retraining" is designed to promote fluent speech in chronic stutterers.

Operant-Interpersonal Treatment for Marital Discord

Interpersonal problems and conflicts in marriage typically cause severe psychological distress among family members, and often result in separation or divorce. The increasing rate of marital dissolutions reflects the fact that spouses often fail to recognize or rectify deficiencies in the degree to which they mutually reward each other. The **operant-interpersonal treatment,** as described by Stuart (1969), involves a sequence of steps in which the marital partners identify specific behaviors that they then agree to perform to please each other. While training and guidance in developing the treatment plan are provided to the couple within the therapist's office, most of the "work" of therapy is carried out by the couple within their natural living situation. These *in vivo* activities include recording the frequencies of the desired behaviors, and then reciprocating each other's efforts for engaging in them. Variations of the approach, which also emphasize the reciprocal application of operant principles, include *contract therapy* (Stern & Marks, 1973), *reciprocity counseling* (Azrin, Naster, & Jones, 1973), and *behavioral marital therapy* (Liberman, Wheeler, & Sanders, 1976). In some approaches the office part of the treatment is conducted with the individual couple; in other approaches it is conducted with groups of couples.

Basic Procedure

In Stuart's (1969) formulation of the operant-interpersonal treatment, there are four basic steps. Initially, the couple is trained in the logic of the approach, which includes two premises. These assert that "the impressions which each spouse forms of the other is based on the behavior of the other [p. 677]," and, "in order to change interaction in a marriage, each partner must assume initiative in changing his own behavior before changes can be expected in his spouse [p. 677]." Next, each spouse is asked to list the three behaviors which he or she would most like to increase in the partner. Stuart (1969) noted some of the difficulties that are often encountered by the couple in formulating this list, including the tendency to focus on negative behaviors that the spouse finds undesirable, rather than focusing on positive behaviors to be increased. The third step of the treatment involves preparing a "behavior checklist" in which the three selected positive behaviors which are to be increased by each partner are posted visibly in the house, and each is instructed to record the frequency with which the other performs the desired acts. Finally, the partners work out a contract in which they agree on the behaviors that they are each going to perform to please the other in reciprocal ways. The basic strategy is sometimes augmented by the use of tokens as rewards to enable each spouse to provide immediate reinforcement for the other's efforts at behavioral improvements.

Variations of the approach depicted by Stuart (1969) have sometimes integrated additional techniques into the treatment strategy. These have included keeping a diary of special joint activities prior to formulating the treatment plan (Crowe, 1973), special training in communication skills using behavioral rehearsal, modeling, prompting, and feedback (Liberman, Levine, Wheeler, Sanders, & Wallace, 1976), supplementary use of communication and sexual skill training (Wieman, Shoulders, & Farr, 1974), and presenting the treatment using nontechnical language while focusing on global sets of responses and reinforcers rather than specific response–reinforcement relationships (Azrin et al., 1973).

Rationale

Stuart (1969) maintains that the operant-interpersonal treatment rests on three assumptions about the nature of marital interaction. The first assumption is that "the exact pattern of interaction which takes place between spouses at any point in time is the most rewarding of all of the available alternatives [p. 675]." The second assumption asserts that "most married adults expect to enjoy reciprocal relations with their partners [p. 675]," the reciprocity referring to an equitable exchange of positive reinforcement. The final assumption maintains that "in order to modify an unsuccessful marital interaction, it is essential to develop the power of each partner to mediate rewards for the other [p. 676]."

In this analysis, "coercion" and "withdrawal" represent two counterproductive patterns of behavioral control which are likely to emerge in disharmonious marriages. In contrast, the successful marriage typically finds both partners working "to maximize mutual reward while minimizing individual costs [Stuart, 1969, p. 676]." Consistent with this perception, the operant-interpersonal approach attempts to improve the marital relationship by teaching the partners to increase the frequency and intensity of mutual positive reinforcement.

Case Example

Wieman *et al.* (1974) employed a multiple baseline design across several behaviors in an attempt to evaluate the effects of an operant-interpersonal approach to the treatment of a young couple having marital difficulties. Mr. B. was a 31-year-old graduate student whose presenting problems of nervousness, ulcers, and school difficulties seemed related to conflicts in his seven-year marriage. He complained of his wife's constant nagging and tearfulness, as well as her disinterest in sexual relations, and was considering leaving her "unless their situation could be altered significantly." Mrs. B., a 30-year-old homemaker, reported feeling neglected and unloved, often "physically miserable" without apparent cause, and complained of being "trapped in a marriage that isolated her geographically from family and friends [p. 292]." The treatment was conducted jointly by male and female cotherapists.

After being introduced to the treatment approach, each spouse selected and operationally defined three behaviors which he or she desired the other to increase. These were paired off and ranked in accordance with their difficulty, beginning with a category of "little things" like favors and compliments. The pair of behaviors representing the middle level of difficulty included the husband's request for an uninterrupted "chance to unwind" when he returns from school, and the wife's desire for an increase in meaningful communication. The third pair of behaviors, representing the most difficult level, concerned the responsibilities of each spouse in attempting to improve their sexual relationship.

The treatment approach included the provision of behavior checklists that the couple used to monitor the target behaviors prior to and throughout treatment, as well as special training in communication and sexual skills when spouses' behavioral repertoires were insufficient for accommodating their mates' requests. In accordance with the multiple baseline design, the couple did not attempt to increase the second pair of behaviors until they had reached an agreed-upon criterion for the first pair. This transpired after the fifth week. The special skill training required for the second and third pairs was conducted prior to attempts to change the corresponding behaviors. Although there was a 4-week treatment interruption related to Mrs. B.'s hospitalization and recuperation from a physical problem, the couple advanced to the third pair of behaviors after the twentieth week of treatment, and therapy was concluded four weeks later. It was noted that "Within 1 month, Mr. B successfully completed his graduate training and, with his wife's encouragement, accepted a position several hundred miles from the Clinic [p. 293]."

As indicated by the authors, the fact that the pairs of behaviors did not improve until they were made the focus of contingent reciprocal reinforcement supports the view that the changes were owing to that feature of the treatment and not to such nonspecific factors as "general client expectancy." In addition to the behavioral evidence of improvement, the couple's verbal reports indicated that "growth in marital satisfaction had been achieved and that this was strongly related to the increased performance of rewarding behaviors [pp. 293–294]."

In reviewing factors which may have been involved in promoting the improvement in this couple, Wieman et al. (1974) commented on the apparent advantages of proceeding in a gradual fashion: "Increasing the rate of simple, easily performed 'little things' early in therapy quickly immersed the B's in the exchange of positive reinforcement, sensitized them to the potential of their actions for eliciting reinforcement from their mates, and set the stage for the later pairing of more difficult behaviors . . . [p. 294]." Also noted was the apparent importance, in this case, of providing special training to rectify deficiencies in communication and sexual skills.

Representative Findings

Several clinical reports in the literature support the efficacy of the operant-interpersonal approach, or variants thereof, in treating couples having marital difficulties. Stuart's (1969) original description of the treatment included results with four couples who had sought therapy "as a last-ditch effort prior to obtaining a divorce [p. 678]." The individuals ranged in age from 24 to 52, in education from high school diploma to Ph.D. degree, and in marital duration from 3 to 23 years. In general, the wives expressed most interest in having their husbands converse more with them, and the husbands expressed interest in having sex more frequently. Seven therapeutic sessions distributed over a 10-week period were held with each couple. The treatment, which included the use of a token system, directed the spouses in carrying out an exchange of positive responses on a reciprocal basis. The effects of this "tit for chat" behavioral exchange were monitored by the spouses, and it was found for each couple that "the rates of conversation and sex increased sharply after the start of treatment and continued through 24- and 48-week follow-up periods [p. 680]." Results of a self-rating inventory indicated that the spouses' subjective marital satisfaction had increased in conjunction with the reported behavioral improvements.

Of four cases described by Liberman (1970) to illustrate a behavioral approach to family therapy, three involved the successful treatment of married couples. The number of sessions ranged from 5 to 15. In discussing the general strategy, Liberman noted "three major areas of technical concern for the therapist . . . (1) *creating and maintaining a positive therapeutic alliance;* (2) *making a behavioral analysis of the problem(s);* and (3) *implementing the behavioral principles of reinforcement and modeling in the context of ongoing interpersonal interactions* [p. 109]."

Further variations on the operant-interpersonal approach were described by Rappaport and Harrell (1972) and by Stern and Marks (1973), each report including a case example. Rappaport and Harrell (1972) characterized their "behavioral-exchange" model as having an educational emphasis, encouraging the spouses "to negotiate their own reciprocal-exchange contracts with decreasing dependency on the counselor–educator [p. 203]." Token economies are not included in their program, which was illustrated in its application to a young married couple with one infant child. The "contract therapy" of Stern and Marks (1973) was employed for 10 hour-long sessions conducted twice a week with a 31-year-old housewife and her 42-year-old husband who were already contemplating separation. The problems of this couple, who had two children, were complicated by the wife's longstanding history of engaging in obsessive–compulsive rituals for which previous attempts at therapy had been unsuccessful. Behavioral improvements were evident in the spouses during the course of treatment, and for the most part these appeared to have been maintained as of 6-week and 12-week follow-ups. Although at a one-year follow-up the wife, attending alone, reported that her husband had recently left her for another woman, the improvement in her obsessive rituals reportedly had been maintained.

Twelve married couples with a mean age of 31 years and an average marriage duration of 9 years served as subjects in a study of "reciprocity counseling" conducted by Azrin et al. (1973). A within-subjects experimental design provided for comparison between the effects of a "catharsis-type" counseling, conducted for three weeks, and the learning-based reciprocity counseling, conducted for the next four weeks. The results indicated that reciprocity counseling increased self-ratings of marital happiness during and following the conclusion of treatment, while catharsis-type counseling did not. According to Azrin et al. (1973):

Ninety-six percent of the clients had an increase of happiness. The increased happiness occurred for each of nine major areas of marital interaction, the greatest increase occurring for the two areas, communication and sex, in which the couples were least happy initially. The specificity of the effect of the procedure was evidenced by the greater increase of happiness in those areas that had been counseled than in the areas for which counseling had not yet been given. Yet, some generalization was evident in that (1) problem areas that had not yet been counseled also did increase [improve] and (2) happiness continued to increase during follow-up when presumably new problems were emerging [p. 380].

Although the reciprocity counseling approach has many basic features in common with Stuart's (1969) operant-interpersonal approach, the former attempts to present the treatment using nontechnical language and focuses on global sets of responses and reinforcers rather than specific response–reinforcement relationships.

A comparative evaluation of behavioral and interactional approaches to marital therapy in groups was reported by Liberman, Levine, Wheeler, Sanders, and Wallace (1976). The participating couples averaged 13 years of education and 14 years of marriage. According to the authors,

> The experimental group of four couples was exposed to behavioral methods based on social learning principles. The primary interventions were (1) training the spouses in discriminating and monitoring the occurrence of pleasing events and behaviors; (2) behavioral rehearsal of communication skills using prompting, modeling, feedback, and "homework" assignments; and (3) contingency contracting. The comparison group of five couples was led in an interactional format with the leaders encouraging ventilation of feelings, problem-solving through discussion, and mutual support and feedback [p. 3].

Treatment of each group consisted of weekly, 2-hour sessions for 8 weeks plus a 1-month follow-up session, with all sessions conducted by the same three therapists—a male psychiatrist, a female psychiatric nurse, and a female social worker. Multiple measures were employed to assess the participants' attitudes and behavior before, during, and after treatment, and at three follow-up intervals. While both groups showed comparable improvements on the self-report measures, direct observational data revealed that "the members in the behavioral group displayed significantly more positive and mutually supportive verbal and nonverbal behaviors in their interaction as a result of treatment [p. 3]." These between-group differences favoring the behavioral approach were attributed to the specific training in communication skills and contingency contracting.

Appraisal

The operant-interpersonal method, and related behavioral approaches, attempt to teach the troubled couple to recognize the behaviors that they appreciate in each other, to monitor them, and to reciprocally reinforce each other for engaging in them. Additional techniques, such as training in improved communication or sexual skills and the use of tokens to reward "contracted" behavior, are also integrated into some behavioral programs. The limited evidence available, consisting of several case reports and a couple of experimental studies, suggests that the basic approach can be very effective in improving marital harmony. Further research is required to evaluate the separate contributions of the treatment components and their variations with a view toward refining the behavioral approach, and then comparing its effectiveness to that of other marriage-counseling approaches (cf. Crowe, 1973). Research designed to identify any characteristics of the couple or their relationship which might indicate or contraindicate a behavioral strategy could also contribute to improving therapeutic outcomes through differential assignment to particular treatments. In this regard, Rappaport and Harrell (1972) noted several "precautions" associated with the behavioral model for marital counseling. Among other things, the requirement that " couples must learn and keep daily behavioral records of their progress in the program [p. 212]" may preclude those who cannot commit themselves to the required effort. It is also maintained that the approach is " not functional for those marriages where one or both spouses are unable or unwilling to compromise and bargain [p. 211]."

While training and guidance in developing and executing the treatment plan are provided to the couple within an office context, it was noted that most of the actual "work" of therapy is carried out by the couple within their natural living situation. This general strategy of preparing and prompting clients to execute behavior-change plans *in vivo* has also been successfully employed with a variety of other instrumental behavior problems. Of particular relevance to the marital area, however, would seem to be the potential applicability of the approach for **preventative** purposes, rather than waiting for conflicts to develop. Viewed within an educational perspective, courses could be offered to newlyweds to alert them to the importance of reciprocal reinforcement in maintaining marital harmony, with *in vivo* "homework" assignments conducted along lines similar to the procedures described above. Since marital problems commonly emerge in the communication and sexual areas, these could receive special attention in such programs. Here, as elsewhere, the possibility of adapting treatment procedures for preventative use requires further exploration.

Metronome-Conditioned Speech Retraining

This approach employs the uniform pattern of beats provided by a metronome to establish fluency in people with severe stuttering problems. The pacing of speech syllables is gradually increased from a slow to a normal rate, and is extended from the office to natural settings through the use of a miniaturized metronome worn behind an ear. The basic procedure has been referred to by such names as **metronome-conditioned speech retraining** (Brady, 1971), and **metronome-conditioning therapy** (Adams & Hotchkiss, 1973). It has been employed successfully with chronic stutterers ranging widely in age, many of whom previously had been treated unsuccessfully by other approaches.

Basic Procedure

A detailed description of metronome-conditioned speech retraining is provided by Brady (1971). The treatment begins by having the client pace his speech to a desk metronome in the therapist's office, under conditions in which almost perfect fluency can be obtained. For example, with a very severe stutterer, this might begin by pacing one syllable of speech to each metronome beat set at a slow speed, while using easy reading material as the source of words. This pacing is also practiced at home. As fluency is attained, the speech rate is increased by gradually and systematically increasing the metronome speed and by pacing longer units of speech to each of the metronome's beats. In addition to gradually increasing the speech rate, the source of words (e.g., conversational speech; spontaneous lecture), and the number and identity of people present during practice sessions (e.g., family, friends, strangers) would be progressively changed to represent more challenging speaking situations. In Brady's (1971) approach: "This phase of treatment is completed when the patient is able to speak with the metronome at a rate within the normal range (100–160 words/minute) with no pronounced blocks in speech and a nonfluency rate that is no more than 20% of the nonfluency rate he exhibited before treatment without a metronome [p. 135]."

It is at this point that the *in vivo* component enters as a major feature of the treatment. The desk metronome, which had been used in office sessions and home practice sessions, is now replaced by a miniaturized, electronic metronome worn unobtrusively behind the ear like a hearing aid. The metronome is very light, and has external controls for turning it on and off, and for regulating the rate and volume of the beats. During this phase, the patient formulates a list of speaking situations he is likely to encounter in daily life, and arranges them in increasing order of anticipated difficulty. He is then instructed to use the metronome in these situations, beginning with the situation expected to cause the least anxiety and stuttering, and gradually progressing up the hierarchy as each situation is mastered. When the client is able to speak in a relaxed and fluent manner in virtually all situations, the use of the metronome is systematically phased out, beginning with the least difficult situation and progressing gradually through the hierarchy. Brady (1971) provides suggestions for helping patients through the occasional setbacks which occur, and indicates that some patients may continue to rely upon the metronome to maintain fluency in their more stressful situations.

Rationale

The behavioral conceptualization of stuttering summarized by Brady (1971) recognizes both operant and respondent factors, the former being involved primarily in the speech nonfluencies and the latter being involved primarily in the anxiety commonly experienced in speaking situations. Consistent with this perspective, the treatment involves both operant and respondent features. While it is not certain how the metronome promotes fluency, its effect in this regard is employed initially to establish fluent verbalizations under nonstressful conditions.

> Once fluent verbalizations can be made, albeit at a low rate and in very particular circumstances, the task is to gradually and systematically "shape" verbalizations to approximate the rate and cadence of normal speech and to help the patient extend this fluency to other situations to which anticipatory anxiety and tension have been conditioned [p. 131].

It is presumed that the positive feelings of self-confidence and relaxation brought about by fluent speech in the presence of the metronome's beats counteract or "reciprocally inhibit" (Wolpe, 1958) the anxiety and tension that previously had characterized such speaking situations. Eventually, the metronomic beats serve as "not only *instructional* stimuli telling the patient when to emit the next syllable or word, but become *discriminative* stimuli, inducing relaxation and fluency [Brady, 1971, p. 131]." It is noted that many patients find it helpful to pace their speech to an imaginary metronome when discontinuing the use of the miniaturized metronome toward the conclusion of therapy. According to Brady (1971), this "may be conceptualized as a gradual 'fading out' of the unnatural cues of the metronome's beats as discriminative stimuli for fluency and hence allowing the cues naturally present in speaking situations to take their place [p. 132]."

Case Example

Adams and Hotchkiss (1973) described the successful use of metronome-conditioning therapy with a 22-year-old college senior who had not profited appreciably from two other treatments. His stuttering was characterized primarily by audible and silent prolongations, accompanied by lip protrusion and tremor, and a forward thrusting of the tongue. On the average, stutterings occurred on approximately 14 words per 100.

Treatment began in the clinic by asking the patient to produce one word with each beat of a desk metronome set at 60 beats per min. During the next several weeks the client made consistent but uneven progress, using a transistorized pacer which had replaced the desk metronome for both clinic and home practice sessions. After 4 months of therapy the client had improved to only 5 stuttered words per 100 while wearing the pacer and engaging in conversational speech with the clinician. The thrusting of the tongue was no longer evident, and the lip protrusion and tremor were reduced.

In view of this progress, the patient was encouraged to wear the pacer outside of therapy and to time his utterances with the device's beat. After a few weeks he reported that his improved fluency in therapy was transferring to a limited degree to everyday speech situations. At this point, the patient moved over 100 miles from the clinic. He continued to employ the pacer, and returned to the clinic once a month. On the sixth of these monthly visits he was met outside the clinic and engaged in extended conversation. He exhibited slightly less than 3 stutterings per 100 words spoken while speaking at the rate of one-phrase-per-beat. No evidence of tongue thrusting, lip protrusion, or tremor was observed. The patient reported that he was enjoying substantial fluency in everyday situations previously characterized by moderate to high levels of stuttering, such as talking on the phone or interviewing for a job. Although he was still reliant on the pacer, the treatment strategy included plans to phase this out in the future.

Representative Findings

It has been known for a long time that the presence of regular metronomic beats at a pace similar to slow speech can be very effective in reducing the amount of stuttering. In fact, Brady (1971) cited an 1831 reference on the use of metronomes in the treatment of stuttering. More recently, Fransella and Beech (1965) experimentally demonstrated the favorable influence of metronomic pacing upon fluency in adult males, and Greenberg (1970) found the same metronome effect with 9- to 11-year-old boys whether or not they were specifically instructed to pace their speech. Despite the well-documented effect of metronomic pacing, the clinical applicability of the technique had, until recently, been limited by the typically poor transfer of fluency from speaking with a metronome to speaking without one.

This problem of transfer decrement was noted by Meyer and Mair (1963), who were among the first to report on the innovative use of a portable metronome device to promote transfer to everyday life situations. The device, which was worn in the ear, represented an integral part of the clinical treatment; it was phased out gradually as the patient achieved fluency in a succession of situations graded in severity. Preliminary results with five clinical patients ranging in age from 19 to 43 revealed appreciable improvements in four of them.

The use of a miniaturized metronome in the context of a gradual *in vivo* shaping treatment received further refinement in the metronome-conditioned speech retraining program described by Brady (1971). The clinical sample consisted of 26 severe stutterers ranging in age from 12 to 53 whose chronic speech problems had not changed much for at least the preceding two years. Of the 26 patients, 23 completed the program and 21 showed a marked increase in fluency and an improvement in their general adjustment. The 23 patients who completed the treatment had received a mean of 11.8 1-hour sessions, and evidenced a 67.3% mean decrease in nonfluency without the metronome. These clinical improvements reportedly were maintained as of follow-ups ranging from 6 months to over 3 years.

In two of three clinical cases described by Adams and Hotchkiss (1973), problems were encountered in the metronome-conditioning program. One of the patients had difficulty monitoring the pacer consistently, and another was unwilling to wear the pacer in public. The authors concluded that stutterers may react on a highly individualized basis to the metronome-conditioning procedures and device; clinicians should be alert to the fact that neither this approach (nor any other) will always be the treatment of choice for all patients.

Appraisal

While the reasons for its effectiveness are not established, the favorable influence of metronomic pacing upon speech fluency appears to be well documented. Furthermore, the longstanding problem of transfer decrement has been alleviated through the use of a miniaturized metronome employed in the context of a gradual *in vivo* behavioral shaping treatment. This is an area where technological advances have facilitated the *in vivo* therapy of a problem which traditionally had been limited to various office treatments, and favorable results have ensued. Several clinical reports have been very encouraging, and there has been little evidence of the high relapse rates that sometimes characterized other approaches. It was noted, however, that not all patients readily adapt to the metronome-conditioning procedures and to the public use of a visible metronomic device. Further research is required to develop variations of the approach which will better accommodate the individual needs of diverse patients. Controlled experiments are also needed to compare the effectiveness of the metronome-conditioning approach to other approaches employed in the treatment of stuttering.

CONCLUDING REMARKS

Most of the *in vivo* therapies reviewed in this chapter are relatively new and, with the exception of contextual therapy, emerged from a behavioristic perspective. While there was at least some supportive clinical evidence concerning the favorable effects of each approach, and experimental evaluations in some cases, a number of unanswered questions were identified to prompt and guide future research efforts. These relate to such concerns as the indications for a particular treatment, the nature and durability of therapeutic gains, and the procedural features responsible for derived benefits. Since these and other issues are relevant also to the *in vivo* therapies examined in the next chapter, they will be considered in more detail at the conclusion of that review.

REFERENCES

Adams, M. R., & Hotchkiss, J. Some reactions and responses of stutterers to a miniaturized metronome and metronome-conditioning therapy: Three case reports. *Behavior Therapy*, 1973, 4, 565–569.
Alberti, R. E., & Emmons, M. L. *Your perfect right: A guide to assertive behavior*. San Luis Obispo, California: Impact, 1970.
Antman, E. M. Flooding *in vivo* for a case of vermiphobia. *Journal of Behavior Therapy and Experimental Psychiatry*, 1973, 4, 275–277.
Axelrod, S. *Behavior modification for the classroom teacher*. New York: McGraw-Hill, 1977.
Ayllon, T., & Azrin, N. *The token economy: A motivational system for therapy and rehabilitation*. New York: Appleton-Century-Crofts, 1968.
Azrin, N. H., Naster, B. J., & Jones, R. Reciprocity counseling: A rapid learning-based procedure for marital counseling. *Behaviour Research and Therapy*, 1973, 11, 365–382.
Azrin, N. H., & Wesolowski, M. D. Theft reversal: An overcorrection procedure for eliminating stealing by retarded persons. *Journal of Applied Behavior Analysis*, 1974, 7, 577–481.
Azrin, N. H., & Wesolowski, M. D. Eliminating habitual vomiting in a retarded adult by positive practice and self-correction. *Journal of Behavior Therapy and Experimental Psychiatry*, 1975, 6, 145–148. (a)
Azrin, N. H., & Wesolowski, M. D. The use of positive practice to eliminate persistent floor sprawling by profoundly retarded persons. *Behavior Therapy*, 1975, 6, 627–631. (b)
Bandura, A. *Principles of behavior modification*. New York: Holt, 1969.
Bandura, A. Psychotherapy based upon modeling principles. In A. E. Bergin & S. L.

Garfield (Eds.), *Handbook of psychotherapy and behavior change: An empirical analysis.* New York: Wiley, 1971.

Bandura, A. Effecting change through participant modeling. In J. D. Krumboltz & C. E. Thoresen (Eds.), *Counseling methods.* New York: Holt, 1976.

Bandura, A. *Social learning theory.* Englewood Cliffs, New Jersey: Prentice-Hall, 1977.

Bandura, A., Blanchard, E. B., & Ritter, B. Relative efficacy of desensitization and modeling approaches for inducing behavioral, affective, and attitudinal changes. *Journal of Personality and Social Psychology,* 1969, *13,* 173–199.

Bandura, A., Jeffery, R. W., & Gajdos, E. Generalizing change through participant modeling with self-directed mastery. *Behaviour Research and Therapy,* 1975, *13,* 141–152.

Bandura, A., Jeffery, R. W., & Wright, C. L. Efficacy of participant modeling as a function of response induction aids. *Journal of Abnormal Psychology,* 1974, *83,* 56–64.

Barlow, D. H., Agras, W. S., Leitenberg, H., & Wincze, J. P. An experimental analysis of the effectiveness of "shaping" in reducing maladaptive avoidance behavior: an analogue study. *Behaviour Research and Therapy,* 1970, *8,* 165–173.

Becker, W. C. *Parents are teachers: A child management program.* Champaign, Illinois: Research Press, 1971.

Bellack, A. S., & Hersen, M. *Behavior modification: An introductory textbook.* Baltimore: Williams & Wilkins, 1977.

Boulougouris, J. C., & Bassiakos, L. Prolonged flooding in cases with obsessive-compulsive neurosis. *Behaviour Research and Therapy,* 1973, *11,* 227–231.

Boylston, W. H., & Tuma, J. M. Training of mental health professionals through the use of the "bug in the ear." *American Journal of Psychiatry,* 1972, *129,* 92–95.

Brady, J. P. Metronome-conditioned speech retraining for stuttering. *Behavior Therapy,* 1971, *2,* 129–150.

Butler, J. F. Toilet training a child with spina bifida. *Journal of Behavior Therapy and Experimental Psychiatry,* 1976, *7,* 63–65.

Clement, P. W. Children as behavior therapists. In A. M. Mitchell & C. D. Johnson (Eds.), *Therapeutic techniques: Working models for the helping professional.* Fullerton, California: Personnel & Guidance Association, 1973.

Clement, P. W. Parents, peers, and child patients make the best therapists. In G. J. Williams & S. Gordon (Eds.), *Clinical child psychology: Current practices and future perspectives.* New York: Behavioral Publications, 1974.

Clement, P. W., Roberts, P. V., & Lantz, C. E. Mothers and peers as child behavior therapists. *International Journal of Group Psychotherapy,* 1976, *26,* 335–359.

Cooke, G. The efficacy of two desensitization procedures: An analogue study. *Behaviour Research and Therapy,* 1966, *4,* 17–24.

Craighead, W. E., Kazdin, A. E., & Mahoney, M. J. *Behavior modification: Principles, issues, and applications.* Boston: Houghton Mifflin, 1976.

Crowe, M. J. Conjoint marital therapy: Advice or interpretation? *Journal of Psychosomatic Research,* 1973, *17,* 309–315.

Crowe, M. J., Marks, I. M., Agras, W. S., & Leitenberg, H. Time-limited desensitization, implosion and shaping for phobic patients: a crossover study. *Behaviour Research and Therapy,* 1972, *10,* 319–328.

Davison, G. C. *Relative contributions of differential relaxation and graded exposure to in vivo desensitization of a neurotic fear.* Paper presented at the national convention of the American Psychological Association, Chicago, Illinois, 1965.

Davison, G. C. Systematic desensitization as a counterconditioning process. *Journal of Abnormal Psychology*, 1968, *73*, 91–99.

Davison, G. C. A procedural critique of "Desensitization and the experimental reduction of threat." *Journal of Abnormal Psychology*, 1969, 74, 86–87.

Deibert, A. N., & Harmon, A. J. *New tools for changing behavior.* Champaign, Illinois: Research Press, 1973.

Eisler, R. M., Hersen, M., & Agras, W. S. Effects of videotape and instructional feedback on nonverbal marital interaction: An analog study. *Behavior Therapy*, 1973, *4*, 551–558.

Eisler, R. M., Hersen, M., & Miller, P. M. Effects of modeling on components of assertive behavior. *Journal of Behavior Therapy and Experimental Psychiatry*, 1973, *4*, 1–6.

Emmelkamp, P. M. G. Self-observation versus flooding in the treatment of agoraphobia. *Behaviour Research and Therapy*, 1974, *12*, 229–237.

Emmelkamp, P. M. G., & Ultee, K. A. A comparison of "successive approximation" and "self-observation" in the treatment of agoraphobia. *Behavior Therapy*, 1974, *5*, 606–613.

Emmelkamp, P. M. G., & Wessels, H. Flooding in imagination vs. flooding *in vivo*: a comparison with agoraphobics. *Behaviour Research and Therapy*, 1975, *13*, 7–15.

Epstein, L. H., Doke, L. A., Sajwaj, T. E., Sorrell, S., & Rimmer, B. Generality and side effects of overcorrection. *Journal of Applied Behavior Analysis*, 1974, *7*, 385–390.

Everaerd, W. T. A. M., Rijken, H. M., & Emmelkamp, P. M. G. A comparison of 'flooding' and 'successive approximation' in the treatment of agoraphobia. *Behaviour Research and Therapy*, 1973, *11*, 105–117.

Folkins, C. H., Evans, K. L., Opton, E. M., Jr., & Lazarus, R. S. A reply to Davison's critique. *Journal of Abnormal Psychology*, 1969, 74, 88–89.

Folkins, C. H., Lawson, K. D., Opton, E. M., Jr., & Lazarus, R. S. Desensitization and the experimental reduction of threat. *Journal of Abnormal Psychology*, 1968, *73*, 100–113.

Foxx, R. M. The use of overcorrection to eliminate the public disrobing (stripping) of retarded women. *Behaviour Research and Therapy*, 1976, *14*, 53–61. (a)

Foxx, R. M. Increasing a mildly retarded woman's attendance at selp-help classes by overcorrection and instruction. *Behavior Therapy*, 1976, *7*, 390–396. (b)

Foxx, R. M., & Azrin, N.H. Restitution: A method of eliminating aggressive-disruptive behavior of retarded and brain damaged patients. *Behaviour Research and Therapy*, 1972, *10*, 15–27.

Foxx, R. M., & Azrin, N. H. The elimination of autistic self-stimulatory behavior by overcorrection. *Journal of Applied Behavior Analysis*, 1973, *6*, 1–14.

Foxx, R. M., & Martin, E. D. Treatment of scavenging behavior (coprophagy and pica) by overcorrection. *Behaviour Research and Therapy*, 1975, *13*, 153–162.

Fransella, F., & Beech, H. R. An experimental analysis of the effect of rhythm on the speech of stutterers. *Behaviour Research and Therapy*, 1965, *3*, 195–201.

Freeman, H. L., & Kendrick, D. C. A case of cat phobia treatment by a method derived from experimental psychology. In H. J. Eysenck (Ed.), *Experiments in behaviour therapy.* New York: Macmillan, 1964.

Garfield, Z. H., Darwin, P. L., Singer, B. A., & McBrearty, J. F. Effect of "in vivo" training on experimental desensitization of a phobia. *Psychological Reports*, 1967, *20*, 515–519.

Gershman, L., & Stedman, J. M. Oriental defense exercises as reciprocal inhibitors of anxiety. *Journal of Behavior Therapy and Experimental Psychiatry*, 1971, 2, 117–119.

Goldfried, M. R., & Davison, G. C. *Clinical behavior therapy*. New York: Holt, 1976.

Goldstein, A. J., Serber, M., & Piaget, G. Induced anger as a reciprocal inhibitor of fear. *Journal of Behavior Therapy and Experimental Psychiatry*, 1970, 1, 67–70.

Goldstein, A. P., Martens, J., Hubben, J., Van Belle, H. A., Schaaf, W., Wiersma, H., & Goedhart, A. The use of modeling to increase independent behavior. *Behaviour Research and Therapy*, 1973, 11, 31–42.

Greenberg, J. B. The effect of a metronome on the speech of young stutterers. *Behavior Therapy*, 1970, 1, 240–244.

Guthrie, E. R. *The psychology of learning*. New York: Harper, 1952.

Hackmann, A., & McLean, C. A comparison of flooding and thought stopping in the treatment of obsessional neurosis. *Behaviour Research and Therapy*, 1975, 13, 263–269.

Hafner, J., & Marks, I. Exposure *in vivo* of agoraphobics: contributions of diazepam, group exposure, and anxiety evocation. *Psychological Medicine*, 1976, 6, 71-88.

Harris, S. L., & Romanczyk, R. G. Treating self-injurious behavior of a retarded child by overcorrection. *Behavior Therapy*, 1976, 7, 235–239.

Hersen, M., Eisler, R. M., Miller, P. M., Johnson, M. B., & Pinkston, S. G. Effects of practice, instructions, and modeling on components of assertive behavior. *Behaviour Research and Therapy*, 1973, 11, 443–451.

Homme, L. *How to use contingency contracting in the classroom*. Champaign, Illinois: Research Press, 1970.

Horan, J. J. Coping with inescapable discomfort through *in vivo* emotive imagery. In J. D. Krumboltz & C. E. Thoresen (Eds.), *Counseling methods*. New York: Holt, 1976.

Hosford, R. E., & Brown, S. D. *Vicarious self observation of appropriate behavior: Using the self-as-a-model*. Paper presented at the Eighth Annual Banff Conference on Behavior Modification, Banff, Alberta, Canada, 1976.

Hosford, R. E., Moss, C. S., & Morrell, G. The self-as-a-model technique: Helping prison inmates change. In J. D. Krumboltz & C. E. Thoresen (Eds.), *Counseling methods*. New York: Holt, 1976.

Jacobson, E. *Progressive relaxation*. Chicago: University of Chicago Press, 1938.

Jersild, A. T., & Holmes, F. B. Methods of overcoming children's fears. *Journal of Psychology*, 1935, 1, 75–104.

Johnson, D. W. *Reaching out: Interpersonal effectiveness and self-actualization.* Englewood Cliffs, New Jersey: Prentice-Hall, 1972.

Jones, M. C. The elimination of children's fears. *Journal of Experimental Psychology*, 1924, 7, 383–390.

Kanfer, F. H., & Goldstein, A. P. *Helping people change*. New York: Pergamon, 1975.

Kanfer, F. H., & Phillips, J. S. *Learning foundations of behavior therapy*. New York: Wiley, 1970.

Kazdin, A. E. *Behavior modification in applied settings*. Homewood, Illinois: Dorsey Press, 1975.

Kazdin, A. E. *The token economy: A review and an evaluation*. New York: Plenum, 1977.

Klinge, V., Thrasher, P., & Myers, S. Use of bed-rest overcorrection in a chronic schizophrenic. *Journal of Behavior Therapy and Experimental Psychiatry*, 1975, 6, 69–73.

Krumboltz, J. D., & Krumboltz, H. B. *Changing children's behavior*. Englewood Cliffs, New Jersey: Prentice-Hall, 1972.

Krumboltz, J. D., & Thoresen, C. E. (Eds.). *Counseling Methods*. New York: Holt, 1976.

Lazarus, A. A. A preliminary report on the use of directed muscular activity in counter-conditioning. *Behaviour Research and Therapy*, 1965, 2, 301–304.

Lazarus, A. A. *Behavior therapy and beyond*. New York: McGraw-Hill, 1971.

Lazarus, A. A., & Abramovitz, A. The use of "emotive imagery" in the treatment of children's phobias. *Journal of Mental Science*, 1962, 108, 191–195.

Leitenberg, H., Agras, W. S., Barlow, D. H., & Oliveau, D. C. Contribution of selective positive reinforcement and therapeutic instructions to systematic desensitization therapy. *Journal of Abnormal Psychology*, 1969, 74, 113–118.

Leitenberg, H., & Callahan, E. J. Reinforced practice and reduction of different kinds of fears in adults and children. *Behaviour Research and Therapy*, 1973, 11, 19–30.

Liberman, R. P. Behavioral approaches to family and couple therapy. *American Journal of Orthopsychiatry*, 1970, 40, 106–118.

Liberman, R. P., Levine, J., Wheeler, E., Sanders, N., & Wallace, C. J. Marital therapy in groups: A comparative evaluation of behavioral and interactional formats. *Acta Psychiatrica Scandinavica*, 1976, *Supplementum 266*, 1–34.

Liberman, R. P., Wheeler, E., & Sanders, N. Behavioral therapy for marital disharmony: An educational approach. *Journal of Marriage and Family Counseling*, 1976, 2, 383–395.

Lick, J. R., & Bootzin, R. R. Expectancy, demand characteristics, and contact desensitization in behavior change. *Behavior Therapy*, 1970, 1, 176–183.

MacDonald, M. L. Multiple impact behavior therapy in a child's dog phobia. *Journal of Behavior Therapy and Experimental Psychiatry*, 1975, 6, 317–322.

MacDonald, M. L., & Bernstein, D. A. Treatment of a spider phobia by *in vivo* and imaginal desensitization. *Journal of Behavior Therapy and Experimental Psychiatry*, 1974, 5, 47–52.

Marks, I. Behavioral treatments of phobic and obsessive-compulsive disorders: a critical appraisal. In M. Hersen, R. M. Eisler, & P. M. Miller (Eds.), *Progress in behavior modification* (Vol. 1). New York: Academic Press, 1975.

Meyer, V., & Mair, J. M. M. A new technique to control stammering: a preliminary report. *Behaviour Research and Therapy*, 1963, 1, 251–254.

Munjack, D. J. Overcoming obstacles to desensitization using *in vivo* stimuli and Brevital. *Behavior Therapy*, 1975, 6, 543–546.

Murphy, C. M., & Bootzin, R. R. Active and passive participation in the contact desensitization of snake fear in children. *Behavior Therapy*, 1973, 4, 203–211.

Naud, J., Boisvert, J., & Lamontagne, Y. Treatment of firearm phobia by flooding *in vivo* and motor activity: A case study. *Journal of Behavior Therapy and Experimental Psychiatry*, 1973, 4, 407–409.

Nay, W. R. *Behavioral intervention: Contemporary strategies*. New York: Gardner Press, 1976.

Nesbitt, E. B. An escalator phobia overcome in one session of flooding *in vivo*. *Journal of Behavior Therapy and Experimental Psychiatry*, 1973, 4, 405–406.

O'Leary, K. D., & Wilson, G. T. *Behavior therapy: Application and outcome*. Englewood Cliffs, New Jersey: Prentice-Hall, 1975.

Patterson, G. R., & Gullion, M. E. *Living with children: New methods for parents and teachers*. Champaign, Illinois: Research Press, 1971.

Peck, C. L. Desensitization for the treatment of fear in the high level adult retardate. *Behaviour Research and Therapy*, 1977, 15, 137–148.

Rachman, S., Hodgson, R., & Marks, I. M. The treatment of chronic obsessive-compulsive neurosis. *Behaviour Research and Therapy*, 1971, *9*, 237–247.

Rainey, C. A. An obsessive-compulsive neurosis treated by flooding *in vivo*. *Journal of Behavior Therapy and Experimental Psychiatry*, 1972, *3*, 117–121.

Rappaport, A. F., & Harrell, J. A behavioral-exchange model for marital counseling. *The Family Coordinator*, 1972, *21*, 203–212.

Rathus, S. A. Instigation of assertive behavior through videotape-mediated assertive models and directed practice. *Behaviour Research and Therapy*, 1973, *11*, 57–65.

Rimm, D. C., & Mahoney, M. J. The application of reinforcement and participant modeling procedures in the treatment of snake-phobic behavior. *Behaviour Research and Therapy*, 1969, *7*, 369–376.

Rimm, D. C., & Masters, J. C. *Behavior therapy: Techniques and empirical findings.* New York: Academic Press, 1974.

Rimm, D. C., & Medeiros, D. C. The role of muscle relaxation in participant modeling. *Behaviour Research and Therapy*, 1970, *8*, 127–132.

Ritter, B. The group desensitization of children's snake phobias using vicarious and contact desensitization procedures. *Behaviour Research and Therapy*, 1968, *6*, 1–6.

Ritter, B. Eliminating excessive fears of the environment through contact desensitization. In J. D. Krumboltz & C. E. Thoresen (Eds.), *Behavioral Counseling*. New York: Holt, 1969. (a)

Ritter, B. Treatment of acrophobia with contact desensitization. *Behaviour Research and Therapy*, 1969, *7*, 41–45. (b)

Ritter, B. The use of contact desensitization, demonstration-plus-participation and demonstration-alone in the treatment of acrophobia. *Behaviour Research and Therapy*, 1969, *7*, 157–164. (c)

Rollings, J. P., Baumeister, A. A., & Baumeister, A. A. The use of overcorrection procedures to eliminate the stereotyped behaviors of retarded individuals: An analysis of collateral behaviors and generalization of suppressive effects. *Behavior Modification*, 1977, *1*, 29–46.

Salter, A. *Conditioned reflex therapy.* New York: Capricorn, 1949.

Schultz, J. H., & Luthe, W. *Autogenic training.* New York: Grune & Stratton, 1959.

Sherman, A. R. Therapy of maladaptive fear-motivated behavior in the rat by the systematic gradual withdrawal of a fear-reducing drug. *Behaviour Research and Therapy*, 1967, *5*, 121–129.

Sherman, A. R. Real-life exposure as a primary therapeutic factor in the desensitization treatment of fear. *Journal of Abnormal Psychology*, 1972, *79*, 19–28.

Sherman, A. R. *Behavior modification: Theory and practice.* Monterey, California: Brooks/Cole, 1973.

Sherman, A. R. Two-year follow-up of training in relaxation as a behavioral self-management skill. *Behavior Therapy*, 1975, *6*, 419–420.

Sherman, A. R., Barone, D. F., & Turner, R. D. *Behavioral self-management of social-effectiveness skills: Assertion, and involvement.* Paper presented at the national convention of the Association for Advancement of Behavior Therapy, Atlanta, Georgia, 1977.

Sherman, A. R., & Plummer, I. L. Training in relaxation as a behavioral self-management skill: An exploratory investigation. *Behavior Therapy*, 1973, *4*, 543–550.

Smith, G. P., & Coleman, R. E. Processes underlying generalization through participant modeling with self-directed practice. *Behaviour Research and Therapy*, 1977, *15*, 204–206.

Stern, R. S., & Marks, I. M. Contract therapy in obsessive-compulsive neurosis with marital discord. *British Journal of Psychiatry*, 1973, *123*, 681–684.

Stuart, R. B. Operant-interpersonal treatment for marital discord. *Journal of Consulting and Clinical Psychology*, 1969, *33*, 675–682.

Sulzer-Azaroff, B., & Mayer, G. R. *Applying behavior-analysis procedures with children and youth*. New York: Holt, 1977.

Thase, M. E., & Moss, M. K. The relative efficacy of covert modeling procedures and guided participant modeling on the reduction of avoidance behavior. *Journal of Behavior Therapy and Experimental Psychiatry*, 1976, *7*, 7–12.

Watson, J. B. *Behaviorism*. New York: Norton, 1930.

Watson, J. P., Gaind, R., & Marks, I. M. Physiological habituation to continuous phobic stimulation. *Behaviour Research and Therapy*, 1972, *10*, 269–278.

Wieman, R. J., Shoulders, D. I., & Farr, J. H. Reciprocal reinforcement in marital therapy. *Journal of Behavior Therapy and Experimental Psychiatry*, 1974, *5*, 291–295.

Williams, J. L. *Operant learning: Procedures for changing behavior*. Monterey, California: Brooks/Cole, 1973.

Wimberger, H. C., & Kogan, K. L. A direct approach to altering mother-child interaction in disturbed children. *Archives of General Psychiatry*, 1974, *30*, 636–639.

Wolpe, J. *Psychotherapy by reciprocal inhibition*. Stanford, California: Stanford University Press, 1958.

Wolpe, J. The experimental foundations of some new psychotherapeutic methods. In A. J. Bachrach (Ed.), *Experimental foundations of clinical psychology*. New York: Basic Books, 1962.

Wolpe, J. *The practice of behavior therapy*. New York: Pergamon, 1969.

Wolpe, J. *The practice of behavior therapy*. New York: Pergamon, 1973.

Wolpe, J., & Lazarus, A. A. *Behavior therapy techniques: A guide to the treatment of neuroses*. Oxford: Pergamon, 1966.

Yeung, D. P. H. Diazepam for treatment of phobias. *Lancet*, 1968, *i*, 475–476.

Yule, W., Sacks, B., & Hersov, L. Successful flooding treatment of a noise phobia in an eleven-year-old. *Journal of Behavior Therapy and Experimental Psychiatry*, 1974, *5*, 209–211.

Zane, M. D. *Contextual therapy and modification of phobic behavior*. Unpublished manuscript, White Plains Hospital (New York), n.d.

Zane, M. D. *Relationships of changing behavior and cognition in children's fears*. Unpublished manuscript, White Plains Hospital (New York), 1976.

3

In Vivo Therapies
for Compulsive Habits,
Sexual Difficulties, and
Severe Adjustment Problems[1]

A. ROBERT SHERMAN
MICHAEL P. LEVINE

INTRODUCTION

The present chapter reviews *in vivo* therapies which have been employed with three categories of psychological disturbance: compulsive habits, sexual difficulties, and severe adjustment problems. Traditional psychotherapeutic interventions have been relatively ineffective in promoting durable improvements in some of the problems represented in these areas, a fact which may have added impetus to the search for *in vivo* alternatives. With the exception of *in vivo* aversion therapy, the present approaches have generally received less systematic empirical

[1] Some of the information presented in this chapter was assembled during a special seminar on *in vivo* therapies conducted by the first author. The contributions of the following students are gratefully acknowledged: Bonnie Gutterman, Janice Hamilton, Laura Hamlin, Janice Jackson, Linda Johnston, Howard Lunche, Lorence Miller, Debbie Mohr, Charles Nasser, Sheri Rego, and Tim Worden.

evaluation than most of the approaches described in Chapter 2. Each approach does have at least some favorable clinical support, however, which justifies its inclusion in this review and should encourage further exploration of its effects and limitations. As in the preceding companion chapter, the presentation of each treatment strategy includes a summary of the basic procedure and its rationale, a case example, representative findings, and an appraisal of its present status.

COMPULSIVE HABITS

Certain persistent behaviors which have immediate pleasurable effects may be maladaptive because of their long-term harmful consequences for the individual. Drug and alcohol addictions are among the most serious of these problems because of their life-threatening potential, but there are other habitual response patterns that may become sufficiently troublesome to warrant treatment. Sometimes a problem emerges after a behavior has been compulsively engaged in over a prolonged time, as when a chronic smoker develops serious respiratory problems. Sometimes a persistent activity develops into a problem because it creates conflict with the law, as when a compulsive gambler accumulates debts that he is unable to repay. Treatment strategies for problems like these often involve the use of noxious stimulation to condition an aversion to the behavior and associated stimuli. When this is conducted in relation to the real behaviors and contexts, it is referred to as "*in vivo* aversion therapy." This approach is reviewed in the present section as it may be applied to a variety of compulsive habits, including deviant sexual behaviors (which are also considered in the next section) and alcoholism (for which the use of "simulated bars" to promote controlled drinking is described separately). Its application to the treatment of enuresis is also presented because, although this is a qualitatively different kind of problem, it represents a difficult clinical challenge which has responded well to *in vivo* aversion therapy.

In Vivo Aversion Therapy

Procedures involving aversive stimuli have been applied in the treatment of certain persistent problems, such as excessive smoking, sexual deviations, alcoholism, gambling, and enuresis, for which the controlling factors cannot always be readily identified or eliminated. Aversion procedures are designed to eliminate the maladaptive behavior by associating it, and related stimuli, with noxious stimulation like electric shocks, emetic drugs, or loud noises. The approach is referred to as *in vivo aversion therapy* when treatment focuses on the real behaviors and contexts rather than their imaginal or symbolic counterparts. Depending on the nature of the behavior and the contingencies through which the noxious stimuli are introduced, there may be two learning processes involved: *classical aversive conditioning*, in which previously attractive items (e.g., cigarettes) become unappealing through contiguous association with noxious stimuli, and *operant punishment*, in which instrumental responses (e.g., taking a cigarette and lighting it) become less probable because they have been followed by noxious events. Since the aversion approach decreases but does not replace maladaptive behavior, it is often coupled with other procedures designed to shape more desirable responses. Barlow (1972) suggested that, for practical and ethical reasons, the use of aversion therapy should be limited to voluntary clients who are capable of understanding and cooperating with the procedures and who have no physical problems which might be exacerbated by the stress of aversive stimulation. While such guidelines usually are appropriate, there are rare occasions when involuntary treatment may be indicated—for example, in managing life-threatening behaviors such as self-mutilation or compulsive vomiting in autistic children, when there are no other effective strategies available.

Basic Procedure

The *in vivo* application of aversion procedures has been conducted in a variety of ways depending upon such things as the nature of the problem, the characteristics of the client, and the type of noxious stimulus. From the standpoint of implementation, an important factor concerns who is responsible for arranging and administering the aversive stimulus. For example, it may be self-administered, therapist-administered, or (in the case of treating nocturnal enuresis in children) parent-administered. Each of these procedures will be presently described.

Self-administered electric shock has been prescribed in the treatment of recurrent and refractory problems, such as sadistic fantasies, hallucinations, nailbiting, and "drug cravings," which cannot be easily or meaningfully reproduced in the therapist's office. Treatment begins with an explanation of the rationale and experimental nature of self-administered shock, a discussion of the necessity for keeping extensive records in order to evaluate the program, and a demonstration of the *in vivo* procedures. The client is instructed to shock himself each time the problematic thoughts or behaviors occur in the course of daily life. The shocks are self-administered using a portable, inconspicuous, and inexpensive shock inductorium (Bucher, 1968; McGuire & Vallance, 1964).

Shock intensity is set by the patient at a level that is subjectively "painful" or "just bearable." Particularly in the early stages of this self-managed *in vivo* treatment, the therapist monitors the client's progress by reviewing the self-monitoring data during weekly office visits and by scheduling daily telephone conversations. These contacts facilitate the client's compliance, help to alleviate procedural or emotional problems associated with the treatment, and may also provide an opportunity for developing adaptive behaviors to replace the undesirable ones.

Enuresis is a condition in which there is an "involuntary discharge of urine in the absence of organic pathology after a child has reached the age of three or four years [O'Leary & Wilson, 1975, p. 111]." In nocturnal enuresis, wetting occurs while the child is asleep. This problem has been construed by psychodynamic theorists as a symptom of intrapsychic conflict, and by behavioral theorists as a habit deficiency that can be rectified by prearranged learning experiences. Within the latter framework, the principal treatment is the "pad–bell" method, an *in vivo* aversive conditioning technique devised by Mowrer and Mowrer (1938).

During the initial consultation, the therapist explains the procedures and rationale to the entire family, provides the parents with instruction booklets and recording forms, and makes arrangements for subsequent visits (usually every other week) and telephone contacts. The parents and the child are also trained to assemble and operate the aversive conditioning apparatus, which is purchased by the family for use in the home. A typical device, which is relatively inexpensive, was described by B. L. Baker (1969):

> The conditioning unit used two foil pads, with holes in the top pad, separated by an absorbent sheet, and placed under *S*'s lower bed sheet. The pads were connected to a white plastic box which contained two 6-v. batteries, a sensitive relay, and a buzzer. Within seconds after the child began to wet, a circuit was completed and the buzzer sounded [p. 43].

This arrangement constitutes *in vivo* aversion therapy because the buzzer, which is triggered by bed-wetting, can be quite loud (up to 105 dB measured at nine feet from the device; Finley, Besserman, Bennett, Clapp, & Finley, 1973) and subjectively obnoxious. It continues to sound until the child or the parents arise and shut it off. At that time, the child is taken to the bathroom to finish voiding, if necessary, and to wash his face, thus ensuring that he is wide awake. The child then returns to the bedroom where he assists in removing the wet sheets, remaking the bed, and resetting the apparatus. To prevent "false alarms" that might result from excessive sweating, the parents are advised to keep the child's bedroom well ventilated and to refrain from using nylon sheets (Taylor & Turner, 1975).

There have been several reports of procedural variations designed to enhance the basic approach described above. Azrin, Sneed, and Foxx (1973, 1974) have developed an operant strategy called the "dry-bed" program which uses the pad–bell apparatus but which emphasizes liberal praise for continence and for correct toileting, verbal reprimands and cleanliness training following an "accident," and concentrated practice in rapid awakening, withholding urination, and correct toileting. Other modifications of the pad–bell procedures are overlearning (Taylor & Turner, 1975) and intermittent association of wetting and the aversive noise (Finley et al., 1973). These will be considered in more detail in the section on Representative Findings.

A final example of in vivo aversion therapy is the use of therapist-administered electric shock in the treatment of transvestism (Blakemore, Thorpe, Barker, Conway, & Lavin, 1963; Marks & Gelder, 1967) and compulsive gambling (Barker & Miller, 1968; Goorney, 1968). Although the treatment sessions are conducted in a hospital, this form of aversion therapy qualifies as in vivo because electric shock is paired with relevant contextual stimuli (e.g., women's undergarments or real gambling machines), mediating fantasies and cognitions, and emission of the actual problematic behavior (e.g., crossdressing or placing coins in a gambling machine). That is, the patient's problem is "treated at all possible points in the sequence from its initiation in internal feelings and imagery to its final expression in overt behavior [Marks & Gelder, 1967, p. 712]."

Typically, aversion sessions are held one to five times per day for a 1- or 2-week period. Electric shock (rather than an emetic drug, for example) is most commonly used as the aversive stimulus because:

1. It is easy to deliver;

2. It permits precision in the timing of delivery, which can be important for obtaining punishment or conditioning effects (e.g., Hull, 1952; Logan, 1970);

3. Many conditioning trials are possible within a single session; and

4. It does not require extensive medical supervision (see Rachman & Teasdale, 1969, pp. 32–38, for a review of these issues).

Blakemore et al. (1963) have noted that the feature of multiple conditioning trials automatically incorporates the potentially therapeutic element of massed practice into the in vivo treatment package.

The proper equipment and specific procedures for safe and effective administration of electric shock are described in detail by Galbraith, Byrich, and Rutledge (1970), Pfeiffer and Johnson (1968), and Butterfield (1975). In general, the inductoria operate from house current or portable batteries and dispense an electric shock via electrodes attached to the fingers, wrist, forearms, legs, or soles of the feet. There is no standard for shock intensity; it has been set at 35 volts (Goorney, 1968), at an amount that is slightly higher than what is experienced as "distinctly unpleasant" (Wolpe & Lazarus, 1966), at a level "sufficient to remove all pleasure" (Marks & Gelder, 1967), and at an intensity that is "sharp and unpleasant" (Blakemore *et al.*, 1963). Often the actual contingencies for shock delivery transcend the simple pairings implied above. For example, Marks and Gelder (1967) included the following arrangement in their *in vivo* treatment of transvestism:

> During practice trials, shocks were given after a warning signal which occurred randomly from 1–120 seconds after the patient started putting on the garments. From one to three shocks were given at random intervals after the signal, ceasing when all the clothes had been discarded. Shocks were omitted from 25 per cent of practice trials in order to produce a partial reinforcement schedule [p. 712].

Rationale

Practitioners of *in vivo* aversion therapy conceptualize self-perpetuating problems like compulsive gambling, transvestism, and enuresis as configurations of specific eliciting (mediating) stimuli, learned behaviors, and powerful conditioned or unconditioned rewards whose immediate effects override delayed aversive consequences (Bandura, 1969). Given this perspective, *in vivo* aversive procedures focus on the actual environmental stimuli (e.g., slot machines, women's shoes) or intraorganismic stimuli (e.g., drug cravings, sadistic fantasies, bladder distention) that mediate problematic sequences of behavior, and on the relationship between those sequences and their immediate consequences. In theory, the attempt to lower **stimulus** valences involves classical aversive conditioning, whereas the arrangement of adverse consequences for deviant **responses** is construed as operant punishment: The former "is designed to make a pleasurable (but undesirable) stimulus object less attractive by pairing it with a noxious stimulus" while the latter "is designed to suppress undesirable instrumental behavior by introducing aversive consequences whenever the behavior occurs [Sherman, 1973, p. 120]." Bucher and Lovaas (1968) maintain that *in vivo* implementation of aversion procedures is desirable because maximum behavior change is achieved when (*a*) aversion procedures mitigate discriminations between the training setting and the actual environment; (*b*) the target behavior is suppressed in the presence of the actual controlling stimuli; and (*c*) the punished sequences are a close approximation to the actual undesirable events.

In actual practice, it is difficult to determine the relative contributions of classical and operant processes to the *in vivo* control of disorders like transvestism and enuresis (Blakemore *et al.*, 1963; Taylor & Turner, 1975; for reviews of the substantial theoretical controversies over the effects of aversive stimulation, see Azrin & Holz, 1966; Campbell & Church, 1969; Rachman & Teasdale, 1969, pp. 119–152; Walters & Grusec, 1977). It is perhaps best to acknowledge that *in vivo* aversion therapy may have multiple effects, as noted by Bandura (1969):

> According to this view, painful stimulation produces both generalized emotional arousal and escape–withdrawal responses, which are usually incompatible with and, therefore, capable of replacing the ongoing behavior. Any environmental stimuli and responses that regularly precede or accompany the aversive experiences acquire, through their contiguous association, the capacity to arouse emotional reactions for some time after punishment is discontinued. In addition to emotional conditioning, any responses that successfully terminate or avoid aversive stimulation are instrumentally reinforced. The punished responses remain suppressed as long as the threatening events maintain their capacity to generate prepotent fear reactions and incompatible avoidance behavior [pp. 297–298]. [From *Principles of Behavior Modification* by Albert Bandura. Copyright © 1969 by Holt, Rinehart and Winston. Reprinted by permission.]

From the clinical standpoint, a primary value of aversive procedures is in achieving control over the problem behaviors long enough to allow new, adaptive behaviors to become established.

Case Example

Barker and Miller (1968) used electrical aversion therapy to treat a 34-year-old man with a 12-year history of compulsive gambling. The client sought treatment because his unsuccessful gambling was putting a severe strain on his marriage and his family. After the rationale and exact techniques were carefully explained to him, the client agreed to be hospitalized and undergo aversion therapy.

The client was hospitalized for 10 days during which he received 12 hours of treatment in 4 distinct 3-hour sessions. To facilitate transfer of conditioning effects, the patient's favorite slot machine was installed in the hospital. The patient set the electric shock level at an intensity sufficient to cause jerking of his arm. The shocks were delivered by a doctor or nurse using a portable shock apparatus like that developed by McGuire and Vallance (1964). Shocks were administered following performance of various segments of the client's actual gambling routine, beginning with the insertion of coins into the machine and concluding with the collection of (apparently rare) payoffs. In the course of treatment the client received a total of 672 shocks.

During the second 3-hour session the client stated that he had developed a revulsion to gambling. Nonetheless, he remained in treatment in order to strengthen the new aversive associations. Since the client had other gambling outlets, shocks were also given contingent upon making out betting slips and reading racing forms. A follow-up over the next 18 months indicated that he had been able to refrain from gambling during the intervening period and that he had been "promoted at work, repaid his debts, purchased a car and his marriage was saved [Barker & Miller, 1968, p. 75]." Shortly after the 18-month follow-up the client began to gamble heavily again, so he was given a 6-hour "booster" session in which his original treatment was repeated. A 2-year follow-up revealed that he had ceased gambling completely.

Representative Findings

The only evaluations of self-administered electrical aversion therapy are clinical reports which, in general, have yielded equivocal results. McGuire and Vallance (1964) found that 10 of 14 "sex perversion" cases demonstrated "good improvement" or "symptom removal" following the association of deviant fantasies and behaviors with self-administered electric shock. Wolpe (1965) reported that nine painful electric shocks, self-administered *in vivo* during the first week of treatment, were sufficient to eliminate a physician's intense craving for demerol for a period of 3 months; subsequently, however, the addictive behavior returned. Bucher and Fabricatore (1970) also reported problems in sustaining adaptive behavior following temporary elimination of obscene and critical auditory hallucinations with self-delivered electric shock. Their *in vivo* procedure resulted in rapid suppression of the voices and the paranoid patient was discharged after 5 weeks. However, shortly thereafter "the patient disappeared for 2 weeks and reappeared disheveled and inebriated. He was suspicious and uncooperative. His voices appeared to have returned [Bucher & Fabricatore, 1970, p. 384]."

In the cases described by Wolpe (1965) and by Bucher and Fabricatore (1970), relapse followed extremely rapid suppression of the target problems. Mees (1966) treated a socially withdrawn young man who was hospitalized because he had assaulted a woman with the intent to carry out a recurrent sadistic fantasy. After a lengthy baseline recording period, the patient was given 2 weeks of therapist-administered aversive conditioning trials in order to initiate the association of the recurrent fantasies with noxious stimulation. Then the patient assumed control over all aspects of the therapy and began self-administering shocks whenever the fantasies occurred and during contrived elicitations. In all, he received 6000 shocks in 65 sessions over a 14-week period. There was no dramatic suppression of sadistic fantasies but rather there was a steady decline in their frequency, an increase in their latency, and an increase in normal sexual fantasies. "Six months following the termination of data collection, the patient was discharged from the hospital. During the intervening period, he had a few abortive sadistic fantasies, but did not use them for masturbation and did not fantasy actually hurting a woman [Mees, 1966, p. 319]."

The *in vivo* treatment of nocturnal enuresis is one of the most heavily researched areas of behavior modification (see O'Leary & Wilson, 1975, pp. 115–123; Taylor & Turner, 1975). Controlled evaluations have indicated that the Mowrer and Mowrer (1938) procedure, which emphasizes *in vivo* use of the pad–bell conditioning device (a) is initially effective for 70–90% of enuretics (e.g., B. L. Baker, 1969; Deleon & Mandell, 1966); (b) requires several weeks or months to produce continence, defined as 14 consecutive dry nights (e.g., B. L. Baker, 1969; Turner, Young, & Rachman, 1970); (c) does not result in "symptom substitution" but rather appears to facilitate emotional and behavioral improvements (B. L. Baker, 1969); and (d) is more effective than no treatment (B. L. Baker, 1969), a placebo attention-control procedure (B. L. Baker, 1969), psychotherapy (Deleon & Mandell, 1966), and drug therapy (Forrester, Stein, & Susser, 1964). However, there is also evidence that the relapse rate for the pad–bell conditioning treatment is approximately 30–40% (Finley, Wansley, & Blenkarn, 1977; Turner, 1973).

Problems with relapse have prompted the investigation of procedures designed to consolidate initial treatment gains. As described previously, the dry-bed program devised by Azrin *et al.* (1973, 1974) combines the pad–bell apparatus with procedures that emphasize the operant and motivational aspects of *in vivo* continence training. Bollard and Woodroffe (1977) compared a dry-bed program to a waiting-list control group and to a modified dry-bed procedure which substituted regularly scheduled nocturnal wakenings for the conditioning device. The 14 children who underwent the dry-bed treatment with the aid of the pad–bell apparatus all reached the criterion of 14 consecutive dry nights and 12 of these children achieved this goal within a month. More importantly, during a 6-month follow-up, only two of these subjects relapsed insofar as they wet more than one night per week. None of the 20 children who received the program without the conditioning device or who received no treatment reached the criterion within the 13-week treatment period.

The other procedural variations involve overlearning, and intermittent association of wetting and the aversive noise. Taylor and Turner (1975) compared these variations with the traditional pad–bell procedure, which uses continuous pairing of wetness and loud noise. Children as-

signed to the intermittent reinforcement condition were unaware that
the apparatus was disconnected 50% of the nights. In the overlearning
condition, as soon as the child had achieved 7 consecutive dry nights, his
fluid intake was increased by 1–2 pints prior to going to bed. Using a
stringent continence criterion of 28 consecutive dry days, the overall
failure was 42.6% and there were no significant differences between
the three treatments. However, the overlearning subjects who had met
the continence criterion had a relapse rate of only 23.1% as compared
to 69.2% and 44.4% for the continuous and intermittent reinforcement
groups, respectively.

Taylor and Turner's (1975) study suggests that intermittent reinforcement was a relatively ineffective procedural modification, promoting only
a small reduction in relapse rate compared to continuous reinforcement.
However, Finley et al. (1977) contended that disconnecting the apparatus
on 50% of the nights is an unacceptable form of intermittent reinforcement because it neglects the fact of multiple wettings, a frequent occurrence in the early stages of treatment. Finley et al. (1977) used "an
automated programmable device which actually provides intermittent
reinforcement within an evening and not simply across evenings [p.
419]." Of the 80 children who received the conditioning treatment on a
preprogrammed intermittent reinforcement schedule, 75 (93.7%)
achieved a criterion of 14 consecutive dry nights. Moreover, the relapse
rate for all age groups combined was 25%, an encouraging figure given
the impressive degree of initial success and the large sample (60 children) for which follow-up data were obtained.

Therapist-administered aversive conditioning of in vivo components
has been used effectively in the treatment of transvestism and fetishism
(Blakemore et al., 1963; Marks & Gelder, 1967). Marks and Gelder
(1967) treated five patients hospitalized for transvestism and/or fetishism of at least 20 years duration in all but one case. All patients were
given a 2-week treatment consisting of daily 2-hour conditioning sessions. Slightly painful electric shocks were administered to the patient's
forearms or legs following production of the deviant fantasies and actual behaviors (e.g., cross-dressing) which comprised the presenting
problem. An impressive feature of this investigation was a within-subject
demonstration that decreases in sexual arousal, as measured by self-reports and changes in penile blood volume, were specific to the article of
clothing worn while the transvestite was shocked. That is, stimuli such
as panties and skirts continued to arouse the patient until they were included in the deviant sequences being associated with shock. This indicated that the noxious stimulation, as opposed to nonspecific aspects of
the therapy, was responsible for the decreases in arousal. At the conclu-

sion of treatment all five patients reported that their deviant thoughts and acts were eliminated. This improvement was maintained by three of the five at a 1-year follow-up, an impressive figure given the chronicity and typical resilience of these target problems.

Appraisal

There is considerable evidence to suggest that *in vivo* aversion therapy may be the most effective method available for eliminating nocturnal enuresis. In this regard, further research is needed to (a) clarify the extent to which the aversive conditioning device is necessary for behavior change—the work of Bollard and Woodroffe (1977) with the dry-bed program indicates that the conditioning device is crucial but Azrin *et al.* (1974) found that an identical dry-bed program in which the alarm rang only in the parents' bedroom was equally effective; (b) isolate the procedural variations (e.g., intermittent reinforcement, practice in withholding urination, increased incentives for continence) and patient variables which facilitate long-term maintenance of continence; and (c) develop special programs for families who otherwise are excluded from data analyses for "lack of cooperation" (see Turner *et al.*, 1970) and for children who have no difficulty in sleeping through a 105 dB noise (see Finley & Wansley, 1977).

The present status of *in vivo* self- and therapist-administered aversion therapy is much more difficult to assess because the case studies are equivocal and there is a paucity of controlled research. It is suggested, therefore, that the following issues merit systematic evaluation: (a) the relative efficacy of therapist-administered aversion therapy in which the problematic behaviors and contexts are presented symbolically versus *in vivo*; (b) the relative efficacy of self-administered noxious stimuli versus self-regulated noxious fantasies such as those used in covert sensitization (Cautela, 1966); and (c) the inclusion of specific procedures for increasing adaptive behaviors to replace the behaviors which are decreased by aversion techniques. This latter issue is particularly important because it has been demonstrated repeatedly that punishment often suppresses undesirable behavior but does not eliminate it, because "relapse" seems to be the rule rather than the exception in the available clinical literature, and because a salient feature of the successful *in vivo* treatments for enuresis (particularly the dry-bed program) is their emphasis on training continence as well as punishing incontinence. In other words, practitioners of *in vivo* aversion therapy must become more aware of the variables which may influence the long-term effectiveness of their procedures for controlling behavior. The most important of these factors is the availability of alternative behaviors. The effectiveness of aversive control techniques "will be maximized and potential problems minimized when they are used in conjunction with other techniques designed to promote more effective behavior patterns [Rimm & Masters, 1974, p. 367]."

Simulated Bars for Training Alcoholics
to Become Controlled Drinkers

Simulated bars have occasionally been used as an integral part of alcoholism rehabilitation programs designed to train patients to become appropriate, controlled drinkers. The actual treatment procedures vary, with some programs emphasizing the use of aversive conditioning techniques to suppress maladaptive drinking habits (e.g., Sobell & Sobell, 1973a) and others emphasizing the shaping of appropriate behaviors through instruction and supervised practice without aversive contingencies (e.g., Strickler, Bigelow, Lawrence, & Liebson, 1976). There are two basic elements which the programs described in this section have in common: the goal of teaching the alcoholic to become a controlled drinker (rather than to become completely abstinent), and the barlike treatment setting designed to resemble the actual situations in which problem drinking usually occurs. Approaches employing simulated bars in alcoholism rehabilitation have been used primarily, but not exclusively, with inpatients; these have usually been chronic alcoholics without histories of psychosis, and without health problems precluding some alcohol consumption.

Basic Procedure

The use of a simulated bar represents the essential feature which several approaches to alcoholism rehabilitation have in common. The facility used at Patton State Hospital in California was described by Schaefer, Sobell, and Mills (1971). The bar and cocktail lounge were located in a large cottage serving as a ward for alcoholics. "The bar itself has a padded, mahogany-finished serving bar complete with a sink and a full-length mirrored bottle display behind. It accommodates nine bar stools. A refrigerator, three circular tables with chairs, and diffuse overhead lighting controlled by a dimmer switch complete the rest of the decor [p. 31]." In addition to video and audio monitoring equipment, provision was made for piping music into the area. The facility also included a simulated home environment located adjacent to the bar and separated from it by floor-length draperies. "It was carpeted and included a sofa, a love seat, a soft chair, two end tables with lamps, two coffee tables, a pole lamp, a television set, and a phonograph [Sobell & Sobell, 1973a, p. 54]." An earlier version of the barroom setting at Patton State Hospital, which included dim blue lighting, beer signs, and fishnets, was described by Vogler, Lunde, Johnson, and Martin (1970).

The simulated bar employed by Strickler et al. (1976) was made to resemble barrooms found in the Southeast Baltimore area: "The facilities consist of an L-shaped bar, with stocked back-bar, cash register, refrigerator, bar stools, tables and chairs, and stereo. The barroom walls were paneled and adorned with beer and whiskey advertisements [p. 284]." A simulated bar setting in a small inpatient facility has also been used for alcoholism research at Rutgers University (Wilson & Tracey, 1976).

The treatment approaches employed in such simulated settings to train alcoholics to become controlled drinkers, as described in several reports (e.g., Mills, Sobell, & Schaefer, 1971; Schaefer et al., 1971; Sobell & Sobell, 1973a; Strickler et al., 1976), have typically included one or more of the following components:

1. Discussion of inappropriate drinking behavior and the circumstances in which it is likely to occur, so that the patient can become more aware of the factors which constitute his problem.
2. Videotape playback of drunken comportment, so that the patient can observe the objectionable aspects of his own excessive drinking.
3. Instruction in appropriate drinking behavior, so that the patient can learn about the behavior patterns he is trying to develop.
4. Training in the recognition of blood alcohol levels, so that the patient will be able to perceive when alcohol ingestion is becoming excessive.
5. Supervised drinking experiences, so that the patient can practice controlled drinking behavior in naturalized settings and learn to resist social pressures to drink excessively.
6. Reinforcement for progress in learning to control drinking behavior, so that the patient will become more likely to exercise such control in the future.
7. Aversive conditioning trials in which a noxious stimulus such as electric shock is administered to the patient contingent upon inappropriate drinking behaviors, so that such behaviors will become less probable in the future.
8. Contingency contracting, in which the patient initially deposits a sum of money which is to be returned to him contingent upon

treatment participation and progress, so that he will be more motivated to continue the program even when the going gets rough.

Rationale

The primary rationale for employing simulated bar settings as an integral part of alcoholism rehabilitation programs is to facilitate treatment
processes and the transfer of improvements to the natural environment.
Moreover, some clinical researchers assume that moderate, controlled
drinking is a more viable goal than total abstinence, since the individual
will invariably encounter social situations in which some drinking is
normally expected. Drinking problems have traditionally been quite resistant to therapeutic change and relapse rates have been relatively high
for a number of reasons, some of which were discussed by Eysenck and
Beech (1971). Although there are maladaptive consequences of excessive
drinking, usually the immediate effects are pleasurable and take place
within a context of social encouragement. When the treatment is conducted in a remote context lacking these features, the patient does not
learn to resist their influence, and any improved drinking habits tend not
to transfer readily to the natural environment. By training appropriate
drinking behavior in the presence of naturalistic stimuli, the probability of transfer decrement is reduced and it is expected that the patient will be better able to maintain the improvements in everyday
situations.

Case Example

As indicated above, there are a variety of procedural components
which may be integrated into an alcoholism treatment program involving simulated bars. Strickler *et al.* (1976) described an innovative program employed in the Baltimore City Hospital system which, unlike
many behaviorally oriented alcoholism treatments, did not include aversive conditioning procedures. Their description of the results with three
volunteer alcohol abusers is summarized here for illustrative purposes.
A 47-year-old married truckdriver, a 57-year-old married realtor, and a
34-year-old divorced salesman, were selected from ten applicants responding to a newspaper article describing the program. All three had
abused alcohol for at least 5 years, had experienced blackouts and disrupted social relationships, and had not responded to prior treatment
attempts.

Upon acceptance into the program the procedures and goals were explained, and a security deposit contingency contract (Tighe & Elliott,
1968) was negotiated. This contract provided for the return of the deposit contingent upon a 6-month self-report follow-up by the participant.

The 7-week training program consisted of 2-hour group meetings twice weekly, for a total of fourteen scheduled sessions. The sessions, which were conducted in a simulated bar setting, were divided into four phases.

The first phase, lasting 2 weeks, required abstinence from drinking. The four sessions "were devoted to discussions and demonstrations of topics useful in increasing subjects' understanding of their own drinking patterns [p. 284]." These topics included a behavioral analysis of each person's drinking, education on alcohol use and abuse, training in relaxation as an alternative to chemically altering internal conditions, and a discussion of guidelines for moderate drinking.

The second phase consisted of supervised practice of moderate drinking habits. During the four sessions, participants were given the opportunity to drink beer while observing the drinking behavior of a model who was adhering to the moderation guidelines. The participants chose the topics of conversation during these sessions in which the time, setting, and atmosphere were similar to an actual barroom situation.

The five sessions constituting the third phase included use of a "breathalyzer" device to help train participants to discriminate blood alcohol levels and to self-regulate alcohol intake accordingly. The one session of the fourth phase consisted of an open-bar party in which alcohol was freely available and many people were actively drinking.

Results of the program indicated that two of the three participants had acquired a moderate drinking style which was maintained during the 6-month follow-up period. These two reported only 1 day and 7 days of excessive drinking during the 6 months, while the third participant, the divorced salesman, reported 47 days of excessive drinking. The failure of the program with the latter person was attributed to his sporadic attendance at treatment sessions, his persistence at drinking between sessions, and "his frequent refusal to alter a life-style (bar-hopping) in compliance with program aims [p. 286]." In contrast, for the two successful participants, the maintenance of moderation was attributed to "attendance and cooperative support of spouse and family members, and behavioral awareness in conjunction with the practice of appropriate drinking [p. 286]."

Representative Findings

Two major investigations of programs involving simulated bars for training alcoholics to become controlled drinkers were conducted at Patton State Hospital in California. In both instances the basic treatments included aversive conditioning components in which electric shocks were administered to patients contingent upon inappropriate drinking behaviors. Unfortunately, no attempt was made to appraise the independent contribution of the simulated barroom setting to the overall effectiveness of the therapy programs. As described below, the drinking behaviors of patients participating in the investigations were followed up for one or two years.

The first study (Mills *et al.*, 1971) was designed "to explore whether bar drinking habits typical of alcoholics (drinking straight liquor in large gulps and large amounts) could be changed to bar drinking habits typical of social drinkers (drinking mixed drinks in small sips and small amounts) [p. 18]." The 13 hospitalized male alcoholics who volunteered to participate had a mean age of 47.5 years and a mean of 6.4 past admissions to institutions for treatment of alcoholism. Located in the center of the ward, the treatment area consisted of a simulated cocktail lounge and bar, with bar stools, a bottle display, mirror, diffuse lighting, refrigerator, and music. Patients were seen in pairs and sat next to each other at the bar, accompanied by one or two female assistants and a "bartender." As a central component of the treatment, brief but painful electric shocks were administered to the patients' nondominant hands when they exhibited drinking behaviors characteristic of alcoholics. The relevant aversive contingencies were explained to the patients prior to the first session and they were also informed that shocks could be avoided by drinking in an appropriately controlled fashion. The bartender and others in the bar gradually increased the amount of social pressure they put on the patients to drink excessively, and verbally praised the patients for successfully refusing to order or consume drinks. There was a total of 14 scheduled sessions, each lasting up to 2 hours.

It was found that 4 of the patients emitted the required repertoire of controlled drinking from the first day, never ordering more than three mixed drinks and consuming these in very small sips. The remaining 9 patients learned these behaviors over a period of 12 to 14 sessions. At the time of a 6-week follow-up, 5 of the 13 treated patients could be classified as either social drinkers or abstinent, while this was true for only 2 of 13 control patients from the same population who had also volunteered for the program but had not received training in social drinking skills. Furthermore, none of the treated patients was reported drunk during this time period, whereas 4 of the controls were in that category. With regard to the possible therapeutic role of the *in vivo* treatment setting, in their discussion, the authors noted that "The use of a simulated bar and cocktail lounge probably facilitated generalization . . . [p. 27]." Follow-up results were subsequently reported by Schaefer (1972) on those patients who were able to be monitored for one year and who were not institutionalized: whereas 7 out of 9 treated patients were either abstinent or drank in socially acceptable ways, this was true for only 2 out of 8 controls.

Sobell and Sobell (1973a) conducted a therapy outcome study with 70 hospitalized male alcoholics. Based upon initial interviews, the patients were assigned to a treatment goal of either controlled drinking or abstinence, whichever seemed most appropriate. Half of the patients within each treatment goal were then randomly assigned to receive a 17-session behavioral therapy program, while the other patients received conventional state hospital treatment oriented toward abstinence (sometimes including group therapy, chemotherapy, Alcoholics Anonymous, and/or physiotherapy).

A variety of procedures were integrated into the behavioral therapy program. These included an explanation of the treatment rationale, instruction in refusing alcoholic beverages, videotape self-confrontation of drunken behavior, and shaping of appropriate controlled-drinking and nondrinking behaviors (depending upon treatment goal) with electric-shock punishment of inappropriate drinking. According to the authors:

> Treatment sessions dealt directly with the inappropriate behavior of excessive drinking and emphasized a patient's learning alternative, more appropriate responses to stimulus conditions which had previously functioned as setting events for his heavy drinking. The treatment took into account the learning history of each individual patient and was specifically tailored to meet each patient's needs [p. 53].

The percentages of patients who were either abstinent or controlled drinkers during the majority of a 6-week interval following hospital discharge were appreciably higher for behaviorally treated patients than for conventionally treated patients. For those who had been behaviorally treated, the figures were 85% for patients with controlled-drinking goals and 73% for patients with nondrinking goals. For those who had been conventionally treated, the figures were 45% and 53%, respectively. Further follow-ups at 1 year (Sobell & Sobell, 1973b) and at 2 years (Sobell & Sobell, 1976) revealed the continued superiority of the behaviorally treated patients. The mean percentages of days of abstinence or controlled drinking during the first 6 weeks, the first year, and the second year, for behaviorally treated patients were 73%, 70%, and 85%, respectively, for those with controlled-drinking goals and 68%, 68%, and 64%, respectively, for those with nondrinking goals. The percentages for their conventionally treated counterparts were 50%, 35%, and 42%, respectively, for those with controlled-drinking goals and 55%, 38%, and 43%, respectively, for those with nondrinking goals.

In addition to supporting the efficacy of the behavioral treatment approach, and in contrast to earlier claims that total abstinence is the only alternative to drunkenness for chronic alcoholics, the results of this research program were interpreted as suggesting that controlled drinking should be considered a feasible treatment goal for some alcoholics. It appears that simulated bars can be employed successfully in therapy programs for alcoholism regardless of whether the goal is to train controlled drinking behaviors, as detailed above, or to condition abstinence (e.g., Vogler *et al.*, 1970; Wilson & Tracey, 1976).

Appraisal

Research in this area has been concerned primarily with evaluating the overall effects of alcoholism treatments conducted in simulated barroom settings, and not the independent contributions of the settings themselves. A variety of procedures have been integrated into such programs, with most treatments including behavioral instruction, supervised practice, and an aversive-conditioning component. While simulated barrooms have been employed successfully in programs directed at conditioning abstinence, they seem especially well-suited to programs designed to train the controlled drinking behaviors which normally occur in bars and cocktail lounges. The limited evidence available suggests that such programs can often promote enduring improvement in the drinking patterns of male patients who had been chronic alcoholics. It is unfortunate that information is not available concerning the role of the simulated bar in the overall efficacy of the therapeutic approach. On theoretical grounds the simulated setting would be expected to facilitate certain treatment processes which involve recognizing, and learning new responses to, stimuli (including social factors) which formerly prompted excessive drinking. Furthermore, the similarity between treatment and natural settings would be expected to facilitate the transfer of behavioral improvements from therapy to the natural environment. Theoretical speculation is no substitute for empirical demonstration, however. Considering the effort and expense required to establish simulated barrooms in therapy settings, it would appear very desirable that research be conducted to ascertain the actual clinical advantages resulting from this *in vivo* treatment component.

SEXUAL DIFFICULTIES

The present section reviews *in vivo* approaches to the treatment of two different categories of sexual difficulties. *In vivo sex therapy* is concerned with the alleviation of anxiety and ignorance about sexual behavior, as well as deficiencies in sexual skills, any or all of which may interfere with sexual performance and pleasure. Common problems in this category include premature ejaculation in males, and difficulty achieving orgasm in females. Sexual education and *in vivo* practice play a central role in this approach, which usually involves the conjoint treatment of both partners. The second category concerns individual sexual practices which are sometimes labeled "deviant" because they normally do not culminate in shared sexual satisfaction between consenting partners. When people derive pleasure from variations in sexual activity which do not harm others, and which they are not ambivalent about, there would clearly be no need for treatment. However, sometimes the person's sexual pleasure becomes dependent upon certain objects or activities which embarrass him, adversely affect other people, and/or violate legal statutes. Examples include *exhibitionism*, which involves sudden exposure of the genitals in public, *transvestism*, which involves dressing in clothes normally worn by the opposite sex, and *voyeurism*, which involves unobtrusively watching other people interacting sexually without their awareness. *Shame aversion therapy*, as described in this section, is a relatively new approach with an *in vivo* emphasis which has been used to help people overcome their compulsive performance of behaviors such as these. While this intervention (and others involving aversion therapy, as described in the preceding section) conditions negative associations to the undesired behavior, the ultimate success may depend upon the individual's acquisition of more acceptable ways of achieving sexual satisfaction.

In Vivo Sex Therapy

In vivo sex therapy is a short-term approach to the treatment of sexual dysfunctions, such as premature ejaculation in males and general or orgasmic dysfunction in females, which are not attributable to disease, substance abuse, physical abnormalities, or severely disturbed social relationships. It is considered most appropriate for the person whose sexual problems are a function of anxiety, ignorance, and/or a lack of sexual skills and who has a partner who is willing to participate in the treatment. In actual practice, it is often found that both partners have difficulties: "Both husband and wife suffered from sexual disorders in 43.7 percent of the couples treated by Masters and Johnson, and 25 percent of the couples in our experience are bilaterally dysfunctional [Kaplan, 1974, p. 468]." While the specific treatment would be dictated by the nature of the problems, the general approach usually involves office-based discussions and skill training together with *in vivo* "homework" assignments directed toward increasing degrees of sexual intimacy

between the partners in their own habitat. According to Kaplan (1974):
"While the incorporation of experiential [*in vivo*] behavior modification
is being explored in some other therapeutic contexts, it finds its fullest
expression in sex therapy, where the sexual tasks constitute a major
essential treatment tool [p. 201]."

Basic Procedure

In vivo sex therapy attempts to eliminate the clients' specific sexual
problems by integrating office-based discussion sessions with highly
structured sexual assignments to be practiced and enjoyed at home. Therapy is generally brief (2 weeks to 2 months) and is often conducted by a
male and female therapist team. The initial meetings are devoted to a
medical examination and to consideration of relevant subjects such as
the clients' sexual histories, their attitudes about their bodies, and their
individual perceptions of the problems. On the basis of this information
the therapists present their treatment plan and specify the shared responsibilities of the therapists and clients in effecting the desired
changes. This arrangement may be formalized in a therapeutic contract
(Kaplan, 1974; Lobitz & LoPiccolo, 1972).

The introductory sessions also prepare the couple for implementing
the program's *in vivo* components. In delivering their diagnosis and in
stipulating the conditions of treatment, the therapists strive to model
openness, trust, and the value of continuous communication in the alleviation of sexual dysfunction. In addition, during this period the therapists often initiate the process of sex education by providing informative literature (e.g., Ellis, 1972), educational films, and discussions of the
physiology and psychology of sex.

Premature ejaculation has been diagnosed on the basis of the latency
of orgasm (LoPiccolo & Lobitz, 1974), on a statistical basis pertaining to
the frequency of the partner's orgasms (Masters & Johnson, 1970), and
on the basis of the male's ability to control the ejaculatory reflex
(Kaplan, 1974). None of these definitions is totally satisfactory but, for
our purposes, "ejaculatory control may be said to be established when
the man can tolerate the high levels of excitement which characterize
the plateau stage of the sexual response cycle without ejaculating re-
flexly [Kaplan, 1974, pp. 290–291]."

The most successful *in vivo* treatment of premature ejaculation, called
the "squeeze technique" (Masters & Johnson, 1970), is modeled after a
"stop–start" method pioneered by Semans (1956). After the couple have
undressed, the male lies on his back and the woman manually or orally
stimulates his penis. The man is told to be utterly selfish and to focus ex-

clusively on the erotic sensations emanating from the penis. When he recognizes "premonitory orgasmic sensations," he signals his partner to stop the stimulation. Semans (1956) and Wolpe (1969) suggest that, at this point, the woman should simply stop stimulating her partner until his erection is lost, and then repeat the entire process again. Masters and Johnson (1970) instruct the partner to squeeze the penis until the urge to ejaculate has subsided. "This is done by placing the index finger of her left hand on the glans just above the coronal ridge; the middle finger is placed just below the coronal ridge and the thumb is placed on the frenulum. In this position she squeezes the penis hard for about 3 to 4 seconds . . . [Runciman, 1975, p. 29]." The procedure does not cause pain or discomfort to the erect penis, but it does delay ejaculation. The entire procedure (either stopping and waiting, or stopping and squeezing) is repeated several times and then the male is allowed to ejaculate. As the male attains more ejaculatory control, subsequent repetitions may use lotions or vaseline to simulate the sensations of the lubricated vagina.

After the man develops the ability to delay ejaculation for increasing periods of time, the couple is instructed to attempt coitus in the female superior position. They are also told that, initially, the female should remain still and allow the man to experience the fundamental sensations of vaginal containment before they begin to increase, very gradually, the level of rocking and thrusting. Whenever the man signals that ejaculation is impending, the woman raises herself off, squeezes the penis, and then inserts it again. This procedure ultimately enables the man to experience 15–20 minutes of thrusting without ejaculating (Runciman, 1975). When ejaculatory control is mastered in the female superior position, the couple practice the technique in side-by-side intercourse for 3–4 weeks before graduating to the male superior position, which provides the most intense penile stimulation.

The woman suffering from "general sexual dysfunction" is unable to be aroused emotionally and has impaired vasocongestive responses (vaginal lubrication and dilation) to sexual stimulation. However, it is more common for a woman seeking sex therapy to report that she becomes sexually aroused but has never achieved orgasm ("primary orgasmic dysfunction") or can achieve orgasm only in specific situations, usually while masturbating ("secondary orgasmic dysfunction").

The *in vivo* treatment of sexually dysfunctional women (and their partners) generally begins with "sensate focus" exercises which (a) assist the woman in identifying and enjoying pleasurable sensations; (b) help her to communicate these discoveries to her partner; and (c) shift the focus of the couple's sexual interaction to giving and receiving pleasure in a nondemanding, sensuous manner. The couple is instructed never to proceed further than is enjoyable for the woman and to avoid doing the exercises when they are anxious or fatigued.

To begin the sensate focus phase the couple undress and find a comfortable and intimate noncoital position in which the man can gently caress the woman's body. At first, he is careful to avoid the breast and genital areas. It is the woman's responsibility to verbally and, more importantly, nonverbally guide her partner's efforts. Nonverbal communication is accomplished by having the woman place her hand over her partner's free hand and thereby use different levels of tactile pressure to convey her feelings of pleasure and displeasure. The woman's other responsibility is to selfishly enjoy the experience without any compunctions about "returning the favor" or not achieving orgasm. When nongenital stimulation can be enjoyed without anxiety, an attempt is made to gradually heighten the erotic tension by using lotions and by including light, teasing genital play. In many instances the man must be taught how to gradually increase the woman's sexual arousal and how to properly lubricate and stimulate her clitoris.

Next, the entire sensate focus sequence is expanded to include "nondemand" coitus. It is crucial that this escalation be initiated by the woman in accordance with her arousal, and not by the man's often incorrect perceptions of her readiness (Kaplan, 1974). To maintain (and heighten) the woman's arousal and concomitantly minimize the conditions for anxiety, it is suggested that coitus proceed with slow exploratory thrusts, rather than demanding and driving movements. The woman is instructed to appreciate the feelings of vaginal dilation, to focus her attention on the sensations of the erect phallus, and to experiment with various contractions of her pubococcyeal muscles while she thrusts at her own rate. To facilitate these desirable experiences, nondemand coitus begins with the female superior position and later is converted to the male superior position in steps analogous to those used in the later stages of the squeeze and stop–start techniques. At any point and in any position, it is entirely up to the woman whether she feels like driving for orgasm. It is important to note that the clients are left to work out the exact details of all sensate focus and coital assignments themselves so that the *in vivo* sexual encounters are realistically "theirs" (Belliveau & Richter, 1970).

Many women who seek sex therapy have no difficulty in becoming sexually aroused but they are either completely unable to achieve orgasm or they can do so only in circumscribed situations (e.g., while masturbating in a special position). *In vivo* sex therapy for these women incorporates the previous exercises but also emphasizes the following:

1. Education of the partner regarding the female orgasmic experience and the proper techniques of sexual behavior;
2. Instruction in the use of fantasy and cognitive self-control techniques which facilitate the dissolution of self-inhibitory defenses such as tiredness or intellectualization;
3. Practice in the proper rhythmic contraction and relaxation of the perineal muscles which are involved in producing sufficient stimulation for orgasm;
4. Helping the totally inorgasmic woman to produce her first orgasm by directed masturbation exercises involving manual and mechanical stimulation; and
5. The use of exercises which include the partner in successive approximations to stimulation of the woman's genitals and to the achievement of coital orgasm (Kaplan, 1974; Kohlenberg, 1974; Lobitz & LoPiccolo, 1972).

Some clients are extremely self-conscious about "letting go" and it may be necessary for them to role-play the overt behavioral and vocal aspects of the orgasmic experience until their anxiety gives way to amusement and, finally, indifference (LoPiccolo & Lobitz, 1974).

The treatment of women who are situationally inorgasmic is quite similar to that for totally inorgasmic women with one notable exception. Quite often the situationally inorgasmic woman has developed a highly ritualized form of masturbation. To break this stimulus control of orgasm the therapists advise the woman not to engage in her habitual pattern. Then they introduce her to different methods of masturbation and gradually "fade" the partner into foreplay and coital interactions (McGovern, Stewart, & LoPiccolo, 1975).

The daily or weekly discussion sessions conducted by the therapist or co-therapists constitute an important adjunct to the *in vivo* sexual exercises. These sessions permit the therapists and the clients to monitor the latter's progress in implementing the sexual assignments and to discuss unforeseen problems, sensitive topics, and new treatment plans. To expedite these functions, clients may be required (via the therapeutic contract) to complete detailed self-monitoring forms concerning their perception and enjoyment of the *in vivo* sexual experiences (LoPiccolo & Lobitz, 1974). The discussions also allow the therapist to observe first-hand any interpersonal behaviors which promote conflict and interfere with expressions of sexuality. Attempts to modify these behavior patterns may include consideration of their probable causes, therapist modeling of appropriate behaviors, role-playing, and the judicious use of therapist self-disclosure (see LoPiccolo & Lobitz, 1974). A concluding feature of the discussion sessions involves preparing the clients to self-manage their sexual problems after therapy is terminated (LoPiccolo & Lobitz, 1974).

Rationale

Most practitioners of *in vivo* sex therapy use a social learning model to conceptualize the etiology and treatment of sexual dysfunction. Human sexual inadequacy is thought to be a function of (*a*) lack of skill and/or ignorance of the physiology of sexual behavior; (*b*) performance-related anxiety compounded by continuing pressure to "perform"; and (*c*) a relationship which does not reinforce sexual expression (Kaplan, 1974; Lobitz & LoPiccolo, 1972; O'Leary & Wilson, 1975). *In vivo* sex therapy seeks to remove these current and specific obstacles to the couple's effective sexual functioning, and not to restructure the personality of a psychologically "inadequate" individual.

The removal of ignorance about sexual functioning is accomplished in a number of ways. The explicit authority of the therapist(s) is used to debunk myths (e.g., masturbation causes insanity) and misconceptions (e.g., the only "real" orgasm is a "vaginal" orgasm). In addition, clients are provided with literature and other graphic aids to understanding sexual functioning. One devastating contributor to ignorance is lack of interpersonal communication. Many couples "may feel deep affection for each other but have difficulty expressing their emotions, initiating and refusing sexual contact, and assertively communicating their likes and dislikes [Lobitz & LoPiccolo, 1972, p. 268]." The behavior of the therapists during the discussion sessions and diagnostic periods is explicitly structured to model open communication about sexual matters, and role-playing exercises conducted in the therapists' office give the clients a chance to practice the skills they observe. Moreover, the *in vivo* exercises are designed in part to encourage body exploration and multi-modal communication.

As noted earlier, *in vivo* sex therapy also attempts to extinguish emotional reactions such as fear, anxiety, or disgust which interfere with effective sexual functioning. The highly structured and graduated *in vivo* exercises are often conceptualized as a form of *in vivo* desensitization (Kaplan, 1974; Lobitz & LoPiccolo, 1972; O'Leary & Wilson, 1975; Rimm & Masters, 1974; Wolpe, 1969). "If while experiencing stimuli usually giving rise to anxiety the person can be made to experience a response [sexual arousal] that inhibits anxiety, the effect will be a reduction in the amount of anxiety elicited by those stimuli [Rimm & Masters, 1974, pp. 76–77]." Wolpe (1969) maintains that the basis for this process is the physiological incompatibility of sexual arousal (which reflects activation of the parasympathetic nervous system) and anxiety (which reflects activation of the sympathetic nervous system), but this explanation is controversial (see Rimm & Masters, 1974). Regardless, the intent is to diminish anxiety and to concomitantly increase sexual arousal with respect to increasingly intimate sexual interactions. This process should undermine the insidious cycle wherein anxiety engenders excessive self-monitoring ("spectatoring"), which leads to diminished excitement and poor performance, which ultimately result in doubt, hostility, and further anxiety in both partners. This perspective is the basis for efforts to insure that all countersexual experiences of pressure, anxiety, and demand are minimized, and for the stipulation that, at any stage in the program of *in vivo* assignments, the individual or couple should proceed no further than is arousing. As the partners become progressively more comfortable and aroused in their interactions, the degree of intimacy and the amount of stimulation is increased until their goals have been achieved.

All of the *in vivo* experiences are viewed as important in the desensitization of performance-related anxiety and the conditioning of arousal, but the sensate focus exercises have four other important functions. First, "basic to the sensate focus is the recognition that touch is a vital part of the personal human communication that gives meaning to sexual responsiveness for both men and women [Belliveau & Richter, 1970, p. 103]." Second, the sensate focus exercises are an antidote to the destructive myth that men know exactly what women want sexually and therefore they should always direct the pace and focus of sexual interaction. One purpose of the sensate focus exercises is "to give the woman a chance to focus on her own sexual feelings, to discover what her preferences are, and to communicate this information to her husband [Belliveau & Richter, 1970, p. 179]." To some extent, masturbation exercises also provide sensory experiences which can be communicated to the partner in order to enhance mutual enjoyment (Kohlenberg, 1974). Third, the exercises are structured to mitigate the couple's excessive preoccupation with orgasm and performance and to reaffirm the sensuousness and excitement of sexuality. And, finally, the exercises provide the woman with direct evidence that the man does not consider his pleasuring of her a chore and that he does not automatically reject a partner who is assertive about her own sexual preferences (Kaplan, 1974).

Increased awareness of (as opposed to obsessive self-monitoring of) sexual arousal is considered one of the principal benefits of the sensate focus experience. Along the same lines, the squeeze technique (or stop–start method) for the treatment of premature ejaculation can be construed as a means of systematically increasing the man's exposure to, and awareness of, the sensory aspects of penile stimulation such that non-anxious cognitive control of the ejaculatory reflex becomes possible (Kaplan, 1974) or learned associations between minimal stimulation, anxiety, and reflexive ejaculation become broken (Lobitz & LoPiccolo, 1972).

Case History

Kaplan (1974, pp. 471–472) reported the successful treatment of a couple, Mr. and Mrs. Y., whose marital relationship was sound but whose sexual interactions were impaired by Mr. Y.'s premature ejaculation and Mrs. Y.'s inability to achieve orgasm in her husband's presence (secondary orgasmic dysfunction). During the initial evaluation it was determined that Mr. Y. "was very cursory in his foreplay, primarily because he was afraid that he would become too aroused and ejaculate even before he could attempt coitus. Therefore, he penetrated her vagina as soon as he had a firm erection and usually ejaculated after two to five thrusts [p. 471]." This problem and Mrs. Y.'s orgasmic inhibitions were exacerbated by Mr. Y.'s guilt over his sexual inadequacy and Mrs. Y.'s embarrassment over asserting her own sexual needs.

The therapist decided to eliminate Mr. Y.'s problem first because otherwise there was insufficient information to establish if Mrs. Y.'s dysfunction was due to inadequate stimulation or psychological conflicts. The couple readily agreed to a treatment plan whereby their situation would be reevaluated after Mr. Y. had attained "ejaculatory continence"; if necessary, the treatment focus could then be shifted to Mrs. Y.'s problem.

The principal mode of treatment for Mr. Y.'s premature ejaculation was *in vivo* implementation of the Semans stop–start method described earlier. "In addition to the Semans procedure . . . [it was] suggested that the couple engage in pleasuring and sensate focus exercises in order to involve Mr. Y. in erotic experiences, as well as for diagnostic purposes to clarify the causes of her [Mrs. Y.'s] unresponsiveness [p. 471]." These *in vivo* exercises were always conducted before or after completion of the Semans procedure. This enabled Mr. Y. to devote full attention to experiencing and attaining mastery over the erotic sensations emanating from his penis during the progressively lengthier stop–start stimulations. After 4 weeks of treatment, Mr. Y. was able to have coitus for 15 min before ejaculating. However, Mrs. Y. remained inorgasmic, except when masturbating alone.

Discussion of the couple's experiences during the sensate focus assignments revealed that Mrs. Y. experienced considerable anxiety when she became very sexually aroused. Several *in vivo* techniques were used to eliminate this response. "Her husband's newly achieved ejaculatory control made possible prescription of the slow, nondemanding coital thrusting, carried out under the woman's control, which is often helpful in the treatment of coital orgastic dysfunction [p. 472]." She was also asked to practice some fantasy techniques that helped her to refrain from engaging in spectatoring when she became intensely aroused. Finally, she was given explicit instructions to "selfishly abandon herself to her own erotic experiences and to disregard her husband's needs temporarily [p. 472]."

The *in vivo* assignments for Mr. and Mrs. Y. were supplemented by "extensive transactional work" which concentrated upon teaching the couple to communicate openly and clearly about their sexual feelings and desires. In the latter stages of treatment special attention was paid to Mrs. Y.'s childhood experiences with prohibitions against sexuality and to her fears of being rejected on the basis of sexual assertiveness.

The treatment of Mrs. Y.'s orgasmic dysfunction was successful in that she became (*a*) more responsive during foreplay; (*b*) multiply orgasmic on clitoral stimulation by her husband; and (*c*) orgasmic during intercourse, provided that her husband concurrently stimulated her clitoris. Mr. and Mrs. Y. were quite satisfied with these outcomes and with Mr. Y.'s attainment of ejaculatory continence.

Representative Findings

There is an impressive array of clinical evidence which suggests that *in vivo* sex therapy is an effective treatment for premature ejaculation in males and primary and secondary orgasmic dysfunction in females. Unfortunately, reports of treatment procedures and outcomes (e.g., Kohlenberg, 1974) usually fail to distinguish between general sexual dysfunction and primary orgasmic dysfunction, despite the seemingly obvious differences between treating someone who cannot be aroused versus someone who cannot achieve orgasm after arousal (see Kaplan, 1974).

The results of programs which emphasize use of the squeeze technique in the elimination of premature ejaculation have been remarkably favorable. Masters and Johnson (1970) reported that 182 of 186 (98%) premature ejaculators were successfully treated with a combination of short-term counseling and the squeeze technique. The criterion for success was ability to delay ejaculation long enough for the partner to achieve orgasm in 50% of coital interactions. A 5-year follow-up revealed that only one man failed to maintain his therapeutic success.

Lobitz and LoPiccolo (1972) were able to eliminate premature ejaculation in all 6 cases treated during a 30-month period at the University of Oregon Psychology Clinic, while Yulis (1976) reported success in 33 of 37 cases (89%).

For the most part, programs which utilize *in vivo* sexual activity as the principal curative element have also been highly successful in treating orgasmic dysfunctions in women. Masters and Johnson (1970) reported that 193 women with primary orgasmic dysfunction (and their partners) were given short-term counseling and instructed to use the sensate focus and graduated coital exercises. The criterion for treatment success was achievement of orgasm in 50% of all coital opportunities. Thirty-two (16.6%) of these couples were considered to be immediate treatment failures. A 5-year follow-up revealed two treatment reversals, but the overall success rate was 82.4%. Masters and Johnson were less successful in eliminating situational orgasmic dysfunction in 149 other women, but the overall success rate after 5 years was still a creditable 72.5%.

LoPiccolo and Lobitz (1974) reported an even greater discrepancy in their treatment outcomes for the two types of orgasmic dysfunction. Therapy included a combination of discussions and social-skills training in conjunction with sensate focus, directed masturbation, and graduated coital assignments. Using the Masters and Johnson criterion, this approach was successful in 13 of 13 cases of primary orgasmic dysfunction, but failed to help 6 of 9 cases of secondary orgasmic dysfunction. However, it may be that the 3 successful cases reflect the effectiveness of a procedural change in which greater emphasis was placed on modifying the marital relationship and on prescribing special masturbation exercises which break the situational specificity of masturbation and facilitate the successful implementation of the exercises leading to coital orgasm (McGovern et al., 1975; Snyder, LoPiccolo, & LoPiccolo, 1975).

An emphasis on the importance of masturbation exercises in the remediation of orgasmic dysfunction is also found in the aggregate case data presented by Kohlenberg (1974). Although the program described by LoPiccolo and Lobitz (1974) reportedly has been highly successful in eliminating primary orgasmic dysfunction, Kohlenberg indicated that a similar program was successful with only 8 of 15 (53%) inorgasmic couples. However, 3 of the initial failures and 4 new couples were later successfully treated with a program which included prescription of extensive *in vivo* masturbation exercises.

The available clinical data suggest that *in vivo* sex therapy is an effective approach to the remediation of premature ejaculation and orgasmic dysfunction (see also Hartman & Fithian, 1972). It is difficult to attribute the reported clinical effects of this therapy solely to "nonspecific" factors such as attention or client expectation. Over 50% of the successful cases reported by Masters and Johnson (1970) had previously undergone some form of psychotherapy which had not alleviated their problems. Furthermore, an evaluation of the effectiveness of psychoanalysis and psychotherapy with coitally inorgasmic women suggested that the approximate "cure" rate with these "*in vitro*" therapies was only 30–40% (O'Connor & Stern, 1972).

The clinical data reviewed above imply that the *in vivo* aspects of sex therapy contribute substantially to its relative effectiveness. This contention was examined by Mathews, Bancroft, Whitehead, Hackmann, Julier, Bancroft, Gath, and Shaw (1976). A 3 × 2 factorial design was used to compare the effectiveness of three treatments administered by either one or two therapists. The treatments, each of which lasted 10 weeks, were (*a*) imaginal and (later) *in vivo* desensitization of performance-related anxiety, plus participation in weekly office-based counseling sessions; (*b*) *in vivo* sexual assignments plus counseling, that is, an adaptation of the Masters and Johnson (1970) program; and (*c*) *in vivo* sexual assignments supervised by weekly correspondence from the therapist(s). The clients were married couples and the most common complaints—premature ejaculation and erectile failure in men, and general sexual dysfunction and primary orgasmic dysfunction in women—were balanced across conditions.

Improvement in sexual functioning was measured by therapist ratings of each couple's general and sexual relationship, similar ratings made by independent assessors, and the clients' reports pertaining to the frequency and enjoyment of varying types of sexual contact. In general,

> Whilst changes in individual outcome measures are limited and do not show highly significant differences between treatments, the consistency of trends is striking, and suggests that Treatment 2 (i.e. directed practice plus counselling) is generally superior to Treatments 1 [desensitization plus counselling] and 3 [directed practice with minimum contact]. This would imply that the components of Treatment 2, directed practice and counselling, are of importance in determining overall outcome [Mathews *et al.*, 1976, p. 435].

There is also some evidence from the independent assessors' ratings that the effects of the directed practice-plus-counseling treatment may be enhanced by the involvement of co-therapists. It should be noted that, although the combination of *in vivo* sexual assignments and weekly counseling sessions tended to be more effective in increasing the frequency of sexual contact and the therapists' ratings of female enjoyment of this contact, all of the treatments were decidedly ineffective in increasing the frequency of orgasms in the sexually dysfunctional inorgasmic women. The extent to which each treatment was successful in alleviating premature ejaculation and erectile failure cannot be determined from the reported data.

Appraisal

The equivocal results reported by Mathews *et al.* (1976) emphasize the necessity of further **controlled** outcome studies which can evaluate the salutary implications of the voluminous clinical data in this area. While certain features of the study by Mathews *et al.* (1976) can serve as a fine model for future research in this area, it is suggested that more attention be given to (*a*) the specification of the demographic characteristics and exact dysfunctions of the treated populations; (b) the use of dependent measures which permit a determination of the extent to which these specific dysfunctions are alleviated; and (*c*) the coordination of assessment and treatment. A good example of this latter feature is the development of the *Sexual Interaction Inventory* (LoPiccolo and Steger, 1974) and the incorporation of information from this and other instruments into a more effective treatment for situationally inorgasmic women (McGovern *et al.*, 1975; Snyder *et al.*, 1975).

While considerable work remains to be done in the refinement and evaluation of *in vivo* sex therapy, recent efforts have contributed substantially to our knowledge about sexuality, and to the alleviation of sexual dysfunctions in many people. The evolving atmosphere of increasing openness about sexual matters also appears to be a refreshing by-product of clinical and experimental work in this area.

Shame Aversion Therapy

Shame aversion therapy, as described by Serber (1970), has been employed successfully with such behaviors as transvestism, exhibitionism, pedophilia, and voyeurism. In this treatment, the person who is embarrassed about his habitual performance of a deviant sexual act is required to perform the act in front of a number of observers in settings resembling the real situations. This is intended to result in a prolonged unpleasant experience which will discourage the person from continuing the behavior in the future. Serber (1970) maintains that the approach will work only with patients who experience shame and self-conscious-ness about being observed performing the deviant behavior, and recommends special caution in the treatment of patients who have a psychotic history.

Basic Procedure

According to Serber (1970), shame aversion therapy "consists of having the subject who is embarrassed or self conscious about the act he performs perform the act on demand in front of a number of observers. The act is made to continue for 15 to 35 minutes and its style kept as close to the *in vivo* situation as is possible. The patient is told simply to observe himself and be aware of being observed [p. 213]." The patient is sometimes required to verbalize his thoughts and feelings during the enactment of the deviant behavior (e.g., Wickramasekera, 1972; Stevenson and Jones, 1972). The observers are usually instructed to appear nonjudgmental (Serber, 1970) and to react with indifference (Reitz & Keil, 1971); they might also be advised to sit expressionlessly and make no comment on the patient's behavior (Wickramasekera, 1972). It is noted that the success of the treatment in promoting enduring improvements may depend upon the individual having alternative, acceptable sexual outlets (Serber, 1970). If the individual does not already have some history of appropriate heterosexual experience, the shame aversion therapy might have to be coupled with a therapy program for establishing appropriate sexual behavior.

Rationale

Shame aversion therapy represents an application of aversive conditioning. With those clients for whom the approach is appropriate, being observed engaging in a sexually deviant act causes unpleasant feelings of anxiety, guilt, or shame. The aim is to have the client "experience the act with little or no reinforcement . . . and mild to moderate punishment from himself [Reitz & Keil, 1971, p. 68]." The dysphoric affect disrupts the sexual arousal usually experienced in the situational context of the act, so that it is not a rewarding experience. In addition, the negative feelings become conditioned to the stimuli and activities involved in the deviant sexual behavior so that the prospect of engaging in the act on future occasions is negatively, rather than positively, arousing. If other, appropriate sexual outlets are available to the client, these become more likely to be pursued and the deviant behavior becomes less and less probable. As with other treatments relying upon the suppressive effects of aversive conditioning, booster sessions may occasionally be required to restore the conditioned aversion which tends to extinguish over time. This would probably be less necessary if the client has found alternative

sexual outlets which are adequately satisfying and thereby alleviate the
need for the deviant behavior.

Case Example

The treatment of a 36-year-old man who had been engaging in exhibitionistic behavior for 25 years was described by Reitz and Keil
(1971). The man, who was married and the father of six girls, estimated
that he had been exposing himself an average of 4 or 5 times per month
in a variety of settings, with a special preference for young girls. He had
received psychodynamic treatment on three prior occasions without
enduring benefit.

The treatment was formulated as follows:

> Four volunteer psychiatric nurses were selected as stimuli. A meeting was
> held with the nurses and the patient to outline the procedure and rationale.
> The office was to be treated as a waiting room. The patient was supplied
> with magazines to read and the nurses were to come in singly for 15
> minutes each. They were to bring "ward work" with them to complete
> during the session. The patient was to exhibit himself as nearly as
> possible as he would in real life.... Conversation was to be avoided....
> The nurses were instructed to react with indifference. They were told to
> "look at him as though he was handling a cigarette" [p. 68].

According to the report, the patient initially had difficulty in exhibiting, but continued despite strong feelings of embarrassment, shame, and
guilt. Treatment had been planned at the rate of two 15-min sessions
per visit, twice a week, and 10 sessions were implemented before the
patient moved to a new house. A similar schedule was continued for
several weeks, and then a tapering off began. In the course of treatment,
which lasted about 6 months, the patient discovered that masturbation reduced his need to exhibit, and was more pleasurable as well as
less socially undesirable; masturbation was therefore encouraged as a
preferable alternative at times when he was tempted to exhibit.

In a follow-up interview some 14 months after treatment was terminated, the patient reported continued freedom from exhibitionistic behavior and a greatly reduced impulse towards it. He also reported continuing to enjoy sexual relations with his wife and increased general
marital satisfaction, as well as a virtual absence of his once characteristic
depression.

Representative Findings

The shame aversion approach is relatively new. It was developed by
Serber (1970) as an incidental result of noting the marked anxiety manifested by a transvestite patient while Serber was attempting to photo-
graph the patient during various stages of his cross-dressing. The still

photographs were to be used in a classical aversion therapy treatment in which electric shock was to be administered to the patient while he was observing the photographed scenes. The patient's apparent distress at being observed and photographed prompted Serber to employ those very conditions as the aversive factor in an *in vivo* treatment. Prior to the treatment, the 23-year-old law student had been practicing transvestism for 11 years, averaging 8–11 occasions per month. The treatment was terminated as successful after three sessions. The client was then given pictures of himself cross-dressing in front of observers and told to look at them if he ever felt the desire to cross-dress again. A 1-year follow-up revealed that the patient had not cross-dressed and denied any urge to do so.

The success of the treatment with that patient prompted attempts to employ shame aversion therapy with others. The initial report (Serber, 1970) presented the results of working with eight male patients (including the first). They ranged in age from 23 to 52, and had been practicing their deviant sexual behaviors an average of 1–15 times per month for 11–30 years. The behaviors included transvestism, pedophilia, exhibitionism, voyeur–exhibitionism, and frotteurism. After two or three sessions of shame aversion therapy, five patients remained free of their asocial behaviors during 6- to 12-month follow-ups, and a sixth patient had only one episode. The two remaining patients, the one frotteur and one of the four transvestites, did not appear to have benefited from the treatment. Given the chronicity of the asocial behaviors, and their considerable resistance to change by other treatments, five or six successes out of eight appears quite impressive. The approach was also very efficient, requiring only two or three treatment sessions.

Other reports on the effects of shame aversion therapy, or variations therefrom, have focused primarily on the treatment of exhibitionism. Wickramasekera (1972) described a modified form of shame aversion therapy which was employed successfully with six exhibitionists who had been practicing the behavior for anywhere from 4 to 40 years. After the treatment, which never exceeded four sessions, none of the patients reported, nor had there been detected, any return of the deviant behavior. Stevenson and Jones (1972) also described the successful treatment of a 33-year-old exhibitionist with a form of shame aversion therapy.

Appraisal

Shame aversion therapy for deviant sexual behavior is a form of aversive conditioning treatment. The aversive effect derives primarily from feelings of shame and anxiety, as evoked by the embarrassment of being passively observed while engaging in the deviant act in settings resembling the real situations. Clinical reports by several practitioners have indicated the treatment's frequent success with such behaviors as transvestism and exhibitionism that have tended to be quite resistant to other forms of therapy. The approach is also relatively efficient in that most successful cases have required only a small number of sessions. There is some indication that it is likely to be particularly effective with patients who experience considerable shame and anxiety when observed engaging in the deviant behavior, who have some history and the present availability of appropriate sexual outlets, and who are not psychotic. The approach needs to be subjected to closer empirical scrutiny to learn more about the characteristics of individual patients that would indicate or contraindicate such treatment, and to provide controlled comparisons of the treatment with others that are employed for the same deviant behaviors.

An important issue which requires discussion in regard to shame aversion therapy concerns the effect of the treatment process upon the observers. Sometimes these people are described as volunteers from the treatment staff (e.g., Reitz & Keil, 1971); at other times the recruitment contingencies or identities of the participant–observers are not indicated. For example, in one case reported by Serber (1970), "an attractive girl was asked to participate, and the frotteur was requested to rub against her just as he would rub against strangers in buses and subways [p. 214]." In treatments like this, it would seem obligatory for therapists to make sure that observers are not coerced into participating, and are not adversely affected by the experience. That such participation could distress observers was noted by Stevenson and Jones (1972). In their treatment of male exhibitionism, men as well as women were eventually included in the audience "because the women team members were apprehensive when on their own and we wished to avoid the subject feeling this apprehension [p. 841]." While the primary intent of the therapists may have been to prevent the client from being reinforced by the audience's apprehensive reaction, this clinical report highlights the need for precautions to assure that the observers themselves are not stressed or harmed by the experience. At the very least, prospective observers should be fully informed in advance of what is to transpire, and should be given ample opportunity to decline to participate without having to justify their reservations.

SEVERE ADJUSTMENT PROBLEMS

Most of the *in vivo* treatments reviewed thus far have focused upon relatively circumscribed problem areas. Sometimes, however, a person's "maladjustment" is so pervasive that independent functioning becomes difficult or impossible. Severe adjustment problems sometimes emerge in people who have had extremely traumatic experiences, in "psychotic" people who lose touch with reality, and in elderly people who suffer losses in their mental and physical abilities. Often the person's family is unable or unwilling to provide the continuing emotional support and custodial care necessary to maintain the person in the home setting, and institutionalization becomes necessary. Depending on the nature and severity of the person's difficulties, different kinds of therapy or rehabilitation programs may be attempted. The present section reviews three categories of intervention programs for severe adjustment problems, each of which has an *in vivo* component. In some cases, attempts are made to treat the person within the family context at home, as an alternative to institutionalization. In other cases, special facilities and procedures are employed to help institutionalized people prepare for and proceed through the difficult transition back to community living. Implicit in such efforts is the goal of trying to help disturbed people attain as high a level of independent functioning as possible. Since the objective is to restore adaptive functioning in natural contexts, it is not surprising that *in vivo* features have been integrated into these treatment programs.

Family Treatment in the Home

In recent years there has been a significant shift in the focus of psychiatry away from the traditional hospital or office-based treatments which emphasize private verbal interactions between "patient" and therapist. Contemporary programs now often include strategies to maintain the severely troubled person in his or her natural setting, to avoid the disruption of family, occupational, and community life, and to discourage the person from assuming a "mental patient" role. Approaches such as *conjoint family therapy in the home* and *social network therapy* reflect this trend. These therapies qualify as *in vivo* approaches because they focus upon social interactions as they transpire in the natural settings. The rationale for family treatment resides partly in the view that certain psychiatric difficulties reflect general family problems that are not intrinsic to a single "sick" person (e.g., Howells, 1976). Family treatment in the home is seen as particularly applicable to (*a*) adolescence adjustment difficulties involving separation from the family; (*b*) marital problems; and (*c*) psychotic conditions such as schizophrenia which have proved refractory to other treatments, and which are characterized by social isolation and an inability to maintain a commitment to outpatient services (Friedman, Boszormenyi-Nagy, Jungreis, Lincoln, Mitchell, Sonne, Speck, & Spivack, 1965; Group for the Advancement of Psychiatry, 1970). Ackerman (1966) listed some contraindications for family therapy, including the presence of a severely paranoid or psychopathic parent, the existence of cultural or religious prejudice against this form of therapy, severe physical disability in an important family member, and the therapist's impression that schisms in the family unit are irreversible.

Basic Procedure

It has been stated that "family therapy today is not a treatment method in the usual sense; there is no generally-agreed-upon set of procedures followed by practitioners who consider themselves family therapists [Group for the Advancement of Psychiatry, 1970, p. 38]." Nonetheless, it is possible to distinguish two major types of family treatment which can be conducted in the clients' home. These are family group therapy and social network therapy.

For family group therapy in the home, the therapist assembles the nuclear family unit for a series of diagnostic and therapeutic conjoint interviews and discussions. This basic arrangement is illustrated in the project reported by Friedman et al. (1965). Their clients were nuclear families, each of which included a schizophrenic young adult who was referred to the Philadelphia Psychiatric Center by an outpatient clinic, family service agency, or psychiatrist in private practice. Each case was evaluated by the entire treatment team, which consisted of four psychiatrists, two clinical psychologists, and two psychiatric social workers; where it seemed appropriate, the parents were then offered family treatment in the home.

The initial home visit, conducted by as many as four members of the treatment team, was devoted to an explanation of the concepts and goals of family therapy and to the collection of further observational data for the formation of a treatment plan. The subsequent sessions, each of which lasted approximately 90 min, were held weekly for periods which varied from several months to several years. Due to the complexity and emotional intensity of the in vivo family therapy experience, these sessions were conducted by two therapists; "we prefer heterosexual therapy teams whenever possible, as this provides a more natural identification model for the family [Friedman et al., 1965, p. 25]."

In general, the therapy teams focused upon inadequate family interactions, including, but not confined to, (a) the formation of dyads which sanction irrational behavior, (b) failures to accept responsibility, (c) collective fears, (d) acting out, and (e) behaviors which discourage meaningful communication. In addition, all the participants discussed nonverbal family interactions, the family's relationships to their possessions and pets, and the occasional absences of family members from the therapy sessions. To stimulate and sustain these emotion-laden discussions, "the therapists' activities include[d], among others: reflecting, interpreting, confronting, active empathic participation, functioning as a communication and problem-solving expert, and providing direct authoritative leadership [Friedman *et al.*, 1965, p. 27]." The integration and ongoing assessment of these functions was facilitated by periodic meetings of the two therapists with the entire treatment unit.

It is apparent that Friedman *et al.* (1965) used an eclectic approach in their implementation of *in vivo* family therapy. Office-based conjoint family therapy has usually been conducted in accordance with psychoanalytic (Framo, 1972), communication systems (Satir, 1964), or behavioral (Liberman, 1970) principles but there is no reason why these strategies could not be used in the clients' home. Regardless of their theoretical orientations, family therapists can utilize their skills and the observational advantages of the home setting to:

1. Make group goals explicit.
2. Establish rapport and communication between the various members of the family and between the family and the therapists.
3. Clarify the group's salient conflicts, particularly as they reflect inappropriate and rigidifying communication and behavioral patterns.
4. Provide emotional support for the activation of whatever coping skills remain available to individual family members or subgroups.
5. Neutralize "processes of prejudicial scapegoating that fortify one part of the family while victimizing another part [Ackerman, 1972, p. 178]."
6. Model appropriate verbal and nonverbal expressions.
7. Assist the family in the formulation of coping behaviors and criteria for self-evaluation.

The procedures reviewed thus far are oriented toward the nuclear family. *Social network therapy* is an innovative approach which expands the target group to include "that group of persons who maintain an ongoing significance in each other's lives by fulfilling specific human needs [Speck & Rueveni, 1969, p. 182]." In general, this network consists of 30–40 people drawn in equal numbers from the spheres of family, friends, neighbors, relatives, and employment (Pattison, Defrancisco, Wood, Frazier, & Crowder, 1975). The goals of social network therapy encompass those delineated for conjoint treatment of the nuclear family but there is additional emphasis upon "enabling people to cope and share their strengths in coping, and also to reap enjoyments and pleasures that restore their potentials and set them up to handle the inevitable next crises of living [Speck & Attneave, 1973, p. 50]."

The criteria for selecting social network therapy from among the array of possible interventions are not clearly specified in the existing literature. Rationales have included the presence of an ongoing "clan" or extended family which is seen as having therapeutic potential (Attneave, 1969), the previous failure of "traditional" dyadic or family therapies to help a disintegrating family (Speck & Rueveni, 1969), and the existence of a crisis which demands an immediate and innovative solution (Rueveni, 1975). Within this approach, the family is given the responsibility for securing appropriate space and for inviting the people whom they consider to be important members of their social network.

The following description of social network therapy procedures represents a synthesis of the techniques described in several articles (Rueveni, 1975; Speck & Attneave, 1973; Speck & Rueveni, 1969). Four-hour sessions are held weekly at different homes of individuals within the network, for a period of 6 weeks. As one therapist cannot possibly comprehend or regulate the complex interactions occurring within such a large group, social network therapy normally is conducted by a treatment team which may include a psychiatrist, a psychologist, a social worker, a medical student, and an activist from another network. This team attempts to insure the evolution of group processes through the six distinct phases which are considered to be necessary for a successful treatment. The first phase, *retribalization*, refers to the "process of reacquaintance and increased awareness" which develops from the "target" family's efforts at coordinating the meetings themselves and from their initially tentative and strained attempts at (re)establishing lines of communication and sensitivity. The second phase, *polarization*, describes the inevitable schisms which occur, particularly along generational lines, as conflicts and inadequacies are exposed. This tension is a crucial motivating force and it may be deliberately heightened by placement of factions into inner and outer circles of seats. The third phase, *mobilization of action*, characterizes the efforts of more dominant members to "mobilize" their own or their subgroup's resources to effect their proposed resolution of the aforementioned polarities.

The fourth phase, *depression*, refers to the frustration and futility which seem to be an inevitable and important result of the network's initially disorganized attempts to resolve the polarities by mobilizing diverse resources. The final two stages are *breakthrough* and *exhaustion–elation* in which group members, utilizing the impressions, encouragement, and direction provided by the treatment team, dissolve the impasses and realize the emotional benefits. At the end of the sixth session the social network is encouraged to continue meeting without the therapists.

Rationale

Conjoint family therapy is a subclass of family psychiatry, that "system of theory and practice of psychiatry whereby the family is taken as the unit to be evaluated and treated [Howells, 1976, p. 8]." The focus in family psychiatry is not upon a "sick" target person who operates within a relatively healthy and cooperative family unit, but upon the family itself as the context of pathology and as the unit of treatment: "there is an increasing awareness that psychiatric problems are social problems which involve the total ecological system [Haley, 1972, p. 270]." This perspective implies that the behavior of any family member often can be understood as a symptom of family pathology, as a stabilizing force in the family's dynamic structure, as a potential "healer of family disorder," and as a symbol of the unit's growth potential (Ackerman, 1972).

Pattison (1973) has maintained that family therapy represents an historical trend away from an insistence upon the unilateral value of the "closed model" of psychotherapy toward an acknowledgment of the value of a complementary "open model." A consideration of the elements of this open model suggests that family therapy in the home is the next logical step in this evolution. According to Pattison (1973), the model emphasizes

1. The reinforcement of adaptive personality structure
2. The maintenance of the "patient" within the social system, as opposed to his extraction for purposes of rehabilitation and/or confinement
3. The inclusion of the therapist in the ongoing social system, as opposed to his sanctioned segregation
4. The integration of psychotherapy with ongoing social processes
5. The belief that office-based conversations between a "therapist" and a "patient" are at best ineffective and at worst antitherapeutic, as opposed to an insistence upon the sacredness of the confidential dyadic interview as a therapeutic technique
6. The catalyzation of the social system as a therapeutic agent with long-term influence, as opposed to focusing upon the development of individual self-direction.

Family therapy in the home represents a synthesis of these elements and, in addition, it offers a number of unique advantages (Friedman *et al.*, 1965; Speck, 1964). Specifically, there may be

1. An opportunity to provide meaningful psychiatric services for people who are too frightened, withdrawn, or resistant to use existing outpatient services
2. A minimization of the well-documented problems associated with becoming a "mental patient"
3. Less chance that family members will adopt a set of stereotypic defenses and deference postures which camouflage important information
4. Less chance that therapy will be sabotaged by absenteeism
5. Tacit recognition that it is the family which has problems, not simply its most salient member
6. An opportunity to include housebound family members in the transactions
7. Considerable general information for a better understanding of the family's "spirit" and of the nature of its functioning

The theoretical rationales for conducting the specific diagnostic and treatment phases of eclectic, psychodynamic, communications-oriented, and behavioral family group therapies have been discussed elsewhere (e.g., Cromwell, Olson, & Founier, 1976; Framo, 1972; Friedman et al., 1965; Howells, 1976; LeBow, 1972; Ritterman, 1977; Sager & Kaplan, 1972; Scheflen, 1972; Zuk, 1971). There also has been considerable sociological and psychological theorizing behind the development of social network therapy (e.g., see Attneave, 1969; Pattison, 1973; Pattison et al., 1975; Ritterman, 1977; Speck & Rueveni, 1969). The principal difference between the rationales of conjoint family therapy in the home and social network therapy is the latter's attention to the ways in which the larger social network mediates the reciprocal influences of its individual constituents, the nuclear family, and the culture at large. It is this perception of the network's role which stimulates the belief that "network intervention may be able to evoke the potential of people to creatively and cooperatively solve their own problems as an antidote to the aura of depersonalized loneliness characteristic of post-industrial society [Speck & Attneave, 1972, p. 438]."

Case Example

Matta and Mulhare (1976) treated a middle-aged black woman, Mrs. L., by family group therapy conducted in the home. Mrs. L. was selected for conjoint family therapy because, although she had been hospitalized six times between 1960 and 1970, the various diagnoses of mild mental deficiency, paranoid schizophrenia, and transient personality disorder were strikingly inconsistent and there were numerous indications of "selective craziness" and of good premorbid adjustment. At the time of referral she was obsessed with the belief that her husband was trying to harm her and to turn her children into animals, a fate which she felt she could forestall only by performing an elaborate set of sorcerous rituals. This obsessive–compulsive behavior irritated and confused her husband and children and their interactions with her appeared to contribute to a cycle of bizarre behavior, hospitalization, apparent rehabilitation, and decompensation upon return to the home.

The authors noted that their "initial objective was to de-emphasize Mrs. L.'s pathology by redistributing the burden of her sickness among the rest of the family members, as well as to examine other processes that were contributing to her illness. This process was accelerated by locating the therapy at home. . . . [They] were able to explore in depth the cultural and environmental factors that had been ignored previously [1976, p. 347]." Conjoint family sessions were conducted by both therapists on a weekly basis for three months and then the frequency of the therapists' "visits" was gradually decreased. The emphasis in the group's interaction was on examination, clarification, and resolution of overt problems and unconscious conflicts relating to Mr. and Mrs. L.'s unexpressed hostility and affection, Mr. L.'s constrictive dominance of the household which began when he retired from his job, and Mrs. L.'s delusions and rituals. The conjoint family therapy enabled the therapists to observe the family as a system, to understand Mr. L.'s contributions to Mrs. L.'s pathology, and to understand "the sociocultural factors that served as the basis for Mrs. L.'s delusions and . . . [accept] them as learned beliefs rather than as psychotic illness [Matta & Mulhare, 1976, p. 348]."

At the conclusion of the 8-month treatment period both Mr. and Mrs. L. were demonstrating improvements in their interpersonal relations, Mr. L. had effected a satisfactory adjustment to retirement, and Mrs. L. had taken a renewed interest in her marked talent for sewing and in an expanding set of social activities. According to Matta and Mulhare (1976), "after a decade of instability and unhappiness, and five years after our home visits took place, they are functioning well as a family [p. 348]."

Representative Findings

Evidence for the effectiveness of family therapy conducted in the home is limited to extensive case examples of the type reported by Matta and Mulhare (1976) and Friedman et al. (1965), and to the "aggregate impressions" of Friedman et al. (1965): "It is our subjective impression that all the families [over 100] who were in treatment gained something of importance from the therapeutic enterprise [p. 175]." It is essential, however, to note the subsequent qualification of this appraisal: "we are not speaking of so-called 'cures,' or implying that the family no longer has any serious problems, or even that a basic structural change has occurred in the family structure [p. 176]." Despite this enigmatic addendum, several of the cases described in detail by Friedman et al. (1965) suggest that family therapy in the home is potentially beneficial for the treatment of families with severely disturbed adolescents.

The work mentioned above involved contact with families for the purpose of long-term assessment and group therapy in the home. Family therapy in the home has also been practiced as but one component of large-scale crisis intervention programs which focus upon the prevention of hospitalization and/or the mobilization of available community services for the psychotic individual (Langsley, Kaplan, Pittman, Machotka, Flomenhaft, & DeYoung, 1968; Langsley, Flomenhaft, & Machotka, 1969; Weiner, Becker, & Friedman, 1967). Langsley and his colleagues assigned 150 families, who had requested hospitalization of a family member with a severe emotional disorder, to receive short-term, crisis-oriented conjoint family therapy. At least one of the treatment sessions took place in the clients' home. The researchers also established a matched control group of 150 families with similarly disturbed members who had been admitted to the hospital as inpatients. Prior to and at several points following this period the target patient within each family was evaluated on a battery of measures pertaining to (re)hospitalization, "days lost from functioning," and social and emotional development.

At the 6-month follow-up evaluation (Langsley et al., 1969) it was found that the patients who had received family-centered therapy had a lower percentage (13% versus 29%) of hospital admissions during the posttreatment to follow-up phase and had a lower median (5 versus 23) of "days lost from functioning" than their matched controls. There were no significant between-group differences in pretest to follow-up changes in the therapists' ratings of the patients' emotional and social functioning, but both groups demonstrated significant within-group improvements on these ratings.

The work of Langsley et al. (1968) suggests that the short-term, crisis-oriented family therapy was successful in diverting 150 acutely disturbed individuals from hospitalization with no loss in therapeutic benefits and with substantial savings to the state's taxpayers. In general, the finding that short-term crisis-oriented family treatment in the home can often make hospitalization unnecessary was the same conclusion reached by Weiner et al. (1967), who evaluated the efficacy of the Psychiatric Home Treatment program established by Boston State Hospital (see also Meyer, Schiff, & Becker, 1967).

There are several case examples which illustrate the successful application of social network therapy to problems such as marital difficulties and adolescent rebellion (e.g., Rueveni, 1975), inadequate maternal behavior (e.g., Attneave, 1969), and schizophrenia (e.g., Speck & Rueveni, 1969). In the latter case, questionnaire responses obtained after the sixth session indicated that at least some of the participants felt that the experience was personally rewarding and that the schizophrenic client had become more sociable.

Appraisal

Family treatment in the home is an *in vivo* therapeutic innovation worthy of further consideration because it reflects important new perspectives in community psychiatry, and it has direct ties to recent theoretical developments in the fields of sociology and small-group communications. Some clinical evidence concerning its therapeutic efficacy is encouraging, and there is substantial evidence that crisis intervention programs which incorporate family treatment in the home can often substitute beneficially for inpatient hospitalization. However, as Skynner (1976) has observed, "family therapists, like most clinicians, have shown little interest in the scientific validation of their results, and while their work has been relatively public and open to examination, and though most practitioners would probably have welcomed outcome research by independent, unbiased assessors, the opportunities have not been taken up [p. 293]." There is a definite need for controlled outcome studies that can

1. Assess the relative merits of social systems therapy in the home as opposed to other treatments.
2. Determine the most influential components of the various family-centered treatments.
3. Establish the contribution, if any, of the home setting.
4. Specify the patient groups and family types with whom family therapy in the home is most effective.
5. Determine the effects of the family-centered therapies on all the family members.

Transitional Living Centers

In assessing the impact of modern psychiatric facilities, Becker and Bayer (1975) observed that "for many patients who have been hospitalized ten or twenty years, the severity of the thought, emotional, and behavioral disorders that initially precipitated hospitalization has diminished. However, because of the debilitating effects of long-term institutionalization . . . these chronic patients are apathetic, inactive, and profoundly deficient in their repertoire of daily living skills [p. 448]." *Transitional living centers* constitute a specialized form of *in vivo* therapy in that ward or residential social structures and activities are programmed to train and motivate the patient toward reentry into the community rather than toward adjustment to an institutional role of passivity and dependence with little opportunity for exercising self-initiative. Although therapeutic communities and halfway houses have been considered potentially beneficial in the rehabilitation of drug addicts (e.g., Glasscote, Sussex, Jaffe, Ball, & Brill, 1972) and alcoholics (e.g., T. Baker, 1972; Rubington, 1967), the results with such recalcitrant populations have not been particularly favorable. The present review therefore focuses on the use of transitional living centers with schizophrenic and other severely disturbed mental patients, where the evidence occasionally has been more encouraging.

Basic Procedure

A transitional living center may be established in the context of an existing hospital ward system (e.g., Childers, 1967), in a special facility on the hospital grounds (e.g., Wiernasz, 1972), or in the community itself (e.g., Scoles & Fine, 1971). Several programs have established a sequence of transitional living units within the hospital and community settings which provide regulated exposure to realistic social and occupational experiences (e.g., Boettcher & Vander Schie, 1975; Brown & Petty, 1966; Shean, 1973).

In general, the emphasis of a hospital-based transitional living center is on "structuring a ward situation so that a community life develops which offers the patients collectively increasing responsibility and authority to solve problems pertaining to their discharge from the hospital and return to community living [Boettcher & Vander Schie, 1975, p. 130]." Specifically, this type of transitional living center is oriented toward:

1. Making discharge the central focus of the patients and staff
2. Maximizing the patients' expectations of discharge
3. Maximizing the patients' involvement in self-direction and minimizing constant interventions by the staff in the patients' daily activities
4. Utilizing the combined influence of the staff and the ward social structure to train the "residents" in self-care, social, and basic occupational skills

5. Desensitizing the patients and the community to the decisions and challenges that the former "mental patient" faces in the transition from a passive–dependent role to an active, self-reliant, and productive role

The pursuit of these ambitious goals has fostered a variety of hospital-based milieu approaches (e.g., Bartz, 1970; Becker & Bayer, 1975; Boettcher & Vander Schie, 1975; Gibson, Marone, Coutu, & King, 1972; Wiernasz, 1972) which owe much of their philosophy and procedures to the influential work of Fairweather and his associates (Fairweather, 1964; Fairweather, Sanders, Maynard, Cressler, & Bleck, 1969). The center described by Childers (1967), who studied Fairweather's program at the Veterans Administration Hospital in Palo Alto, California, will be presented to illustrate the *in vivo* elements of a transitional living center.

The four most important features of Childers' (1967) program were:

1. A progress-level contingency system wherein the patients' responsibilities and rewards were hierarchically arranged in the direction of increasing their involvement with the outside community;
2. A carefully engineered social structure which demanded that patient subgroups meet regularly, without staff intervention, to make recommendations and decisions about the conduct of the group's members and to facilitate the discharge process;
3. A communication network in which both the staff's and patients' requests, complaints, suggestions, and decisions were clarified and expedited by the use of standardized notes and deadlines for correspondence; and
4. A system of multiple-level planning for discharge in which the staff virtually insisted upon progress toward this goal as they gradually transferred to the patient the responsibility for making the final decision to leave the hospital.

At the outset all the psychiatric patients were given complete oral and written descriptions of the program's composition and the staff's expectations for their progress. Then the staff determined each patient's initial competencies and needs and assigned him to the appropriate one of four graduated levels of responsibilities and concomitant privileges. For example, patients assigned to the first (lowest) level were required to attend all group meetings, perform basic housekeeping chores on the ward, participate in one hour of off-ward duties daily, and cooperate with ward regulations. If the patient accepted these responsibilities and performed the duties satisfactorily, he was permitted to use the hospital grounds in the company of a fourth-level patient and to receive $5 in cash per week from his own funds. Fourth-level patients were required to perform 4 hours of off-ward assignments daily, participate in group meetings, help orient new first-level patients, demonstrate the capacity to handle money wisely, and actively pursue the fourth-level group's and staff's approval of a self-designed discharge plan. Performance of these diverse functions was rewarded with a grounds and off-grounds pass for use during any free time, long weekend passes, and unrestricted funds up to $50 per week.

This systematic encouragement of hospital- and community-related self-management and occupational responsibilities is an important *in vivo* feature of the transitional living center. Equally crucial are the progress-level groups which, in this program, consisted of 15 to 25 patients each. These groups, each directed by a different elected patient, were entrusted with the functions of interpreting program requirements, coordinating requests for work and recreational assignments, and insuring that all their members actively work toward advancement through the responsibility–privilege levels. The groups were also responsible for requesting additional medical or psychiatric attention for their members if this was deemed necessary. With respect to this function, Childers (1967) noted that "although there is little time for traditional therapy in the groups, there is a great deal of therapeutic interaction among group members. Some patients take a particular interest in helping regressed members of their group and . . . a great deal of informal interaction continues outside the meetings [p. 292]."

The groups convened for six mandatory meetings each week, four unsupervised and two with the staff present. However, in general, the staff's interference with the groups' dynamics was intentionally minimal. The staff offered requested suggestions, acted upon the groups' recommendations, and mitigated the groups' often excessively punitive reactions to lack of cooperation with the program's goals and requirements; group leaders were reminded that the goals of the project were rehabilitation and release, not simply regimentation and behavior management. The staff also met once each week to formally evaluate each group's performance. A (rare) unsatisfactory rating resulted in automatic disapproval of that group's most recent recommendations, suspension of all its members' immediate access to higher responsibility–privilege levels, and, if its functioning was particularly poor, restriction of community passes. This contingency was an attempt to insure that each patient would take his role in the small groups seriously and that each group would not deviate from its intended purposes.

Preparing the patient for a successful reentry into the community requires a different type of staff involvement, much as it necessitates a different reorganization of basic ward activities and regulations. The extensive influence of the small groups, the explicit nature of the contingencies for progress toward discharge, and the aforementioned written communication system combine to relieve the staff of many of its previous, poorly coordinated duties in the area of patient supervision. Thus, the staff can devote substantially more time to individualized therapy and to representing and advising the patients during their interaction with family members, landlords, community service workers, and other people who will undoubtedly figure heavily in a smooth transition from the hospital to the community.

The transitional living centers which operate within the confines of a psychiatric hospital make numerous provisions for their residents' interaction with the "outside world." However, some people who are ready to be discharged do require further nonthreatening opportunities to refine their social and occupational skills. These needs are met by residential or nonresidential transitional living centers located in the community itself (e.g., Brown & Petty, 1966; Scoles & Fine, 1971; Shean, 1973). The setting for a residential center can vary from an urban apartment to a suburban home to a large boarding home arrangement. These social units, consisting of 3–26 adults, are semiautonomous democracies in which the participants have equal responsibility for self-care, formulation and implementation of house rules, distribution of chores, and for the support and education of other group members. Participants are informed that they must comply with house rules and goals in order to retain the use of the facilities, but the extensive system of contingencies which operate in the ward living center are omitted in a further effort to promote effective personal autonomy.

In a nonresidential transitional living center (e.g., Scoles & Fine, 1971; Wolkon & Tanaka, 1966) the professional and paraprofessional staff offer individualized counseling and a protective atmosphere for the functioning of self-governed client groups. Like their counterparts on the ward and in the residential units, these groups provide informal therapy and social support. Moreover, the groups also supervise programs for learning social skills, for discussing current events, for recreation, and for acquiring specific occupational skills related to sewing, cooking, and handicrafts. Scoles and Fine (1971) noted that the "emphasis is on making objects or giving services that can be sold at a specific price. . . . The matter of payment is taken quite seriously because no single factor is more important in the total picture of rehabilitation than to discover that one is being paid for ability rather than disability [p. 78]." The staff may also work closely with the patient's family and the operators of board and care facilities to insure that these important people understand the patients' problems and reinforce their inchoate social and occupational skills.

Rationale

It has been observed that, for the most part, recent developments in psychotherapy and rehabilitation have neglected the chronically ill mental patient (Becker & Bayer, 1975; Paul, 1969). This oversight is particularly appalling because there exists substantial documentation that the predominant treatment, hospitalization, may itself contribute to the psychosocial problems which isolate the "mental patient" from effective contact with society (Goffman, 1961; Querido, 1956; Stanton & Schwartz, 1954).

Transitional living centers have been developed to (*a*) mitigate the effects of long-term hospitalization; (*b*) redirect the chronically ill patient's attention to getting out of the hospital; (*c*) provide *in vivo* training for the self-care, interactional, and occupational skills necessary for self-management in the community; and (*d*) dissolve the atmosphere of suspicion, mistrust, and fear which often characterizes the community's reactions to "mental patients."

Boettcher and Vander Schie (1975) have noted that "ironically, sound medical routines on a ward and adequate occupational, recreational, and educational supports often reinforce dependence on the hospital and weaken the patient's motivation to plan for discharge. But if sound routines and supports are not present, patients tend to regress socially, be apathetic to hospital life, and [be] poorly motivated for discharge [p. 130]." Transitional living centers attempt to solve this conundrum by arranging for the staff and the patient groups to reinforce the expectation that each patient can work toward discharge, and by shaping the behaviors necessary for achieving this goal. As chronically ill mental patients initially may be frightened by the prospect of returning to a hostile society, transitional living centers use a hierarchy of responsibility–privilege contingencies which punish disorganized and dependent behavior and reward increasing involvement in self-care, sheltered workshops, social outings, and general community activities.

As a result of their interpersonal deficiencies, many chronic psychiatric patients have surrendered their capacities to make basic decisions and to solve their own problems. The transitional living center's utilization of the contingencies and the small groups format constitutes an *in vivo* approach to inculcating or restoring these functions. That is, the center offers an environment which is protective but which, nevertheless, insists that the patient and his group assume responsibility for each member's acquisition of decision-making skills which will promote personal planning for reentry into the community.

Patients who have successfully completed a hospital-based program may still encounter problems when it comes time to actually leave the hospital. It is unfortunate that, all too often, the community presents rehabilitated and remotivated people with a limited number of available placements for family care, a limited range of jobs for which they are qualified, and a limited amount of empathy and understanding. As noted previously, the heavily programmed structure of the transitional living center enables the staff professionals to abandon their traditional roles as custodians and instead become role models, experienced advisors, and active advocates. This metamorphosis is very important for insuring that the longstanding promise of discharge will not be an empty one for those patients who adhere to the center's philosophy and contingencies.

Case Example

Shean (1973) reported the case of a 51-year-old woman who benefited greatly from involvement in both hospital-based and residential transitional living centers. As a young woman the patient had functioned fairly well but gradually she became emotionally and socially withdrawn, occasionally experiencing episodes of violent behavior and paranoid delusions. She was admitted to Virginia's Eastern State Hospital at age 24 with a diagnosis of catatonic schizophrenia. A year later she was released but she returned within several months following two suicide attempts.

During her 27 years of hospitalization the woman became apathetic and indifferent. A few routine housekeeping chores constituted the extent of her participation in hospital activities. She presented no management problems but she was seen as unlikely ever to leave the hospital of her own accord.

When the hospital, in conjunction with Virginia's Department of Vocational Rehabilitation, began a "community living project" in 1969, the patient and nine other schizophrenic women were placed in a semiautonomous living unit on the hospital grounds. It cannot be determined from Shean's (1973) report whether participation was voluntary or dictated by the staff. For 5 months the patient and her group received vocational and social training. After this period, the women were transferred to a 5-bedroom house in Williamsburg, Virginia, which was rented for them by the Department of Vocational Rehabilitation. A board of directors, consisting of 10 community people from the legal, medical, financial, and administrative professions, was established to oversee the intricate financial aspects of this arrangement. For tax purposes the program was conducted as a nonprofit corporation and this feature necessitated extramural control of much of the group's funds. It cannot be determined to what extent the residents participated in the financial administration of this corporation; it is clear that they exercised considerable independence in the organization of shopping, cooking, and housekeeping assignments, in addition to their daily affairs. Thus the women who occupied this residential transitional living center lived as a small, self-governing unit which received weekly counseling on practical or personal matters from a consulting psychologist.

Initially, the patient in question had difficulty in working quickly enough to retain a maid job which she had apparently secured through her own efforts. However, unspecified "special training efforts" by both the Department of Vocational Rehabilitation and her peers helped her to locate and hold another job. Eventually, she found a permanent job in the kitchen of a rest home. At this point the woman left the transitional living unit and moved to a boarding home where she "has continued to make a satisfactory adjustment [Shean, 1973, p. 98]."

Representative Findings

It is difficult to provide truly representative findings regarding the efficacy of rehabilitation programs which include transitional living centers. There is considerable variability in the patient samples, in the implementation of the various procedures outlined previously, and in the criteria for determining effectiveness. Nonetheless, uncontrolled evaluations of hospital-based transitional living centers for chronic mental patients report recidivism rates of 12% (Becker & Bayer, 1975; Wiernasz, 1972), 23% (Gibson *et al.*, 1972), and 39% (Bartz, 1970) for follow-up periods of at least 1 year. In general, these figures compare favorably with the array of baseline recidivism rates which are available (e.g., 60%, Fairweather & Simon, 1963; 85%, Paul, 1969; 37%, Scoles & Fine, 1971; 41% and 52%, Wolkon & Tanaka, 1966).

The implication that hospital-based transitional living units for chronically ill mental patients are more effective than traditional rehabilitation efforts was not supported by Ellsworth's (1965) controlled evaluation of Childers' (1967) program. At the outset of the project the patient populations of three physically comparable hospital wards were equated on the basis of age, chronicity, marital status, and behavioral adjustment. Then one ward was randomly designated as a transitional living center and the remaining two as control conditions. The comparative statistic was the percentage of patients who, following discharge, were able to remain 90 continuous days in the community (i.e., to achieve a "first significant release"). The data suggest that in its second year of operation the transitional living ward was considerably more effective in the rehabilitation of semichronic schizophrenics (54% versus 19% and 19%), slightly more effective for acute schizophrenics (84% versus 74% and

64%) and nonpsychotics (91% versus 82% and 81%), and **not** very effective, in either relative or absolute terms, for chronic schizophrenics (18% versus 18% and 5%) or geriatric patients (13% versus 14% and 25%). It is unfortunate that data concerning recidivism or employment were not provided.

Although Ellsworth's (1965) assessment does not support the view that hospital-based transitional living units are particularly effective in the rehabilitation of chronic mental patients, a later report by Brown and Petty (1966) does. These investigators presented the preliminary results of a center which was established on the grounds of Milledge-ville State Hospital in Georgia. At some unspecified follow-up period the first 50 participants had, relative to unmatched but comparable controls, more subsequent work or training experience (94% versus 24%), more ratings of at least good "stability" (68% versus 36%), and more jobs considered as their best ever (44% versus 4%). Moreover, the recidivism rate for the target group was 10% as compared with 34% for the controls.

Shean (1973) reported that Eastern (Virginia) State Hospital's sequential hospital-based and residential living units were effective in promoting community reentry. Of 25 chronic schizophrenic women who had returned to the community via these centers, 52% were living and working independently and only 12% were subsequently rehospitalized. Stronger evidence for the relative efficacy of a "small-group ward-and-lodge treatment subsystem" was provided by Fairweather et al. (1969). These investigators found that, compared to matched controls who participated in traditional community mental health programs, participants in their living centers remained in the community substantially longer, obtained many more jobs, and were more satisfied with community living. However, a recent assessment of a similar program by Boettcher and Vander Schie (1975) noted that, while the recidivism rate at 16 months was low (approximately 16%), 67% of the 75 patients were discharged on "convalescent leave." That this phrase could imply a transfer of some patients to other institutions is suggested by the absence of data on subsequent employment.

Several attempts to evaluate the effectiveness of nonresidential transitional living centers have also produced positive but somewhat equivocal results. Wolkon and Tanaka (1966) conducted a study of Hill House, a nonresidential center in Cleveland. Clients who persisted in utilizing the center had a recidivism rate of only 9%, although 19% of the original sample terminated at intake and 41% dropped out of the program against the advice of the staff. Overall, of the 118 people (85% schizophrenic) who attended at least one session at the center, 27% were rehospitalized in the 1-year period following initial discharge. This figure, while not outstanding, did compare favorably with the 52% recidivism rate of control patients who were refused service on a random basis and with a 41% rate reported for a large number of clients from the Cleveland Psychiatric Institute (Wolkon & Tanaka, 1966). Even more encouraging findings were reported by Scoles and Fine (1971), who followed the progress of 100 participants (81% schizophrenic) in the West Philadelphia Mental Health Consortium's two "after-care" programs. After 18 months only 9% of the clients were rehospitalized. No employment data were reported but, interestingly, a review of prescriptions at 18 months indicated that 63% of the people were on "substantially smaller doses [p. 81]."

The results of these studies with mental patients, while not overwhelming, are more encouraging than the results of transitional living centers with drug addicts. Smart (1976) reviewed the evaluations of such independent therapeutic communities as Daytop (Casriel & Amen, 1971; Collier, 1971) and Phoenix House (Brown, 1972; Nash, Waldorf, Foster, & Kyllingstad, 1971) and of several halfway houses which are affiliated with correctional institutions. In general, although a variable percentage (33–92%) of the "graduates" of these milieu programs discontinued drug usage, more than 50% of the successful participants did not find employment in the community; instead, many were assimilated into drug treatment and other social service programs. Moreover, it appears that a conservative estimate of the median dropout rate from transitional living centers for narcotics addicts is 60%. A further contribution to this discouraging picture comes from two controlled outcome evaluations of halfway houses connected with correctional institutions (Berecochea & Sing, 1972; Miller, Himelson, & Geis, 1967). These studies suggest that there is no difference in opiate drug use or subsequent incarceration between those assigned on a random basis to a halfway house or to regular parole. Smart (1976) concluded that (a) there is little evidence that transitional living centers for narcotics addicts are more beneficial than probation or no treatment at all, and (b) there is a glaring need for controlled evaluations of therapeutic communities such as Synanon (Volkman & Cressey, 1963; Yablonsky, 1962), Daytop, and Phoenix House.

Appraisal

The preceding review of representative findings basically supports the contention that transitional living centers, with their focus on *in vivo* development of self-care, interpersonal, and occupational skills, can obviate the insidious effects of prolonged hospitalization and, for many chronic mental patients, facilitate meaningful reentry into the community. Moreover, there is evidence that the programs can be implemented at low cost to the supporting agencies without any sacrifice of professional services (Becker & Bayer, 1975; Fairweather *et al.*, 1969, pp. 210–211; Scoles & Fine, 1971; Shean, 1973). Becker and Bayer (1975) reported that in 1973 the special treatment activities in their multi-stage transitional living project were instituted at an additional average monthly cost of only $1.52 per patient!

It is hoped that future descriptions and evaluations of transitional living centers will address a number of procedural, assessment, and research issues unexplicated in most existing reports (the study by Fairweather *et al.*, 1969, being a notable exception). Procedural difficulties include: (*a*) motivating initially apathetic or recalcitrant patients or staff (Bartz, 1970; Boettcher & Vander Schie, 1975; Wiernasz, 1972); (*b*) coordinating searches for employment and convincing prospective employers that former "mental patients" are suitable for more than menial jobs (Boettcher & Vander Schie, 1975; Shean, 1973); and (*c*) educating the community toward enhanced understanding and acceptance of rehabilitated mental patients (Childers, 1967; Scoles & Fine, 1971; Wiernasz, 1972). In the area of assessment, considerable work needs to be done in specifying and reporting the social, occupational, and temporal criteria for determining successful reentry. When these basic evaluative requirements are fulfilled, future investigations can identify the demographic and psychosocial characteristics of those mental patients and drug addicts who benefit most from transitional living centers, the effective components of these programs (e.g., Hersen & Bellack, 1976), and the legal and institutional limitations on their implementation.

Reality Orientation Therapy

It has been estimated that approximately 1 million elderly people in the United States reside in old-age homes (Kramer, Taube, & Redick, 1973). Many of these people have physical and psychological problems which until recently have been viewed as the inevitable accompaniments of aging. These patients are often diagnosed as having "organic (chronic) brain syndrome," a collection of deficits which includes lability and shallowness of affect, and impairment of attention, memory, intellectual functioning, and judgment (Suinn, 1975). Traditionally, the treatment of disoriented elderly patients usually has been custodial at best and the prognosis pessimistic. **Reality orientation therapy** was developed to initiate the rehabilitation of patients with moderate to severe degrees of cerebral deficits (Folsom, 1967). It consists of several procedures which emphasize the systematic and consistent involvement of staff in providing patients with information and guidance concerning daily-life events and activities. The object is to promote the return of reality awareness and basic functions of self care and initiative through repetition, encouragement, and reinforcement. The continual focus on real-life facts and activities constitutes the *in vivo* essence of reality orientation therapy. It is considered to be appropriate for any individual with the aforementioned symptoms but the majority of people requiring it are aged. Further, the therapy is conceived of as preparation for participation in more complex treatments such as remotivation therapy, occupational therapy, or speech therapy (Folsom, 1967).

Basic Procedure

A complete reality orientation program uses three components to accomplish its goal of reorienting the confused patient. The three elements are (*a*) 24-hour reality orientation; (*b*) classroom reality orientation; and (*c*) attitude therapy. The 24-hour component requires that the staff "use every contact [they] make with [the patient] as a part of the process—in the routine activities of daily living as well as the occupational and corrective therapy programs on the ward [Folsom, 1967, p. 210]." Initially, this focuses upon stimulating the confused patient by repeating what Phillips (1973) calls "basic motifs" such as the client's name, his room number, his age, the date, and other simple facts about his current situation. For example, when the client is taken to bathe, the staff member continually addresses the client by name, carefully explains what day and time it is, where they are going and why, what they see and do in transit, and what they do when they arrive. The patient is given as much latitude as possible in choosing courses of action and is encouraged to say and do as much as he can. Verbal reinforcement is provided liberally for all appropriate responses.

Interpersonal stimulation is supplemented by environmental supports such as pocket and wall calendars, name tags, large clocks, and the "reality orientation board"; the latter is a prominent display which presents basic information such as the day of the week, the weather, the nurse's name, the prospective menu, and upcoming institutional activities (Taulbee & Folsom, 1966). It should be noted that while implementing 24-hour reality orientation, the staff are required to behave calmly, consistently, and respectfully toward all patients (Shannon, 1972).

While the 24-hour component establishes the supportive, informative, and consistent milieu necessary for reorienting the patient, the reality orientation classroom allows for individualized instruction and reintegration into group activities (Barnes, 1974). A trained instructor meets with five patients for 30 min per session, five times per week. The sessions consist of any academic or social exercises (e.g., talking, identifying pictures, reading simple words, spelling, writing) which are potentially valuable in furthering the orientation process for each "student." The instructor minimizes frustration by asking questions which the patient can deal with, by speaking clearly without being patronizing, by allowing the patient adequate time to respond, and by providing immediate verbal reinforcement for correct performances. When the patient shows signs of having mastered basic information, he is placed in an advanced class. When this second phase is completed formal graduation ceremonies are held.

The third element of reality orientation therapy is attitude therapy. On the basis of each patient's particular deficiencies one of five attitudes is adopted by the staff. These attitudes are active friendliness, passive friendliness, matter-of-fact, kind firmness, and no-demand (The Treatment Team, 1965). Active friendliness is the foundation of 24-hour reality orientation and it is described as being a "supportive ego-building attitude that helps the patient to feel that he is worth something after all, that someone cares, that life has not passed him by [Veterans Administration Hospital, 1970, p. 1]." Often the matter-of-fact attitude is adopted toward manipulative patients who demand assistance with activities which they are actually capable of performing alone and toward helpless patients who have simply given up. This attitude conveys the explicit expectation that the patient is capable of accepting responsibility for basic self-care functions such as eating and grooming. These preselected attitudes, if implemented in the context of the guidelines for 24-hour reality orientation, stand in marked contrast to the mixture of bullying, patronizing, and bribing tactics occasionally used by inadequately trained staff to control residents' behaviors in some convalescent homes.

A final procedural note concerns the patient's family. The Veterans Administration Hospital (1970) recommends that families be given an explanation of reality orientation principles, that they be encouraged to apply them in their interactions with the patient, and that they be encouraged to visit the patient often during regular hours and, with permission, during reality orientation classes.

Rationale

Three basic assumptions appear to underlie reality orientation therapy. The first is that often behavioral and psychological deficits in the elderly are a product of their uncertain role in the American family structure and the retiree's inability to meet the challenge of developing new activities and interests. This perspective implies that the problems which characterize the "brain syndromes" are reversible learned responses. Folsom, the developer of reality orientation therapy, states that "old age is inevitable if one lives long enough, but 'oblivion' in the sense of being out of touch with reality is not [in Shannon, 1972, p. 1]."

Many experts agree that all too often well-intentioned relatives and poorly trained hospital personnel exacerbate the deterioration of mental processes (Citrin & Dixon, 1977; Folsom, 1968; Harris & Ivory, 1976). The second postulate of reality orientation therapy is that the convalescent hospital experience need not add insult to cerebral injury; rather, it can be used to arrest this tragic process and help the elderly person regain at least some of his lost capacities. It was in this spirit that the approach was designed as a milieu therapy in which the institution's social organization is structured

> so that residents are encouraged and allowed to behave in a more oriented fashion. The key to the successful implementation ... is in training staff members to be more aware of individual resident behavior and to use their own behavior patterns to reinforce desired behavior on the part of the resident. By providing residents with repeated cues about spatio–temporal events in their environment, the staff is arranging the milieu so that residents become aware of this basic information which is so essential to daily functioning [Citrin & Dixon, 1977, p. 42].

It is this emphasis on the fundamental features of the naturalistic environment which constitutes the *in vivo* dimension central to reality orientation therapy.

The third basic assumption is that the inactivity, confusion and aura of helplessness shown by many elderly patients is in part the result of the inconsistent and disorganized quality of many people's responses to them. Some are solicitous, some are suspicious, and a majority are simply insensitive. Consequently, it is imperative that an intensive and integrated 24-hour approach be adopted which utilizes the therapeutic potential of virtually all staff.

Case Example

Folsom (interviewed by Shannon, 1972) described the case of a 77-year-old man admitted to the Veterans Administration Hospital in Tuscaloosa, Alabama. The patient had retired from his job 8 years earlier and since that time suffered two heart attacks and a series of strokes. His wife and daughter tried valiantly to care for him but he was admitted to the hospital in a state of near vegetation. The patient was mute, disoriented, nonambulatory, and incontinent.

Reality orientation therapy was begun immediately. Every member of the hospital staff who spoke with the patient addressed him by name and told him their names. Further, they each provided other information regarding the date, the room he was in, and the type of activity the patient and the staff member were engaging in. The patient was also given the opportunity to feed and shave himself regardless of how messy or halting these efforts initially were. A physical therapist spent considerable time helping him to walk again. The patient was also encouraged to wear his regular clothes instead of his drab, overused pajamas.

Two months after admission the patient left the hospital. Two years later a relative reported that the patient had taken up gardening and was still able to walk without the use of a cane.

Representative Findings

The evaluation of the effectiveness of reality orientation therapy began with publication of impressive case histories (e.g., Folsom, 1968) and uncontrolled examinations of large groups exposed to this treatment (e.g., Folsom, 1967; Letcher, Peterson, & Scarbrough, 1974; Phillips, 1973; Stephens, 1969). Letcher et al. (1974) examined the effects of the complete reality orientation program on 125 males with a mean age of 82.8 years admitted over a 5-year period to a large Veterans Administration Hospital. The final sample was heterogeneous for a number of demographic variables but a sizable proportion were unskilled laborers with little formal education. Slightly over 60% of the men were diagnosed as having some form of brain damage. In order to evaluate changes in the amount of disturbance as a function of treatment, four levels of severity were defined on the basis of the amount of nursing care required. Improvement was defined as a reduction in severity of at least one level.

Approximately 32% of the patients improved, 67% remained at their initial level of functioning, and 1% regressed. Of 39 patients who improved, 10 improved two levels and 6 progressed from the fourth level (requiring total nursing care) to the first level (requiring minimal nursing care). The variables showing significant statistical association with improvement were amount of time spent in the treatment (greater than 18 months) and level of self-sufficiency prior to treatment (first two levels).

The first study employing a no-treatment control group was conducted by Harris and Ivory (1976). Fifty-eight females, 40% of whom had some sort of brain syndrome, were randomly assigned to receive either the complete reality orientation program or regular hospital care. The treatment lasted 5 months. The dependent measures consisted of pre- to posttreatment changes in scores on the three domains of the Florida State Hospital Behavior Rating Sheet: (a) ward behavior; (b) verbal orientation; and (c) observations and impressions of aide-therapists. The ratings were made by resident psychiatric aides who also served as therapists. They received 11 hours of training for these functions.

The analysis of the changes in behavior ratings revealed little except that the measure was reactive, unreliable, and generally invalid. However, in the other two domains the superiority of the reality orientation group was demonstrated. On 6 of 9 categories using the patients' verbal responses to structured questions, aides rated this group as being significantly more oriented. The aides' general impressions supported these findings.

Although this study has severe methodological deficiencies, it suggests that reality orientation therapy may have a major effect only on verbal orientation measures closely approximating the actual focus of therapy. This impression has been corroborated by Citrin and Dixon (1977) using a slightly older patient population and a more valid measure of behavioral competency. Also worth noting is a study by Barnes (1974) suggesting that classroom reality orientation by itself does not promote lasting improvements.

Appraisal

Reality orientation therapy was designed as a milieu approach to the rehabilitation of patients suffering from the psychological confusion and behavioral disorganization attendant to many of the diseases of aging. Given the pessimistic prognosis for most patients subjected to the typical form of custodial care given in today's geriatric institutions, it would seem that this approach deserves consideration as an initial step in a general rehabilitation program.

It is apparent, however, that the systematic evaluation of reality orientation therapy has been deficient in many respects. Among other things, there is no unequivocal evidence that the *in vivo* milieu focus of the treatment facilitates the development and generalization of behavioral and emotional benefits. Prominent among the methodological flaws in the research reviewed are the absence of long-term follow-up evaluations, the lack of structured, valid behavioral tests for assessing improvement in nonverbal areas, the use of the same personnel both as administrators and as evaluators, and the lack of adequate controls for the effects of attention and expectancy on patients and raters alike. While the issue of generalization is important, it must be remembered that reality orientation therapy is intended primarily as a prelude to more complex therapies (Folsom, 1968); therefore, failure to find profound generalization may not be an indictment of the treatment itself.

Finally, it is hoped that future researchers will also address important issues related to the effective training of staff, the involvement of the family, the isolation of beneficial components of the therapy, and the identification of any patient variables which might contraindicate this form of treatment.

CONCLUDING REMARKS

Some of the limitations of traditional office psychotherapy are well documented (e.g., see reviews by Bergin, 1971; Eysenck, 1966). Few would disagree that, at the very least, there is considerable room for improvement in increasing the efficacy of treatments for psychological problems. One response to this therapeutic challenge has been the recent emergence of interventions which attempt to focus directly on the problems as they are manifested in reality, either by conducting the treatment in the client's natural problem setting or by simulating the central problem features within an office setting.

The logic behind this *in vivo* strategy was expressed by Goldstein, Heller, and Sechrest (1966) in a discussion of treatment features expected to enhance the transfer of psychotherapeutic learning to the patient's real-life environment. It was hypothesized that transfer would be facilitated "when the therapy stimuli are representative of extratherapy stimuli [p. 226]," "if therapy is conducted outside an office in a variety of situations in which the patient will ultimately have to respond [p. 227]," and "if therapy is provided by more than one therapist [p. 231]."

As most of the work on *in vivo* therapies reviewed in this chapter and the preceding one was conducted since the publication of the book by Goldstein *et al.* (1966), it could be hypothesized that they were either very influential on subsequent developments in the field, good predictors of such developments, or lucky at guesswork. The complex research problems that would be encountered in attempting to evaluate these hypotheses, which are neither mutually exclusive nor exhaustive, resemble the kinds of problems associated with evaluating the therapies themselves: It is not yet possible to identify all of the factors which influence behavior, let alone to isolate all of the interrelationships among them.

The fact that complete knowledge may be an unrealistic goal does not mean that advancing knowledge is an unworthy pursuit. On the contrary, only through systematic research will it be possible to continue to develop and refine more effective methods for helping people psychologically. While there is at least some supportive clinical evidence concerning the *in vivo* approaches reviewed here, there remain numerous open questions. Many of these were discussed in relation to particular treatments in the Appraisal sections which accompanied the reviews of each therapy approach. For present purposes, an overview of some general issues which emerged frequently throughout the reviews may assist further in prompting and guiding future research efforts. There are a number of basic issues in the practice and evaluation of psychological therapies which need to be confronted by practitioners and investigators alike. These include questions related to identifying the objectives, specifying the procedures, and assessing the effects (cf. Sherman, 1973, pp. 9–10). Some of these and others prompted by the present analysis are reviewed below as they apply to the *in vivo* therapies:

1. Diagnostic assessment and treatment selection. What are the demographic and behavioral characteristics (see problem classification schema formulated by Kanfer & Grimm, 1977) which would recommend or contraindicate the selection of a particular *in vivo* treatment approach? In most of the treatments reviewed here, little information was discovered concerning contraindications for particular approaches, or reasons for selecting one approach over others intended for the same kind of problem. Research is needed in this area to provide guidelines to practitioners in formulating optimal intervention programs for their clients.

2. Nature and durability of treatment effects. What are the positive and negative effects of the treatment, how well do the improvements transfer to the natural environment, how long are they maintained, and how do they relate to the original objectives of therapy? While all of the *in vivo* therapies presented here were supported by at least some evidence, there was considerable variability in the extent to which data were available concerning multiple dimensions of possible treatment impact, behavior in real-life settings, and long-term maintenance of improvements. Certainly it is difficult to obtain unobtrusive measures of behavior changes in natural living situations, but this is essential for the evaluation of certain *in vivo* interventions because the effects of office or laboratory treatments involving simulations of problem features do not always transfer readily to the real-life environment (cf. Sherman, Mulac, & McCann, 1974). Assessment of transfer is especially relevant here because the phenomenon of "transfer decrement," which has often been found to limit the value of other therapeutic approaches, represented a major rationale for the development of *in vivo* procedures.

3. Effective treatment components. What are the effective components of the *in vivo* treatment strategies, and how can they be further enhanced? The therapies reviewed here all have in common an *in vivo* component, but in very few instances were there experimental evalua-

tions of the separate contributions of this component to the overall efficacy of the treatment. In fact, the *in vivo* component itself can be constituted in several ways, ranging from treatment in the natural environment to varying degrees of simulation in an office setting. Research is needed to identify all effective treatment components as well as their limitations, and to clarify the mechanisms involved, with a view toward the continued development of increasingly effective interventions.

4. Comparative outcome research. Do clients who receive *in vivo* therapies show more improvement than people with comparable problems who receive other interventions, or no treatment at all? Most of the evaluations of the *in vivo* therapies have been based upon clinical studies of one or several clients. While such examples serve an important function in illustrating the application of innovative treatments, they alone cannot establish the relative efficacy of those treatment approaches. The fact that successful cases are much more likely to appear in the literature than unsuccessful ones can further obscure the picture. Only controlled research can provide the information necessary to assess the relative efficacy of *in vivo* therapies compared to other interventions.

This brief analysis attempted to summarize some of the basic areas in which research could substantially advance our understanding of the *in vivo* treatments, and enhance their therapeutic impact. The fact that so much remains to be done should not be construed as an indictment of the *in vivo* approach: Considering that most of the work in this area was conducted within the past decade, it is rather remarkable how much has already been accomplished. Hopefully, the favorable reports will encourage continued research so that the strengths and limitations of *in vivo* procedures can be identified and translated into more effective treatments. Close scrutiny will also help to assure that only effective procedures are retained, thereby protecting the present *in vivo* therapies from the ignoble fate of "functional autonomy" which is alleged to characterize certain other psychotherapeutic approaches (Astin, 1961).

REFERENCES

Ackerman, N. W. *Treating the troubled family.* New York: Basic Books, 1966.
Ackerman, N. W. Family psychotherapy—theory and practice. In G. D. Erickson & T. P. Hogan (Eds.), *Family therapy: An introduction to theory and technique.* Monterey, California: Brooks/Cole, 1972.
Astin, A. W. The functional autonomy of psychotherapy. *American Psychologist,* 1961, *16,* 75–78.
Attneave, C. L. Therapy in tribal settings and urban network intervention. *Family Process,* 1969, *8,* 192–210.

Azrin, N. H., & Holz, W. C. Punishment. In W. K. Honig (Ed.), *Operant behavior: Areas of research and application.* New York: Appleton-Century-Crofts, 1966.

Azrin, N. H., Sneed, T. J., & Foxx, R. M. Dry bed: A rapid method of eliminating bedwetting (enuresis) of the retarded. *Behaviour Research and Therapy,* 1973, 11, 427–434.

Azrin, N. H., Sneed, T. J., & Foxx, R. M. Dry-bed training: Rapid elimination of childhood enuresis. *Behaviour Research and Therapy,* 1974, 12, 147–156.

Baker, B. L. Symptom treatment and symptom substitution in enuresis. *Journal of Abnormal Psychology,* 1969, 74, 42–49.

Baker, T. Halfway houses for alcoholics: Shelters or shackles? *International Journal of Social Psychiatry,* 1972, 18, 201–211.

Bandura, A. *Principles of behavior modification.* New York: Holt, 1969.

Barker, J. C., & Miller, M. E. Some clinical applications of aversion therapy. In H. Freeman (Ed.), *Progress in behavior therapy.* Bristol, England: Wright, 1968.

Barlow, D. H. Aversive procedures. In W. S. Agras (Ed.), *Behavior modification: Principles and clinical applications.* Boston: Little, Brown, 1972.

Barnes, J. A. Effects of reality orientation classroom on memory loss, confusion and disorientation in geriatric patients. *The Gerontologist,* 1974, 14, 138–144.

Bartz, W. R. A small-group approach on state hospital wards. *Hospital and Community Psychiatry,* 1970, 21, 390–393.

Becker, P., & Bayer, C. Preparing chronic patients for community placement: A four-stage treatment program. *Hospital and Community Psychiatry,* 1975, 26, 448–450.

Belliveau, F., & Richter, L. *Understanding human sexual inadequacy.* Boston: Little, Brown, 1970.

Berecochea, J. E., & Sing, G. E. The effectiveness of a halfway house for civilly committed narcotics addicts. *International Journal of the Addictions,* 1972, 7, 123–132.

Bergin, A. E. The evaluation of therapeutic outcomes. In A. E. Bergin & S. L. Garfield (Eds.), *Handbook of psychotherapy and behavior change: An empirical analysis.* New York: Wiley, 1971.

Blakemore, C. B., Thorpe, J. G., Barker, J. C., Conway, C. G., & Lavin, N. I. The application of faradic aversion conditioning in a case of transvestism. *Behaviour Research and Therapy,* 1963, 1, 29–34.

Boettcher, R., & Vander Schie, R. Milieu therapy with chronic mental patients. *Social Work,* 1975, 20, 130–134.

Bollard, R. J., & Woodroffe, P. The effect of parent-administered dry-bed training on nocturnal enuresis in children. *Behaviour Research and Therapy,* 1977, 15, 159–165.

Brown, I. F. *Phoenix House: The Featherstone Lodge project, annual report, 1971–1972.* London: Management Committee, Featherstone Lodge Project, 1972.

Brown, R., & Petty, W. A state hospital vocational rehabilitation center. *Hospital and Community Psychiatry,* 1966, 17, 52–55.

Bucher, B. A pocket-portable device with application to nailbiting. *Behaviour Research and Therapy,* 1968, 6, 389–392.

Bucher, B., & Fabricatore, J. Use of patient-administered shock to suppress hallucinations. *Behavior Therapy,* 1970, 1, 382–385.

Bucher, B., & Lovaas, O. I. Use of aversive stimulation in behavior modification. In M. R. Jones (Ed.), *Miami symposium on the prediction of behavior, 1967: Aversive stimulation.* Coral Gables, Florida: University of Miami Press, 1968.

Butterfield, W. H. Electric shock—Safety factors when used for the aversive-conditioning of humans. *Behavior Therapy*, 1975, *6*, 98–110.

Campbell, B. A., & Church, R. M. (Eds.). *Punishment and aversive behavior.* New York: Appleton-Century-Crofts, 1969.

Casriel, D., & Amen, G. *Daytop: Three addicts and their cure.* New York: Hill and Wang, 1971.

Cautela, J. R. Treatment of compulsive behavior by covert sensitization. *Psychological Record*, 1966, *16*, 33–41.

Childers, B. A ward program based on graduated activities and group effort. *Hospital and Community Psychiatry*, 1967, *18*, 15–21.

Citrin, R. S., & Dixon, D. N. Reality Orientation: A milieu therapy used in an institution for the aged. *The Gerontologist*, 1977, *17*, 39–43.

Collier, W. V. *An evaluation report on the therapeutic programs of Daytop Village, Inc., for the period 1970–1.* New York: Research Division, Daytop Village, 1971.

Cromwell, R. E., Olson, D. H., & Founier, D. Tools and techniques for diagnosis in marital and family therapy. *Family Process*, 1976, *15*, 1–49.

Deleon, G., & Mandell, W. A comparison of conditioning and psychotherapy in the treatment of functional enuresis. *Journal of Clinical Psychology*, 1966, *22*, 326–330.

Ellis, A. *The sensuous person: Critique and corrections.* Secaucus, New Jersey: Lyle Stuart, 1972.

Ellsworth, R. B. *Patient and staff perception of relatively effective and ineffective psychiatric treatment programs.* Paper presented at the Veterans Administration Tenth Annual Conference on Cooperative Studies in Psychiatry, New Orleans, March 1965.

Eysenck, H. J. *The effects of psychotherapy.* New York: International Science Press, 1966.

Eysenck, H. J., & Beech, H. R. Counterconditioning and related methods. In A. E. Bergin & S. L. Garfield (Eds.), *Handbook of psychotherapy and behavior change.* New York: Wiley, 1971.

Fairweather, G. W. (Ed.). *Social psychology in treating mental illness: An experimental approach.* New York: Wiley, 1964.

Fairweather, G. W., Sanders, D. H., Maynard, H., Cressler, D. L., & Bleck, D. S. *Community life for the mentally ill: An alternative to institutional care.* Chicago: Aldine, 1969.

Fairweather, G. W., & Simon, P. A further follow-up comparison of psychotherapeutic programs. *Journal of Consulting Psychology*, 1963, *27*, 186.

Finley, W. W., Besserman, R. L., Bennett, L. F., Clapp, R. K., & Finley, P. M. The effect of continuous, intermittent, and "placebo" reinforcement on the effectiveness of the conditioning treatment for enuresis nocturna. *Behaviour Research and Therapy*, 1973, *11*, 289–297.

Finley, W. W., & Wansley, R. A. Auditory intensity in the conditioning treatment of enuresis nocturna. *Behaviour Research and Therapy*, 1977, *15*, 181–185.

Finley, W. W., Wansley, R. A., & Blenkarn, M. M. Conditioning treatment of enuresis using a 70% intermittent reinforcement schedule. *Behaviour Research and Therapy*, 1977, *15*, 419–427.

Folsom, J. C. Intensive hospital therapy for geriatric patients. *Current Psychiatric Therapies*, 1967, *7*, 209–215.

Folsom, J. C. Reality orientation for the elderly mental patient. *Journal of Geriatric Psychiatry*, 1968, *1*, 291–307.

Forrester, R. M., Stein, Z., & Susser, M. W. A trial of conditioning therapy in nocturnal enuresis. *Developmental Medicine and Child Neurology,* 1964, *6,* 158–166.

Framo, J. L. (Ed.). *Family interaction: A dialogue between family researchers and family therapists.* New York: Springer, 1972.

Friedman, A. S., Boszormenyi-Nagy, I., Jungreis, J. E., Lincoln, G., Mitchell, H. E., Sonne, J. C., Speck, R. V., & Spivack, G. *Psychotherapy for the whole family.* New York: Springer, 1965.

Galbraith, D. A., Byrick, R. J., & Rutledge, J. T. An aversive conditioning approach to the inhibition of chronic vomiting. *Canadian Psychiatric Association Journal,* 1970, *15,* 311–313.

Gibson, R., Marone, J., Coutu, E., & King, E. A rehabilitation program for chronically hospitalized patients. *Hospital and Community Psychiatry,* 1972, *23,* 381–383.

Glasscote, R., Sussex, J. N., Jaffe, J. H., Ball, J., & Brill, L. *The treatment of drug abuse: Programs, problems, prospects.* Washington, D.C.: Joint Information Service of the American Psychiatric Association and National Association for Mental Health, 1972.

Goffman, E. *Asylums: Essays on the social stimulation of mental patients and other inmates.* Chicago: Aldine, 1961.

Goldstein, A. P., Heller, K., & Sechrest, L. B. *Psychotherapy and the psychology of behavior change.* New York: Wiley, 1966.

Goorney, A. B. Treatment of a compulsive horse race gambler by aversion therapy. *British Journal of Psychiatry,* 1968, *114,* 329–333.

Group for the Advancement of Psychiatry. *Treatment of families in conflict: The clinical study of family process.* New York: Science House, 1970.

Haley, J. Family therapy. In C. J. Sager & H. S. Kaplan (Eds.), *Progress in group and family therapy.* New York: Brunner/Mazel, 1972.

Harris, C. S., & Ivory, P. B. C. B. An outcome evaluation of a reality orientation therapy with geriatric patients in a state mental hospital. *The Gerontologist,* 1976, *16,* 496–503.

Hartman, W. E., & Fithian, M. A. *Treatment of sexual dysfunction.* Long Beach, California: Center for Marital and Sexual Studies, 1972.

Hersen, M., & Bellack, A. S. Social skills training for chronic psychiatric patients: Rationale, research, and future directions. *Comprehensive Psychiatry,* 1976, *17,* 559–580.

Howells, J. G. *Principles of family psychiatry.* New York: Brunner/Mazel, 1976.

Hull, C. L. *A behavior system.* New Haven, Connecticut: Yale University Press, 1952.

Kanfer, F. H., & Grimm, L. G. Behavioral analysis: Selecting target behaviors in the interview. *Behavior Modification,* 1977, *1,* 7–28.

Kaplan, H. S. *The new sex therapy: Active treatment for sexual dysfunctions.* New York: Brunner/Mazel, 1974.

Kohlenberg, R. J. Directed masturbation and the treatment of primary orgasmic dysfunction. *Archives of Sexual Behavior,* 1974, *4,* 349–356.

Kramer, M., Taube, C. A., & Redick, R. W. Patterns of use of psychiatric facilities by the aged: Past, present, and future. In C. Eisdorfer & M. P. Lawton (Eds.), *The psychology of adult development and aging.* Washington, D.C.: American Psychological Association, 1973.

Langsley, D. G., Flomenhaft, K., & Machotka, P. Follow-up evaluation of family crisis therapy. *American Journal of Orthopsychiatry,* 1969, *39,* 753-760.

Langsley, D. G., Kaplan, D. M., Pittman, F. S., Machotka, P., Flomenhaft, K., & DeYoung, C. D. *The treatment of families in crisis.* New York: Grune & Stratton, 1968.

LeBow, M. D. Behavior modification for the family. In G. E. Erickson & T. P. Hogan (Eds.), *Family therapy: An introduction to theory and technique.* Monterey, California: Brooks/Cole, 1972.

Letcher, P., Peterson, L., & Scarbrough, D. Reality orientation: A historical study of patient progress. *Hospital and Community Psychiatry,* 1974, *25,* 801–803.

Liberman, R. Behavioral approaches to family and couple therapy. *American Journal of Orthopsychiatry,* 1970, *40,* 106–118.

Lobitz, W., & LoPiccolo, J. New methods in the treatment of sexual dysfunction. *Journal of Behavior Therapy and Experimental Psychiatry,* 1972, *3,* 265–271.

Logan, F. A. *Fundamentals of learning and motivation.* Dubuque, Iowa: Brown, 1970.

LoPiccolo, J., & Lobitz, W. Behavior therapy of sexual dysfunction. In L. A. Hammerlynck, L. C. Handy, & E. J. Mash (Eds.), *Behavior change: Methodology, concepts, and practice.* Champaign, Illinois: Research Press, 1974.

LoPiccolo, J., & Steger, J. C. The Sexual Interaction Inventory: A new instrument for assessment of sexual dysfunction. *Archives of Sexual Behavior,* 1974, *3,* 585–595.

Marks, I. M., & Gelder, M. G. Transvestism and fetishism: Clinical and psychological changes during faradic aversion. *British Journal of Psychiatry,* 1967, *113,* 711–729.

Masters, W., & Johnson, V. *Human sexual inadequacy.* Boston: Little, Brown, 1970.

Mathews, A., Bancroft, J., Whitehead, A., Hackman, A., Julier, D., Bancroft, J., Gath, D., & Shaw, P. The behavioral treatment of sexual inadequacy: A comparative study. *Behaviour Research and Therapy,* 1976, *14,* 427–436.

Matta, S., & Mulhare, M. T. Breaking a cycle of hospitalization through the psychiatric house call. *Hospital and Community Psychiatry,* 1976, *27,* 346–348.

McGovern, K., Stewart, R., & LoPiccolo, J. Secondary orgasmic dysfunction. I. Analysis and strategies for treatment. *Archives of Sexual Behavior,* 1975, *4,* 265–275.

McGuire, R. J., & Vallance, M. Aversion therapy by electric shock: A simple technique. *British Medical Journal,* 1964, *1,* 151–153.

Mees, H. L. Sadistic fantasies modified by aversive conditioning and substitution: A case study. *Behaviour Research and Therapy,* 1966, *4,* 317–320.

Meyer, R. E., Schiff, L. F., & Becker, A. The home treatment of psychotic patients: An analysis of 154 cases. *American Journal of Psychiatry,* 1967, *123,* 1430–1438.

Miller, D. E., Himelson, A. N., & Geis, G. Community's response to substance misuse: The East Los Angeles Halfway House for felon addicts. *International Journal of the Addictions,* 1967, *2,* 305–311.

Mills, K. C., Sobell, M. B., & Schaefer, H. H. Training social drinking as an alternative to abstinence for alcoholics. *Behavior Therapy,* 1971, *2,* 18–27.

Mowrer, O., & Mowrer, W. M. Enuresis: A method for its study and treatment. *American Journal of Orthopsychiatry,* 1938, *8,* 436–459.

Nash, G., Waldorf, D., Foster, K., & Kyllingstad, A. *The Phoenix House program: The results of a two year follow-up.* New York: Phoenix House, 1971.

O'Connor, J. F., & Stern, L. O. Results of treatment in functional sexual disorders. *N. Y. State Journal of Medicine,* 1972, *72,* 1927–1934.

O'Leary, K. D., & Wilson, G. T. *Behavior therapy: Application and outcome.* Englewood Cliffs, New Jersey: Prentice-Hall, 1975.

Pattison, E. M. Social system psychotherapy. *American Journal of Psychotherapy,* 1973, *17,* 396–409.

Pattison, E. M., Defrancisco, D., Wood, P., Frazier, H., & Crowder, J. A. A psychosocial kinship model for family therapy. *American Journal of Psychiatry,* 1975, *132,* 1246–1251.

Paul, G. L. Chronic mental patient: Current status—future directions. *Psychological Bulletin,* 1969, *71,* 81–94.

Pfeiffer, E. A., & Johnson, J. B. A new electrode for the application of electrical shock in aversive conditioning therapy. *Behaviour Research and Therapy,* 1968, *6,* 393–394.

Phillips, D. F. Reality orientation. *Hospitals, Journal of the American Hospital Association,* 1973, *47,* 46–49.

Querido, A. Early diagnosis and treatment services. In *Elements of a community mental health program.* New York: Milbank Memorial Foundation, 1956.

Rachman, S., & Teasdale, J. *Aversion therapy and behaviour disorders: An analysis.* Coral Gables, Florida: University of Miami Press, 1969.

Reitz, W. E., & Keil, W. E. Behavior treatment of an exhibitionist. *Journal of Behavior Therapy and Experimental Psychiatry,* 1971, *2,* 67–69.

Rimm, D. C., & Masters, J. C. *Behavior therapy: Techniques and empirical findings.* New York: Academic Press, 1974.

Ritterman, M. K. Paradigmatic classification of family treatment theories. *Family Process,* 1977, *16,* 29–46.

Rubington, E. The halfway house for the alcoholic. *Mental Hygiene,* 1967, *51,* 552–560.

Rueveni, U. Network intervention with a family in crisis. *Family Process,* 1975, *14,* 193–203.

Runciman, A. Sexual therapy of Masters and Johnson. *The Counseling Psychologist,* 1975, *5,* 22–30.

Sager, C. J., & Kaplan, H. S. (Eds.). *Progress in group and family therapy.* New York: Brunner/Mazel, 1972.

Satir, V. *Conjoint family therapy: A guide to theory and technique.* Palo Alto, California: Science & Behavior Books, 1964.

Schaefer, H. H. Twelve-month follow-up of behaviorally trained ex-alcoholic social drinkers. *Behavior Therapy,* 1972, *3,* 286–289.

Schaefer, H. H., Sobell, M. B., & Mills, K. C. Some sobering data on the use of self-confrontation with alcoholics. *Behavior Therapy,* 1971, *2,* 28–39.

Scheflen, A. E. Human communication: Behavioral programs and their integration in interaction. In G. E. Erickson & T. P. Hogan (Eds.), *Family therapy: An introduction to theory and technique.* Monterey, California: Brooks/Cole, 1972.

Scoles, P., & Fine, E. Aftercare and rehabilitation in a community mental health center. *Social Work,* 1971, *16,* 75–82.

Semans, J. H. Premature ejaculation, a new approach. *Southern Medical Journal,* 1956, *49,* 353–358.

Serber, M. Shame aversion therapy. *Journal of Behavior Therapy and Experimental Psychiatry,* 1970, *1,* 213–215.

Shannon, M. Return to reality. *Atlanta Journal and Constitution Magazine,* January 9, 1972, pp. 1–3.

Shean, G. An effective and self-supporting program of community living for chronic patients. *Hospital and Community Psychiatry*, 1973, 24, 97–99.

Sherman, A. R. *Behavior modification: Theory and practice.* Monterey, California: Brooks/Cole, 1973.

Sherman, A. R., Mulac, A., & McCann, M. J. Synergistic effect of self-relaxation and rehearsal feedback in the treatment of subjective and behavioral dimensions of speech anxiety. *Journal of Consulting and Clinical Psychology*, 1974, 42, 819–827.

Skynner, A. C. R. *Systems of family and marital psychotherapy.* New York: Brunner/Mazel, 1976.

Smart, R. G. Outcome studies of therapeutic community and halfway house treatment for addicts. *International Journal of the Addictions*, 1976, 11, 143–159.

Snyder, A., LoPiccolo, L., & LoPiccolo, J. Secondary orgasmic dysfunction. II. Case study. *Archives of Sexual Behavior*, 1975, 4, 277–283.

Sobell, M. B., & Sobell, L. C. Individualized behavior therapy for alcoholics. *Behavior Therapy*, 1973, 4, 49–72. (a)

Sobell, M. B., & Sobell, L. C. Alcoholics treated by individualized behavior therapy: One year treatment outcome. *Behaviour Research and Therapy*, 1973, 11, 599–618. (b)

Sobell, M. B., & Sobell, L. C. Second year treatment outcome of alcoholics treated by individualized behavior therapy: Results. *Behaviour Research and Therapy*, 1976, 14, 195–215.

Speck, R. V. Family therapy in the home. *Journal of Marriage and the Family*, 1964, 26, 72–76.

Speck, R. V., & Attneave, C. L. Social network intervention. In C. J. Sager & H. S. Kaplan (Eds.), *Progress in group and family therapy.* New York: Brunner/Mazel, 1972.

Speck, R. V., & Attneave, C. L. *Family networks.* New York: Pantheon Books, 1973.

Speck, R. V., & Rueveni, U. Network therapy—a developing concept. *Family Process*, 1969, 8, 182–190.

Stanton, A. H., & Schwartz, M. S. *The mental hospital: A study of institutional participation in illness and treatment.* New York: Basic Books, 1954.

Stephens, L. P. *Reality orientation: A technique to rehabilitate elderly and brain-damaged patients with a moderate to severe degree of disorientation.* Washington, D.C.: American Psychiatric Association, 1969.

Stevenson, J., & Jones, I. H. Behavior therapy technique for exhibitionism: A preliminary report. *Archives of General Psychiatry*, 1972, 27, 839–841.

Strickler, D., Bigelow, G., Lawrence, C., & Liebson, I. Moderate drinking as an alternative to alcohol abuse: A nonaversive procedure. *Behaviour Research and Therapy*, 1976, 14, 279–288.

Suinn, R. M. *Fundamentals of behavior pathology* (2nd ed). New York: Wiley, 1975.

Taulbee, R. N., & Folsom, J. C. Reality orientation for geriatric patients. *Hospital and Community Psychiatry*, 1966, 17, 23–25.

Taylor, P. D., & Turner, R. K. A clinical trial of continuous, intermittent and over-learning 'bell and pad' treatments for nocturnal enuresis. *Behaviour Research and Therapy*, 1975, 13, 281–293.

Tighe, T. J., & Elliott, R. A technique for controlling behavior in natural life settings. *Journal of Applied Behavior Analysis*, 1968, 1, 263–266.

The Treatment Team (Tuscaloosa Veterans Administration Hospital). Attitude therapy and the team approach. *Mental Hospitals*, 1965, 16, 307–323.

Turner, R. K. Conditioning treatment of nocturnal enuresis: present status. In I. Kolvin, R. C. MacKeith, & S. R. Meadow (Eds.), *Bladder control and enuresis.* London: Heineman Medical Books, 1973.

Turner, R. K., Young, G. C., & Rachman, S. Treatment of nocturnal enuresis by conditioning techniques. *Behaviour Research and Therapy,* 1970, *8,* 367–381.

Veterans Administration Hospital. *Guide for reality orientation.* Unpublished manuscript. Tuscaloosa, Alabama, 1970.

Vogler, R. E., Lunde, S. E., Johnson, G. R., & Martin, P. L. Electrical aversion conditioning with chronic alcoholics. *Journal of Consulting and Clinical Psychology,* 1970, *34,* 302–307.

Volkman, R., & Cressey, D. R. Differential association and the rehabilitation of drug addicts. *American Journal of Sociology,* 1963, *69,* 129–142.

Walters, G. C., & Grusec, J. E. *Punishment.* San Francisco: Freeman, 1977.

Weiner, L., Becker, A., & Friedman, T. T. *Home treatment: Spearhead of community psychiatry.* Pittsburgh: University of Pittsburgh Press, 1967.

Wickramasekera, I. A technique for controlling a certain type of sexual exhibitionism. *Psychotherapy: Theory, Research, and Practice,* 1972, *9,* 207–210.

Wiernasz, M. Quarter-way house program for the hospitalized mentally ill. *Social Work,* 1972, *17,* 72–77.

Wilson, G. T., & Tracey, D. A. An experimental analysis of aversive imagery versus electrical aversive conditioning in the treatment of chronic alcoholics. *Behaviour Research and Therapy,* 1976, *14,* 41–51.

Wolkon, G., & Tanaka, H. Outcome of a social rehabilitation service for released psychiatric patients: A descriptive study. *Social Work,* 1966, *11,* 53–61.

Wolpe, J. Conditioned inhibition of craving in drug addiction: A pilot experiment. *Behaviour Research and Therapy,* 1965, *2,* 285–288.

Wolpe, J. *The practice of behavior therapy.* New York: Pergamon, 1969.

Wolpe, J., & Lazarus, A. A. *Behavior therapy techniques: A guide to the treatment of neuroses.* New York: Pergamon, 1966.

Yablonsky, L. *The tunnel back: Synanon.* New York: Macmillan, 1962.

Yulis, S. Generalization of therapeutic gain in the treatment of premature ejaculation. *Behavior Therapy,* 1976, *7,* 355–358.

Zuk, G. H. *Family therapy: A triadic-based approach.* New York: Behavioral Publications, 1971.

4

Family Therapies

WILLIAM R. McPEAK

Family therapy legend (see Bodin, 1968) has it that until recently there was a centuries-old tradition in the Hawaiian Islands, called *O' Ho Puna Puna*, where a particular female of the tribe was designated to assist families in stress. Her task was to gather immediate, and if necessary more distant, kin together to deal with family issues and any individual grievances. In this story, we have both an ancient version of a recent style of family therapy, namely, network therapy (Speck & Attneave, 1973), and an example of one of the main tenets of family therapy, that is, "treat 'em where they get troubled and stay troubled."

The basic theory of family therapy describes emotionally disturbed and mentally ill individuals in terms of their responses to dysfunctional aspects of their families (e.g., roles, affects, communication patterns). A primary hypothesis for family therapy is that the "self" and the attitudes and behaviors characterizing that self, is primarily developed and maintained in interpersonal contexts, the most significant and powerful of which is the family. This further suggests that psychotherapeutic treatment requires some degree of active engagement of family members, so that the presumedly distressing context can be altered. The therapists' intent is to change the *ways* in which family members define themselves and each other, handle individuation and togetherness and respond to each other, so that overt difficulties in one or more members will be modified and more functional mutual patterns of behavior will be developed and/or enhanced.

Because family therapy intends to alter the actual interpersonal context of troubled individuals by treatment of the whole family, (as will be noted below, family therapists differ in defining "whole family"), it is assumed that we no longer need be as worried about the transfer of behaviors from the "office" to the "home" as family therapy seeks to blend those two worlds. The daily manifestations of depression, anxiety, and anger that are presenting problems can and do appear in their precipitating and preserving contexts in treatment sessions, and can be altered by the participants with the guidance of the therapist. These generalizations about the value of a family therapy approach admittedly can not fully deal with the issue of transfer, as there are additional or different stimuli and meanings present in families without the therapist(s), and in their homes, and there are other potent interpersonal contexts that distress individuals, although the family is traditionally considered to be the most significant of these. However, each of the different family treatment approaches discussed below have demonstrated, with varying degrees of rigor, that interventions made with the family have produced substantial and nontransient changes both in the targeted individual or client and in his relationships with other family members.

To achieve these changes, the family therapist focuses on the ways in which the members in a powerful emotional field such as a family handle their interactions. These "ways" are known to family therapists as *process*, and a more complete explication of this concept will be given below. The major implication here is that alteration of the usual patterns of social and emotional interchange, which patterns are studied and modified as they occur between and among the ongoing participants in the therapeutic session, will result in changed functioning in the nontreatment settings in which these participants function. The likelihood of these changes should increase to the degree that the participants individually define and mutually negotiate acceptable behaviors, and then positively experience these changes. "Homework" assignments, and ex-

plicit definition by the therapist of initial behaviors that trigger dysfunctional patterns, such that participants can change and produce more
desirable patterns, should further assist transfer.

BASIC CONCEPTS OF FAMILY THERAPY

The task of defining what is meant by *family* has been accepted by
several different disciplines, each of which offers an important perspective to the family therapist. Anthropology describes families in terms of
relationship structure, using terms such as *polyandrous, patrilineal,* and
affinal, and in terms of properties such as sexual access and economic
roles (Nimkoff, 1965; Zelditch, 1964) which differ from one culture to
another. Sociologists, such as symbolic interactionists, define the family
as "a unity of interacting personalities" (Burgess, 1926), and interpret
family phenomena in terms of roles and statuses, and communication and
decision-making patterns (Stryker, 1964). Laing (1969), a psychiatrist,
has distinguished between family as a sociological collection of individuals and "family" as a set of individualized perceptions and internalized
relationships. Family theorists influenced by general systems theory (e.g.,
Jackson, 1957, 1965) have described families in phrases such as "transactional causality" (i.e., causality is circular not just lineal or undi-
rectional), "homeostasis" (i.e., a family seeks equilibrium, using rules
and meta-rules as corrective mechanisms), "open versus closed" families,
"process" focus (i.e., what is the family **doing**) and "synergy" (i.e., the
behavior of a system is more complex and different than the behavior of
its individual parts).

A second basic concept, *family therapy,* has been defined as a systematic method of psychotherapeutic intervention into the multiple, in-
terlocking, emotional disorders of a family group (Ackerman, 1971).
Perhaps the best known definition comes from Satir (1963) who described
family therapy as a method in which all family members are seen at the
same time by the same therapist, "based on the theory that the mentally
ill member, whom we designate as 'identified patient' (IP), by means of
his symptoms, is sending a message about the sick condition of his
family [p. 34]." Satir, and her colleagues such as Jackson and Haley,
also led a major theoretical thrust of the developing field, as they conceptualized and described the "systems" aspect of the family. They
focused on the family's interactive qualities in the development and
maintenance of individual symptoms, and used interventions focused
on the verbal and nonverbal communication patterns of families through

which the family promulgates and enforces rules about its functioning (see Ford & Herrick, 1974), and teaches social perceptions, expectations, role behaviors, handling of feelings, and a sense of one's "self."

More recent definitions of the field continue this basic emphasis on systems intervention. Bloch and LaPerriere (1973) have defined family therapy as follows:

> face-to-face psychotherapy of a natural system, natural in contrast to a group formed specifically for the purpose of therapy. The therapist, or team of therapists, directly engages the family, or some substantial element of the family, of the index patient.... What unites all family therapists is the view that change, which is significant to the psychotherapeutic endeavor, takes place in the family system. With this unifying thread, they may vary considerably as to the size of the elements of the family they engage, the techniques they employ, and the theory to which they adhere [p. 1].

Foley (1974) has also emphasized the centrality of the concept of the family as a system, and has added this comment:

> We see then that in family therapy a new *gestalt* is formed with the family in the foreground and the individual member in the background, reversing the more traditional way of seeing the individual person as sick and of prime concern and the family only as background. This new picture leads to new ways of doing therapy [p. 3].

Haley (1972) has stated that the experienced family therapist increasingly sees family therapy "not as a method but as a new orientation to the area of human problems [p. 154]." With the belief in the family as a system, the therapist sees psychopathology as a relationship problem, and focuses all diagnosis and any treatment on the processes between and among people.

A third basic concept in family therapy is that of the family as a *system*. The family is viewed as a social unit with specific and relatively constant patterns and characteristics, some of which have already been noted. The parts (individuals) are studied as they operate in relation to one another, and to other external systems (e.g., schools or parental employment). Causality is circular, since a response to a stimulus becomes a stimulus to a further response. All individuals in a family participate in its process, and a change by any one member has an impact on the whole family. When change occurs in a family, upsetting the usual balance or homeostasis, compensating factors (e.g., strong affects) occur to regain balance.

History of Family Therapy

The recognition of the homeostatic characteristic of families, seen in relatively rapid resumption of earlier symptomatic behavior when a "cured" inpatient returned to his family, was one of the major reasons leading early practitioners like Jackson to begin to see whole families in therapy.

Before 1950, there were a few practitioners such as Ackerman, Sullivan, and Whitaker who were trying to conceptualize and/or work with the interactive field of the family, based on their evolving belief in the significance of the family environment in the development and maintenance of psychopathology. Concepts such as "schizophrenegenic mothering" were attempts to describe interpersonal causation, although generally they were unidirectional (e.g., mother stressing child) rather than reciprocal (e.g., a mutually distressing system between mother and child, and eventually between mother and father, and other children, etc.).

In the 1950s, two general schools emerged—one more influenced by traditional psychodynamic thinking and the other more influenced by general systems theory. The psychodynamic school was represented by people such as Giffin, Johnson, and Litin (1954) who discussed "superego lacunae" and Lidz and his co-researchers at Yale (Lidz, Cornelison, Fleck, & Terry, 1957) who described "schismatic" and "skewed" families. Each group used intrapsychic concepts and language to describe the interactional patterns they were observing in families, the former discussing the unconscious transmission of delinquent behaviors from parent(s) to child by permissiveness and/or disciplinary inconsistency, while the latter group described marriages and families split by chronic frustration and hostility (schismatic), or dominated by the serious psychopathology of one parent (skewed).

Practitioners such as Jackson who were influenced by systems and communication theory attempted to apply those concepts to family functioning (e.g., seeking homeostatic mechanisms) and began to describe certain dysfunctional family processes (e.g., the "double bind" theory of schizophrenia by Bateson, Jackson, Haley, & Weakland, 1956). It is interesting to note that in the 1950s both the psychodynamic and systems thinkers, as well as Bowen, Wynne, Laing and others, were generally looking at families with a schizophrenic member, which suggests that many of our early ways of describing and treating (e.g., Satir 1964) family interaction were primarily based on a particular type of psychopathology.

In the 1960s there was an attempt to describe more clearly the ways to
do family therapy (e.g., Satir's *Conjoint Family Therapy*, 1964 and
Ackerman's *Treating the Troubled Family*, 1966) and some beginning
efforts to compare and contrast styles (e.g., Haley and Hoffmans' *Techniques of Family Therapy*, 1967, and Beels and Ferber's "Family Therapy: A View," 1969). The book *Families of the Slum* by Minuchin and
his co-researchers (Minuchin, Montalvo, Guerney, Rosman, & Schumer,
1967) was significant during this time both because a nonschizophrenic
population was studied and described, and because the researchers attempted to identify **types** of family structure and the accompanying implications for treatment for each type.

Two other important events in the 1960s were the founding in 1962
of the major journal in the field, *Family Process*, as a joint venture of the
Ackerman-led and Jackson-led training centers, and the effort by Framo
(1972) in 1967 to engage the prominent family researchers and family
therapists in a productive dialogue. A general effect of these efforts was
increased dialogue between the psychodynamically oriented family therapists and those influenced by family systems theory, and a gradual mutual enrichment of their work. The late 1960s also witnessed a greater
use of family therapy with poor white and nonwhite families (e.g.,
Minuchin & Montalvo, 1967), more conceptualization and use of short-
term therapy (e.g., Barten & Barten, 1972).

Other more recent developments have been the increase in family
therapy training centers and greater attention to training issues and
methods (e.g., Constantine, 1976; McPeak, 1975). Another has been the
encouragement from Bowen and his disciples to "study one's own family" (e.g., Guerin & Fogarty, 1972), which is similar to the psychoanalytic
training method of a didactic analysis, used to heighten one's own self-
awareness and to minimize countertransference problems in therapy.

The past few years also have seen renewed efforts to define "types" of
families (e.g., Alexander, 1973; Ford & Herrick, 1974). Special populations, such as the black family, are being studied (e.g., Willie, 1974),
and special techniques or programs such as family therapeutic camping
(Clark & Kempler, 1973), and sensitivity exercises for families (e.g.,
Satir, 1972) are being offered. Newer psychotherapeutic methods, such
as *Reality Therapy* (e.g., Glasser, 1973) and *Gestalt Therapy* (e.g.,
Kempler, 1974), are being adapted to work with families. Ethical issues
such as the release of aggressive affects within families are being discussed (e.g., Straus, 1974). An important publication in 1970 was an
article on the use of behavior modification techniques in family therapy
by Liberman (1970). Others who had been researching and writing in
this area were O'Leary, O'Leary, and Becker (1967) and Patterson and

his associates at the Oregon Research Institute (e.g., Patterson, Ray, & Shaw, 1968). An important book which emerged from the Oregon group was *Families: Applications of Social Learning to Family Life* (Patterson, 1971), as well as a recent teaching film (Oregon Research Institute, 1974) entitled *Childhood Aggression: Social Learning Approach to Family Therapy*.

A COMPARATIVE FRAMEWORK

As is true of the general field of psychotherapy, there is no **one** way to do family therapy. As Block and LaPerriere suggested, there is a unifying thread in the belief in the family as a system, but many variations as to how a therapist or team of therapists will attempt to alter a dysfunctional system. There have been a variety of attempts (Beels & Ferber, 1969; Foley, 1974; Group for the Advancement of Psychiatry [GAP], 1970; Haley, 1976) to view differences in theoretical approaches and styles of intervention, usually involving some types of polarities and the placement of various therapists along a particular continuum. Such continua may also be useful for a systematic assessment of the general style of one's own and others' practice of therapy, whether with individuals, groups, or families.

The following continua are offered to characterize differences among family therapists. Placement on a particular end or "extreme" does not imply a value judgment of better or worse.

1.   *All* - - - - - - - - - - - - - *One*

This continuum is concerned with how family therapists define *family* for purposes of treatment. As will be true of most of the continua, the majority of family therapy practice probably occurs around the midpoint, that is, in this instance, most therapists will tend to see the nuclear family (see GAP, 1970), or "ma, pa, and the kids."

The *all* extreme is represented by therapists such as Speck and Attneave, (1973) who expand *family* vertically into the different generations and horizontally into the various significant relationships in a family's "network" such as family friends, teachers, etc. When he sees that other generations or significant people are deeply involved in the life of the family, Minuchin (1974), as part of "structural family therapy" will seek to involve them. Another position, involving at least three generations of a family, is likely to be taken by therapists who are influenced by the writings of Boszormenji-Nagy and Spark (1973), on the importance of conceptualizing generational transmission of family problems and stating a preference to involve family members such as grandparents whenever possible.

The *one* end of the continuum is occupied almost exclusively by Bowen (e.g., 1966, 1976) who frequently seeks out the "strongest" in a family in order to help that person with the process of differentiation from his family. The assumption is made that the changes which that person makes will have an impact on the rest of the family system, and thereby readjust previously dysfunctional relationships. Other individually oriented psychotherapists, from Freud on (e.g., the case of Little Hans), have coached individuals on how to deal with their part in the family problems. Bowen's contribution has been to develop family systems concepts such as "triangulation" (the introduction of a third person, or a distracting preoccupation, to stabilize a distressed dyad) to bring order and direction into such work, and also point out the complexity of this task as the system responds by trying to regain homeostasis.

2.   *Model* - - - - - - - - - - - - - *Contract*

The basic intent of a *model*-focused therapist is to move the family toward a way or ways of functioning which the therapist believes is "best" for them, while the *contract*-focused therapist seeks to implement the goals and therapeutic directions which the family has. Therapists such as Satir have clear models of how a family should look, sound, and function, and they proceed in therapy to realize such models. Haley, and the behaviorists, are more likely to spend considerable time and effort to define and negotiate the directions which the family members wish to go, and then to apply their expertise to help achieve those goals.

3.   *Behavior* - - - - - - - - - - - - - *Feelings*

The struggle between these two poles has long been a major issue in the general field of psychotherapy. Therapists focused on behavior change hold that if new ways of relating to other family members are begun, then changes in feelings and attitudes will follow. Other therapists agree, for example, with marital partners who are concerned that they cannot show affection or cooperation or trust when they "don't feel it," because they assume that true behavior change cannot occur unless the underlying attitudes and feelings are changed. The first group of therapists will tend to subscribe to communicational and behavioral theories, while the others will focus, with Ackerman and Satir, on a general psychodynamic or phenomenological approach which emphasizes the perceptions and emotional reactions of each family member.

4.   *Past* - - - - - - - - - - - - - *Present*

Education and training in any of the mental health professions has tended to stress review of a patient's past, whether this is done in terms of early childhood experiences with parents or peers, or a behavioral conditioning history. Many psychotherapists, with some exceptions such as Perls' Gestalt therapy, attempt to systematically gather and study data from the past for purposes of diagnosis, and often proceed to deal in the treatment with this type of material. Among family therapists, many do take various types of histories, such as Satir's interest in the development of the parents' marriage or Bowen's focus on the intergenerational transmission of certain types of family issues and conflicts. Psychodynamically oriented practitioners study history to understand the development of symptomatic behavior. Practitioners such as Haley will minimize the importance of history, seeking instead for current patterns of interaction (see Haley's initial interview below), assuming this to be the material for family work.

5.   *Compliance* - - - - - - - - - - - - - *Opposition*

Most family therapists, while aware of ambivalence and resistance as important concepts in therapeutic work, assume that the family generally will give its cooperation (e.g., in receiving and acting on the therapist's suggestions). Ackerman and Satir were warm and rather charismatic figures who gave their good will to the family in supportive and yet challenging interchanges, and expected their good will to be reciprocated. Haley, Jackson, Wynne, and Whitaker, expecting resistance, used techniques to explore and manage the issues of power that they see as central to therapy, and may, like Whitaker, suggest co-therapists to help each other in the face of the family's power to extrude them. Increasingly we are discovering that we can expect opposition from the more rigid and enmeshed families, as individual and family change seems more threatening to them.

6.   *Conduct* - - - - - - - - - - - - - *React*

This distinction comes from Beels and Ferber (1969). The conductor is seen as a dominant leader and organizer of the family session, who may also use various types of special techniques (e.g., videotapes or family sculpturing). The Beels and Ferber listing of such therapists includes Ackerman, Bowen, Minuchin, and Satir.

The reactors tend to be less active and controlling of the situation. They watch the family interact, and make interventions in more subtle and complex ways, (e.g., the power-highlighting moves of Haley, 1963). They tend to adopt roles more like outside experts or consultants. In addition to Haley and Jackson, Boszormenji-Nagy, Whitaker, Wynne and Zuk are included here.

The issue of whose style is "best" will probably never be resolved.

What may occur is general agreement that some one theory of causative interrelationships between family dynamics and symptomatic manifestations accounts more fully for what therapists and researchers observe than other theories. Also, some related theory may provide therapeutic guidelines for interventions into various **types** of families and family problems.

Such relatively comprehensive theories may hopefully integrate concepts such as intergenerational influences, the need for generational boundaries, the relationships between interpersonal transactions in families and the intrapersonal issues of family members, the nature and use of *process* within a family, the role of communication, the task of individuation while maintaining connectedness, and the changing nature of families because of interactions with the broader society and because of intrafamilial stages of development. These concepts seem to be found in some way in most writing about family therapy.

Guidelines for family therapy may require a broad working knowledge of various styles of family intervention. Reflecting the research in the field of individual psychotherapy, efforts may be made to identify certain core conditions, which are "necessary but not sufficient," for effective interventions into various troubled families (see Carkhuff & Berenson, 1967; Strupp, 1973), followed by more specific prescription of terminal and implementing goals and relevant methods, for a particular family group. It seems likely that the various approaches to family therapy will struggle with issues of "matching," that is, what style of therapy and sets of intervention techniques will best "fit" this family, and its style and problems at this time? (See Goldstein & Stein, 1976.)

A "PROCESS" ORIENTATION

One of the main insights which Jackson (e.g., 1954) took from general systems theory and applied to family therapy was the sense of flow and ways of exchange between and among different interacting parts. Family therapists have termed this *process*, that is, the "how" or ways of a family's operation. The "what" about which a family is concerned (e.g., who will do the dishes, where a family will go for vacation) is known as *content*.

There are some family therapists who see their role as content-focused. They function more as judges and decision makers who hear various parties to a dispute and then render a hopefully fair decision. Such intervention may be motivated by a variety of factors such as believing this is a severely disorganized family over which one may temporarily need to take charge, or experiencing an inner need to save families by being a wise grandparent. The difficulty of this approach is that the family carries home no new skills for its own problem solving, though they may have a solution to a particular problem.

A process focus, however, assumes that once a family has learned different and more effective ways to deal with problems, then most content areas can be resolved. To that end, the therapist's constant focus is on the *patterns of interaction* between and among family members in their positions as spouses, siblings, parents and children, and even as members of the extended family.

What Does Process Look Like:

It was from this new system's perspective that the early family therapists and researchers tried to view the development and maintenance of psychopathology. Attempts were made to develop concepts and language to describe interactive events, usually occurring over a long period of time, a condition, of course, that is present in families.

Perhaps the best known interactional concept from the early development of the field was the "double bind." Bateson *et al.* (1956) studied schizophrenics and their families from the perspectives of communication theory, especially in terms of logical types and different levels of abstraction (see Watzlawick, 1966). The primary characteristics of the double-bind interaction pattern were seen as follows:

1. Two or more persons in ongoing interaction
2. Similar repeated experience of:
    a. A primary negative injunction
    b. A secondary injunction conflicting with the first at a more abstract level, and, like the first, enforced by punishments or other signals that threaten survival
    c. A tertiary negative injunction prohibiting the victim from leaving the field of interaction

Such an interactional pattern, especially when occurring between parent and child, was seen as destructive to the degree that the victim needed the intense relationship, wanted to perceive correctly and communicate back appropriately, and was prevented from commenting on the mixed message by fear of loss of the relationship and/or denial of his reality.

Laing (1969), who has noted his interest in the work of the Bateson research group discussed his concept of "invalidation," which has some similarities to the double-bind process. He stated that where one's wishes, feelings, desires, hopes, fears, perceptions, imaginations, memory, and dreams do not correspond with what significant others say they should be, such phenomena are "outlawed and excommunicated" by public definers of experience (e.g., parents, psychiatrists). Thus excommunicated, such phenomena do not cease to exist, but undergo secondary transformations which takes forms which society has chosen to define usually as mental illness. Laing and Esterson's (1964) earlier descriptions of their family research give examples of this process (e.g., Maya Abbott and her parents).

There were other interactional processes in families hypothesized. One of the first was the concept of "superego lacunae," first described by A. Johnson and Szurek (1952) and later by Giffin et al. (1954). Parents were described as seeking vicarious gratification of their own poorly integrated forbidden impulses in the acting-out of the child, using their unconscious permissiveness or inconsistency toward the child in certain areas of behavior to reinforce the behavior. The child's superego lacunae, that is, circumscribed defects in an otherwise strong and healthy superego, correspond to similar defects of the parent's superego, which, in turn, were derived from the conscious or unconscious permissiveness of their own parents. The careful investigation of processes between parents and children demonstrated that such behaviors as truancy, stealing, and sexual misconduct were encouraged subtly by parents by their excessive attention and warnings, fascinated probings, and other inconsistent and ambivalent value inculcation in order to satisfy their own needs. Parents frequently say that the child will outgrow a symptom, only to counteract this indifference by guilt, alarm, and punishment when criticism comes from external sources such as school personnel.

Another concept was "scapegoating." Based on their earlier research, Vogel and Bell (1960) suggested that a disturbed marital dyad develops an equilibrium which minimized contact with each other, and any expression of affect, especially hostility. In projecting their marital conflict onto an unconsciously selected child, his resulting dysfunction channels family tensions and provides a basis for solidarity. They described some of the factors in the selection of such a child (e.g., an eldest child who was first on the scene to receive parental conflict) and noted an induction process which involves explicit punishment with implicit approval, using indifference to or acceptance of the symptoms, unusual interest in the deviation, special attention, or exemption of the child from responsibilities. Often one parent may encourage one type of behavior while the other encourages another. The parents are able to see themselves as victims of the child's behavior, thus alleviating guilt at victimizing the child.

Based on their NIMH studies of families of schizophrenics, Wynne and his co-researchers (Wynne, Ryckoff, Day, & Hirsch, 1958) discussed

the concept of "pseudomutuality." Pseudomutual families were characterized as preoccupied with family harmony, with any divergence among
family members and/or attempts at individuation perceived as threatening the family relationships. The dilemma of such families is that divergence is viewed as leading to disruption of the family, but avoidance
of difference makes individual and family growth impossible. The result
of pseudomutuality in families was seen as an absence of spontaneity,
humor, and zest, and an abundance of rigidity, seriousness, and tension.

As the field developed, these concepts attempted to describe dysfunctional characteristics and patterns within families (see also "schism and
skew" by Lidz et al., 1957), and to move psychiatric thinking past an
exclusive focus on the intrapersonal dynamics of distressed behavior.

Bowen (1966, 1976) has been interested in a more extensive description of the system's qualities of families, especially a view which can
define the chain of mutually influencing behaviors, rather than the more
unidirectional early concepts (e.g., parents causing schizophrenia). One
of his basic concepts is "fusion–differentiation," describing individuals in
a system in terms of their use of emotions and intellect in relationships.
The former characteristic involves dominance by the emotional system,
while the latter implies the ability to separate intellectual and emotional
functioning in times of stress. Another of his basic concepts has been the
process of "triangulation" which describes the breakdown of an emotional process between two people and a resulting move to stabilize that
process by forming a triangle with a third person. Triangulation may
take place by the active movement of one or both parties to triangle a
third, or by the third party being caught up by the anxiety in the un-
stable dyad and entering the emotional process as a stabilizer. The
dysfunctional aspect of this process is that it prevents the emotional
process between two people from being worked out, and impedes personal, one-to-one open relationships with mutual sharing of thoughts
and feelings. An earlier Bowen concept was "undifferentiated family ego
mass," which described characteristics such as unclear expectations, anticipated rather than stated needs, indefiniteness of generational boundaries, and conflicts unresolved with one's own parents in the family of
origin. This latter characteristic also was a part of his concept of a
"multi-generational transmission system," where unresolved conflicts
and problems are passed from generation to generation.

How to Find Process: The Initial Interview

There are many ways to gain entry and gather diagnostic information
about a troubled family. Generally, the method one uses depends on
one's belief about what causes individual symptoms in a family context

and on one's style in attempting to relieve family stress. As already suggested, most interview styles should have a strong *process* focus, since the intent is to find both functional and dysfunctional patterns and to assist the family to make the corrections that will then become a part of their everyday life together.

A number of articles (e.g., Franklin & Prosky, 1973) and books (e.g., Satir 1964) have described styles for the initial interview with a family. Two such styles will be described briefly below, noting the points where the therapist is focusing on the interactional patterns.

The Watzlawick (1966) interview has been described both as a clinical tool, and as a research tool for measurement of family interaction. He suggests that its relative simplicity, its brevity, and the significance of its results are the factors which most recommend it.

In the first stage of the interview one asks each member individually and separately what he perceives as the "main problem" in his family. When the family is later brought together, they are told that their individual responses revealed some differences of opinion, and they are asked to come to some agreement among themselves, without the interviewer, as to what the major problems are.

The second stage consists of asking the family members to "plan something together." In this instance, both the actual content of the decision and the manner (process) of decision making are seen as important, though the latter is seen as more significant for the purposes of therapy.

The third stage occurs with the parents, but without the children. They are asked "How did you two meet and get together?" As in the second stage, the interviewer is interested both in the content of their recollections and in the manner of their relating to each other in the context of the interview.

With the children still outside the interview room, the fourth stage begins with the parents being given a proverb such as "a rolling stone gathers no moss." The parents are asked to discuss the meaning of the proverb between themselves, and then to call their children in after five minutes to teach them its meaning. The agreements and disagreements, the focus on the literal or metaphorical, and the degree of logical interpretation are studied by the interviewer, as well as the way in which they decide to teach the children and how this proceeds.

The final stage of the structured interview is to have all family members write down the "main fault" of the person on their left. The interviewer arranges special seating for this task, and introduces statements of his own, without the family's knowledge. The statements are shuffled by the interviewer and the whole family is asked to respond to each card, being asked, "To whom do you think this applies in your family?"

The responses reveal data on scapegoating, and assignment of blame in a family, as well as issues of favoritism and alliances.

Once the structured interview is completed, it is assumed that the assigned therapist, who has been viewing the family through a one-way mirror, can begin actual work with the family with a clearer knowledge of the family's dynamics and patterns of interaction.

The Haley (1976) interview can also be viewed in stages. The first is the "social" stage, where the whole family is greeted and made comfortable. After having them determine their seating arrangement, the therapist makes a social contact (e.g., name, grade in school) with each member to impress upon them that each person is important and will be involved. The mood of the family is assessed, as well as the general patterns of parent–child, spouse–spouse, and parent–therapist relationships that begin to be evident.

The next phase of the interview is the "problem" stage. The therapist describes briefly what he knows about the family, and explains why he wanted everyone in the family to be present. Asking questions such as "What is the problem?" or "What do you want from our clinic?" he usually begins with the adult who seems least involved in order to engage that person by underlining the need for his/her perceptions and assistance. Facts and perceptions about the problematic situations are sought at this time from all family members.

In the "interaction" stage, the therapist moves out of an active role, and asks the family members to talk about the types of disagreements that have emerged. Staying in charge by continually turning them back to each other, he watches patterns of interaction, the generational boundaries that may be violated, and the coalitions that seem to be present in the family. The therapist may even ask that the family's problem situations be acted out in the interview room, so that behavioral sequences become clearer and so that the family is actively engaged in beginning work on their own daily difficulties.

The final stage is that of developing a contract for further work. Clear statements about the changes that each member seeks are gathered, and specific goals for treatment set. Arrangements are made for the time and place for the next interview, and, perhaps, other significant people are identified who may be important to the further work of therapy.

What to Do with Process: A Communication Approach

If operating from a *model* position, the therapist may have a set of principles and procedures for the family to learn and probably practice, both within the treatment session, and at home. The therapist believes that the interpersonal techniques and interactive styles suggested, if accepted and used by the family, will be helpful not only at times of stress but also in their everyday functioning.

Satir (1964) discussed a variety of ways for families to communicate. She encouraged, and modeled in her own behavior with family members, clarity, specificity, congruence, and directness as the individuals endeavored to exchange informations about themselves and their needs, and about their perceptions of others and about life in general. In order to avoid some of the affective traps that family members set for each other, she would assist them to minimize or eliminate the assignment of blame and the use of words such as "always" or "never." It was her experience that such statements tended to sidetrack the basic communication activity; the one accused used his energy to marshall evidence about why one's accuser was wrong, listing the occasions when certain things did or did not occur, thus "proving" the other wrong. Rather than continue the original dialogue, a separate process would begin, focused on personalities instead of issues and understanding, and leaving one or both parties feeling unheard, angry, and hurt.

The sequence just outlined is a highly familiar one in marriages, and has its counterpart in other important relationships, including those of parents and children. An example of a process sequence in a parent–child dyad would be a child who does not tell the truth. Exploration of the sequence shows the gradual shutdown of the child in giving potentially negative information about himself as he anticipates or receives an angry reaction from his parent. The withholding of information, especially if the parent suspects what has really happened, serves only to increase the parent's frustration and loss of trust. This often leads to parental anger, which further reinforces the child's lying to protect himself. In both of these examples we experience the emotional reactiveness of the parties to a dialogue, which reactiveness seems to increase in proportion to the emotional investment and survival meaning of the relationship. This aspect of communication has been referred to as part of the "context" of a communication sequence, that is, the emotional meanings, both historical and current, that the relationships have for its participants.

The pathway out of these interactional traps and vicious cycles is a careful retracing of the steps that create them. The therapist can assist the family by first creating a therapeutic atmosphere in which each person feels safe with himself, with the therapist, and with the intimate others who are present in the sessions. Such safety is the result of feeling that what you say or feel will not be judged only negatively by another, that it will not automatically end a significant relationship, and that some ways can be evolved to help the parties grow as individuals **and** as a couple or family unit, though knowing that this growth process will almost always be painful because it brings changes in the relationship system.

The next therapeutic step is the careful retracing of the sequences and assumptions that are currently a problem. Knowing that this process will be relatively constant, although the content may vary widely, the therapist works to increase each person's awareness of the words and actions that tend to short-circuit communication and prevent the mutually satisfying resolution of issues. As this awareness increases, efforts may or may not be made to facilitate understanding of the origins and meanings of the dysfunctional patterns. Some therapists, such as Haley (1976), believe this historical understanding to be unnecessary, while others, such as Bowen (1976), believe that earlier relationships—especially in one's family of origin—need not only to be understood but also corrected before one is free to connect fully and effectively in one's current intimate relationships.

Once the dysfunctional patterns are made clear, efforts are begun to define the ways that each participant in a transaction would prefer to be heard and dealt with, and to find points of communality and points of compromise. The therapist may also present some suggestions as to how their interchanges might better occur. Where individuals' positions are far apart, the work begins by negotiation of needs and wants, perhaps trying a variety of new ways of responding to and meeting perceived needs. Participants are also asked to give feedback about the effects these new behaviors have on them.

The next step is to practice the more desirable alternatives that have been defined. This can usually occur in the therapeutic sessions themselves, where old content and issues are processed through new interactional pathways. There will be some new behaviors, such as the sensate focus exercises of Masters and Johnson (1970) in changing a couple's sexuality, that should be tried in the privacy of the home. But where legitimate privacy issues are not involved, such in-session practice can be an important step in the development of new behaviors.

The final step, which most specifically relates to transfer of training, is to utilize the new communicative process and interactional behaviors in the everyday life of the family. Since these have already been practiced in the therapeutic sessions, generally only the physical setting will be changed; this may have some impact of its own, but generally it is a minor one. A more significant factor may be the absence of one party in the "safety" issue, namely, the therapist. Depending on the nature of the changes sought, and the threat factors to the relationship they may involve, some new behaviors may be more difficult to implement without the security of the therapist's presence. This leads us to another necessary part of the process: to review the incident and ease of the changes in subsequent sessions, and to explore the resistances that arise. This may lead to new interpersonal understanding and possibly some modifications in the new processes being developed.

Knowing that the likelihood of having new behaviors continue is a function of the type and frequency of reinforcement that occurs after the presentation of a behavior, the therapist also helps the individuals to understand the need for encouragement and to define what each prefers for reinforcement. In the earlier stages, when individual needs were being explored and new and more pleasing behaviors selected and established, we assume that each person was at least implicitly defining attitudes or behaviors that would feel better to him if presented by the other, as well as defining current behaviors that one or the other perceives as noxious. In these instances, the removal of existing undesirable behaviors is also received positively.

What to Do with Process: A Structural Approach

The work of Minuchin (e.g., 1974) and his colleagues at the Philadelphia Child Guidance Center has come to be known as *structural family therapy*. The structure of the family is defined in terms of its boundaries (i.e., factors such as generational lines that limit a system), its alignments (i.e., ties between and among people for affection, support, etc.), and its balance (i.e., forces such as dependency or overinvolvement which operate to continue dysfunctional boundaries and/or alignments). The family is also assessed according to its general developmental stage (e.g., a first child entering adolescence) and its place in the larger social network (ecology) of schools, churches, health care, etc.

The intent of the therapist is to effect behavioral changes by planned manipulations of existing interactional patterns so that the dysfunctional mutual processes are permanently changed and new role behaviors are developed. This structural approach in its earlier form (Minuchin *et al.*, 1967) was seen as possibly effective with low-income families with delinquent children. More recently, as its goals and methods have been more clearly developed, its value with anorexia nervosa (Rosman, Minuchin, & Liebman, 1975) and with psychogenic pain (Liebman, Honig, & Berger, 1976) has been demonstrated.

In their discussion of the "family lunch session," Rosman *et al.* (1975) state, "eating lunch with the family provides exceptional opportunities for the therapist to observe family members' transactions around eating, and to make on-the-spot interventions to change the patterning of these transactions. This session also serves broader diagnostic purposes, since structural and dysfunctional characteristics of the family are more readily apparent in this context [p. 847]." This procedure obviously relates to *in vivo* concerns and transfer of training issues. The slices of family living selected offer the opportunity to observe more directly the methods that spouse pairs, parent–child pairs, and sibling units use to interact with each other, and to make changes in the sequences that occur.

While Minuchin (1974) has been careful to point out that the addition of a therapist to a family system does alter that system, he assumes that the family is transmitting reasonably valid messages about its everyday functioning, and that his interventions into that functioning can be effective. The lunch session intervention is chosen because of its clear relevance to the problem of anorexia nervosa, and because some substantial resolution of the presenting problem can free the family to view more basic areas of conflict. Liebman *et al.* (1976) note that the subsequent work of such therapy is to change the more basic patterns in the family and the extrafamilial environment that tend to reinforce the presenting symptoms, and, finally, "to promote lasting disengagement of the patient in order to prevent a recurrence of the symptoms or the development of a new symptom-bearer by resolving chronic marital conflicts [p. 401]."

The first step for the therapist is to change the status and the role of the identified patient in those cases by having the parents make deliberate but frustrated attempts to pressure the child into eating thereby highlighting his power, and their impotence, rather than the child's sickness, or by engaging the parents in the discussion of more basic concerns in their marriage and/or their family, thereby removing the major attention from the child's presenting symptom. These, and other similar redefining moves (also, see following section on a Strategic Approach), move the family to the second stage which is to define the eating or other problem as one of interpersonal dysfunctioning, which has been obscured by the focus on the index patient's symptom.

As the therapist has been observing the family in action, his attention has been focused on understanding the interactional processes, though such understanding is not seen as necessary for the family members. Once the therapist attains this goal, a variety of directives may be given (e.g., "Let your husband handle that discipline problem" or "I will work with your son on controlling his temper so you don't have to worry about it"), to begin to change the boundaries (e.g., to disengage a mother from overinvolvement with a child and connect up the father instead) that control access to family members and to define the problems as those of interpersonal functioning and not of a "sick" individual. Once the systems or interactional perspective is made clear and beginning moves made to change the process, the therapist can work with the family to resolve the longstanding conflicts that may be present—especially in the marriage. Some of these more basic areas are marital or parent–child communication, struggles over individuation, and control or power concerns.

What to Do with Process: A Strategic Approach [1]

An increasing amount of attention (e.g., Haley, 1973, 1976; Palazzoli, Boscolo, Cecchin, & Prata, 1974) is being given to the active influencing of a dysfunctional system by a therapist's use of direct suggestion, or indirect means such as prescription of seemingly counterproductive or paradoxical behaviors, (i.e., the therapist requests that the family try "illogical" behaviors that to them would seem only to worsen the problem) or by the therapists' defining as positive and helpful those behaviors that family members have been experiencing negatively.

The use of paradox in interactional therapies arises because, for many families—especially those that have more rigid and resistant systems— the notion of change is threatening and attempts to help often are met with familial sabotage of the therapist's best efforts. In general, strategic therapy assumes that common sense solutions have already been tried and found ineffective, and, therefore, continued efforts in those directions will only increase frustration and dysfunction. The therapist instead studies the ways that the system manages to maintain symptoms, and may push further in those directions, relabeling them as positive intents and efforts by family members.

Haley (1976) discusses the therapist's active use of directives, that is, the assignment of relatively specific tasks which he believes will relatively quickly produce changed behaviors in a family, with resulting changed subjective experiences. The therapist first needs to motivate family members to follow these directives, and can best do this by convincing each of them of the personal and familial benefits that will result. Once motivated, understandable and specific instructions are given to do something different in the everyday sequences of behavior. In general, all family members should be involved in the task(s) assigned, and all

---

[1] While Haley (e.g., 1973) defines "strategic therapy" as any method where the therapist accepts responsibility for problem-definition, goal settings, use of specific interventions, and evaluation of treatment, the viewpoints and methods he advocates are, in general, those noted here.

should know both their specific roles in the change, and be prepared to report in a subsequent session on the way they did (or perhaps did not do) their assignment.

Haley also discusses the use of metaphors, selected for their relevance to the nature of the family's struggles, as ways to deal with problems. The intent is to select a task or activity which is related symbolically to their problem, but is less threatening and therefore more likely to change. The hope of the therapist is that changes made in one sphere of a family's life will be carried over into the more immediate problems, and either be spontaneously resolved or at least made less threatening so that more direct work can be done with the presenting symptoms.

Weakland, Fisch, Watzlawick, and Bodin (1974), using a therapeutic style similar to Haley's, report significant success in approximately three-fourths of their family treatment cases. Initial steps involve the explicit definition of the presenting complaint(s), followed by explication of the behaviors in the system that are maintaining the presenting problems. Asking family members to relate what they have been doing, in concrete terms, to deal with the problem, is often sufficient.

Once dysfunctional behaviors have been specified, observable, realistic, and concrete goals are established both as mutually-agreed-upon (by family members and therapist) foci for change and as measures for evaluation of success. The means to reach these goals involve several of the methods already discussed, namely, the relabeling of noxious behaviors as beneficial, the use of paradox to highlight symptoms and/or to induce a resistant patient to change to prove the therapist wrong, or the use of directives to alter sequences of behavior. The prescription of tasks, paradoxical or not, often requires that they be carried out in settings outside the consulting room. Termination occurs within 10 sessions, and focuses on the gains made through the efforts of the patient and on further ways that changes can be maintained and/or enhanced.

What to Do with Process: A Behavioral Approach

Research and application in the field of behavior modification is increasingly characterized by its attention to families, especially in the area of parent training. As Mash, Hamerlynch, and Handy (1976) note:

> This emphasis is based on the assumption that behavior is maintained by contemporaneous events in the natural environment, and it is through the alteration of the events that behavior change is achieved. This assumption leads directly to the utilization of family members in mediating behavior

> change, and has served as the basis for the multitudinous number of
> "parent training" programs which have developed [p. xiv].

They further offer some observations on the characteristics of past research, including its predominant focus on pathology rather than prevention, and a focus on a child as the target of change, usually by training parents to systematically alter the child's environment through contingency management. They also define as a currently underdeveloped area assistance to families with "special" situations such as single parenthood, child abuse, or communal family living.

As discussed elsewhere in this volume, behavioral approaches have long been focused on training parents as contingency managers and on defining specific antecedents, current and more desirable behaviors, and types and frequency of reinforcers, as a behavior modification program moves closer to natural environments from a more artificial clinical situation. A very good review of the research concerned with parents as mediators, generalization, and self-control strategies can be found in Conway and Bucher (1976), while Patterson (1976) provides an extensive discussion of the family systems aspect in behavior modification programs with aggressive children, and describes an intervention program and its outcomes. Patterson and his colleagues (Arnold, Levine, & Patterson, 1975) have also demonstrated that training given to parents in contingency management has favorable effects not only on the "deviant" child but also on his siblings whether or not the siblings were involved as target children. Such findings have increasingly convinced Patterson's group of the advantage, and necessity, of conceptualizing the family as an interactive and mutually influencing system, and on the generalization effects that occur in parent training programs.

The primary focus of the Patterson group continues to be on developing or enhancing parenting skills in order to resolve deviant child behaviors, training parents in behavioral observation and record keeping, in withdrawal of reinforcement for punishment of coercive behaviors, and in use of positive reinforcers for desirable behaviors. Their home treatment program begins by having parents study a programmed text (e.g., Patterson, 1971) on social-learning–based child management methods. Parents are then taught to define, follow, and record deviant and/or desirable child behaviors, and then are assigned to training groups where modeling and role-playing are used to develop skills in withholding reinforcement for deviant behaviors and in providing reinforcement for desirable behaviors. Following this, parents learn to devise contracts with clear contingencies, both points and social reinforcers for specific behaviors. The program discussed above (Patterson, 1976) also involved classroom intervention for some of the boys, using the experimenters as behaviors managers rather than additionally burdening the teachers.

The research showed significant changes in coercive behaviors for the majority of the boys and generally for their siblings, though less clear changes for coercive behaviors by parents. Patterson suggests that, while a behavior management program is often sufficient for some families, many of them need additional treatment efforts. He cites development of negotiation skills and partial resolution of marital conflicts and depression as the most common foci for such intervention.

CONCLUSION

A major strength of family therapy is that it seeks to alter those sequences of behavior which occur between and among ongoing social participants such as spouses or parents and children. While research into the effectiveness of family therapy has been hampered by the conceptual and methodological problems that have attended much of the research on psychotherapy (see Wells, Dilkes, & Trevelli, 1972), sufficient strides have been made to justify our continued optimism that:

1. A family systems perspective will increasingly be a major framework of diagnosing and treating individual psychopathology.
2. Family intervention methods will continue to be refined and made more specifically applicable to different types of distressed families at different stages of their development.
3. The effectiveness of family intervention methods will be demonstrated because of growth in our therapeutic sophistication and in our research methodology.

The evaluative research to this point is sparse, as the major energy in the field has gone into defining the variety of diagnostic and treatment issues, describing the types of individual and family problems encountered in clinical practice, and beginning to come to some consensus on the similarities and differences among ideas and styles of the thousands of practicing family therapists. The earlier work of practitioners such as the Denver crisis group (Langsley, Flomenhaft, & Machotka, 1969; Langsley, Pittman, Machotka, & Flomenhaft, 1968) and Minuchin et al., 1967 suggested the potential value of family therapy. Spurred by the review of Wells et al. (1972), recent research has been more attentive to the significant methodological issues in psychotherapy research. The studies of the Philadelphia Child Guidance Center group (e.g., Rosman *et al.*, 1975) cited earlier have been less global and more rigorous, defining more clearly the theory and the methods that seem therapeutically useful. In addition, there are now more carefully designed outcome studies in other areas, such as the recent work of Ro-Trock, Wellisch, and Schoolar (1977) which showed more rapid return to community functioning and lower rehospitalization rates for those adolescents receiving family therapy compared to those receiving individual therapy, after a three month follow-up. Still unanswered for the field are the more specific questions of what types of family intervention are more effective for which client families. Careful clinical hunches and observations, followed by collegial discussion and sound research will help us further in the direction of specificity.

REFERENCES

Ackerman, N. W. *Treating the troubled family.* New York: Basic Books, 1966.
Ackerman, N. W. The growing edge of family therapy. *Family Process*, 1971, *10*, 143–156.
Alexander, J. Defensive and supportive communication in family systems. *Journal of Marriage and the Family*, 1973, *35*, 613–617.
Arnold, J., Levine, A., & Patterson, G. Changes in sibling behavior following family intervention. *Journal of Consulting and Clinical Psychology*, 1975, *43*, 683–688.
Barten, H., & Barten, S. (Eds.). *Children and their parents in brief therapy.* New York: Behavioral Publications, 1972.
Bateson, G., Jackson, D., Haley, J., & Weakland, J. Toward a theory of schizophrenia. *Behavioral Science*, 1956, *1*, 241–264.
Beels, C., & Ferber, A. Family therapy: A view. *Family Process*, 1969, *8*, 280–318.
Bloch, D., & LaPerriere, K. Techniques of family therapy: A conceptual frame. In D. Bloch (Ed.), *Techniques of family psychotherapy: A primer.* New York: Grune & Stratton, 1973.
Bodin, A. Conjoint family therapy. In W. E. Vinacke (Ed.), *Readings in general psychology.* New York: American Book, 1968.
Boszormenji-Nagy, I., & Spark, G. M. *Invisible loyalties: reciprocity in intergenerational family therapy.* New York: Harper & Row, 1973.
Bowen, M. The use of family theory in clinical practice. *Comprehensive Psychiatry*, 1966, *7*, 345–374.
Bowen, M. Theory in the practice of psychotherapy. In P. Guerin (Ed.), *Family therapy: Theory and practice.* New York: Gardner Press, 1976.
Burgess, E. The family as a unity of interacting personalities. *The Family*, 1926, *7*, 3–9.
Carkhuff, R., & Berenson, B. *Beyond counseling and therapy.* New York: Holt, 1967.
Clark, J., & Kempler, H. Therapeutic family camping: A rationale. *The Family Coordinator*, 1973, *22*, 437–442.
Constantine, L. Designed experience: A multiple, goal directed training program in family therapy. *Family Process*, 1976, *15*, 373–387.
Conway, J., & Bucher, B. Transfer and maintenance of behavior change in children:

A review and suggestions. In E. Mash, L. Hamerlynck, & L. Handy (Eds.), *Behavior modification and families.* New York: Brunner/Mazel, 1976.

Foley, V. *An introduction to family therapy.* New York: Grune & Stratton, 1974.

Ford, F., & Herrick, J. Family rules: Family life styles. *American Journal of Orthopsychiatry,* 1974, *44,* 61–69.

Framo, J. (Ed.). *Family interaction: A dialogue between family researchers and family therapists.* New York: Springer, 1972.

Franklin, P., & Prosky, P. A standard initial interview. In D. Bloch (Ed.), *Techniques of family psychotherapy: A primer.* New York: Grune & Stratton, 1973.

Glasser, W. Reality therapy in child and marital counseling. *Audio-Digest Psychiatry,* 1973, *2*(17). (Audiotape)

Goldstein, A., & Stein, N. *Prescriptive psychotherapies.* New York: Pergamon Press, 1976.

Giffin, M., Johnson, A., & Litin, E. Specific factors determining antisocial acting-out. *American Journal of Orthopsychiatry,* 1954, *24,* 668–684.

Group for the Advancement of Psychiatry. *Treatment of families in conflict.* New York: Science House, 1970.

Guerin, P., & Fogarty, T. Study your own family. In A. Ferber, M. Mendelsohn, & A. Napier (Eds.), *The book of family therapy.* New York: Science House, 1972.

Haley, J. *Strategies of psychotherapy.* New York: Grune & Stratton, 1963.

Haley, J. Beginning and experienced family therapists. In A. Ferber, M. Mendelsohn, & A. Napier (Eds.), *The book of family therapy.* New York: Science House, 1972.

Haley, J. *Uncommon therapy: The psychiatric techniques of Milton H. Erickson, M.D.* New York: Norton, 1973.

Haley, J. *Problem solving therapy.* New York: Jossey Bass, 1976.

Haley, J., & Hoffman, L. *Techniques of family therapy.* New York: Basic Books, 1967.

Jackson, D. The question of family homeostasis. *Psychiatric Quarterly Supplement,* 1957, *31,* 79–90.

Jackson, D. Family rules: Marital quid pro quo. *Archives of General Psychiatry,* 1965, *12,* 589–594.

Johnson, A., & Szurek, S. The genesis of antisocial acting out in children and adults. *Psychoanalytic Quarterly,* 1952, *21,* 323–343.

Kempler, W. *Principles of gestalt family therapy.* Salt Lake City: Deseret Press, 1974.

Laing, R. D. *The politics of the family and other essays.* New York: Pantheon, 1969.

Laing, R., & Esterson, A. *Sanity, madness and the family.* New York: Basic Books, 1964.

Langsley, D., Flomenhaft, K., & Machotka, P. Follow-up evaluation of family crisis therapy. *American Journal of Orthopsychiatry,* 1969, *39,* 753–760.

Langsley, D., Pittman, F., Machotka, P., & Flomenhaft, K. Family crisis—results and implications. *Family Process,* 1968, *7,* 145–158.

Liberman, R. Behavioral approaches to family and couple therapy. *American Journal of Orthopsychiatry,* 1970, *40,* 106–118.

Lidz, T., Cornelison, A., Fleck, S., & Terry, D. The intrafamilial environment of schizophrenics: Marital schism and marital skew. *American Journal of Psychiatry,* 1957, *114,* 241–248.

Liebman, R., Honig, P., & Berger, H. An integrated treatment program for psychogenic pain. *Family Process,* 1976, *15,* 397–405.

Mash, E., Hamerlynck, L., & Handy, L. (Eds.). *Behavior modification and families*. New York: Brunner/Mazel, 1976.

Masters, W., & Johnson, V. *Human sexual inadequacy*. Boston: Little, Brown, 1970.

McPeak, W. *Design, delivery, and evaluation of an introductory course in family therapy*. Unpublished doctoral dissertation, Syracuse University, 1975.

Minuchin, S. *Families and family therapy*. Cambridge, Massachusetts: Harvard University Press, 1974.

Minuchin, S., & Montalvo, B. Techniques for working with disorganized, low socioeconomic families. *American Journal of Orthopsychiatry*, 1967, 37, 880–887.

Minuchin, S., Montalvo, B., Guerney, B., Rosman, B., & Schumer, F. *Families of the slums*. New York: Basic Books, 1967.

Nimkoff, M. (Ed.). *Comparative family systems*. Boston: Houghton Mifflin, 1965.

O'Leary, K., O'Leary, S., & Becker, W. Modification of a deviant sibling interaction pattern in the home. *Behavior Research and Therapy*, 1967, 5, 113–120.

Oregon Research Institute (Producer) *Childhood Aggression: A Social Learning Approach to Family Therapy*. Champaign, Illinois: Research Press, 1974. (Film)

Palazzoli, M. S., Boscolo, L., Cecchin, G. F., & Prata, G. The treatment of children through brief therapy of their parents. *Family Process*, 1974, 13, 429–442.

Patterson, G. *Families: Applications of social learning to family life*. Champaign, Illinois: Research Press, 1971.

Patterson, G. The aggressive child: Victim and architect of a coercive system. In E. Mash, L. Hamerlynck, & L. Handy (Eds.), *Behavior modification and families*. New York: Brunner/Mazel, 1976.

Patterson, G., Ray, R., & Shaw, D. Direct intervention in families of deviant children. *Oregon Research Institute Research Bulletin*, 1968, 8, (9).

Ro-Trock, G., Wellisch, D., & Schoolar, J. A family therapy outcome study in an inpatient setting. *American Journal of Orthopsychiatry*, 1977, 47, 514–522.

Rosman, B., Minuchin, S., & Liebman, R. Family lunch session: An introduction to family therapy in anorexia nervosa. *American Journal of Orthopsychiatry*, 1975, 45, 846–853.

Satir, V. Quest for survival: Training programs for family diagnosis and treatment, *Acta Psychotherapeutica*, 1963, 11, 33–38.

Satir, V. *Conjoint family therapy: A guide to therapy and technique*. Palo Alto, California: Science and Behavior Books, 1964.

Satir, V. *Peoplemaking*. Palo Alto, California: Science and Behavior Books, 1972.

Speck, R., & Attneave, C. *Family networks*. New York: Pantheon, 1973.

Straus, M. Leveling, civility and violence in the family. *Journal of Marriage and the Family*, 1974, 36, 13–29.

Strupp, H. On the basic ingredients of psychotherapy. *Journal of Consulting and Clinical Psychology*, 1973, 41, 1–8.

Stryker, S. The interactional and situational approaches. In H. Christensen (Ed.), *Handbook of marriage and the family*. Chicago: Rand McNally, 1964.

Vogel, E., & Bell, N. Emotionally disturbed child as the family scapegoat. In N. Bell & E. Vogel (Eds.), *A modern introduction to the family*. Glencoe, Illinois: Free Press, 1960.

Watzlawick, P. A structured family interview. *Family Process*, 1966, 5, 256–271.

Weakland, J., Fisch, R., Watzlawick, P., & Bodin, A. Brief therapy: Focused problem resolution. *Family Process*, 1974, 13, 141–168.

Wells, R., Dilkes, T., & Trevilli, N. The results of family therapy: A critical review of the literature. *Family Process*, 1972, 11, 189–207.

Willie, C. Black family and social class. *American Journal of Orthopsychiatry*, 1974, *44*, 50–60.

Wynne, L., Ryckoff, I., Day, J., & Hirsch, S. Pseudomutuality in the family relations of schizophrenics. *Psychiatry*, 1958, *21*, 205–220.

Zelditch, M., Jr. Cross-cultural analyses of family structure. In H. Christensen (Ed.), *Handbook of marriage and the family*. Chicago: Rand McNally, 1964.

II

TRANSFER-ENHANCEMENT
BASED ON
SELF-GENERATED PROCESSES

5

Self-Management:
Strategies and Tactics

FREDERICK H. KANFER

INTRODUCTION AND CONCEPTUAL ISSUES

A perennial problem in assessing the effectiveness of psychotherapeutic techniques lies in the diversity of objectives associated with different theoretical approaches. Dynamic and psychoanalytic models stress
the reconstruction of personality and the alteration of intrapsychic
processes as success criteria. Therefore their natural basis for assessment
is the therapist's evaluation of the patient's progress, both in adjustment
and personal growth, supplemented by the patient's indication of his
comfort, understanding, and acceptance of himself. A changed self-
concept, the remission of symptoms in the cognitive, affective, or perceptual areas, and increased self-understanding were both the objectives
and the success criteria for psychotherapy until less than two decades
ago. Although earlier writers have frequently emphasized the importance
of increased subjective comfort, reduction of anxieties, and increased

interpersonal skills, these changes were seen primarily as by-products of fundamental changes in the psychological processes which control emotional states and behaviors.

With the advent of behaviorally oriented therapies the focus shifted abruptly to the other extreme of the intrapersonal-process versus observable behavior continuum. Change in selected target behaviors, reduction of anxiety in the presence of specific stimuli, and acquisition of well-defined and socially desirable skills became the primary criteria for evaluating effectiveness of treatment. In the former approach, questions about the generalization of treatment effects beyond the locus and time of treatment were relatively irrelevant. When changes occurred at the affective, cognitive or intrapersonal level, it was clearly presumed that a changed perception of the environment and a healthier personality organization would enable the individual to handle later living problems, regardless of their content or locale. In its early stages, the conditioning therapies also showed little concern about the generalization of treatment effects. Generalization was considered to be a **passive** phenomenon. Extinction, reconditioning, or acquisition of new responses was assumed to be controlled not only by the specific elements present in the training program, but also by members of a larger class of stimuli, responses and reinforcers resembling the elements utilized in treatment. Stokes and Baer (1977) characterized this expectation neatly by saying, "generalization was something that happened, not something produced by a procedure specific to it [p. 349]."

During the last 25 years, the field of psychotherapy has undergone, and is still undergoing, a significant dialectic process. The earlier stress on intrapsychic processes and the corresponding efforts to alter the organization of the self-system (personality) in treatment resulted in a revolutionary shift by the new behavior therapists toward focusing on environmental controlling variables. The earliest behavioral programs were devoted to the engineering of behavior changes by reconstructing environments. With operant conditioning as a vehicle, they relied mainly on response contingencies and stimulus control to eliminate or replace symptomatic behavior. The pioneering programs by Lindsley (1956), King, Armitage, and Tilton (1960), and Ayllon and Haughton (1962) represent this shift.

The behavior modifier's antithesis embodied a rejection of concern with subjective experiences, cognitive and perceptual phenomena, patient-generated covert events, and all other events that were neither publicly observable nor easily accessible to control by environmental stimuli and reinforcers. In behavioral programs that specifically aimed at changing target responses, the generalization by small and unprogrammed fluctuations during the reconditioning process, both in the environment and in the client, were *unprogrammed* events; or they were viewed as distant consequences of the change program.

To learning-oriented therapists, it became clear that such situation-specific techniques would have to be supplemented, theoretically and in practice, by programming for transfer and durability of therapeutic effects. Interestingly, early demonstration of the effects of conditioning therapies were conducted within an ABA design. In this design, a baseline is first established (A), a treatment is then administered (B), and again withdrawn (A). Demonstration of the return of the undesirable behavior to pretreatment levels has frequently been cited as an indication of the therapeutic power of the treatment variable. In practice, of course, it is exactly the opposite effect that is desired. Namely, the most powerful and beneficial therapeutic technique would be one that produces **persistent** effects, even after treatment is stopped.

The last few years have witnessed the synthesis stage of the dialectic in several directions. First, a rapidly increasing number of behavioral therapists has begun to explore, study, and utilize treatment methods that include the intrapersonal repertoire in the target domain. Development of the broadly labeled cognitive-behavioral approaches, utilization of patient's self-report both for assessment and treatment, and modification of such covert behaviors as thinking, planning, problem-solving, fantasizing, and decision making, have been incorporated both as treatment targets and as treatment modes. The evolving synthesis also includes the incorporation of self-administered and self-generated programs within the operant framework (Kanfer, 1975; Mahoney & Thoresen, 1974), and the development of learning-based methods for training of behavioral skills that become relatively independent of external control (e.g., Goldstein, Sprafklin, & Gershaw, 1976; Mahoney, Moura, & Wade, 1973). Thus the rift between the insight and intrapsychically oriented clinicians and their rigorous behavior-oriented colleagues is giving rise to a synthesis that barely resembles the earlier approaches of either group. Nonbehavioral clinicians are adopting the technology of behavioral approaches and applying them to both observable and covert behaviors, while behavioral clinicians are concerning themselves increasingly with self-control methods, training of general imitative processes, and establishing effective self-regulatory functions. It should be clearly noted, however, that this trend does not seem to represent a rapprochement between opposing theoretical camps. Rather, it is a true dialectic synthesis that should result in the eventual abandonment of both prior positions.

The increasing interest in incorporating cognitive behaviors and processes into the social learning model (Bandura, 1977; Kanfer, 1970, 1977b; Mischel, 1973) spurred behavior therapists to develop methods aimed at changing cognitive behaviors. But, since such target behaviors often are regarded as mediators for action, greater trans-situational generality is expected. What can be changed are not specific responses in given situations, but *strategies* or behavioral conduct rules, applicable in many different situations. As a result, not only environmental contingency programs but also interview-mediated methods came under the purview of behavioral techniques. What were considered distinctly different approaches in theory *and* method a decade ago are often integrated programs today that combine methods derived from different schools of therapy under one broad theoretical umbrella.

Treatment Strategies

In an earlier paper (Kanfer & Phillips, 1966) we have differentiated between four basic strategies for behavior change:

1. *Interactive therapy.* It is characterized by use of dyadic interactions in which the relationship with a therapist is viewed as the critical vehicle for change. The major mark of interactive therapy is the catalytic role of the therapist in altering patients' understanding of the causal relationships between their past history and current behaviors, their perception of themselves in relation to others, their recognition of the repetitive nature of interpersonal themes as they unfold and recur in therapy sessions, and the subsequent reorganization of the patients' perceptions and emotional reactions to conflicts and personal experiences. Verbal exchange is the sole treatment mode in this approach. Despite the variations in theoretical explanations for how the corrective experience comes about, all who use this strategy share the common assumption that the patient's new outlook will permit him to engage in new learning and growth, free of emotional inhibitions and distortions. It is further assumed that this underlying change permits improved handling of conflict situations, acquisition of new skills and general enrichment of personal experiences without further need for therapist-supervised guidance in acquiring and maintaining the new behavioral repertoires. Thus, if a transfer of skills and knowledge acquired in therapy is programmed at all, it is instrumented only in the broad sweeping coverage of various life experiences during treatment. Generalization is presumed to occur because the determinants of the patient's behavior in all life situations have been radically altered. Natural psy-

chological growth processes are said to account for increased and enduring effectiveness after the termination of treatment.

2. *Instigation therapy.* This strategy presumes that behavior change occurs **between** therapy sessions and that the "talk sessions" serve mainly to explore objectives, train the client in methods, and motivate him to modify his extra therapeutic environment and to apply learning techniques to his own behavior. In this sense the patient learns to become his own therapist. During sessions, assigned tasks are practiced, tactics are discussed, and a favorable orientation toward change is created. Instigation therapy reduces the need for generalization since the behavior changes are programmed for occurrence in the natural environment and since in-session efforts are focused on altering the client's self-management techniques. Therapists who utilize this strategy may at times fit the pattern of the interactive therapist or the behavior modifier. For example, primary emphasis may be given to altering cognitive processes and self-regulating techniques during the dyadic interaction. These methods are then utilized in everyday behavior to remove symptomatic behaviors or to increase behavioral efficiency (e.g., Ellis, 1962, 1974); or the instigation therapist may train patients in self-administration of conditioning techniques and detailed step-by-step programs, resembling the mode of action of intervention therapists (Harris & Hallbauer, 1973; Richards, 1975, 1976; Sherman & Plummer, 1973). The patient may also be guided in engineering environmental changes that would cue and reinforce new behaviors. In any case, however, instigation therapy strategy attends to *both* the interactional and preparatory phase during the treatment *and* the execution of specific activities outside the sessions. An essential problem in generalization lies in the fact that the motivational components of the therapeutic relationship must be transferred both to the patient and to the environment to maintain treatment effectiveness after termination. Therefore, efforts to help the client assume responsibility for change process play a central part in this strategy.

3. *Replication therapy.* This strategy encompasses techniques for changing behavior which attempts to replicate critical segments of the patient's life in the therapy setting. This strategy can be carried out in both institutional and dyadic settings. In the former, efforts are made to simulate as closely as possible, within the walls of the institution, life settings to which patients return. In the latter, contrived role-play, miniature life situations, or representations of life experiences by imaginal techniques are used. Generalization is programmed by replicating close similarity to natural life events, and by developing behavior repertoires and relating them to the wide set of contextual determinants that cover

the most likely problem situations the patient encounters in everyday life.

4. *Intervention therapy.* This strategy is characterized by the direct application of behavior change techniques in the setting in which the problem occurs. In contrast to the preceding strategies, the patient often assumes a passive role in treatment. Characteristic tactics of this approach are reflected in the token economy. Frequently, parents or other family members participate in training and become the therapeutic agents who conduct the actual intervention. Problems in the generalization to new situations and the transfer to similar response classes have been frequently noted (Marholin, Siegel, & Phillips, 1976; Stokes & Baer, 1977; Wahler, 1969).

The strategies described above tend to correlate with different theoretical explanations of the change process and to employ different tactics. However, combinations of the strategies are becoming increasingly common. The major distinction between the strategies thus lies in the emphasis and priority, and not on the exclusiveness of the methods used.

Issues in Combining Verbal and Nonverbal Modes of Treatment

The present chapter discusses therapeutic approaches that can be best characterized as instigation therapy. Emphasis will be given to the ingredients that attempt to extend the utility of therapy beyond the time, place, and focus of treatment by deliberate programming of tactics that foster behavior changes both in and outside the therapeutic sessions from the beginning of treatment. The first section describes some representative theoretical positions on the nature of the change processes which the approach utilizes. The second section deals with specific tactics and methods.

Essentially, we have chosen one framework, developed and applied in the clinic by the author and his associates, as representative of this strategy. While it overlaps with many other approaches that have been called cognitive-behavioral, it does not claim to be either comprehensive or exclusive. Indeed, variation in therapists' style and minor shifts in direction toward emphasis on modification of specific behaviors or psychological processes have given rise to distinctive labels among several approaches which share a common strategy. Further, the present survey of available methods and their related research and theoretical formulations is selective rather than comprehensive. Differences in patients and variations in the context in which treatment is carried out result in unique combinations of the various treatment methods in a single case.

A vast literature has documented the changeability of human behavior when strong control over environmental variables permits the engineering of a highly structured and responsive environment.

The functional relationships between parameters of the learning situation, the learner, and the learning task are well known and have enabled us to develop many methods for maximizing acquisition and performance. The extant learning models are less satisfactory, however. What occurs in learning has been expressed in models and analogues ranging from neurophysiological explanations to complex information processing structures. Yet, there is only incomplete understanding of memory processes and the manner in which a person selectively attends to information, integrates it with previous experiences and retrieves it at the proper moment. But it is just this understanding of our capacities and functions to combine old and new experiences and to relate the products to future events that is involved in human thought and in complex learning. Strict behaviorists circumvent the questions by restricting themselves to a descriptive level. Theorists of other persuasions build models by inference and proceed to acquire more or less faith in the reality of their verbal-symbolic constructions. Pragmatists use admittedly limited models for heuristic purposes and gauge the values by their contribution toward solving a given problem. All admit both the importance of such events as thinking, language usage, or imagery and the inadequacies of their explanations.

In his introduction to a sophisticated survey of cognitive behaviors and processes, Posner (1973) succinctly describes the current status in discussing the contents of his book. "[Thus] the material is objective in the sense of being based upon experiments which can be repeated freely and openly. It is subjective only in the sense that *inferences* are drawn about processes inside the organism (Preface)." The explanation of cognitive behavior, defined above as the organization and integrated use of old and new knowledge, would be especially useful in understanding how patients learn to discriminate and generalize single acts-in-specific-situation beyond the original training conditions; and how they can transcend even the time and content of the newly learned responses by learning rules and conditional operations that further regulate such behavior. It is obvious that our framework is tentative and heuristic. It is a patchwork of related empirical facts and logical inferences and speculations, held together by practical experiences that give it some credence and utility.

Leaving aside the controversy about the nature of the learning process, several other critical issues remain before a learning model can be translated to clinical problems. First, behavior change is performance change.

Although a person may have the potentialities for carrying out certain behaviors, various conditions may need to be altered in order to realize such potentialities in actual performance. Thus, a basic feature of behavior change programs is the induction or maintenance of motivation that enables the patient to carry out the behaviors of which he is capable. Second, it is obvious that everyday learning does not involve the acquisition of all the myriads of specific responses of which an adult is capable. Consequently, a limited behavior change program must concentrate on altering those behavioral acts which have the most far-reaching significance, or which can activate a large preexisting repertoire of responses. Third, the behavior of talking **about** an act is not equivalent to the act. Knowing what one should say to assert one's rights when under attack is not equivalent to doing so. How can knowledge be translated into skill? Fourth, under tutelage of the therapist a patient can begin to act a certain way, at least on a few occasions. Under duress a child can confess to wrong doing and promise to make amends. In the absence of adult supervision, however, the child may or may not fulfill the promise. Therapeutic effectiveness requires that the new response become independent of external pressure. Thoughts and fantasies about oneself and the world can facilitate or interfere both in learning and in the later execution of the response. These and numerous other observations about human behavior have led to questions about the adequacy of a linear S–R model. Our knowledge of the supplementary variables that alter the simple input–output relationship, and of the biological characteristics of the human organism that enable us to process information, to translate thoughts into action, and to utilize symbolic processes is by far incomplete.

Since the entire rationale of self-management strategies rests on the assumption that persons can be taught to acquire new patterns of thinking, fantasizing, planning, and initiating behaviors, some available options for conceptualizing such processes have been selected for discussion. The research associated with them forms some basis, albeit a very tenuous one, for the rationale underlying many of the procedures discussed here. Essentially, these theories deal with psychological processes in the cognitive realm and in the motivational domain. They attempt to explain how various private events modify our reactions to environmental influences and complicate our prediction and modification of behavior on the basis of situational variables alone.

The simplest model for explaining private events is one that deals with such events in the same way as with observable behaviors. This continuity assumption has been proposed by Skinner (1953, 1963), Bandura (1969), Kanfer and Phillips (1970) and many others. The approach makes the heuristic assumption that the same analysis that is applied to external stimuli, responses, and reinforcements can be extended to cover self-generated stimuli, responses, and reinforcements. The model does not account for the particular structural features of private events that may control organization of such stimuli and responses but prescribes a pragmatic approach to training covert behaviors. Homme (1965) expressed this view by suggesting that private events form a special class of operants—which he called coverants—and that conditioning methods can be applied to them. This conceptualization has resulted in the development of such therapeutic techniques as covert sensitization, covert modeling, and thought stopping. The concept of covert conditioning (Cautela, 1971) offers little explanation on how this learning process occurs but reflects the basic belief that an extension of learning principles to private events can be made by applying operations comparable to conditioning procedures to self-reported or inferred private events. Although this approach bypasses many of the methodological problems encountered in dealing with unobservable events, it has provided a pragmatic base for modifying fantasies, thoughts, and self-statements.

A more elaborate model has been developed by social learning theorists (Bandura, 1969, 1971; Kanfer, 1971; Kanfer & Karoly, 1972; Mischel, 1971, 1973). This cognitive-mediational model is similar to the covert conditioning model in that it utilizes the same methodological approaches as proposed for observable behaviors. But it attempts to describe the operation of specific processes by which an individual integrates incoming information, reacts to his own behavior and provides cues and reinforcers for both his observable and private actions. Bandura (1977) explains the need for describing cognitive controlling mechanisms as due to the fact that "cognitive factors partly determine which external events will be observed, how they will be perceived, whether they leave any lasting effects, what valence and efficacy they have, and how the information they convey will be organized for future use [p. 160]." Kanfer (1970, 1971) describes these processes as self-regulatory mechanisms which involve the attainment of information, the evaluation and reinforcement of current behaviors, and the establishment of goals for future behaviors. All behavior is determined by the joint action of variables located in the environment, in the biological nature of the organism, and in the self-generated behavioral processes that result from past social and personal experiences (Kanfer, 1977a,b). Thought processes are believed to be modifiable both by personal experiences and by modeling the behavior of others.

Because of the easy manipulation of symbolic acts, thought processes have long been given a central role (Dollard & Miller, 1950). They are viewed as important cues for action, as instrumental behaviors (such as in problem solving) and as potential representations of future outcomes that can serve incentive and reinforcing value for action. Most important is their relative freedom from specific situations and their transposability from one content area to another. For example, rule learning (Goldiamond, 1966) permits the acquisition of a highly sophisticated behavioral skill that can be applied under appropriate circumstances to a wide variety of situations. Once a person has acquired skills in solving mathematical problems or rules for interpersonal conduct with intimate friends, the same behavior can be applied with minor modification to innumerable situations. Aided by a person's potential for self-correction, these rules can further be modified for increased generality or to include specific conditional parameters that can alter the rule in a given case.

A critical facilitator of rule learning is the use of language. And after early childhood, the use of thinking or private speech is pivotal in developing shorthand rule summaries. Kohlberg, Yaeger, and Hjertholm (1968) presented a series of experiments that suggest that the precursors of thinking undergo specific developmental stages, progressing from audible to inaudible or private speech. Similarly, Pavlov has suggested the importance of speech and thought in human behavior. According to Pavlov, the simple conditioning reflex system in animals that determines the relationship between inputs and outputs is supplemented at the human level by the second signaling system. In this system, linkages, mainly based on speech, mediate between external signals and immediate reactions. The system abstracts and organizes incoming signals and inhibits reflex actions. The process "creates a new information-system within which each signal presented to the subject now operates [Luria, 1961, p. 44]." To Pavlov and his followers, the interposition of the second signal system represents a considerable discontinuity in reflexology for learning in animals and men. Essentially, the second signaling system permits the organization of incoming information in such a way that differential reactions to various signal combinations are made according to rules that have previously been acquired. Verbal skills facilitate such organization. The Pavlovian approach corresponds closely to more recent statements of social learning theorists of the priority of self-generated rules and reinforcers over external contingencies. As Luria (1961) describes it: "Whereas in animals eliminating the reinforcement means the gradual extinction of the link established, no such phenomenon is observed in man; having formulated a given rule, man no longer needs the constant external reinforcement. The coincidence of the reaction with the behavior rule as formulated now becomes the reinforcement [p. 45]." Thus, "man's behavior takes on the character of the 'highest self-regulating system' described by Pavlov [p. 45]." Research by Luria, Vygotsky and other Russian investigators attempted to examine the development of this process, the transition from training of the child by modeling and reinforcement for appropriate verbal statements to the internalization of self-regulatory behaviors.

Two questions are of special concern for application to behavior change processes. First, what variables facilitate a person's development of rules of conduct? If overt rehearsal and shaping are necessary and sufficient for eventual utilization of such responses by the individual without continuing external triggers, the obvious treatment of choice would be the supervised training of the particular verbal sequences that one hopes a patient will eventually adopt. Indeed, if this were sufficient, changing cognitive behaviors would simply involve careful shaping of appropriate verbal response sequences. Unfortunately, there is considerable evidence that, while this process might be a basic one, numerous variables may interfere with the smooth transition from rehearsal to "internalization." For example, Collins (1976) has suggested that the techniques most effective in producing externally controlled behavior may actually be least effective in fostering internal regulation. The opportunity to choose among several courses of action, the utilization of self-generated criteria as incentives, or low extrinsic reinforcement might be detrimental for learning of behavior under public control. However, these same variables may facilitate the emission of such behaviors under self-regulation. Clearly, any therapeutic effort that succeeds in training individuals to self-generate appropriate rules of conduct or self-instructions would go a long way toward maintenance and transfer of treatment effects.

Assuming that such cognitive behavior changes can be achieved, the second critical question concerns their effectiveness in cueing appropriate observable behaviors. Recently, numerous investigators have attempted to show, primarily in children, the utility of training rules of conduct or cognitive strategies on later overt behavior. For this process as well, careful arrangement of facilitating variables may be necessary to result in a rule application under appropriate circumstances. For example, the transition from knowing how to be assertive or how to approach a problem, to implementation of this knowledge may require therapeutic attention (MacDonald, 1975). In this respect, behavioral approaches differ from therapeutic methods that are based on a rational model of man. In the latter, it is assumed that knowledge about how to behave and removal of emotional blocks toward execution of such behavior is sufficient to eventuate in appropriate responding. A behavioral approach also works on the second problem by attempting to train actual rule applications in as many instances as possible under favorable conditions. As Skinner (1966) has suggested, knowledge of contingencies and experience of such contingencies are not identical. Thus it would seem that the training of cognitive behaviors in therapy requires an essential follow-up step in providing appropriate contingencies for their actual application.

A major disagreement among current therapists concerns the sequence in which changes occur. Authors who remain behaviorally focused have tended to suggest that cognitive changes **follow** behavioral changes. Bem (1972) has suggested that a later alignment of cognitive behaviors is brought about by the person's changed self-perception as he observes his own behavior. Others stress the importance of reconstructing cognitive behaviors and suggest that overt behaviors more easily follow the new perceptions and self-reactions of the client.

Cognitive mediational models cover a broad range. While some authors see mediational processes only as an extension—albeit covert—of a chain of simple responses triggered by external stimuli and resulting in observable action, other authors speak of fairly elaborate cognitive structures (e.g., Beck, 1976; Ellis, 1970; Mischel, 1973). The practicing clinician requires some theoretical framework for selection of appropriate therapeutic techniques. However, he must also be pragmatic. His choice among competing theories is based on their respective effectiveness in guiding him toward methods that produce lasting behavior changes. At the present time, claims of success have been made by persons who use different process models. Analysis of their techniques, however, suggest frequent convergence in operations. In effect, most reports suggest the cognitive-behavior therapists focus at least on both the cognitive behaviors and the everyday actions which flow from them. Some emphasize further the need for changing interactions in both directions and strengthen cognitive behaviors both as antecedents **and** consequences of observable target behavior.

Motivational Sources

As we have mentioned previously, behavior can be shaped and maintained without much difficulty, once an organism is under strong environmental control. But a critical problem is the maintenance of the patient's motivation for continuing the therapeutic work and maintaining the changes that have been accomplished after external reinforcement by the therapist is no longer available. To overcome this difficulty, the focus of self-management and instigation therapies has been on helping the patients to develop responsibility for initiating and sustaining actions, thus freeing themselves from dependence on external supports. An important task of the therapist lies in the development of the patient's motivation to strive for and maintain new behaviors and life patterns. Numerous recent experiments and case histories illustrate these attempts at transfer of control from the environment to the person himself by training in self-control, self-regulation, or self-reinforcement.

In addition to change of the locus of control, however, a significant feature appears to be the patient's belief that he has control over his own behavior and that behavioral changes are indeed attributable to his own actions. Two large bodies of literature have addressed themselves to these questions, the research and theories on the effects of freedom of choice and on causal attribution. Limiting ourselves primarily to pragmatics, a series of studies has indicated that persons who believe that they have control over their own behavior or that they can choose among alternatives in determining their own destiny show greater behavioral efficiency. For example, students who were given a choice in selecting different types of classroom sections did significantly better on exams and reported greater satisfaction with their sections and class leaders in comparison to no-choice subjects (Liem, 1975). Residents in a home for the aged who were given greater personal responsibility and choice in daily routines improved significantly more than control subjects in alertness, active participation and self-rated well-being (Langer & Rodin, 1976). Further, an 18-month postintervention evaluation indicated sustained beneficial effects (Rodin & Langer, 1977). Belief that one has some control over an outcome can also influence a tolerance of aversive events (Averill, 1973; Kanfer & Seidner, 1973; Langer, Janis, & Wolfer, 1975). Choice of the order of taking a number of tests can reduce anxiety (Stotland & Blumenthal, 1964). College students who perceived that they had a choice in a training procedure for improved reading speed showed significantly greater improvement than subjects deprived of choice (Kanfer & Grimm, 1978). The empirical evidence strongly suggests that therapeutic settings in which clients perceive themselves as exerting some control over treatment objectives and methods, or, at least, see themselves as active participants in the process, should enhance motivation toward change. Such increased motivation toward change can also be utilized for improving the likelihood that posttreatment gains are maintained.

Some empirical support for these expectations comes from a study on adult phobics (Bandura, Jeffery, & Gajdos, 1975). Snake phobic subjects were treated by a participant modeling procedure. Half the group also spent an hour in "self-directed performance." During this time they could independently practice any of the activities which had previously been executed with the therapist's assistance. The therapist was present but did not contribute in any way. The self-directed performance group was further divided into two halves. The free interaction with the phobic object occurred either with a boa constrictor, the same animal with which treatment had been conducted, or with both the boa and an unfamiliar king snake. Follow-up assessment occurred 1 month and 1 year after training. In addition, questionnaires were mailed 6 months after treatment to assess self-rated changes in snake related activities. All groups showed improvement in approach behavior. But the self-directed treatments produced significantly greater generalized changes on posttest and follow-up. The most important finding, however, concerns the effects on a wide range of skills and situations not obviously related to the snake phobia. Subjects who had the self-directed experience showed greater fear reduction, higher levels of self-competency and less fear of threats beyond the specifically treated phobia. In contrast, participant-modeling alone weakened only the intensity of the animal fears. Self-directed performance with a familiar threat, however, extinguished fears more thoroughly than did the experience with the familiar and unfamiliar snakes. The self-reports also indicated that 44% in the self-directed boa-plus-king-snake group and 22% in the boa-only group used the treatment procedures occasionally to cope with other anxiety situations. The authors conclude, "the overall evidence indicates that the successful transfer effects resulted from stimulus generalization, enhancement of self-adequacy, and acquisition of a generalizable skill for coping with fear-provoking situations [p. 141]." The study lends strong support to the thesis that training of coping strategies and anxiety reduction in one area can have far-reaching effects if it includes some practice in self-initiated therapeutic efforts.

In a study on the effectiveness of training programs for male college students with dating problems, Glass, Gottman, and Shmurak (1976) compared a response acquisition treatment with a cognitive self-statement modification treatment. The results indicated that students trained in cognitive self-statement modification showed significantly better performance in role-play situations for which they had not been trained, made significantly more phone contacts and made a significantly better impression on the women than subjects in other groups. The effects were maintained in a 6-month follow-up assessment. In fact, the cognitive self-statement group improved on the role-play measures from posttreatment to follow-up. Thus, subjects who received some form of cognitive self-statement training showed significantly better improvement in dating-relevant behaviors, both in the laboratory and outside.

In a review of research on the role of attribution, Kopel and Arkowitz

(1975) concluded that "the basic principle suggested by this research is that self-attributed behavior change is maintained to a greater extent than is behavior change which is attributed to an external agent or force [p. 183]." The authors explain this effect as due to the availability of information in self-attribution that permits new self-inferences about the person's ability and motivation. In contrast, external attributions permit only inferences about external situational factors. Self-attributions facilitate new self-inferences that can cut across settings and over time, "while the inferences arising from external attribution may only be relevant to the setting and time during which the external conditions are present [p. 184]." Somewhat indirect evidence for these self-attribution hypotheses comes from the area of research on extrinsic versus intrinsic motivation (Deci, 1975). Although questions have been raised concerning the adequacy of the various theoretical explanations offered (Levine & Fasnacht, 1974; Reiss & Sushinsky, 1975), the empirical evidence suggests that the imposition of external reinforcement contingencies on a behavior that has a fairly high initial frequency can further increase the response frequency. However, termination of external reinforcement tends to reduce the frequency of the behavior **below** the initial level. An extrapolation of these data to the clinic suggests that therapists refrain from assuming excessive control over client behaviors. In fact, continuing independence and emphasis on client responsibility should work toward prolonging durability of treatment gain. The direct attack on target behaviors by reassessing and reassigning their causes is a technique described as reattribution therapy (Kopel & Arkowitz, 1975).

In summary, it appears that therapeutic gains are strongest and most enduring when the therapist can help the client to have some confidence that he is an active participant in the therapeutic process, that he can exert some control over his own behavior, that he can practice and experience a behavior change without excessive supervision. Furthermore, transfer and generalization should be facilitated when it is the client who provides incentives and reinforcers for achieving and maintaining an improved level of behavioral effectiveness and when the client can ascribe the behavior change to his own actions.

Two recent conceptualizations of self-regulatory processes suggest that self-generated reinforcement may be effectively used not only for specific behaviors but as a general source of motivation. Bandura (1977) has suggested that the likelihood and strength of the person's effort to overcome obstacles and cope with problems is a function of the person's expectations of his personal efficacy. The model suggests that the effectiveness of various therapeutic treatments is related to their potential in creating and strengthening expectations of self-efficacy. This construct is

described as the conviction that one can successfully execute the behaviors required to produce a desired outcome. The expectations of self-
efficacy are derived from information about one's accomplishments,
from vicarious experiences, from the effects of verbal persuasion, and
from physiological states. The model suggests that any component of
the therapeutic operation that enhances expectations of self-efficacy
should also increase client participation and performance.

The proposed model further suggests the strong dependence of behavioral performances on the person's cognitive processing of information relevant to self-efficacy. Furthermore, differences in individual experiences influence the magnitude and direction of information as they
contribute toward expectations of personal efficacy. Unlike momentary
biological states or emotional arousal states, the self-efficacy motive is
multiply determined and develops slowly. Expectations that have been
supported for many years prior to the patient's entry into therapy may
require many counteracting experiences before a change occurs. Bandura's paper also suggests that therapists should not expect success experiences alone to alter the patient's self-efficacy expectation. It is the
mastery of challenging tasks and the rate and pattern of their attain-
ments that furnishes information for judging personal efficacy. The
Bandura model is consistent with the basic concepts of self-management
therapy that require patients to experience the entire range of self-regulatory processes with at least some success in achieving objectives which
are important to them and for which instrumental behaviors are
available.

Kanfer's (1971) self-regulation model suggests an inherent motivational component in the self-regulation system. Confirmatory evidence of
achieving self-generated criteria should not only reinforce the behaviors
that have been used to reach the objective but should also enhance the
self-regulatory process per se. The importance of positive self-evaluation as an enhancer of self-esteem has frequently been stressed by therapists. The theoretical model points to the importance of helping a client
toward establishing performance criteria that gradually increase in difficulty but are within range of attainment in order to yield confirmations of
his potentials for successful self-regulation in coping with life's problems. It is logical, therefore, to select therapeutic techniques with two
goals in mind. First, to bring about immediate changes in behavioral
problems, and second, to strengthen the entire self-regulatory process in
coping with challenging or conflictful events.

The motivational models described here are consistent with the ver-
nacular concepts of self-confidence and ego strength, expressing the importance of a person's ability to engage in behavior change with some

anticipation of success. Strengthening a patient's cognitive and behavioral skills that are needed to analyze and tackle problem situations would thus be a desirable outcome of therapy. This strategy should extend the content-specific treatment gains to other areas and to future situations.

METHODS FOR ENHANCING TRANSFER EFFECTS

Recent cognitive-behavioral techniques have integrated procedures derived from laboratory research with others that have long been in the repertoire of practicing clinicians. Essentially, they can be categorized into four clusters on the basis of their main objectives:

1. Techniques in which specific problem-related behaviors are the target of treatment
2. Methods that train individuals in coping skills designed to handle the current problem-related behavior as well as future occurrences of similar instances
3. Methods for altering self-regulatory processes, designed to modify the current problem and to prevent future occurrences by retraining of a person's cognitive behaviors
4. Strategies in dyadic therapy that aim to facilitate specific behavior changes, as well as to develop skills in taking responsibility for changing and to initiate problem-avoiding and self-correcting behaviors

Most proponents of these approaches subscribe to a general model of behavior that presumes the concurrent influences of situational, self-generated and biological variables (Kanfer, 1977a,b). In this model there is clear recognition of the importance of situational influences on behavior. However, it is also hypothesized that both the situations themselves and their potential impact on the individual can be altered within limits by interpolation of self-generated cues, actions, and reinforcers. Finally, although biological variables have often been considered as either fixed or amenable to change only through physiochemical operations, recent research and clinical work in the areas of anxiety reduction and biofeedback have suggested that even the biological variables can be influenced by self-generated (cognitive) action.

The major threat to sustaining effective behaviors developed during therapy comes from two sources: First, from changes in situational cues as the patient moves from the therapeutic environment to his natural environment or as natural situations change along some dimension (stimulus generalization); second, from the need to vary selection among members of a response class as situational demands change (response generalization). Numerous studies have suggested the necessity of programming for the shift in stimulus control from the therapeutic to the natural environment. Among the possible strategies for avoiding excessively narrow stimulus control is the increase in self-generated stimulus control. When a patient can be helped to greater reliance on self-generated rather than on externally provided stimuli, his behavior can become increasingly independent of fluctuations in the natural environment. Consequently, behaviors acquired during therapy with specific persons, under highly restricted training conditions or in clearly defined institutional settings, can be maintained across many situations and over a longer time if the individual can be trained to generate appropriate cues for such behaviors. In some cases, abstracting significant aspects of environmental settings may be needed as a signal for the individual to engage or not engage in the acquired behaviors. In other cases, self-generated cues can be tied to changes in interoceptive stimulation or chained to other verbal responses. The main practical principle in all these techniques is to shift behavioral control from external to self-generated variables. When response generalization is required, similar training of cognitive behaviors can assist the individual toward a closer match between the situational demand and the required response. Finally, self-generated control can also help the individual to select among environments which present the most advantageous stimulation or reinforcement for desirable behaviors. For instance, unwanted stimulus control can be broken by a former drug addict through continuing avoidance of his former circle of friends and other social and physical cues associated with his habit. Development of drug-competing behaviors can be facilitated by selecting friends and living conditions in which modeling and reinforcement of desirable behaviors occurs frequently. And maintenance of the competing behaviors can be fostered by self-reinforcement for specific behaviors and for achievement of the challenge to maintain drug-free behavior.

A second general principle underlying many of the following procedures concerns the development of skills for generating goals and motivations so that the patient can continue to pursue activities consistent with a newly established life pattern or self-attitude. Training in self-regulatory behaviors serves to ease continuing growth and development. Combined with the direct training of such cognitive skills is the underlying effort to help the patient develop increased responsibility for his own actions and greater skills in analyzing, solving, or avoiding future problems.

Finally, many of the strategies employ the principle that response specificity due to physical limitations of the training environment can be bridged by use of role-play, imagery, or cognitive rehearsal which permits practice of the target behavior "as if" it were in the setting in which it eventually must occur. In addition to specific training procedures and change methods that have been proposed to achieve the goal of transferring newly acquired behaviors from the protective therapeutic environment, facilitation of transfer effect can also be obtained by various dyadic strategies and structure of the therapy relationship. The latter practices attempt to structure the change process from the very beginning as one in which the therapeutic setting only serves to analyze, plan, and rehearse natural life events and behaviors. Such a properly established structure avoids excessive expectations of the patient so that the therapist and his techniques will produce effortless change without further independent practice.

Development of Coping Skills

In the last ten years, a series of procedures has been developed that is based on training clients to recognize stress-related cues, to anticipate emotional arousal and to apply methods for tolerating or reducing the stress. The diverse procedures include the learning of self-instructional statements, self-induced relaxation, self-generated goal setting, and rehearsal of potential escape responses. Proponents of coping skill techniques believe that these methods promise a higher degree of treatment generalization than other anxiety reduction techniques such as systematic desensitization, because they are not closely tied to specific elements of the anxiety-arousing situation. Instead, they utilize either situational or internal cues only as a trigger for bringing into play similar self-generated behaviors that can be applied across a wide range of situations.

In an early paper, Sipprelle (1967) described the use of *induced anxiety* to alter coping with stress. The subjects are first relaxed and asked to attend to internal cues associated with anxiety, fear or any intense feelings resulting in disruption of effective behaviors. The therapist initially strengthens the emission of behaviors usually associated with anxiety, such as physical tension, rapid breathing, swallowing, crying. After the patient has reached a high degree of anxiety and emits verbal statements associated with the heightened state of emotionality, he is repeatedly relaxed while instructed to think of the anxiety-associated stimuli (Jordan & Sipprelle, 1972). According to the authors, this procedure produces a new pairing of stimuli and affect in which calmness is substituted for agitation as a response to the internal and verbal cues related to the heightened emotional state. The procedure aims to produce at first a state of anxiety arousal in which stimuli characteristically evoking such anxiety can be verbalized and clearly discriminated. The introduction of the relaxation response to countercondition the anxiety results in decreased heart rate and respiration, and a GSR pattern characteristic of a calm state (Ascough & Sipprelle, 1968; Boer & Sipprelle, 1969; Jordan & Sipprelle, 1972). The technique is marked by the deliberate induction of anxiety and the pairing of relaxation responses, **not** to the external stimuli but to the perceived internal cues and verbal reports of the subjective experiences. In this way, the relaxation response is relatively independent of particular precipitating situations. It is conditioned directly to the consequences of the presentation of emotional stimuli rather than to the stimuli themselves. A recent study (Ollendick & Nettle, 1977) employed a modification in which the relaxation stage was omitted. This procedural variant did not reduce treatment effectiveness. The authors suggest that extinction alone—without systematic counterconditioning—may suffice for reducing anxiety.

A similar anxiety management procedure has been reported by Suinn and Richardson (1971). The client is told about the approach and is given relaxation training. The client is then trained to visualize anxiety arousing scenes, scenes associated with relaxation, and scenes describing competency reactions. After all of these scenes can be easily visualized, a rapid shift from anxiety arousal and anxiety control is repeatedly practiced. The authors base their method on the theory that anxiety responses can serve as discriminative stimuli, and clients can be conditioned to these cues with competing responses that remove the stimuli by reciprocal inhibition. The relaxation responses are attached to identified anxiety cues and their recognition serves as a signal to shift instantly to relaxation or competency responses, incompatible with the anxiety. The authors suggest that these procedures are especially useful for coping with present or future fear situations in which the specific stimuli are not clearly identifiable, or in dealing with general anxiety in which innumerable situational cues evoke heightened emotional tension.

Goldfried (1971) suggested some modifications in systematic desensitization with the purpose of offering the client a broader skill rather than reducing anxiety associated with particular situations. Basing his conceptualization on a mediational interpretation, Goldfried suggests that a client be taught to "become sensitive to his proprioceptive cues for tension, and to react to these cues with his newly acquired skill in muscular relaxation. He is also taught to differentiate the proprioceptive feedback associated with tension from that associated with relaxation, and to identify this feeling of 'calm' with the state of muscular relaxation [pp. 228–229]." The client learns to cope actively with anxiety and becomes less dependent on a passive process that reduces the fear arousing properties of specific aversive stimuli. The procedural variant from desensitization is shared by other similar techniques. It includes giving the client a rationale to try to relax when a feeling of tenseness is first noted. During relaxation training, the initial tensing of muscles is offered as a signal for use of relaxation and as a means for practicing repetition of proprioceptive feedback associated with tension. The procedure also reduces the need for careful construction of hierarchy items and instructs the client to maintain visualization of an anxiety producing scene when experiencing anxiety. Instead of terminating the imagined scene, the client is helped to continue a relaxed state as long as possible. In our own use of similar procedures, we also instruct clients to verbalize their imagery and to rehearse appropriate controlling statements, such as positive self-statements about their ability to cope with the anxiety. Instrumental escape responses which the client can execute at any time "at will" are also practiced in imagination. Other variations of Wolpe's basic systematic desensitization procedure that include training in coping are found in clinical reports and laboratory studies.

These techniques are used primarily with patients who experience anxiety and are intended to extend therapeutic effects beyond the specific fear situations which the client has experienced in the past. They also call for the development of coping techniques in the presence of either the fear arousing stimuli or internal cues indicating tension or emotional arousal. Another series of methods are characterized by their emphasis on preparing a client for future stress experiences. Training is conducted in the absence of the anxiety reducing cues or setting. These prophylactic or preventive methods are based on the inherent rationale that training general coping skills provides the client with a repertoire that can be applied to later situations, even though the parameters of the future stress are unknown. Meichenbaum (1977) has suggested stress inoculation for phobic reactions (Meichenbaum & Cameron, 1972), anger control (Novaco, 1975, 1977), and pain control (Meichenbaum & Turk, 1976). The stress inoculation procedures are primarily derived from basic research on the variables that maintain self-control either in the presence of noxious stimulation or strongly tempting stimuli. Self-generated cognitive controlling responses that alter response probabilities are viewed by many as especially important determinants of other behavior when strong momentary environmental cues or reinforcers invite responses that can result in later aversive consequences for the client or others (e.g., Bandura, 1977; Kanfer, 1971; Mischel & Mischel, 1976).

Stress inoculation training generally begins with discussion of the conceptual framework. In this structuring process, the therapist emphasizes the importance of introducing constructive self-statements in a stress situation to reiterate the person's potentials to cope with the stress. The listing of many possible instrumental responses and the generation of self-reinforcements for successful coping are included in the procedure. During the actual training, a series of coping techniques are learned. Among them are: relaxation, adaptive self-instructions, directions for realistic appraisal of the stressor, and self-motivating statements toward handling the problem situation. An important component of the training includes practice in actual situations in which the client can utilize the newly learned coping responses. This latter stage permits transfer of training to a wide variety of situations in the client's daily life.

On the basis of an analysis of decisional conflict resolution studies on stress, Janis (1958, 1959, 1967) and Mann (1972) have developed clinical procedures for "emotional inoculation" by systematic shaping of cognitive and motivational procedures. An analysis of decisional conflicts (Janis & Mann, 1976) suggests that stress can arise from the anticipation of some loss when a choice must be made, and from the threat to self-esteem as a competent decision maker. Their conflict model of decision making postulates that coping with a difficult choice is affected by awareness of the risks involved, the hope of finding a better solution, and the time available in which to make the decision. An experiment by Langer et al. (1975) illustrates the interrelationships between the reactions to stress and preparation for the experience by cognitive reappraisal, additional information, and later cognitive control during the stress experiences. The subjects were hospital patients awaiting major surgical operations. The coping device involved encouraging an optimistic reappraisal of anxiety-provoking events in order to build up hope in the realistic possibility of dealing effectively with setbacks that might be encountered. In counseling sessions, patients were trained to think of the positive consequences of their decision to undergo surgery and were instructed to rehearse these consequences when starting to feel upset about the unpleasant aspects of surgery. Persons who were trained to use these coping devices later scored lower on nurses' ratings of preoperative stress and on postoperative requests for sedatives and pain relievers. Janis and Mann also suggest that awareness of an impending stress situation allows a person to anticipate his actions and to make plans for more adequate coping. In a study with surgical patients (Janis, 1958), patients who were given little information and were unaware of the unpleasant consequences of a course of action had little preoperative stress but later expressed regrets, refused routine postoperative treatments, and generally reacted strongly to setbacks during the postdecisional period. In all, the extensive work by these investigators suggest that stress reactions can be reduced by preparing the client with accurate information, a reappraisal of the stress situation, and the provision of coping responses for use during stress.

Behavior Rehearsal

A common practice in treatment sessions has been the simulation of important life experiences in the consultation room. Essentially, behavioral rehearsal and role-play techniques can be used to achieve several different purposes. First, the client can practice newly acquired responses in a protected setting and under guidance of the therapist. Second, the clinician can obtain information for diagnostic judgments and evaluate the client's capability to carry out new behaviors. Third, behaviors can be gradually refined and shaped. Finally, the client obtains systematic preparation of a scenario prior to engaging in an important activity, making a decision, or implementing a newly learned rule of conduct. All of these functions are based on the logical assumption that the rehearsal experience or *prehearsal* prepares the client not only for handling an important life event but also generalizes to alter her style of dealing with future interactions and decisions by careful cognitive and actual practice. The concept of behavior rehearsal underlies many of the current skill development techniques. Programs in assertion training, in social skills training, in problem solving, and in training of parenting skills utilize behavior rehearsal as an important component in the total program. Rehearsal during treatment sessions can also be used as a preparation for carrying out therapeutic assignments outside of treatment. Behavior rehearsal techniques have also been used to alter a person's reactions toward herself, especially when they are coupled with assignments to observe other people's reactions to the person's new "role."

A variation of the role rehearsal technique has been suggested by Lazarus (1971). The client is asked to think of a person whom he admires or whose behavior he wishes to adopt. An exaggerated version of the desirable features of the behavior is then practiced in the therapy sessions and encouraged in the naturalized setting. Initial exaggeration of a new behavior pattern is expected to result in eventual change toward the appropriate behavior. Kelly's (1955) fixed role therapy and applications of role theory (Sarbin & Allen, 1968) utilize behavior rehearsal on an assumption that even if a client deliberately role plays new behaviors, these new behaviors will ultimately become part of her daily repertoire. There have been reports in the social psychology literature that counter-attitudinal role-playing can result in attitude changes under some conditions (Harrison, 1976). However, some writers have pointed out that the "mere" role-playing of the particular behavior is not sufficient to guarantee that the content which it represents will eventually become part of the natural (internalized) repertoire of the client (Collins, 1976; Kazdin & Bootzin, 1972). Goldfried and Davison (1976) suggest that "behavior rehearsal should most appropriately be viewed as providing an intermediate step in changing behavior, with the eventual behavior change occurring as the client tries out the new role *in vivo* [p. 157]."

Behavioral rehearsal requires a considered plan for its successful application. Goldfried and Davison (1976) have suggested four general stages for effective behavioral rehearsal: (*a*) preparation of the client; (*b*) selection of the target situation; (*c*) behavior rehearsal proper; and (*d*) practice of the new behavior in life situations. Discussion of the client's experience in subsequent therapy sessions, further refinement of the specific behaviors, and evaluation of other people's reactions and other consequences of the newly rehearsed behavior serve to bolster the client's readiness to adopt the new role in future interactions. In our experience, an important motivational feature of the rehearsal procedures seems to lie in the client's new awareness that he is indeed capable of carrying out certain behaviors, even if in artificial settings or by deliberate effort, and that the anticipated negative consequences for such behaviors (e.g., assertiveness) fail to occur. Thus it is likely that the carefully conducted behavior rehearsal procedure can serve to alter expectations of aversive outcomes. It can facilitate the patient's positive attitude toward a change process and can thereby affect a much wider range of behaviors than those which are specifically rehearsed.

Problem-Solving Methods

Problem-solving has been viewed as a type of thinking in which the person proceeds through various stages in arriving at a solution. The stages which have been described differ, but essentially include the formulation of the problem, the organization of a plan, the selection among various plans, the execution of the plan, and the test of its utility in arriving at an acceptable solution. These stages have been the basis for discussion of various aspects of problem-solving, although it is doubtful that they occur in the proposed order in actual problem-solving (Poser, 1973). Some S–R theorists have defined problem-solving as a complex form of discriminational learning and have dealt with the behavior in terms of habit family hierarchies, chains of associations, or ideational responses (e.g., Cofer, 1957; Kendler & Kendler, 1962; Maltzman, 1955). More recently, attempts at an operant analysis of problem-solving have been offered (Goldiamond, 1966; Skinner, 1966) and at the same time computer programming has provided an impetus for developing information processing theories (Newell & Simon, 1961, 1962, 1972). It is not surprising to find a reawakening of interest in problem-solving as contemporary research shifts toward investigation of cognitive processes. Recent work goes beyond the earlier attempts to study the naturalistic sequence of events in problem-solving (e.g., Duncker, 1945). The development of models for the operations applied to the problem situation and terminating with the acceptance of a solution as adequate is the goal of much current research.

Almost all the work on problem-solving was conducted with impersonal tasks (Duncan, 1959; Duncker, 1945; Maier, 1940). Application of the problem-solving approach to interpersonal problems is relatively recent. A general rationale for the application of problem-solving models to clinical situations has been presented by D'Zurilla and Goldfried (1971). A series of experiments by Spivack and his coworkers (Shure, Spivack, & Jaeger, 1971; Spivack, Platt, & Shure, 1976; Spivack & Shure, 1974) have resulted in the development of detailed programs for training problem-solving skills to children, adolescents, and adults. The problem-solving procedure can be applied either directly to the problem associated with the client's difficulties (e.g., Sarason & Ganzer, 1969), or by developing some vehicle in which problem-solving is taught indirectly, not by modeling or instruction but by the demands of the training task (e.g., Blechman's family contract game, 1974). Since the particular examples chosen for the training programs can range widely, emphasis is put on learning the process rather than the specifics of a given situation. It is hoped that problem-solving skills would be applied by clients to actual problems as they arise in the future. The relationship between the training procedures and the specific processes that operate to enhance generalization are not quite clear. As in many other situations in which behavioral components are learned separately, the entire sequence is not carried out as orderly and systematically as the practice exercise. As Spivack et al. (1976) suggest, "the actual practice probably involves jumping back and forth between a solution and possible consequences, jumping back to another solution, and even reassessing and perhaps redefining the problem itself [p. 165]." Perhaps the most significant feature of problem-solving training procedures is to help the client to interpose some cognitive behaviors rather than to accept solutions or engage in critical behaviors spontaneously.

While different component skills are required for different types of problems and different components require differential attention as a function of age, some standardized programs have been prepared for general use. The Spivack *et al.* (1976) program for adults contains 19 units. The early units stress the notion of problem-solving as an important element in interpersonal relationships and are aimed at training of basic skills. The second half of the program is designed to train a person to implement these skills. The units emphasize the importance of generating alternatives, of recognizing how people feel, and of learning all the facts necessary to work toward a solution. In contrast to the relative flexibility of this program in combining components that train interpersonal sensitivity with problem-solving, a more behavioristically oriented approach (Goldfried & Goldfried, 1975) presents a program guide in which steps in problem analysis and solution are systematically taken up, discussed and rehearsed with the client. Goldfried and Goldfried suggest a program that includes five specific steps. They are: general orientation, problem definition and formulation, generation of alternatives, decision making, and verification.

Self-Regulatory Methods

Social learning theorists have worked toward conceptualization of self-processes with the explicit purpose of understanding how persons free themselves from total dependence on momentary environmental controlling and reinforcing stimuli. It is presumed that individuals have the potential for generating self-corrective reactions to their own behavior, for discriminating among environments that signal the opportunity for certain favorable consequences, and for engaging in cognitive behaviors that rehearse and anticipate behavioral outcomes at a symbolic level without the inherent risk of failure if they were executed immediately *in vivo* (Bandura, 1977; Mischel, 1973). When the therapeutic objective is a change in the cognitive variables that intervene between inputs and outputs, it is based on a diagnosis of similar maladaptive behaviors that recur across different situations and over time. If cognitive behaviors are altered, it is expected that the client will apply his new cognitive repertoire in many new situations. Consequently, transfer and generalization effects are inherently built into the training procedures. What is learned is not a specific response to a given stimulus but a new set of behaviors used in evaluating the environment and one's own personal reactions; a behavioral sequence in establishing situation-specific goals; a self-corrective technique for enhancing progress toward these goals on the basis of evaluating one's present performance; and finally, a technique for maintaining the entire sequence by self-generated material or symbolic reinforcing contingencies.

We have already noted Bandura's (1977) view that different therapeutic change methods may achieve their effects through a common cognitive mechanism called self-efficacy. In this model the experience of personal mastery, that is a person's conviction of her own effectiveness, serves both to initiate and maintain coping behavior and to increase efforts to resolve conflicts or handle stressful situations. Among the many factors that affect self-efficacy is the knowledge derived from personal mastery experiences. Such knowledge requires both observation and assessment of one's performance. Together with information obtained from others, self-generated reactions and feedback from one's level of physiological arousal, these sources of information affect perceived self-efficacy. In turn, they influence the person's behavior by providing the motivational conditions for execution of self-corrected or newly learned repertoires. The Bandura position implies that a therapeutic approach that is directed toward strengthening of perceived self-efficacy would be expected to produce relatively enduring behavioral changes in a wide variety of situations.

A study by Bandura, Adams, and Beyer (1977) illustrates the clinical application of this approach. It compared the effects of participant modeling (in which subjects assume gradually increasing initiative in treatment) and modeling (in which subjects passively observed the therapist perform the problematic behavior). Snake-phobic volunteer adults thus either engaged in self-directed performance giving them mastery experiences or in observation that gave them vicarious experiences. The authors reason that the latter should yield lower efficacy expectations, therefore poorer improvement and lower and weaker generalized expectancies. These expectations were confirmed. The authors further report that a self-report measure of efficacy expectations was a good predictor of performance, regardless of treatment groups to which subjects were assigned. In 1-month and 6-month follow-ups, the durability of treatment benefits and generalization of effects were demonstrated. This study further corroborates the findings of the study on snake phobics mentioned on pages 197–198 (Bandura *et al.*, 1975).

A recent study (Moss & Arend, 1977) extended the concept of self-directed mastery one step further. Bandura *et al.* (1975) demonstrated that participant modeling was more effective when **followed** by self-directed experiences. Moss and Arend modified the procedure to allow subjects control over their experience from the start of treatment. Snake phobic college students were assigned to self-directed treatments in which they used a manual to engage nonfearful friends or strangers to act as their therapists for two sessions. The manual allowed subjects to control the rate and procedures of the nonfearful therapist model at first. At the end of the sequence, the subject assumed complete control over the snake. Basically, the manual "described how the subject might teach a nonfearful individual how to act as his or her (the subject's) therapist [p. 732]." In comparison to a therapist-controlled contact desensitization procedure, subjects in self-directed treatment groups improved as much as those in therapist-directed groups on pre- to posttest changes in approach behavior and fear survey schedule scores. Unfortunately, the study did not include follow-up assessment of the treatment effects. However, it points to the hitherto poorly explored potentials of self-directed treatment procedures that could be combined with less frequent therapist interactions. Research on such a treatment combination appears to be of great practical and theoretical importance, since economic benefits of partially "pre-packaged" self-directed programs could increase clinical efficiency. From a theorist's view, supportive research could shift our conceptualization of some therapy cases more toward a joint client–therapist endeavor in which therapists serve as consultants and guides to active self-directed clients. Translated into clinical practice, the theoretical model and the associated techniques suggest that the opportunity to practice newly acquired responses under conditions in which the person can ascribe success to enhance personal efficacy rather than to external factors can materially strengthen not only immediate therapeutic effectiveness but also long-term effects of treatment. It also suggests the viability of methods that give clients greater responsibility in directing their own treatment than has previously been considered.

Strong emphasis on the importance of cognitive social learning variables has also been given by Mischel (1973). The author suggests the following person variables as critical for study:

1. The individual's competencies to generate diverse behaviors
2. The individual's encoding and catagorization strategies, that is the ways in which information from stimulus inputs is grouped
3. The expectancies of behavioral outcomes (the relationship between behavioral alternatives and their probable consequences) and the expectancies of stimulus outcomes (the probable correlation among various stimulus events)
4. The subjective value of the outcomes for various stimuli
5. The self-regulatory system which has at its core the subject's adoption of contingency rules that guide behavior independent of external events

Mischel's position suggests that therapeutic interventions aimed at affecting these five proposed cognitive processes would produce performance changes that should be relatively enduring.

Kanfer (1970, 1971) suggested a three stage model of self-regulation. According to this model, self-regulatory processes are cued by any event that disrupts the smooth flow of behavior, such as unexpected events, high emotional arousal, or new learning. The first stage consists of the person's self-monitoring of his performance and his emotional reactions. This stage is followed by self-evaluation, in which a comparison is made between the information obtained from the monitoring stage and the performance criteria which the person has generated for the specific situation. This evaluation is followed by the reinforcement stage. If performance has matched or exceeded the criteria, positive self-reinforcement may occur. Poor performance may elicit a repetition, self-criticism or, if too discrepant from the standard, an abandonment of the behavioral sequence. The model suggests that remediation of deficits or distortions in the self-regulatory system represent an important therapeutic objective. Further, the modification of any of these self-regulatory components, for example alleviating a self-monitoring deficit or reassessing inappropriate performance criteria, should permit behavioral changes in a wide range of situations and across many responses that are dependent on self-regulatory processes.

A clinical application of the self-regulation model is illustrated in a study by Fuchs and Rehm (1977) with depressed patients. The component processes have been thoroughly studied and widely applied. Self-monitoring procedures have been used as assessment techniques and as a means for behavior change (Kanfer, 1975; Kazdin, 1974; Nelson, 1977). The pivotal role of self-monitoring in enhancing the durability of treatment effects lies in the expectation that the client's increased skill and awareness in observing the context and consequences as well as the substance of his own behavior provides a skill that is basic to self-diagnostic and self-corrective processes. Regardless of the particular repertoire that has been acquired in therapy, continuing self-monitoring should alert the client to the necessity for introducing such coping responses as relaxation, problem-solving, or self-control techniques. In a sense, the client is thus able to perform the therapist's function in terms of knowing when his behavior requires attention or change. The increased self-awareness should permit the client to apply what he has learned in therapeutic sessions, or to trigger a self-reinforcing sequence that would strengthen desirable behaviors in new situations. From this point of view, proper self-monitoring equips the client to assume an important function of the therapist, that of probing and examining his own behavior and its context without external guidance.

Training in the second stage of self-regulation, the comparison between current performance and previously learned performance criteria, is also intended to help clients to undergo continuing reevaluation of their self-generated criteria and to examine their progress in achieving them. As is the case with other components, the training in self-evaluation should enable clients to apply a previously learned behavioral repertoire to a multitude of situations which may be unrelated to the original complaint for which therapeutic assistance was sought. Self-evaluative processes have also been suggested as representing conditioned reinforcers for maintaining behavior (Johnson & Martin, 1973).

Because of early recognition that behavioral change cannot be continually maintained economically by external reinforcement, considerable efforts have been devoted to developing clinical techniques in the use of self-reinforcing procedures (Bandura, 1977; Jones, Nelson, & Kazdin, 1977; Kanfer, 1975; Kanfer & Marston, 1963; Marston, 1965). Since self-reinforcing operations require the individual to establish her own response contingencies, the operations are difficult to separate from the establishment of performance criteria on which the reinforcing operation is contingent. Furthermore, self-administration of a reinforcing event implies that the individual has free access to that event. When the person postpones delivery until the criterion is met, she is engaging in self-control. Additional conceptual complications relate to the question of whether external factors ultimately are necessary to maintain the entire self-reinforcing operation. In fact, some critics (e.g., Catania, 1975; Gewirtz, 1971) have questioned the necessity of distinguishing between self-reinforcing and other reinforcing operations. Nevertheless, clinical and analogue studies with a wide range of problems support the general conclusion of the efficacy of such self-generated operations, both in the acquisition and maintenance of target behaviors. Clinical reports indicate that clients utilize self-reinforcing operations in situations that are unrelated to the treated behavioral problem, and that there are long-term effects for treatment methods that employ self-reinforcement.

Other self-regulatory techniques include training of individuals to arrange their physical environment in such a way that it either facilitates or retards a target response. The methods of stimulus control fall into the category of intervention methods that may be applied for a specific problem. By appropriate training during instigation therapy, their application can be broadened by training clients to utilize general strategies of rearranging their environment that transcend the context of treated behavior.

Various authors (Cautela, 1971; Kazdin, 1975; Mahoney, 1974; Rimm & Masters, 1974) have reported a series of different procedures that commonly have been described as covert conditioning. In essence, these methods attempt to parallel many operant and classical conditioning procedures by substituting self-generated or imaginal stimuli, responses and reinforcements for the experimenter or therapist-manipulated operations. The specific clinical techniques include covert sensitization, covert reinforcement, covert extinction, and covert modeling. The common feature of all these methods is the client's freedom to practice and apply these techniques without therapeutic supervision. Consequently they are available for utilization in different situations and beyond the therapeutic intervention, if the client has learned to apply them effectively and has sufficient sophistication to make use of them when needed.

Another group of self-regulatory techniques involves the utilization of self-instruction for increased behavioral effectiveness. In principle, self-instructional techniques are similar to those described under problem-solving. In both techniques, the client is taught to verbalize a series of directives that permit systematic execution of some desirable behavioral sequence (Meichenbaum, 1975; Meichenbaum & Goodman, 1971; Palkes, Stewart, & Kahana, 1968). Programs vary for different client populations and target behaviors. Essentially, they involve the modeling of overt self-instructional behaviors by the therapist, with increasing demands on the client to imitate the same verbalizations first overtly, then covertly. The content of self-instructions can be formulated to help the client to approach problems systematically, to attend to critical cues in his environment or in his own behavior, or to carry out a behavioral sequence of proven effectiveness. The self-instructional techniques often form components of the stress inoculation programs described above and other cognitive behavior modification methods.

All the methods which we have described under this section are intended first to bring a person's behavior under her own control, thereby freeing her from dependence on the therapist. Secondly, the particular content of these techniques can be expanded by the therapist so that the client learns a broad behavioral rule rather than a response to a specific situation. Finally, as indicated in our discussion of the conceptual base of these methods, they are often directed at those cognitive behavior patterns that are believed to determine a variety of different specific responses in divergent situational contexts. These three features represent the main contributions of the cognitive techniques toward increased durability and generality of treatment effects. Unfortunately, there is a very limited data base from which we can ascertain whether such techniques have an appreciably longer life span than other behavior change programs, both of the operant and dynamic varieties. Justification for use of these methods is based primarily on logical and theoretical grounds and on the inherent assumption that alteration of cognitive behaviors, in turn, can result in large changes in the execution

of observable behaviors which are controlled by the former. In contrast
to earlier dynamic approaches that attempted to modify internal psychological processes, the techniques presented in this chapter have either
been derived from laboratory work or from the body of general psychological knowledge and research. Among the numerous questions that
need to be resolved before they can be credited with strong and lasting
posttreatment effects are those concerning the fate of the practiced
techniques after treatment is terminated. Do clients indeed continue to
use self-management skills which they have learned in treatment? Even
if the initially detailed and systematic form of the newly learned cognitive skills decays, is there such residual effect on later handling of
problem situations? To what extent do self-initiated techniques remain
independent of external reinforcement? Until these questions are resolved by supporting data, these methods take their place among many
other clinical procedures whose use is based as much on clinical experience and faith as it is on indisputable scientific evidence. After a
review of the use of self-control procedures for response maintenance
and transfer of training, Kazdin (1975) concludes "the effects of self-
reinforcement and self-instructional training on long-term response
maintenance and transfer of training have not been thoroughly assessed.
Intuitively, self-control is a viable approach to achieving these goals
[p. 226]." The currently available studies lend some justification to the
hopes that further exploration of these techniques represent a most
fruitful area in the clinician's quest for attaining long-term effects of
therapeutic interventions.

DYADIC STRATEGIES FOR GENERALIZATION

In addition to the use of specific methods and the organization of
the content in treatment, an overall structure of the therapeutic interaction can be developed to enhance durability and generality of treatment effects. In this section we will describe several tactics and
considerations used in our own approach. Both draw heavily on the writings of numerous therapists but differ in an attempt to provide an
integrated model that stresses a tripartite therapeutic process. The objectives of the therapist's activities and strategies are to accomplish
changes at three different levels:

1. To formulate for the therapist tentative hypotheses, to test and
   confirm or reject hypotheses, to strengthen or reinforce successful

steps in the behavior change process and to continually evaluate the direction and utility of the enterprise.

2. At the same time, as much as possible, the therapist models his own cognitive behaviors for the client so that he can apply the approach to the **defined** problem. Additionally, the therapist guides the client in adoption of the approach to the specified problem situation.

3. However, throughout the sessions the therapist continues to attempt instigation of the client's application of the newly learned strategies and behaviors to **other** problem situations and to develop **general rules** for coping with problems.

Numerous specific tactics are available for this purpose. They include an emphasis on overt verbalization of the clinician's thinking whenever it can assist the client in learning a more effective problem approach; the continuing challenge to the client to attempt similar tactics in daily living experiences that have not been specifically discussed in therapy; the encouragement of the client to search for similarities and differences between problematic situations and to develop coping procedures for **classes** of events rather than specific events.

The collaboration between therapist and client is encouraged by the use of the *negotiation model* for therapy (Kanfer & Phillips, 1970). This stresses the importance of client participation and responsibility in defining problems and objectives, and in establishing mutual agreements or contracts both for long-term strategies and the steps taken in the change process. Through use of the negotiation model in the sessions, it is expected that the client will also learn similar interpersonal tactics in other life situations and in later treatment stages. In this model the therapist describes possible alternatives, objectives and procedures, indicates probable costs and consequences, and challenges the client to establish firm commitments toward the chosen objectives.

Implementation of the client's newly learned coping behaviors involves the rehearsal of tactics for dealing with future events, the planning of cognitive and overt behaviors to avoid stress situations or to handle them appropriately, and the reinforcement of the client, first by the therapist then by self-generated reinforcements. This future-oriented broadscale approach is implemented primarily in the interview. The therapist's main emphasis may be on any one of the three levels (the therapist's formulation, the client's attack of a specific problem, or the client's generalized learning) depending on the nature and severity of the difficulty. As a general rule, greater urgency of a specific problem or severity of a disturbance shifts the priority toward the first two levels. With clients whose difficulties are less threatening to their current life situations, greater attention can be given to training in general cognitive strategies and behavioral techniques that have broad applicability. Consistent with the previously discussed self-management principles, the therapist attempts to help the client to develop consistent self-attributions for behavioral choices and consequences. Motivation of continuing self-monitoring and self-change is also encouraged by asking the patient to take an active role in preparing practice assignments, in suggesting alternate objectives or behaviors, and in reporting relevant events or actions.

In practice, the essence of this approach lies in continuously activating the client to work toward several therapeutic tasks:

1. To observe and analyze current and past events in order to provide information for hypotheses and for a formulation of action plans
2. To search for possible favorable outcomes of the change process and to accept necessary limitations and setbacks
3. To assume responsibilities for continuation of change strategies and for motivating himself toward continuing change
4. To search in his daily environment for means and situations that would try out the instigated changes and procedures discussed during treatment sessions
5. To attempt application of the already learned techniques to new problem areas

This overall conceptualization of the therapeutic interviews presumes that both cognitive and behavioral changes can be initiated and rehearsed during the sessions but neither can be maintained by the therapist's efforts alone. It also assumes that what is learned are both specific methods for reducing current problems and general procedures for use after therapy terminates and in areas that are not specifically discussed in therapy. The goals of self-management therapy are inconsistent with some clients' expectations of a passive role in treatment. For these reasons, the numerous techniques discussed by therapists of all persuasions for counteracting resistance to changes and to assumption of responsibility are employed in the dyadic situation.

The attempts to integrate the theoretical formulations about human change processes derived from laboratory research with clinical tactics derived from the content of human experiences are in their early development. Due to their complexity, it has been difficult to examine in research designs combinations of well-substantiated change methods and clinical strategies that attempt to maximize their effectiveness. Nevertheless, introduction of cognitive change methods, the programming of self-generated motivation to change and the strong emphasis on training clients to think and behave differently, not only in the current problem situation but also in other experiences, appears to be a promising approach for maximizing treatment effects. It remains for future outcome research to indicate whether this blend of behavioral methodology, empirical laboratory data and clinical judgment is indeed effective in producing long-term changes in human behavior.

REFERENCES

Ascough, J. C., & Sipprelle, C. N. Operant verbal conditioning of autonomic responses. *Behaviour Research and Therapy*, 1968, *6*, 363–370.

Averill, J. R. Personal control over aversive stimuli and its relationship to stress. *Psychological Bulletin*, 1973, *80*, 286–303.

Ayllon, T., & Haughton, E. Control of the behavior of schizophrenic patients by food. *Journal of Experimental Analysis of Behavior*, 1962, *5*, 343–352.

Bandura, A. *Principles of behavior modification*. New York: Holt, 1969.

Bandura, A. Vicarious and self-reinforcement processes. In R. Glasser (Ed.), *The nature of reinforcement*. New York: Academic Press, 1971.

Bandura, A. *Social learning theory*. Englewood Cliffs, New Jersey: Prentice-Hall, 1977.

Bandura, A., Adams, N. E., & Beyer, J. Cognitive processes mediating behavioral change. *Journal of Personality and Social Psychology*, 1977, *35*, 125–139.

Bandura, A., Jeffery, R. W., & Gajdos, E. Generalizing change through participant modeling with self-directed mastery. *Behaviour Research and Therapy*, 1975, *13*, 141–152.

Beck, A. T. *Cognitive therapy and the emotional disorders*. New York: International Universities Press, 1976.

Bem, D. J. Self-perception theory. In L. Berkowitz (Ed.), *Advances in experimental social psychology* (Vol. 6). New York: Academic Press, 1972.

Blechman, E. A. The family contract game. *The Family Coordinator*, 1974, *23*, 269–281.

Boer, A. P., & Sipprelle, C. N. Induced anxiety in the treatment for LSD effects. *Psychotherapy and Psychosomatics*, 1969, *17*, 108–113.

Catania, A. C. The myth of self-reinforcement. *Behaviorism*, 1975, *3*, 192–199.

Cautela, J. R. Covert conditioning. In A. Jacobs & L. B. Sachs (Eds.), *The psychology of private events: Perspectives on covert response systems*. New York: Academic Press, 1971.

Cofer, C. N. Reasoning as an associative process: III. The role of verbal responses in problem solving. *Journal of General Psychology*, 1957, *57*, 55–68.

Collins, B. E. *Internalization: Toward a micro-social psychology of socialization or enduring behavior control*. Unpublished manuscript, University of California, Los Angeles, 1976.

Deci, E. L. *Some thoughts on the internal state called internal motivation.* Paper presented at the meeting of the American Psychological Association, Chicago, September, 1975.

Dollard, J., & Miller, N. E. *Personality and psychotherapy.* New York: McGraw-Hill, 1950.

Duncan, C. P. Recent research on human problem-solving. *Psychological Bulletin,* 1959, *56,* 397–429.

Duncker, K. On problem solving. *Psychological Monographs,* 1945, *58* (5, Whole No. 270).

D'Zurilla, T. J., & Goldfried, M. R. Problem solving and behavior modification. *Journal of Abnormal Psychology,* 1971, *78,* 107–126.

Ellis, A. *Reason and emotion in psychotherapy.* New York: Lyle Stuart, 1962.

Ellis, A. Rational emotive therapy. In L. Hershen (Ed.), *Four psychotherapies.* New York: Appleton-Century-Crofts, 1970.

Ellis, A. *Humanistic psychotherapy.* New York: McGraw-Hill, 1974.

Fuchs, C. Z., & Rehm, L. P. A self-control behavior therapy program for depression. *Journal of Consulting and Clinical Psychology,* 1977, *45,* 206–215.

Gewirtz, J. L. The roles of overt responding and extrinsic reinforcement in "self-" and "vicarious-reinforcement" phenomena and in "observational learning" and imitation. In R. Glaser (Ed.), *The nature of reinforcement.* New York: Academic Press, 1971.

Glass, C. R., Gottman, J. M., & Shmurak, S. H. Response acquisition and cognitive self-statement modification approaches to dating-skills training. *Journal of Counseling Psychology,* 1976, *23,* 520–526.

Goldfried, M. R. Systematic desensitization as training in self-control. *Journal of Consulting and Clinical Psychology,* 1971, *37,* 228–234.

Goldfried, M. R., & Davison, G. C. *Clinical behavior therapy.* New York: Holt, 1976.

Goldfried, M. R., & Goldfried, A. P. Cognitive change methods. In F. H. Kanfer and A. P. Goldstein (Eds.), *Helping people change: A textbook of methods.* New York: Pergamon, 1975.

Goldiamond, J. Perception, language and conceptualization rules. In B. Kleinmuntz (Ed.), *Problem solving: Research method and theory.* New York: Wiley, 1966.

Goldstein, A. P., Sprafkin, R. P., & Gershaw, N. J. *Skill training for community living: Applying structured learning therapy.* New York: Pergamon, 1976.

Harris, M. B., & Hallbauer, E. S. Self-directed weight control through eating and exercise. *Behaviour Research and Therapy,* 1973, *11,* 523–529.

Harrison, A. A. *Individuals and groups: Understanding social behavior.* Monterey, California: Brooks/Cole Publishing Company, 1976.

Homme, L. E. Perspectives in psychology: XXIV. Control of coverants, the operants of the mind. *Psychological Record,* 1965, *15,* 501–511.

Janis, I. L. *Psychological stress.* New York: Wiley, 1958.

Janis, I. L. Motivational factors in the resolution of decisional conflicts. In M. R. Jones (Ed.), *Nebraska symposium on motivation* (Vol. 7). Lincoln: University of Nebraska Press, 1959.

Janis, I. L. Effects of fear arousal on attitude change: Recent developments in theory and experimental research. In L. Berkowitz (Ed.), *Advances in experimental social psychology* (Vol. 3). New York: Academic Press, 1967.

Janis, I. L., & Mann, L. Coping with decisional conflict: An analysis of how stress affects decision-making suggests interventions to improve the process. *American Scientist,* 1976, *64,* 657–667.

Johnson, S. M., & Martin, S. Developing self-evaluation as a conditioned reinforcer. In B. Ashem & E. G. Poser (Eds.), *Behavior modification with children*. New York: Pergamon, 1973.

Jones, R. T., Nelson, R. E., & Kazdin, A. E. The role of external variables in self-reinforcement: A review. *Behavior Modification*, 1977, *1*, 147–178.

Jordan, C. S., & Sipprelle, C. N. Physiological correlates of induced anxiety with normal subjects. *Psychotherapy: Theory, Research, and Practice*, 1972, *9*, 18–21.

Kanfer, F. H. Self-regulation: Research, issues and speculations. In C. Neuringer & J. L. Michael (Eds.), *Behavior modification in clinical psychology*. New York: Appleton-Century-Crofts, 1970.

Kanfer, F. H. The maintenance of behavior by self-generated stimuli and reinforcement. In A. Jacobs & L. B. Sachs (Eds.), *The psychology of private events*. New York: Academic Press, 1971.

Kanfer, F. H. Self-management methods. In F. H. Kanfer & A. P. Goldstein (Eds.), *Helping people change: A textbook of methods*. New York: Pergamon, 1975.

Kanfer, F. H. The many faces of self-control, or behavior modification changes its focus. In R. B. Stuart (Ed.), *Behavioral self-management*. New York: Bruner/Mazel, 1977 (a).

Kanfer, F. H. Self-regulation and self-control. In H. Zeier (Ed.) *Die Psychologie des 20. Jahrhunderts*. Vol. 4. Zurich, Switzerland: Kindler Veriag, 1977 (b).

Kanfer, F. H., & Grimm, L. G. Freedom of choice and behavioral change. *Journal of Consulting and Clinical Psychology*, 1978, *46*, 873–878.

Kanfer, F. H., & Karoly, P. Self-control: A behavioristic excursion into the lion's den. *Behavior Therapy*, 1972, *3*, 398–416.

Kanfer, F. H., & Marston, A. R. Conditioning of self-reinforcing responses: An analogue to self-confidence training. *Psychological Reports*, 1963, *13*, 63–70.

Kanfer, F. H., & Phillips, J. S. Behavior therapy: A panacea for all ills or a passing fancy? *Archives of General Psychiatry*, 1966, *15*, 114–128.

Kanfer, F. H., & Phillips, J. S. *Learning foundations of behavior therapy*. New York: Wiley, 1970.

Kanfer, F. H., & Seidner, M. Self-control: Factors enhancing tolerance of noxious stimulation. *Journal of Personality and Social Psychology*, 1973, *25*, 381–389.

Kazdin, A. E. Self-monitoring and behavior change. In M. J. Mahoney & C. E. Thoresen (Eds.), *Self-control: Power to the person*. Monterey, California: Brooks/Cole, 1974.

Kazdin, A. E. Covert modeling, imagery assessment, and assertive behavior. *Journal of Consulting and Clinical Psychology*, 1975, *43*, 716–724.

Kazdin, A. E., & Bootzin, R. R. The token economy: An evaluative review. *Journal of Applied Behavior Analysis*, 1972, *5*, 343–372.

Kelly, G. *The psychology of personal constructs*. New York: Norton, 1955.

Kendler, H. H., & Kendler T. S. Vertical and horizontal processes in problem solving. *Psychological Review*, 1962, *69*, 1–16.

King, G. F., Armitage, S. G., & Tilton, J. R. A therapeutic approach to schizophrenics of extreme pathology: An operant-interpersonal method. *Journal of Abnormal and Social Psychology*, 1960, *61*, 276–286.

Kohlberg, L., Yaeger, J., & Hjertholm, E. Private speech: Four studies and a review of theories. *Child Development*, 1968, *39*, 691–736.

Kopel, S., & Arkowitz, H. The role of attribution and self-perception in behavior change: Implications for behavior therapy. *Genetic Psychology Monographs*, 1975, *92*, 175–212.

Langer, E. J., Janis, I. L., & Wolfer, J. A. Reduction of psychological stress in surgical patients. *Journal of Experimental Social Psychology*, 1975, *11*, 155–165.

Langer, E., & Rodin, J. The effects of choice and enhanced personal responsibility for the aged: A field experiment in an institutional setting. *Journal of Personality and Social Psychology*, 1976, *34*, 191–198.

Lazarus, A. A. *Behavior therapy and beyond*. New York: McGraw-Hill, 1971.

Levine, F. M., & Fasnacht, G. Token rewards may lead to token learning. *American Psychologist*, 1974, *29*, 816–820.

Liem, G. R. Performance and satisfaction as affected by personal control over salient decisions. *Journal of Personality and Social Psychology*, 1975, *31*, 232–240.

Lindsley, O. R. Operant conditioning methods applied to research in chronic schizophrenia. *Psychiatric Research Reports*, 1956, *5*, 118–139.

Luria, A. R. *The role of speech in the regulation of normal and abnormal behavior*. New York: Liveright Publishing Corporation, 1961.

MacDonald, M. L. Teaching assertion: A paradigm for therapeutic intervention. *Psychotherapy: Theory, Research and Practice*, 1975, *12*, 60–67.

Mahoney, M. J. *Cognition and behavior modification*. Cambridge, Massachusetts: Ballinger, 1974.

Mahoney, M. J., Moura, N. G. M., & Wade, T. C. Relative efficacy of self-reward, self-punishment, and self-monitoring techniques for weight loss. *Journal of Consulting and Clinical Psychology*, 1973, *40*, 404–407.

Mahoney, M. J., & Thoresen, C. E. *Self-control: Power to the person*. Monterey, California: Brooks/Cole, 1974.

Maier, N. R. F. The behavior mechanisms concerned with problem solving. *Psychological Review*, 1940, *47*, 43–58.

Maltzman, I. Thinking: From a behavioristic point of view. *Psychological Review*, 1955, *62*, 275–286.

Mann, L. Use of a "balance-sheet" procedure to improve the quality of personal decision-making: A field experiment with college applicants. *Journal of Vocational Behavior*, 1972, *2*, 291–300.

Marholin II, D., Siegel, L. J., & Phillips, S. Treatment and transfer: A search for empirical procedures. *Progress in Behavior Modification*, 1976, *3*, 293–342.

Marston, A. R. Self-reinforcement: The relevance of a concept to analogue research in psychotherapy. *Psychotherapy: Theory, Research and Practice*, 1965, *2*, 1–5.

Meichenbaum, D. Theoretical and treatment implications of developmental research on verbal control of behavior. *Canadian Psychological Review*, 1975, *16*, 22–27.

Meichenbaum, D. *Cognitive-behavior modification: An integrative approach*. New York: Plenum, 1977.

Meichenbaum, D., & Cameron, R. *Stress inoculation: A skills training approach to anxiety management*. Unpublished manuscript, University of Waterloo, 1972.

Meichenbaum, D., & Goodman, J. Training impulsive children to talk to themselves: A means of developing self-control. *Journal of Abnormal Psychology*, 1971, *77*, 115–126.

Meichenbaum, D., & Turk, D. The cognitive-behavioral management of anxiety, anger and pain. In P. Davison (Ed.), *The behavioral management of anxiety, depression and pain*. New York: Bruner/Mazel, 1976.

Mischel, W. *Introduction to personality*. New York: Holt, 1971.

Mischel, W. Toward a cognitive social learning reconceptualization of personality. *Psychological Review*, 1973, *80*, 252–283.

Mischel, W., & Mischel, H. N. A cognitive social-learning approach to morality and self-regulation. In T. Likona (Ed.), *Moral development and behavior: Theory, research, and social issues.* New York: Holt, 1976.

Moss, M. K., & Arend, R. A. Self-directed contact desensitization. *Journal of Consulting and Clinical Psychology,* 1977, *45,* 730–738.

Nelson, R. O. Methodological issues in assessment via self-monitoring. In J. D. Cone & N. P. Hawkins (Eds.), *Behavioral assessment: New directions in clinical psychology.* New York: Bruner/Mazel, 1977.

Newell, A., & Simon, H. A. The simulation of human thought. In W. Dennis (Ed.), *Current trends in psychological theory.* Pittsburgh: University of Pittsburgh Press, 1961.

Newell, A., & Simon, H. A. Computer simulation of human thinking. *Science,* 1962, *134,* 2011–2017.

Newell, A., & Simon, H. A. *Human problem solving.* Englewood Cliffs, New Jersey: Prentice-Hall, 1972.

Novaco, R. W. *Anger control: The development and evaluation of an experimental treatment.* Lexington, Massachusetts: Lexington Books, 1975.

Novaco, R. W. Stress inoculation: A cognitive therapy for anger and its application to a case of depression. *Journal of Consulting and Clinical Psychology,* 1977, *45,* 600–608.

Ollendick, T. H., & Nettle, M. D. An evaluation of the relaxation component of induced anxiety. *Behavior Therapy,* 1977, *8,* 561–566.

Palkes, H., Stewart, M., & Kahana, B. Porteus maze performance of hyperactive boys after training in self-directed verbal commands. *Child Development,* 1968, *39,* 817–826.

Posner, M. I. *Cognition: An introduction.* Glenview, Illinois: Scott, Foresman, 1973.

Reiss, S., & Sushinsky, L. W. Overjustification, competing responses, and the acquisition of intrinsic interest. *Journal of Personality and Social Psychology,* 1975, *31,* 1116–1125.

Richards, C. S. Behavior modification of studying through study skills advice and self-control procedures. *Journal of Counseling Psychology,* 1975, *22,* 431–436.

Richards, C. S. Improving study behaviors through self-control techniques. In J. D. Krumboltz & C. E. Thoresen (Eds.), *Counseling methods.* New York: Holt, 1976.

Rimm, D. C., & Masters, J. C. *Behavior therapy: Techniques and empirical findings.* New York: Academic Press, 1974.

Rodin, J., & Langer, E. J. Long-term effects of a control-relevant intervention with the institutionalized aged. *Journal of Personality and Social Psychology,* 1977, *35,* 897–902.

Sarason, I. G., & Ganzer, V. J. Social influence techniques in clinical and community psychology. In C. D. Spielberger (Ed.), *Current topics in clinical and community psychology* (Vol. 1). New York: Academic Press, 1969.

Sarbin, T. R., & Allen, V. L. Role theory. In G. Lindzey & E. Aronson (Eds.), *The handbook of social psychology* (Vol. 1, 2nd ed.). Reading, Massachusetts: Addison-Wesley, 1968.

Sherman, A. R., & Plummer, I. L. Training in relaxation as a behavioral self-management skill: An exploratory investigation. *Behavior Therapy,* 1973, *4,* 543–550.

Shure, M. B., Spivak, G., & Jaeger, M. A. Problem-solving thinking and adjustment among disadvantaged preschool children. *Child Development,* 1971, *42,* 1791–1803.

Sipprelle, C. N. Induced anxiety. *Psychotherapy: Theory, Research, and Practice,* 1967, *4,* 36–40.
Skinner, B. F. *Science and human behavior.* New York: Macmillan, 1953.
Skinner, B. F. Operant behavior. *American Psychologist,* 1963, *18,* 503–515.
Skinner, B. F. An operant analysis of problem solving. In B. Kleinmuntz (Ed.), *Problem solving: Research, method and theory.* New York: Wiley, 1966.
Spivak, G., Platt, J. J., & Shure, M. B. *The problem-solving approach to adjustment.* San Francisco: Jossey-Bass, 1976.
Spivak, G., & Shure, M. B. *Social adjustment of young children: A cognitive approach to solving real-life problems.* San Francisco: Jossey-Bass, 1974.
Stokes, T. F., & Baer, D. M. An implicit technology of generalization. *Journal of Applied Behavior Analysis,* 1977, *10,* 349–367.
Stotland, E., & Blumenthal, H. The reduction of anxiety as a result of the expectation of making a choice. *Canadian Journal of Psychology,* 1964, *18,* 139–145.
Suinn, R. M., & Richardson, F. Anxiety management training: A non-specific behavior therapy program for anxiety control. *Behavior Therapy,* 1971, *2,* 498–510.
Wahler, R. G. Setting generality: Some specific and general effects of child behavior therapy. *Journal of Applied Behavior Analysis,* 1969, *2,* 239–246.

6

Instigation Therapy:
Using Therapeutic Homework
to Promote Treatment Gains

JOHN L. SHELTON

Instigation therapy refers to the systematic use of therapeutic home-work assignments planned jointly by the professional and the client which are completed in the client's natural environment. As originally discussed by Kanfer and Phillips (1966, 1969), this approach requires the client to instigate new behavior away from the therapy session in a primarily client controlled generalization of behavior previously re-hearsed. Instigation therapy puts clients to work outside the therapy hour in an effort to increase efficiency, to enhance self-regulatory skills and to promote transfer of training.

Instigation procedures result in a number of benefits. For example, Secord and Bachman (1964) noted the increase in self-control skills acquired by clients who perceive themselves as the principle agent of behavior change while in therapy. Whereas Phillips and Johnson (1972) suggested that the clients who help design and carry out treatment are more motivated to change their behavior. In this general vein, Davison

(1968) demonstrated that clients who were involved in their own treatment planning were more likely to maintain therapy gains over time.

This latter finding is closely related to the transfer of training phenomenon so noticeably lacking in psychotherapy research. Since many prescribed assignments are mobile and can be practiced anywhere, the likelihood of positive transfer is enhanced when instigation therapy is employed. Thus, the client who practices a learned skill in a number of settings and with a number of targets is more likely to experience positive transfer than the client who practices a newly acquired skill in the presence of one therapist working in a single treatment setting.

A WORD ABOUT HISTORY

Although, in this writer's opinion, few traditional psychotherapists make adequate use of homework, the basic notions surrounding instigation therapy are not new. Especially likely to use assigned activities are behavior therapists who recognize the gains in efficiency, and so forth, that result when clients are able to work on their problems in the other 167 hours of the week not devoted to formal therapy.

However, even before the arrival of modern behavior therapy, some psychotherapists were discussing homework in their writing. Among the first of these were Dunlap (1932), Herzberg (1941), and Karpman (1949), all of whom pointed out the advantage that comes from putting clients to work outside the therapy hour. For the most part, their work consisted of client regulated extinction trials conducted outside the consulting hour as an adjunct to psychotherapy.

From a historical perspective, the work of George Kelly (1955) represents a cornerstone for all recent work done in the area of prescribed assignments. As contrasted to those who had preceded him, Kelly integrated homework into therapy rather than use it as a tacked on afterthought as it was used previously. Kelly's work consisted of urging clients to define appropriate target roles and then to act those roles out in the natural environment. In part, the assumption underlying his work was that reinforcement from the natural environment would maintain the new behavior, once emitted.

A history of homework-focused therapy would be incomplete without mention of the contributions of Albert Ellis (1961). Although known primarily for the development of rational emotive therapy, Ellis and other rational emotive therapists such as Maultsby (1971) have played an important role in advancing the notion that clients need to become involved in practice outside the therapy hour. Maultsby (1971) in particular should be singled out for his work in developing systematic instigation procedures since he has produced the only known empirical study addressed exclusively to the gains accrued by using homework.

Despite the work of Kelly, Ellis, and Maultsby, the use of prescribed outside activities did not begin to realize full potential until recently. Since then, three developments have transpired which have taken homework and prescribed activities from the occasionally used adjunct to the point where it is **the** central focus of treatment around which all intervention within the office are aimed.

The Work of Kanfer and Phillips

The first of the three developments was the work of Kanfer and Phillips (1966, 1969). These writers provided the crucial first step in the development of homework-based therapy by providing the conceptual model around which the technique could develop. Their writing provided the theoretical underpinnings for what is now recognized as behavioral self-control. These writers coined the term "instigation therapy," contrasted it with other forms of therapy, and argued that clients could learn to regulate their own environment, thereby modifying their own behavior. They wrote persuasively that in some instances prescribed outside activities could and should be the entire focus of therapy.

Sex Dysfunction Therapy

Whereas Kanfer and Phillips provided the crucial conceptualization of the role of homework in behavior therapy, it remained for researchers such as Masters and Johnson (1970) to translate these principles into action. Sex dysfunction researchers such as those just mentioned were among the first to introduce *systematic* homework assignments into their work with clients. The word "systematic" implies that homework is an integral part of therapy which is planned in a careful step-by-step manner. Thus, the sex dysfunction professionals made prescribed activities a focus of treatment as Kelly had done but added the additional dimension of systematization. Researchers in this important area provided a model of homework utilization which transcended the previous mode of giving homework in a hit or miss, haphazard way with little attention given to careful planning and integration.

The Work of Shelton and Ackerman

The most comprehensive focus on prescribed outside activities is the work of Shelton and Ackerman (1974) and their associates. For these writers, systematic homework is **the** core of successful behavior therapy interventions. Based on the conceptual model provided by Kanfer and Phillips (1969), their first major publication took the abstract notion of instigation therapy and translated it into more than 150 examples of homework assignments useful with several common behavioral disorders. Their work was the first to address to itself to homework per se and discussed the format by which homework should be given, counterindications for its use, and provided detailed examples of how to integrate homework into behavior therapy.

Since then, Shelton has written a number of articles aimed at demonstrating the importance of prescribed activities on treatment outcome. In a recent article, Shelton and Levy (in press) surveyed all the behavior therapy oriented journals published in the United States. Their search was devoted to discovering whether or not homework assignments were used in articles involving adult outpatient treatment. They discovered that homework played an enormous role in treatments reported in sampled journals. In fact, 59% of all outpatient treatment articles published in behavioral journals in the last 5 years used outside practice assignments to promote behavior change!

Other studies have been devoted to showing the efficacy of using homework in clinical settings. For example, Shelton (1973) demonstrated the positive impact of homework assignments involving relaxation practice and cognitive control procedures in reducing the stress experienced on a college campus as a result of a homicide committed on a coed. In another study, Shelton (1975) used systematic homework assignments involving speech shadowing to eliminate a chronic stuttering problem. In a more elaborate study, Chesney and Shelton (1976) used homework assignments involving relaxation practice to enhance the treatment effects of biofeedback training. They were able to show that biofeedback with relaxation practice exercises were more effective than biofeedback alone in reducing the frequency and duration of tension headaches. In another study, Shelton (in press) demonstrated the effectiveness of homework exercises utilized in the treatment of conditioned urinary retention. This study revealed that clients bothered by an inability to urinate in public restrooms found significantly quicker relief when treated by homework assignments involving self directed practice then those clients who received the same office treatment but who were not given homework. Although both groups profited from treatment, the group receiving outside practice assignments got much better faster than the control group.

OVERVIEW OF INSTIGATION THERAPY

This writer believes psychotherapy to be primarily an educational, skill building endeavor. Thus, the more clients participate in the endeavor, the greater their chances of making desired changes. Having decided on therapy goals, the client and therapist coparticipate in treatment; they work together in an atmosphere of empathy, warmth and genuine caring (Truax & Carkhuff, 1967). Besides conveying empathy, warmth and respect, the effective instigation therapist is an active, directive teacher, expert in skill training and cognitive control. A friend to the client, the professional also guides the client toward attitudes and behaviors that will increase the client's ability to live a more satisfying life. Under the direction of the therapist, homework provides an ideal vehicle for clients to extend the practice of new skills and attitudes from the therapy hour to the outside world in which they live.

The above beliefs about psychotherapy lead this writer to follow a particular sequence in conducting therapy. The sequence consists of six steps:

1. The careful identification of client problems
2. A precise definition of therapy objectives in behavioral terms
3. A contractual agreement between the client and therapist to work toward these objectives
4. A rank ordering of the therapeutic intervention so that the first objective pursued will make the most difference to the client and is, in the judgement of the therapist, technically the most feasible to pursue
5. Selection of skills and methods of skill-training acceptable to the client and effective for working toward the first behavioral objective
6. Systematic skill-training using homework assignments as integral parts of behavioral skill-building

The remainder of this chapter is addressed to specific principles which enhance the effectiveness of instigation therapy. The first involves self-recording.

Homework Involves Self-Observation

The first step in instigation therapy is diagnostic. Frequently instigation procedures begin with gathering information regarding the frequency, duration, and magnitude of target behaviors. In addition, effort is expanded to identify critical events antecedent to the appearance of the problem which may have caused the problem to develop and current events which may help to maintain the problem.

Because many client problems are too private, too infrequent, or too situation-specific to be observed by the professional, the behavior therapist must rely on the client to obtain this information. Without the client's help, helping professionals may not fully understand the problem and, as a result, may be unsuccessful in their treatment interventions.

Aside from formal interviews, data regarding the client can be obtained by asking the client to complete psychometric self-report inventories or by engaging in self-observation. Regarding the former procedure, the behavior therapist using instigation procedures can give the client suitable inventories to take home and complete. Many initial therapy sessions end with prescribed activities involving the completion of these paper and pencil tests. These inventories, which are extensively reviewed in behavior therapy journals, are completed and discussed during the next sessions during which time clients can elaborate upon items significant for treatment planning.

Because self-report inventories do not exist for all problem areas or are limited in what information they yield about any specific targeted behavior, the behavior therapist must frequently rely on self observation recording procedures by the client as a means to gathering important information. Since these recording procedures have been reviewed extensively by Hall (1971) and others, they will not be elaborated upon at this time. It is worth stating, however, that self-observation is made more reliable by using standard recording formats such as frequency, interval, time sample, and duration recording systems. Commercial counting devices also improve accuracy.

Despite using commercial recording devices and standard counting formats, the accuracy of self-recorded data varies dramatically across subject, situation, target behavior, and recording system used (Mahoney and Thoreson, 1974). For example, this writer has observed that the immediacy, mobility, and conspicuousness of the recording system, as well as the recording format used, alter the reliability of self-observation. To make matters more complex, the reader is undoubtedly well aware that the act of counting a behavior alters the response being counted (Mahoney, 1974). Unfortunately, treatment gains accruing from counting do not seem to maintain over time (Mahoney & Thoreson, 1974).

Regardless of the problems associated with the use of self-observation, instigation procedures often involved its use. For this reason, the competent professional is well advised to take steps to make self-observation as valid and reliable as possible. As has already been indicated, commercial recording devices can help immensely. For this reason, many instigation therapists have a stock of mechanical counters available for rent or loan to their clients. In addition, standard recording formats such as those just mentioned can be easily taught to most clients.

However, despite the availability of commercial counters and standardized recording formats, the competent instigation therapist is well advised to spend some in-office time teaching self observation skills to the client. Training in self observation can be accomplished by using the following procedure:

First: Modeling the skill
Second: Prompting the skill
Third: Shaping the client's response
Fourth: Giving prescribed practice assignments in self observation

The first step in teaching self observation skills is to provide a model for the client to imitate. This is done by the professional emitting some high frequency, discrete behavior such as coughing or clearing one's throat. The therapist then counts aloud and punches a mechanical clicker or similar device each time the behavior occurs. Using this same highly discrete behavior as a prompt, the professional then asks the client to count along with him as the therapist gradually fades out his count. Reinforcement is then given for the client's ability to attend to, discriminate, and record the target behaviors. As the client catches on to the procedure, the frequency, discreteness, etc., can be altered to gradually conform to the realistic demands of the self observation situation.

In addition to the methods just reviewed, this writer urges the reader to recognize that counting behavior may not transfer to the natural environment unless appropriate self-observation homework assignments are made. As a result, a good gambit to follow with the novice self-recorder is to ask them to record only discrete, high frequency (more than five an hour) behaviors at first. The behavior being counted may or may not be related to the target behavior.

In many instances it may be advisable to go with the client into the natural environment where continued modeling and imitation can occur. Paraprofessionals can serve handsomely in this regard. Even the professional in private practice should consider *in vivo* outside practice with the client. If that is not possible, frequent phone calls during this phase of treatment will help to maintain the counting behavior.

Another important intervention that serves to maintain counting behavior is to ask the client to self-reinforce after each recording attempt. Covert positive self-reinforcement is especially useful in this regard. After 2 or 3 days of practice, the client is usually ready to proceed in self-observation of target behaviors.

Successful Homework Involves a Sound Conceptualization

To be effective, prescribed activities must be closely integrated with treatment. Successful homework is the outgrowth of well planned treatment. Without careful preparation, the best intentioned behavioral prescriptions are likely to be relatively useless and in some cases dangerous.

The effective use of prescribed activities in behavior therapy is firmly grounded in a sound conceptualization of the target presented problem. Such a conceptualization allows the professional to translate therapy objectives in behavioral terms and consequently generate treatment plan.

A review of the literature contained in behavior therapy publications represents a wide range of varied conceptualizations. Many are highly worthwhile. However, from this writer's personal viewpoint, the conceptual model which yields the most thorough understanding of the presenting problem, generates treatment and homework plans is the BASIC ID formulation of Arnold Lazarus (1976). Lazarus' plan asks the behavior therapist to define therapy objectives in terms of the client's behaviors, affect, sensations, imagery, cognitions, interpersonal relations, and drugs. Each of these variables is an important part of the client's total being. The last variable, drugs, refers to the organic or biochemical processes that influence behavior. An example of the BASIC ID formulation used for the behavioral diagnosis of a recent client follows in Table 6.1.

Using Lazarus' paradigm allows the therapist to bring the client's troubles into clear focus. After establishing those goals, treatment interventions can be designed for each identified problem. Homework activities can in turn be generated from the treatment plan.

How to Give Homework

When client and therapist agree upon the behavioral objectives of the therapy contract, work toward attaining these begins. The therapist directs the latter portion of most therapy hours so that a precise set of

TABLE 6.1
A Behavioral Diagnosis of Nonassertive Behavior Using BASIC ID

Behavior:	The client cannot say "no," ask "why," or accept compliments.
Affect:	The client is anxious much of the time.
Sensations:	The client suffers from tension headaches.
Imagery:	The client obsesses about an earlier bad marriage.
Cognitions:	The client believes that she is dumb and that she must never make her husband angry.
Interpersonal:	The client seldom speaks in groups and has few close friends.
Drugs.	No organic problem present.

homework instructions is written before the sessions end. At that time, the reason for and nature of the homework is carefully explained to the client by the therapist. Summarized homework instructions usually are written on NCR (no carbon required) paper so both therapist and client have a copy. The homework provides continued practice for the client in acquiring the knowledge, attitudes or skills upon which the therapy session was focused.

The format for homework includes one or more of the following instructions:

1. A *do* statement. "Read, practice, observe, say, count, . . . some kind of homework."
2. A *quantity* statement. "Talk three times about . . . ; Spend thirty minutes *three* times . . . ; Give *four* compliments per day . . . ; Write a list of at least *ten* . . ."
3. A *record* statement. "Count and *record* the number of compliments; Each time he hits, *mark* a —— on the chart; Whenever that thought comes to you, *write* a —— on the . . ."
4. A *bring* statement. "*Bring* . . . your list; the chart; the cards; your spouse . . . to your next appointment."
5. A *contingency* statement. "Call for your next appointment after you have done . . . ; For each activity you attend, one dollar will be deducted . . . ; Each minute spent doing —— will earn you ——; One-tenth of your penalty deposit will be forfeited for each assignment completed."

An example of this format as written on NCR paper, is the following:

Homework for John and Sally:
1. Both read two marital papers.
2. Discuss 3x for 15–30 minutes each time.

3. Write separate lists of at least 3 behaviors you want *more of* from
   spouse. (These are positive behaviors, *not* negatives.)
4. Make next appointment after above is done.
5. Bring lists with you to next appointment.

The therapist should give manageable amounts of homework. Early
in therapy, especially following the first session, a single item of homework may be enough. As the professional becomes more acquainted
with the client's attitudes, expectations, and habits, the amount and
complexity of homework may be increased. Excessive amounts of homework require too much planning time, may frustrate the client, and
simply not get done.

Homework assignments should be written in down-to-earth simple
language. Since one major cause for assignments going awry is poor
communication, the use of NCR paper helps overcome any misunder-
standing or problems due to forgetting the assignments. Each session
should end by asking the client to paraphrase the homework assignment
agreed upon.

Homework Is Reinforced

The importance of "doing his homework" is emphasized to the client
at the time the homework is assigned. The contingency statement in
the homework format is one way of assuring that the homework will
be completed—rather than seeing the client on an interval schedule of
appointments, say Tuesdays at 10:00; the client is not scheduled for his
next appointment until he or she calls to say the homework is done.
This contingency is based upon three assumptions: Clients accept the
homework as relevant to their needs, find it manageable in quantity,
and share enough rapport with the therapist that they will do the
homework in order to again see the therapist.

Other reward contingencies can be made as well. For example, this
writer has observed that some behavior therapists in private practice
have given a money "rebate" contingent upon attempts with the client
homework. Other therapists make regular appointments with the client
but reduce part of the hour if the client doesn't attempt the homework.
Phone calls also provide a handy and easy way to reinforce efforts and
are especially useful when homework is potentially dangerous and
should be monitored frequently by the therapist.

Another successful means of insuring completion of assignments is
to involve other members of the family in prompting, assisting and
reinforcing the clients in their efforts to do homework.

Each Session Begins and Ends with Prescribed Activities

Earlier, this writer mentioned that therapy sessions begin and end with discussions on prescribed activities. A word or two more about this process may be in order. After initial greetings, therapy sessions begin with a quick review of the homework assigned. The client is asked to describe his experience with his homework. If written homework or data are part of the assignment, the client is asked to present it to the therapist. As stated in the previous section, smiles and verbal approval accompany the therapist's examination of the homework. It is important to reinforce the client for having done his homework whether the data indicate program success or a need for revision.

The use of written homework assignments can provide advantages to the therapist in conducting psychotherapy. A quick review of his copy of the homework reminds him of the topic of focus when the last therapy hour ended. Combined with brief progress notes, the written homework minimizes the warm-up time necessary for the therapist and client to reestablish therapy goals and direction; as a result, therapy flows more smoothly toward evaluation of progress in the current step of skill training and toward identification of the next step in therapy. Since each therapy hour culminates in a written homework assignment precise therapy contract definition, control of rambling onto side issues, and maintenance of coparticipation in therapy are facilitated in an optimal use of therapy sessions.

The therapist can prompt and facilitate completion of homework by providing the client with easy access to required homework materials. Printed assignment devices, books, pamphlets or papers, graph paper, cassette tapes, wrist counters, or special devices such as enuresis blankets, electric shockers, or tape recorders can be loaned, rented, or sold to the client. Some instigation therapists make extensive use of books in their treatment approach and develop a lending library or make special arrangements with local booksellers and other merchants to keep certain items in stock. In addition, instigation therapists continue to watch for new materials that will facilitate the conduct of therapy through the use of better homework for their clients. This necessitates being on the mailing lists of as many equipment suppliers and book publishers as one can digest.

For many, the written word has exceptional authority and consequently can present a powerful stimulus for change. Another advantage of homework employing bibliotherapy is its economy and the facility with which it can be accomplished. Clients using bibliotherapy are free to read at their own pace and can mull over ideas presented in the book.

However, it is not enough to ask clients to merely read the material. To be most effective, assigned readings must be done in such a way as to insure comprehension and retention. To accomplish these goals, clients are asked whether or not they like to read. Equally important is the assessment of the patient's reading ability. Bibliotherapy should be avoided for clients who read very slowly or who find reading an ordeal.

An attempt is made to insure reading retention by several means. In some cases written tests are prepared which the client must "pass" in order to continue in therapy. In other instances, especially those concerning marital or family discord, clients are asked to read at the same pace and have scheduled times in which to discuss their understanding of the readings. In addition, a few minutes of each therapy hour are taken to discuss the client's reading. The advantage of this approach is that it affords the client a first-hand opportunity to discuss potentially important material with the therapist.

The therapist deciding to use bibliotherapy must overcome the problem of what book for which client. Based on this writer's observations, no systematic method exists to assess the client's needs; as a result, the psychotherapist must rely on past experiences to guide him in assigning books. Consequently, trial and error will play an important role in bibliotherapy.

Despite the many precautions the therapist might take, instigation therapy assignments are not always completed. When the clients have not done their homework the reasons are quickly sought. Initially, the therapist should assume that the error is his own. For example, not all homework is assigned clearly or proves to be relevant to the needs of the client. If the therapist has failed to explain the homework clearly and the homework still is current and relevant, it is reassigned with more clarity. New homework is selected for those occasions that the client becomes aware of different needs than those perceived during the previous session. But when the homework is relevant and clearly assigned, yet not done because of illness or more important business, its importance to progress in therapy should be emphasized. Depending on the client and his problem, some contingency may be established between homework completion and the next therapy session. Unless the client and therapist have a positive relationship, or the client thinks he will benefit from continuing to see the therapist, the contingency may provide the client with the excuse he needs for terminating therapy. Hence, early in therapy when the client is still sizing him up, the therapist must be particularly sensitive to his client's needs and expectations and assign homework only after clearly explaining to the client its value to him. At all times the homework must be assigned with clarity; we double-check the client's understanding of the homework assignment by having him read the homework sheet written by the therapist before leaving the therapy session. In addition, clients are invited to telephone if they have any problems in doing the homework.

INSTIGATION THERAPY INVOLVES PLANNING FOR TRANSFER

As writers such as Eysenck (1964) and Holmes (1971) have observed, few professionals plan for transfer of training during their work with clients. Most mental health workers do not appear to be aware of the importance of programming transfer or assume like Wolpe (1958) that skills learned during their particular treatment intervention automatically transfer to the natural environment.

The fact that transfer of training does not typically occur during psychological treatment is now well established (Gruber, 1971). Thus the fact that behaviors are usually emitted only in the environment in which they were originally learned has serious implications for treatments that involve skill training in the presence of only one therapist working in a single environment.

Despite these admonitions, relatively little has appeared in the literature regarding methods of improving transfer of skills and attitudes learned during therapy to the outside world. Although definitive research is lacking, it appears that systematic homework assignments have the potential for increasing transfer of therapy gains. As a result, a few notions regarding transfer as it relates to systematic homework are worth mentioning.

Homework tasks can purposely be programmed to occur in different settings. Almost any setting is better than the consulting room for promoting transfer. In fact, after initial skill acquisition has occurred it may be advisable to design homework assignments that prompt that client to practice newly acquired skills in a variety of situations and with a number of people. Of course, this particular approach does present problems for the private practitioner working alone. But for those who work in agencies such as mental health clinics and counseling centers, such manipulations are relatively easy to accomplish.

An example of programmed transfer of this kind is the work of Pendleton, Shelton, and Wilson (1976) involving treatment of social inhibition. Their work took place in a college counseling center and involved training a number of undergraduate paraprofessionals to work with socially inhibited men and women. The program functioned by first doing skill training with the clients and then giving them homework assignments involving practice of those skills with the paraprofessionals. Simultaneously, the paraprofessionals met in a group and were briefed on the specific skills being taught to the treatment group that particular week. The paraprofessionals were then briefed on troubles the client might have and ways for overcoming them. Each paraprofessional then was randomly assigned a client to meet with for several hours during the week. The location of the meeting place was changed each week as well. As a result of this practice, each socially inhibited client had experienced outside practice assignments with a new person in a new environment each week.

As Deese and Hulse (1967) have noted, regardless of the particular methods chosen to promote transfer, practice is crucial. Recall that individuals lose 50% of what they learn during the day following the learning trial (Cain & Willey, 1939). As a result, much valuable therapist material is forgotten soon after the therapist session has occurred. Practice is the one way to overcome this problem. Thus, the client who practices what has been learned in therapy begins to overlearn the materials and retention is greatly enhanced.

Of course, practice can also be practiced covertly. As Meichenbaum (1969) has shown, covert practice of trained responses transfers across both time and space. Cautela's work (1966) has also shown that covert modeling allows almost unlimited practice with new CRs in countless environments. In summary, regardless of whether the practice is overt or covert, programmed rehearsal of learned skills is crucial because weak CRs limited to little practice will extinguish beyond a single setting.

Assigned Homework Can be Risky

Can you imagine the possible consequences of an assertive response from a woman whose letter was recently published in *Dear Abby:*

> DEAR ABBY: I am 25 and my ex-husband is 33. We have been divorced for 14 months but we're still living together. I just never got up the nerve to kick him out because he's kind of helpless. He doesn't want me to have any friends. In fact, he yells if I leave the house. I am an excellent cook and housekeeper and serve him three hot meals a day. I do all the yard work and even the painting and house repairs. All he wants to do after work is sit in front of the T.V. and drink beer.
>
> We were married for four years and never had any kids. (He can't stand them.)
>
> He hardly ever makes love to me, and when he does he satisfies only himself. If I complain, he gets mad.
>
> He never compliments me and never wants to take me out. But he runs with his friends whenever he feels like it.
>
> Don't tell me to leave him, Abby. I love him.
>   RUSSELLVILLE, ARK.

Although one cannot predict with certainty, it appears likely that newly acquired assertive responses—especially of a confrontive nature—might elicit a potentially destructive retaliation from her ex-husband. Although this case might be a bit extreme, the fact remains that presented activities are potentially risky for the client.

The nature of the treatments such as those for nonassertiveness, social inhibition, marital conflicts and depression will occasionally have adverse consequences as a result of prescribed activities. This general finding appears to be true for behaviors that are not readily reinforced and maintained by the natural environment such as assertive responses.

The problem with many prescribed activities is that the response of the target cannot be controlled. Although some work, such as that by Pendleton *et al.* (1976), has attempted to overcome the problem by "programming" trained targets in the natural environment, most mental health practitioners are at the mercy of the target response to their client.

Although the instigation therapist cannot control the consequences that may befall the client when conducting a homework assignment, he can take precautionary measures that will minimize the danger. Some of the most important precautions follow:

Related to negative consequences is the danger associated with giving homework assignments to clients who do not possess the skills to behave appropriately. The potential for a disaster is increased if the client is skill deficient in behaviors crucial to the success of the homework. As a result, the therapist can decrease the likelihood of adverse consequences by engaging in skill training **prior** to the prescribed activity. Such a simple suggestion may be taken for granted by the reader, however, in this writer's opinion, all too many professionals urge behavior change without first being certain that the clients have the behavior repertoire vital for success.

A detailed discussion of skill training is beyond the scope of this chapter. However, a few words may prove instructive to the novice professional who may not be completely aware of skill training strategies. This writer prefers to conduct skill training in a step by step fashion in the order that follows:

1. Skill Preparation
  (*a*) *Bibliotherapy.* This procedure affords the therapist and client a common language with which to discuss the problem. More important, if chosen carefully, it typically becomes an important source of motivation for the client since most bibliotherapy exhorts behavior change and points out the many negative conse-

quences of the particular behavior in question. Furthermore, bibliotherapy provides a good measure of commitment to change since clients for whom the prognosis is bad often do not complete the readings assigned.

(b) *Modeling*. Clients learn from watching their therapist engage in appropriate target behaviors.

(c) *Imitation*. After having watched the therapist model behavior the client now copies what he or she observed.

(d) *Coaching*. The client's behavior is now critiqued with reinforcement being given for successful approximations and hints being given for improving deficits.

2. *Covert Practice*. After the client has progressed to the point where he can emit the correct response, the therapist should assign practice assignments in which the client imagines himself engaging in the correct target response with positive consequences occurring. This procedure is similar to what Suinn (1972) called visual motor behavior rehearsal (VMBR) and continues up to the instance of actual overt behavior. In fact the client shall be instructed to engage in VMBR before any instance of prescribed activity. VMBR works by asking the client to:

First: *Relax*
Second: *Visualize* the correct response
Third: *Do* the correct response

3. *Client Veto Power* Another way in which the potential bad effects of homework can be reduced is by giving the client veto power of any particular assignment. This particular writer thinks that the client is typically the best judge of whether or not they are capable of engaging in the behavior in question. If they are immobilized by the homework then the instigation procedures have not been given in small enough steps. As is the case with systematic desensitization, if the client becomes so anxious that she can't proceed then it is typically the therapist's fault. As a result, clients should be given the power to veto any and all procedures which seem beyond their capacity.

4. *Start with a Success Task* One way to enhance the confidence that clients have in the advisability of prescribed activities is to ensure that the first homework assignment be a successful one. The success of the first homework assignment can be enhanced by adequate skill training, and picking a particularly innocuous target. In some cases, the therapist may go along with the client during the first few trials much like *in vivo* desensitization. Frequent phone calls may also help the client at first by providing support and badly needed reminders of guidelines to follow when completing the homework.

Regardless of these efforts, all behavior therapists have found from time to time that their clients have suffered as a result of homework gone wrong. Despite the professional's many efforts, disaster cannot always be prevented. As a result, the competent therapist is wise to consider teaching cognitive control procedures to help soften the impact of failure when it occurs.

In regard to preparing the client for occasional misadventures which occur as a result of prescribed activities, many cognitive coping strategies exist (Mahoney, 1975). However, this writer has discovered that the model proposed by Casey and McMullin (1976) is an excellent one with much utility value.

COUNTERINDICATIONS FOR USING INSTIGATION THERAPY

Not every client can profit from instigation procedures. Many clients expect and need a relationship with a professional which focuses on understanding the causes of target behaviors. Other individuals seek out a relationship with the professional in which the therapy relationship is the central focus and all significant behavior change occurs as a result of open and honest discussion of feelings and thoughts between the two participants. This "here and now" relationship would flounder badly if the therapist gave homework assignments or imposed a contingency on the client such that homework would have to be done before the next appointment occured. To many clients and therapists, any hint of a contingency interjected into therapy is suggestive of lack of unconditional positive regard and is therefore to be disdained.

Some clients come to therapy with other expectations, overt or covert, well-defined or diffuse, and wish to be served in other ways. For example, clients may simply wish to ventilate and to be heard attentively and without interruption. They may want to present their viewpoint to one who will accept that viewpoint without argument.

Some clients have magical expectations. They come to be "treated" by a doctor, a healer who will work some medical, technological or mystical miracle. This client is after eloquent assurances or pills, or even the laying-on of hands. Healing comes from the therapist, occurs during the therapy hour or soon after, and is medicine of which the treated is the passive recipient. The client's contribution to treatment is not homework, but keeping the appointment; faith; acceptance of the cure; and, hopefully, the payment of the fee.

Another type of client who is a perverted relative of the seeker-of-magic is the hard-headed business man. "Psychology is bunk," he says. "But my wife thinks I have a problem, and you can do something about it. Well, I'll give you a chance. Go to it." Frequently this client will not do his homework.

This brief list of the types of clients seeking a therapy who will not complete homework assignments is not exhaustive. There are many other cognitive sets that clients bring to therapy which counterindicate the assignment of systematic homework. One of the most common sets, though one not stated overtly by clients, is that homework makes therapy too much work. An hour of work per week on changing their feelings is what they seek, not more. They are too busy with other matters when away from therapy. The completion of homework is of lower priority than the other activities that are done in its place. Such clients may agree to do the homework but return with it uncompleted. They often explain how they had the best of intentions, but "things came up." When this occurs time after time, the client's attitude regarding therapy should be reexamined.

Another reason that clients do not do their homework can be that they are unable to start and complete it in their home setting due to competing, stronger stimuli. Much like the failure of New Year's resolutions, homework may represent a set of behaviors so incompatible with those the home environment maintains that a therapist's instructions are insufficient to give the client control over the home environment. A careful analysis of setting variables may be necessary before lead-in procedures of sufficient potency to start the homework are identified and planned. Most new behaviors require a set of skills, a place, and a time so that they may be practiced. Unless these are present for homework, it may never get "turned on."

A good example of competing stimuli is the client's family. Patterson and Gullion (1968) describe some families as having a "diffusion environment." There seems to be little consistency and regularity in the discipline of children; many competing cues and consequences surround behaviors, and behavior is erratic. Such a disorganized family environment may exist in the homes of clients unable to do their homework. Much work with the client in planning pro-homework antecedents may be necessary for it to occur in the face of all the home distractions.

Retarded or psychotic clients may present the therapist with special problems in selecting homework that they can, and will, initiate and complete. It is necessary to program small, concrete steps; involve other members of the family in facilitating homework; and devote much time to planning pro-homework antecedent controlling events. Instigative homework requires considerable client ability to absorb verbal instructions and use them as homework facilitating. Thus the client with below average intelligence will have difficulties following homework assignments. In addition, the behavior therapist is not present to observe homework and deliver reinforcing consequences. This drawback often makes instigative therapy ineffective when working with retarded or psychotic individuals who may respond only to direct intervention in the problem setting.

To a certain degree, the addicted are only marginally responsive to self-managed cues assigned as homework and designed to prevent their excessive consumption of food, drugs, cigarettes, or alcohol. A very careful analysis of the controlling cues is necessary so that antecedents to the problem behavior may be eliminated and incompatible behaviors are strengthened. Since addictions are, in the short run, strongly reinforcing, the therapist attempts to aid the client to manipulate antecedents which he often "doesn't want to" manipulate. As a result, homework often fails. In all instigation therapy, involving the use of homework assignments, the therapist relies on silent observation, recording and reporting of behaviors that are not directly observable by the therapist. The usual criticisms can be leveled regarding the unverified nature of most client data. Dishonest clients can pad data. Clients who wish to please a therapist who wants to see improvement may report more improvement than an independent observer would record. Unmotivated clients who find homework too much work will not do it, or they may use uncompleted homework as an excuse to not return to their next appointment with the therapist. The "free spirit" who values immediate, gut-level feeling may see homework, or behavioral rehearsal, as contrived, mechanistic, regimented, and unspontaneous. Self-collection of data does require a systematic, precise, organized approach to problem-solving. If the "free spirits" do collect data in the first place, they may have many errors in their data. Before homework is assigned we believe it important to determine whether a client accepts the behavioral approach, and has the behavioral repertoire necessary to successfully do homework of a particular level of complexity, for example, the illiterate should not be given a book to read.

To whatever extent practical, data involving independent verification should be obtained. For example, the successful dieter should weigh less on the office scales, and Mrs. Jones should not see her husband smoke if his data show that he has stopped. But it is this writer's belief that therapy is not the same as "hard data" research; clients who come to pay for help with a problem are, in the final analysis, the customers to be satisfied. While their data may sometimes be inaccurate, insensitive attempts to insure data validity can undermine therapist–client rapport.

Implicit questioning of honesty or excessive recording are not appreciated. A balance between certifiability and trust, precision and ease, must be established.

REFERENCES

Cain, L. F., & Willey, R. The effect of spaced learning on the curve of retention. *Journal of Experimental Psychology*, 1939, *25*, 204–214.

Casey, W., & McMullin, R. *Talk sense to yourself*. Champaign, Illinois: Research Press, 1976.

Cautela, J. R. Treatment of compulsive behavior by covert sensitization. *Psychological Record*, 1966, *16*, 33–41.

Chesney, Margeret, & Shelton, John L. A comparison of muscle relaxation and electromyogram biofeedback treatments for muscle contraction headaches. *Behavior Therapy and Experimental Psychiatry*, 1976, *7*, 221–226.

Davison, G. Systematic desensitization as a counter conditioning process. *Journal of Abnormal Psychology*, 1968, *73*, 91–99.

Deese, J. & Hulse, S. H. *The Psychology of Learning*. New York: McGraw Hill, 1967.

Dunlap, K. *Habits, their making, and unmaking*. New York: Liveright, 1932.

Ellis, Albert. *A guide to rational living*. Englewood Cliffs, New Jersey: Prentice-Hall, 1961.

Eysenck, H. J. *Experiments in Behavior Therapy*. Oxford: Pergamon Press, 1964.

Gruber, R. P. Behavior therapy: Problems in generalization. *Behavior Therapy*, 1971, *2*, 361–368.

Hall, R. Vance *Managing behavior, behavior modification: Basic principles*. Lawrence, Kansas: H & H Enterprises, 1971.

Herzberg, A. Short treatment of neurosis by graduated tasks. *British Journal of Medical Psychology*, 1941, *19*, 36–51.

Holmes, David S. R. R. therapy: A technique for implementing the effects of psychotherapy. *Journal of Clinical and Consulting Psychology*, 1971, *37*, 324–331.

Kanfer, F., & Phillips, J. A survey of current behavior and a proposal for classification. *Archives of General Psychiatry*, 1966, *15*, 114–128.

Kanfer, F., & Phillips, J. A survey of current behavior therapies and a proposal for classification. In C. M. Franks (Ed.), *Behavior therapies: Appraisal and status*. New York: McGraw-Hill, 1969.

Karpman, B. Objective psychotherapy. *Journal of Clinical Psychology*, 1949, *5*, 140–148.

Kelly, G. A. *The psychology of personal constructs*. New York: Norton, 1955.

Lazarus, A. A. *Multi-model behavior therapy*. New York: Springer, 1976.

Mahoney, M. Research issues in self-management. *Behavior Therapy*, 1972, *3*, 45–63.

Mahoney, M. *Cognition and behavior modification*. Cambridge, Massachusetts: Ballinger, 1974.

Mahoney, M. J. The self-management of covert behavior: A case study. *Behavior Therapy*, 1971, *2*, 575–578.

Mahoney, M., & Thoreson, C. *Self-control: Power to the person*. Monterey, California: Brooks-Cole, 1974.

Masters, W., & Johnson, V. *Human sexual inadequacy*. Boston: Little, 1970.

Maultsby, M. Systematic written homework in psychotherapy. *Rational Living,* 1971, *6,* 17–23.

Meichenbaum, D. Cognitive modification of test anxious college students. *Journal of Consulting and Clinical Psychology,* 1972, *39,* 370–380.

Pendleton, L. R., Shelton, J. L., & Wilson, S. E. Social interaction training using systematic homework. *The Personnel and Guidance Journal,* May, 1976, *54*(9), 484–491.

Phillips, R., & Johnson, G. Self-administered systematic desensitization. *Behavior Research and Therapy,* 1972, *10,* 93–96.

Secord, P. F., & Bachman, C. W. *Social psychology.* New York: McGraw-Hill, 1964.

Shelton, John L. Murder strikes and panic follows—can behavioral modification help? *Behavior Therapy,* 1973, *4,* 706–708.

Shelton, John L. The elimination of persistent stuttering by the use of homework assignments involving speech shadowing. *Behavior Therapy,* 1975, *6,* 392–393.

Shelton, John L. Prescribed homework assignments for the treatment of conditioned urinary retention: An instigation therapy procedure. *Behavior Medicine,* in press.

Shelton, J., & Ackerman, J. M. *Homework in counseling and psychotherapy: Examples of systematic assignments for therapeutic use by mental health professionals.* Springfield, Illinois: Thomas, 1974.

Shelton, John L. & Levy, Rona. Instigation therapy: A survey of the reported use of assigned homework activities in contemporary behavior therapy literature. *Journal of Applied Behavior Analysis,* in press.

Suinn, R. Removing emotional obstacles to learning and performance by visuo-motor behavior rehearsal. *Behavior Therapy,* 1972, *3,* 308–310.

Truax, C. B., & Carkhuff, R. R. *Toward effective counseling and psychotherapy: Training and practice.* Chicago: Aldine, 1967.

Wolpe, J. *Psychotherapy by reciprocal inhibition.* Stanford: Stanford University Press, 1958.

III

TRANSFER-ENHANCING ENVIRONMENTS

7

Parents as Real Life Reinforcers: The Enhancement of Parent-Training Effects across Conditions Other than Training[1]

W. ROBERT NAY

INTRODUCTION

The recent past has witnessed the training of a wide variety of non-professionals to serve as change agents for an equally varied population of clients. Terms like "nonprofessional," "paraprofessional" or some variation upon the professional label (e.g, "psychologist assistant") have been employed to describe these persons. While some of these extra-professional behavior change agents (BCAs) are trained for continuing careers at the para- or nonprofessional levels, many are trained with short-term, rather delimited goals in mind: to deal with some specific person, population or class of problem that they are best equipped to deal with. Within this category, parents have frequently served as mediators for their own children (Patterson, 1971; Pawlicki, 1970; Berkowitz & Graziano, 1972; O'Dell, 1974; Sloop, 1975); however, the

[1] The author wishes to thank Paul Turner and Gail Hamel for their contributions.

MAXIMIZING TREATMENT GAINS:
Transfer Enhancement in Psychotherapy

notion that the parent should be **trained** in parenting is not a new one. Within the turn-of-the-century extended family, a variety of senior family members (e.g., grandparents, aunts, and the like) were available to train prospective parents in the "art" of child rearing; and certainly this training involved heavy doses of modeling, practice and instructions, perhaps in the form of occasional admonitions.

Parent training took place in the home and the trainers were present on a full-time basis to provide training, feedback, and social or other consequences for the parents' performance. In addition, each child was exposed to the behavior of the trainee (parent) as well as the trainer and as new siblings were "born into" the family one would expect that expectations and methods would remain relatively fixed. In the absence of teams of grandparents who could be encouraged to live in the modern-day home, the contemporary BCA typically works with the parent in the clinical environment and often does not have access to both parents, let alone to the family as a functioning system. When parent training occurs at home (which is rare), it is certainly limited by a variety of practical considerations (e.g., available BCA time). These limitations suggest that a major goal of contemporary parent training is to ensure that skills and knowledge acquired in training are employed by the parents in the ordinary home setting when the BCA is not present, and ultimately, after intervention is terminated. Other intervention goals frequently include hoped-for parental administration of methods to alternative problem behaviors currently displayed by the "referred" child, as well as to unforeseen, novel behaviors as they emerge in future times. In addition, the BCA may hope that a parent who cannot, or will not, endure parent training will in some way learn more appropriate methods through exposure to the trained parent. Finally, the BCA may hope that the trained parent will be able to effectively manage children other than the referred child, given the interdependent nature of behaviors displayed by members of the interpersonal system we call a "family." It is immediately obvious that the modern-day BCA is at a real disadvantage when compared to his extended-family counterpart who was in the home on a continuous basis. In compensation, specific steps must be taken to ensure that these various goals are met.

Parent training has drawn the vast majority of its procedures from the social learning or behavior modification literature which is largely identified with an emphasis upon systematic evaluation of methods. BCAs within this camp have frequently criticized more "traditional" BCAs for their failure to assess whether or not behavior change instigated within the clinic generalizes to alternative conditions and is durable over time. In fact, those writers who have examined outcome within the behavioral intervention literature have found a large proportion of these reports to also be wanting with respect to outcome assessments. For example Keeley, Shemberg, and Carbonell (1976) reviewed 146 "operant" projects described in "leading behavioral journals [p. 293]" for the years 1972–1973 in a critical evaluation of outcome methodology. In assessing the durability of effects the authors found that only 17 studies reported "long-term follow-up" data (6 months or more), and that this represents only 11.6% of all articles analyzed. Of these, only 9 presented *hard* data (systematic observations) and of that subsample, only four were judged as "qualified or marginal successes [p. 294]." The authors found that the vast majority of studies displayed significant problems of methodology or were single case reports that did not permit a meaningful interpretation of outcome. With regard to what the authors termed *stimulus generalization,* 15 studies or 10.3% of the total sample presented hard data to show change across treated and nontreated settings. Of these, 7 were characterized as failures of stimulus generalization and 4 were judged successes, with the remaining reports falling at some point in between. Finally, the authors found that only 13 studies (or 8.9% of the total sample) reported hard *response generalization* data: behavior change across targeted and nontargeted behaviors. Of these, 2 were judged successes, 6 failures, and 7 were characterized at some point in between. The authors concluded that while these studies frequently show short-term success, they say little about "enduring, and/or generalizable changes to an unprogrammed setting [p. 302]," with few investigations even looking at the durability of effects beyond the period of 6 months.

In an exhaustive review of the methods of child behavior modification, Marholin, Siegel, and Phillips (1976) noted that the terms "stimulus generalization" and "transfer of training" have frequently been employed in an interchangeable fashion within the literature. The authors proposed that most investigators are in fact interested in promoting transfer, and that stimulus generalization applies to the more delimited goal of "finding that a response conditioned in the presence of one stimulus also occurs in the presence of other physically different, although related stimuli [Nevin, 1973, pp. 116–117]." While not specifically focused upon the issue of durability or maintenance of effects, a number of the methods that the authors discuss are clearly designed to enhance maintenance in extratherapy environments. Based upon their findings, the authors suggested that the extratherapy or criterion environment must provide avenues of incentives for behavior learned within training for transfer to occur. The authors criticized the brief follow-up periods and general lack of rigor in methodology across the various studies that they reviewed.

Thus, two recent reviews of the behavioral intervention literature, one specifically addressed to child intervention, have assessed the current state of the art and found it to be wanting. With specific regard to parent training a multitude of reviewers have drawn similar conclusions. For example, O'Dell (1974) points out that effective parent training requires three steps. Parents "must acquire the modification skills and changes in their own behavior, changes must be implemented with the child and changes must generalize and persist. Of these three steps only the implementation phase with the child has received sufficient attention [p. 430]." A review by Forehand and Atkeson (1977) specifically focused upon what they term the "generality" of treatment effects within parent training. Temporal generality was defined as the "maintenance of treatment effects following termination of treatment [p. 575]," while setting generality involves the "occurrence of treatment effects in settings other than the therapeutic one." Behavioral generality describes "changes in behaviors not targeted for treatment" while sibling generality involves "changes in the behaviors of the treated child's sibling [p. 576]." The authors summarize the status of the literature as follows:

> If one chose to disregard method of data collection and number of generalization measures (which is probably an unwise decision), a number of studies have presented support for temporal generality and setting generality from clinic to home. Generality from home to school and behavioral generality are the two areas in which the least compelling evidence is available. Few studies have investigated sibling generality, but those which have examined this area have generated data suggesting positive change in the untreated siblings. [pp. 589-590]

The authors emphasized that because **child** behavior change, supposedly related to changes in the parents' behavior, has been the criterion measure for assessing the generality, the effects of parent training can only be inferred. Therefore they urge investigators to assess the parents' behavior within the criterion setting as a routine part of assessment. Finally, while agreeing with all reviewers that parent training can produce positive outcomes within the training setting if not elsewhere, Forehand and Atkeson (1977) emphasized the need for investigation of specific components of treatment that may enhance generalization. It would be a fair summary to say that replicable correspondences between methods for programming extra-training behavior change and particular outcomes across times, settings, targets, or persons have yet to be demonstrated.

One thing that is obvious from the foregoing is the multitude of terms that writers have employed to describe behavior change beyond the strict conditions of training. This is not only confusing but may also be misleading, given that terms like transfer and generalization (generality) imply specific mechanisms of behavior change. For example, most BCAs initially focus upon helping the parent(s) change the frequency of some specific behavior (the *target*) as a means of fostering practice of methods learned within training. The same change in behaviors other than these initial targets might be variously attributed to response generalization (Keeley *et al.*, 1976), generalization (Wiltz & Patterson, 1974), behavioral generality (Forehand & Atkeson, 1977) or transfer of training (Marholin *et al.*, 1976). In fact, this behavior change could be the result of one or more of a variety of mechanisms. First, the parent(s) may indeed directly apply newly learned management skills to nontargeted behaviors and in this case transfer of training (from the conditions of training, i.e., a particular target, to other conditions, i.e., other nontargeted behaviors) has occurred. In contrast, if the term *generalization* has any meaning in this context it derives from the phenomenon of *response generalization* originally described in the animal learning laboratory. According to Hall (1966): "Most contemporary investigators who have examined response generalization have adopted an empirical definition of the concept: If Response B is associated with Stimulus A, other responses similar to B have a greater than chance probability of being elicited by A [pp. 433–434]." This suggests that behaviors similar (e.g., topographically) to the target may change merely as a function of some stimulus (e.g., parent behavior) causing the target to change. As will be pointed out in a later section, nontargeted behavior change may also occur via mechanisms other than transfer and generalization. For example, reduction of a given targeted behavior (e.g., whining; destructive–assaultive acts) may alter the child's possibilities for other behavior (e.g., **playing** with other children who now are willing to approach the child). If the BCA is to enhance extra-training behavior change, it is clear that the mechanisms of such change must be clearly understood.

The goal of this chapter is to explore those mechanisms by which behavior change instigated by parent training can be maintained over time and shown across certain extra-training conditions. To avoid confusion, specific methods for accomplishing these goals will be linked to a proposed mechanism of change. Because variants of the term generalization or transfer define particular mechanisms of change and are inappropriate when applied to all cases, this chapter will employ the acronym COT (conditions other than training) to define the general goal of enhancing behavior change beyond the strict conditions of training.

In order to obtain a clear picture of the current state of the art and to provide a data base for presenting and evaluating methods that might enhance some category of COT change, the author reviewed reports of parent training for the years 1972–1977. Earlier reports, reports of a technical nature, reviews of the literature and analogue experiments not directed toward instigating clinical behavior change may be discussed but are not included in a final sample of 37 reports that will repeatedly be referred to.[2]

The author was immediately faced with the question of how to organize the varied and in some cases unique methodologies that have been employed to enhance some category of COT. Previous authors have organized the literature around a sequential presentation of method categories, with examples from the literature illustrating each (e.g., Marholin, Siegel, & Phillips, 1976), while others have discussed methods within the context of categories of COT to which they have been applied (e.g., Forehand & Atkeson, 1977). Given that a particular clinical decision (e.g., training within the home versus the clinic; treating the family at large versus a parent–child dyad) may very well predict the goals for behavior change beyond training conditions and may also limit methodological possibilities, it would seem fruitful to employ the methodological choices/decisions made by the BCA as major sign posts for organizing the material that follows. Following a brief discussion of each major method option, the implications of that option for COT enhancement will be discussed within the context of the sample studies. Mechanisms by which COT change may occur will be offered, followed by a review of enhancement methods employed within the literature. In some cases findings derived from "nonclinical" disciplines within psychology (e.g., the experimental or social psychological laboratory) will be specifically referred to in offering methodological suggestions for future research.

INSTIGATING BEHAVIOR CHANGE IN THE HOME

The first step in any program of training is to insure that the trainee has in fact acquired knowledge or mastered a targeted skill within the

[2] Four earlier studies are included in the sample due to their frequent citation in the literature and relevance to this chapter. Sample studies are rated by an asterisk in the reference section for this chapter.

training environment. In fact, all of the studies within our sample employed some form of pre–post assessment of mastery, although assessment methods varied from paper and pencil reports to observations using a formal coding system. While it is the parent who is trained, the criteria for mastery are most often behavioral changes on the child's part presumably mediated by the parent's behavior change. This supports Forehand and Atkeson's (1977) finding that few BCAs attempt to systematically link the child's behavior to training-instigated parent behavioral change. Certainly child behavior change **outside of** parent behavior change is difficult to explain from within the parent-training paradigm, and may reflect factors other than training.

Once the parent demonstrates mastery within the training setting the BCA must insure that mastery criteria are met within the criterion setting, which is typically the home. If the home is selected as the locus of training this obviates the necessity of fostering behavior change from the clinic or laboratory to the home setting, eliminating one domain of COT that the BCA must plan for in designing training. Given this initial advantage, it should also be noted that home training may add to the costs of intervention and may be impractical for many BCAs who are unable to expend time necessary for travel and visits within the home. In fact, only 19% of the sample investigators trained parents exclusively within the home environment. It should also be noted that regardless of the training site, the home is often visited by observers for assessment purposes, and the role that these persons may play in providing inadvertent feedback or avenues of training to the parents is frequently not clear in methodological reports.

All of the sample reports of home-based training are case studies, treating families using a gamut of training procedures such as verbal instruction, modeling, role playing and feedback (sometimes via cues) as reported elsewhere (O'Dell, 1974; Berkowitz & Graziano, 1972; Pawlicki, 1970; Sloop, 1975; Johnson & Katz, 1973). Given the cost of traveling to the parent's home, it is interesting to note that most of the investigators spent considerable periods of time in providing training and ongoing feedback to parents. For example, Lavigueur (1976) employed 30 sessions of approximately 45 min each to train two sets of parents to reduce the negative verbalizations, noncompliance and aggressive behavior of their children, while Resick, Forehand, and McWhorter (1976) employed 55 home sessions to train a parent to use time out procedure to increase her child's compliance with requests. Other efforts range from four and seven sessions of about 30 to 60 minutes to train two sets of parents in the use of time out procedure (Wahler, 1969) to 28, 1-hour sessions (Zeilberger, Sampen, & Sloane, 1968), and

20 to 24 sessions of 20 minutes each (Colletti & Harris, 1977). While all of these studies report a successful outcome, it is obvious that this represents quite a time investment for the BCA.

If the BCA decides to conduct parent training within the clinic or laboratory setting, the question of enhancing concomitant behavior change in the home immediately arises. Of those studies that employed clinic-based training, a full 60% assessed pre–post behavioral change on the part of the referred child or parent within the home. In all cases, observable single-case behavior change or statistically significant behavior change across subjects was found immediately following clinic training. The remainder of the sample failed to assess parent or child behavior in the home which is rather remarkable given the emphasis upon evaluation and accountability within the behavioral intervention literature. It should be noted that some investigators, while not conducting home assessments, train and assess parents within clinic-based analogues that simulate the home setting in some fashion (e.g., Forehand & King, 1977; Budd, Green, & Baer, 1976; Gardner, Forehand, & Roberts, 1976). For example, Forehand and his associates employ standardized situations in which the parent is observed while playing a game or making a request of the child. Along these lines, it is comforting to note that 53% of all studies employing clinic-based treatment supplemented parent reports and written assessments with systematic observations of some kind, either conducted within the clinic or the home proper. The length of training varied quite considerably across investigations, ranging from 1 hour (Herbert & Baer, 1972) to 106 hours, 5- to 20-min sessions across 25 weeks (Budd et al., 1976). Thirteen (43%) reports of clinic treatment employed the group as a vehicle for training, with group meetings ranging from 1 highly focused session (Nay, 1975) to 16, 3-hour sessions directed toward general principles as well as personalized intervention targets (Hall, Axelrod, Tyler, Grief, Jones, & Robertson, 1972).

Few investigators made specific reference to COT enhancement in describing clinic treatment methods even though fostering extra-training change is an implicit goal for virtually any therapeutic transaction that occurs outside of the criterion environment. Of course, the very act of training the parent as BCA is an attempt to foster extra-clinic change (Forehand & Atkeson, 1977). The parent, once trained, is present in the home on a full-time basis to serve as mediator, and presumably is motivated to see things change. In addition, it has already been pointed out that seemingly regardless of methodology, parents are very likely to be able to display newly found skills within the home immediately following training; perhaps leading BCAs to assume that specific steps at enhancement are unnecessary.

Enhancement procedures most often attempt to foster transfer of training from clinic to home by encouraging the parent to practice skills learned within the training setting at home, and ensuring that positive consequences for instigating newly learned skills are present within the home environment. While not often employed, environmental and stimulus manipulations designed to increase stimulus generalization across the training and criterion (home) environments will also be described.

The "Homework" Assignment

While some investigators report that parents are given assignments to complete at home during training, this author would not be surprised to find that the employment of homework assignments is even more widespread than reported. The rationale for homework is to get the parent to transfer the employment of novel procedures to the home **as training proceeds,** rather than relying upon immediate transfer following training. A major advantage is that the BCA can focus training around areas of difficulty that emerge from the parent's report of homework completion. Assignments typically involve the parent's monitoring of the child's or the parent's own behavior, or the practice of certain procedures (e.g., praising appropriate behavior; employment of time-out procedure).

With regard to self-monitoring, a wide variety of investigators have found that an individual's behavior frequently changes merely as a function of monitoring (see Kanfer, 1970; Kazdin, 1974; Nay, 1979 for reviews). The well-known parent-training program developed by Gerald Patterson and his colleagues was among the first to employ parent record keeping as a standard training procedure (see Patterson, Cobb, & Ray, 1973 for an excellent overview of this program). Patterson (1971) provides an explicit description of the kinds of instructions provided to parents for data collecting:

> On this data recording sheet you put the date and the time that you start. If it is something that you do not do all day, then you record here the time when the kids get up, or whenever it is that you begin to observe. Write the beginning time down here; and then also write down when you stop. For example, bed time. Write that down here. That way we can figure out total time in minutes ... and the number of whatever you count is over here, just a plain tally. You should have your piece of paper and pencil someplace where it is convenient for you to use it; or you might use this golf counter so you won't have to worry about the paper and pencil. [pp. 754–755]

For parents who experience difficulty in carrying out the task, Patterson reports that daily telephone calls are used to prompt data recording and provide verbal reinforcement for the parent's efforts. Patterson and his colleagues hope that self-monitoring will improve the precision with which parents describe the behavior of their children and teach them to better observe important events as they occur. Along similar lines, Johnson (1971) trained two parents to record the number of minutes during meal time that their children engaged in inappropriate behavior, while Bernal (1969) asked for daily notes of "conflicts" ("what the child and mother did and said, and how the conflict ended. [p. 377]") as a means of defining goals for intervention. An explicit account of the procedures employed to train these parents to self-monitor is not provided by these authors and this is typical within the literature. In contrast to its use as an adjunctive procedure, Herbert and Baer (1972) studied the role of self-recording of contingent attention as a primary parent-training method. Two parents were trained within a 1-hour orientation session in definitions for attention and "appropriate" child behavior (a total of 70 behaviors on the parents' lists were defined as either appropriate or inappropriate) and asked to begin counting appropriate behavior in the home using wrist counters. Independent home observations showed that with the implementation of self-recording, the percentage of maternal attention to appropriate behavior increased as did the child's appropriate behavior. When the parent was asked to stop counting, the percentage of appropriate behaviors displayed by the child did not revert to former conditions, but remained stabilized. When the parents were again asked to count, the percentage of child appropriate behavior continued to climb to about 85% of the time. Follow-ups at 4 and 24 weeks posttraining indicated that treatment gains were maintained by both parents. It is interesting to note that the two parents made these gains even though they showed only 46% and 72% agreement, respectively, when their records were compared to those of independent observers.

Johnson, Christensen, and Bellamy (1976) required parents within five families to systematically record the frequency and/or duration of a targeted behavior of their choosing 1 week prior to intervention, and during intervention for as long as the behavior remained a focus for treatment. In contrast to many reports, the authors employed parent data as one of an array of multiple criteria (see Eyberg & Johnson, 1974) for evaluating the impact of intervention. Parent-collected data on a mean of 6.8 problems across the families showed an average reduction (from baseline to the last 3 weeks of active treatment) of 77%, with a range of 58–91%. Thus parent records, when employed with multiple modalities of measurement (e.g., independent observations, parent-written self-reports, the reports of significant others) can provide a comprehensive data base for evaluating outcome. Eyberg and Johnson (1974) made therapist time contingent upon parent home data collection. The therapist would contact the parent via telephone to determine whether or not data had been collected for a given week. If not, the therapist immediately cancelled the treatment session and restated the contingency. Thus the parents' home efforts were readily monitored and reinforced by the therapist, and similar procedures could of course be applied to any homework task. If parent record keeping holds some therapeutic benefit for parents, we would hope that parents continue to monitor once formal treatment is terminated. One study that investigated the durability of monitoring found that only 1 parent in 20 continued to keep records at an 8-month follow-up (Boren & Jagodzinski, 1975). Methods that might be employed to enhance continued parent employment of newly learned procedures will be the subject of a later section.

As an example of homework that involves the practice of intervention procedures, Rinn, Vernon, and Wise (1975) report that the admission of some 1130 parents over a 3-year period to each of five weekly training classes was contingent upon the mastery of five discreet steps for changing their children's behavior. These steps involved specifying the behavior to be changed, measuring its base rate and setting a goal for intervention, identifying rewards and punishers, developing a program for changing the consequences of the behavior, and measuring the consequated behavior. The homework ensured that once a procedure had been practiced in the clinic session, it would be practiced at home prior to moving on to additional steps within training. An "instructor's assistant" kept track of the parents' completion of homework assignments and made constructive criticisms of "program sheets" that each parent completed to show that homework goals had been met. The authors report that 79% of all single parents and couples completed their program sheets throughout the course of the 3-year period. As another example, Forehand and King (1977) trained mothers within standard laboratory situations to learn basic skills involving verbal rewards and use of time out procedure. Following each mother's interaction with her child in the laboratory situation, she was instructed to practice at home for two 5-min periods each day. An additional homework assignment required parents to identify 10 verbal rewards that they could employ with their children. Unfortunately, assessment of outcome was conducted within the clinical setting, so that the transfer of parent and child behavior change to the home is unknown.

Reinforcement for Extra-Setting Instigation

If transfer is to occur it would seem to be critically important that the parent's initial efforts at employing newly learned skills be supported by the home environment. A later section of this paper will document the general failure of BCAs to provide for avenues of support other than BCA-mediated praise and feedback. The BCA should be sure to examine potential avenues of reinforcement that exist within the home and attempt to identify any impediments to home use of procedures. Along these lines it is most important that all adults who would serve as mediators within the home have a clear understanding of methods prior to initiating their use. Whenever possible, both parents (or other relevant adults or siblings) should be included within training. Frequently, an untrained parent fails to understand or misinterprets instructions given to the trained parent. Minimally, this parent may fail to provide a "consistent front" in supporting the trained parent's efforts; at worst, this parent may actively attempt to sabotage the trained parent's efforts, particularly if parent training is overlaid upon a marital communication system that is poor or a marriage that we might describe as troubled. This speculation is supported by the findings of Reisinger, Frangia, and Hoffman (1976) who found that mothers who did not report difficulties in their marriages attended to 33% more cooperative and 50% less oppositional behavior following parent training and reported more frequent use of procedures in other environments and with other children and behaviors than their troubled counterparts. It is worth reporting the authors' hypotheses regarding these findings:

> The oversimplistic explanation for the preceding training outcome differences might be attributable to paternal "support." That is, the most successful mothers had husbands who purportedly reinforced the learning and usage of differential reinforcement techniques. Husband-supplied reinforcement took the form of repeated, voluntary visits to the clinic and praise of their wives during the mothers' training period. Less successful mothers reported little or no husband reinforcement, occasional punishment (i.e., verbal disapproval directed to the mother when using techniques in the home), frequent (i.e., bi-weekly) arguments, and some extra-marital relationships. The effects of such interactions are probably detrimental to therapeutic efficacy [p. 339].

The authors suggest that systematic research might evaluate the specific point at which marital status contributes to outcome and note the need for an evaluation of the marriage as a part of pretreatment assessment. Patterson et al. (1973) report upon the need for individuation of their parent training procedures when marital difficulties exist, and, as a result, Patterson has also developed a program for marital intervention (e.g., Patterson & Hops, 1972).

If both parents cannot be present within training, the BCA would do well to consider instructing the trained parent in ways of presenting child management procedures to the untrained parent; in a sense, to train the parent to train others. As an additional bonus, the trained parent must carefully rehearse learned procedures in order to be able to train others in their use. When both parents actively employ the procedures they are more likely to be employed consistently, to be noted and commented upon by the alternative parent, and to be reinforced within the parents' ordinary interactions. The author believes that we so frequently see immediate transfer to the home because the BCA provides a rich schedule of positive feedback for the parent's efforts within the context of monitoring homework assignments and successes and failures at home intervention. Because intervention will not be judged a success unless the parent's efforts at home are maintained over time, the BCA would do well to build in avenues of support and reinforcement for the parent that are likely to be present on a continuous and ongoing basis. It is most unfortunate that such procedures are rarely described within the literature.

Enhancing Stimulus Generalization

Within the animal and human learning literatures, generalization of responding from one set of stimulus conditions to some other set of conditions is typically related to the similarity between training and criterion stimuli (see Nevin, 1973; Hall, 1966). In the child behavior modification literature this often takes the form of creating a training environment that, in its physical characteristics, approximates some criterion environment (e.g., classroom, home, cottage). Or characteristics of trainers may be varied to ensure similarity with the persons present (e.g., teachers, parents) in the criterion setting. For example, in training a 9-year-old child to reduce self-injurious behavior, Reiss and Redd (1970) found that this behavior increased in frequency when a new therapist was introduced. To enhance generalization across BCAs the authors decided to systematically introduce multiple trainers. After the fourth and fifth novel trainer was introduced the child was found to maintain low levels of the target. In a real sense, this child was now failing to discriminate between the distinctive characteristics of trainers. Along similar lines, Barrett and McCormack (1973) have employed multiple tutors in training children to perform certain academic tasks. Finally, Goldstein (1973) and Goldstein, Heller, and Sechrest (1966) have recommended the employment of more than one psychotherapist as a means of fostering extrasetting generalization.

With regard to the physical characteristics of the setting, Griffiths and Craighead (1972) decided to vary the locus of training to include a therapy room as well as a cottage, and found that the employment of multiple training settings led to increased generalization of the child's behavior to a novel classroom. Emshoff, Redd, and Davidson (1976) successfully obtained generalization outside of the training setting by varying multiple factors present within training: the trainer, the activity, as well as the setting itself.

In contrast to the literature describing therapist training of children, this author found only two reports of parent training that explicitly employed stimulus manipulations as a means of fostering extrasetting generalization. Wiltz and Gordon (1974) constructed an apartment-like setting within the clinic to train the parents of a 9-year-old hyperactive, aggressive youngster to cope with a variety of the child's acts (e.g., urinating over the toilet facilities and walls; throwing eggs; lighting matches; locking himself in the bathroom; throwing fruit). A three-bedroom apartment was devised that permitted observational access to this family via microphones and one-way mirrors when the family interacted within the living room, kitchen and one bedroom. While the authors provide a rather vague description of training procedures, it is clear the family lived within the apartment for a period of 5 days, frequently receiving training and feedback from the BCAs. The authors report a significant reduction in destructive acts during training which continued into the home environment. Unfortunately, data collected by the parents at home was not supplemented by independent observations, although the authors did provide continued supervision via telephone. Hanf and Kling (1973) also report the use of a simulated home environment within the clinic. The parent was asked to interact with her child within this environment while the authors provided feedback via a bug-in-the-ear device. Unfortunately, independent observations were not carried out within the home to assess generalization.

At present the efficacy of varying elements of trainer-in-setting to foster stimulus similarity with the criterion environment is questionable and further research would be a desirable addition to the literature.

MAINTAINING CHANGE ACROSS TIME

Given that the parent can display trained behaviors and is able to employ them in the criterion-home setting, a question immediately arises:

How can the current and presumably desirable frequency of the parent's newly learned behavior be maintained over time following formal training? This period of time is frequently referred to as the *follow-up* within the literature. In contrast to the recommendations of virtually every reviewer of the parent-training literature (e.g., O'Dell, 1974; Berkowitz & Graziano, 1972), only 19 studies, or 51% of the sample, reported follow-up data beyond 4 weeks posttreatment. Of those investigators who did employ the follow-up, a full 37% failed to report the *hard* data used as a criterion by Keeley *et al.* (1976) in their review of the "operant" literature. For example, Bernal (1969), Wagner (1968), and Boren and Jagodzinski (1975) interviewed the parent following intervention, while Wiltz and Gordon (1974) employed parent-collected data as a criterion for successful follow-up. Along similar lines, Rinn *et al.* (1975) and Ferber, Keeley, and Shemberg (1974) employed a telephone interview. While Ferber *et al.* (1974) did employ coding procedures similar to those used by Patterson (Patterson, Ray, Shaw, & Cobb, 1969) for five follow-up observations during the first 2 months following intervention, a 12-month follow-up was conducted via a telephone inquiry that inquired: "How is the child presently functioning? What behavior modification strategies are you now using? What are you doing differently because of the program? [p. 416]." Finally, Glogower and Sloop (1976) assessed the maintenance of group parent training at a 5-month follow-up by employing a written analogue that required parents to write down what they would say and/or do in response to described situations involving children.

The most extensive follow-ups are reported by Patterson and his colleagues (e.g., Arnold, Levine, & Patterson, 1975; see Patterson *et al.*, 1973) using the well-known Behavioral Coding System (BCS) employed by well-trained, professional observers. Significantly, Arnold *et al.* (1975) conducted a total of 15 follow-up observations within the home: 12 during the first 6 months and 3 over the remaining 3 months of the follow-up year. The authors reported successful maintenance of effects over the first 6 months, however, notable attrition in the sample was observed at 12 months follow-up. Unaccounted-for families contained more deviant siblings at baseline than those families who were available for follow-up observations. It is frequently difficult to obtain the cooperation of families for extensive follow-ups, and thus most important to examine the characteristics of the follow-up sample in qualifying results.

The remaining investigators who employed home observations at follow-up conducted significantly fewer observations over a more restricted period of time. For example, Bernal (1970); Forehand, Sturgis, Aguar, Green, McMahon, and Wells (1976); Herbert and Baer (1972);

Karoly and Rosenthal (1977); Miller and Cantwell (1976); and Colletti and Harris (1977) all performed only one or two follow-up probes conducted within the first 6 months following intervention. Johnson and Christensen (1975) conducted two observational follow-ups at 3 and 8 months, respectively, while Reisinger et al. (1976) conducted three follow-up observations at 12 months. It is interesting to note that Johnson and Christensen also report significant differences in their original and follow-up samples and this author suspects that this is frequently the case. Assessments were undertaken in the clinical setting, by Forehand and King (1977) and Budd et al. (1976) who employed systematic observations within clinic-standardized or analogue situations to demonstrate successful maintenance of parenting skills over 3 and 4 months, respectively. While observations within the home would of course be desirable, the analogue assessments provide an additional data channel beyond the parent's self-report or responses to paper and pencil stimuli and should certainly be encouraged in future investigations. Eyberg and Johnson (1974) present an example of the employment of home and analogue-collected observational data as two of a series of information categories assessed within parent training, and illustrate how any one channel (e.g., observations in the home) may produce misleading results if evaluated in isolation.

It should be noted that all of these investigations reported maintenance of treatment effects at follow-up, as indicated by visual inspection of case study findings or statistical criteria, with the exception of Ferber et al. (1974) and the previously noted lack of maintenance of parent self-monitoring found by Boren and Jagodzinski (1975). Ferber et al. (1974) found children in only one of seven families continued to show high levels of compliance to parental requests at 12 months. In contrast, half of the families had shown desirable change during a 3-month follow-up. These two negative results are based upon data collected via the telephone, whereas all investigators who employed independently gathered observation data for follow-up report positive results.

In summary, of roughly 50% of the total sample that report follow-up data, a significant portion employ interviews performed directly or via the telephone, or very limited occasions of observation conducted during the first 6-month period as criteria for success. While many positive findings are reported, it would be safe to say that the **long-term** effects of parent training upon the family have yet to be documented. If the specific elements of training that can be related to successful maintenance are to be unearthed, systematic and scheduled follow-ups—using multiple and divergent data channels—must be undertaken to obtain a comprehensive picture of change within the family system over time. Patterson (1974) encourages investigators to replicate their methods across multiple groupings of families and points out the importance of dismantling the multi-faceted technology that has been applied to parent training in order that specific components can be related to outcome:

> It is imperative that an analysis be made of the contribution of various aspects of the treatment procedures. It is not at all clear which of the treatment components are essential, if indeed any of them are. Analyses of this kind would probably underline the fact that some of the components require a good deal of professional time, but contribute very little to the overall treatment effectiveness [p. 319].

Those investigators who take the time to assess the durability of parent and/or child behavior change rarely report specific steps taken to enhance maintenance; they attempt to explain its occurrence in post-hoc fashion. In presenting those procedures that might be employed to enhance maintenance this author has included methods that represent a best guess based upon a kind of face validity decision process. These methods fall into the following categories: (a) the act of follow-up itself, as a tool for prompting and reinforcing the parent's efforts; (b) avenues of retraining; (c) systematically fading out the BCA as trainer; and (d) attempts to somehow reprogram the home environment to provide continued avenues of support and reinforcement for the parent's efforts. The first two categories have received considerably more attention in the literature.

BCA Contacts at Follow-up

It has been noted that approximately 50% of reports of parent training include some provision for contact with the parents following termination of treatment. While these contacts are typically aimed at assessment, it is obvious that this monitoring might in itself prompt parents to continue using the intervention strategies learned within training. Given the fact that the BCA will be privy to information collected within these probes, and that the parent in some fashion values the BCA or wishes to present a positive picture, it would seem likely that parents might well be vigilant in carrying out procedures at least when the assessments are made. Johnson and Bolstad (1975) are among investigators who have shown that parents can manipulate their children's behavior to look "good" or "bad" if they are motivated to do so, and an entire body of literature suggests that persons (e.g., observers) who are aware that their actions are being assessed behave in a more task-congruent fashion (in line with the assessor's expectations) than when they are unaware of assessments (e.g., Reid, 1970; Kent, O'Leary, Diament, & Dietz, 1974). It is a short step to generalize these findings to parent behavior in the home under well-defined, delimited, and highly salient conditions of assessment across the months of follow-up.

Obviously, this issue calls into question the validity of data obtained under obtrusive observational assessment. One would imagine that parents who are made aware that an assessment is imminent, perhaps some weeks in advance, might make preparations to present themselves in a positive light, perhaps even instructing family members to behave in a particular, task-consonant fashion. It would certainly be possible for many families to maintain this pose during the abbreviated (typically 1–2 hour) observation sessions that take place on rare and irregular occasions. It is also important to note that many families do not permit such follow-up assessments (a portion of the attrition within the sample). One possible explanation is that they are either dissatisfied with the services provided (perhaps due to outcome?), or are unwilling to show themselves in a poor light given the failure of intervention gains to be maintained. While these are rather discouraging possibilities, they are certainly well within the realm of possibility. In fact, Kent (1976) has called into question the findings reported by Patterson (1974) due to the attrition present in Patterson's follow-up sample and other methodological inadequacies (see Reid & Patterson, 1976 for a rebuttal). The employment of assessments across interview, written, self- and independent-observational methodological facets on a more continuous basis following intervention would seem to go a long way toward ensuring a more comprehensive and representative sample of the behavior of family members. While this author would commend the BCA for performing multiple follow-up assessments, the issues raised would suggest that additional enhancement methods should be employed to ensure parent performance of procedures outside of assessments and to ensure the maintenance of gains once the follow-up assessment period (often quite abbreviated within the literature) is ended. Another method, that is related to the follow-up assessment, is the provision of periodic retraining or "booster" sessions.

Periodic Retraining

One way of ensuring the maintenance of treatment gains is to systematically gate those parents who display "drift" (from employing

methods as originally taught) or other difficulties back into the therapeutic environment for additional training. This training might occur
either within the home or clinical setting, and would ideally be specifically focused upon those problems of implementation that emerge from
follow-up assessments. Patterson and his colleagues have been fore-
most in employing avenues of retraining to parents once intervention
is terminated (see Patterson *et al.*, 1973 for a detailed account). These
investigators employ written handouts for parents to refresh their
memory as to program procedures (the "Vest Pocket Refresher Course"),
as well as readmission to individual or group intervention as defined
by the parents' behavioral assets and deficits. Because of the extensiveness of follow-up assessments within the Patterson program (up to 15
over the first year), these BCAs are in an excellent position to detect
problems in implementation as they emerge and tailor avenues of
remediation (from simple verbal feedback to extensive modeling and
role playing) to the parent's behavioral needs. The limited follow-ups
performed by other investigators would certainly restrict possibilities
for retraining, unless the BCA merely programs future "reunion"
meetings among individuals or group members at the time of termination. When extensive follow-up assessments are not undertaken it would
seem that contracts between the BCA and parents to discuss progress
at certain prearranged times would be a minimally acceptable means
of ensuring that necessary retraining occurs.

   Other examples of retraining include the work of Bernal (1970) and
Kogan and Gordon (1975). Bernal describes a series of individual cases
of parent training involving a multitude of standard procedures already discussed. For one case, a follow-up at 60 weeks showed that
the mother was still not employing some of the procedures taught
within training to deal with her physically aggressive son. The author
provided specific instructions to the parent to assist her in training her
child to discriminate those occasions when physical aggressiveness is
appropriate (e.g., when he was hit by another boy of his own size)
and those occasions when he could not hit back. It is obvious from
Bernal's case description that she had a very warm relationship with
this parent which facilitated the parent's acceptance of additional training and would presumably increase the possibility that a parent would
let the BCA know if things were not going well. Kogan and Gordon
(1975) constructed a parent training program modeled after that of
Hanf and Kling (1973) to train 30 mothers to increase their repertoire
of skills for interacting with their children. Following 8 weeks of instruction, 8 weeks of no contact with family members was followed
by an additional two sessions during which feedback was provided to

the parents on an individual problem-tailored basis. Unfortunately, no follow-up beyond this period is reported, making it impossible to evaluate the efficacy of this booster session.

Fading Procedures

Within the animal and human learning literatures, a continuous and often rich schedule of reinforcement is employed to systematically "shape" the frequency of a targeted behavior to some desired level, followed by a schedule that involves providing reinforcements on a less than continuous schedule. In some cases, a time interval defines when reinforcements will be offered, while in other cases, reinforcements are offered after some fixed number of correct responses (interval versus ratio schedules). In addition, the schedule itself may be fixed or varied with respect to time or number of correct responses between reinforcements, and a vast variety of investigators have found variable schedules to increase the number of responses offered during extinction when all reinforcement is terminated (see Nevin, 1973; Ferster & Skinner, 1957). A central notion for explaining this phenomenon is that a partial schedule of reinforcement makes it difficult for the subject to clearly discriminate between training and criterion conditions, thus enhancing stimulus generalization between the two.

Within the child behavior modification literature, varied schedules of reinforcement are typically employed with young children in a highly controlled learning environment. The impact of schedule manipulations within training upon the maintenance of adult behavior outside of the training environment has not been demonstrated and this approach has rarely been employed within parent training. Instead, a variant upon the theme, namely, the systematic fading out of the BCA (and BCA mediated reinforcement) or the management methods themselves, has been reported by a few authors. For example, in a study previously described, Herbert and Baer (1972) trained two parents to use a golf counter to record each instance of attention to appropriate behavior with the observer present, and also for 1 hour each day at a time when they were not observed as a means of promoting "generality of any changes in the mother's behavior that might occur with counting [p. 143]." This intervention resulted in a change in the percentage of child appropriate behavior within the home which seemed to closely approximate changes in the mother's **attention** to appropriate behavior as a result of the monitoring. In an attempt to "promote the maintenance of the improvements in maternal attention" the authors instructed one mother to employ the golf counter on an intermittent basis (3 days out of a 21-day period), programmed in advance. Follow-up observations made over the next 5 months showed these behavioral gains to be maintained. Along similar lines Hall *et al.* (1972) trained a mother to decrease the frequency of performance checks which resulted in monetary pay-offs for her child from five times per day to once per day to once every 2 weeks. Treatment gains were maintained over that period of time.

Wiltz and Gordon (1974) trained the parents of a 9-year-old hyperactive, aggressive boy to employ a token economy that made points earned contingent upon the child's compliance and appropriate behavior. The authors trained the parents to gradually increase the amount of time the child had to display appropriate behavior in order to earn points, employing a variable schedule of reinforcement. Unfortunately, the authors' procedural description is quite vague, and of course the intermittent schedule was not applied to the parents but by the parents to the child. Finally, Eyberg and Johnson (1974) described the individualized training of 17 families characterized as having a child with *active behavior problems* (aggressiveness, destructiveness, disobedience, hyperactivity, temper tantrums or high rate activity with annoyance value). The authors provide a rather limited description of the specific parent training procedures employed (patterned after Patterson *et al.*, 1973) but do make the point that parents became increasingly responsible for program modification. The authors report that in every case, "parents became increasingly more responsible for the design, modification, and fading of treatment programs [p. 598]." Specific criteria by which the therapist was faded out are not reported.

In fading out the role of the BCA, avenues of BCA reinforcement for the parent's efforts are also placed on a more intermittent schedule, perhaps reducing the formal distinction between training and termination, and follow-up (which might also involve delimited amounts of BCA supervision and support). At present the few and distinctly different variants of fading employed within parent training make it most difficult to evaluate the promise of fading as a COT enhancing procedure.

The Family as a Consequation System: Implications for Maintenance of Parent Behavior

Most reports of parent training include a description of avenues of verbal and physical, and in some cases material reinforcement supplied by parents to their children, contingent upon appropriate behavior. Along similar lines, negative consequences, in particular, time-out procedure, are frequently employed as a means of reducing classes of inappropriate child behavior. Given this emphasis upon consequation as a means of instigating and maintaining behavior, one would imagine that systematic avenues of consequation are frequently provided to encourage the maintenance of the **parents'** behavior. Reviewing the sample studies, this author found only 16 reports (about 43%) that included a specific account of consequences made contingent upon the parent's behavior. Nine of these defined the BCA's actions (e.g., praise) as the sole locus of reinforcement, while others employed variants of a token economy or contracting, with a monetary deposit frequently made contingent upon parent attendance and/or carrying out of training procedures (Eyberg & Johnson, 1974; Bernal, 1970; Peine & Munro, 1973; Wagner, 1968; Rinn et al., 1975; Glogower & Sloop, 1976; and Hall et al., 1972). In all cases, consequences were provided by the BCA **during** the course of training. No investigator reported systematic procedures for reinforcing parents' management efforts **following** termination; that is, no reinforcement was provided for maintenance. Before suggesting possible avenues of support for the parent's efforts it may be useful to examine the interdependent system of persons that makes up the family; the medium within which a newly trained parent must translate the fruits of training into behavior change. The author will attempt to illustrate that the family system may not passively tolerate change instigated from outside. The ways in which families might initially deal with change should also say something about potential strategies for enhancing long-term change.

While the cast of characters may vary across families, the trained parent (single parent or married) is a member of an ongoing system; a system that has evolved over a period of time that is considerably longer than time spent within parent training; a system within which certain roles have been defined for parents and children that involve expectancies to behave in a particular way; a system where established lines of authority may already exist as communications are passed from parent to parent, parent to child or among siblings. Parent's expectancies for children's behavior and development at a given age, their communication styles and consequation emphasis (e.g., negative versus positive), as well as their current repertoire of management methods have evolved from long exposure to parental models as well as previous trial and error behavior with their own children. For the child's part, expectations have developed regarding how the parent will likely behave in response to certain child behaviors; and depending upon the age of the child, such expectations may be well-established via a long learning history. Also, the child has learned how other family members expect him to behave via the rules, implicit norms and traditions that have evolved within the family's history. In addition to behavioral norms for self and parent, each sibling within the family certainly holds expectancies for and has developed characteristic ways of communicating with other siblings (e.g., Watzlawick, Beavin, & Jackson, 1967; Haley, 1963, 1976; Sullivan, 1953). The foregoing suggests that exposure to information and alternative management strategies within parent training is in fact overlaid upon a well-established learning history and ongoing family system. To the extent that the parent trainers' conceptualization of parent–child behavior is consonant with the parents', and that assigned tasks and behavioral goals of training mesh with the goals and expectations of family members, one would expect that immediate behavior change as well as maintenance of change would be much easier for the BCA to instigate. If this is not so, it is not hard to imagine that the BCA will meet with some degree of failure which may be labeled as "resistance."

Let us imagine a typical scenario: A mother from within an intact family system attends a "child-management" group for parents. Within the first two meetings she is exposed to lists of verbal and material reinforcements that she is expected to consider employing with her child, as well as modeling videotapes that show parents providing rich regimens of praise and some form of token currency (e.g., coins, marks on a chart, stars) that can be traded in for "rewarding activities" selected by the child. The parent is provided with a homework assignment that involves spending 15–20 min each evening in rewarding the targeted child with a game or other activity of the child's choosing, and encouraged to employ a similarly rich schedule of rewards when the child is caught being "good." With some modification, the reader would probably agree that these are components of many parent training programs. Now let us also assume that within this family there is, at present, little in the way of positive feedback for appropriate behavior provided by members to other members along verbal or material lines. Both parents emerged from families within which children were provided with very explicit expectations and role definitions for their own behavior (e.g., "seen and not heard"; "respect your elders") and both parents, particularly the father, received frequent spankings that were loosely contingent upon a wide variety of events. Both of these parents can recall few instances of their own parents telling them that they had done a "good job" or providing "a rich schedule" of verbal rewards; in fact, their parents rarely showed signs of approval or affection to one another. Within our present parents' marriage both partners feel that they are "more liberal" than their own parents and yet they behave in much the same manner: Appropriate and rule-consonant behavior is expected and is part of one's responsibilities as a family member and is rarely attended to in any way by the parents or by other siblings. In contrast, violations of the rules, "disrespect," or "backtalk" are among categories of negative behavior that are frequently met with verbal reprimands, orders to "go to one's room" and slaps and hits about the face and behind (depending upon the severity of the act, as judged by the parents at the moment). Family members tend to show affection toward one another in nonverbal ways. For example, these parents are very apt to attend the children's Little League games, participate in Boy Scouts, and to help the children with their homework, and in some cases physical affection is transmitted by a push, blow to the arm or other physical communication. The author and the reader can well imagine the impact of this mother coming home from a second group meeting to implement the present homework assignment. This assumes that she has not dropped out of the group upon being asked to engage in behavior that is quite beyond her ordinary repertoire and is very likely to meet with negative consequences when she attempts to explain the assignment to her husband. Assuming she decides to remain within the group, trusting in the wisdom of the BCA, it is likely that she will receive little support for behavior that may well be viewed by the husband as "bribery" or "spoiling" the children, even though these parents are experiencing difficulty in their current methods of managing the children. This husband could well believe that such verbal praise should be employed exclusively for outstanding acts (as was typical of his own parents' view) and may actually view his wife's performance as belittling her position of authority within the family. This would be particularly true if this father's role construction of a parent involves elements like being "forceful," "firm," or "a person of authority." Not only is this mother likely to receive little support and perhaps much negative feedback from her husband for changing her ordinary style, but this change might be misinterpreted by the children in any one of a variety of ways, given the context of their former expectations. While it may be difficult for us to believe that verbal praise could hold negative properties for the recipient, these children may in fact view their mother's behavior as "phony," "different," or perhaps may even feel that they are being "singled out" in some ill-defined fashion for later punishment. In addition, if the children were to view this behavior as a sign of lenience on the mother's part (which is possible in the context of previous parental communications and expectations) the children might well engage in inappropriate behavior as a means of testing the limits and redefining and exploring the "new" nature of things. If the father is motivated to do so, he might view such a change in the children's behavior as evidence of the inadequacy of the procedures.

This example has emphasized in a rather extreme way how a given change in the behavior of one member of a family system might lead to outcomes that are much beyond the BCA's expectations. Patterson and his colleagues (Patterson & Reid, 1970; Patterson, 1976) have systematically evaluated the functional relationships between certain classes of communication on the part of members of troubled families. Among other things, such analyses have shown that negative coercion seems to be a primary means of communication, with negative communications spiralling upward in level of intensity as a multitude of demands are made by family members upon other members. In fact, many families rarely employ positive categories of communication. While standard parent-training efforts **may** succeed in causing a chain reaction that in fact results in alterations within the family structure along more positive lines (Patterson & Reid, 1970; see also Patterson, 1971), it would seem that a variety of negative possibilities for outcome also exist when a family is treated as a collection of isolated persons, and single elements within that system are altered outside of the context of the family as a system.

A comprehensive assessment of the family as a system would seem to ideally include, at minimum, the following elements:

1. *Each parent's theory or conceptualization of child behavior;* that is, to what factors (e.g., child, themselves, environment) do the parent attribute "good" and "bad" child behavior? One means of getting at this is to collect comprehensive case history data from each of the parents, with special emphasis upon interactions that each parent had with his own parents, and the philosophy of child-rearing that existed within the parent's own family. The author has described an outline for case history assessment elsewhere (Nay, 1979). In addition, it is useful to learn about those age or sex norms that each parent holds for children's behavior. Are the parents' norms appropriate given what we know about child development?

2. The specific *expectations that each parent has for the behavior of each of the children within the family,* and that parent's view of how those expectations have or have not been met in the past. Within this exploration, the BCA should seek to determine what each child contributes to the family and how that child might be expected to behave; in essence, the "role" that the child plays within the family system. Often, an exploration of the child's "strengths" provides useful infor-

mation that helps to place the child's "problems" or "weaknesses" within a contextual framework, and also provides clues to potential avenues of reinforcement that may be employed in intervention.

3. *Each parent's current repertoire of management procedures and knowledge of human learning.* At this point, the BCA should be well versed in the parent's general views of the parent-child relationships within the context of the parent's history. Now it is important for the BCA to explore, perhaps via observation of parent-child behavior or self-reported examples from the immediate past, how each parent specifically goes about managing each child's behavior. Often, much useful information can be obtained by exploring how the parent handles certain developmental phenomena like toilet-training, as well as how ordinary problems of "bed time," "eating," "carrying out of regular household duties" (e.g., keeping the room clean), as well as episodes of noncompliance and destructive behavior are dealt with. In addition, if the parent proclaims that a given method has been a success or failure the BCA should explore the specific criteria the parent has employed in labeling this outcome. This may hold important implications for the manner in which the parent views success or failure once the BCA begins intervention and it may be that the parent's and BCA's criteria are quite divergent.

4. *Each child's view of his parents: how the child expects each parent to behave in response to certain situations.* Given that the child is old enough to handle an interview, the BCA might well explore what the child sees each of his parents as "being like," and what the child thinks each parent would do in response to certain, hypothetical situations involving both appropriate and inappropriate child behavior. Discrepancies between the child's view of the parent and the manner in which the parent describes himself will offer many further assessment questions to the BCA, and may reveal that one or more family members are poor self-observers or that particular family members are attempting to present a rather distorted view of things. In addition, the BCA should explore the child's likes and dislikes for possible categories of incentives which may be used within intervention, and in general obtain an assessment of the child's communicative and other social skills.

5. *An evaluation of the physical environment* within which the family functions. If the BCA is invited into the home, the home environment should be examined as a potential facilitator or inhibitor of intervention goals. For example, if the family is crowded into a small home or several children are placed in a single bedroom, this may be predictive of troubled communications and antagonism (e.g., fights between sib-

lings over territory) as it is difficult to find privacy. While the family may be unable to alter their living environment, this evaluation helps the BCA to better understand the resources the family brings to bear upon the problem, and may assist the BCA in making recommendations for reassigning family members to locations within the home that may be more conducive to the family goals.

6. An *evaluation of the family's ordinary communications* under analogue conditions (see Hanf & Kling, 1973; Haley, 1963; Watzlawick *et al.*, 1967) within the clinical setting and/or home observations along the lines suggested by Patterson and his colleagues (Patterson *et al.*, 1973). Because formal, predefined observation categories may not be sensitive to communicative and/or other behaviors viewed as problematic by family members (see Eyberg & Johnson, 1974 for an excellent discussion of this), the BCA would do well to begin by specimen recording (Wright, 1967) in a comprehensive fashion, all of the behavior that occurs to the extent possible. From these records specific targets may emerge that can be focused upon using more formal avenues of event or time sampling, and the functional relationships between various events may be more fully understood. As opposed to writing down all the information, a specimen observer may employ written symbols, coding language, speak into an audiotape recorder, or merely video- or audiotape the family's interactions as a means of obtaining a comprehensive record that can later be analyzed in a number of ways (e.g., number of events of some behavior; functional relationships between behaviors). A host of methodological options for performing independent observations have been reviewed by this author (see Nay, 1979) and by a host of others (see Jones, Reid, & Patterson, 1974; Hersen & Bellack, 1976; Ciminaro, Calhoun, & Adams, 1977).

In evaluating observation data, the BCA should specifically focus upon the organization of the family in terms of each member's role in making decisions, initiating as well as receiving communications, and in mediating disputes. In addition, evidence of coalitions between particular members within the family, the isolation of particular family members from ordinary and ongoing communications, as well as notable repetitive negative or positive interactions between particular family members should be noted. The BCA should explore the manner in which family members communicate positive as well as negative feelings to one another (e.g., verbally versus nonverbally, or perhaps not at all), and obtain some sense of the family's repertoire of communicative skills. In particular, paralinguistic and kinesic (body language)

behavior that is not consonant with the denotative message of communications should be carefully considered, particularly when the BCA
suspects that family members are attempting to portray themselves in
a favorable light. Finally, the BCA should assess whether or not family
members are able to function as a unit in performing a task in a
standardized situation in the clinic or home setting (e.g., reaching
consensus on a topic), and particularly, how the mother and father
tend to work (e.g., together or as independents) in accomplishing the
task.

This information is certainly not meant to be exhaustive, but provides
a framework for evaluating something other than the child behaviors
(targets) to be changed that seems to so preoccupy the assessment
decision-making of many behaviorally oriented BCAs. In answering the
above questions the BCA can obtain some notion of the likely responses
of family members to particular modes of intervention, and the BCA
is in a position to present methods using a vocabulary and currency
that makes sense to the family and is not likely to violate those expectations and traditions that **can** reasonably stand, given the BCA's
methodology for change. In a very real sense the BCA (at least this
author's view of him) wishes to offer the family alternative approaches
to dealing with problem events as they emerge without radically changing the family in ways that members find intolerable. As the assessment
outlined above is accomplished, the BCA will also have occasion to
meet and get to know each member of the family. In some cases the
BCA may wish to focus upon the family system rather than individual
members as the target for intervention.

The foregoing assessment should assist in promoting transfer to the
home as well as maintenance, given that potential avenues of resistance
on the part of family members are understood and hopefully reduced
and the resultant program best fits with the family's goals and expectations. Even if this is so, one would suspect that previous "ways of
doing things" which have become much ingrained due to the family
history, may be employed again, particularly when the family is placed
under stress, or when the children's behavior becomes noticeably improved and the parents explicitly or implicitly decide to "slack off."
This author would suggest that specific steps be taken to ensure that
there is support and reinforcement for the parents in carrying out program procedures. Such avenues of support will be increasingly important as the BCA terminates his relationship with the family.
Approaches to providing ongoing reinforcement for the parent's efforts
as mediator will now be discussed.

Consequenting the Parent's Behavior

While it is certainly important that the BCA provide praise and encouragement for the parent's efforts, it has already been pointed out that this rarely occurs beyond the termination of intervention. One possibility described elsewhere in this chapter is to arrange in advance, perhaps via a written contract, for the BCA and client to discuss the progress of the family at certain follow-up times. This may occur within or outside of ordinary, systematic schedules for home observation or other assessments. The BCA could collect a monetary deposit from the parents following intervention that could be systematically distributed at certain follow-up points, contingent upon the parent's efforts. This approach has frequently been successfully employed as a means of encouraging attendance to parent group meetings and participation in therapeutic assignments (e.g., Eyberg & Johnson, 1974) and could reasonably be employed within a follow-up contract. Alternatively, the BCA might consider training a nonprofessional volunteer (perhaps from a local community agency or university undergraduate course offering) in program procedures, and arrange to have that individual meet with the family on a regular basis to provide ongoing support and reinforcement for intervention efforts. For example, Ferber et al. (1974) employed "trained undergraduate behavior analysts" (BAs) to assist them in meeting with parents in the home during parent training proper. Within those communities that contain a college, university, or extension service, course credit could be provided to the nonprofessional for carrying out support and follow-up with family members. In other cases, senior citizen volunteers, "housepersons," and other volunteers might provide a pool from which the BCA could enlist regular and systematic reinforcement for the parent's efforts. As a variant, such persons could be trained **along with the parents,** with parent and nonprofessional forming a support dyad; and this dyad could be maintained over the first year or more following intervention, as the nonprofessional systematically fades out supervision. These approaches would seem to meet the manpower needs faced by many BCAs in an economical fashion.

Along similar lines, parents who have participated in training could be systematically yoked to parent trainees. The trained parents could perhaps earn a modest salary for providing ongoing monitoring, feedback, and support for the trainee's efforts. As an alternative, trainees themselves could be formed into support systems. For example, a large parent group, perhaps containing 20 or more members, could be broken up into dyads or triads, and these units could function as the training, support and/or follow-up unit outside of the ordinary group situation. Parents with similar backgrounds and presenting problems could be encouraged to meet together following training as a kind of support group. As an alternative, parents could bring a friend, relative or neighbor (who does or does not seek parent training) to the training environment to participate along with the parent. This "participant" would be present on an ongoing basis following intervention to support the parent's efforts and provide positive and negative feedback. In many community catchment areas preexisting groups (e.g., within the church, fraternal and social organizations) already exist, and the BCA has only to capitalize upon these social systems to develop avenues of support during and following training.

With regard to support systems that can be developed within the family proper, it is perplexing that very few writers have discussed the possibility of programming a husband and wife, or parent and other family member to systematically monitor and provide reinforcement to one another. This author found only one BCA, Wagner (1968), who provided explicit instructions to parents to reinforce one another for their efforts at changing the child's behavior. In treating an 11-year-old child referred for "severe" school and home problems, Wagner trained the parents to alter the consequences for the child's behavior, and carefully defined avenues of reinforcement and punishment they could employ. In these instructions, the author asked the parents to pay attention to each other's behavior in the following fashion:

> Parents must work together at noticing what the other is doing. Reinforce each other when a good reinforcement of daughter's behavior is seen. Ask each other how to reinforce a particular behavior (if stuck, write it down and we'll go over it). Father: Note particularly mother's criticism, and positively reinforce her when she could have been critical and wasn't. Mother: Note particularly when father is giving in to whining. Make a friendly comment or praise when he doesn't. Both: Reinforce each other's efforts to let her do things on her own. Talk to brothers about what to do and the need for their active cooperation. [p. 455]

To make each parent's role explicit, the BCA might encourage the spouses to contract with one another verbally or in writing to monitor and perhaps even chart certain behaviors on the other party's part, with contingencies decided in advance. The best kind of contractual agreement would not be a *quid pro quo* (if Mother does X, Father will do Y), given the possibility of negative control (if Mother doesn't do X, Father won't do Y). Instead, the contract should specify divergent and perhaps unrelated outcomes that each parent finds rewarding contingent upon their efforts, as well as (optionally) negative outcomes that might realistically be imposed in order to encourage both partners to carry out program procedures. Even if parents are somewhat haphazard in their monitoring of the other's behavior and occasionally fail to be systematic in delivering outcomes, a monitoring and support system at least encourages some measure of vigilance and may well maintain the parents' efforts. A number of investigators have discussed the importance of defining the status of the marriage as a prelude to intervention (e.g., Bernal, 1970; Johnson & Lobitz, 1974; Reisinger *et al.*, 1976). Certainly a reciprocal monitoring and reinforcement system should be imposed upon a troubled marriage only after careful consideration.

Another approach would employ siblings within the family to serve as contingency managers for the parents' behavior, while the parents serve as contingency managers for the children's behavior. Using this approach, all family members would agree in advance upon behavioral goals for the parents as well as for each of the children within the family. This approach encourages all the members within the family system to monitor other members' behavior, and to serve as both the initiator and recipient of consequation. Such an approach may prove to be particularly acceptable to families that operate along more democratic or egalitarian lines, and may be especially appropriate to families containing older siblings, who tend to be less responsive to the parent as the sole locus of reinforcement. This is not a new approach, and a variety of reports attest to the utility of a family contract of family "council" approach to intervention (e.g., Phillips, 1975).

A final approach involves establishing a system of self-mediated consequences for the parent's behavior.

Self-Systems of Reinforcement

In some cases, it may be impossible to employ family members or others within a support system. For example, many contemporary families contain only two or three members. With our current divorce rate approaching 40 percent of marriages, the BCA is quite likely to see single parent families, and in many cases support from other persons is not available. In this case, training the parent to systematically self-consequate his or her own behavior may be particularly advantageous. The idea of self-reinforcement is probably not new to the reader and has been discussed at length elsewhere (e.g., Kanfer & Phillips, 1970; Kanfer, 1975; Bandura, 1969; Goldfried & Merbaum, 1973; Mahoney, 1974). The interested reader is also referred to Chapter 5 by Kanfer in the present text.

Basically, this approach would involve training the parent to systematically *self-monitor* the employment of program procedures, to
provide the parents with *criteria for self-evaluating performance,* and
to provide avenues by which the parent can *consequate* himself if
criteria are met or fail to be met. Criteria for reinforcement might range
from the performance of simple acts (e.g., "Did I use time out today
when Billy failed to comply?"; "Did I play with Billy using interactive
play for 15 minutes today?") to complex criteria involving parental
self-ratings of performance. Self-mediated consequences might involve
extrinsic items (e.g., a restaurant meal, purchasing a desired stereo
album, the acquisition of an article of clothing, spending money) or
intrinsic phenomena (e.g., saying something positive to characterize
one's behavior; imagining a positive, gratifying scene). The procedures
of self-control would seem to be particularly valuable for maintaining
a parent's behavior during periods when the BCA or other persons are
not available to provide monitoring and support. Given this, it is perplexing that not one of the reviewed studies included training in self-
control as a part of parent training.

CHANGE ACROSS NONTARGETED BEHAVIORS

To this point we have considered methods and issues having to do
with establishing enduring parent behavior change within the home
environment. In most cases the parent's initial intervention efforts are
directed toward a specific, focal child ("referred," the "target") and
within the child, one or more behavors become the initial focus for
behavior change. The BCA may wish to know whether the parent is
able to apply parenting skills to alternative behaviors displayed by the
referred child, or to alternative siblings within the family. This section
will refer to the first of these two questions.

The introductory portion of this chapter suggested that non-tar-
geted behavior change may result from the parent's direct application
of management skills to those behaviors (transfer of training) or via
avenues of response generalization. We might ask how nontargeted
behaviors might change outside of these mechanisms. One possibility
is that changing a targeted behavior increases the possibility that the
environment will encourage some other class of behavior, illustrating
a kind of interaction or reciprocity between behavior and environment.
For example, reducing a child's temper tantrums may also have the
effect of increasing the number of social contacts that the child has
with siblings or peers who previously avoided the child due to the

tantrums. Along similar lines, a child's attention to academic tasks may increase merely as a function of increasing in-seat behavior within the classroom situation, given that the child's fixed position places him in a better position to pay attention to material presented. Increasing in-seat behavior might also reduce the frequency of inappropriate verbalizations, given reduced child access to alternative peers. Thus, when certain targets are changed, the behavioral possibilities of the child may be altered. Environmental contingencies that were in effect may be changed to elicit nontargeted repertoire or even novel behaviors on the child's part.

Along these lines, Lichstein and Wahler (1976) have found evidence for consistent relationships between child behaviors with respect to change. The authors employed a multivariate coding system (Wahler, House, & Stambaugh, 1976) to observe the behavior of an autistic child across three settings: home, school structured (formal class), and school unstructured (e.g., during play). Sixteen distinctive child and six adult and peer behaviors were observed over a 6-month period. The authors found that certain behaviors "clustered" together—covarying in response to adult behaviors. Thus change shown for one behavior within a cluster would be coupled with concomitant change shown for other cluster behaviors. The composition of 22 identified clusters varied considerably across the settings and only one appeared in more than one setting, illustrating that observations of adult–child behavior in any one setting would not necessarily be generalizable to other settings. Such behavior–behavior relationships are perhaps mediated by response generalization and/or behavior–environment reciprocity. The implications of clustering for enhancing nontargeted behavior change will be discussed in a later section.

The foregoing suggests that change on the part of nontargeted behaviors may be due to one or more of a variety of mechanisms. When we better understand the nature of phenomena that are responsible for such change following intervention we will be in a more effective position to enhance its occurrence. Theoretical issues aside, there is very little evidence for nontargeted behavior change following parent training, regardless of its supposed genesis. Of the sample studies, only 13.5% present data for nontargeted behaviors, and of that grouping, only a study by Wiltz and Patterson (1974) specifically hypothesized that parents would "generalize the procedures" to modify nontargeted, deviant behaviors. In evaluating the results of training specifically designed to enhance "generalization," the authors found that significant decreases in targeted deviant behaviors from baseline to five weeks of intervention were not accompanied by statistically significant decreases in nontargeted behaviors, although a trend of deceleration was present. Unfortunately, the authors fail to discuss possible reasons for these results. The remaining studies found evidence for nontargeted behavior change. Three employed behavioral observation data as a criterion (Zeilberger *et al.*, 1968; Forehand *et al.*, 1976; Lavigueur, 1976) while Glogower and Sloop (1976) assessed parental responses to written hypothetical situations. With the exception of Glogower and Sloop (1976) these reports failed to provide a critical discussion of these findings, nor was nontargeted behavior change expected or preprogrammed. Glogower and Sloop compared parent training in general principles plus instruction focused upon a particular target, with instruction directed only at a particular target (specific instruction). From the authors' rationale for this study it is obvious that they expected training in general principles to enhance a parent's ability to apply management technology to multiple targets.

Thus the vast majority of investigators fail to take specific steps to program nontargeted behavior change and rarely assess its occurrence. While there is some support for occurrence of changes in nontargeted behaviors, results often seem more serendipitous than planned for and certainly do not represent systematic attention to COT enhancement. The current state of the art noted, it is difficult to rationally present a compendium of methods that might predictably foster change on the part of nontargeted behaviors. The following represent methods discussed in the literature as well as the author's suggestions. Methods will be divided into several categories: (*a*) providing the parent with general versus specific management skills; (*b*) training in multiple applications of parenting skills; and (*c*) selection of targets that are likely to facilitate change shown by certain nontargeted events of interest to the BCA.

Training in General Versus Specific Management Skills

Providing parents with methods focused upon some specific category of behavior would seem to reduce the likelihood that parents will possess skills relevant to changing alternative classes of behavior. For example, teaching a parent to employ time-out procedure to reduce the frequency of noncompliant behavior might not equip the parent to deal with other categories of child problems (e.g., social isolation; bedtime or eating problems) as they emerge. In contrast, exposing the parent to general principles or to a compendium of varied approaches to understanding and managing behavior would seem to prepare the parent to deal with a heterogeny of problem classes. Given this speculation, it is interesting to note that 37% of the sample studies provided training in general principles. Of this subgroup, nine studies provided general and individualized, focused instruction which would seem to capitalize upon the advantages of both strategies (e.g., Eyberg & Johnson, 1974; Walter & Gilmore, 1973; Wiltz & Patterson, 1974; Patterson, 1974; Arnold *et al.*, 1975; Bernal, 1970; Glogower & Sloop, 1976; Hall *et al.*, 1972; Mash, Lazere, Terdal, & Garner, 1973).

The Glogower and Sloop (1976) study already mentioned provides the only systematic evaluation of the impact of general versus problem-focused training upon outcome. The authors composed two groups of 4 mothers from a file of approximately 75 who had requested aid in managing their children (the authors' criteria for selection are not included). The group that exposed parents to general principles and also to specific strategies for particular targets was called the *combination training* group. The other four parents constituted the *specific focus* group and their sessions dealt exclusively with modifying particular behaviors. Members of both groups attended weekly, 2-hour sessions over a 10-week period. During the first 4 weeks of training, the combination group members were exposed to "general concepts of behavior modification," including reinforcement principles, schedules of reinforcement and systematic recording and shaping of child behavior. In addition, each parent was asked to collect 2 weeks of base rate data for one targeted behavior selected for increase and one for decrease in frequency and ultimately to develop programs for dealing with those targets. In contrast, the specific focus mothers learned observation procedures and were then asked to baserate two targeted behaviors and to bring these records to the group. Remaining sessions focused upon developing programs for these behaviors. The authors specifically hpothesized that "combination mothers would be better able to generalize their knowledge to different situations and children [p. 180]" than specific focus mothers. Following the group all parents completed the Behavioral Vignettes (Smith & Smith, 1966) which require parents to write down how they would respond to a series of hypothetical situations involving children. The authors' hypothesis was confirmed in that the combination group mothers showed significantly greater improvement than specific focus mothers. In addition, the improvements achieved by the combination group were found to be maintained over a 5-month period as indicated by paper and pencil measures. While the Behavioral Vignettes perhaps do assess a parent's ability to transfer *knowledge* to different children and targets, they provide no assessment of the parent's ability to apply newly learned skills to alternative child behaviors within the home. While the sample was small and assessments limited to parental report and written assessments, this is an example of the kind of components analysis of specific parent training procedures that needs to be performed more frequently and in a more sophisticated fashion within the literature.

Multiple Applications of Management Technology

Many investigators have required parents to develop, with assistance or on their own, management programs for behaviors not initially targeted for intervention. This strategy places the BCA in a position to evaluate transfer of parent application of skills across behaviors within the clinic or home setting under more systematic and controlled conditions **in advance,** rather than assuming that the parent will be able to adequately handle novel and perhaps distinctly different problem situations as they occur. For example, Wiltz and Patterson (1974) composed groups of up to five sets of parents (and four therapists) that spent 30 min each week assisting parents in designing a behavior modification program for a target of their selection. Both the BCAs as well as other parents provided feedback to each parent during this 30-min period. Although it is not clear whether this occurred within the five weeks of group meetings, the authors also required each parent grouping to self-record and to modify a second behavior by designing a program independent of the BCA's assistance. The authors state: "It was felt that training was not complete until parents could demonstrate competence in applying the principles on their own. Parents were asked to set up and run the second program using the experience gained in the group and through reading the book (*Living with children*, Patterson & Guillion, 1974) [p. 217]." As already mentioned, these authors failed to find statistically significant evidence for nontargeted behavior change. Along similar lines, Lavigueur (1976) trained parents at home (via instructions and hand cueing) to systematically reinforce positive child verbalizations while ignoring or applying time-out to inappropriate child verbalizations. During a later phase, the parents were instructed to reinforce a second appropriate behavior ("offering help" in one family, "helping" in another) and to ignore or time-out a second inappropriate behavior (aggression and noncompliance respectively). While the authors do not provide a specific rationale for requiring multiple applications of skills, it is likely that this training expanded the parent's understanding of procedures.

Gardner, Forehand, and Roberts, (1976) employed clinic-based training to enhance parents' repertoire of rewarding behaviors, while teaching them to ignore or use time-out procedure to decelerate inappropriate behaviors. Each mother was required to develop programs to be used outside of the clinic, and to employ those programs to increase the frequency of at least two appropriate child behaviors. Other than a brief description, the authors are vague as to the rationale and the manner in which these "programs" were monitored by the BCA and employed within training. Glogower and Sloop (1976) required parents to select two targeted behaviors, to "base rate" those behaviors over a 2-week period and to develop programs for each of the targets with the help of other parents in the group. An important feature of this approach is that each parent was exposed to programs for ten targeted behaviors (e.g., two targets for each of the five parents). Patterson (1974) reports that group attendance is optional for parents once they have presented their own program to other members. It would seem that this would remove a potentially valuable source of learning for parents, although the efficacy of exposure to other parents' programs as a means of enhancing transfer to nontargeted behaviors remains to be empirically demonstrated.

As another option, the BCA might compile a "library" of programs developed by other parents to deal with diverse child problem behaviors and encourage parent trainees to learn about intervention strategies related to current or potential problems within their own families. The parent would thus be provided with ideas related to classes of child problematic behavior that may not be directly dealt with in training. Finally, support dyads or groups composed of parents and volunteers or other parents might be a source of ideas for parents in dealing with novel child problems as they emerge. If nothing else, support persons might provide a "sounding board" for the parent's ideas. This author and his colleagues have recently employed "problem-solving" skills with groups of divorced single parents, requiring all parents to assist in "brainstorming" potential solutions to the problems of individual members. We have found that the group is able to generate large numbers of credible and workable solutions, and it is obvious that brainstorming procedures would be most suitable for a support group that continues to meet once formal parent training has ended.

Systematic Selection of Targets

This chapter has emphasized that behavior change displayed by one member of a family system is likely to have an impact upon other family members; that a child's behavioral possibilities and avenues of reinforcement from the environment may be altered when some aspect of his behavior is modified. Also, it was pointed out that some behaviors tend to covary when assessed under baseline conditions (e.g., Lichstein & Wahler, 1976) and that merely changing one behavior within a behavioral cluster may have an impact upon one or more additional behaviors that are highly correlated with the target. It may be that through artful selection of targets for intervention the BCA can promote change on the part of alternative targets via one of these avenues. Thus behaviors that are most likely to increase a child's possibilities to engage in other desirable behaviors (e.g., entry into the group) might be selected as targets over behaviors that are likely to have a delimited and isolated impact upon the child. Along similar lines, a behavior that seems to be particularly central within a cluster of behaviors might be selected as a target in the hopes that other behaviors within that cluster will show concomitant behavior change. Unfortunately, the rationale for selecting targets for intervention is rarely reported by investigators.

CHANGE ACROSS NONFOCAL FAMILY MEMBERS

While a given child or parent may become the initial focus for intervention, the BCA may also wish to instigate behavioral change on the part of other family members. In a recent analysis of his own research and that of others, Patterson (1976) suggests that the referred child may in fact be "victim" as well as architect of a troubled family system; a system characterized by high rates of negative/coercive behavior on the part of all members. An obvious implication of this hypothesis, which has been stated elsewhere in somewhat different ways (e.g., Haley, 1963; 1976; Bateson, Jackson, & Weakland, 1956), is that the behavior of multiple members of the family system who may serve to elicit and/or reinforce the target's behavior must also be changed to effect a long-term successful outcome. A discussion of mechanisms that might explain change on the part of untreated family members will be followed by a presentation of methods that might be employed to enhance family systems change. It should be noted at the outset, however, that few reports of parent training assess the behavior of persons other than the targeted child (only 8% of our present sample) and few BCAs seem to be influenced by a "systems" view of the family in their rationale and methods for training. When nontargeted family members are assessed, the untreated sibling is most often the focus. An analysis of transfer or generality across trained and untrained **adult** family members is rarely reported. We will thus focus upon sibling behavior change following parent training, keeping in mind that many of the methods and issues to be discussed are applicable to explaining or instigating change on the part of adult family members as well.

Virtually all investigators assume that behavior change on the part of untreated siblings is due to the trained parent's ability to transfer employment of newly learned skills to other siblings. If this is an accurate view of the mechanism for change in the family, then we should expect to see change displayed **by the parent,** followed by change on the part of a succession of children in the family. In agreement with Forehand and Atkeson (1977), this author found that the child's behavior is the exclusive training criterion reported by most BCAs (e.g., Arnold *et al.*, 1975; Resick *et al.*, 1976; Lavigueur, 1976) making it impossible to support or defend this notion. In addition to changes in the parent's behavior vis-à-vis nontargeted siblings, there are other mechanisms by which sibling behavior might change.

The *reciprocity and coercion* hypothesis developed by Patterson and Reid (1970), posits that the behavior of members within an interdependent family system (e.g., mother–father, mother–child, child–child) is, in fact, reciprocal with respect to classes of reinforcers and punishers that members deliver to one another. Growing out of behavioral exchange theory within social psychology (see Thibaut & Kelly, 1959) the authors define reciprocity as a "balance of trade" that exists within most social interactions:

> Specifically, the term refers to an equity in the giving and receiving of positive and aversive consequences which occur in most social interactions. The first hypothesis refers to the assumption that reciprocity in fact exists, in most dyadic interactions. This would require that, over a series of interactions, two persons reinforce or punish each other for approximately the same proportion of behaviors. For example, if Person A reinforces B for 50 percent of the interactions which B has with A, then A, in turn, will receive about the same proportion of positive reinforcers from B [p. 13].

In addition, the authors suppose that the targeted child within a troubled family receives much reinforcement from parents and siblings (e.g., in the form of attention and giving in) for *manding* behavior: coercive verbal and nonverbal demands. The child learns to be coercive because the parents do not provide rich schedules of reinforcement for appropriate behavior, and in fact may fail to provide much attention at all to a child. Such coercive behavior makes it impossible for the child to become a part of reciprocal avenues of positive exchange with other family members.

The reciprocity hypothesis suggests that if the parents succeed in reducing the frequency of the targeted child's negative communications, this child may now be more approachable by other siblings (e.g., less aversive to them) and in a position to enter into positive and reciprocal interactions that should become balanced over time. The sibling may now find himself involved in fewer verbal and/or physical aggressive communications and is programmed to display increasingly positive communications in response to the targeted child's behavior. Obviously, the phenomenon of reciprocity would hold implications for virtually every member within an interdependent family system. In reviewing data collected by Arnold *et al.* (1975) for 27 trainees, Patterson (1976) found support for the reciprocity hypothesis in the coercive exchanges between the targeted child and siblings and fathers, but not for the targets' interactions with their mothers. In addition, the reciprocity hypothesis would predict that as the targeted child's behavior is brought under control, coercive behavior on the part of other family members would be reduced as well, finding a point of equilibrium. Data from Patterson's original sample of 27 families show a trend from baseline to termination of treatment which supports the hypothesis. Only pre–post behavior change for siblings, however, was significant, as was that for the targeted children. Patterson (1976) concludes that "some aspects of the system were altered [p. 305]," while pointing to the poor prognosis for long-term maintenance for those families where significant across-person changes did not occur.

Finally, social learning theory (Bandura & Walters, 1963; Bandura, 1969) would suggest that changing the behavior of family members whose behavior is systematically attended to by other members might promote behavioral change via some category of observational learning. Changing the behavior of the targeted child could alter the behavior of other siblings in at least three ways. First, nontargeted siblings may learn novel behaviors (outside of their current repertoire) by attending to some new category displayed by the targeted sibling (perhaps never before displayed to other siblings). Second, the frequency of some current repertoire behavior on the part of the child-observer may be increased or decreased via avenues of inhibitory or disinhibitory effects. Regarding inhibitory effects, a nontargeted child may observe the parent employing a punishment procedure contingent upon the targeted child's behavior. If the observer reduces the frequency of that same behavior following observation, we would say that he has been inhibited; his behavior has been decelerated merely by observing the targeted child receive negative consequences. In contrast, disinhibitory effects would apply to sibling behavior that has been previously punished by the parent or others. If the sibling observes the targeted child engage in this behavior *without receiving negative consequences* from his environment, the sibling may now display this behavior at an increased frequency; the sibling-observee has been disinhibited vicariously. Finally, social facilitation has to do with behavior in the nontargeted child's repertoire that has not been previously associated with punishment. Such behavior may increase in frequency on the sibling's part merely as a function of observing the targeted child display it. The transactions between parent and targeted child often occur in the presence of siblings who may not be directly treated. The possibilities for vicarious learning would seem to be extensive and might well be capitalized upon by the BCA who wishes to instigate multiple person change within the family.

Thus change on the part of untreated siblings may occur via parent transfer of training to alternative siblings, systems change toward an equilibrium of positive–negative behaviors and/or social learning processes. We will now explore methods that hold demonstrated or potential utility for enhancing such change.

Direct Training

One obvious approach to enhancing sibling change is to systematically train and/or supervise parents in applying newly-learned skills to nontargeted children within the family. The BCA is afforded an opportunity to evaluate the parent's ability to transfer knowledge and skills to nontargeted children **prior to termination** in the controlled training situation, where immediate feedback and remediation can be provided if necessary. In fact, few investigators have employed this remarkably good idea. A notable exception is the report of Arnold *et al.* (1975). The parents of 27 "pre-delinquents" were trained in social learning procedures as described by Patterson elsewhere (Patterson *et al.*, 1973). In addition to these targeted children, the authors were interested in evaluating behavioral change on the part of 55 siblings also present within these families. Specifically, the authors compared behavioral change on the part of siblings whose parents were either "involved," that is supervised in sibling management, to that of siblings whose parents were "uninvolved"; not provided with intentional supervision by the BCAs. Unfortunately, it is not clear from the author's report what "supervision" involved in terms of the number of therapist contacts, specific methodology employed, and consistency of approach across parents. The authors found no significant differences between the identified "problem" children and their siblings at baseline supporting Patterson's ideas about reciprocity already discussed. Following 4 intervention weeks, the average targeted child showed a significant reduction in deviant behavior, coupled with an average reduction of 36% in sibling deviant behavior. Because data were unavailable for a large proportion of the families (better than 40%) for observations collected between 6-months and 1-year follow-up, the authors placed emphasis upon observations collected during the first 6 follow-up months, which represent 74% of the original sample. The authors do not describe the 26% of families who were unavailable at 6 months but do say that those families who were available for the 1-year follow-up contained siblings who were less deviant at baseline than the sub-sample who failed to participate. Given these qualifications, the authors conclude that the siblings' treatment effects were "maintained over the first six months following intervention [p. 687]" based upon a statistical comparison of siblings at termination and follow-up (defined as the average of months 1 through 6). Unfortunately, an analysis of sibling behavior between baseline and follow-up is not provided. While the "magnitude" of the treatment effect appeared larger for the "involved" subset of siblings, statistical analyses revealed no significant differences between siblings whose parents were supervised and siblings whose parents were not so trained.

If parents can be successfully trained to manage the behavior of the targeted child it only makes sense that direct training in sibling management should prove to be equally successful. Unfortunately, since it is not clear how Arnold et al. (1975) employed "supervision," it is difficult to critically evaluate their negative finding.

Enhancing the Impact of the Target Child as Model

This author could find only one set of investigators who attempted to systematically enhance the likelihood that untreated siblings would vicariously learn from the behavior of the targeted child. Resick et al. (1976) trained a mother to employ praise for compliance, and time-out for noncompliance with two young siblings, Glenn and Keith. Employing a multiple baseline design, the authors began by treating Glenn who was considered to be less "problematic" by the parent. The parent was not required to employ these procedures with Keith. Significantly, the authors required that Keith be present at the initiation of treatment for Glenn, to hear as well as see any consequences that the parent applied to the younger child's behavior. Thus while the parent directly applied treatment to Glenn's room cleaning, Keith was exposed to the parent's efforts in an exclusively vicarious fashion. Results showed a marked increase in Glenn's cleaning once intervention was initiated, along with associated increments in the frequency of Keith's cleaning behavior.

When treatment was initiated for a second behavior on Glenn's part (bath taking) no change was noted for a second target defined for Keith (kitchen clean-up). The authors concluded that the similarity and location of expected performance of tasks performed by the trained and untrained child may be crucial to instigating comparable behavior change across siblings. In addition, the authors note that the effects upon the untreated child may not have been due to modeling but to subtle changes in the mother's behavior or reduced sibling reinforcement for behavior that interfered with task completion, and emphasized that future research must identify the mechanisms responsible for their results.

It is puzzling that few investigators have attempted to systematically program vicarious learning on the part of untreated siblings, particularly given the "social learning" orientation of most parent-training programs. A review of the extensive social learning literature (e.g., Bandura & Walters, 1963; Bandura, 1969) provides the BCA with a number of ideas as to how such programming might be accomplished. For example, the primary prerequisite for modeling seems to be that the observer systematically attend to the model, and research has shown that models who in some way control the outcome of observers, are of high status or competence, and who might generally be defined as being "similar" to the observer, tend to increase the probability of discriminated attention and thus modeling (e.g., Mischel & Grusec, 1966; Mischel & Liebert, 1967; Bandura & Whalen, 1966; Baron, 1970; Rosekrans, 1967). In addition, the BCA should insure that the model's behavior occurs under conditions that are likely to *enhance the observer's attention*. Thus, as for Resick *et al.* (1976), the parent could require that siblings be present to witness treatment administered to the targeted child, and provide explicit instructions for attending. In addition, the BCA and parent could explore avenues of reinforcement for a sibling's attending to the targeted child's appropriate behavior. Research findings would also suggest that the BCA should carefully select a particular sibling to be the focus of intervention, given that certain siblings within the family may elicit higher degrees of attending from other siblings via their status, role within the family, perceived competence, age or some other characteristic. Often, older siblings are idolized by younger children and assume a training role (often to the older child's regret), and the BCA might capitalize upon this phenomenon by selecting an older child of high status to be the target. This enhances the possibility that behavioral change displayed by the targeted child (as a result of direct parent intervention) may be vicariously learned by other siblings within the family. The author hopes that the utility of systematically enhancing modeling effects as a means of instigating change across persons will be evaluated in future studies. Obviously the promotion of modeling effects can be a primary strategy or be employed as an adjunct to other procedures.

Along similar lines, the attractiveness of certain family members might be assessed as a prelude to selecting a target for intervention. Social psychological research indicates that certain group members are more likely to be communicated with or selected to be with when each group member is asked to make a choice and sociometric procedures have been developed for evaluating such choices in a systematic way (e.g., Walster, 1966). It might be useful to examine the sociometrics of a family as a means of defining certain siblings whose behavior is maximally likely to influence (e.g., via instructions, modeling, positive and negative control) change on the part of other siblings. Parenthetically, it is worth noting that the behavior change displayed by a less powerful sibling may be punished or, at minimum, ignored by more powerful family members. The manner in which such social–psychological factors as leadership (e.g., Raven & French, 1958; Mausner, 1954), attractiveness, (family) norms, conformity (e.g., to positive or negative behavior displayed by another sibling) might be capitalized upon in order to enhance systems change within the family might prove to be a fruitful avenue for future research.

Training the Sibling as BCA

The procedure most frequently employed to encourage sibling behavior change has been to train siblings to serve as trainers for targeted siblings within the family. Miller and Cantwell (1976) have described some of the advantages of employing a sibling as BCA. First, because older siblings frequently "teach" younger siblings, it may be possible to employ this natural tendency to systematically encourage certain appropriate behaviors on the targeted child's part. Also, the training of siblings ensures consistency in employing management skills, as all family members react to the targeted child in a similar fashion. In addition, the authors feel that many siblings have a negative reaction to the attention received by the targeted child as a result of parent training. The sibling, as BCA, is forced to spend more time with the targeted child under conditions where "successful, positive experiences together [p. 449]" are possible. Finally, the authors suggest that involving siblings in training "might help prevent the development of behavior problems in the siblings themselves [p. 450]," particularly if the sibling's problem behavior is related to the targeted child (e.g., fighting, name calling). The authors present case evidence for positive benefits accruing to an older sibling who served as therapist for a younger child.

Lavigueur (1976) describes the employment of siblings as "therapeutic aides" within two families experiencing similar problems. Following the usual baseline observations within the home, the first five training sessions involved the BCA's training of the parents to systematically reinforce the targeted child's "positive verbalizations," while ignoring or timing-out "negative verbalizations." During the next five sessions the parents continued to differentially reinforce the targeted child's behavior and in addition, a sibling (aged 10 in both families) was instructed by the parents to carry out the same treatment strategy. The author reports:

> With the experimenter present, the sibling was told that his brother (or sister) was currently having conduct problems which might get him in trouble and that the sibling could help him overcome these problems. The parents role played positive and negative verbalizations and how the sibling should respond to these behaviors. It was emphasized that, in the future, the sibling might have similar problems and that the targeted child might then help him. Parents were encouraged to praise the sibling for carrying out his work, letting him know specifically how he was being helpful [p. 604].

Additional experimental phases involved training the parents first to deal with an additional target ("offering help" and "helping" across the two families), followed by the siblings again being trained to employ the procedures along with the parents. The behavior of both the targeted children and their sibling-trainers was systematically monitored across the sessions. The author reports that significant behavioral change for the targeted child in the first family was accompanied by concomitant changes in the same targets for the sibling who served as trainer. Thus both the targeted child and the sibling showed increased positive verbalizations, decreased negative verbalizations, and increased occasions of help offering. Importantly, the sibling's behavior change did not occur until that sibling was specifically trained to deal with the targeted child's behavior. With some exceptions, the sibling in the second family showed similar behavioral changes concomitant with changes in the targeted child's behavior. In addition, the author reports that the siblings and targeted children interacted more frequently and in a more positive way. He hypothesizes that this finding may be due to reduced jealousy, in that parents who are worrying about the development or behavior of a particular targeted child may tend to ignore other siblings "whose adjustment . . . is more assured [p. 612]." Siblings cooperating within treatment are provided with more attention from the parents. Among problems encountered, Lavigueur (1976) notes that the sibling within the second family was "inconsistent" in carrying out training over time, and this would suggest that the BCA and parents must carefully and continuously monitor the sibling-trainer's efforts to ensure maintenance.

Along similiar lines, Colletti and Harris (1977) trained a 10-year-old female sibling to systematically train her 9-year-old, autistic sister to string beads (the rationale for this is not clearly provided), while also instructing the 12- and 11-year-old siblings in a second family to train a neurologically-impaired 9-year-old brother to carry out addition problems and appropriately print letters. Using an A-B-A-B reversal design, the authors showed that the siblings had gained control of the targeted child's behavior. While providing further support for the potential efficacy of siblings as trainers, this study does not speak to therapeutic benefits accruing to the sibling-trainer.

Miller and Cantwell (1976) present issues attendant to employing a sibling as therapist. First, the sibling's responsibilities should be presented within training sessions that augment didactic teaching with active role playing and behavioral rehearsal, with the length of sessions and content of procedures geared to the developmental stage and abilities of the sibling. Also, the authors emphasize the potential for inconsistency in the sibling's performance during initial stages of training, and suggest careful supervision (e.g., writing down required assignments), perhaps with mother or father serving in the role of "manager" of the program. Next the authors report that many siblings feel quite uncomfortable in a BCA role and may be loathe to discuss the behavior of other family members. The authors suggest that rules be established at the outset to ensure that the behavior of all family members is open to discussion within family meetings. Among other potential problems, the present author would suppose that certain combinations of sibling-trainer and targeted child should be avoided (e.g., a sibling who abuses his power as trainer to dominate a younger trainee).

The few preceding case studies suggest that siblings may indeed be capable of serving as mediators for other children within the family and that the sibling-trainer may benefit as much as the focal child. In placing a sibling in the role of BCA the parents may come to expect behavior consonant with this supervisory–teaching role (e.g., responsible; behaves in accordance with positive behavior taught to child-trainee; maturity and so forth) and these expectations may well influence their behavior toward the child (e.g., Johnson & Bolstad, 1975). This new role may not only alter the way the parents respond, but also alter the sibling's constructs for viewing himself (e.g., Kelly, 1955; 1970). According to Kelly's personal construct theory, forcing the sibling to play an alternative role may well provoke change consonant with that new role. While a number of writers have emphasized the roles that family members play (e.g., "sick," "well") in their speculations about the nature of severely troubled families (e.g., Watzlawick, 1967; Bateson *et al.*, 1956) little systematic research has been directed toward evaluating the genesis of role constructs or the impact of role change upon the functioning of a family exposed to some variant of parent training.

SUMMARY

As indicated by a variety of criteria, parents can indeed learn and apply novel child management skills immediately following training. The myriad combinations of written materials, lectures, instructions, episodes of modeling, role-playing, feedback–cueing, and other methodologies that so frequently result in child behavior change within the home suggest that either a variety of methodologies can independently lead to the same outcome, or that a common core of methodology (including certain nonspecifics that have yet to be documented within the literature) is responsible. Significantly, immediate, positive change in the home seems to occur regardless of methodology and few investigators take active steps to enhance transfer of training or generalization. This chapter has repeatedly emphasized the need for a more thorough and comprehensive description of operations employed within parent training in order to determine those training components necessary and sufficient for these long-term positive outcomes.

With regard to the maintenance of parent and/or child behavior, it is surprising that many investigators fail to carry out follow-up assessments, particularly given the imploring remarks of a variety of reviewers (e.g., O'Dell, 1974; Berkowitz & Graziano, 1972; Sloop, 1975) regarding the importance of follow-up evaluations. Of those investigators who provide follow-up data, most report some category of evidence for the maintenance of the child's behavior at follow-ups ranging up to the period of 6 months, with few investigators (Patterson and his associates are an exception) reporting follow-up assessments beyond that period. Unfortunately, the vast majority of investigators report fewer than four follow-up probes, often carried out within a single, "one-shot" interview and/or observation occasion within the home. In addition, the criteria for evaluating behavior change at follow-up varies from clinic interviews and telephone reports to the systematic employ-

ment of multivariate coding systems like the BCS (Patterson *et al.,*
1973; Jones, Reid, & Patterson, 1975). While a few recent reports have
emphasized the divergent findings that may result when multiple criteria
(interview, written, observational) are employed, few investigators assess multiple response channels (e.g., parent, targeted child, siblings)
using multiple methods. Finally, even the most systematic follow-ups,
as carried out by Patterson and his colleagues, frequently report extensive attrition on the part of the population of families originally trained,
and often the specific reasons for attrition are not reported. This is
frequently the case when follow-ups are extended beyond the period
of 6 months and some findings suggest that those families who are
unavailable for evaluation may indeed represent a much different population from those who are available. With regard to the effects of parent
training upon nontargeted behaviors for the referred child and across
persons present within the family (parents as well as untreated siblings)
a number of investigators have developed innovative and quite promising methods, often within single case reports. These methodologies
await further, more systematic exploration within the literature. In
summary, a literature that is most promising with respect to immediate
posttraining behavior change inspires less confidence when maintenance
beyond brief follow-up periods and change across alternative, nontargeted behaviors and family members is assessed.

This report has described a number of terms that are employed to
account for behavioral changes displayed outside of the immediate conditions of training. Unfortunately, the same term (e.g., transfer, behavioral generality, generalization) is frequently employed to describe
behavioral change that may be mediated by a variety of potential
mechanisms, many of which are not clearly understood. Given the
mechanisms described in previous sections that may explain such
change, it is obvious that the BCA must systematically tailor enhancement methods to a particular mechanism, and describe such change in
language that is operationally descriptive. The mechanisms and methodologies described for enhancing COT change in the previous sections
are a step in the direction of linking outcome to specific change phenomena. Repeatedly the author has emphasized that the family, regardless of its composition, must not be viewed as a passive respondent to
whatever manipulation the BCA introduces via the trained parent. The
notion of the family as a system of interdependent members is certainly not a new one, and has frequently been discussed within other
contexts and particularly by writers who adopt a communications
model of behavior change (e.g., Haley, 1963). In addition, the contributions of Patterson and his colleagues toward a more comprehensive

view of those system elements that may influence how family members respond to parent-training methods have repeatedly been cited. The importance of standing back from a strict behavior modification ("rewards, time-out and count it") perspective to scrutinize what other disciplines may have to offer in understanding the family has been underscored repeatedly in discussions of the mechanisms and methods of COT enhancement.

The last 10 years has witnessed the development of a technology fully capable of changing the behavior of parents and their children across a wide variety of investigators, settings and family descriptions. Now that it is demonstrated that we can get parents to behave in alternative ways and this often leads to desirable behavioral change on the part of referred children, it is time to deliberately turn our attention toward a systematic analysis of how such change can be maintained and promoted across behavior and person domains. It is this author's contention that the place to begin is in better understanding those processes that occur within families, to better understand the interdependent system into which we introduce our technology. This will require that we carefully observe and describe family constellations that vary with respect to demography, composition and other dimensions as a prelude to constructing treatment regimens.

REFERENCES

Arnold, J. E., Levine, A. G., & Patterson, G. R. Changes in sibling behavior following family intervention. *Journal of Consulting and Clinical Psychology*, 1975, *43*, 683–688.

Bandura, A. *Principles of behavior modification*. New York: Holt, 1969.

Bandura, A., & Walters, R. *Social learning and personality development*. New York: Holt, 1963.

Bandura, A., & Whalen, C. The influence of antecedent reinforcement and divergent modeling cues on patterns of self-reward. *Journal of Personality and Social Psychology*, 1966, *3*, 373–382.

Baron, R. Attraction toward the mode and model's competence as determinants of adult imitative behavior. *Journal of Personality and Social Psychology*, 1970, *14*, 345–351.

Barrett, B. M., & McCormack, J. E. Varied-teacher tutorials: A tactic for generating credible skills in severely retarded boys. *Mental Retardation*, 1973, *11*, 14–19.

Bateson, G., Jackson, J., & Weakland, J. Toward a theory of schizophrenia. *Behavioral Science*, 1956, *1*, 251–264.

Berkowitz, B. P., & Graziano, A. M. Training parents as behavior therapists: A review. *Behaviour Research and Therapy*, 1972, *10*, 297–317.

Bernal, M. E. Behavioral feedback in the modification of brat behaviors. *Journal of Nervous and Mental Disease*, 1969, *148*, 375–385.

Bernal, M. E. Training parents in child management. In R. Bradfield (Ed.), *Behavior modification and the learning disorders*. New York: Academic Therapy Publications, 1970.

Bernal, M. E., Williams, D. E., Miller, W. H., & Reagor, P. A. The use of videotape feedback and operant learning principles in training parents in management of deviant children. In A. Rubin, & C. M. Franks, (Eds.), *Advances in behavior therapy* (Vol. 3). New York: Academic Press, 1972.

Boren, J. J., & Jagodzinski, M. G. The impermanence of data-recording behavior. *Journal of Behavior Therapy and Experimental Psychiatry*, 1975, 6, 359.

Budd, K. S., Green, D. R., & Baer, D. M. An analysis of multiple misplaced parental social contingencies. *Journal of Applied Behavior Analysis*, 1976, 9, 459–470.

Ciminaro, A. R., Calhoun, K. S., & Adams, H. E. *Handbook of behavioral assessment*. New York: Wiley, 1977.

Coletti, G., & Harris, S. L. Behavior modification in the home: Siblings as behavior modifiers, parents as observers. *Journal of Abnormal Child Psychology*, 1977, 5, 21–29.

Emshoff, J. G., Redd, W. H., & Davidson, W. S. Generalization training and the transfer of pro-social behavior in delinquent adolescents. *Journal of Behavior Therapy and Experimental Psychiatry*, 1976, 7, 141–144.

Eyberg, S. M., & Johnson, S. M. Multiple assessment of behavior modification with families: Effects of contingency contracting and order of treated problems. *Journal of Consulting and Clinical Psychology*, 1974, 42, 594–606.

Ferber, H., Keeley, S. M., & Shemberg, K. M. Training parents in behavior modification: Outcome of and problems encountered in a program after Patterson's work. *Behavior Therapy*, 1974, 5, 415–419.

Ferster, C. B., & Skinner, B. F. *Schedules of reinforcement*. New York: Appleton-Century-Crofts, 1957.

Forehand, R., & Atkeson, B. M. Generality of treatment effects with parents as therapists: A review of assessment and implementation procedures. *Behavior Therapy*, 1977, 8, 575–593.

Forehand, R., & King, H. E. Noncompliant children: Effects of parent training on behavior and attitude change. *Behavior Modification*, 1977, 1, 93–108.

Forehand, R., Sturgis, E., Aguar, D., Green, K., McMahon, R., & Wells, K. *Generality of treatment effects resulting from a parent-training program to modify child noncompliance*. Paper presented at the meeting of the Association for the Advancement of Behavior Therapy, New York, 1976.

Gardner, H. L., Forehand, R., & Roberts, M. Time-out with children: Effects of an explanation and brief parent training on child and parent behaviors. *Journal of Abnormal Child Psychology*, 1976, 4, 277–288.

Glogower, F., & Sloop, E. W. Two strategies of group training of parents as effective behavior modifiers. *Behavior Therapy*, 1976, 7, 177–184.

Goldfried, M., & Merbaum, M. (Eds.). *Behavior change through self-control*. New York: Holt, 1973.

Goldstein, A. P. *Structured learning therapy: Toward a psychotherapy for the poor*. New York: Academic Press, 1973.

Goldstein, A. P., Heller, K., & Sechrest, L. B. *Psychotherapy and the psychology of behavior change*. New York: Wiley, 1966.

Griffiths, H., & Craighead, W. E. Generalization in operant speech therapy for misarticulation. *Journal of Speech and Hearing Disorders*, 1972, 37, 485–494.

Haley, J. *Strategies of psychotherapy*. New York: Grune & Stratton, 1963.

Haley, J. *Problem solving therapy*. San Francisco: Jossey-Bass, 1976.

Hall, J. F. *The psychology of learning*. Philadelphia: Lippincott, 1966.

Hall, R. V., Axelrod, S., Tyler, L., Grief, E., Jones, F. C., & Robertson, R. Modification of behavior problems in the home with a parent as observer and experimenter. *Journal of Applied Behavior Analysis*, 1972, 5, 53–64.

Hanf, C., & Kling, F. *Facilitating parent-child interaction: A two-stage training model*. Unpublished manuscript, University of Oregon Medical School, 1973.

Herbert, E. W., & Baer, D. M. Training parents as behavior modifiers: Self-recording of contingent attention. *Journal of Applied Behavior Analysis*, 1972, 5, 139–149.

Hersen, M., & Bellack, A. *The behavior therapy handbook*. New York: Pergamon, 1976.

Johnson, C. A., & Katz, R. C. Using parents as change agents for their children: A review. *Journal of Child Psychology and Psychiatry*, 1973, 14, 181–200.

Johnson, J. M. Using parents as contingency managers. *Psychological Reports*, 1971, 28, 703–710.

Johnson, S. M., & Bolstad, O. D. Reactivity to home observations: A comparison of audio recorded behavior with observers present or absent. *Journal of Applied Behavior Analysis*, 1975, 8, 181–185.

Johnson, S. M., & Christensen, A. Multiple criteria follow-up of behavior modification with families. *Journal of Abnormal Child Psychology*, 1975, 3, 135–154.

Johnson, S. M., Christensen, A., & Bellamy, G. T. Evaluation of family intervention through unobtrusive audio recordings: Experience in "bugging" children. *Journal of Applied Behavior Analysis*, 1976, 9, 213–219.

Johnson, S. M., & Lobitz, G. K. Parental manipulations of child behavior in home observations. *Journal of Applied Behavior Analysis*, 1974, 7, 23–31.

Jones, R. R., Reid, J. B., & Patterson, G. R. Naturalistic observation in clinical assessment. In P. McReynolds (Ed.), *Advances in psychological assessment* (Vol. 3). San Francisco: Jossey-Bass, 1975.

Kanfer, F. H. Self-monitoring: Methodological limitations and clinical applications. *Journal of Consulting and Clinical Psychology*, 1970, 35, 148–152.

Kanfer, F. H. Self-management methods. In F. H. Kanfer & A. P. Goldstein (Eds.), *Helping people change*. New York: Pergamon, 1975.

Kanfer, F. H., & Phillips, J. S. *Learning foundations of behavior therapy*. New York: Wiley, 1970.

Kazdin, A. E. Reactive self-monitoring: The effects of response desirability, goal setting, and feedback. *Journal of Consulting and Clinical Psychology*, 1974, 42, 704–716.

Karoly, P., & Rosenthal, M. Training parents in behavior modification: Effects on perceptions of family interaction and deviant child behavior. *Behavior Therapy*, 1977, 8, 406–410.

Keeley, S. M., Shemberg, K. M., & Carbonell, J. Operant clinical intervention: Behavior management or beyond? Where are the data? *Behavior Therapy*, 1976, 7, 292–305.

Kelly, G. A. *The psychology of personal constructs*. New York: Norton, 1955.

Kelly, G. A. A brief introduction to personal construct theory. In D. Bannister (Ed.), *Perspectives in personal construct theory*. New York: Academic Press, 1970.

Kent, R. N. A methodological critique of "Interventions for boys with conduct problems." *Journal of Consulting and Clinical Psychology*, 1976, 44, 297–299.

Kent, R. N., O'Leary, K. D., Diament, C., & Dietz, A. Expectation biases in observational evaluation of therapeutic change. *Journal of Consulting and
   Clinical Psychology*, 1974, 42, 774–780.
Kogan, K. L., & Gordon, B. N. A mother-instruction program: Documenting change
   in mother–child interactions. *Child Psychiatry and Human Development*,
   1975, 5, 189–200.
Lavigueur, H. The use of siblings as an adjunct to the behavioral treatment of
   children in the home with parents as therapists. *Behavior Therapy*, 1976, 7,
   602–613.
Mahoney, M. J. *Cognition and behavior modification*. Cambridge, Mass.: Ballinger,
   1974.
Marholin II, D., Siegel, L. J., & Phillips, D. Treatment and transfer: A search for
   empirical procedures. In M. Herson, R. M. Eisler, & P. M. Miller (Eds.),
   Progress in Behavior Modification (Vol. 3.), New York: Academic Press, 1976.
Mash, E. J., Lazere, R., Terdal, L., & Garner, A. Modification of mother–child
   interactions: A modeling approach for groups. *Child Study Journal*, 1973, 3,
   131–143.
Mausner, B. The effect of one partner's success in a relevant task on the interaction of observer pairs. *Journal of Abnormal and Social Psychology*, 1954,
   49, 557–560.
Miller, N. B., & Cantwell, D. P. Siblings as therapists: A behavioral approach.
   American Journal of Psychiatry, 1976, 133, 447–450.
Mischel, W., & Grusec, J. Determinants of the rehearsal and transmission of neutral
   and aversive behaviors. *Journal of Personality and Social Psychology*, 1966,
   3, 197–205.
Mischel, W., & Liebert, R. The role of power in the adoption of self-reward pat-
   terns. *Child Development*, 1967, 38, 673–683.
Nay, W. R. A systematic comparison of instructional techniques for parents. *Be-
   havior Therapy*, 1975, 6, 14–21.
Nay, W. R. *Multimethod clinical assessment*. New York: Gardner Press-Wiley,
   1979.
Nevin, J. A. (Eds). *The study of behavior: Learning, motivation, emotion, and
   instinct*. Glenview, Ill.: Scott, Foresman, 1973.
O'Dell, S. Training parents in behavior modification: A review. *Psychological
   Bulletin*, 1974, 81, 418–433.
Patterson, G. R. Behavioral intervention procedures in the classroom and in the
   home. In A. E. Bergin & S. L. Garfield (Eds.), *Handbook of psychotherapy and
   behavior change*. New York: Wiley, 1971.
Patterson, G. R. Interventions for boys with conduct problems: Multiple settings,
   treatments, and criteria. *Journal of Consulting and Clinical Psychology*, 1974,
   42, 471–481.
Patterson, G. R. The aggressive child: Victim and architect of a coercive system.
   In E. J. Mash, L. A. Hammerlynck, & L. C. Handy (Eds.), *Behavior modifica-
   tion and families*. New York: Brunner/Mazel, 1976.
Patterson, G. R., & Gullion, M. E. *Living with children*. Champaign, Ill.: Research
   Press, 1974.
Patterson, G. R., Cobb, J. A., & Ray, R. S. A social engineering technology for
   retraining the families of aggressive boys. In H. E. Adams & I. P. Unikel
   (Eds.), *Issues and trends in behavior therapy*. Springfield, Ill.: Thomas, 1973.
Patterson, G. R., & Hops, H. Coercion, a game for two: Intervention techniques for

marital conflict. In R. Ulrich & P. Mountjoy (Eds.), *The experimental analysis of social behavior.* New York: Appleton-Century-Crofts, 1972.

Patterson, G. R., Ray, R. S., Shaw, D. A., & Cobb, J. S. *Manual for coding of family interaction* (Document #01234). New York: ASIS/NAPS, 1969.

Patterson, G. R., & Reid, J. B. Reciprocity and coercion: Two facets of social systems. In C. Neuringer & J. D. Michael (Eds.), *Behavior modification in clinical psychology.* New York: Appleton-Century-Crofts, 1970.

Pawlicki, R. Behaviour-therapy research with children: A critical review. *Canadian Journal of Behavioural Science,* 1970, *2,* 163–173.

Peed, S., Roberts, M., & Forehand, R. Evaluation of the effectiveness of a standardized parent training program in altering the interaction of mothers and their noncompliant children. *Behavior Modification,* in press.

Peine, H. A., & Munro, B. C. Behavioral management of parent training programs. *The Psychological Record,* 1973, *23,* 459–466.

Phillips, D. The family council: A segment of adolescent treatment. *Journal of Behavior Therapy and Experimental Psychiatry,* 1975, *6,* 283–287.

Raven, B., & French, J. R. P. Group support, legitimate power, and social influence. *Journal of Personality,* 1958, *26,* 400–409.

Reid, J. B. Reliability assessment of observation data: A possible methodological problem. *Child Development,* 1970, *41,* 1143–1150.

Reid, J. B., & Patterson, G. R. Follow-up analyses of a behavioral treatment program for boys with conduct problems: A reply to Kent. *Journal of Consulting and Clinical Psychology,* 1976, *44,* 299–302.

Reisinger, J. J., Frangia, G. W., & Hoffman, E. H. Toddler management training: Generalization and marital status. *Journal of Behavior Therapy and Experimental Psychiatry,* 1976, *7,* 335–340.

Reiss, S., & Redd, W. H. Suppression of screaming behavior in an emotionally disturbed, retarded child. *Proceedings of the American Psychological Association,* 1970, 741–742.

Resick, P. A., Forehand, R., & McWhorter, A. The effect of parent treatment with one child on an untreated sibling. *Behavior Therapy,* 1976, *7,* 544–548.

Rinn, R. C., Vernon, J. C., & Wise, M. J. Training parents of behaviorally disordered children in groups: A three years' program evaluation. *Behavior Therapy,* 1975, *6,* 378–387.

Rosekrans, M. Imitation in children as a function of perceived similarity to a social model. *Journal of Personality and Social Psychology,* 1967, *7,* 306–315.

Sloop, E. W. Parents as behavior modifiers. In W. D. Gentry (Ed.), *Applied behavior modification.* St. Louis: Mosby, 1975.

Smith, J., & Smith, D. E. D. *Child management: A program for parents and teachers.* Ann Arbor, MI: Ann Arbor Publishers, 1966.

Sullivan, H. S. *The interpersonal theory of psychiatry.* New York: Norton, 1953.

Thibaut, J. W., & Kelly, H. H. *The social psychology of groups.* New York: Wiley, 1959.

Wagner, M. K. Parent therapists: An operant conditioning method. *Mental Hygiene,* 1968, *52,* 452–455.

Wahler, R. G. Oppositional children: A quest for parental reinforcement control. *Journal of Applied Behavior Analysis,* 1969, *2,* 159–170.

Wahler, R. G., House, A. E., & Stambaugh, E. E. *Ecological assessment of child problem behavior: A clinical package for home, school, and institutional settings.* New York: Pergamon Press, 1976.

Walster, E. Assignment of responsibility for an accident. *Journal of Personality and Social Psychology,* 1966, *3,* 73–79.

Walter, H. I., & Gilmore, S. K. Placebo versus social learning effects in parent training procedures designed to alter the behavior of aggressive boys. *Behavior Therapy,* 1973, *4,* 361–377.

Watzlawick, P., Beavin, J., & Jackson, D. *Pragmatics of human communication.* New York: Norton, 1967.

Wiltz, N. A., & Gordon, S. B. Parental modification of a child's behavior in an experimental residence. *Journal of Behavior Therapy & Experimental Psychiatry,* 1974, *5,* 107–109.

Wiltz, N. A., & Patterson, G. R. An evaluation of parent training procedures designed to alter inappropriate aggressive behavior of boys. *Behavior Therapy,* 1974, *5,* 215–221.

Wright, H. F. *Recording and analyzing child behavior: With ecological data from an American town.* New York: Harper & Row, 1967.

Zeilberger, J., Sampen, S. E., & Sloane, H. N. Modification of a child's problem behaviors in the home with the mother as therapist. *Journal of Applied Behavior Analysis,* 1968, *1,* 47–53.

8

The Role of Stimulus
Control and
Response Consequences

DAVID MARHOLIN II
PAUL E. TOUCHETTE

There are two major influences that determine the probability of behavior. The first is that of the behavior's consequences, well known
as the reinforcement principle or the law of effect. The second influence
is less well understood; it involves the precursors of behavior and is
generally discussed under the rubric of stimulus control.

When any consideration is given to making behavior robust and
likely to occur outside a therapeutic environment, the emphasis has
traditionally focused on consequences. This chapter will consider both
the antecedent conditions and consequences which are likely to affect
behavior in extratherapy environments. Without consequences adequate
to maintain it, the new behavior will deteriorate. Without the antecedent
conditions necessary to provoke it, the behavior may not occur at all.
Both antecedent conditions and consequences must be considered when
the target is the transfer of behavior to environments over which therapists have no direct control.

We will use the term **transfer** to refer to the probability that a desired

MAXIMIZING TREATMENT GAINS:
Transfer Enhancement in Psychotherapy

response will occur in a new environment at a rate above zero. Once the behavior occurs, it must be reinforced in order to be strengthened or maintained. We will use the term **maintenance** to refer to the probability that the behavior will continue unabated in a new environment after its initial occurrence. Transfer is prerequisite to maintenance. Maintenance contingencies must be in effect if the behavior which transferred is to continue.

Some comments about the scope, organization, and style of this chapter are in order. The scope is purposely quite limited. The chapter is primarily an excursion into the separate but related notions of transfer and maintenance of therapy-induced behavior change. Although many authors have addressed themselves to broad issues of generalization, few have attempted to analyze the critical components responsible for transfer **and** maintenance of behavior change. We feel that such a chapter is a needed and useful addition to the literature in this area. We do not have all of the answers. We think the chapter provides a frame of reference from which an analysis of transfer and maintenance may be developed.

The emphasis of the chapter is on techniques that are practical, empirically supported, and open to replication. There are four main sections. First, an operational distinction is made between the concepts of transfer and maintenance. Then an analysis of stimulus control is presented as a theoretical underpinning of transfer. This is followed by a series of practical stimulus control techniques that include procedural descriptions, case examples, and a short commentary about each technique. The final portion of the chapter is devoted to maintenance factors. Sections are devoted to an analysis of environmental contingencies and types of target behaviors likely to lead to maintaining reinforcement contingencies. As in the stimulus control technique section, descriptions of procedures, case examples, and commentaries are included to demonstrate maintenance enhancing techniques.

The style of the theoretical sections is somewhat technical, but we expect that the language and concepts used are familiar to clinicians who use operant conditioning procedures. The technique sections of the chapter are written in a rather informal and nontechnical style.

TRANSFER AND MAINTENANCE

Three assumptions are commonly made concerning behaviors acquired in the course of therapeutic intervention. First, changes effected in the treatment environment are expected to be paralleled by changes in extratherapy settings (Kazdin, 1977a; Marholin, Siegel, & Phillips, 1976). Second, when a new behavior is strengthened, similar behaviors are also expected to occur more frequently. Finally, the stability of behavior following treatment is often taken for granted.

The goals of most interventions involve transfer and maintenance of behavior. Change achieved in a group home, clinic, school, or other therapy setting is expected to carry over to less accessible environments. It is not uncommon, however, that changes in behavior brought about in one environment remain specific to that environment (e.g., Redd, 1969; Redd & Birnbrauer, 1969; Wahler, 1969).

Behavior changed by the application of effective contingencies of reinforcement is likely to become tied to stimuli associated with the setting in which the change occurred. Newly acquired behavior may then fail to occur in extratherapy settings that do not contain these stimuli. Conversely, stimuli in the extratherapy environment may control behavior incompatible with that achieved in therapy. These stimuli may have been associated with the reinforcement of undesireable behavior, or with the extinction and punishment of the desired response pattern.

The extent to which behavior transfers from treatment programs to other settings is rarely evaluated. The term most often applied to this phenomenon is "generalization." A laboratory based definition of generalization emphasizing minor stimulus changes within stable environments and reinforcement contingencies can be misleading. The relevant foci in therapy include both response maintenance and transfer of stimulus control (Kazdin, 1977a; Marholin et al., 1976) in settings which are rarely well specified and never completely stable.

It is important to distinguish between transfer and maintenance. They represent two separate problems of analysis. What does it mean when a client in a token economy program evaluated 6 months after placement in the community is found not to be performing behaviors acquired during his stay in the program? The stimulus conditions in the community may be inadequate to provoke transfer from the token setting. It may be, however, that behavior did transfer from the token setting to the community, but it was not reinforced in the community. It may not be a desirable behavior in that environment. Reinforcement may be explicitly withheld and delivered contingent on other behaviors.

A ghetto youngster who is taught to articulate in middle class fashion during his stay at a residential treatment program may use his new speech patterns in the ghetto; but ghetto dwellers are likely to reinforce only ghetto talk. The "transfer environment" may provoke behavior patterns that are stronger to begin with and better maintained than patterns established in a therapeutic environment. A drug addict

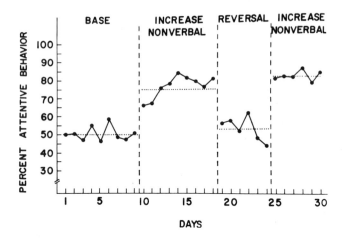

Figure 8.1 Mean daily rate of attentive behavior in the class. Base represents the baseline conditions; Increase Nonverbal represents the treatment condition during which nonverbal teacher attention was contingent on attentive student behavior; and Reversal represents a return-to-baseline condition. (Note. From "The effect of nonverbal teacher approval on student attentive behavior" by A. E. Kazdin and J. Klock, *Journal of Applied Behavior Analysis*, 1973, 6, 643–654. Copyright 1973 by The Society of the Experimental Analysis of Behavior. Reprinted by permission.)

may exhibit socially desireable behaviors at a detoxification center where drugs are inaccessible, but may fail to emit these same appropriate behaviors in a community where drugs are readily available. As a clinician, and as an applied researcher, it is important to recognize that the reduced frequency of behavior that was at high strength in a treatment setting may result from the failure of behavior to transfer, the failure of the environment to provide supporting contingencies or a combination of influences. The failure of desired behavior to transfer from treatment to real world environments is demonstrated by the research methodology used in behavior therapy.

Reversal and multiple-baseline designs are generic in behavior therapy research. Both rely on a demonstration of transient intervention effects.[1] Reversal designs demonstrate the effect of treatment by alternately presenting and removing treatment over time (see Figure 8.1). The sequence usually begins with an assessment of baseline rates of behavior. After baseline, treatment is implemented. Treatment is continued

---

[1] For a more detailed description of typical experimental designs in behavior therapy research, the reader is referred to the following: Baer, Wolf, and Risley, 1968; Hersen and Barlow, 1976; Kazdin, 1977b; and Kazdin and Marholin, 1978.

until behavior stabilizes. At this point, treatment usually is withdrawn and baseline conditions are reinstated. Typically, behavior returns or approaches baseline levels of performance. The return-to-baseline demonstrates that behavior may revert when treatment contingencies are dropped. The competing interest in demonstrating experimental effects (e.g., showing that a specific intervention technique produces behavior change) and maintenance of behavior (e.g., showing that the change produced is durable) has depressed interest in nonreversible changes (Emery & Marholin, 1977; Kazdin, 1977a). For example, Bijou, Peterson, Harris, Allen, and Johnston (1969) have recommended that treatment phases be brief so that behavior is unlikely to be maintained when the intervention is withdrawn.

Multiple-baseline designs rely on the behavior being tied to particular settings and people in order to demonstrate the influence of treatment. In these designs, effects are shown by introducing treatment at different points in time across different baselines (see Figure 8.2). The design is referred to as a multiple-baseline design because data are gathered across two or more baselines. One version of the design is the multiple-baseline across settings. Baseline data are gathered on one behavior in two or more settings. When data baselines have stabilized, treatment is implemented in one location while data are gathered in both. When treatment in the first setting is completed, intervention is begun in the second. Data continued to be gathered in both environments. The behavior is manipulated in each setting sequentially.

This experimental design depends on situational specificity of behavior. It is often used as a demonstration of experimental stimulus control, and relies on the failure of transfer from one setting to another. If behavior change were reflected in all settings before formal treatment was initiated in the second setting, ambiguity would be introduced in the experimental evaluation. Thus, failure of transfer and maintenance are so prevalent that they form the basis of two designs commonly used to evaluate behavioral intervention.

STIMULUS PROPERTIES OF THE ENVIRONMENT

The benefits of stimulus control are evident when Tom stops at a red light as he passes through Picayune, Mississippi; when Sophie opens a refrigerator to seek out a snack in a friend's home; when Andy circles the bases in proper order after hitting a baseball over the center field fence in a recently opened stadium; and when a psychologist greets a new client with a smile and a handshake. Stopping at the red

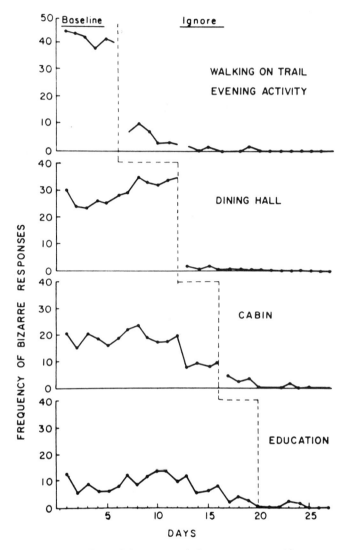

Figure 8.2 Daily number of bizarre verbalizations in specific camp settings. (Note. From "Case study: Implementation of behavior modification techniques in summercamp setting" by G. J. Allen, *Behavior Therapy*, 1973, 4, 570–575. Copyright 1973 by *Behavior Therapy*. Reprinted by permission.)

light in a novel city, opening the refrigerator in a strange room, circling the bases on a never-before-seen field, and shaking the hand of the new client occur because stimuli are present to indicate the high probability of reinforcement available contingent on specific behavior (avoiding an accident, finding food, scoring a run, and receiving a hand-shake, smile, and fee in return).

A less desirable feature of stimulus control is evident when desirable behaviors are left behind in the therapy setting. Stimuli that have been shown to acquire strong control over behavior during or subsequent to therapy are the therapists themselves (Marholin & Steinman, 1977; Marholin, Steinman, McInnis, & Heads, 1975; Redd, 1970; Risley, 1968); specific reinforcement contingencies (Meichenbaum, Bowers, & Ross, 1968; Redd & Birnbrauer, 1969; Harris & Romanczyk, 1976; Wahler, Steinman, McInnis, & Heads, 1975; Rabin & Marholin, 1978; Redd, 1972); and incidental physical features of the training environment (Pomerantz & Redd, 1977; Rincover & Koegel, 1975). What we mean to suggest is that acquisition of control by stimuli specific to the treatment situation may explain many instances of failure of transfer. As we will explain later, a functional analysis of the controlling relation can lead to strategies which incorporate these stimuli and provoke transfer (Marholin *et al.*, 1976; Rincover & Koegel, 1975).

A Theoretical Framework of Stimulus Control

Our analysis of stimulus control proceeds within a theoretical framework. The frame of reference which follows has emerged from a laboratory based experimental analysis which is readily applied in therapy settings.

Ferster and Skinner (1957) stated that "The effect of reinforcement is maximally felt when precisely the same conditions prevail. Thus, if a response is reinforced in the presence of stimulus A, any increase in frequency will be maximal in the presence of stimulus A [p. 8]." This early formulation suggests that single-stimulus training, without explicit differential reinforcement, will produce stimulus control. Laboratory research suggests that single-stimulus training is not always sufficient (e.g., Peterson, 1962). On the other hand, differential reinforcement training does not guarantee stimulus control either (e.g., Newman & Baron, 1965; Ray, 1967; Reynolds, 1961). Reinforcement procedures themselves do not generate stimulus control, but strengthen and maintain it once it occurs (Ray & Sidman, 1970). Establishment and maintenance of stimulus control are separate problems. Both must be considered in planning for transfer and maintenance of therapeutic gains. Given that a controlling relation between a stimulus and response somehow occurs (establishment of stimulus control), immediate reinforcement of the controlling relation should make it more likely to occur again (maintenance of stimulus control).

One problem clarified by the distinction between the emergence and maintenance of stimulus control is that of measurement. Although the human eye will usually suffice to determine changes in response topography during shaping, it is often impossible to "see" developing stimulus control. The clinician can evaluate a controlling relation between a stimulus and a response only by systematically altering the stimulus. If a stimulus–response relation exists, there will be corresponding changes in the response.

To reiterate, there are two primary influences on the occurrence of behavior. A stimulus must initiate a behavior in a particular environment, and a reinforcing consequence must follow that behavior. In addition to initiating and consequating stimuli, a third class of stimuli must be taken into account, those which control competing behaviors. There are often a substantial number of stimuli which may disrupt fragile, new, desireable behavior. For example, academic behaviors may be taught to a child in a one-to-one situation. The child may then respond consistently to teacher-delivered instructions. Sudden introduction of other children into this situation would most likely disrupt the performance. Gradual introduction of disruptive influences would, on the other hand, help maintain the performance while the more normal one-to-ten teacher to pupil ratio was approximated. Starting with the one-to-one situation the next step might be one-to-two, then one-to-four, one-to-six, and finally one-to-ten (e.g., Koegel & Rincover, 1974, Exp. 2; Pomerantz & Redd, 1977). The technique of gradual stimulus change is a method of eliminating the devastating effects of environmental features which control behavior incompatible with the desired repertoire. In addition, gradual stimulus change provides "a parsimonious combination of stimulus-control measurement and maintenance of controlling relations [Ray & Sidman, 1970, p. 197]."

Precise definition of the controlling relation itself is another problem area. "All stimuli are compound, in the sense that they have more than one element, or aspect, to which a subject may attend. To ask that an experimenter (clinician) be aware of all the possibilities is already, perhaps, an impossible demand. To ask, further, that the experimenter (clinician) arrange conditions so that no undesired stimulus response correlation is ever reinforced sets a truly impossible task [Ray & Sidman, 1970, p. 199]." Rincover and Koegel (1975) provide an example of the difficulty in determining specific stimulus response relations on an a priori basis. John, an autistic youngster, was taught to imitate in an experimental room. In another setting (outside on the lawn) with a strange adult, John seemed to have lost the behavior acquired in the experimental setting. When the original therapist replaced the strange adult in the transfer setting, responding did not recover. John was placed back in the treatment setting with the novel adult; again, no responding occurred. While observing training sessions, it was noted that the therapist showed John a piece of candy before the start of each trial. Specifically, the therapist started each trial by placing his own hand in his lap and holding a piece of candy. Next, he raised the hand and candy until it was directly in front of John's mouth. Finally, he said, "Touch your chin [Koegel & Rincover, 1977, p. 240]." The incidental hand movement was introduced into the transfer setting (outside), and John's responses were recorded. The stranger started a trial by raising his hand (without candy) from his side until it was directly in front of John's mouth. Then the stranger gave the command, "Touch your chin." No candy was present, so one could rule out the possibility of John's responding to the candy. John responded appropriately. The session was then repeated without the hand movement. John again failed to respond. When the hand movement was included again, John responded. A stimulus incidental to the training procedure had come to control John's behavior. Examples such as this suggest that we may rarely know precisely what stimulus combinations control behavior in real world settings.

STIMULUS CONTROL TECHNIQUES

This section deals with techniques that have been used to establish, transfer, and maintain behavior change. Each will be introduced by a brief procedural description, followed by several examples and a short commentary.

Multiple Therapists

Principle

As many individuals as possible should carry out the treatment program in order to prevent a single therapist from inadvertently becoming the major stimulus for desired behavior. The problem of the therapist serving as a controlling stimulus is apparent when the client acts appropriately in the presence of his or her therapist, but in the therapist's absence the newly acquired behavior is absent. Stimulus control specific to the therapist was reported by Risley (1968) who shocked an autistic child contingent on climbing and rocking. Both of these behaviors were rapidly eliminated in the therapy setting. Control was restricted, however, to the experimenter's presence. Climbing and rocking occurred when the experimenter was absent. The therapist's presence is especially likely to gain control when punishment contingencies are in effect.

A therapist's presence may also acquire strong control when associated with reinforcement contingencies. Marholin and Steinman (1977), and Marholin, Steinman, McInnis, and Heads (1975) have formally observed a familiar schoolroom phenomenon. When a teacher reinforces appropriate classroom behavior, the students may behave in the desired fashion only in the teacher's presence.

Clients often behave differently in the presence and absence of their therapist. Data suggest that the control of desirable behavior beyond a particular therapist is more likely if clients interact with several therapists (Goldstein, 1973; Goldstein, Heller, & Sechrest, 1966; Kazdin, 1977a; Marholin et al., 1976; Marholin & Siegel, 1978).

Case Example

Stokes, Baer, and Jackson (1974) present an instance of encouraging generalization using multiple trainers. Four institutionalized, retarded youngsters were taught to wave their hand when adults approached. All four youngsters rapidly learned the greeting when nonverbal prompts and shaping contingencies were applied. The authors were interested in discovering whether handwaving would occur in other places and in the presence of other adults. Data were collected when as many as 14 staff members daily approached the trainees. For three of the four children handwaving occurred only in the presence of the individual who conducted the training sessions. A second trainer was added to the training sessions, and handwaving subsequently occurred with up to 20 individuals who had not been associated with training.

Commentary

Frequently treatment is carried out on a one-to-one basis (Marholin & McInnis, 1978). Although treatment procedures may be designed to be carried out by all staff in residential settings, maintaining certain critical contingencies is usually the responsibility of a single staff member. Treatment decisions not clearly defined by a therapy program may await discussion between one particular staff member (e.g., counselor, team coordinator, social worker, psychologist) and the client. Thus the client may unintentionally come under the specific control of that staff member. Treatment programs that allow for multiple staff decision making concerning contingencies not clearly covered by the written program aid in avoiding this problem.

However, using multiple therapists may adversely influence the rate at which a client acquires new behavior. The more people involved in a treatment program, the less consistent that treatment program is likely to be. If the program is not consistent, acquisition of target behaviors may be retarded. To overcome this potential drawback, programs can begin with a limited number of therapists. After the client makes substantive progress, additional therapists can be added. When Stokes *et al.* (1974) taught handwaving to retarded children, it took the addition of only one staff to produce transfer of the trained response. Consistency among multiple therapists can be enhanced by providing well defined tasks for the therapists and explicit contingencies on staff behavior (McInnis, 1976, 1978).

Studies using multiple therapists as facilitators of maintenance and transfer of treatment effects include: Barrett and McCormack, 1973; Emshoff, Redd, and Davidson, 1976; Garcia, 1974; Kale, Kaye, Whelan, and Hopkins, 1968; Koegel and Rincover, 1974; and Lovaas and Simmons, 1969.

Rehearsal in the Natural Environment

Principle

Client–therapist interactions are often limited to a therapist's office. Unless the therapist designs his or her treatment program to encourage the client to practice behaviors outside of the office, they may not occur elsewhere. In most cases, behavior must occur and be reinforced outside of the therapy setting to be truly useful.

To test whether behavior established in treatment will transfer to a client's natural environment, a therapist should first instruct the client to try out the behavior in the real world. If the client successfully engages in the behavior outside of the therapist's office, all is well and good. If, however, the client reports that he was unable to carry out the behavior in the natural environment, additional support is necessary. This support may take the form of rehearsal and desensitization. Therapists may design homework assignments and place contingencies on the client for carrying them out (Kanfer, 1975) in order to encourage practice of new behaviors. If the target behavior is well selected, the presence of reinforcing consequences will shift control to features of the client's natural environment.

Case Examples

Clients who are in need of assertiveness training often begin by learning to be more assertive in a client–therapist dyad. Assertive behavior can be shaped with comparative ease in an office or hospital situation, but the target is the transfer of assertive behavior to the client's natural environment. Eisler (1976) discusses the case of Mr.

Jones, a 39-year-old black bricklayer who had been hospitalized with complaints of sleeplessness, tension headaches, and tachycardia. A behavioral assessment revealed that Mr. Jones, who had recently been promoted by his white boss to a supervisory position, lacked assertive skills necessary for performing his supervisory functions. Rather than reprimand his six subordinates for poor performance, Mr. Jones worked extra hours himself to make sure each job would be finished on time. The few times that he attempted to assert his proper authority, his subordinates complained that he was an Uncle Tom and a slave driver. He subsequently allowed himself to be bullied by his subordinates for fear of offending them. Through role playing with a therapist, Mr. Jones acquired assertive skills relevant to his job demands in five training sessions. During training Mr. Jones imagined scenes from his work situation. For example, he was requested to imagine a scene in which the subordinates were taking an exceptionally long break. The therapist modeled, and then Mr. Jones role played and practiced the following assertive reply: "Don't give me that slave-driver business. You guys have had your break twice over. If you don't give me some cooperation in getting this job done, I'll have to deduct the time from your paychecks. I'd like you to get back to work right now [Eisler, 1976, p. 33]." Transfer to real life situations was enhanced by **asking** Mr. Jones to practice the skills acquired during the assertive training sessions in actual real-life encounters. As Mr. Jones practiced newly learned assertiveness in his natural environment, stimulus control was successfully switched from the in-office role playing to the job situation. Falling behind schedule became a stimulus sufficient to provoke assertive behavior previously provoked only by the therapist. The responsiveness from his subordinates served to reinforce the stimulus control exerted by cues such as falling behind schedule.

In an example of using practice assignments or "homework," McGovern and Burkhard (1976) present the case of Art, a 21-year-old male, university student. At the time of initial contact with a psychologist, Art indicated that he had not had any dates during high school and college. He also told the psychologist that he was "extremely anxious, could not interact effectively in most heterosexual social situations, and needed basic information about heterosexual dating [McGovern & Burkhard, 1976, p. 38]." As part of therapy, Art read a social skills training manual (McGovern, 1972) containing six sections: "Initiating Brief Conversations," "Relevant Information about Developing Heterosexual Relationships," "Maintaining an Effective Conversation," "Personal Attractiveness," "Positive and Negative Social Behaviors," and "An Invalid Fear of Rejection." Art and his female therapist then role played a variety of conversations involving dating. Following several sessions of behavioral rehearsal in a clinic setting and in the natural environment (a college pub), Art was given weekly homework assignments. "During the first week of these assignments, Art was told to say 'Hello' to 20 college women a day. During the second week, he was instructed to continue saying 'hello'; in addition, he was to initiate brief conversations with two women each day. For example, he would say: 'Hello, my name is Art. I just transferred here from the state university. Could you tell me where the clinical services building is?' " Following each conversation, Art was asked to record what had occurred in a diary he carried. For example, after the first day, he wrote, "Thank God I got that over with." The second day he wrote, "A good day. I really timed my smiles well." Each week the assignments became more difficult. That is, Art was asked to maintain each conversation for a longer period of time. After 4 weeks of these assignments, Art was initiating and maintaining at least two 7-min conversations a day. In fact, on several days he decided to spend several hours talking to a number of college women at different locations around the campus. The assignments in combination with other procedures were successful in increasing the amount of heterosexual contact.

Commentary

A number of points should be considered. Homework assignments must be "doable" and highly likely to produce a positive result at least most of the time (Krumboltz & Thorensen, 1976). Art, for example, when asked to say "hello" to 20 women was almost guaranteed some warm greetings in return, along with a few cold stares, which were noncatastrophic. If Art's therapist had first asked him to engage in twenty 5-min conversations, Art probably would have been unsuccessful.

The client must have the desired behavior in his repertoire before he is asked to perform it outside of the therapy setting. This can be established in the therapeutic environment, as behaviors are role played, rehearsed, and discussed in detail prior to execution eleswhere. It is then important for the therapist to reinforce the client for carrying out assignments. A vital step in the transfer of stimulus control from the therapist to features of the natural environment is therapist-delivered reinforcement contingent on the client's execution of the assigned task (Kanfer, 1975). The therapist usually cannot monitor the client directly. However, asking him to bring in a specific record of events in the environment related to the assignment (e.g., a data sheet recording the number of different people talked to during a 1-hour period in a bar) has served to provoke the desired behavior in many cases. As the client completes assignments from which desirable natural environmental consequences result, the therapist may begin to fade his instructional control as natural environmental stimuli come to control the client's behavior.

Case studies which illustrate variations of rehearsal and assignments in the natural environment include: Marholin and Kanfer (1977)—increasing social skills of a woman reporting a phobia of the Catholic host; Youell and McCullough (1975)—decreasing colitis; McCullough, Huntsinger, and Nay (1977)—decreasing aggression in a 16-year-old; Meyers, Farr, and Craighead (1976)—eliminating female organismic dysfunction; Karoly (1974)—overcoming fear of flying; Melamed and Siegel (1975)—reducing ritualistic checking behavior; and Scheiderer and Bernstein (1976)—treatment of marital problems and chronic back pain.

Multiple Settings

Principle

Train new behaviors in a variety of settings. This procedure is actually a corollary and extension of behavioral rehearsal. Although it is usually practical to train new behaviors in only one setting, it is desirable to have the client practice in a number of environments where the behavior will be immediately reinforced. This precludes the formation of a conditional discrimination which could tie the behavior to features of the therapeutic environment (e.g., Harris & Romanczyk, 1976; Wahler, 1969).

Case Example

In an effort to correct the articulation problems of a retarded woman residing in an institution, Griffiths and Craighead (1972) reinforced approximations to proper articulation. All speech therapy sessions were carried out in the "speech therapy room." The training procedures were effective in correcting the client's misarticulation. However, when she returned from speech therapy to her cottage or classroom, she still spoke incomprehensibly. Speech patterns acquired in the speech therapy room did not transfer. Providing contingent reinforcement for correct articulation in the cottage quickly established good articulation in that setting. Reinforcement in the second environment (cottage) resulted in untrained transfer of appropriate speech to a third environment (classroom).

Commentary

The formation of situation-specific discriminations by clients is a frequently observed clinical phenomenon. The problem is most common among the severely and profoundly retarded and autistic youngsters. These discriminations may occur with other populations such as delinquents and adult prisoners especially if they have been confined to institutions for prolonged periods. For these populations it becomes critical that training initiated in specific settings be carried out in environments outside of the original training setting regardless of the efficiency with which the behavior was occurring in the original training setting.

Several good examples of multiple training settings used to provoke transfer have been reported: Allen (1973); Emshoff *et al.* (1976); Griffiths and Craighead (1972); Koegel and Rincover (1974, Exp. 2); Lent (1968); and Rubin and Stolz (1974).

Preprogrammed Controlling Stimuli

Principle

During training, an object, task, or word may be established as a controlling stimulus for the desired behavior. Preprogrammed stimuli (e.g., assignments) which provoke previously low probability behaviors in posttreatment settings allow for reinforcement and consequent strengthening of the desired behavior and subsequent development of more appropriate controlling stimulus–response relations. In the absence of a specific controlling stimulus, the target behavior may never occur in the natural environment regardless of the contingencies of reinforcement.

Redd (1970) taught four retarded children to play cooperatively. Two adults participated in the training sessions. One adult was designated as the "contingent adult"; in his presence, cooperative play was reinforced with M&M candies. The second adult was designated as the "noncontingent adult"; in his presence, the children were not reinforced regardless of whether they engaged in cooperative play. The contingent adult acquired stimulus control over cooperative play. Several probes were then conducted in a novel setting, a large playroom. When the noncontingent adult entered the playroom, he had no effect on the children's behavior. When the contingent adult entered the playroom, however, the children immediately began to play cooperatively. Finally, both the contingent and noncontingent adults entered the playroom without the cup that had held the M&Ms. Under these conditions, the children failed to play cooperatively for either the noncontingent or contingent adult. When the noncontingent adult entered the playroom with the reinforcement cup, the children failed to play cooperatively. Only the preprogrammed combination of contingent adult and reinforcement cup controlled the target behavior in the new setting.

Case Examples

Marholin, Steinman, McInnis, and Heads carried out a series of studies aimed at designing procedures for teachers to use to transfer the control of social and academic behaviors of their students from the teacher to other naturally occurring stimuli (Marholin & Steinman, 1977; Marholin, Steinman, McInnis, & Heads, 1975). When a student leaves special management systems used in the therapeutic classrooms and returns to regular classes, it is not unusual to find a marked deterioration in the child's behavior. Deterioration of student behavior upon withdrawal of classroom contingency management systems has been observed in several studies (Broden, Hall, Dunlap, & Clark, 1970; Marholin & Townsend, 1978; McArthur & Hawkins, 1975; Meichenbaum et al., 1968; O'Leary, Becker, Evans, & Saudargas, 1969).

If an adult has been established as a controlling stimulus for reinforced behavior, the presence of that adult will increase that behavior and his absence will decrease it (Redd, 1974, 1976; Steinman, 1970a, 1970b, 1977). It is likely that the teacher will develop stimulus control over a variety of behaviors such as sitting quietly, working independently, asking questions, and so on. To the extent that the teacher's presence is necessary both to monitor and reinforce the child's classroom behavior, it should be expected that the child's appropriate classroom behavior may decrease in the teacher's absence. The student will simply learn a conditional discrimination in which responding appropriately to various classroom stimuli is only functional when the teacher is present. The student may sit quietly, work independently, and ask questions only when the teacher is present. A controlling relation exists between the teacher's presence, the child's behavior, and adequate teacher-delivered reinforcement. Without any of these components, the controlling relationship breaks down, and the student's behavior deteriorates.

In most classrooms contingencies are applied to increase task-oriented behavior and to decrease disruptive behavior (e.g., Winett & Winkler, 1972). Because of the nature of the behaviors being manipulated, the teacher's presence is necessary to observe the occurrence of these behaviors and to deliver appropriate consequences. It is therefore likely that her presence will develop precise stimulus control over the student's appropriate classroom behavior. However, since delivery of consequences never occurs in the teacher's absence, appropriate behaviors are not likely to be maintained under this condition.

A class of behaviors can be reinforced in a classroom which does not require direct, on-the-spot observation by the teacher. This class of behaviors includes permanent measures of rate and accuracy of academic performance. Marholin and Steinman (1977) tested the hypothesis that reinforcing rate and accuracy would establish academic materials as controlling stimuli rather than the teacher. The study was conducted in a classroom of 19 highly disruptive elementary children. It compared reinforcing task-oriented and nondisruptive behavior alone (B) and reinforcement for accuracy and rate of work (C). A baseline (A) BCBC reversal design was used to evaluate the effects of reinforcing directly observed social behavior versus permanent project targets. The teacher was absent from the classroom for 3 consecutive days at the end of each condition. In the teacher's absence, task-oriented behavior was markedly reduced, and disruptive behaviors were markedly increased, regardless of the reinforcement condition in operation. In addition, the teacher's absence resulted in a marked reduction in academic accuracy and rate. However, the extent to which the children became disruptive in the teacher's absence was decreased when reinforcement was made contingent on the accuracy and rate of the children's academic performance. Reinforcing a permanent product (e.g., correct problem solution) maintained the frequency of task-oriented behavior and the rate of attempted problems to a greater degree than reinforcing task-oriented behavior alone. A controlling relation was established between the academic materials and desired classroom behaviors.

Rabin and Marholin (1978) demonstrated how an arbitrary stimulus could be programmed as a controlling stimulus during training and later introduced as a controlling stimulus in both the training setting in the trainer's absence and in a novel extratherapy setting in the trainer's absence. Michael, a severely retarded, institutionalized adult, was given ice cream and social praise when he placed cubes in a pair of plastic receptacles. During a discrimination training phase, a signal light was placed on a table in front of Michael. The teacher working with Michael could turn the light on or off. When the light was on, Michael would receive reinforcement for working. When the light was off, Michael would not be reinforced regardless of whether he worked or not. Two-minute light-on and light-off periods were alternated during 12-minute training sessions. Michael worked faster during the light-on periods when reinforcement was available, and slower during the light-off periods when reinforcement was not available. Two types of generalization tests were then carried out. The trainer left Michael alone in the room where he had been taught to work independently, with instructions to complete the same task assigned during the training sessions. Michael's work might drop off markedly when the adult who had trained Michael left (Meddock, Parsons, & Hill, 1971; Peterson, Merwin, Moyer, & Whitehurst, 1971; Redd & Wheeler, 1973). What effect would the light have in the trainer's absence? The light controlled Michael's rate of work as it had during the training sessions. The adult's absence had no effect.

The second test was to move to a building located about one-half mile from the room in which the trainer-present and trainer-absent tests had been conducted. Michael had never previously seen this building. He was taken to a classroom, seated at a table with his work materials and the light apparatus, and instructed by the trainer to complete the task in a normal manner. Then the trainer left Michael alone in the room. When the light was on, Michael worked as efficiently as he had during the original training sessions. When the light was off, Michael's performance dropped dramatically. The programmed discriminative stimulus controlled Michael's behavior in the training setting with the trainer absent and in a novel setting with the trainer absent. A similar demonstration of transfer with the controlling stimulus present in a novel (untrained) setting is provided by Page, Iwata, and Neef (1976).

Commentary

Establishing behavior in extra-treatment settings through the use of specific preprogrammed stimuli is a different approach but compatible with methods discussed earlier. The use of multiple therapists, multiple settings, and behavioral rehearsal attempt to expand stimulus control. Establishing preprogrammed controlling stimuli utilizes narrowing of stimulus control to a stimulus complex which can be systematically presented to provoke appropriate behavior.

In the first case example presented, Marholin and Steinman (1977) encouraged the reinforcement of permanent products of client behavior (i.e., a certain number of completed math problems) rather than behavior associated with the attainment of permanent products (i.e., task orientation). By reinforcing permanent products, events prerequisite to generating the product rather than attainment-associated behaviors become controlling stimuli for performance of desired behavior. In the natural environment it is more likely that stimuli associated with a permanent product are going to be present than those persons who have reinforced behaviors associated with the attainment of permanent products. For example, the artist is continually surrounded by his brushes, paints, canvasses, and sketch pads, but less frequently sees either his buyer or teacher who reinforced his artistic development. The research psychologist is immersed in books, journals, published articles, note pads, typewriter, and laboratory equipment, but less often is in the presence of his colleagues, department chairman, mentors, or dean. If the painter wishes to maintain a high frequency of artistic creation, and the psychologist frequent high quality publication, it might be more effective to provide effective reinforcers contingent on acceptable paintings and articles rather than on painting and writing behavior.

The second example demonstrated the programming of arbitrary controlling stimuli which control behavior in a novel environment. Such stimuli are readily associated with specific training procedures in practical ways. A ring, for example, might be used as a controlling stimulus for "no nail biting," a picture of fruit or other nonfattening foods posted on a refrigerator door as a controlling stimulus for not eating high caloric foods, and so on. Each of these controlling stimuli could be established during a formal therapy program. Then the controlling stimuli would be placed in the client's natural environment.

It has been suggested that covert stimuli such as visual images can control the execution of specific behaviors. The work of Cautela (1971) and Kazdin (1977c) exemplifies this approach. During therapy sessions, an alcoholic client may be asked to imagine a scene in which he raises a glass full of his favorite drink to his lips (Kanfer, 1975). Then the client is asked to imagine an aversive event such as getting sick and vomiting. When the client appears to be truly experiencing the aversive image, the therapist suggests to the client that he imagine himself immediately leaving the bar. When he leaves the bar, he imagines some positive event (e.g., the smell of fresh air, an attractive young woman smiling at him). Then the therapist helps the client develop effective self-statements such as "Why do I do silly things like drinking, it only gets me sick. No, I won't take any alcohol [Kanfer, 1975, p. 344]." The client is then encouraged to use these covert images and self-instructions in real world problem situations (e.g., at a bar, at a party) as controlling stimuli for abstaining from drinking.

Once a controlling stimulus is established during training, the therapist may choose to gradually withold its presentation or he may attempt to increase the probability of the stimulus appearing in relevant environments. The light that was established as a controlling stimulus for Mike might gradually be faded from a transfer environment. Once Mike successfully performed work behaviors in an extratherapy environment under the control of the bright light, the trainer could slowly fade the brightness of the light. At the same time Mike would receive reinforcement for producing in the work environment. Finally, the light might be completely faded, and the natural contingencies in the workshop setting would come to maintain Mike's hard working behavior; new controlling stimuli would then be in operation (e.g., foreman, work bench, peers). A second strategy might simply attempt to devise a practical way for the client to carry the controlling stimulus around with him or for the controlling stimulus to be naturally present in most relevant environments. Goldiamond, for example, instructed his stuttering clients to carry a small button around with them that had been established as a controlling stimulus for smooth uninterrupted speech.

Peer Control

Principle

Stimulus control may be broadened by having peers administer consequences. Peers, especially children, have been used with increasing frequency as major or adjunct agents of behavior change (e.g., Bailey, Timbers, Phillips, & Wolf, 1971; Fixsen, Phillips, & Wolf, 1973; Harris & Sherman, 1973; Kazdin, 1971; Phillips, Phillips, Wolf, & Fixsen, 1973; Siegel & Steinman, 1975). If children are successful in modifying their peers through direct reinforcement procedures, the peers themselves are likely to become controlling stimuli for appropriate behavior when adult therapists are not around (Kazdin, 1975; Marholin & McInnis, 1978). Their presence in various extratherapy settings will then lead to performance of the behaviors acquired during training. Peers have several advantages over other agents. First, peers are likely to be present in a number of situations in the natural environment. Second, if several are used to carry out a particular program, it is likely that peers in general, rather than one specific peer-therapist, will become a controlling stimulus for desired behavior. If the behavior normally occurs in the presence of others, stimulus control will be extended to any situation in which a peer is present.

Case Example

Johnston and Johnston (1972) used peers to encourage generalization. Each of two 8-year-old girls with articulation deficits were trained to monitor the correct and incorrect speech sounds of the other. For example, one child was taught to say to the other child within 1 or 2 sec of her articulating her speech sound incorrectly: "You said *fish* wrong," or "That was a bad 'f' in fish," or saying to the other child within 1 or 2 sec of her pronouncing her speech sound correctly: "That was a good 's' sound," or "You said *snake* right that time [p. 241]." Peer delivered feedback led to a rather rapid reduction of incorrect speech sounds. Transfer was assessed by bringing other children into the training setting. When the two children who had monitored and reinforced correct speech of each other were together, their rates of misarticulation were markedly lower than when they were placed with other peers who had never monitored their speech. In an earlier experiment in the same study, adults carried out the same speech program for two other children. Although the adult program was effective in decreasing incorrect speech, there was virtually no transfer from training to nontraining conditions. Stokes and Baer (1976) reported a case study which replicated Johnston and Johnston's findings. Had Stokes and Baer (1976) or Johnston and Johnston (1972) used more than one peer as a behavior change agent during the training phase, transfer of the target response might have occurred in the presence of novel peers. Multiple peer-therapists increase the probability that peers in general will become a controlling stimulus for reinforcing consequences.

Commentary

Peers as behavior change agents have recently been used in residential and outpatient therapy programs as data collectors (Siegel & Steinman, 1975), reinforcement deliverers (Axelrod, Hall, & Maxwell, 1972; Graubard, Rosenberg, & Miller, 1971; Solomon & Wahler, 1973), or participants in group contingencies (Marholin, Plienis, Harris, & Marholin, 1975; Medland & Stachnik, 1972; Patterson, Cobb, & Ray, 1972). For example, additional time at recess for an entire elementary class was made contingent upon the total number of points earned by a single class member (Patterson *et al.*, 1972). The contingencies were initially tailored in such a manner that on the first trial the child obtained the requisite points to earn recess time for all of his classmates. Gradually the contingencies were altered to require greater amounts of appropriate behavior from the target child. Similar procedures making reinforcement for a group contingent upon the performance of a single child (e.g., Barrish, Saunders, & Wolf, 1969; Walker & Buckley, 1972), a part of a group (e.g., Harris & Sherman, 1973), or the entire group (Marholin, Steinman, McInnis, & Heads, 1975; Packard, 1970) have been successfully used. In such a situation, each member of the peer group may encourage the desired behavior of the target client or clients in order to acquire reinforcers. It is also possible that they will employ censure and reprimands in order to control their peer's behavior (Axelrod, 1973). Given that the peers are successful change agents because they can dispense reinforcement or punishment, they may become controlling stimuli for appropriate behavior in other situations. The probability of the target behavior in extratherapy situations is increased. This notion is supported by a study of group reward versus individual reward with two groups of hyperactive elementary school children (Rosenbaum, O'Leary, & Jacob, 1975). Children's behavior in the group-reward condition was maintained for a longer period of time than the behavior of those in the individual-reward condition.

Multidimensional Stimulus Control

Principle

Vary as many irrelevant stimulus conditions as possible during training to prevent any one stimulus from acquiring control of the behavior. The stimulus control procedures heretofore presented (the use of multiple trainers and multiple settings) have been shown to be effective in their own right. The most effective treatment program would vary multiple stimulus conditions during training to blur the distinction between training and nontraining situations.

Case example

Emshoff et al. (1976) have reported an excellent example of varying multiple stimuli during training. These authors wanted to develop generalizable positive interpersonal comments among institutionalized, delinquent adolescents. Four adolescents from a residential home for delinquent and disturbed children were nominated by staff members as those most likely to remain in the home for an extended time. During a 2-week baseline period the students were observed during recreational activities such as basketball and ping-pong, meetings, shopping trips, meals, and informal relaxation periods in the lounges to ascertain the frequency with which positive or negative comments were made concerning the behavior or character of other peers or adults. Subsequently, the youngsters participated in seven 30-min therapy sessions over a 14-day period. Training consisted of an activity during which they received points and verbal praise from adult counselors for each positive comment. At the end of each session, the children received 3 cents per point. Two of the four youngsters were trained under "constant stimulus conditions." All sessions involved the same therapist, the same activity (ping-pong), the same location, and the same time (in the recreation room after the evening meal). The other two children received generalization training. The following conditions were varied during successive sessions: activity, trainer, location, and time. Activities included basketball, ping-pong, a trip for ice cream, a word game, a card game, and a discussion of life at home, dinner, and swimming. Several counselors were used as therapists, the location changed with the activity, and the time of the activities were widely varied. Both sets of students dramatically increased their rate of positive comment during the 2-week treatment period. Generalization tests were conducted (a) in the same activity but with new trainers and noncontingent reinforcement; (b) with a new activity, setting, and trainers with noncontingent reinforcement; and (c) in the residential home setting during daily activities. For each of the test situations it was shown that the two individuals who received generalization training maintained high rates of positive comments; the other two clients, who received training in the same setting, in the same activity, at the same time, and by the same trainer, exhibited lower rates of positive comments. Varying the stimulus conditions associated with training increased the transfer of the newly-acquired behavior to nontraining settings and previously unknown adults.

Commentary

Instructional and/or therapeutic sessions are often conducted one-to-one, with a therapist who uses idiosyncratic methods. Neither therapist nor contingencies are usually present in the natural environment (Pomerantz & Redd, 1977). Because the therapeutic environment may be relatively "distraction free," the client often does not have the opportunity to be exposed to conditions which may occasion responses incompatible with the target behavior(s) of therapy. When the individual returns to various natural settings, he may fail to emit his newly acquired behavior because of the absence of controlling stimuli and the presence of distractions.

One approach to teaching a client to ignore irrelevant distracting stimuli is to keep the controlling stimulus for the target behavior constant and to gradually introduce a distracting stimulus into the therapy setting.

By consistently reinforcing the desired target behavior only when the relevant stimuli are present, without regard to the presence or absence of distracting stimuli, the client can learn to ignore distractions and focus on the relevant stimuli. Goocher and Ebner (1968) applied this approach to academic behavior taught to a special education class. Following acquisition of selected behaviors, distractions were introduced into the classroom including a television set and other children. The behavior acquired in the training classroom transferred to the children's regular classroom, presumably because of the distractions introduced in the treatment setting. Other psychologists have reported adding distractors systematically during training in an effort to facilitate transfer of newly learned behavior. The distractors used have included peers, new instructors, group lessons, children playing (Pomerantz & Redd, 1977), classroom activities, other class members, and class instructional sessions (Jackson & Wallace, 1974).

Although using multiple therapists and settings and adding distracting stimuli to a training situation will generally increase the probability of transfer of behavior from one environment to another, these procedures are best used late in training. Varying stimulus conditions early in treatment might retard the client's rate of change. Early in training it is usually desirable to limit stimulus variations in order to facilitate acquisition of clinically desirable behavior. Once the client has acquired the target behavior and his performance has become somewhat stable, the therapist should vary stimulus conditions while continuing to monitor the client's rate and accuracy. A dramatic drop in performance indicates that the target behavior was not sufficiently well established prior to introduction of stimulus variations. This suggests that the therapist should refrain from adding additional stimulus variations until the performance is stable and satisfactory. Stimulus variations can be introduced later as the therapist continues a titration process.

MAINTENANCE

Transfer of stimulus control from a carefully designed therapy situation to the real world must occur if durable responding is desired. However, reliable occurrence of the target behavior is not assured when the stimulus that controlled it in the treatment situation is present in a desirable real world setting. The target behavior may fail to occur because more powerful controlling stimuli are present; in this case, behavior other than the desired target behavior will occur. For example, a red place mat on a dining room table may have been established as a controlling stimulus in a weight loss program (Ferster, Neuringer, & Levitt, 1962). Perhaps the red place mat was established as a controlling stimulus while a seriously overweight client was an inpatient in a residential setting. During treatment, the red place mat indicated the time and place of eating and the type and amount of food to be eaten. When the client returned to his home, he was instructed to take the red place mat and place it on his dining room table. However, the client's wife may serve as an even more powerful controlling stimulus for eating at other times (snacks) and at other places (in front of the television, in bed, and on the porch), and eating less desirable foods (chocolate sundaes, pizza). Although the controlling stimulus (red place mat) may be present in a desirable environment, it may not exert sufficient control over the client's behavior.

Even if a previously established controlling stimulus is present in an environment where one wishes a behavior to occur and more powerful competing controlling stimuli are not present, the desired behavior may still not continue. Once stimulus control has been achieved, the stimulus–response relationship must be reinforced to be maintained in the natural environment. Let us return to the example of the seriously overweight client. At the end of treatment the red place mat had come to control a variety of behaviors associated with eating (time, place, type, and quantity of food) in the controlled treatment setting. Initially, the place mat in the client's home might control these same behaviors. However, the client's wife could either reinforce or punish the controlling relation. That is, she might eat with her husband at the dining room table, make pleasant conversation with him during meals, and generally encourage his adherence to the treatment program. This might result in the maintenance of the controlling relation between the place mat and the client's appropriate eating behavior. On the other hand, his wife might fail to eat with him at the dining room table, encourage him to eat with her in the living room while watching the evening news, and generally ridicule his adherence to the treatment program; this might result in the weakening of the controlling relation between the place mat and his appropriate eating behavior.

The preceding portion of this chapter emphasized the establishment of a controlling relation between a stimulus and some target behavior. A theoretical analysis of stimulus control was presented, and a series of practical clinical procedures were offered to enhance the probability of transfer from the therapy situation to the client's natural environment. The following section will emphasize reinforcement and maintenance. Once stimulus control is established and transferred to an appropriate environment, the clinician must concentrate his efforts on increasing the likelihood of that environment possessing consequences which will maintain the relationship between the controlling stimulus and the target response. In any clinical endeavor, stimulus control must first be established, then contingent reinforcement must be provided to maintain it. Without stimulus control, the desired behavior will never occur in the target environment. Without sufficient reinforcement, the controlling relation will cease to occur.

CHANGING ENVIRONMENTAL CONTINGENCIES

Some features of the natural environment will support desirable behavior established under therapeutic conditions. The opposite, however, is often the case. Desirable behavior may be inconsequential or discouraged while undesirable behavior may be reinforced. For example, Walker and Buckley (1971) and Hall, Lund, and Jackson (1968) reported that inappropriate behavior receives at least as much reinforcement from the teacher as appropriate behavior in many classrooms. Walker and Buckley (1971) found that one teacher attended to inappropriate behavior 74% of the time and to appropriate behavior only 26% of the time. Attention contingencies in this classroom encouraged inappropriate behavior. This poses a dilemma for the clinician. A specially designed environment may increase desired behaviors only to have the contingencies prevailing in the child's classroom result in the weakening of desired behaviors and strengthening of undesirable ones.

One solution is to change the natural environment in such a manner that prevailing contingencies are used to support desired stimulus–response relationships. This requires shifting emphasis from an analysis of the individual client to the client's social environment. Instead of conceptualizing clinical intervention in terms of a dyadic model (therapist to client), it becomes necessary to conceptualize treatment in terms of a broader social model (Tharp & Wetzel, 1969; Weathers & Liberman, 1978). This approach involves multidirectional relationships among therapist (or consultant), mediator, and client. A careful analysis will serve to guide the organization of and techniques for intervention. The relevant behavioral analysis identifies reciprocal sources of stimulus control and maintaining contingencies (Patterson & Reid, 1970). The mediator is the central figure of the model. The mediator is the intermediary between the therapist and the target client. The mediator must (a) possess the target's reinforcers and (b) be able to dispense them contingent on the target's behavior. Any number of individuals occupying any number of social roles might serve as mediator: father, teacher, sister, minister,

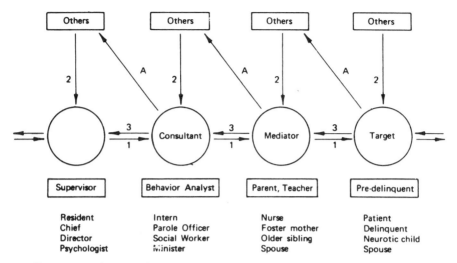

Figure 8.3 The consultative triad embedded in the social environment. (Note. From *Behavior modification in the natural environment* by R. G. Tharp and R. J. Wetzel, New York: Academic Press, 1969, p. 59. Copyright 1969 by Academic Press. Reprinted by permission.)

mother, employer, friend, or psychotherapist. Indeed, the same is true of the functions of either consultant or target.

In using the model in a positive manner, the therapist can arrange the relationship to encourage behavioral change in the system that will be maintained. Therapist, mediator, and client have clear and powerful controls over each others' behavior. Establishment and maintenance of desirable change requires that each participant be adequately rewarded for his efforts. If reinforcing consequences are not forthcoming, the multiple relationship will become dysfunctional or terminate.

The special feature of this approach is that the therapist's goal is to modify the behavior of a mediator. The therapist or consultant must establish mediator behaviors which will, in turn, result in the desirable modification of the client's behavior. If the therapist attended only to the client's behavior, he would be making serious errors. First, he will have failed to "modify the maintaining stimuli for the target's (client's) misbehavior; thus the target (client) would revert to misbehavior upon the withdrawal of the consultant [Tharp & Wetzel, 1969, p. 57]." Second, he would find it most difficult to alter the behavior of the client directly, because it is the mediator and not the consultant who controls the most powerful reinforcers for the client. Finally, it is important to recognize that the mediator and client can exert contingent control over the consultant. Client and mediator behavior change can be used to maintain desirable consultant behavior.

The objective of the triadic model is to arrange contingencies that strengthen desirable behavior of all parties concerned, and weaken undesirable behavior. The therapist prompts and reinforces behavior of the mediator (e.g., a mother of a tantrumming 7-year-old). Altered mediator behavior leads to a desirable change in the child's behavior, fewer tantrums. The change in the child's behavior results in reinforcement for the mediator (e.g., less frequent tantrums, more frequent pleasant interactions with her son). This, in turn, results in reinforcement for the therapist as the result of changes in both the child's and mother's behavior. Another important contribution of the triadic model is that it requires the therapist or consultant to analyze and possibly modify the environment in which clients reside. If the therapist's analysis of functional relationships was correct, the modified environment should subsequently result in the production and maintenance of desirable changes in the client's behavior.

Case Examples

Weathers and Liberman (1978) reported successful use of the triadic model in a community mental health center. Two cases involving parents follow.

Case 1. Mrs. F. (mediator) complained to a workshop leader (consultant) that her boys (target clients) would not mind her. The workshop leader subsequently asked Mrs. F to count the number of requests made of all her boys; responses were to be divided into immediate compliance, delayed compliance, and noncompliance. During a 2-week baseline, the boys complied immediately to only 7% of the mother's requests. As a therapeutic intervention, the workshop leader helped Mrs. F design a token system to use in the home. Rather than yelling and coercing her children into compliance, as was the pretreatment pattern, the token system stressed reinforcing compliant behavior. The mother was to award points in the home in the following way: immediate compliance (within 1 min of request) earned six points, delayed compliance (by the end of the day) earned two points, noncompliance earned no points. These points could be exchanged as follows: four points for one-half hour of TV viewing, four points for one-half hour of outside play, one point for 15¢. When the token system was instituted in the home by the mother, a six-fold increase in the rate of immediate compliance occurred; the children were now immediately compliant 42% of the time. The children were reinforced by the mother for compliant behavior; the mother was reinforced by the workshop leader for carrying through the token system and by the children (increased compliance, absence of yelling); the workshop leader was reinforced when the mother carried out the program and when the children became increasingly more compliant.

Case 2. Mr. and Mrs. B expressed concern to the workshop leader that their children were not very communicative. They were especially worried about the high rate of tantrums exhibited by their youngest son. After discussing their problem with the workshop leader, an initial goal was established as increasing the rate that Mr. B dispensed social reinforcers to his wife and children. It was thought that if the father modeled more positive verbal behavior and praised the family members more often, communication would increase and tantrums would decrease. Individual self-reinforcement contingencies were devised for Mr. B. The workshop leader and Mr. B decided upon a predetermined rate of compliments for specific consequences to occur. Shaving, ice cream, naps, watching television, a special breakfast, and bowling were the reinforcers used by Mr. B to successfully increase his rate of complimenting his family. Communication within the family increased, and the youngest son's tantrums decreased. In terms of reciprocal reinforcement, it may be assumed that Mr. B reinforced his wife and children when he delivered compliments; the wife and children reinforced Mr. B for delivering compliments by their communicative responses and by the youngest son's decrease in tantrums; Mr. B received self-delivered reinforcers for increasing his rate of compliments; and the consultant was reinforced by the father and children's success.

Walker, Hops, and Johnson (1975) illustrate contingency management using the triadic model. Eight highly deviant youngsters were referred to a contingency management classroom due to high rates of disruptive behavior in their regular public school classroom. The contingency management classroom involved a token economy combined with an intensive remedial program in reading, mathematics, spelling, and vocabulary. The token economy used social reinforcement, contingent points backed up by a variety of privileges, and response cost. Following treatment in the special token program, four of the children were merely returned to their regular classrooms. For the other four children, a consultant met with the teachers on a weekly basis to discuss student progress, training was provided for the regular class teachers, the consultant delivered weekly feedback on child and teacher performance, and positive consequences were delivered to the teachers contingent on their performance and the target child's performance. Teacher training and feedback focussed on the consistent use of social reinforcement contingent on desired social and academic behaviors of the target child. The teachers were also enrolled in a college course with the consultants. They received 6 hours of course credit for attending weekly feedback meetings and reading and mastering a text on basic reinforcement principles. Another reinforcer was made contingent on the child's behavior and indirectly, the teacher's. The teacher's course grade was contingent on how well the child's behavior was maintained compared to performance levels achieved in the contingency management classroom. Not surprisingly the four children, who returned to classrooms without intervention aimed at the teachers, failed to maintain treatment gains in appropriate behavior; the four children, who returned to classrooms in which maintenance procedures were initiated, maintained treatment gains. More importantly, 4 months after all contingencies were discontinued, the four children whose teachers had been trained as mediators still had higher rates of appropriate behavior than the controls.

The program for the four children, who maintained their treatment acquired behavior, can be discussed in terms of the triadic model. The teachers were selected as mediators. They controlled reinforcers for their students in the form of social reinforcement. The consultants placed contingencies on the teachers for improving their skills in the classroom including the consistent reinforcement of appropriate student behavior. Maintaining improved levels of client behavior (students) resulted in reinforcing consequences for the mediators (better grades, approval, and praise from the consultants and school administrators). Finally, the consultants were reinforced for their part in the program (observing teachers, attending training and feedback sessions) when the children's and teacher's desired behaviors increased and when the paper describing the maintenance procedures was published.

Commentary

Even in the earliest examples of behavior therapy, there was an implied commitment to training "significant others" as behavior change agents (e.g., Williams, 1959). Training significant others has received a considerable amount of research attention (cf. O'Dell, 1974; Patterson, 1971). The primary focus of research in this area has not been directed to the issue of transfer of treatment effects. However, the data suggest that encouraging significant others in the natural environment to reinforce controlling relations between certain stimuli and resulting desirable behavior serves to enhance the likelihood of the maintenance of behavior change even after the treatment program per se has been discontinued. One example frequently cited as evidence for the efficacy of training significant others involves the work of Lovaas and his colleagues (Lovaas, Koegel, Simmons, & Long, 1973). They followed the progress of 20 autistic children who were clients in their well-known intensive treatment program for psychotic youngsters at UCLA's Neuropsychiatric Institute. Some of the children discharged from the program were returned to various institutions. Other children were returned to their natural families. For the children returned to their families, an effort was made to train their parents in basic behavior modification techniques. Follow-up measures taken from 1 to 4 years after discharge showed that significant differences existed between children whose parents were trained in behavior modification techniques as compared to children who were institutionalized. It was noted by these authors that people in the institutional environments probably failed to reinforce newly acquired behavior (e.g., free play, appropriate speech, social behavior) while providing intermittent reinforcement for inappropriate behavior (e.g., self-injury, echolalia). In contrast, the parents trained in behavioral techniques probably provided sufficient contingent reinforcement to maintain appropriate behaviors while extinguishing inappropriate behavior.

When training mediators, it is critical to carefully weigh the target behavior of the client and the reinforcing consequences for the client and the mediator. The target behavior selected for the client must be reinforcing, when emitted, to the mediator. Only if excellence in school is important to a particular parent, will a program which increases a youngster's grades in school result in reinforcing consequences for that parent. It is important to analyze the consequences for the mediator as well as the target client.

Finally, the consultant or therapist must carefully assess the mediator's repertoire prior to suggesting changes in his behavior aimed at modifying the behavior of the target client. The consultant should not assume that a mediator can spontaneously change his behavior any more than one could assume that the client could. The mediator's behavior must often be shaped. A parent may be asked to ignore tantrums of a child in order to reduce their frequency. However, the parent may not have the self-controlling responses to ignore the behavior. Rather than ignore the behavior, the parent might remain silent for 15 sec and finally scream at the child, "Be quiet!" Thus, it would be the consultant's task to help the mediator develop strategies to carry out "ignoring" more effectively. The consultant might suggest that the mediator monitor his own behavior so that he could recognize when he was "losing his cool," walk out of the room in which the child was tantrumming, and possibly call a friend on the telephone. In other words, the behavioral repertoire of the mediator may have to be shaped as systematically as that of the target client.

The preceding portion of this chapter emphasized the analysis of reinforcement contingencies operating in a client's natural environment. Once a behavior has been taught and brought under appropriate stimulus control in a training and/or transfer setting, the environment must produce sufficient reinforcing consequences to maintain it. Training significant others to reinforce desired target behaviors in a client's natural environment was suggested as one useful maintenance enhancing technique. In addition to attending to the distributors of reinforcement, the functional utility of selected target responses must be analyzed.

THE FUNCTIONAL UTILITY OF BEHAVIOR CHANGE

Selecting Behaviors Likely to be Reinforced

Procedure

One strategy to enhance the probability of maintenance of any stimulus–response relationship is the purposeful selection of target behaviors that are likely to be reinforced by events which occur reliably without therapeutic intervention (Ayllon & Azrin, 1968; Kazdin, 1977a; Marholin et al., 1976; Stokes & Baer, 1977).

This strategy has been called the "Relevance of Behavior Rule" that states, "Teach only those behaviors that will continue to be reinforced after training [Ayllon & Azrin, 1968, p. 49]." The relevance of behavior rule stresses the importance of selecting target behaviors that are relevant in the setting in which the client will ultimately reside after treatment. Teaching adherence to institutional routines (e.g., attending group therapy sessions, participating in scheduled activities) might develop responses that are functional in the treatment setting but not in the client's natural environment. It is important to select target behaviors that will result in positive consequences for the client outside of the treatment program. Behaviors which are likely to generate their own reinforcing consequences include social skills, job skills, and even self-care behaviors.

Case Examples

An example of a training program designed to teach skills that are functional and likely to be maintained by natural consequences is provided by Marholin, O'Toole, Touchette, Berger, and Doyle (1978). They were interested in increasing access skills of institutionalized adults. They taught community skills including the use of public transportation, stores, and restaurants. Using prompting, modeling, corrective feedback, social reinforcement, and rehearsal as instructional procedures, four retarded adults learned to ride a bus to a predetermined destination, select and purchase an item from a store, and purchase a meal in a McDonald's restaurant. Training was carried out in the community. The likelihood of the skills taught during training being maintained by natural contingencies is quite high. That is, asking a salesperson for help is likely to be reinforced by the final acquisition of a desired product, asking a bus driver for the bus's destination would be reinforced by arriving at the destination, ordering a Big Mac would be reinforced by eating it, and so on.

In a second example, Seymour and Stokes (1976) taught a group of institutionalized, delinquent girls to recruit their own reinforcement. Prior to intervention the staff of the institution displayed little or no systematic attempts to reinforce desirable behaviors. Using an ecological approach (Graubard, Rosenberg, & Miller, 1971; Gray, Graubard, & Rosenberg, 1974), the girls were taught to modify the behavior of the staff. Whenever the girls had performed well, they were encouraged to prompt the staff by saying such things as "Am I working well?", "Look how much work I've done," "How's that, Miss . . .?" The girls' prompting was successful in increasing the amount of contingent praise delivered by the staff. Thus, "in theory, this new skill (cueing the staff) should have obviated the need for further experimental reinforcement, for the praised evoked should have functioned to maintain both the girl's work and cueing, and the cueing, in turn, should have functioned to maintain staff praise [Stokes & Baer, 1977, p. 354]."

Commentary

Selecting target behaviors that are relevant and functional is good clinical practice. Unfortunately, the therapist rarely knows beforehand what behaviors are relevant for a particular client in his idiosyncratic environment. Encouraging a husband to assist his wife in keeping their apartment tidy might be reinforced by a wife who values a neat apartment but extinguished or even punished by a wife who finds the activity disruptive. Travel skills might be reinforced in many major cities but would probably be extinguished in Oreana, Illinois, which is devoid of stores and restaurants. The clinician must be able to assess in some way the appropriateness of potential target behaviors for his clients. If a behavior is unlikely to be reinforced in the client's natural environment, it is not a valid solution to the client's problem.

The clinician can assess how valid and thus useful the intervention effects have been in two ways which might be referred to as the *social comparison* and *subjective evaluation* methods (Kazdin, 1977d). Social comparison involves determining whether the client's behavior before and after treatment is distinguishable from the behavior of his or her peers. For example, Walker and Hops (1976) assessed a group of "deviant" primary grade students and found that they exhibited markedly lower rates of appropriate classroom behavior (e.g., following instructions, working on assignments) than did their "nondeviant peers." The deviant children were placed in a special token economy classroom. Various appropriate classroom behaviors increased in frequency. Subsequently, the deviant children were returned to their regular classroom whereupon their appropriate behavior was compared to that of their peers. Their behavior was found to be indistinguishable from that of their nondisruptive peers. Thus, if appropriate behaviors were reinforced in the classroom, the clinician could be confident that the performance of the deviant students would be maintained.

A second method, subjective evaluation, involves judgments of behavior that has been changed by individuals who interact with the client or represent a certain segment of society (e.g., policemen, judges, high school students, businessmen, etc.). At Achievement Place, predelinquent boys were trained to interact more positively with police officers (Werner, Minkin, Minkin, Fixsen, Phillips, & Wolf, 1975). Because many youthful offenders get themselves in or out of trouble depending on how they handle interactions with police officers, Dr. Werner and his colleagues developed a training package including modeling, practice, and feedback to teach important youth–police interactions (e.g., facing the officer, giving polite short answers, expressing a desire to reform, cooperation, politeness). Operational measures of performance increased dramatically. The authors then assessed subjective evaluations of police, citizens of the boys' community, and college students as they viewed videotapes of boys who had and had not been trained. The trained boys were judged to interact more appropriately than the nontrained boys in areas such as suspiciousness, cooperativeness, and politeness. Thus, the training program developed important clinical changes based on the subjective assessment of those likely to come into contact with the youth in the future. Subjective assessments do not assure the therapist that newly acquired behaviors will be reinforced in the client's natural environment, but they do provide useful clinical insights concerning the clients and those who are likely to function as mediators of positive and negative consequences.

Numerous investigations and case studies report teaching skills that are expected to produce reinforcing consequences. Some of the better ones include teaching conversation skills to delinquent females (Maloney, Harper, Braukmann, Fixsen, Phillips, & Wolf, 1976); public speaking behavior to normal adults (Fawcett & Miller, 1975); job interview skills to delinquent youths (Braukmann, Maloney, Fixsen, Phillips, & Wolf, 1974); problem-solving strategies to members of a community board (Briscoe, Hoffman, & Bailey, 1975); assertive behavior to a university clinic population (Kazdin, 1976); independent eating skills to retarded residents of an institution (O'Brien & Azrin, 1972); social skills to with-drawn children (O'Connor, 1969, 1972); hypertensive patients to reduce their blood pressures (Elder, Welsh, Longacre, & McAfee, 1977); the conservation of electric power (Hayes & Cone, 1977); the elimination of chronic pain (Fordyce, Fowler, Lehmann, DeLateur, Sand, & Triesch-mann, 1973); basic pedestrian skills to retarded adults (Page *et al.*, 1976), a retarded boy to walk on crutches (Horner, 1971); a "blind" retarded male to discriminate visual stimuli (Stolz & Wolf, 1969); and social skills to chronic psychiatric patients (Hersen & Bellack, 1976; Wil-liams, Turner, Watts, Bellack, & Hersen, 1977).

Incompatible Behaviors

Procedure

A treatment program devoted exclusively to the elimination of prob-lem behavior is not likely to be successful. If a client employs socially in-appropriate behavior to obtain reinforcers from his environment, inter-vention will usually attempt to strengthen acceptable behavior which achieves the same objective. "Incompatible behaviors" can lead to the same reinforcers as the socially undesirable behavior. They may not be physically incompatible. Several reports of successful classroom rein-forcement programs accelerated a behavior incompatible with disruption (i.e., academic output). Desired academic behavior increased, disruptive behavior decreased and academic production transferred to other periods of the school day when therapeutic contingencies were not in effect (Marholin & Steinman, 1977; Marholin, Steinman, McInnis, & Heads, 1975). New academic productivity produced intermittent reinforcement and made disruptive behavior unnecessary.

Behavioral intervention programs with delinquents often attempt to strengthen a variety of responses incompatible with the socially unac-ceptable behavior designated as delinquency (Emery & Marholin, 1977). Delinquent behavior is aversive to society as a whole (Morris, 1978). In attacking the problem, society may demand that delinquent behaviors be directly suppressed. Punishment might temporarily alleviate the social problem, but a long range solution requires an alternative way for de-linquent youths to gain reinforcers. "If stealing and property damage are reduced in delinquents, but no alternative skills exist in them for gaining the same reinforcers, then they can only become examples of no response and although we may no longer consider them a delinquency problem, we surely find that they are now a welfare problem or a retardation problem [Baer, 1975, p. 28]."

Rather than attempt to suppress delinquent behaviors per se, delinquency programs have targeted behaviors which are believed to be incompatible with delinquency (e.g., Bassett, Blanchard, & Koshland, 1975; Phillips, 1968; Willner, Braukmann, Kirigin, & Wolf, 1978). The belief on which this approach rests is that skills of gaining reinforcers legally will eliminate the need for a program to punish stealing and property destruction after the fact. "Those undesirable responses may simply fall into disuse, displaced by the desirable (and more profitable) skills [Baer, 1975, p. 28]." Is it possible to reduce or eliminate delinquency through encouraging "more profitable" behaviors which are not directly related to the problem? The delinquency example points out the necessity of empirically determining what type of target behaviors are likely to be reinforced in the real world. This is necessary to predict likely maintenance of the behaviors taught to any client. If potentially incompatible behaviors are taught and not reinforced in natural settings, they will quickly extinguish.

Case Example

Bassett and his colleagues provide an excellent example of this approach. They taught inmates at the Shelby County Penal Farm behaviors that might achieve reinforcers equally as potent as those achieved through illegal behaviors (Bassett et al., 1975). Virtually ignoring the behaviors that resulted in incarceration, a token economy program was developed to teach "free world" behaviors which had potential value for the inmates once they returned to the outside world. Targets included increased television news watching and increased attending to and understanding of the content of the news. They also attempted to increase voluntary attendance at a remedial education center during free-time periods. It was hypothesized that both of these behaviors would be useful in the free world and would have some adaptive value. "Thus, being informed of current events from having watched the news would seem to lead to being a better citizen more in tune with society's values. Furthermore, spending free time in educational or other self-improvement pursuits would also seem to lead to being a better and potentially more productive citizen [Bassett et al., 1975, p. 640]."

Target behaviors were increased in a cross section of Penal Farm inmates when point contingencies were established. Points could be spent on telephone calls, additional visiting hours, participation in special outings, baseball games, and access to a television set, magazines, games, and a stereo. Ideally, the increased rates in the target behaviors achieved while the inmates were incarcerated should persist after their release. These newly acquired behaviors could form a base for acquiring reinforcers. A job might be easier to obtain for an inmate who had earned a high school diploma at the remedial education center. The job might then provide access to monetary reinforcement that was previously attainable only through illicit means.

Commentary

The assumption in the incompatible behavior approach is that the program designer knows of approved behaviors which lead to the same consequences as did prior unacceptable behaviors. It is rare indeed that one is certain which functional response–reinforcer arrangements were and will be relevant. In the case example, the inmate may leave the Penal Farm with increased academic skills and even a high school diploma. He may, however, return to the free world and continue to engage in illegal behaviors (e.g., robbery) rather than seek a job. The academic skills acquired in prison, may, in fact, aid the individual in his pursuit of reinforcement through robbery. He may now become a more proficient thief who reads books about locks and plans more complex robberies. For this individual, academic skills may not be incompatible with the antisocial behavior that led to incarceration.

Behaviors such as housekeeping, grooming, polite speech, job skills, academic repertoires, and negotiation skills cannot be assumed to be related to problems such as arrests, court contacts, and institutionalization on an a priori basis. Increase in "incompatible" behaviors should be functionally related to a decrease in measures of deviance (e.g., number of arrests).

The hypothetical experimental analysis in Fig. 8.4 involves two groups of delinquents. In one group, five incompatible behaviors are analyzed and modified, while no intervention takes place for the second group. Pre- and postmeasures of delinquency are collected for both groups.

> If the five responses are, indeed, an analysis of the problem, then in the first group there should result a clear decline in delinquency, while in the second group (for whom the five responses were not altered), no such change could be seen. That would constitute an analysis of the problem, in that it would have shown where the five responses were altered, the problem was solved, but where the five responses were unchanged, so was the problem [Baer, 1975, p. 28].

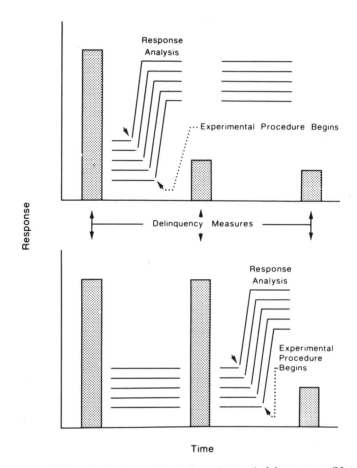

Figure 8.4 A hypothetical experimental analysis of delinquency. (Note. From "In the beginning, there was the response" by D. M. Baer, in E. Ramp and G. Semb (Eds.), *Behavior analysis: Areas of research and application,* Englewood Cliffs, New Jersey: Prentice-Hall, 1975, p. 29. Copyright 1975 by Prentice-Hall. Reprinted by permission.)

The same analysis of the five targeted behaviors could then be carried out on the second group who would have twice demonstrated their delinquency. Should change in the five behaviors be followed by a decrease in the measure of delinquency for this second group, the analysis would be replicated. This analysis and replication supports a conclusion that a positive change in a set of target behaviors caused a decrease in delinquency.

The relationship between teaching incompatible target behaviors and subsequent reduction in delinquency may raise questions concerning additions or deletions to the list of target behaviors to produce more efficient combinations of incompatible behaviors. In a recent review of the literature of behavioral approaches to delinquency all of the studies reported detailed data on subordinate target behaviors, but not one established a relationship of changes in these behaviors to delinquency (Emery & Marholin, 1977). Numerous behaviors have been modified in delinquent populations without evidence that these changes have led to a decrease in delinquency. Recently, however, the Achievement Place Research Group has begun to analyze delinquency measures subsequent to modification of specific target behaviors (Braukmann, Kirigin, & Wolf, 1976). Although their data are far from complete, results suggest a concurrent decrease in measures of delinquency, for at least one set of target behaviors taught to Achievement Place residents (e.g., Phillips, 1968; Willner *et al.*, 1978; Wolf, Phillips, & Fixsen, 1972). Currently, the clinician is left only with clinical judgment in trying to establish what is an incompatible behavior for a particular client. Even after specific empirical relationships are demonstrated between target behaviors and problems, the clinician will still be required to conduct a thorough behavioral analysis of each client's idiosyncratic environment (e.g., Kanfer & Saslow, 1969; Marholin & Bijou, 1977, 1978).

Other interesting controlled studies demonstrating the teaching of probable incompatible behaviors include instructing predelinquent youths and their parents to negotiate conflict situations (Kifer, Lewis, Green, & Phillips, 1974); teaching oppositional children to be more compliant (Wahler, 1969); instructing alcoholics to imagine pleasurable scenes when they feel an urge to drink (Hay, Hay, & Nelson, 1977); the teaching of appropriate sibling interaction skills in high-conflict families (Leitenberg, Burchard, Burchard, Fuller, & Lysaght, 1977); encouraging disruptive or hyperactive children in a classroom to quietly raise their hands and sit in their seats (Marholin & Steinman, 1977); and reinforcing aggressive siblings to play cooperatively (O'Leary, O'Leary, & Becker, 1967).

CONCLUSION

Behavior recently established in therapeutic settings is often subject to very high density reinforcement and specially designed artificial contingencies. Making the consequences of therapeutically-induced behavior less predictable and more "natural" renders the behavior more resistant to extinction. Space limitations do not allow us to deal with the variety of reinforcement features which facilitate the maintenance of behavior in extratherapy settings (e.g., fading contingencies, increasing delay of reinforcement parameters, thinning schedule of reinforcement, and so forth). They have been discussed elsewhere (cf. Kazdin, 1977a; Marholin et al., 1976; Stokes & Baer, 1977).

Stimulus control, like its sister concept, reinforcement, is a functional relationship. In the case of stimulus control, the relationship is between the antecedent of behavior and its subsequent likelihood of occurrence; in the case of reinforcement, the relationship is between the consequences of behavior and its likelihood. Antecedents are more likely to affect transfer, and consequences are more likely to affect maintenance of behavior.

If the presence or intensity of a stimulus accurately predicts the probability of the response, stimulus control is evident. In a pigeon study, control by the color red is demonstrated if the rate of pecking is high when red is displayed and low when other colors appear. The laboratory experimenter holds environmental features constant and presents the experimental stimuli in random order, making it easy to observe reliable relations between red and a pattern of responding. Careful, detailed, well-controlled stimulus manipulations carried out in a laboratory environment reveal the extraordinary power of controlling relations between stimuli and the likelihood of a particular response. In multiple schedule studies, for example, pigeons change their response patterns reliably before the various schedules of reinforcement come to bear when the visual stimulus associated with that stimulus appears (Ferster & Skinner, 1957; Skinner, 1969). Similar results have been obtained with human subjects in laboratory settings (Bijou & Baer, 1966). These effects occur outside of the laboratory as well. They account for a variety of response patterns characteristic of human behavior. We can only suggest the power of this laboratory–society analogy; rarely can it be tested directly.

We are convinced that stimulus control is the major element which influences the transfer of treatment induced behavior. Laboratory procedures and results provide a working frame of reference for this analysis. More often than not the therapist cannot identify stimuli which control behaviors of interest. Moreover, the client may not be of much help. Being under the control of a stimulus does not mean that the individual so controlled can verbalize what is going on. Applied behavior analysis offers some hope of clarifying this as yet murky area. As researchers in this field analyze stimulus control and transfer phenomena, we can begin to generate a list of transfer enhancing techniques.

Critics of behavioral approaches to behavior dysfunctions frequently suggest that failure to transfer indicates that treatment was inappropriate. When behavioral therapies are proposed, it has become commonplace to be faced with a hostile "but will it transfer to other environments?" The question is a good one. The assumption that a failure to answer it with predictive accuracy indicates incompetence or inadequacy of technique is absurd. Any number of factors may be responsible for the failure of transfer. Competing behavior may be more likely in extra therapy environments as a result of powerful contingencies of reinforcement associated with special features of that environment. Stimuli associated with extinction may be present. Selective attention may result in a client's failure to observe the stimuli which would provoke the desired behavior, or, as we have emphasized throughout, unanalyzed critical stimuli thought to be incidental during therapy may not be present in the transfer environment.

There are no guarantees of transfer or maintenance of therapy gains. The individual clients bring their unique learning history and genetic predispositions to therapy. These unique characteristics will determine the precise conditions which promote or retard transfer. The therapist concerned with assuring extratherapy gains must be committed to engage in a training-testing-retraining-retesting series until the target behavior is considered to be sufficiently unlikely in yet unencountered situations.

Numerous attempts may be required in order to achieve the desired robustness of therapy induced behavior patterns. In cases where accessible transfer targets can be specified, the therapist may make a best guess about the most effective approach and measure the outcome directly. If the initial strategy is not successful, the situation can then be reanalyzed and another approach tried until success is achieved. Persistence, accurate observation, and an imaginative application of behavioral principles are all that this problem demands. On the other hand, some behavioral intervention targets involve transfer to currently inaccessible environments. Common problems involve unspecified or unknown residences, work placements or other physical and social environments. The question then amounts to, will the target behavior remain in place no matter what happens? The answer is assuredly NO. The malleability of behavior which allowed the therapeutic changes to take place will also allow them to be displaced. The competency of the clinician as a predictor of transfer and maintenance is roughly comparable to that of a weather forecaster. They both know what many of the relevant variables are, but neither discipline has advanced to the point of being able to make completely accurate forecasts.

REFERENCES

Allen, G. J. Case study: Implementation of behavior modification techniques in summer camp settings. *Behavior Therapy*, 1973, 4, 570–575.

Axelrod, S. Comparison of individual and group contingencies in two special classes. *Behavior Therapy*, 1973, 4, 83–90.

Axelrod, S., Hall, R. V., & Maxwell, A. Use of peer attention to increase study behavior. *Behavior Therapy*, 1972, 3, 349–351.

Ayllon, T., & Azrin, N. H. *The token economy: A motivational system for therapy and rehabilitation*. New York: Appleton-Century-Crofts, 1968.

Baer, D. M. In the beginning, there was the response. In E. Ramp & G. Semb (Eds.), *Behavior analysis: Areas of research and application*. Englewood-Cliffs, New Jersey: Prentice-Hall, 1975.

Baer, D. M., Wolf, M. M., & Risley, T. R. Some current dimensions of applied behavior analysis. *Journal of Applied Behavior Analysis*, 1968, 1, 91–97.

Bailey, J. S., Timbers, G. D., Phillips, E. L., & Wolf, M. M. Modification of articulation errors of predelinquents by their peers. *Journal of Applied Behavior Analysis*, 1971, 4, 265–281.

Barrett, B. H., & McCormack, J. E. Varied-teacher tutorials: A tactic for generating credible skills in severely retarded boys. *Mental Retardation*, 1973, 11, 14–19.

Barrish, H. H., Saunders, M., & Wolf, M. M. Good-behavior game: Effects of individual contingencies for group consequences on disruptive behavior in a classroom. *Journal of Applied Behavior Analysis*, 1969, 2, 119–124.

Bassett, J. E., Blanchard, E. B., & Koshland, E. Applied behavior analysis in a penal setting: Targeting "free world" behaviors. *Behavior Therapy*, 1975, 6, 639–648.

Bijou, S. W., & Baer, D. M. Operant methods in child behavior and development. In W. K. Honig (Ed.), *Operant behavior: Areas of research and application*. New York: Appleton-Century-Crofts, 1966.

Bijou, S. W., Peterson, R. F., Harris, F. R., Allen, K. E., & Johnston, M. S. Methodology for experimental studies of young children in natural settings. *Psychological Record*, 1969, 19, 177–210.

Braukmann, C. J., Kirigin, K. A., & Wolf, M. M. *Achievement Place: The researchers' perspective*. Paper presented at the meeting of the American Psychological Association, Washington, D.C., September 1976.

Braukmann, C. J., Maloney, D. M., Fixsen, D. L., Phillips, E. L., & Wolf, M. M. An analysis of a selection interview training package for predelinquents at Achievement Place. *Criminal Justice and Behavior*, 1974, 1, 30–42.

Briscoe, R. V., Hoffman, D. B., & Bailey, J. S. Behavioral community psychology: Training a community board to problem solve. *Journal of Applied Behavior Analysis*, 1975, 8, 157–168.

Broden, M., Hall, R. V., Dunlap, A., & Clark, R. Effects of teacher attention and a token reinforcement system in a junior high school class. *Exceptional Children*, 1970, 36, 341–349.

Cautela, J. R. Covert conditioning. In A. Jacobs & L. B. Sachs (Eds.), *The psychology* of private events: Perspectives on covert response systems. New York: Academic Press, 1971.

Eisler, R. M. Assertive training in the work situation. In J. D. Krumboltz & C. E. Thoresen (Eds.), Counseling methods. New York: Holt, 1976.

Elder, S. T., Welsh, D. M., Longacre, A., & McAfee, R. Acquisition, discriminative stimulus control, and retention of increases/decreases in blood pressure of normotensive human subjects. Journal of Applied Behavior Analysis, 1977, 10, 381–390.

Emery, R. E., & Marholin II, D. An applied behavior analysis of delinquency: The irrelevancy of relevant behavior. American Psychologist, 1977, 32, 860–873.

Emshoff, J. G., Redd, W. H., & Davidson III, W. S. Generalization training and the transfer of prosocial behavior in delinquent adolescents. Journal of Behavior Therapy and Experimental Psychiatry, 1976, 7, 141–144.

Fawcett, S. B., & Miller, L. K. Training public-speaking behavior: An experimental analysis and social validation. Journal of Applied Behavior Analysis, 1975, 8, 125–135.

Ferster, C. B., Neuringer, J. L., & Levitt, E. B. The control of eating. Journal of Mathetics, 1962, 1, 87–107.

Ferster, C. B., & Skinner, B. F. Schedules of reinforcement. New York: Appleton-Century-Crofts, 1957.

Fixsen, D. L., Phillips, E. L., & Wolf, M. M. Achievement Place: Experiments in self-government with predelinquents. Journal of Applied Behavior Analysis, 1973, 6, 31–47.

Fordyce, W. E., Fowler, R. S., Lehmann, J. F., DeLateur, B. J., Sand, P. L., & Trieschmann, R. B. Operant conditioning in the treatment of chronic pain. Archives of Physical Medicine and Rehabilitation, 1973, 54, 399–408.

Garcia, E. The training and generalization of a conversational speech form in nonverbal retardates. Journal of Applied Behavior Analysis, 1974, 1, 137–149.

Goldstein, A. P. Structured learning therapy: Toward a psychotherapy for the poor. New York: Academic Press, 1973.

Goldstein, A. P., Heller, K., & Sechrest, L. B. Psychotherapy and the psychology of behavior change. New York: Wiley, 1966.

Goocher, B. E., and Ebner, M. A. A behavior modification approach utilizing sequential response targets in multiple settings. Paper presented at the meeting of the Midwestern Psychological Association, Chicago, May 1968.

Graubard, P. S., Rosenberg, H., & Miller, M. B. Student applications of behavior modification to teachers and environments or ecological approaches to social deviance. In E. Ramp & G. Semb (Eds.), New direction in education: Behavior analysis, 1971. Lawrence: The University of Kansas Support and Development Center for Follow Through, Department of Human Development, 1971.

Gray, F., Graubard, P. S., & Rosenberg, H. Little brother is changing you. Psychology Today, 1974, 7, 42–46.

Griffiths, H., & Craighead, W. E. Generalization in operant speech therapy for misarticulation. Journal of Speech and Hearing Disorders, 1972, 37, 485–494.

Hall, R. V., Lund, D., & Jackson, D. Effects of teacher attention on study behavior. Journal of Applied Behavior Analysis, 1968, 1, 1–12.

Harris, S. L., & Romanczyk, R. G. Treating self-injurious behavior of a retarded child by overcorrection. Behavior Therapy, 1976, 7, 235–239.

Harris, V. W., & Sherman, J. A. Effects of peer tutoring and consequences on the math performance of elementary classroom students. Journal of Applied Behavior Analysis, 1973, 6, 587–598.

Hay, W. M., Hay, L. R., & Nelson, R. O. The adaptation of covert modeling procedures to the treatment of chronic alcoholism and obsessive-compulsive behavior: Two case reports. *Behavior Therapy*, 1977, *8*, 70–76.

Hayes, S. C., & Cone, J. D. Reducing residential electrical energy use: Payments, information, and feedback. *Journal of Applied Behavior Analysis*, 1977, *10*, 425–436.

Hersen, M., & Barlow, D. H. *Single case experimental designs: Strategies for studying behavior change.* New York: Pergamon, 1976.

Hersen, M., & Bellack, A. S. A multiple-baseline analysis of social skills training in chronic schizophrenics. *Journal of Applied Behavior Analysis*, 1976, *9*, 239–245.

Horner, R. D. Establishing use of crutches by a mentally retarded spina bifida child. *Journal of Applied Behavior Analysis*, 1971, *4*, 183–189.

Jackson, D. A., & Wallace, R. F. The modification and generalization of voice loudness in a fifteen-year-old retarded girl. *Journal of Applied Behavior Analysis*, 1974, *7*, 567–576.

Johnston, J. M., & Johnston, G. T. Modification of consonant speech-sound articulation in young children. *Journal of Applied Behavior Analysis*, 1972, *5*, 233–246.

Kale, R. J., Kaye, J. H., Whelan, D. A., & Hopkins, B. L. The effects of reinforcement on the modification, maintenance, and generalization of social responses of mental patients. *Journal of Applied Behavior Analysis*, 1968, *1*, 307–314.

Kanfer, F. H. Self-management methods. In F. H. Kanfer & A. P. Goldstein (Eds.), *Helping people change.* New York: Pergamon, 1975.

Kanfer, F. H., & Saslow, G. Behavioral diagnosis. In C. M. Franks (Ed.), *Behavior therapy: Appraisal and status.* New York: McGraw-Hill, 1969.

Karoly, P. Multicomponent behavioral treatment of fear of flying: A case report. *Behavior Therapy*, 1974, *5*, 265–270.

Kazdin, A. E. Toward a client administered token reinforcement program. *Education and Training of the Mentally Retarded*, 1971, *6*, 52–55.

Kazdin, A. E. *Behavior modification in applied settings.* Homewood, Illinois: Dorsey, 1975.

Kazdin, A. E. Developing assertive behavior through covert condition. In J. D. Krumboltz & C. E. Thoresen (Eds.), *Counseling methods.* New York: Holt, 1976.

Kazdin, A. E. *The token economy.* New York: Plenum, 1977. (a)

Kazdin, A. E. Methodology of applied behavior analysis. In T. A. Brigham & A. C. Catania (Eds.), *The handbook of applied behavior research: Social and instructional processes.* New York: Irvington Press/Halsted Press, 1977. (b)

Kazdin, A. E. Research issues in covert conditioning. *Cognitive Therapy and Research*, 1977, *1*, 45–58. (c)

Kazdin, A. E. Assessing the clinical or applied importance of behavior change through social validation. *Behavior Modification*, 1977, *1*, 427–452. (d)

Kazdin, A. E., & Klock, J. The effect of nonverbal teacher approval on student attentive behavior. *Journal of Applied Behavior Analysis*, 1973, *6*, 643–654.

Kazdin, A. E., & Marholin II, D. Program evaluation in clinical and community settings. In D. Marholin II (Ed.), *Child behavior therapy.* New York: Gardner, 1978.

Kifer, R. E., Lewis, M. A., Green, D. R., & Phillips, E. L. Training predelinquent youths and their parents to negotiate conflict situations. *Journal of Applied Behavior Analysis*, 1974, *7*, 357–364.

Koegel, R. L., & Rincover, A. Treatment of psychotic children in a classroom environment: I. Learning in a large group. *Journal of Applied Behavior Analysis*, 1974, *7*, 45–59.

Koegel, R. L., & Rincover, A. Research on the difference between generalization and maintenance in extra-therapy responding. *Journal of Applied Behavior Analysis*, 1977, *10*, 1–12.

Krumboltz, J. D., & Thoresen, C. E. (Eds.). *Counseling methods*. New York: Holt, 1976.

Leitenberg, H., Burchard, J. D., Burchard, S. N., Fuller, E. J., & Lysaght, T. V. Using positive reinforcement to suppress behavior: Some experimental comparisons with sibling conflict. *Behavior Therapy*, 1977, *8*, 168–182.

Lent, J. R. Mimosa cottage: Experiment in hope. *Psychology Today*, 1968, *2*, 50–58.

Lovaas, O. I., Koegel, R., Simmons, J. Q., & Long, J. S. Some generalization and follow-up measures on autistic children in behavior therapy. *Journal of Applied Behavior Analysis*, 1973, *6*, 131–165.

Lovaas, O. I., & Simmons, J. Q. Manipulation of self-destruction in three retarded children. *Journal of Applied Behavior Analysis*, 1969, *2*, 143–157.

Maloney, D. M., Harper, T. M., Braukmann, C. J., Fixsen, D. L., Phillips, E. L., & Wolf, M. M. Teaching conversation-related skills to predelinquent girls. *Journal of Applied Behavior Analysis*, 1976, *7*, 371.

Marholin II, D., & Bijou, S. W. A behavioral approach to the assessment of children. *Child Welfare*, 1977, *56*, 93–106.

Marholin II, D., & Bijou, S. W. Behavioral assessment: Listen when the data speak. In D. Marholin II (Ed.), *Child behavior therapy*. New York: Gardner Press, 1978.

Marholin II, D., & Kanfer, F. H. *A functional analysis of a phobia of the Catholic Host: A case study*. Manuscript submitted for publication, 1977.

Marholin II, D., & McInnis, E. T. Treating children in group settings: Techniques for individualizing behavioral treatment programs. In D. Marholin II (Ed.), *Child behavior therapy*. New York: Gardner, 1978.

Marholin II, D., O'Toole, K. M., Touchette, P. E., Berger, P. L., and Doyle, D. "I'll have a Big Mac, large fries, large coke, and apple pie ..." or teaching adaptive community skills. *Behavior Therapy*, 1978, in press.

Marholin II, D., Plienis, A. J., Harris, S., & Marholin, B. L. Mobilization of the community through a behavioral approach: A school program for adjudicated females. *Criminal Justice and Behavior*, 1975, *2*, 130–145.

Marholin II, D., & Siegel, L. J. Beyond the law of effect: Programming for the maintenance of behavioral change. In D. Marholin II (Ed.), *Child behavior therapy*. New York. Gardner, 1978.

Marholin II, D., Siegel, L. J., & Phillips, D. Treatment and transfer: A search for empirical procedures. In M. Hersen, R. M. Eisler, & P. M. Miller (Eds.), *Progress in behavior modification* (Vol. 3). New York: Academic Press, 1976.

Marholin II, D., & Steinman, W. M. Stimulus control in the classroom as a function of the behavior reinforced. *Journal of Applied Behavior Analysis*, 1977, *10*, 465–478.

Marholin II, D., Steinmann, W. M., McInnis, E. T., & Heads, T. B. The effect of a teacher's presence on the classroom behavior of conduct-problem children. *Journal of Abnormal Child Psychology*, 1975, *3*, 11–25.

Marholin II, D., & Townsend, N. M. An experimental analysis of side effects and response maintenance of a modified overcorrection procedure: The case of the persistent twiddler. *Behavior Therapy*, 1978, 9, 383–390.

McArthur, M., & Hawkins, R. P. The modification of several behaviors of an emotionally disturbed child in a regular classroom. In R. Ulrich, T. Stachnik, & J. Mabry (Eds.), *Control of human behavior: Behavior modification in education* (Vol. III). Glenview, Illinois: Scott, Foresman, 1975.

McCullough, J. P., Huntsinger, G. M., & Nay, W. R. Self-control treatment of aggression in a 16-year-old male. *Journal of Consulting and Clinical Psychology*, 1977, 45, 322–331.

McGovern, K. *The development and evaluation of a social skills training program for college male non-daters.* Unpublished doctoral dissertation, University of Oregon, 1972. (University Microfilms No. 737929)

McGovern, K. B., & Burkhard, J. Initiating social contact with the opposite sex. In J. D. Krumboltz & C. E. Thoresen (Eds.), *Counseling methods.* New York: Holt, 1976.

McInnis, T. Training and maintaining staff behaviors in residential treatment programs. In R. L. Patterson (Ed.), *Maintaining effective token economies.* Springfield, Illinois: Thomas, 1976.

McInnis, T. Training and motivating staff members. In D. Marholin II (Ed.), *Child behavior therapy.* New York: Gardner, 1978.

Meddock, T. D., Parsons, J. A., & Hill, K. T. Effects of an adult's presence and praise on young children's performance. *Journal of Experimental Child Psychology*, 1971, 12, 197–211.

Medland, M. B., & Stachnik, T. J. Good-behavior game: A replication and systematic analysis. *Journal of Applied Behavior Analysis*, 1972, 5, 45–51.

Meichenbaum, D. H., Bowers, K., & Ross, R. R. Modification of classroom behavior of institutionalized female adolescent offenders. *Behaviour Research and Therapy*, 1968, 6, 343–353.

Melamed, B. G., & Siegel, L. J. Self-directed in vivo treatment of an obsessive-compulsive checking ritual. *Journal of Behavior Therapy and Experimental Psychiatry*, 1975, 6, 31–35.

Meyers, A. W., Farr, J. H., & Craighead, W. E. Eliminating female orgasmic dysfunction through sexual reeducation. In J. D. Krumboltz & C. E. Thoresen (Eds.), *Counseling methods.* New York: Holt, 1976.

Morris, E. K. A brief review of legal deviance: References in behavior analysis and delinquency. In D. Marholin II (Ed.), *Child behavior therapy.* New York: Gardner, 1978.

Newman, F. L., & Baron, M. R. Stimulus generalization along the dimension of angularity: A comparison of training procedures. *Journal of Comparative and Physiological Psychology*, 1965, 60, 59–63.

O'Brien, F., & Azrin, N. H. Developing proper mealtime behaviors of the institutionalized retarded. *Journal of Applied Behavior Analysis*, 1972, 5, 389–399.

O'Connor, R. D. Modification of social withdrawal through symbolic modeling. *Journal of Applied Behavior Analysis*, 1969, 2, 15–22.

O'Connor, R. D. Relative efficacy of modeling, shaping, and the combined procedures for modification of social withdrawal. *Journal of Abnormal Psychology*, 1972, 79, 327–334.

O'Dell, S. Training parents in behavior modification: A review. *Psychological Bulletin*, 1974, 81, 418–433.

O'Leary, K. D., Becker, W. C., Evans, M. B., & Saudargas, S. A. A token reinforcement program in a public school: A replication and systematic analysis. *Journal of Applied Behavior Analysis*, 1969, *2*, 3–13.

O'Leary, K. D., O'Leary, S., & Becker, W. C. Modification of a deviant sibling interaction pattern in the home. *Behaviour Research and Therapy*, 1967, *5*, 113–120.

Packard, R. G. The control of "classroom attention": A group contingency for complex behavior. *Journal of Applied Behavior Analysis*, 1970, *3*, 13–28.

Page, T. J., Iwata, B. A., & Neef, N. A. Teaching pedestrian skills to retarded persons: Generalization from the classroom to the natural environment. *Journal of Applied Behavior Analysis*, 1976, *9*, 433–444.

Patterson, G. R. Behavioral intervention procedures in the classroom and in the home. In A. E. Bergin & S. L. Garfield (Eds.), *Handbook of psychotherapy and behavior change*. New York: Wiley, 1971.

Patterson, G. R., Cobb, J. A., & Ray, R. S. Direct intervention in the classroom: A set of procedures for the aggressive child. In F. Clark, D. Evans, & L. Hammerlynck (Eds.), *Implementing behavioral programs for schools and clinics.* Champaign, Illinois: Research Press, 1972.

Patterson, G. R., & Reid, J. B. Reciprocity and coercion: Two facets of social systems. In C. Neuringer & J. L. Michael (Eds.), *Behavior modification in clinical psychology.* New York: Appleton-Century-Crofts, 1970.

Peterson, N. Effect of monochromatic rearing on the control of responding by wavelength. *Science*, 1962, *136*, 774–775.

Peterson, R. F., Merwin, M. R., Moyer, T. S., & Whitehurst, G. J. Generalized imitation: The effect of experimenter absence, differential reinforcement, and stimulus complexity. *Journal of Experimental Child Psychology*, 1971, *12*, 114–128.

Phillips, E. L. Achievement Place: Token reinforcement procedures in a home-style rehabilitation setting for predelinquent boys. *Journal of Applied Behavior Analysis*, 1968, *1*, 213–223.

Phillips, E. L., Phillips, E. A., Wolf, M. M., & Fixsen, D. L. Achievement Place: Development of the elected manager system. *Journal of Applied Behavior Analysis*, 1973, *6*, 541–561.

Pomerantz, D. J., and Redd, W. H. Programming generalization through stimulus fading with retarded children. Unpublished manuscript, University of Illinois at Urbana-Champaign, 1977.

Rabin, E. M., & Marholin II, D. Programming transfer of treatment effects: A case study of a stimulus control procedure. *Journal of Behavior Therapy and Experimental Psychiatry*, 1978, in press.

Ray, B. A. The course of acquisition of a line-tilt discrimination by rhesus monkeys. *Journal of the Experimental Analysis of Behavior*, 1967, *10*, 17–33.

Ray, B. A., & Sidman, M. Reinforcement schedules and stimulus control. In W. N. Schoenfeld (Ed.), *The theory of reinforcement schedules*. New York: Appleton-Century-Crofts, 1970.

Redd, W. H. Effects of mixed reinforcement contingencies on adults' control of children's behavior. *Journal of Applied Behavior Analysis*, 1969, *2*, 249–254.

Redd, W. H. Generalization of adult's stimulus control of children's behavior. *Journal of Experimental Child Psychology*, 1970, *9*, 286–296.

Redd, W. H. Attention span and generalization of task-related stimulus control: Effects of reinforcement contingencies. *Journal of Experimental Child Psychology*, 1972, *13*, 527–539.

Redd, W. H. Social control of adult preference in operant conditioning with children. *Journal of Experimental Child Psychology*, 1974, 17, 61–78.

Redd, W. H. The effects of adult presence and stated preferences on the reinforcement control of children's behavior. *Merrill-Palmer Quarterly*, 1976, 22, 93–98.

Redd, W. H., & Birnbrauer, J. S. Adults as discriminative stimuli for differential reinforcement contingencies with retarded children. *Journal of Experimental Child Psychology*, 1969, 7, 440–447.

Redd, W. H., & Wheeler, A. J. The relative effectiveness of monetary reinforcers and adult instructions in the control of children's choice behavior. *Journal of Experimental Child Psychology*, 1973, 16, 63–75.

Reynolds, G. S. Attention in the pigeon. *Journal of the Experimental Analysis of Behavior*, 1961, 4, 203–208.

Rincover, A., & Koegel, R. L. Setting generality and stimulus control in autistic children. *Journal of Applied Behavior Analysis*, 1975, 8, 235–246.

Risley, T. R. The effects and side effects of punishing the autistic behaviors of a deviant child. *Journal of Applied Behavior Analysis*, 1968, 1, 21–34.

Rosenbaum, A., O'Leary, K. D., & Jacob, R. G. Behavioral intervention with hyperactive children: Group consequences as a supplement to individual contingencies. *Behavior Therapy*, 1975, 6, 315–323.

Rubin, B. K., & Stolz, S. B. Generalizations of self-referent speech established in a retarded adolescent by operant procedures. *Behavior Therapy*, 1974, 4, 93–106.

Scheiderer, E. G., & Bernstein, D. A. A case of chronic back pain and the "unilateral" treatment of marital problems. *Journal of Behavior Therapy and Experimental Psychiatry*, 1976, 7, 47–50.

Seymour, F. H., & Stokes, T. F. Self-recording in training girls to increase work and evoke staff praise in an institution for offenders. *Journal of Applied Behavior Analysis*, 1976, 9, 41–54.

Siegel, L. J., & Steinman, W. M. The modification of a peer-observer's classroom behavior as a function of his serving as a reinforcing agent. In E. Ramp & G. Semb (Eds.), *Behavior analysis: Areas of research and application*. Englewood Cliffs, New Jersey: Prentice-Hall, 1975.

Skinner, B. F. *The contingencies of reinforcement*. New York: Appleton-Century-Crofts, 1969.

Solomon, R. W., & Wahler, R. G. Peer reinforcement control of classroom problem behavior. *Journal of Applied Behavior Analysis*, 1973, 6, 49–56.

Steinman, W. M. Generalized imitation and the discrimination hypothesis. *Journal of Experimental Child Psychology*, 1970, 10, 79–99. (a)

Steinman, W. M. The social control of generalized imitation. *Journal of Applied Behavior Analysis*, 1970, 3, 159–167. (b)

Steinman, W. M. Generalized imitation and the setting event concept. In B. C. Etzel, J. M. LeBlanc, & D. M. Baer (Eds.), *New developments in behavioral research: Theory, method and application. In honor of Sidney W. Bijou*. Hillsdale, New Jersey: Erbaum, 1977.

Stokes, T. F., & Baer, D. M. Preschool peers as mutual generalization-facilitating agents. *Behavior Therapy*, 1976, 7, 549–556.

Stokes, T. F., & Baer, D. M. An implicit technology of generalization. *Journal of Applied Behavior Analysis*, 1977, 10, 349–367.

Stokes, T. F., Baer, D. M., & Jackson, R. L. Programming the generalization of a greeting response in four retarded children. *Journal of Applied Behavior Analysis*, 1974, 7, 599–610.

Stolz, S. B., & Wolf, M. M. Visually discriminated behavior in a "blind" adolescent retardate. *Journal of Applied Behavior Analysis*, 1969, 2, 65–77.

Tharp, R. G., & Wetzel, R. J. *Behavior modification in the natural environment.* New York: Academic Press, 1969.

Wahler, R. G. Oppositional children: A quest for parental reinforcement control. *Journal of Applied Behavior Analysis,* 1969, 2, 159–170.

Walker, H. M., & Buckley, N. K. *Investigation of some classroom control parameters as a function of teacher dispensed social reinforcers.* Unpublished manuscript, University of Oregon, 1971.

Walker, H. M., & Buckley, N. K. Programming generalization and maintenance of treatment effects across time and across settings. *Journal of Applied Behavior Analysis,* 1972, 5, 209–224.

Walker, H. M., & Hops, H. Use of normative peer data as a standard for evaluating classroom treatment effects. *Journal of Applied Behavior Analysis,* 1976, 9, 159–168.

Walker, H. M., Hops, H., & Johnson, S. M. Generalization and maintenance of classroom treatment effects. *Behavior Therapy,* 1975, 6, 188–200.

Weathers, L. R., & Liberman, R. P. Modification of family behavior. In D. Marholin II (Ed.), *Child behavior therapy.* New York: Gardner, 1978.

Werner, J. S., Minkin, N., Minkin, B. L., Fixsen, D. L., Phillips, E. L., & Wolf, M. M. "Intervention package": An analysis to prepare juvenile delinquents for encounters with police officers. *Criminal Justice and Behavior,* 1975, 2, 55–84.

Williams, C. D. The elimination of tantrum behavior by extinction procedures. *Journal of Abnormal Psychology,* 1959, 59, 269.

Williams, M. T., Turner, S. M., Watts, J. G., Bellack, A. S., & Hersen, M. Group social skills training for chronic psychiatric patients. *European Journal of Behavioural Analysis and Modification,* 1977, 4, 223–229.

Willner, A. G., Braukmann, C. J., Kirigin, K. A., & Wolf, M. M. Achievement Place: A community treatment model for youths in trouble. In D. Marholin II (Ed.), *Child behavior therapy.* New York: Gardner, 1978.

Winett, R., & Winkler, R. Current behavior modification in the classroom: Be still, be quiet, be docile. *Journal of Applied Behavior Analysis,* 1972, 5, 499–504.

Wolf, M. M., Phillips, E. L., & Fixsen, D. L. The teaching family: A new model for the treatment of deviant child behavior in the community. In S. W. Bijou & E. Ribes-Inesta (Eds.), *Behavior modification: Issues and extensions.* New York: Academic Press, 1972.

Youell, K. J., & McCullough, J. P. Behavioral treatment of mucous colitis. *Journal of Clinical and Consulting Psychology,* 1975, 43, 740–745.

On November 22, 1978 David Marholin II died of leukemia at the age of 29. All of us who knew him respected his work, but more importantly we respected him as a kind and gentle person with truly humanitarian motives. His concern for those who need help and guidance stands as a model for every professional psychologist. We miss him deeply.

PAUL E. TOUCHETTE
ARNOLD P. GOLDSTEIN
FREDERICK H. KANFER

9

The Effects of Social Support: Prevention and Treatment Implications

KENNETH HELLER

The terms *social support* and *support networks* are currently in vogue. They were given recent prominence by both Gerald Caplan (Caplan, 1974; Caplan & Killilea, 1976) and Seymour Sarason (Sarason, 1976; Sarason, Carroll, Maton, Cohen, & Lorentz, 1977); and emerged as a major theme of the recent Austin Conference on Community Psychology (Iscoe, Bloom, & Spielberger, 1977). Facilitating the development of community support networks could represent an important new direction for both clinical and community psychology, with potential for both preventive and therapeutic functions. On the preventive side, the possibility exists for increasing coping capacity and reducing the need for professional psychological help among large segments of the population. Equally attractive is the possibility of providing current or former patients with community supports that could help reduce the intensity and duration of disability while aiding in the maintenance of newly established therapeutic changes. Thus the promise of community support networks as a new helping modality seems enormous.

MAXIMIZING TREATMENT GAINS:
Transfer Enhancement in Psychotherapy

While much of positive value probably can be achieved by the creative use of community support networks, a note of caution is in order in that we should be wary of the uncritical acceptance of panaceas. This is an acute problem in the mental health fields which in the past have been scarred by the wholesale adoption of unproven fads (R. B. Caplan, 1969; Heller & Monahan, 1977). Disillusionment sets in as accomplishment falls short of what has been promised, with the unfortunate consequence that what might have been of value in the rejected fad also is discredited. Furthermore, there can be an erosion of public confidence in the credibility of a profession that in following what is faddish, appears to respond more to social and personal whim than to the accumulation of evidence.

The purpose of this chapter is to review the evidence concerning social support in a more objective manner than has been done in the past, highlighting unanswered questions and the directions that research in this new area might take. If social support does have positive effects, we need to know its most crucial and potent ingredients, the social conditions under which positive effects are facilitated, and the types of persons for whom social support would be beneficial or contraindicated. The need is for more specific knowledge, a need that has been recognized several times in the past concerning other helping modalities (Goldstein & Stein, 1976; Heller & Monahan, 1977; Strupp, 1971).

A Social Support Paradox: Are Close Ties to Others Sources of Strength or of Stress?

As one begins to review this area, a paradox becomes apparent. Close interpersonal ties have been described in the literature in both positive and negative terms. The family, in particular, has been cited as a source of stress (Croog, 1970) or as facilitative of psychological growth and development (G. Caplan, 1976).

Originating from the experiences of practicing psychotherapists, the traditional view in clinical psychology was to emphasize the liabilities in family life. As patients with severe and incapacitating symptomatology recounted instances of traumatic family experiences, it was quite natural for these to appear more important than the prosocial but prosaic aspects of family life that may have been occurring simultaneously. Clinicians became more interested in looking for traumatic experiences, and these very quickly became prominent features of clinical theory. A stance toward family members evolved in which they were seen as "culprits" against whom developing individuals (patients) required protection. Some therapists began to see their job as requiring patients to be freed from family influences.

As long as attention remained focused on mental patients, with the only source of information about family life coming from persons whose perceptions of family members were primarily negative, it is not surprising that the dysfunctional aspects of close family ties were continually noted. However, a different perspective was obtained when the views of other informants were obtained, as in family therapy, or when the social life of nonpatients was studied. Sociologists, observing broader segments of the population, were quick to recognize the positive functions of close ties to kin and community. The supportive effects of social networks were described in the sociological literature in the 1950s (Axelrod, 1956) and in the next two decades the links between mental health and support networks were noted frequently (Blackman & Goldstein, 1968; Fox, 1960; Gans, 1969; Hughes, Tremblay, Rapoport, & Leighton, 1960; Leighton, 1959; Lewis, 1966; Weiss & Bergen, 1968). Mechanic (1974a) best summarizes the major theme of this body of literature in his comment that "the ability of persons to maintain psychological comfort will depend not only on their intrapsychic resources, but also—and perhaps more importantly—on the social supports available or absent in the environment [p. 33]."

It is of some historical interest that the early sociologists, while recognizing the importance of functional ties to family and community, predicted widespread disruption in social life as a result of massive industrialization. As Fischer (1975) has noted:

> Sociology evolved centrally around a concern for the consequences of the Great Transformation. The discipline's pivotal question was and largely still is: How can the moral order of society be maintained and the integration of its members achieved within a highly differentiated and technological social structure [pp. 67–68]?

The expectation was that the Industrial Revolution and the subsequent growth of large cities would irreparably harm social life whose form initially developed in small village communities. Isolation and anomie were seen as necessary consequences of city life and its specialized technological structures that demanded highly compartmentalized and fragmented social roles. For example, the fear was that there would be neither supports nor restraints on the urban dweller as ties to clan and church became dispersed and amorphous. Urban ethnographers seemed to validate these negative expectations in that instances of urban decay and social disintegration were not difficult to discover. Yet, the basic question remained. Was social disintegration a necessary concomitant of urbanization? The surprise was that while indices of anomie could be found in numerous communities, social life in cities flourished in ways unaccounted for by sociological theory. For example, many urban migrants from rural areas were not isolated or disoriented in large cities. Despite the dispersion of kin across large geographic areas, ties to primary groups flourished (Craven & Wellman, 1974). The development of network theory in sociology and anthropology (Mitchell, 1969, 1974) has been one recent attempt to account for the retention of social ties despite migration and urbanization.

As can be seen from the above comments, the two conceptions of close interpersonal ties as either stressful or supportive came from different sources of evidence. Family members have not changed; the change has been in how we have viewed them. It is apparent that interpersonal relations can be either supportive or stressful. What is crucial is discovering the conditions that can lead either to positive or negative outcomes.

What is Social Support?

As is true for other concepts in psychology, what may appear to be a simple term with a commonly accepted meaning, reveals ambiguities in definition upon closer examination. A major problem with the concept "social support" is in defining the behaviors to be classified as supportive. One view is to consider all forms of close interpersonal ties as social support. If this strategy is adopted, the term becomes synonymous with "positive interpersonal relationships" and probably loses any unique utility. Some writers have attempted to increase the specificity of the concept by defining support as involving linkages to key groups, while still others require more specific exchanges of information, action or material aid (Carveth & Gottlieb, 1977).

Kahn and Quinn (1977) define social support as an interpersonal transaction consisting of:

> the expression of positive *affect*, including liking, admiration, respect, and other kinds of positive evaluation;
> the expression of *affirmation*, including endorsement of an individual's perceptions, beliefs, values, attitudes or actions; or
> the provision of *aid*, including materials, information, time, and entitlements.

Cobb (1976) provides a similar definition, but one that emphasizes *information* that allows an individual to become oriented in a social matrix for the satisfaction of personal needs. According to Cobb, social support is conceived to be information belonging to one or more of the following classes:

> information leading the subject to believe that he is cared for and loved; information leading the subject to believe that he is esteemed and valued; information leading the subject to believe that he belongs to a network of communication and mutual obligation [Cobb, 1976, p. 300].

G. Caplan (1974) agrees that support provides informational feedback that increases the capacity of the individual to satisfy basic psychological and social needs. Caplan defines support systems as:

> continuing social aggregates that provide individuals with opportunities for feedback about themselves and for validations of their expectations about others.... People have a variety of specific needs that demand satisfaction through enduring interpersonal relationships.... Most people develop a sense of well-being by involving themselves in a range of relationships that in toto satisfy these specific needs ... [pp. 4–5].

G. Caplan (1976) suggests that a second characteristic of support systems is reciprocity of need satisfaction. There is mutuality in a supportive relationship. The system is perpetuated over time because an exchange in need gratification is occurring for the parties involved.

The reciprocal nature of social support is emphasized by the term *network*. Mitchell's (1969) definition, which is generally accepted in the field, states that a social network is a "specific set of linkages among a defined set of persons, with the additional property that the characteristics of these linkages may be used to interpret the social behavior of the persons involved [p. 2]." A network may connect individual persons or larger social units such as families, work groups, business corporations or agency linkages. Network relationships can be represented in matrix format (Craven & Wellman, 1974) or by the use of graph theory and smallest space analysis (Laumann & Pappi, 1973), which all provide mathematical tools with which the formal characteristics of networks can be studied and compared. Network analysis has been used extensively by social anthropologists working in small, often rural societies (Mitchell, 1969) but applications to personal and group networks in urban settings also have been undertaken (Craven & Wellman, 1974; Wellman, Craven, Whitaker, Stevens, Shorter, DuToit, & Bakker, 1973). Measures such as density, range, reciprocity, and frequency of contact, etc., can be obtained for any group of interest. Thus a new set of descriptive tools has become available. However, it is important to recognize that network analysis does not represent a "theory" as much as a set of descriptors whose usefulness depends upon the conceptual templates to which they are attached—most prominent among which are exchange and role theories. As Mitchell (1974) points out, there is no network "theory" in the sense of a set of tight, logically related notions "which may be used deductively to analyze field material relating to social interaction." However, "that propositions may be derived from a consideration of the characteristics of social networks" is evident from a review of the literature (Mitchell, 1974, pp. 282–283).

The substantive problems investigated with network concepts have varied from a description of coalitions among community power elites (Laumann & Pappi, 1973) to the development of helping networks for mental patients (Garrison, 1974). In the latter instance, the screening-linking-planning conference, originally developed by Norris Hansell (1967), was elaborated as a method for helping retain disturbed patients in the community. The procedure involves convening an extended family network capable of strengthening the nuclear family during particularly stressful times. Concentration on family pathology is specifically avoided as the network coalesces and develops a self-sustaining support atmosphere.

In this chapter, the emphasis will be on the uses of support systems (as above) with less emphasis on sociological description of networks. We will examine the purported effects of support in terms of facilitation of role performance and coping with stress. The chapter ends with a review of needed future directions for research on social support.

THE EFFECTS OF SOCIAL SUPPORT

The commonly accepted belief is that the beneficial effects of social support are self-evident. Humans have been described as social animals who are more comfortable and productive living with companions than in isolation. It is not surprising that numerous studies have found that productivity, morale, and satisfaction are all enhanced by positive affiliation with others.

While the importance of group ties no longer is in dispute, it is time to go beyond the simple truism that social support is beneficial, to an examination of the conditions and mechanisms by which support operates most optimally. The methodological flaws in the existing research must be examined closely so that future research does not simply repeat these weaknesses. As Rabkin and Struening (1976) point out with regard to the life events literature relating social factors to illness, when new studies simply repeat both the findings and the flaws of earlier ones, the development of systematic knowledge is delayed. Thus it is important to review, not only the established evidence, but the methodological weaknesses in that evidence and the unresolved issues that still need research attention.

The literature concerning the effects of social support come from a variety of sources. Most frequently cited are the naturalistic studies claiming that social support protects or "buffers" an individual against the adverse effects of stress. A second group of naturalistic studies deals with the consequences of loss of support among individuals previously supported. This research suggests that loss of support is a risk factor in the development of later symptomatology. Least known by mental health practitioners is a third group of experimental studies on social facilitation and affiliation—that is, the effects of a social audience on performance. Here the most relevant studies are experiments investigating reactions to stress as a function of the presence or absence of a companion. Each of these three areas will be reviewed in turn, highlighting significant findings, methodological problems, and unanswered questions to be addressed by future research.

Naturalistic Studies of the "Buffering" Hypothesis

Does social support buffer individuals against the deleterious effects of stress? What seems to be a straightforward question cannot be answered unequivocally based upon current research.

Let us start with the often quoted association between stressful life events and the development of various somatic and psychological disorders. It is generally accepted that stressful events play some role in the development of disability (Dohrenwend & Dohrenwend, 1974), but the extent of that role still is open to dispute. One problem is the magnitude of the correlation between number and nature of life events and subsequent episodes of illness. Rabkin and Struening (1976) estimate that correlations generally are below .30, indicating that life events at best may account for only 9% of the variance in illness. A more basic problem concerns the very correlational nature of the evidence itself. A positive association between events and disability cannot be interpreted as indicating that events are responsible for the formation of symptomatology. For example, Hinkle (1974) reported that telephone operators who were frequently ill had less benign social histories than more healthy co-workers. "Ill" telephone operators also found their work more confining and boring, and in general were more dissatisfied with their lot. It would be extremely difficult to untangle these correlations and use them as evidence for a causative relationship. Does a deprived social history lead to illness, or do chronic illnesses lead to poorer coping ability so that minor life events take on crisis proportions? Is the relationship between life events and crisis mediated by some subjective attributional process (Mechanic, 1974b) such that unhappy and discontented workers report more illness because taking refuge in a "sick role" allows one to take time off from disliked work? Furthermore, since chronic illness is a slowly developing process whose onset may be subtle and gradual, it becomes very difficult to say which came first—crisis events or incipient disorder.

This same problem can be found in studies purporting to show the buffering effects of social support. For example, Brown, Bhrolchain, and Harris (1975) reported that psychiatric disorder, particularly depression, was more likely among urban women who lacked an intimate, confiding relationship with a husband or boyfriend. Lack of support from a partner may lead to vulnerability for depression but it is equally likely that depressed women may perceive and report fewer intimate relationships even if they did exist. In this case, the disability may be responsible for the low levels of reported support.

A similar methodological problem can be found in the frequently quoted study by Nuckolls, Cassel, and Kaplan (1972) claiming evidence for the buffering hypothesis. Nuckolls et al. studied life stress events and "psychosocial assets" for women during pregnancy. Results indicated that women most likely to develop complications during pregnancy and delivery were those with many stress events and low assets. In contrast, women with high life stress events scores but reporting many assets, had as few pregnancy complications as women with low stress events scores. Thus it would appear that stress events lead to complications only in the absence of assets. Since assets included perceived social support, this study has been interpreted as indicating that social support buffers pregnant women against stress.

There are two problems with this study that argue against the conclusion stated above. The first is that psychosocial assets, as measured in this study, was not a pure measure of social support. Also included were questions relating to personality factors such as positive self concept and ego strength. The subject's self perception and the perception of support from others were confounded. It is quite possible that those with good self concepts are likely to perceive higher levels of support than those with poor self-concepts. Furthermore, even with a pure measure of support, the naturalistic and correlational nature of the data do not allow the rejection of important plausible rival hyptheses (Campbell & Stanley, 1963). The most likely rival hypothesis is *social com-*

petence. It is possible that competent persons, who are more immune to the adverse effects of stress, are also more likely to have well developed social networks as a direct result of their more general social competence. The often repeated finding in naturalistic studies that persons with established support networks are in better mental and physical health than are the unsupported (Caplan, Cobb, French, van Harrison, & Pinneau, 1975; Cassell, 1975; Dean & Lin, 1977; de Araujo, van Arsdel, Holmes, & Dudley, 1973; Gore, 1973; Ludwig & Collette, 1970; Phillips, 1967, 1969; Segal, Weiss, & Sokol, 1965) may be due to the operation of variables other than social support.

The Gore research deserves special note because the study's methodology involved a longitudinal, quasi-experimental design. As part of a broader study of the effects of unemployment on health (Kasl & Cobb, 1970; Kasl, Cobb, & Brooks, 1968; Kasl, Gore, & Cobb, 1975; Slote, 1969), physiological and psychological data were collected from men whose jobs were abolished. Data collection was conducted by public health nurses who visited the men after the work shutdown had been announced but before job termination and at regular intervals 6, 12 and 24 months thereafter. The terminated men lived in one of two settings: a specific urban or rural community. A comparison group was formed consisting of continuously employed men who worked for different companies but whose jobs were similar to those of the terminees under study.

The initial studies in this series revealed that the stress of job loss was associated with physiologic changes in blood pressure (Kasl & Cobb, 1970) and serum uric acid levels (Kasl *et al.*, 1968). Gore was interested in discovering whether support from friends and family could ameliorate these effects. She found that supported men reported less depression and fewer complaints of illness and in addition had less elevated cholesterol level at termination than did the unsupported. However, the association between support and low levels of depression and complaints is ambiguous as to causality since, as we have seen before, the correlation may represent the effects of depression, not support, that is, depression-prone individuals are more likely to complain of illness and perceive their environment as less supportive.

Other difficulties cloud data interpretation with regard to the finding concerning the buffering effects of support on cholesterol levels. It was the unsupported men, without prospects for new jobs who showed the greatest elevation in cholesterol at job termination. However, this finding was confounded with rural–urban differences in social support. Men who perceived support from spouse and friends were more likely to come from rural communities. Thus, while rural men may have been receiving greater support, they also may have been living in a less stressful environment. That supported men react less adversely to un-employment stress may be a function of the lower overall stress among rural men, and/or the likelihood that job loss in a homogeneous rural community is inherently less stressful.

Once again, we are faced with suggestive evidence for the buffering hypothesis, which, because of the correlational nature of the data, leaves final interpretation ambiguous. Some might argue that the accumulation of studies each imperfect by itself, should indicate a strong overall finding. This position would be more persuasive were it not for the fact that the methodological weaknesses tend to be similar and are repeated in subsequent studies.

Loss of Support

Loss of support occurs with greatest impact through death of a loved one. In scaling life events, Holmes and Rahe (1967) asked subjects to rank a series of events in terms of the degree of adjustment required by the event. In various studies (summarized by Holmes & Masuda, 1974) the item consistently ranked as requiring the greatest adjustment was "death of a spouse." The items ranked next most severe were "divorce" and "marital separation." Thus, from the point of view of subjective distress, the most upsetting items involved loss of support of a marital partner.

Clinical and epidemiological studies have implicated loss of support as a risk factor for subsequent mental health problems (Ludwig & Collette, 1970) particularly depression and suicide (Maris, 1969; Moss & Hamilton, 1956). Social losses have been related to pessimism about the future among the widowed (Gurin, Veroff, & Feld, 1960) and low morale among the aged (Lowenthal & Haven, 1968).

That the young are not immune to the effects of loss of support can be seen in a startling epidemiological study by Kraus and Lilienfeld (1959) who analyzed mortality rates reported in the 1950 census for age and sex patterns. As expected, frequency of death increased with age, but among young adults (ages 20–34) the death rate was highest for the nonmarried. This increased vulnerability was found for a wide variety of physical illness categories regardless of sex or race. The group with the highest vulnerability were young widowed males whose death rate was 2½ to 4 times that of married males of comparable ages. The authors discuss several factors that could have accounted for their findings, such as the mutual selection of poor risk mates (e.g.,

those with physical handicaps might tend to marry similarly handi-
capped individuals); or, the action of illness causing environments to
which both partners are equally exposed and vulnerable. While neither
of these possibilities can be discounted, Kraus and Lilienfeld demonstrate that they are not completely satisfactory and furthermore they
do not explain why males should show greater vulnerability than
females. Kraus and Lilienfeld do not provide a definitive explanation
of their data. Instead, they leave the reader to speculate as to why
widowhood should pose a greater psychosocial threat to the young
than to the old, or to young men more than young women. Perhaps
one factor may be that young men have the least developed networks
of social ties that they can access freely in time of need.

It is important to note that while the evidence concerning the deleterious effects of **loss** of support is fairly strong, it is not necessarily
the case that those who have always lived alone, that is, lifelong
isolates, are equally vulnerable. If single status is a result of voluntary
choice, lifelong isolates are not necessarily more prone to develop
mental disorders (Lowenthal, 1964). That the never-married generally
are over represented in mental hospital admission rates (Levy &
Rowitz, 1973) again can be interpreted in part as a function of social
competence. A number of the never-married may be lacking in the
social skills necessary to initiate and maintain meaningful interpersonal
relationships that could eventuate in marriage. This is particularly true
for single men who, in our culture, have the responsibility to initiate
heterosexual relationships. In their study of community prevalence
rates for psychological symptomatology in midtown Manhattan, Strole,
Langner, Michael, Kirkpatrick, Opler, and Rennie (1962) found that
impairment rates for single and married women were indistinguishable.
However, psychological impairment rates for bachelors at all ages were
considerably higher than those for married men or for women regardless of marital status. Similarly, death rates from physical illnesses are
somewhat higher for single men than for single women (Kraus & Lilienfeld, 1959). Again, social competency may be implicated in a lower
ability to engage needed medical care and a greater neglect of personal
well-being.

The literature on loss of support as a risk factor in subsequent
maladjustment does not confront the buffering hypothesis directly. One
cannot infer that support buffers an individual against the adverse effects of stress simply by noting that maladjustment is likely to increase
for those who have lost significant close ties. Loss also involves the
production of disequilibrium and the disruption of established relation-

ship patterns (Fried, 1963). Thus, while losing friends may be disruptive, the presence of supportive others does not automatically confer invulnerability.

The presence of others on reactions to stress has been investigated in the experimental literature, and it is to this body of research that we now turn. As we shall see, the experimental work offers a promising **beginning** towards understanding the parameters of the support phenomenon.

Experimental Studies of Social Facilitation and Affiliation

There are two subareas within social psychology particularly germane to our concerns with social support. These can be found in the literature on **social facilitation** (Zajonc, 1965) and **affiliation** (Schachter, 1959).

The social facilitation research deals with the effects of mere presence of others (i.e., a social audience) on learning and performance and has been summarized on several occasions (Cottrell, 1972; Epley, 1974; Geen, 1976; Geen & Gange, 1977; Zajonc, 1965). Zajonc established the field on a firm theoretical structure and in his 1965 paper, concluded that the presence of others functions as a source of arousal or drive. As such, the presence of others facilitates the performance of already learned dominant responses, but impairs the learning of still unpracticed behaviors. Subsequent research has indicated that in humans, social facilitation has arousal properties only when the individual experiences evaluation apprehension—the fear that others will negatively evaluate his performance (Cottrell, 1972; Geen, 1976). When the audience is seen in more positive terms, as for example in observing behavior for the purpose of providing future help, the effects of audience on performance are greatly mitigated.

The social facilitation paradigm described by Zajonc typically involves placid subjects who become aroused by the presence of others. However, if the focus shifts to stress situations, we find the opposite conditions—namely, stress aroused individuals motivated to reduce arousal. What effects does a social audience have on individuals experiencing arousal emanating from environmental stress? Schachter's (1959) work on social affiliation is relevant to this topic.

Schachter demonstrated that a preference for being with others could be induced in aroused subjects. Under threat of shock or during experimentally induced hunger, subjects preferred waiting in the company of others rather than waiting alone, regardless of whether communication among waiting subjects was allowed.

Subsequent experimental research has generally confirmed the affiliation effect although with some qualification (Epley, 1974). Affiliation tendencies under stress have been found to be stronger for first born than for later born individuals (Wrightsman, 1960) probably because first born initially respond to stress with higher levels of anxiety (Schachter, 1959). The desire to affiliate with others has been found to occur not only for subjects exposed to fear stimuli (Sarnoff & Zimbardo, 1961; Schachter, 1959) but also for those aroused by hunger (Schachter, 1959). Interestingly, subjects in whom embarrassment was induced preferred isolation to affiliation (Buck & Parke, 1972; Sarnoff & Zimbardo, 1961). Furthermore, the desire to affiliate under stress was stronger when others were described as similar in personality to the subject (Miller & Zimbardo, 1966).

The above studies dealt with attitudinal preferences for affiliation. There is further evidence that affiliation under stress improves performance and reduces psychphysiological reactivity. Affiliation under stress was found to improve complex verbal learning (Amoroso & Walters, 1969), lower heart rate (Amoroso & Walters, 1969; Angermeier, Phelps, & Reynolds, 1967), and reduce autonomic (GSR) reactivity (Kissel, 1965). The effect of affiliation on autonomic reactivity was found to be stronger if others were known to the subject (Kissel, 1965), were seen as occupying a supportive social role such as that of a hospital nurse (Davidson & Kelley, 1973) and were not seen as potential competitors (Angermeier et al., 1967).

At a more theoretical level, there is continued debate concerning the psychological processes producing the affiliation phenomenon. Schachter (1959) posited that his results could be explained by a social comparison process. Aroused subjects, placed in an ambiguous situation, seek cues that can explain their feelings and that can serve as a guide to appropriate behavior. This view implies a cognitive appraisal process that may be occurring during arousal. However, Schachter's results also are consonant with a motivational explanation—namely, that positive affiliation serves to reduce arousal states directly.

Other explanations of arousal have employed the concepts of interference and distraction. A companion can lead the individual to orient away from the anxiety producing properties of the stimulus situation. Perhaps, the simplest explanation of affiliation is that of imitation. A companion who responds calmly to a threatening situation can induce similar behavior from an observer subjected to the same stress (Epley, 1974).

At this point, although the affiliation phenomenon seems fairly well documented, no one explanation has received undisputed acceptance.

Given the theoretical ambiguity, is there sufficient empirical evidence that would allow affiliation to serve as an analogue base for social support? If "mere presence" of others, with only minimal or no interaction allowed, can affect individuals under stress at attitudinal, behavioral and physiological levels, should not active positive support do more? The dilemma is, as we have pointed out earlier, that close ties with others can be sources of stress as well as support. Indeed, the social facilitation literature indicates that others can **increase** arousal when they are perceived as threatening or negatively evaluative (Geen, 1976). To understand when ties to others are likely to produce beneficial results requires more detailed experimental research than presently exists concerning social support. How significant others are perceived, their actual behaviors and the quality of the relationship are basic aspects of social support that require systematic study. We should not continue to champion the unequivocal value of social support until we more fully understand its basic parameters.

NEEDED DIRECTIONS FOR FUTURE RESEARCH: CLARIFYING THE POTENT FACTORS IN SOCIAL SUPPORT

Given the incomplete state of knowledge about the ingredients in social support and their effects, how should we proceed? What types of research are necessary to clarify the active factors in the support phenomenon? Basically, two classes of research are needed; (a) laboratory studies investigating the parameters of support; and (b) field research in which support programs are tested in controlled demonstration projects. Both of the above steps can be considered "bridging research" between hypothesis and application and are similar to the steps previously advocated (Heller, 1969) as essential in understanding the active ingredients in psychotherapy. Figure 9.1 and its accompanying description describe these steps more fully:

Figure 9.1 The research steps needed between the discovery of psychological change factors and their clinical application.

As illustrated in Figure 9.1, therapeutic hypotheses may be derived from clinical experience (their traditional source) or from behavior change research in other areas of psychology. Regardless of their source, factors thought to be responsible for change should be identified and studied in controlled laboratory settings that approximate clinical interactions. The purpose of clinical laboratory research is to determine what factors produce change, under what conditions they operate best, and how they should be combined to produce an effective therapeutic package. The therapeutic agents thus identified can then be studied in clinical field research to obtain information about the interaction of therapeutic ingredients with personality and setting characteristics that are part of actual treatment. Finally, the practitioner is in a position to apply this knowledge to individual patients with some degree of confidence in the expected outcome. Also, he can use the information gained from practice to develop further hypotheses about the relevant factors in the change process.

The sequence in which the research steps between hypothesis and application are carried out is not at issue. What is important is that all are accomplished.

Needless to say, the above description does not represent the usual manner in which research in psychotherapy is conducted. Clinicians most often move directly from clinical hypotheses to clinical trials. Little attention is given to determining the exact factors that produce change in complex therapeutic procedures, or to the conditions under which each therapeutic ingredient is optimized. Therapeutic strategies are often expected to apply regardless of patient, therapist, or setting characteristics (Kiesler, 1966). Unfortunately, only after a therapeutic approach has become entrenched as a "school" with disciples committed to its perpetuation, do researchers begin to question the value of some of its therapeutic ingredients [Heller, 1969, pp. 524–525].

With regard to social support, the parameters that should be studied to better understand the process can be listed as follows:

1. The relationship between the individual and supportive others
2. The behavior of supportive companions and the content of support
3. Personality, demographic characteristics and role behavior that influence the receptivity to support
4. The skills necessary to access and maintain supportive relationships
5. Environmental structures that are conducive to the establishment and maintenance of support systems

What follows is a brief review of each of these topics, highlighting relevant research already completed.

The Relationship between the Individual and Supportive Others

Variables such as reciprocity and the balance of expectations and demands between members of a relationship seem prime candidates for investigation. Informal helping relationships have been described as reciprocal in nature. The individual who receives support on one occasion can reciprocate by offering support at subsequent times. In many ways, reciprocal support bears some similarity to the *helper therapy* principle described by Riessman (1965) in which people can solve their own problems in the process of attempting to help others. Reciprocal support allows the giver and the recipient to alternate their role relationships for maximal mutual benefit.

Despite the repeated suggestions in the literature highlighting reciprocity as an active ingredient in social support, it is noteworthy that professional support is marked by asymmetry in role relationships. The very concepts, "client" and "helper," define and maintain asymmetry throughout the course of the relationship. When is reciprocity to be preferred and when is going to an "expert" more beneficial? The field has always assumed that professional relationships by their very nature are "better." Indeed, while most people use informal helpers more frequently for common problems and "recent concerns" (Clifford, 1976); the use of formal helpers (particularly doctors and ministers) increases for more severe life crises (Warren, 1976). Yet we have also seen that nonprofessional workers have managed to produce competent results in functions previously reserved for the "properly qualified" credentialed professional. As Heller and Monahan note:

> Nonprofessional competency challenges the very definition of "helping service." For example, is professionally administered psychotherapy unique, or can similar effects be produced by others regardless of the status of the helper? If nonprofessionals can provide significant help, perhaps similar effects can be produced by friends and neighbors. Social support from peers such as these, because it is constantly available, may have greater utility than help provided by a formal practitioner regardless of his professional status. Thus, a change in service provider while of less import by itself, can lead to stimulating new questions. When is the treatment of choice psychotherapy; and under what conditions does a more optimal treatment strategy involve the development of alternatives such as support networks? ... For example, forming a supportive relationship with a client may be less valued by professionals than dynamic psychotherapy, yet at times the former may be the treatment of choice. Dreiblatt and Weatherley (1965) reported that newly admitted mental hospital patients responded much more favorably to brief, friendly contact than they did to more problem-focused discussions. The authors speculate that non-symptom-oriented friendly contacts convey a feeling of support and interest not available in more structured symptom-oriented interactions [Heller & Monahan, 1977, pp. 324–325].

The Behavior of Supportive Companions and the Content of Support

The experimental studies of social facilitation and affiliation reviewed earlier were concerned with "mere presence" of a companion. However, it is clear that others are sought out for much more than their physical presence. In a 1976 replication of the "Americans View their Mental Health" survey, Veroff, Douvan, and Kulka (personal communication, 1977) found that while "listening" was the most frequent activity of both formal and informal helpers, persons who just "listened" were rated as least helpful by respondents. Helpers were rated as considerably more valuable when they engaged in activities involving affective support (cheering and comforting) and active coping (helping take action).

In a survey of college students, Liem and Liem (1976) found that emotional support and material aid had independent effects on levels of reported distress. Emotional support and encouragement provided by friends were inversely related to reported depression and inadequacy; the greater the emotional support the less intense the feelings of distress. However, tangible support showed the opposite relationship: the more tangible support provided, the **greater** the reported psychological symptomatology. The Liems explain this apparent paradox by noting that students receiving tangible support, most often money, were more likely to be financially destitute. They argue that it is not unreasonable to assume that students who perceive their financial resources to be inadequate are likely to feel more pressure in college and hence are more likely to report psychological distress.

An additional finding by the Liems is that support from family members was associated with **physical** well-being while availability of friends in a support network was related to **psychological** well-being. Thus the role relationships between individuals and network members also needs explication. More generally, it would seem that the few examples cited thus far would indicate that we need to look for specific effects. The specific components of support cannot be assumed to affect outcome measures in the same way. It is not the case that all behaviors considered "supportive" are perceived as helpful by the recipients of intended support.

The Personality, Demographic Characteristics, and Role Behaviors Influencing Receptivity to Support

Most probably, social support is not needed to the same degree by all. But what are the characteristics of individuals for whom it is most beneficial? Gruen (1975) developed an interesting therapeutic program for acute heart attack patients that emphasized emotional support and the encouragement of active coping. While the therapeutic regimen had positive effects, Gruen reported that both therapy and control groups contained a small subsample of patients "who possessed such a storehouse of inner resources that they did not require the treatment [Gruen, 1975, p. 226]." Gruen did not provide data on the characteristics of these natural copers; and the literature is generally sparse in identifying the characteristics of copers who are seemingly "invulnerable" to stress. However, there are a few leads that point to variables that may be of some importance in mediating reactions to stress.

Antonovsky (1974) describes resources for stress resistance as including *homeostatic flexibility*, that is, the ability to accept alternative roles and values. Hinkle (1974) believes that a nonreactive emotional disposition is a crucial ingredient in invulnerability, and indeed, defense mechanisms such as denial appear repeatedly in the clinical literature (Monat & Lazarus, 1977). Whether denial is adaptive probably depends upon the type of stress and whether the role behavior of the stressed individual allows active coping (Averill, 1973; Lazarus, Averill, & Opton, 1974). When stress is unavoidable, denial can be ego protective; when direct forms of coping are possible, denial is more likely to be maladaptive. For example, the Chinese citizens stranded in this country when the Communists gained control of China, faced a stressor that was beyond their control, namely, separation from family members. Hinkle (1974) observed that the healthiest members of this group seemed to show little reaction to loss or isolation. On the other hand, denial of the early signs of cancer, for example, a lump in a woman's breast, is clearly maladaptive. Katz, Weiner, Gallagher, and Hollman (1970) found this type of denial coupled with postponement of a visit to a physician was a frequent response among women eventually hospitalized for breast tumor biopsy. Thus, Katz *et al.* (1970) conclude that a psychologically effective defense (e.g., denial) is not necessarily a healthy, reality oriented one.

There are other dispositional characteristics associated with receptivity to the warning signs of approaching stress (Averill, 1973). Andrew (1970) studied patients in a Veterans hospital about to undergo hernia surgery. Patients were classified according to coping style and then were presented with taped information about the operation that they were about to undergo. Results indicated that the midgroup on the coping style variable, those classified as "nonspecific defenders" improved most, recovering in less time and with least medication when instructed than when not instructed. Patients whose personality style was to avoid or deny threatening emotions required **more** pain-killing medication when instructed than when not, while those subjects who were sensitive to and readily acknowledged threatening feelings showed no effect for instruction. Andrew suggests that this latter group of "sensitizers" had already prepared themselves for the operation so that the taped information did not provide them with incentive for additional preparation.

Similar results indicating an interaction between personality attributes and the utility of preparing for stress were obtained by DeLong (1970) and by Auerbach, Kendall, Cuttler, and Levitt (1976). "Sensitizers" recovered more quickly from surgery when given specific information but less quickly when given general information (DeLong, 1970). Similarly, dental surgery patients with an internal locus of control orientation showed better adjustment during surgery after viewing a preparatory film with specific rather than general information. In both studies, "avoiders" (DeLong, 1970) and "externals" (Auerbach et al., 1976) showed a better reaction to general rather than specific information. Internals and "sensitizers" were more inclined to seek out specific information to cope with the impending stress of surgery by engaging in "the work of worrying [Janis, 1958]."

The studies cited in this section indicate that procedures designed to aid in preparation for stress vary in effectiveness depending upon personality attributes of stressed individuals. The relevance of this work for social support is in the design of support programs. There is probably no one "best" set of support procedures. Effectiveness will probably depend upon the type of stress and how it is responded to by individuals of different dispositional characteristics. It is in this sense that specificity of support effects should be expected and built into future research and evaluation studies.

The Skills Necessary to Access and Maintain Supportive Relationships

As we have pointed out in a previous section of this chapter, the relationship between social isolation and admission rates to psychiatric treatment facilities found in previous studies may be a function of lack of social competence. The socially isolated may lack the skills to access and maintain supportive relationships. This possibility resonates with a major theme in the recent psychotherapy literature involving the remediation of skill deficits for a variety of clinical problems. For example, McFall (1976) has suggested that many individuals behave maladaptively simply because they lack the necessary skills to do better. We need not join the debate as to whether skill deficits, by themselves, are sufficient to account for the etiology of various behavior disorders (Buchwald & Young, 1969) to recognize that regardless of the reasons for onset, behavioral techniques can modify the nature, duration, and frequency of psychological deficits. If teaching social skills can increase social competency, might not a skills approach help individuals maintain themselves more appropriately in a supportive environment?

In recent years, problems of shyness (Twentyman & McFall, 1975), nonassertiveness (McFall & Twentyman, 1973), alcoholism (Lloyd & Salzberg, 1975), delinquency (Sarason & Ganzer, 1973; Freedman & McFall, 1977), and chronic schizophrenic reactions (Goldsmith & Mc-

Fall, 1975; Goldstein, 1973) have all been approached from a skills training perspective. The most dramatic work has been done with the latter
group and thus deserves additional emphasis.

Leff (1976) presented data indicating that, rather than being supportive, the family environment of schizophrenic patients may be one factor
contributing to continued poor adjustment. Leff developed an index of
"expressed emotion" consisting of variables such as critical comments
and overinvolvement by family members and found that relapse rates
among schizophrenics were related to these measures of emotional climate in the home. Even with behavioral disturbance levels of patients
partialed out and controlled statistically, there was a sizable significant
correlation ($r = .52$) between expressed emotion by family members and
patient relapse rate. The data further indicated that patients living in
high expressed emotion homes were made less vulnerable by drug therapy and/or **reduced** face-to-face contact between patient and family
members. Leff hypothesized that the social withdrawal exhibited by
many schizophrenic patients may function as a "protection" against excessive and disturbing social stimulation.

Given these circumstances, what should be the appropriate rehabilita-
tive strategy? Should patients be allowed to live in isolation, or should
programs be mounted to train patients in improved social skills and
coping techniques (Goldsmith & McFall, 1975; Goldstein, 1973)? Should
family members be encouraged to be more tolerant and supportive (Garrison, 1974; Speck & Attneave, 1973), or should alternative structures
be established (e.g., Fairweather, *et al.*, 1969) to provide the positive
support missing from patient-family interactions?

Both Leff (1976) and Test and Stein (1977) are pessimistic about
modifying long standing maladaptive family relationships involving
chronic mental patients. Test and Stein believe that the best approach
often is one of "constructive separation." Their experience in implementing a Community Living Program for chronic mental patients was
that families needed help in responding to the patient "as a responsible
adult rather than as a sick child [Test & Stein, 1977, p. 12]." In their
view, patients had learned to become aggressively dependent on family
members and hence were unmotivated to learn independent living skills
as long as they could arrange (through a display of helplessness and
symptomatology) to have others care for them. There was no doubt that
patients usually had an extremely limited repertoire of skills needed for
daily living in the community; but they would only begin to learn appropriate self care skills if pathological dependence on family members
and/or mental hospital tenure could be broken. Thus, Test and Stein
might argue that while skill training for community living is important,

it is insufficient if not accompanied by independence from family members and temporary but extremely active outreach support from project staff members. In order for community adjustment to succeed, chronic mental patients need to be linked to supportive structures in the community, but only to those that can accept and encourage independent, responsible behavior.

Environmental Structures Conducive to the Establishment and Maintenance of Supportive Relationships

There are a number of ways in which environmental support can be provided. That work on this topic is still sparse, in part, reflects the recency of interest in community approaches to psychological problems. In psychology, so much emphasis has been placed on individual predispositions and capacities that the social context often has been neglected. To be sure, successful coping depends upon individual capacities and motivation. But as Mechanic points out, an individual's ability to cope also depends upon "the efficacy of the solutions his culture provides [Mechanic, 1974a, p. 33]." Coping skills, motivation, and psychological comfort all depend upon the incentives and social supports provided by the environment. Not only does culture shape the form that adaptation will take, more basically, whether coping behavior appears at all, also depends on societal practices.

There are a number of examples in the literature of approaches taken to increase the supportiveness of social environments. The most direct tactic is to change the impact of social institutions by modifying the nature of institutional programs. For example, schools can decrease alienation by opening their facilities to citizens of all ages for extra curricular educational, vocational and recreational programs. An early program of this sort, staffed by volunteer "teachers" from the community, was established in the public schools of Gary, Indiana at the beginning of this century (Levine & Levine, 1970). Currently, the concept of school or library as community center is returning in popularity and like the settlement house of a previous era, a structure is being provided for group cohesion and support that can be accessed freely by all. One need not become the client of a social service agency to participate in parent effectiveness classes, social skill training, assertiveness enhancement, death and dying seminars, or various focused support groups that could be offered by such centers.

Another alternative involves the training of a new cadre of community support agents. These could be formal employees of social service or mental health agencies (e.g., outreach workers; or therapists trained to access and utilize family networks) or indigenous community members chosen for special characteristics and experience. For example, Silverman (1969, 1976) trained widows to work as widow-aides and provide support for the newly bereaved. Collins and Pancoast identified naturally helpful neighbors to whom others turned in time of crisis, and provided them with extra consultation and backup training. Both projects employed sensitive indigenous personnel capable of generating and sustaining helpful relations on their own with minimal supervision. As the self-help movement has amply demonstrated (G. Caplan & Killilea, 1976; Levy, 1976, 1978), meaningful social support does not require professional credentials.

Given that we understand how to increase the supportiveness of community institutions and train supportive community personnel, why have so few of the projects described in this chapter been adopted on a wider scale? The most immediate response might be that the effectiveness of the projects have not been demonstrated adequately. Indeed, in each case, questions of effectiveness and generalizability can be raised. For example, the Gary public school program, while increasing citizen morale, apparently did not affect student academic achievement, and, in addition, was involved in considerable public controversy in its day. In terest in the Gary system declined when its supporters in New York City, hoping to transpose the plan to their schools, were defeated in the mayorality election of 1917 (Levine & Levine, 1970).

The other programs cited also lack adequate control comparisons and the exact effective ingredients in the support package often are unknown. For example; it would be useful to know for whom a widow-to-widow project would be most beneficial and for whom it might be superfluous; or, what structural changes in the program would be necessary for widowers to become as involved and accepting of support as widows seem to have been. So, while the need for further research is apparent, better research, by itself, is not the answer in explaining utilization of research findings or its lack.

At the beginning of this chapter, we warned against the wholesale adoption of unproven fads and pointed to the political and social forces that often are involved in the pressure for premature acceptance of new ideas. Similarly, we must now recognize that these same factors are responsible for nonadoption as well. Good ideas that do not resonate with political and social values often lie fallow. While some might argue that social support is a concept whose time has come, at least among mental health professionals, it must be recognized that changes in **community** attitudes and mores are not so easily modifiable. A major impediment to public acceptance of social support programs can be traced to the laissez faire tradition in this country with its emphasis on personal initiative and individual freedom of action. As a society we tend to downplay the need for others and tend to value a cultural norm of privacy, "the right and privilege of each person, and family, in a free society to mind his own business and have others mind theirs [Bower, 1969, p. 233]." The institutionalization of social support programs would require a shift in this value toward the usefulness of interpersonal support as a key ingredient in the maintenance of psychological well-being. While such a shift in values is possible, its occurrence cannot be taken for granted and requires active attitude change and dissemination efforts.

CONCLUSION

In a book about maximizing therapeutic gain through transfer enhancement, it would be fitting to close with suggestions for the clinical use of social support. However, the level of research in this field is such that detailing the ingredients in a social support treatment package would be premature at this time.

There is an abundance of *naturalistic* and *correlational* research highlighting the beneficial effects of social support. In these studies, those with social ties have been found to show less vulnerability to stress and improved social adjustment. Even for mental patients initiating psychotherapy, the unaffiliated and those with weak social ties have been found to be more likely to drop out of treatment in **every** study in which social ties have been investigated (Baekeland & Lundwall, 1975). Thus it would appear that social support available in the environment is a key ingredient in effective adjustment and in the maintenance of the therapeutic contract itself.

The difficulty in accepting the above conclusion rests with the correlational nature of the evidence, and the similarity in designs and measures used in different studies that leaves this body of research vulnerable to validity threats from competing hypotheses. *Social competence* is the most prominent and reasonable alternative that would account for these results. It may be that deficits in social competence produce the poorer levels of adjustment reported for unsupported individuals, as well as accounting for the lower levels of social support they receive. Those with low levels of social competence are likely to be less able to access and maintain supportive relationships, even those readily available in the environment.

The primary recommendation at this time is for greater effort in basic research focused upon clarifying the most potent support factors and their interaction with person, relationship and setting variables. Determining the specific operative factors in the support phenomenon is important in deciding upon the most appropriate social intervention. For example, if the unaffiliated simply are lacking in appropriate supportive environmental structures, a program to provide the missing support networks might be all that is needed. However, if basic skills needed to access and maintain interpersonal relationships are absent, linking individuals to supportive environments is not likely to succeed without prior programs emphasizing social skills training.

Even for those **with** adequate social skills, the key ingredients in optimizing psychological growth and development by means of supportive relationships are still unclear. Very little research has been done on the structural aspects of support networks. Variables such as the density and extensiveness of network relationships, and reciprocity among network members only recently have been identified as of potential importance. How support should be structured, the content of support and the interaction of person variables with content and structure to determine optimal receptivity to support all need further examination in basic research.

After decades of naturalistic clinical studies, the call for more specific knowledge has been a recurring theme in the psychotherapy literature. Fortunately, basic experimental research in psychotherapy and behavior change has been accumulating to explicate some key therapeutic ingredients, and advances in the development of new therapeutic programs has occurred over the last two decades. It is time for the area of social support to receive similar experimental focus.

ACKNOWLEDGEMENTS

This chapter was begun while the author was on sabbatical leave as Visiting Scholar at the Institute for Social Research, University of Michigan. Financial support for the research leave came from Indiana University and from an NIMH postdoctoral fellowship award (IF32 MH05727–01). The author would like to thank Stephen B. Withey, Director of the Survey Research Center for his hospitality and help during the year. Special thanks also are extended to the following individuals who very generously shared their own research ideas with the author and who aided in establishing a facilitative climate for scholarly work: Edward Bordin, Nathan Caplan, Robert Caplan, David Clifford, Elizabeth Douvan, John R. P. French, Jr., Edward Jacobson, Jerome Johnston, Richard Kulka, Melvin Manis, Richard Price, and Joseph Veroff.

REFERENCES

Amoroso, D. M., & Walters, R. H. Effects of anxiety and socially mediated anxiety reduction on paired-associate learning. *Journal of Personality and Social Psychology*, 1969, *11*, 388–396.

Andrew, J. M. Recovering from surgery, with and without preparatory instruction, for three coping styles. *Journal of Personality and Social Psychology*, 1970, *15*, 223–226.

Antonovsky, A. Conceptual and methodological problems in the study of resistance resources and stressful life events. In B. S. Dohrenwend & B. P. Dohrenwend (Eds.), *Stressful life events: Their nature and effects*. New York: Wiley, 1974.

Angermeier, W. F., Phelps, J. B., & Reynolds, H. H. Verbal stress and heart-rate in humans exposed in groups. *Psychonomic Science*, 1967, *8*, 515–516.

Auerbach, S. M., Kendall, P. C., Cuttler, H. F., & Levitt, N. R. Anxiety, locus of control, type of preparatory information and adjustment to dental surgery. *Journal of Consulting and Clinical Psychology*, 1976, *44*, 809–818.

Averill, J. R. Personal control over aversive stimuli and its relationship to stress. *Psychological Bulletin*, 1973, *80*, 286–303.

Axelrod, M. Urban structure and social participation. *American Sociological Review*, 1956, *21*, 14–18.

Baekeland, F., & Lundwall, L. Dropping out of treatment: A critical review. *Psychological Bulletin*, 1975, *82*, 738–783.

Blackman, S., & Goldstein, K. M. Some aspects of a theory of community mental health. *Community Mental Health Journal*, 1968, *4*, 85–90.

Bower, E. M. Primary prevention of mental and emotional disorders: A conceptual framework and action possibilities. In A. J. Bindman & A. D. Spiegel (Eds.), *Perspectives in community mental health*. Chicago: Aldine, 1969.

Brown, G. W., Bhrolchain, M. H., & Harris, T. Social class and psychiatric disturbance among women in an urban population. *Sociology*, 1975, *9*, 225–254.

Buchwald, A. M., & Young, R. D. Some comments on the foundations of behavior therapy. In C. M. Franks (Ed.), *Behavior therapy: Appraisal and status*. New York: McGraw-Hill, 1969.

Buck, R. W., & Parke, R. D. Behavioral and physiological response to the presence of a friendly or neutral person in two types of stressful situations. *Journal of Personality and Social Psychology*, 1972, *24*, 143–153.

Campbell, D. T., & Stanley, J. C. *Experimental and quasi-experimental designs for research*. Chicago: Rand McNally, 1963.

Caplan, G. *Support systems and community mental health: Lectures on concept development*. New York: Behavioral Publications, 1974.

Caplan, G. The family as a support system. In G. Caplan & M. Killilea (Eds.), *Support systems and mutual help: Multidisciplinary explorations*. New York: Grune & Stratton, 1976.

Caplan, G., & Killilea, M. (Eds.). *Support systems and mutual help: Multidisciplinary explorations*. New York: Grune & Stratton, 1976.

Caplan, R. B. *Psychiatry and the community in nineteenth century America: The recurring concern with the environment in the prevention and treatment of mental illness*. New York: Basic Books, 1969.

Caplan, R. D., Cobb, S., French, J. R. P., Jr., VanHarrison, R., & Pinneau, S. R., Jr. Job demands and worker health: Main effects and occupational differences. HEW Publication No. 75–160. Washington, D.C.: U.S. Government Printing Office, 1975.

Carveth, W. B., & Gottlieb, B. H. The role of social support in mediating stress among new mothers. Paper presented at the Convention of the Canadian Psychological Association, Vancouver, B.C., 1977.

Cassel, J. Social science in epidemiology: Psychosocial processes and "stress" theoretical formulation. In E. L. Struening & M. Guttentag (Eds.), *Handbook of evaluation research* (Vol. I). Beverly Hills, California: Sage Publications, 1975.

Clifford, D. L., A comparative study of helping patterns in eight urban communities. Unpublished doctoral dissertation, University of Michigan, 1976.

Cobb, S. Social support as a moderator of life stress. *Psychosomatic Medicine*, 1976, *38*, 300–314.

Collins, A. H., & Pancoast, D. L. *Natural helping networks: A strategy for prevention*. Washington, D.C.: National Association of Social Workers.

Cottrell, N. B. Social facilitation. In C. G. McClintock (Ed.), *Experimental social psychology*. New York: Holt, 1972.

Craven, P., & Wellman, B. The network city. In M. P. Effrat (Ed.), *The community: Approaches and applications*. New York: Free Press, 1974.

Croog, S. H. The family as a source of stress. In S. Levine & N. A. Scotch (Eds.), *Social stress*. Chicago: Aldine, 1970.

Davidson, P. O., & Kelley, W. R. Social facilitation and coping with stress. *British Journal of Social and Clinical Psychology*, 1973, *12*, 130–136.

Dean, A., & Lin, N. The stress-buffering role of social support: Problems and prospects for systematic investigation. *Journal of Nervous and Mental Disease*, 1977, *165*, 403–417.

de Araujo, G., van Arsdel, P. P., Holmes, T. H., & Dudley, D. L. Life change, coping ability and chronic intrinsic asthma. *Journal of Psychosomatic Research*, 1973, *17*, 359–363.

De Long, D. R. Individual differences in patterns of anxiety arousal, stress-relevant information and recovery from surgery. Unpublished doctoral dissertation, University of California, Los Angeles, 1970.

Dohrenwend, B. P., & Dohrenwend, B. S. Social and cultural influences on psychopathology. *Annual Review of Psychology*, 1974, *25*, 417–452.

Drieblatt, I. S., & Weatherley, D. An evaluation of the efficacy of brief-contact therapy with hospitalized psychiatric patients. *Journal of Consulting Psychology*, 1965, *29*, 513–519.

Epley, S. W. Reduction of the behavioral effects of aversive stimulation by the presence of companions. *Psychological Bulletin*, 1974, *81*, 271–283.

Fairweather, G. W., Sanders, D. H., Maynard, H., & Cressler, D. L. *Community life for the mentally ill: An alternative to institutional care*. Chicago: Aldine, 1969.

Fischer, C. S. The study of urban community and personality. *Annual Review of Sociology*, 1975, *1*, 67–89.

Fox, J. R. Therapeutic rituals and social structure in Cochiti Pueblo. *Human Relations*, 1960, *13*, 291–303.

Freedman, B. J., & McFall, R. M. A social-behavioral analysis of skill deficits in delinquent adolescent boys. Unpublished manuscript, University of Wisconsin, 1977.

Fried, M. Grieving for a lost home. In L. J. Duhl (Ed.), *The urban condition: People and policy in the metropolis*. New York: Basic Books, 1963.

Gans, H. *The Levittowners: Ways of life and politics in a new suburban community*. New York: Vintage, 1969.

Garrison, J. Network techniques: Case studies in the screening-linking-planning conference method. *Family Process*, 1974, *13*, 337–353.

Geen, R. G. The role of the social environment in the induction and reduction of anxiety. In I. G. Sarason & C. D. Spielberger (Eds.), *Stress and anxiety, Vol. 3*. Washington, D.C.: Hemisphere, 1976.

Geen, R. G., & Gange, J. J. Drive theory of social facilitation: Twelve years of theory and research. *Psychological Bulletin*, 1977, *84*, 1267–1288.

Goldsmith, J. B., & McFall, R. M. Development and evaluation of an interpersonal skill-training program for psychiatric inpatients. *Journal of Abnormal Psychology*, 1975, *84*, 51–58.

Goldstein, A. P. *Structured learning therapy: Toward a psychotherapy for the poor.* New York: Academic Press, 1973.

Goldstein, A. P., & Stein, N. *Prescriptive psychotherapies.* New York: Pergamon, 1976.

Gore, S. The influence of social support and related variables in ameliorating the consequences of job loss. Unpublished doctoral dissertation, University of Pennsylvania, 1973.

Gruen, W. Effects of brief psychotherapy during the hospitalization period on the recovery process in heart attacks. *Journal of Consulting and Clinical Psychology*, 1975, *43*, 223–232.

Gurin, G., Veroff, J., & Feld, S. *Americans view their mental health: A nationwide interview survey.* New York: Basic Books, 1960.

Hansell, N. Patient predicament and clinical service: A system. *Archives of General Psychiatry*, 1967, *17*, 204–210.

Heller, K. Effects of modeling procedures in helping relationships. *Journal of Consulting and Clinical Psychology*, 1969, *33*, 522–526.

Heller, K., & Monahan, J. *Psychology and community change.* Homewood, Illinois: Dorsey Press, 1977.

Hinkle, L. E., Jr. The effect of exposure to culture change, social change and changes in interpersonal relationships on health. In B. S. Dohrenwend & B. P. Dohrenwend (Eds.), *Stressful life events: Their nature and effects*. New York: Wiley, 1974.

Holmes, T. H., & Masuda, M. Life change and illness suspectibility. In B. S. Dohrenwend & B. P. Dohrenwend (Eds.), *Stressful life events: Their nature and effects*. New York: Wiley, 1974.

Holmes, T. H., & Rahe, R. H. The social readjustment rating scale. *Journal of Psychosomatic Research*, 1967, *11*, 213–218.

Hughes, C., Tremblay, M., Rapoport, R., & Leighton, A. *People of cove and woodlot: Communities from the viewpoint of social psychiatry. The Stirling County Studies* (Vol. II). New York: Basic Books, 1960.

Iscoe, I., Bloom, B. L., & Spielberger, C. D. *Community psychology in transition: Proceedings of the National Training Conference in Community Psychology.* Washington, D.C.: Hemisphere, 1977.

Janis, I. L. Emotional inoculation: Theory and research on effects of preparatory communications. In G. Róheim (Ed.), *Psychoanalysis and the social sciences.* New York: International Universities Press, 1958.

Kahn, R. L., & Quinn, R. P. Mental health, social support, and metropolitan problems. Research proposal, University of Michigan, 1977.

Kasl, S. V., & Cobb, S. Blood pressure changes in men undergoing job loss: A preliminary report. *Psychosomatic Medicine*, 1970, *32*, 19–38.

Kasl, S. V., Cobb, S., & Brooks, G. W. Changes in serum uric acid and cholesterol levels in men undergoing job loss. *Journal of the American Medical Association*, 1968, *206*, 1500–1507.

Kasl, S. V., Gore, S., & Cobb, S. The experience of losing a job: Reported changes in health, symptoms and illness behavior. *Psychosomatic Medicine*, 1975, *37*, 106–122.

Katz, J. L., Weiner, H., Gallagher, T. F., & Hellman, L. Stress, distress and ego defenses: Psychoendocrine response to impending breast tumor biopsy. *Archives of General Psychiatry*, 1970, *23*, 131–142.

Kiesler, D. J. Some myths of psychotherapy research and the search for a paradigm. *Psychological Bulletin*, 1966, *65*, 110–136.

Kissel, S. Stress-reducing properties of social stimuli. *Journal of Personality and Social Psychology*, 1965, *2*, 378–384.

Kraus, A. S., & Lilienfeld, A. M. Some epidemiologic aspects of the high mortality rate in the young widowed group. *Journal of Chronic Disease*, 1959, *10*, 207–217.

Laumann, E. D., & Pappi, F. U. New directions in the study of community elites. *American Sociological Review*, 1973, *38*, 212–230.

Lazarus, R. S., Averill, J. R., & Opton, E. M. Jr. The psychology of coping: Issues of research and assessment. In G. V. Coelho, D. A. Hamburg, & J. E. Adams (Eds.), *Coping and adaptation*. New York: Basic Books, 1974.

Leff, J. P. Schizophrenia and sensitivity to the family environment. *Schizophrenia Bulletin*, 1976, *2*, 566–574.

Leighton, A. *My name is Legion. The Stirling County studies* (Vol. I). New York: Basic Books, 1959.

Levine, M., & Levine, A. *A social history of helping services: Clinic, court, school and community*. New York: Appleton-Century-Crofts, 1970.

Levy, L. H. Self-help groups: Types and psychological processes. *Journal of Applied Behavioral Science*, 1976, *12*, 310–322.

Levy, L. H. Self-help groups viewed by mental health professionals: A survey and comments. *American Journal of Community Psychology*, 1978, *6*, 305–313.

Levy, L., & Rowitz, L. *The ecology of mental disorder*. New York: Behavioral Publications, 1973.

Lewis, C. E. Factors influencing the return to work of men with congestive heart failure. *Journal of Chronic Diseases*, 1966, *19*, 1193–1209.

Liem, J. H., & Liem, R. Life events, social supports and physical and psychological well-being. Paper presented at the meetings of the American Psychological Association, September, 1976.

Lloyd, R. W. Jr., & Salzberg, H. C. Controlled social drinking: An alternative to abstinence as a treatment goal for some alcohol abusers. *Psychological Bulletin*, 1975, *82*, 815–842.

Lowenthal, M. F. Social isolation and mental illness in old age. *American Sociological Review*, 1964, *29*, 54–70.

Lowenthal, M. F., & Haven, C. Interaction and adaptation: Intimacy as a critical variable. *American Sociological Review*, 1968, *33*, 20–30.

Ludwig, E. G., & Collette, J. Dependency, social isolation and mental health in a disabled population. *Social Psychiatry*, 1970, *5*, 92–95.

Maris, R. The sociology of suicide. *Social Problems*, 1969, *17*, 132–149.

McFall, R. M. *Behavioral training: A skill-acquisition approach to clinical problems*. Morristown, New Jersey: General Learning Press, 1976.

McFall, R. M., & Twentyman, C. T. Four experiments on the relative contributions of rehearsal, modeling, and coaching to assertion training. *Journal of Abnormal Psychology*, 1973, *81*, 199–218.

Mechanic, D. Social structure and personal adaptation: Some neglected dimensions. In G. V. Coelho, D. A. Hamburg, & J. E. Adams (Eds.), *Coping and adapta-*

tion. New York: Basic Books, 1974. (a)

Mechanic, D. Discussion of research programs on relations between stressful life events and episodes of physical illness. In B. S. Dohrenwend & B. P. Dohrenwend (Eds.), *Stressful life events: Their nature and effects.* New York: Wiley, 1974. (b)

Miller, N., & Zimbardo, P. G. Motives for fear-induced affiliation: Emotional comparison or interpersonal similarity. *Journal of Personality,* 1966, *34,* 481–503.

Mitchell, J. C. (Ed.). *Social networks in urban situations.* Manchester, England: University Press, 1969.

Mitchell, J. C. Social networks. *Annual Review of Anthropology,* 1974, *3,* 279–299.

Monat, A., & Lazarus, R. S. *Stress and coping.* New York: Columbia University Press, 1977.

Moss, L. M., & Hamilton, D. M. Psychotherapy of the suicidal patient. *American Journal of Psychiatry,* 1956, *112,* 814–820.

Nuckolls, K. B., Cassel, J., & Kaplan, B. H. Psychosocial assets, life crisis and the prognosis of pregnancy. *American Journal of Epidemiology,* 1972, *95,* 431–441.

Phillips, D. L. Social participation and happiness. *American Journal of Sociology,* 1967, *72,* 479–488.

Phillips, D. L. Social class, social participation and happiness: A consideration of "interaction-opportunities" and "investment." *Sociological Quarterly,* 1969, *10,* 3–21.

Rabkin, J. G., & Struening, E. L. Life events, stress, and illness. *Science,* 1976, *194,* 1013–1020.

Riessman, F. The "helper" therapy principle. *Social Work,* 1965, *10,* 27–32.

Sarason, I. G., & Ganzer, V. I. Modeling and group discussion in the rehabilitation of juvenile delinquents. *Journal of Counseling Psychology,* 1973, *20,* 442–449.

Sarason, S. B. Community psychology, networks and Mr. Everyman. *American Psychologist,* 1976, *31,* 317–328.

Sarason, S. B., Carroll, C., Maton, K., Cohen, S., & Lorentz, E. *Human services and resource networks.* San Francisco: Jossey-Bass, 1977.

Sarnoff, I., & Zimbardo, P. G. Anxiety, fear and social affiliation. *Journal of Abnormal and Social Psychology,* 1961, *62,* 356–363.

Schachter, S. *The psychology of affiliation: Experimental studies of the sources of gregariousness.* Stanford, California: Stanford University Press, 1959.

Segal, B. E., Weiss, R. J., & Sokol, R. Emotional adjustment, social organization and psychiatric treatment rates. *American Sociological Review,* 1965, *30,* 548–556.

Silverman, P. R. The widow to widow program: An experiment in preventive intervention. *Mental Hygiene,* 1969, *53,* 3.

Silverman, P. R. The widow as a caregiver in a program of preventive intervention with other widows. In G. Caplan & M. Killilea (Eds.), *Support systems and mutual help: Multidisciplinary explorations.* New York: Grune & Stratton, 1976.

Slote, A. *Termination: The closing at Baker plant.* Indianapolis: Bobbs-Merrill, 1969.

Speck, R. V., & Attneave, L. L. *Family networks.* New York: Random House, 1973.

Strole, L., Langner, T. S., Michael, S. T., Kirkpatrick, P., Opler, M. K., & Rennie, T. A. C. *Mental health in the metropolis: The midtown Manhattan study.* New York: McGraw-Hill, 1962.

Strupp, H. H. *Psychotherapy and the modification of abnormal behavior.* New York: McGraw-Hill, 1971.

Test, M. A., & Stein, L. I. A community approach to the chronically disabled patient.

Social Policy, 1977, *8,* 8–16.

Twentyman, C. T., & McFall, R. M. Behavioral training of social skills in shy
  males. *Journal of Consulting and Clinical Psychology,* 1975, *43,* 384–395.

Warren, D. I. Neighborhood and community contexts in help seeking, problem
  coping, and mental health: Data analysis monograph. Unpublished manuscript, University of Michigan, 1976.

Weiss, R. J., & Bergen, B. J. Social supports and the reduction of psychiatric disability. *Psychiatry,* 1968, *31,* 107–115.

Wellman, B., Craven, P., Whitaker, M., Stevens, H., Shorter, A., DuToit, S., &
  Bakker, H. Community ties and support systems: From intimacy to support.
  In L. S. Bourne, R. D. MacKinnon, & J. W. Simmons (Eds.), *The form of cities
  in central Canada: Selected papers.* Toronto, Canada: University of Toronto
  Press, 1973.

Wrightsman, L. S., Jr. Effects of waiting with others on changes in level of felt
  anxiety. *Journal of Abnormal and Social Psychology,* 1960, *61,* 216–222.

Zajonc, R. B. Social facilitation. *Science,* 1965, *149,* 269–274.

10

The Social Ecology
of Treatment Gain

RICHARD H. PRICE

MAXIMIZING TREATMENT GAIN FROM THE PERSPECTIVE OF RESEARCH ON THE SOCIAL ENVIRONMENT

From the point of view of researchers who have been interested in measuring the characteristics of effective treatment settings, perhaps one of the most sobering findings was that of Ellsworth, Foster, Childers, Arthur, and Kroeker (1968). In an important early study of the milieu characteristics of treatment programs they found that, although milieu characteristics were strongly associated with patient status upon discharge, they were only weakly associated with a more important measure of effectiveness, length of stay in the community. Thus Ellsworth *et al.* (1968) added still another bit of evidence indicating that gains associated with the immediate impact of a treatment environment had little transfer to the later community settings in which the patient resided. Although Ellsworth's findings were confined to research to inpatient psy-

MAXIMIZING TREATMENT GAINS:
Transfer Enhancement in Psychotherapy

chiatric treatment settings, similar findings in a variety of outpatient treatment settings have been accumulating over the last 20 years.

Because researchers and practitioners have been impressed with the immediate impact of treatment interventions, they have tended to underestimate the impact of other subsequent social environments on behavior. Clearly, it is time to demystify ourselves and to broaden our conceptualization of the "treatment environment" beyond the immediate treatment milieu of the client.

It is the thesis of this chapter that a conceptualization of effective treatment must extend beyond the immediate treatment setting to the broader social ecology in which the client lives and works. Only by broadening our vision and our measurement techniques to account for the larger social ecology of the client will we be able to enhance the transfer of immediate therapeutic gains to the rest of the life space of the individual.

In this chapter it is argued that the enhancement of initial therapeutic gains requires a four step process. First, a workable conceptualization of the social environment is required. Second, measurement strategies based on this conceptualization must be developed that will provide useful tools to measure the major elements of the social environment thought to be of importance in behavior change. Third, the researcher or practitioner must have in mind a clear action goal to be maximized whatever the initial conceptualization and measurement strategy. The goal to be proposed here involves the concept of person–environment congruence. That is, the researcher or practitioner must consider the degree of congruence or *fit* between the individual's needs or goals and the demands of the social environment. Finally, a set of specific strategies for altering the social environment of the client is necessary. The development of such strategies requires thoughtful, data based planning early in the course of therapeutic intervention.

In this chapter, three perspectives on the social environment will be reviewed that provide useful initial conceptualizations of the nature and impact of the social environment. The three perspectives to be reviewed are (a) the social climate perspective; (b) the human aggregate perspective; and (c) the undermanning perspective. Measurement techniques associated with each of these three conceptual approaches will be reviewed. Following this, the person–environment congruence conception will be examined as a guide to action. Finally, three major strategies for maximizing treatment gains will be considered. The three strategies— setting selection, setting change, and setting creation—all focus on altering the social ecology of the client in order to maximize initial treatment gains.

THREE PERSPECTIVES ON THE SOCIAL ENVIRONMENT

Currently, there exists no single generally accepted theoretical approach to conceptualizing the nature and impact of the social environment. Instead, a review of the literature suggests that there are a number of perspectives or approaches to this problem. Each of them selects some aspects of the social environment as most salient and minimizes the importance of others. At this early stage of our knowledge, we have no clear basis for choosing one over another. Since both practitioners and researchers may find one approach more congenial than others, we will consider three approaches in the following discussion.

The Social Climate Perspective

The social climate approach argues that it is possible to conceive of social environments in much the same way that traditional descriptions of personality have been used. As Moos (1976) notes,

> The social climate perspective assumes that environments, like people, have unique "personalities." Social environments can be portrayed with a great deal of accuracy and detail. Some people are more supportive than others. Likewise some social enviromnents are more supportive than others. Some people feel a strong need to control others. Similarly, social environments can be extremely rigid, autocratic, and controlling. Order, clarity, and structure are important to many people. Correspondingly many social environments strongly emphasize order, clarity and organization. People made detailed plans regulating and directing their behavior. Likewise, environments have overall programs that regulate and direct the behavior of people within them [p. 320].

Moos and his colleagues have conducted a substantial amount of research based on this conceptualization (Moos, 1974, 1975, 1976). These researchers argue that three major dimensions of social climate can be found in a wide variety of different social environments. One set of dimensions is described as **relationship oriented.** They focus on various aspects of the interpersonal relationships that exist between people in the setting. A second major set of dimensions is described as **personal development.** These dimensions focus on the various aspects of the social environment that are designed to change or develop the abilities and the behaviors of people within the setting. Finally, Moos argues that a third set of dimensions which he calls **system maintenance** and **system change** can be isolated. These dimensions focus on those aspects of the social environment that are designed to maintain the setting and to plan changes within it.

Moos (1976) has summarized a wide variety of research concerning the impact of these dimensions on the behavior and attitudes of setting participants. In summarizing overall findings Moos argues that settings which are high on relationship dimensions tend to produce higher satisfaction among setting inhabitants, lower anxiety and depression, higher self-esteem, and lower feelings of irritability. Personal development dimension, on the other hand, tend to produce more positive attitudes to staff, higher levels of skill learning and in some cases higher levels of tension among setting inhabitants. System maintenance dimensions tend in general to have positive effects when they focus on program clarity and order and organization within the setting. Controlling elements of system maintenance dimensions, especially in therapeutic environments, tend to have negative effects on morale.

Thus, in brief, the social climate conceptualization argues that environments have personalities just like people, and that major dimensions of the "personality of the environment" have differential effects on the behavior of setting inhabitants.

Measurement and Application

Moos (1976) and his colleagues have developed a number of different social climate scales designed to measure various dimensions of the social environment in different types of settings. Of interest in the present context are the Ward Atmosphere Scale designed to measure inpatient treatment programs, the Community Oriented Program Environment Scale designed to measure community based treatment programs, the Correctional Institutions Environment Scale designed to measure juvenile and adult correctional facilities. In addition, the University Residents Environment Scale is designed to measure student living groups in the university. The Classroom Environment Scale is designed to measure the social climate of the family.

Each of these instruments consists of 90 to 100 true–false items which fall on 9 or 10 dimensions intended to describe major characteristics of the particular setting under investigation. In order to gain a clearer idea of the structure of social climate instruments, consider the Community-Oriented Programs Environment Scale (COPES) shown in Table 10.1. In this illustration the overall dimensions, specific subscales, and typical items from each scale are shown.

In order to illustrate how social climate scales can be used to characterize social environments, let us consider a study conducted by Price and Moos (1975). In this study a national sample of 144 inpatient treatment programs were assessed using the Ward Atmosphere Scale. The resulting profiles were classified using cluster analysis (Carlson, 1972)

TABLE 10.1

Community-Oriented Programs Environment Scale (COPES) [a]

Broad dimensions of social climate	Description of subscales	Typical items
Relationship oriented dimensions	1. *Program involvement:* measures how active members are in day-to-day functioning of program— enthusiasm, self-initiated efforts. 2. *Support:* measures how supportive members are to each other and how supportive staff is to members. 3. *Spontaneity:* measures the extent to which the program encourages members to act openly and express feelings openly.	+ "Members put a lot of energy into what they do around here." − "Very few members ever volunteer around here." + "Staff always compliment a member who does something well." − "Staff have relatively little time to encourage members." + "Members are strongly encouraged to express feelings." − "Members are careful about what they say when staff are around."
Personal development dimensions	4. *Autonomy:* assesses how self-sufficient members are encouraged to be in personal decisions and staff relationships. 5. *Practical orientation:* assesses extent to which the members' program orients toward release re: job attaining, goal orientation. 6. *Personal problem orientation:* measures extent to which members are encouraged to focus on and understand own problems. 7. *Anger and aggression:* measures extent to which a member is encouraged to argue, become openly angry or otherwise aggressive.	+ "Members can leave the program when they want to." − "There is no membership government in this program." + "Members are taught specific new skills in this program." − "Staff care more about how members feel than about practical problems. + "Staff are mainly interested in learning about members' feelings." − "Members are rarely encouraged to discuss personal problems." + "Staff here think it is a healthy thing to argue." − "Members here rarely become angry."

(continued)

[a] From Moos 1974.

TABLE 10.1 (*continued*)

Broad dimensions of social climate	Description of subscales	Typical items
	8. *Order and organization:* measures how important order and organization are in the program and in member and setting appearance.	+ "Members here follow a regular schedule every day." − "Things are sometimes very disorganized around here."
System maintenance and system change dimensions	9. *Program clarity:* measures extent to which members know what to expect and how explicit rules and procedures are.	+ "If a member breaks a rule, he knows the consequences." − "People are always changing their minds here."
	10. *Staff control:* assesses extent to which staff uses means to control members; e.g., control of relationships, resources.	+ "Staff make and enforce all the rules here." − Staff do not order members around."

yielding six distinctive types. The average WAS profile for each type is shown in Figures 10.1, 10.2, and 10.3.

We called the first type we observed **the therapeutic community type.** This cluster of 19 programs shown in Figure 1 was distinguished by having relatively high scores on all relationship oriented and treatment program dimensions of the Ward Atmosphere Scale but being much lower than average on dimensions measuring system maintenance and control. This program type tended to emphasize patient involvement, open expression of feelings, active preparation for patient release, and concern about the personal problems of patients. It did not, however, emphasize clear goal expectations or staff enforcement of rules. We called this particular cluster the therapeutic community type because it resembled the description of therapeutic communities, offered by Jones (1953).

A second cluster of programs included 38 that we described as **relationship oriented programs.** This group of programs, shown in Figure 10.1, also emphasized relationship and treatment program variables, but tended to be only average in its emphasis on patient expressions anger and aggression. This type also placed a very strong emphasis on program clarity. The relationship between patients and staff in these programs tends to be both explicit, clear and supportive and is probably the active therapeutic ingredient in this program type.

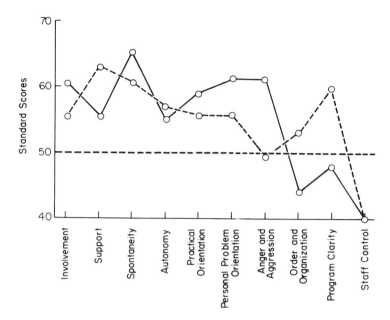

Figure 10.1 Inpatient treatment programs using the Ward Atmosphere Scale. O——O is the therapeutic community (N = 19 programs); O- - - -O is the relationship-oriented (N = 35 programs).

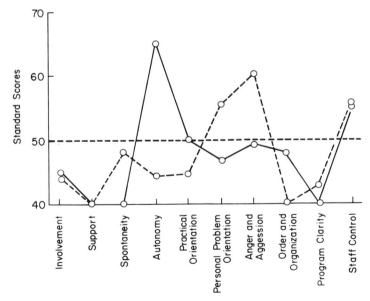

Figure 10.2 Inpatient treatment programs using the Ward Atmosphere Scale. O——O is the action-oriented (N = 5 programs); O- - - -O is the insight-oriented (N = 21 programs). [Figures 10.1 and 10.2 from R. H. Price and R. H. Moos, Toward a taxonomy of treatment environment. Copyright 1975 by the American Psychological Association. Reprinted by permission.]

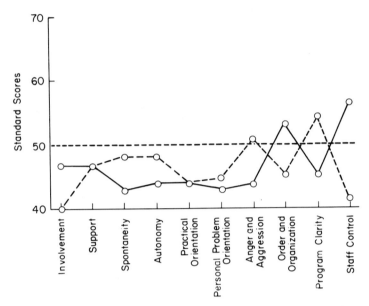

Figure 10.3 Inpatient treatment programs using the Ward Atmosphere Scale.
O——O is the control-oriented ($N = 50$ programs); O- - - -O is the disturbed behavior ($N = 11$ programs). [From R. H. Price and R. H. Moos, Toward a taxonomy
of treatment environment. Copyright 1975 by the American Psychological Association. Reprinted by permission.]

A small but distinct program type that emerged in our analysis we
called **action oriented programs** (Figure 10.2). This program type is most
strikingly distinguished by its emphasis on patient autonomy and its
simultaneous emphasis on staff control. In this type of program patients
are encouraged to make active individual plans to leave the program,
and to be independent and self sufficient in their planning for the future.
With their simultaneous emphasis on staff control and patient independence, these programs may minimize the "secondary gain" frequently
found in inpatient treatment settings (Price, 1972; Zussman, 1973).

Still another distinctive program type in our analysis involved **insight
oriented programs**. These programs displayed a high degree of encouragement and acceptance of open expressions of anger and aggression by
patients. Although staff control was also marked in these programs, their
primary focus appeared to be to encourage cathartic expressions of feelings on the part of patients.

By far the largest cluster of programs in our sample were most strikingly characterized by their orientation toward patient control (Figure
10.3). In these **control oriented programs,** strict rules for patient be-

havior and staff determination of those rules are the norm. This program type resembles the "total institution" type of treatment setting described by Goffman (1961). Active orientation toward treatment or relationships with patients seems to be minimized while control of patient behavior is the major focus.

The last cluster of programs discovered in our sample, we called **disturbed behavior programs**. It appears (Figure 10.3) to be composed primarily of programs that are designed to handle acutely disturbed and aggressive patients. Its major focus is on clear rules and routines for patients and the treatment milieu is also characterized by a substantial amount of anger and aggression among patients.

Thus the social climate scales appear to capture distinctive characteristics of social environments. Obviously, the classification approach we have used is not confined to inpatient treatment settings but can also be used in describing a wide range of classrooms, the family, halfway houses, work environments, and others.

Since we will consider a number of specific applications of the social climate scales to the problem of maximizing treatment gain, it is useful to describe briefly some details of administration and application at this point. Typically, members of the setting complete items on the questionnaire in a true or false fashion according to their own perception of the setting. Scores for each dimension are then obtained and a profile describing the social climate or "personality" of the setting is computed based on the average perceptions of the setting participants.

Although this form of administration is most commonly used, it is also possible to train observers to use the social climate scales as basis for rating the social environment rather than relying exclusively on the perceptions of participants in the setting. The perceptions of participants themselves and those of outside observers can then be compared in conducting an assessment of social climate of a particular setting. In addition, each social climate scale has a "real" form that requires that the observer or setting participant respond to the questionnaire in terms of their current perceptions of the social environment.

An "ideal" form is also available that allows setting participants to respond to the scale in terms of their idea of an ideal social environment. That is, respondents are instructed to answer the social climate scales in terms of the setting as they would ideally like it to be. This procedure allows the researcher to obtain information on the values and goals of setting participants. And, perhaps more important, one can examine the discrepancies between the perceptions of the setting as it currently exists and the setting as participants in it would like it to be. As we shall see, the discrepancies between the real and ideal forms of the various social climate scales provide an important point of entry into setting selection, setting change, and setting creation strategies for maximizing treatment gains.

There are a variety of practical applications of data obtained from social climate assessments (Moos, 1976). We will briefly mention several of them here and consider them in more detail later in the chapter. First, social climate measures can be used for describing the current perceptions of existing social environments from the point of view of various participants. For example, one might wish to know how staff and program members see the program of a halfway home and examine differences where they exist. Similarly, one might wish to compare the ideal perceptions of staff and program members in order to determine where members and staff goals for the program differ.

Another possible strategy for using these instruments is to compare different settings of the same general type. Thus, for example, one may wish to compare the degree to which an inpatient and half-way house treatment environment differ in their social climate, since these differences may have important implications for the degree to which treatment gains are maintained.

Still another use of social climate scales is in assessing program change. One can answer questions such as : "What is the effect of a staff training program on the social environment of the program?" Assessments made before and after the institution of a staff training program may reflect important changes in the social milieu. For example, one may ask the question: "Does the social environment of the treatment program change when a token economy is instituted within the program?"

The social climate scales can also be used as a basis for program selection. Typically, in deciding about the referral of clients to community based programs, a great more is known about the characteristics of the individual than about the characteristics of the program that they enter. Profiles of various treatment environments can be used as a basis for selecting treatment programs for individuals with particular needs.

Finally, the social climate scales can be used as a data base for program development. As we shall see, social climate data fed back to program participants, especially when real and ideal discrepancy data is available, can provide an effective beginning point for program change and program development efforts. Thus the social climate scales can provide a moderately flexible set of descriptive instruments for various social and treatment environments that have real practical implications for maximizing treatment gains.

The Human Aggregate Perspective

A second major perspective on the nature of social environments focuses on those aspects of the social environment that are determined by the similarity in individual characteristics of its members. The human aggregate perspective on social environments argues that important environmental features are determined by the average background characteristics of its members (Bromet & Moos, 1976). This perspective on the social environment suggests that social characteristics such as age, sex, race, social class, educational level, and other personality or attitudinal characteristics of groups *when they are aggregated across the individuals in the setting* provide a basis for conceptualizing the character and impact of that environment.

Even casual observation suggests that the characteristics of the members of various social groups and settings are not distributed randomly throughout the population of settings. On the contrary, some settings consist primarily of children, others of adults, some settings are predominantly male, others predominantly female. Other individual characteristics such as race, educational background, value orientation, interest patterns, and socioeconomic status tend in many cases to be quite homogeneous within a given setting. A number of researchers (Bromet & Moos, 1976; Holland, 1966; Mechanic, 1975) have suggested that this important social fact is a major determiner of the nature and impact of social settings.

People tend to select settings in which to work or live partly on the basis of the similarity of the characteristics or interests of the people in the setting to their own pattern of characteristics and interests. Mechanic (1975) notes that social selection is a major field of study that has been substantially ignored. Social selection, he notes, is one of the most pervasive processes characteristic of human communities, and its study concerns the identification of underlying principles by which the sorting and resorting among social groups occurs. It is presumably this process of social selection according to individual characteristics that leads many social settings to have their relatively homogeneous character. Bromet and Moos (1976) suggest that the average background characteristics of a social environment directly affect the social climate of a setting and that the climate produced in turn has major implications for the behaviors and attitudes encouraged or discouraged within the setting itself.

Whether or not one chooses to think of social climate as the mediator of effects of aggregated individual characteristics, it is clear that the human aggregate perspective asserts that a process of social selection increases the homogeneity of background characteristics in the setting. It is this homogeneity then, that finally produces predictable effects on the behavior and attitudes of the people within the setting. This is, in effect, one mechanism whereby the "culture" of the setting is transmitted from person to person.

Furthermore, a reasonable inference from the human aggregate perspective is that the culture of the setting can be maintained in at least three ways. First, recruitment into the setting is likely to be on the basis of similarity in aggregated characteristics. Second, the homogeneity of attitudes of characteristics is likely to shape the behavior and attitudes of people in the setting in the direction of the prevailing norms. Finally, persons whose individual attitudes are at substantial variance with those of the setting are more likely to leave the setting because of the lack of "fit" between their own background characteristics and those of other setting participants.

This is an intuitively appealing idea and seems consistent with our everyday observations. But we may ask, is there evidence that the average background characteristics of a particular setting do, in fact, have an impact on the behavior of participants within the setting? In their review of this perspective on social environments, Bromet and Moos (1976) cite several studies that would suggest that this is indeed the case.

One approach to studying this problem is to examine the congruence between the individual characteristics or interest patterns of particular individuals as they enter a setting and those of the setting itself. If settings with a particular pattern of background characteristics do indeed affect the behavior of individuals once they enter the setting, then one would expect behavior and attitudes to change in the direction of the modal characteristics of the setting.

Holland (1963) has found that students who entered a university in which their major field resembled that of the majority of students in the university tended to have more stable goals and higher achievement than students who had incongruent interests and goals. Astin and Panos (1969) conducted an extremely large scale study involving 246 institutions of higher education and 36,000 students. They found that students career choices tend to conform over time with the more popular choices existing in a particular university. They call this phenomenon the **process of progressive conformity.**

Although these studies are of some interest in supporting the idea that the average background characteristics of individuals will affect later occupational and career choices, they are essentially correlational in nature. One can always raise the question of whether students with incongruent initial vocational choices were somehow different from those with congruent choices. For example, perhaps they were less sure of their initial decision and thus more likely to change later. What is needed is an experimental study that more directly demonstrates the impact of settings as a consequence of average background characteristics of its members.

One such study was conducted by Brown (1968). Brown experimentally formed "minority group" members in assigning humanities and science majors to different floors of a freshman residence hall. Brown's strategy was to pair 44 humanity students with 44 science students and assign 11 roommate pairs to each of 4 floors in the residence hall. Brown then created two floors of predominantly humanities students and 2 floors of predominantly science oriented students. Thus, in this cleverly conceived experiment, "minority group" students could be either humanities or science students on floors having the opposite orientation. The findings were reasonably clear cut. Humanities majors on science dominated floors tended to change their majors in the direction of the majority or became more uncertain of their initial choice during the school year. The same effect occurred in the opposite direction for science students who were living on floors dominated by humanities students. Furthermore, "minority" students of both types expressed less satisfaction with residence hall life than did majority group members.

Whether such findings occur in settings other than the university is not as easily demonstrated using experimental studies. But this research and numerous correlational studies seem to suggest that the average background characteristics of a social setting can have substantial impact of the behavior and attitudes of both new entrants with congruent background characteristics and on those whose characteristics are incongruent with the majority within the setting. If, as these data suggest, aggregated background characteristics of setting participants are a powerful source of behavior shaping, then this perspective on the nature of social environments should have genuine implications for maximizing treatment gains in the social ecology of the individual client.

Measurement and Application from the Human Aggregate Perspective

Perhaps the most serious and extensive attempt to use the concept of average background characteristics of setting participants as a basis for characterizing social environment has been conducted by Holland

(1973) and by Astin and Holland (1961). Holland conducted his initial research in the area of vocational choice.

In his early work Holland developed a theory that suggested that most inventories of vocational choice were actually personality questionnaires. These instruments typically asked the respondent to choose activities or jobs which they most preferred.

Holland believed that the reason these inventories were able to predict job success and individual satisfaction was that people were more likely to choose activities and environments that were similar to their own patterns of interest and behavior. Thus people with particular orientations were more likely to choose particular activities and settings. People with artistic interests and characteristics, for example, were more likely to choose settings and activities that were congruent with these basic characteristics of their personality. Holland argued "because people in a vocational group have similar personalities, they will respond to many situations and problems in similar ways, *and they will create characteristic inter-personal environments* [1973, p. 9]."

Thus, although Holland was primarily interested in vocational choice and satisfaction, he extended his thinking to encompass the idea that vocational choice and its personality correlates could create settings with distinctive characteristics when people were grouped on this basis.

Astin and Holland used research on vocational choice and the choice of major fields to develop a typology of personalities and environments based on this logic. Six major orientations emerged from this research and provide a major approach to classification of personalities and environments. This classification system is shown in Table 10.2. It can be seen in Table 10.2 that a personality description of a particular type of individual is offered, and with it there is a corresponding description that attempts to capture the "character" of the social or work environment in which such people are likely to be found.

Thus, the average background characteristics of individuals provide a basis for developing a typology of social settings. But how may the characteristics of such settings be measured? Astin and Holland (1961) have developed a method which they call **environmental assessment technique.** Their goal was to measure the characteristics of various college environments, but the principle underlying the approach could easily be extended to other settings. The strategy is simply to conduct a census of the choices of major fields in a particular college population. These choices are then placed in the six categories shown in Table 10.3 and the proportion of students falling in each of the six categories is recorded.

The product of this strategy is a "profile" of a particular college en-

TABLE 10.2

Holland's Classification of Personalities and Social Environments [a]

Orientation	Personality descriptions	Environmental descriptions
Conventional	Prefers structured numerical and verbal activities and subordinate roles; conforming; identifies with power, externals and status	Stimulates conventional activities, rewards people for conventional values, and reinforces conscientiousness, obedience, control, efficiency, orderliness
Artistic	Asocial; avoids problems that are highly structured or require gross physical skills; need for individualistic expression	Stimulates artistic activities, rewards people for artistic values, and reinforces emotionality, independence, nonconformity, introspection, originality
Realistic	Masculine, materialistic, unsociable, aggressive, stable, uninsightful, practical, persistent	Stimulates realistic activities, rewards people for conventional values, and reinforces conformity, thrift, pragmatism, stability, shyness
Investigative	Task-oriented, introspective, asocial, prefers to think through rather than act out; needs to understand	Stimulates investigative activities, rewards people for investigative values and reinforces precision, rationality, introspection, pessimism
Enterprising	Verbal skills for dominating, selling, leading others; verbally aggressive	Stimulates enterprising activities, rewards people for enterprising values, reinforces ambition, self-confidence, acquisitiveness, flirtation, arguments
Social	Sociable, responsible, feminine; needs attention; avoids intellectual problem-solving; dependent	Stimulates social activities, rewards people for social values and reinforces friendliness, responsibility, tact, femininity, kindness, insight

[a] Adapted from Moos, 1976, p. 288–289.

TABLE 10.3

Hypothetical College Environment Profile Based on Proportion of
Students Choosing Majors in Each of Holland's Six Major Orientations

Orientation	Proportion of student choices
Conventional	5
Artistic	42
Realistic	8
Investigative	9
Enterprising	15
Social	21
Total	100

vironment based on the proportion of majors falling in each category.

Studies of the concurrent validity of this technique suggests that it predicts other characteristics of the environment of colleges and universities measured by such instruments as the College Characteristic Inventory (Astin & Holland, 1961), the College and University Environment Scale (Pace, 1967), and the University Residence Environment Scale (Hearn & Moos, 1976).

For our present purposes it is most important to recognize that, although the social environment in university settings is characterized by the choice of college major, other background characteristics could be equally effective in characterizing the social environment. Profiles of social settings based on sex, age, race, interest patterns, stage in the life cycle, or other variables could be generated that would provide important information about the impact of social settings and its implications for maximizing treatment gains.

The Undermanning Perspective

Still a third conception of the social environment is based neither on the social climate, nor the aggregated characteristics of individuals, but on the relationship between the number of roles available in a setting and the number of people available to fill them. The research on this perspective has been summarized by Barker (1960, 1968), Wicker (1973), and Price (1976).

Barker's (1960) original theory was stimulated in part by a comparison of two small towns, one in Kansas ("Midwest") and one in Yorkshire, England ("Yoredale"). A number of striking differences emerged from this cross-cultural study, but among the most interesting was the fact that although Midwest had a considerably smaller population than Yoredale, it had approximately 1.2 times as many behavior settings such as social clubs, classes, programs, meetings, fairs, and conferences. In addition, residents of Midwest performed at least three times as often in their behavior settings as residents of Yoredale did in theirs. Barker reasoned that, in order to maintain the more numerous settings in Midwest, the residents were required to accept more positions of responsibility and to include in the settings larger proportions of people who were only marginally qualified to function in those settings. Thus Barker argued that the behavior settings of Midwest were "undermanned," at least when compared with those of Yoredale.

Since there were relatively fewer people available to maintain the settings, Barker concluded that Midwest residents needed to participate in a wider variety of settings if the settings were to be maintained. In fact, according to the theory, a larger number of behaviorial consequences should occur for individuals participating in undermanned settings. Barker hypothesized that undermanned settings made a greater "claim" on people both by requiring greater effort and because relatively more difficult and more important tasks would be assigned to their occupants.

In addition, the range and direction of forces acting on individual occupants was hypothesized to be greater. For example, a wider variety of activities would be required of each occupant and, because every individual in the setting was crucial for the maintenance of the setting, there would be less sensitivity to, and evaluation of, differences among people. Furthermore, since performers in the settings would be required to carry out a variety of different tasks, it was expected that there would be a lower level of maximum performance for occupants of the setting. Since many setting occupants would have to carry out a number of different tasks, it seemed unlikely that any single occupant would achieve great proficiency at any one task.

The joint influence of greater strength of forces on occupants of undermanned settings, as well as a greater range of forces, would result, Barker surmised, in each individual having greater functional importance within a setting, more responsibility, and a greater feeling of functional self-identity. There would also be lower standards and fewer tests for admission to the setting. There would also be greater feelings of insecurity since each person would be in more jeopardy of failing to carry through the tasks assigned him. Finally, Barker predicted that undermanned settings should produce more frequent occurrences of success and failure.

Thus, if a behavior setting is to be maintained, and few people are available to perform in that setting, very real forces will operate on the occupants of the setting. These forces will push the individual into roles of greater responsibility and participation, but at the same time, undermanned settings will also create greater insecurity and more opportunities for failure. As Barker (1960) put it: "The underpopulated setting is one where self-esteem and social status can both flourish, and also wither [p. 33]."

Table 10.4 provides a summary of the hypothesized effects of under-manned settings on the behavior of setting participants.

Examination of these predicted effects suggests that undermanned settings may indeed have implications for maximizing treatment gains, but let us first consider some of the evidence for the impact of under-manned settings on behavior.

In an initial exploration of the undermanning hypothesis Barker and Gump (1964) compared large and small schools. They found that com-pared with large schools, students in small schools: (a) participated in a wider variety of settings; (b) acted as performers (rather than ob-servers) in twice as many settings; and (c) experienced satisfactions associated with competence development and cooperation rather than vicarious satisfactions, associated with being merely an observer.

In a later investigation, Baird (1969) studied 21,371 students from large and small schools and found that small school students did indeed participate in a wider range of activities at both the high school and

TABLE 10.4

Hypothesized Effects of Undermanned Settings on the Behavior of Behavior Setting Participants [a]

---

1. Greater effort to support the setting and its functions, either by "harder" work or by spending longer hours.
2. Participation in a greater diversity of tasks and roles.
3. Involvement in more difficult and more important tasks.
4. More responsibility in the sense that the setting and what others gain from it depend on each individual occupant.
5. Viewing oneself and others in terms of task-related characteristics, rather than in terms of social-emotional characteristics.
6. Greater functional importance of individuals within the setting.
7. Less sensitivity to and less evaluation of differences between people.
8. Setting of lower standards and fewer tests for admission into the setting.
9. A lower level of maximal or best performance.
10. Greater insecurity about the eventual maintenance of the setting.
11. More frequent occurrences of success and failure, depending upon the out-come of the setting's functions.

---

[a] From Wicker, 1975.

college level. In a study of large and small churches Wicker (1969) found that members of small churches participated in more different kinds of activities, had more positions of leadership, spent more time in the activities, attended church more often, and contributed more money. Still another measure used by Wicker (1969) involved the examination of archival data on a much larger sample of 104 churches. These data also showed that support of church activities was much greater in smaller churches.

These findings are of real interest, but do not tell us anything about marginal members of the setting. From the point of view of research relevant to maximizing treatment gains, evidence of this sort would be particularly important. Willems (1967) has addressed this question in a study of school size as it affects the sense of obligation to high school activities felt by marginal and regular students. In two field studies, Willems demonstrated that small schools produced a much higher average sense of student obligation, and that the difference between marginal and regular students in small schools with respect to their sense of obligation was virtually nonexistent. In large schools, on the other hand, marginal students felt a much lower sense of obligation when compared with regular students. As Willems puts it: "It would appear that the small school marginal students were not experientially and behaviorally marginal, while their large school counterparts were a group of relative outsiders [Willems, 1967, pp. 1257–1258]." Willems replicated these original findings reported in 1961 in a larger sample of schools obtained in 1965 (Willems, 1969).

Measurement and Application from the Undermanning Perspective

Thus far, we have treated the concept of undermanning as if it was equivalent to the number of participants in the setting. A moment's reflection, however, will suggest that is only a crude measure of the degree of manning of a setting. For two settings requiring the same number of roles, the setting with fewer inhabitants will probably be undermanned relative to the setting with more inhabitants. However, adequate tests of the undermanning hypothesis and for application to actual settings a more precise approach to measurement is needed.

Wicker (1973) have offered a more precise definition of the manning concept. In this formulation they offer three basic definitions. The first is the *maintenance minimum,* which is the minimum number of persons required for the setting to be maintained. The second definition is that of *capacity,* which is the maximum number of persons that the setting can accommodate. Finally they define the concept of *applicants.* The total number of persons who seek to participate and who meet the eligibility requirements of the setting is considered the number of applicants to the setting.

In addition, a distinction is made between two kinds of setting occupants: *performers* and *nonperformers*. This distinction between the roles potentially existing in any behavior setting is derived from Barker's earlier formulation. The advantage of differentiating between two roles which occupants may take, and adding the concept of capacity, is that behavior settings may then be described as either undermanned or overmanned in terms of either performer or nonperformer roles.

In the context of this new formulation, whether a setting is undermanned, adequately manned, or overmanned depends of the relationship between the number of applicants (either performers or nonperformers) relative to the maintenance minimum and capacity of the setting for either performers or nonperformers. Thus, if the number of applicants falls below the maintenance minimum, the setting is defined as undermanned. If, on the other hand, the number of applicants falls somewhere between the maintenance minimum and the capacity one can specify the setting as being adequately manned. Overmanning occurs when there are more applicants than the capacity of the setting.

THE CRITERION OF PERSON–ENVIRONMENT CONGRUENCE

Before discussing specific strategies for the application of social environmental information to the problem of treatment gain, we need to consider one crucial issue. *Environmental data are not automatically transformed into treatment gains.* In order to transform information about the social environment into treatment gains, some general conception of the relationship between individual needs and behavior on the one hand, and characteristics of the social environment on the other must be established. Put another way, we need a general action goal for using individual difference data and social environmental data. These data are, in themselves, essentially neutral. But their application is never value free.

Ideally, such a conception should be a **general** one that transcends the particular perspective and data base being used to measure environmental variables. In addition, the conception should treat environmental variables and individual characteristics in *commensurate* terms. That is, it should allow a matching or translation of individual differences or needs into comparable environmental data. Henry Murray has offered one set of commensurate terms when he suggested a relationship between individual "needs" and the "press" of the social environment. Thus a person may have a strong need for affiliation or achievement and settings may or may not have a corresponding "press" for these characteristics.

In addition, the conception we use to guide the application of social environmental data should take account of the growing body of research (e.g., Endler, Hunt, & Rosenstein, 1962; Moos, 1969; Pervin, 1968; Price, 1974; Price & Bouffard, 1974) that indicates that variation among settings, among individuals, and their interaction are all important sources of variance in predicting a variety of behavioral outcomes.

One such general conception is that of *person–environment congruence*. This conception argues that it is possible to identify combinations of individual differences and social settings that provide a good "fit" relative to other combinations. Thus, presumably, persons in need of support "fit" better in settings that are capable of supplying that need. Similarly, people with a strong need for achievement "fit" better in settings that encourage that need and may languish in settings that do not provide such opportunities or challenges. It is likely that most people operate as if they have an intuitive understanding of the congruence idea, seeking settings that meet their own needs and avoiding or ultimately leaving settings in which the fit is less than optimal.

When considering the question of using the social environment as a means of maximizing treatment gains, the person–environment congruence conception is particularly useful. In general, it suggests that a guideline for choosing, shaping, or creating social settings with a potential for maximizing treatment gains can be based in part on an inventory of the existing needs or abilities of the client. Furthermore, the inventory can include not just existing needs but also areas for further development.

Another important advantage of the person–environment congruence conception is that it avoids two ideologically loaded errors common to thinking about the nature and determinants of disturbed or disturbing behavior. The first of these errors has been called "victim blaming" (Ryan, 1971; Rappaport, Davidson, Mitchell, & Wilson, 1975). Briefly, this view attributes individual failings to intrinsically inferior qualities of the individual. And, of course, it suggests that it is the individual who must somehow be changed to conform to the demands of the setting.

The second error can be described as "system blaming" (Rappaport et al., 1975) or perhaps as naive environmental determinism. This view asserts that individual failings and vulnerabilities are a consequence of a stressful or discriminatory environment and that environmental reform is the only means of alleviating victimization.

Of course, neither of these views is capable of capturing the complexity of person–environment interactions and their myriad outcomes. It is interesting to reflect on the fact that although almost no social scientist would accept either of these views when put so baldly,many do unwittingly act as if they adhered to one or the other of them (Caplan & Nelson, 1973) when we examine their tactics of individual rehabilitation or social reform.

Nothing like a mechanical formula is now available for applying the person–environment congruence idea to the problem of maximizing treatment gains. Rather, it remains a theoretical guide against which our efforts to use environmental information can be compared. It is possible, however to pose some orienting questions based on the congruence conception that may be useful in transforming the concept into clinical operations in a particular case.

One set of questions involves the issue of need satisfaction. We may ask, "Are there client needs that can be identified by the client, the treatment agent, or both that a social setting should supply in order to maintain existing treatment gains?" Similarly with regard to settings we can ask, "Are there settings in the social ecology of the client that could be selected, shaped, or created to meet those needs?"

A second set of questions involves the issue of competence building. Here we can ask, "Can we identify client behaviors and skills that are considered desirable by the client, the treatment agent, or both that could be promoted by a particular social environment in order to maximize treatment gains?" If so, then we can ask further, "Are there settings in the social ecology of the client that can be selected, shaped, or created to promote these behaviors and skills?"

The answers to these questions require, of course, an inventory of individual needs and skills, something the clinician should have readily available, and a knowledge of the existing settings that might meet those needs or promote those skills. This latter information may be less readily available.

If we draw on our previous discussions of the social climate, human aggregate, and undermanning views some general guidelines for seeking person–environment congruence can be derived. From the social climate perspective, we can identify client needs or desired competencies by examining ideal social climate profiles generated by both the client and clinician. Such profiles might emphasize specific relationship dimensions or particular personal growth dimensions of settings that are congruent with client needs or goals. From the human aggregate perspective, guidelines might involve matching individual client characteristics, attitudes, or interests with the aggregate characteristics of particular settings. Application of the undermanning perspective might suggest matching clients with a need for acceptance and involvement with undermanned settings since undermanned settings appear to possess lower criteria of acceptance and high involvement as salient attributes.

The actual application of the congruence idea will of necessity be partly intuitive and far from mechanical. Still, it is argued here that it may be the failure to use **any** data-based measure of congruence that produces many of the losses of initial treatment gain. In the following section we will examine some concrete tactics for maximizing treatment gain that implicitly use the congruence conception.

THREE STRATEGIES FOR USING INFORMATION ABOUT THE SOCIAL ENVIRONMENT TO MAXIMIZE TREATMENT GAINS

Thus far, we have examined three general perspectives on the social environment. The social climate approach focuses upon the perceived characteristics of the social environment and how they affect the behavior of setting participants. The human aggregate approach considers the aggregated characteristics of individuals as a characteristic of the social environment or group itself. Finally, the undermanning approach emphasizes the relationship between the number of people in a setting and the number of roles or tasks required to make the setting function effectively. We have also discussed the concept of person–environment congruence as a general organizing principle that can aid us in the conceptualizing how we wish to use social environmental information to maximize treatment gains.

In the present section we will explore three general strategies for using the social environment to maximize treatment gain. The approaches are: (a) setting selection; (b) setting change; and (c) setting creation. Each of these general strategies can be used from a variety of environmental perspectives. And of course, none of them is restricted to the three perspectives that we have discussed thus far.

Before considering each of these strategies in more detail, we should make several general comments about all three of them. First, all three of these approaches require that we broaden our perspective beyond the immediate social and treatment environment of the client to consider the current and possible social environments that the person may enter. Thus, we might consider the person's family environment, the work environment, recreational environments, and any other important aspects of the "ecological niche" of the individual. This is an important conceptual reorientation for most professionals concerned with the individual treatment of clients.

Second, each of these strategies already exist as naturally occurring processes. That is, they can and do occur in the natural social environment of the individual with or without the active intervention of the therapist. In fact, it is probably the case that much of the loss of initial treatment gains results from the fact that therapists do not take an active role in helping clients select, shape, or change the social settings that they enter subsequent to formal treatment.

Third, as we examine each of these strategies we will note that each of them has implicit in it the idea of person–environment congruence. The idea of congruence remains the conceptual touchstone. That is, in the case of setting selection, setting change and setting creation, the fit or lack of optimal fit between the person's characteristics or needs and that of the social environment remains a critical issue.

Fourth, each of these approaches requires that we have available a means of maximizing the information available to us about the social environment. Too frequently, unwarranted assumptions about the social ecology of the client are made, or no active attempt is made to systematically assess that social environment for the purposes of constructive setting selection, change or creation.

Fifth, there is a sense in which these three strategies can be thought of as serial in nature. From the point of view of efficiency it is probably the case that a clinician concerned about maximizing treatment gains will first want to ask the question, "Are there settings in the natural social environment of this person that, if we knew about them, could be used to maximize earlier gains?" If the answer to that question is "no," then the second logical question to ask is, "Are there existing settings that, if we could introduce changes into them, would alter those settings so that they would be more likely to maximize gains?" Finally, if neither setting selection nor setting change is a viable strategy, then setting creation becomes a third option. In this case the question is, "Can settings be created in the social environment of the person that are likely to maximize treatment gains?"

Before we turn to a more detailed discussion of each of these general strategies, it is important to note that simply providing the client with *environmental information by itself* can, in some cases, provide a useful adjunct to treatment. Two examples are relevant here. Bromet and Moos

(1976) have pointed out that the simple fact of knowing that other people share certain problems or experiences can provide a more balanced perspective. They note that Zimbardo, Pilkonis, and Norwood (1975) have surveyed 800 high school and college students about the problem of shyness. Forty-two percent of the students considered themselves shy, and two-thirds of these students felt that their shyness was a problem. As Bromet and Moos note, the knowledge that one's peers are also shy may, in itself, alleviate some of the distress associated with shyness. Another example is provided by the research of Bloom (1971) who developed a pilot program to prevent college dropout. Bloom's strategy was to survey students in the freshman class and to feed the data about various college problems common to freshmen back to the students presumably providing a "we're all in the same boat" message. Because pluralistic ignorance about personal problems tends to prevail in almost any setting, providing normative information about common problems or stresses may reduce the distress associated with feelings of competition, inadequacy, or fear of failure.

Let us now turn to our discussion of setting selection, setting change, and setting creation as environmental strategies for maximizing treatment gain. We will consider each of these strategies from each of the three perspectives on the social environment discussed earlier. The resulting nine tactics for maximizing treatment gains are summarized briefly in Table 10.5.

In some cases, these tactics have already been worked out in considerable detail and research evaluating their effectiveness can be found in the literature. In other cases, the proposed tactics are largely speculative. The practitioner concerned with using any of the strategies of setting selection, change, or creation would probably do well to incorporate methods and ideas from each of the perspectives in designing their own approach to using environmental information to maximize treatment gains.

Setting Selection

For the purposes of our present discussion, we can define setting selection as that process whereby the client or treatment agent, individually or in collaboration, scans the social environment of the client to make a decision about subsequent social settings that the client may enter and participate in to maximize client needs or gains.

This is a somewhat abstract definition and several comments are in order. Perhaps the most common setting selection strategy adopted by many clients is to drop out of treatment. This is *setting selection by*

TABLE 10.5

Setting Selection, Change, and Creation Strategies for Maximizing
Treatment Gain from Three Environmental Perspectives

	Setting selection	Setting change	Setting creation
Social climate perspective	Select settings that match ideal social climate profiles	Feedback real and ideal social climate data to setting participants as a basis for setting change	Use ideal social climate profiles as a guide to setting creation
Human aggregate perspective	Select settings with aggregate characteristics matching client goals or needs	Alter selection criteria for setting participants to increase commonality in selected group aggregate characteristics	Create settings to respond to needs reflected in average background characteristics of the client group
Undermanning perspective	Select undermanned settings to promote commitment and decrease marginality	Alter the manning characteristics of the setting by increasing roles, tasks; altering capacity, or "double" casting	Plan undermanning as a characteristic of new settings

default and usually represents a case which the client finds the current treatment environment does not meet his needs, or has found another setting that does. From a more positive perspective, the strategy of setting selection in clinical terms is usually called "referral." Unfortunately, referral is seldom done in ways that maximize treatment gains. This is primarily because both the treatment agent and the client lack adequate information about the potential social environments that the client may enter.

Setting selection is probably the most common strategy adopted by clients in making free choices about the treatment or living settings they wish to enter. It is also probably the case that setting selection is the most underrated approach to maximize treatment gains in terms of its potential power and efficiency. Setting selection is a pervasive phenomenon, but its power is underrated partly because the choices of potential settings that clients may subsequently enter is not known to the clinician.

Setting selection also has the highly desirable characteristic of providing relatively free choice to the client. Once environmental information is made available, the client may choose the living or treatment setting which he feels best fits his needs or may make self-conscious decisions in collaboration with the practitioner about the settings that they wish to enter.

As we noted before, people are continually engaging in setting selection to maximize the fit between their own needs and the characteristics of the social setting. An example of this process is provided by Eddy and Sinnett (1973). These investigators examine the behavior of 46 client members of a rehabilitation living unit in a large university. Each student was evaluated using activity records which provided a chronological account of the behavior of each student and the setting in which it had occurred. Each student was also evaluated using clinical judgments and personality variables and the types of social settings in which the students chose to spend their time. They found that extroverted, action-oriented people tended to spend considerably more time in settings that provided opportunities for social interaction. Introverted students spent considerably less time in such settings. Measures of ego strength tended to be related to whether students engaged in work activities on the weekend and the type of recreation they chose. Sex differences were also important with female students spending more time in shopping activities, grooming activities, and visiting in other students rooms. Thus Eddy and Sinnett were able to show important relationships between individual characteristics and setting characteristics that were based on the ways in which people select settings to meet their own needs and match their own personality characteristics.

In a very different context, Leff (1976) has shown that there is a strong relationship between the likelihood of relapse among schizophrenics and the degree of expressed emotionality in the families to which they return after hospitalization. Families with social environments high in negative social expression tended to create an environment that was highly stressful to schizophrenics and produced significantly higher rates of relapse. Leff also suggests that the high degree of emotional sensitivity of recovering schizophrenic patients leads them in many cases to seek social environments that are not emotionally demanding. Frequently, these people choose to live alone in order to avoid the stressful social environment of family thus engaging in a natural process of setting selection to preserve their own tenuous emotional stability.

These studies illustrate how individuals naturally engage in setting selection to maximize personal outcomes. Let us now turn to tactics of setting selection suggested by each of the perspectives on the social environment that we have described.

Social Climate Tactic: Select Social Settings that Match Ideal Social Climate Profiles Generated by Referral Agent or Client

From the social climate perspective there may be a number of instances in which social climate measures can be used as a guide to setting selection. One possible procedure would involve generating an ideal social climate profile for a particular type of setting such as a foster home, a classroom, or work group. Ideally the referral agent and the client would generate the ideal profile in collaboration. Settings would then be selected for the client to enter which match the ideal social climate profile as closely as possible.

An example of this tactic is being developed by Cherniss (1977). Cherniss argues that youths who are to be placed in foster homes in the community can be more effectively placed in these settings if social climate profiles of the available homes are first collected. This constitutes the sample of homes available for choice and may vary on the extent to which they emphasize relationship dimensions, personal growth dimensions, and system maintenance or system change dimensions. Ideal profiles are then generated by referral agents in collaboration with the children and a choice of homes is made based on the best fit between the ideal profile and those available. A similar tactic is advocated by Murrell (1973).

Cherniss notes that other factors, such as the pressure to fill existing openings in some homes, may impede the use of this tactic and that such barriers to implementation cannot be ignored. Thus, although this tactic is clearly limited by the range of choice settings in the community, it does have the clear advantage of using available environmental information for the purposes of setting selection and increases the chance of treatment gain based on maximizing person–environment congruence.

Human Aggregate Tactic: Select Settings with Aggregate Characteristics Matching Client Goals or Needs

Settings may also be on the basis of using aggregated characteristics of settings or groups. In this case, the procedure involves surveying appropriate community settings that may match or enhance client goals or needs. Information from the survey can then be used in planning referral of clients, again preferably in collaboration with the client, to meet particular goals and needs.

Politser and Pattison (1976) have done considerable research on the characteristics of various community groups and voluntary associations that would serve this purpose nicely. Politser and Pattison surveyed voluntary community groups in one large community and identified five major types. **Self-interest groups** are concerned with promoting some cause common to the group and include groups such as the National Organization of Women, and various minority and liberation groups that are seen as providing a foundation of support for similar individuals. **Self-help groups,** on the other hand, are focused on changing individual characteristics of the person and include groups like Alcoholics Anonymous and Recovery Incorporated. These groups are seen as replacing other naturally occuring social systems for individuals in need of support in coping with a specific problem. A third type, **social communion groups** tend to be social groups for the aged, or women's prayer groups which are usually large undemanding settings offering a replacement of family supports. **Civic development groups,** on the other hand, such as the Kiwanas or Lions tend to provide nonsupportive and relatively demanding environments that foster personal development. Finally, **recreational groups** such as chess clubs or folk dancing clubs provide low pressure environments for superficial involvement and social interaction.

Politser and Pattison have found that each of these different types of groups have strikingly different membership characteristics, group functions, and group structures. Using this typology of community groups as a guide it should be possible to survey the community groups in the community and to choose a type of social group that meets the client's goals and needs.

Undermanning Tactic: Select Undermanned Settings to Promote Commitment and Decrease Marginality

In reviewing the research literature on undermanned settings, we noted that these settings can be particularly effective in requiring participation in a greater diversity of tasks and roles, require high levels of responsibility, emphasize greater functional importance of individuals in the settings, and are less sensitive to evaluation of differences between participants in the setting. Because they are undermanned, these settings also frequently have lower standards of performance and fewer tests for admission into the setting. Thus, for individuals requiring increased involvement and for whom increased commitment in the setting is important, selection of undermanned settings may maximize treatment gain.

A procedure to be followed in selecting undermanned settings such as classrooms, work environments, or even recreational settings might begin by screening the available settings on the basis of absolute size.

Smaller settings of the same type are more likely to be undermanned than larger settings. But as we have noted, Wicker has produced a more precise reformulation of undermanning involving an assessment of the maintenance in which the number of applicants is lower than the maintenance minimum with the expectation that increased commitment, lower rates of drop-out, and increased involvement would result.

Thus the selection of undermanned settings, or at the very least the screening out of overmanned settings for clients with a tendency to be marginal in social settings should provide a setting selection strategy for maintaining or maximizing initial treatment gains.

Setting Change

In the present context, we can define the setting change strategy as an approach in which information about posttreatment social settings is gathered and evaluated in comparison with the needs or goals of the client. When there is incongruence between the features of the social environment desired by the client and the actual features of the environment, some intervention process is initiated to alter the social environment so that it is more congruent with the needs and goals of the client. Targets for change may be work settings, family settings, recreational settings, educational settings, or any other setting that is prominant in the ecology of the individual client.

Frequently, attempts to change social environments so that they are more consistent with the needs of the client take the form of requests for alterations or changes in the setting, or actual advocacy for setting change based on some existing dissatisfaction. Clinicians may often engage in setting change efforts in the role of consultant operating either inside a particular setting or as an outside change agent. Examples of such strategies for program consultation are described by Heller and Monahan (1977). Efforts of this sort are not to be undertaken lightly and may meet with considerable resistance, as Heller and Monahan note.

However, it is argued here that adequate environmental information about the current features of the social setting and its potential for change are a necessary prerequisite for the implementation of setting change strategies. In our subsequent discussion of examples of setting change strategies we will note that some conceptual framework and method of assessment of the social environment is used as a basis for planning effective setting change for the purpose of maximizing treatment gains. As we noted before, setting change strategies require considerably more effort than setting selection, but where setting selection is limited, setting change strategies to alter characteristics of the social setting so that they are more congruent with client needs may be worth the effort.

Social Climate Tactic:
Feedback Real and Ideal Social Climate Data to Setting
Participants as a Basis for Setting Change

Survey feedback technology has been developed to a considerable degree and a number of organizational development studies (Bowers, 1973; Coughlan & Cooke, 1974) have demonstrated the effectiveness of this setting change technique in large work organizations and school settings.

The application of survey feedback techniques to change a community based residential treatment setting is nicely illustrated by Moos, and Otto (1972) and Moos (1975). The basic strategy for program change can be summarized in four stages as shown in Table 10.6.

An interesting feature of this particular application of the survey feedback technique is that both "real" and "ideal" forms of the social climate scale are used in the initial assessment stage. The real form requires that residents and staff in the setting complete a scale describing their own treatment environment as they currently perceive it. The ideal form, on the other hand, requires that residents and staff complete the instrument describing the treatment environment as they would ideally like it to be. Thus data involving *discrepancies* between actual and ideal perceptions of the program can be used for the purposes of problem identification and to point out potential areas for programmatic change.

The second stage of the process involves sessions in which the data is "fed back" to program members and staff usually by a trained facilitator or consultant. Discussions are held in which discrepancies between real and ideal profiles are interpreted and used as a basis for identifying specific features of the program that are agreed to require change.

Stage three in the process involves the planning and implementation of actual change strategies. In this author's experience, it is frequently worthwhile to capitalize on the skills and change styles already existing within a particular program. For example, programs that have a viable self-governing structure may wish to use the patient government meeting as a vehicle for change efforts. Programs that are behaviorally oriented may wish to plan new behaviorally oriented components to respond to perceived needs.

Whatever the method chosen for change, after its implementation, a fourth stage involving reassessment of the program is typically under-

TABLE 10.6

A Data-Guided Program Development Strategy for Treatment Environments

	Stage 1	Stage 2	Stage 3	Stage 4
Stages of program development	Initial assessment of the program environment (Week 1)	Data feedback sessions with members and staff of the program (Weeks 2–3)	Planning and implementation sessions with members and staff focused on specific program changes (Weeks 4–5)	Reassessment of the program environment (Weeks 10–12)
Questions asked at each stage of the development process	How do members and staff perceive the *current* social climate of the program? What would the social climate of an *ideal* program look like to members and to staff? Additional measures of program environment?	What do staff and member profiles look like? Where are the *real–ideal* discrepancies in climate profiles for staff? for members? What do these profiles and discrepancies indicate about *specific features* of this particular program?	How can the program environment be changed or developed to reduce *real–ideal* discrepancies for both members and staff? Specific changes relevant to issues identified during feedback sessions?	Did the desired changes occur?

Operations performed at each stage to answer questions	Administer assessment instruments	Data feedback sessions	Program development methods implemented	Readminister social climate scales and other program measures
	Real and ideal forms of social climate scales administered to residents and staff. Additional program measured process and outcome.	Discuss and interpret social climate profiles with staff and members. Staff and members compare and discuss discrepancies in real and ideal profiles. Staff and members identify specific issues, strengths, and areas needing work indicated by profile discrepancies.	Methods are variable depending on the goals, values, philosophy, and skills existing in the program, for example: a) develop new roles with members and staff. b) token economy: contingency contracts. c) group meetings and committee structure changes. d) introduce new activities. e) new learning programs	Pre–post comparisons a) *real* vs. *ideal* changes in staff and members. b) behavior changes. c) unobtrusive program measures. d) outcome measures.

415

taken. It is also important to remember that in assessing program changes, data **other than** that used for the purpose of feedback should be collected. Data fed back and discussed by program members will be familiar and is likely to be subject to bias in the direction of apparent programmatic change. Thus it is important to collect other independent measures documenting degree of programmatic change obtained.

This particular methodology has certain advantages that recommend it for program development and change with treatment environments. First, collecting information bearing on ideal environments as perceived both by residents and staff, highlights the importance of potential differences in needs and values among staff and patients. In developing effective program change these issues cannot be ignored. Second, the strategy allows for a broad range of different styles and ideologies of treatment to be incorporated within it. Although it is a data based approach, the survey feedback strategy is general enough to be useful in settings that are widely divergent with respect to their value orientation. A third advantage of the survey feedback strategy is that it allows broad participation in the change process. As noted earlier, broad participation is frequently valuable in promoting effective programmatic change.

Moos and Otto (1972) have reported the successful application of this method in both hospital based inpatient treatment programs and in community based residential treatment programs for youth. Cherniss, Perkins, Shinn, and Price (1976) have adapted the survey feedback strategy for use in community based treatment programs for youth and are currently engaged in a systematic evaluation of the effectiveness of the method for program change and development.

Human Aggregate Tactic:
Alter the Selection Criteria for Setting
Participation to Increase Commonality in the Group

Frequently, commonalities in a group along religious, racial, educational, or interest dimensions can also create feelings of support and solidarity within the group. Community groups (Politser & Pattison, 1976), in particular, often assort themselves naturally in this fashion to promote commonality in interests and concerns. A treatment agent can in some cases play a role in increasing the similarity of group members with respect to average background characteristics. The social environment of group settings can be altered by altering the selection criteria for entrance to the setting. Thus group settings which have been heterogenous in the average background characteristics of participants can be made more homogeneous.

An example of this strategy is illustrated by the work of DeCoster (1966) who assigned 50% concentrations of high-ability students to some residence halls and assigned others as controls to other halls in lower concentrations. Concentrated high-ability students showed higher levels of achievement, more satisfaction, and shared study skills with each other to a greater degree than did scattered high ability students.

Similarly, clients attending support groups following intensive treatment may be assigned on the basis of common background characteristics. Relatively homogeneous groups of this kind are likely to be experienced by participants as more supportive and more relevant to their own needs. Common problems confronted by people with similar average background characteristics are likely to emerge as part of the group process and active coping with these problems is more likely to result. For example, students who are members of a minority group within the university environment are likely to perceive and experience similar problems in relation to the majority group. Group consensus about the nature of these problems and strategies for coping with them are more likely to emerge than in settings which are relatively homogeneous and in which a single member of the minority group is placed in a student support group containing only majority members.

Of course, the strategy of altering setting characteristics on the basis of average background characteristics of the individual participants is not limited to minority groups. Students with similar majors, rural or urban background, elderly widows, or other client groups can also be systematically selected into particular settings so that congruence between individuals group members needs and goals and those of the group is enhanced.

Another example of this strategy is the choice of children for community based youth homes on the basis of age groupings. This author has noted that particularly effective directors of group homes make careful and self-conscious choices about the age groupings of children to be placed in foster care facilities and tend to place younger adolescent children in separate facilities from those of older children. When asked about this strategy, one director suggested that the marked developmental differences and concerns of 12- and 13-year-olds as opposed to 16- and 17-year-olds created a distinct problem for the younger group when children from both groups were placed together. Thus the decision was made to separate children on the basis of age and developmental status.

Much of the research on the effects of peer group influence and group homogeneity has been conducted in the context of college and university settings and its generalizability to other settings is not well established. It is likely that in considering the task of enhancing treatment gains that other issues may arise that require thoughtful and cautious application of this tactic. Common perspectives on problems to be dealt with may indeed emerge in groups that are relatively homogeneous, but it is not as clear that unique or creative solutions will also emerge.

Undermanning Strategy: Alter the Manning Characteristics of the Setting

Knowledge about the manning characteristics of settings can also be used as a basis for altering those settings. As we have noted, settings which are overmanned are likely to be considerably less supportive, particularly to marginal members of the setting, and will encourage less commitment of those members to the setting. Willems (1969) research suggests marginal members of schools are much less likely to drop out of undermanned school settings then overmanned school settings. Thus it may be possible to increase member commitment to settings by changing the setting itself to produce undermanning where optimal or overmanning previously existed. Based on what is known about the parameters of manning (Wicker, 1973) let us consider some tactics for producing a state of undermanning in settings.

First in most settings of a given size it is possible to *increase the number of functional roles* available to be performed by doing a careful analysis of tasks required to maintain the setting. Tasks that have been previously assigned to staff may be assigned to setting participants. New tasks can be created in the setting which increase the number of required roles for performance. Complex tasks can be broken into separate components and assigned to marginal members. A second strategy for producing undermanning is to maintain the size of the setting but *increase the number of tasks* to be carried out. This increased task load will, by definition, produce undermanning if the number of participants remains constant. A third strategy for undermanning is to self consciously *change the capacity of the setting*. A decision to lower the number of participants in a setting would also create an undermanned setting since the ratio of persons available to carry out existing roles will change as a consequence. Still a fourth strategy for changing the manning characteristics of setting can be described *double casting*. This tactic, sometimes used to increase the number of active participants in, for example, play involves casting two individuals in each role and having each complete cast perform the plan on a succeeding night. A similar strategy can be used in a variety of tasks oriented groups.

This last setting change strategy it should be noted, is equivalent to creating an additional setting and thus falls midway between setting change strategies and setting creation strategies to which we now turn.

Setting Creation

For our present purposes, we can define setting creation as the process whereby individuals create a new social setting or group in the social environment of the client which is expressly designed to meet the needs and goals of the client or client group. It is important to note that most new settings are created because of dissatisfaction with the limitations of available social settings, or because the social settings that already exist may promote other undesirable processes such as stigmatizing of the client as deviant (Price & Denner, 1973; Denner & Price 1973).

Although setting creation is not yet a well understood process, numerous examples exist. When alternative schools are developed to meet the special needs of children not being adequately served by the public school system, we are observing setting creation. When social scientists attempt to maximize the strength of a particular social group or community by creating settings based on those strengths, we are observing setting creation in process (Rappaport et al., 1975). The development of parallel institutions (Heller & Monahan, 1977) is an important alternative strategy for meeting the needs of specific populations and may result in the creation of daycare centers, schools, or cooperative work settings.

Although new settings are continually being created for various purposes, the theory and technology of setting creation is still in its infancy. However, Sarason (1972) has discussed the dynamics of setting creation in considerable detail and has identified a number of critical issues in the developmental process of creating new settings.

Sarason considers a new setting to be created whenever two or more people come together in new relationships over a sustained period of time to achieve certain goals. He also suggests a number of issues that must be made explicit. Creators of new settings must also be aware of the myth of unlimited resources and the danger of the leader becoming out of touch with the core group. Ideally, external critics of the new setting should be brought in to aid in providing other perspectives on the goals and processes of the new setting. Sarason notes too, that settings are always in process. The problems of settings are never solved, but are continually in evolution. With these cautions in mind, let us suggest some concrete tactics for setting creation and some examples that have the potential of maximizing treatment gain.

Social Climate Tactic: Use an Ideal Social Climate
Profile as a Guide in Setting Creation

From the social climate perspective one point of departure in the creation of a new setting is to develop a shared conception of the social
climate of the planned setting. One procedure for accomplishing this
using social climate scales might be to ask the leader and core group to
complete the ideal form of a social climate so that it reflects their individual conceptions of the characteristics of the setting to be created.
The planning group could then compare the resulting individually generated ideal profiles and develop agreements where discrepancies initially
emerged. Such a strategy will have the advantage of raising critical issues
for the planners of the new setting and allow the discussion before any
actual "creation" has been carried out.

Once consensus has been developed on the ideal nature of the new
setting, features of the social climate profile that are particularly striking
should be noted. Thus, for example, if agreement emerges that relationship variables are particularly important in this new setting, specific
rituals and mechanisms for enhancing the relationship oriented qualities
of the setting can be planned such as peer support groups, social gather-
ings, or other socially oriented activities. Similarly, if it is decided that
program clarity is an important social climate dimension in the newly
created setting, some regular process for informing new entrants into
the setting about the program goals of the setting can be developed to
enhance perceived program clarity.

To the author's knowledge, social climate instruments have not been
used in this way to help plan the creation of new settings. In planning
new settings to maximize treatment gains this tactic might be particularly useful since there already exists research information on the effects
of settings high in either relationship dimensions, personal growth dimensions or system maintenance and change dimensions (Moos, 1976).
Thus, in creating a new group home, or support group, or some other
setting, the issue of congruence of client needs and the critical features
of the setting to be created can be addressed directly.

Human Aggregate Tactic:
Create Settings to Respond to the Needs Reflected in Average
Background Characteristics of the Client Group

Information about the average background characteristics of certain
client groups can be used as a basis for creating settings which will respond more effectively to the needs of those groups. Thus, for example,
long term institutionalized individuals being discharged from a hospital

have certain average background characteristics that are likely to make independent living in the community extremely difficult. However, transitional groups can be created that have characteristics that respond to the needs of such a group.

An example of this strategy of setting creation is reported by Hansell (1967). Hansell's wish to create "spin-off" groups that would aid in preparation for leaving hospital settings and in continuing aftercare group membership. He has noted that many of these people were not members of small group systems such as families, friends, or work groups and found it extremely difficult to develop such group systems on their own. He argues that such groups could provide experience in testing social skills, developing competence, and using peer counseling during the period of reentry into ordinary social life.

The overall strategy of the spinoff group involves a group leader who initially meets for 10 meetings with a small group of six to eight members in order to teach the group a structure, a set of roles, and a set of guiding principles by which they sanction and support each others' behavior. After 10 meetings the professional group leader leaves the group, which "spins off" and continues to function as an independent support group. From that point on, the group interacts with the professional group convener only through a single individual called a "communicator." Spin-off groups are intended to be reality bound, task-oriented, skill-oriented groups managing life problems.

The initial sequence of meetings revolves around the question "Shall we be a group?" The group leader acts vigorously to obtain a commitment to the idea of forming a group. Once an initial commitment has been made, subsequent meetings are devoted to the assignment of offices and roles. Among the roles involved are those of convener, recorder, timekeeper, treasurer, social chairman, arrangements chairman, contact person, projects chairperson, and "aid and comfort" chairperson who expresses the groups' concern about absent members and uses a variety of means to keep the group together. The group is taught to develop their own language including phrases such as "problem-solving," "task-oriented," "doing your job," and "carrying out your role," "expressing concern," and other sanctioning terms and concepts.

Hansell suggests that groups with the average background characteristics we have described experience a number of crises in the initial development of a group, but that each of these crises is resolved in the direction of enhancing individual and group competence. Among the crises are the fact of being faced with a demand to form a group; being asked to make group decisions; being asked to stay together despite some initial conflict; assuming a variety of responsible roles; helping each other be responsible in these roles; and ultimately developing independence from the initial convener.

Hansell notes that once these spin-off groups have become independent, they frequently maintain a relationship with their original hospital setting but one that is very different from their original relationship. Frequently, group members become volunteers associated with a local mental health setting and are thus able to provide help to others rather than merely being the recipients of help and support.

Thus, the spin-off group provides an example of setting creation initiated by a professional care giver, but where the setting ultimately becomes independent and serves the purpose of maximizing treatment gains.

Undermanning Tactic:
Plan Undermanning as a Characteristic of New Settings

Just as undermanning can be selected if undermanned settings can be located in the ecology of the client, or characteristics of a setting can be altered to reduce overmanning or enhance undermanning, settings can be self-consciously created which have undermanned characteristics.

Typically, in the creation of new settings, little attention is given to the question of the number of participants in the settings. Frequently, the enthusiasm and zeal of the creators of new settings (Sarason, 1972) will lead to substantial optimism about the growth of the setting. And in fact, if little consideration is given to the question of the number of participants in new settings and the resources needed to maintain them, overmanning may result with a variety of negative congruencies for participants.

Planners can make decisions about the absolute size of settings before the setting is even created. Being aware of the relationship between setting capacity and the number of roles to be filled could lead planners to actually plan undermanning characteristics into new settings. Similarly, if it becomes clear in the course of setting creation that overmanning is a possibility, planners could cope with this eventuality by using a number of the tactics for setting change described earlier including creating new roles, double casting, adding new tasks to the setting, or controlling the number of new entrants to the setting.

In the example of spin-off groups offered by Hansell (1967) above, one can note that explicit concern is given to the number of participants (six to eight) in the group and careful specification of the number of roles is made so that the setting is at least optimally manned. In research reviewed by Moos (1974) on the effects of treatment setting size, a number of negative effects of treatment unit size have been noted including increased dropout rates from the setting. Thus early decisions about the capacity of the setting, if they are made and if pressures for increased size are resisted, can produce manning qualities that have the potential for maximizing treatment gain. Setting creators may indeed ultimately discover that "small is beautiful [Schumacher, 1973]."

A FINAL WORD

In this chapter, I have argued that the effective use of information about the social environment of the client has the potential to maximize treatment gains. Indeed, it may be that the **failure** to creatively use such information is a major reason for the finding that hard won initial gains are not maintained. Use of information about the social ecology of the client requires that we broaden our view beyond that of the consulting room to ask how work settings, families, or community groups in the clients social environment can be selected, changed, or created to provide contexts for continued growth and development.

Although three distinctive perspectives on the social environment have been offered as a framework for our inquiry, other frameworks may be equally useful. Indeed, a recurrent theme in this chapter is that people **already** make intuitive use of their knowledge about the nature and impact of social settings in engaging in natural processes of setting selection, change and creation. Thus, in some sense, it is true that each of us, client, helper, professional, or spouse, is a social ecologist.

What then should distinguish between the efforts of a psychologist using information about the social ecology and others in attempting to maximize treatment gains? The answer is, I think, the systematic collection and use of information about the social ecology of the person. As Sarason (1976) puts it in another context, it is environmental information "more consciously and expertly applied."

REFERENCES

Astin, A., & Holland, J. The Environmental Assessment Technique: A way to measure college environments. *Journal of Educational Psychology*, 1961, *52*, 308–316.

Astin, A., & Panos, R. *The educational and vocational development of college students.* Washington, D.C.: American Council on Education, 1969.

Baird, L. L. Big school, small school: A critical examination of the hypothesis. *Journal of Educational Psychology*, 1969, *60*, 253–260.

Barker, R. G. Ecology and motivation. In M. R. Jones (Ed.), *Nebraska symposium on motivation*. Lincoln: University of Nebraska Press, 1960.

Barker, R. G. *Ecological psychology*. Stanford, California: Stanford University Press, 1968.

Barker, R. G., & Gump, P. V. *Big school, small school*. Stanford, California: Stanford University Press, 1964.

Bloom, B. L. A university freshman preventive intervention program. *Journal of Consulting and Clinical Psychology*. 1971, 37, 235–242.

Bowers, D. G. OD techniques and their results in 23 organizations: The Michigan ICL study. *Journal of Applied Behavioral Science*, 1973, 9, 21–43.

Bromet, E., & Moos, R. H. The human aggregate. In R. H. Moos, (Ed.), *The human context*. New York: Wiley, 1976.

Brown, R. Manipulation of the environmental press in a college residence hall. *Personnel and Guidance Journal*, 1968, 46, 555–560.

Caplan, N., & Nelson, S. D. On being useful: The nature and consequences of psychological research on social problems. *American Psychologist*, 1973, 28, 199–211.

Carlson, K. A. A method for identifying homogeneous classes. *Multivariate Behavioral Research*, 1972, 7, 483–488.

Cherniss, C. Personal communication. 1977.

Cherniss, C., Perkins, D., Shinn, B., & Price, R. H. *The Youth Home Development Project*. Mimeograph, University of Michigan, 1976.

Coughlan, R. J., & Cooke, R. A. *The structural development of educational organizations*. Unpublished manuscript, Institute of Social Research, University of Michigan, 1974.

DeCoster, D. Housing assignments for high ability students. *Journal of College Student Personnel*, 1966, 12, 10–22.

Denner, B., & Price, R. H. (Eds.). *Community mental health: Social action and reaction*. New York: Holt, 1973.

Eddy, G. L., & Sinnett, R. Behavior setting utilization by emotionally disturbed college students. *Journal of Consulting and Clinical Psychology*, 1973, 40, 210–216.

Ellsworth, R. B., Foster, Leslie, Childers, B., Arthur, G., & Kroeker, D. Hospital and community adjustment as perceived by psychiatric patients, their families and staff. *Journal of Consulting and Clinical Psychology*, 1968, 32.

Endler, N. S., Hunt, J. McV., & Rosenstein, A. J. An S–R inventory of anxiousness. *Psychological Monographs*, 1962, 76(17, Whole No. 536).

Goffman, E. *Asylums: Essays on the social situations of mental patients and other inmates*. Garden City, New York: Doubleday, 1961.

Hansell, Norris. *Predischarge groups: Transitional type and spin-off type*. Northwestern University Medical School Department of Psychiatry, Curricular Reprint Series No. 29.

Heller, K., & Monahan, J. *Psychology and community change*. Homewood, Illinois: Dorsey Press, 1977.

Holland, J. Explorations of a theory of vocational choice and achievement: II. A four-year predictive study. *Psychological Reports*, 1963, 12, 547–594.

Holland, J. *The psychology of vocational choice: A theory of personality types and model environments*. Waltham, Massachusetts: Blaisdell, 1966.

Holland, J. *Making vocational choices: A theory of careers*. Englewood Cliffs, New Jersey: Prentice-Hall, 1973.

Jones, M. *The therapeutic community: A new treatment in psychiatry*. New York: Basic Books, 1953.

Leff, J. P. Schizophrenia and sensitivity to the family environment. *Schizophrenia Bulletin*, 1976, 2, 566–574.

Mechanic, D. Sociocultural and social-psychological factors affecting personal responses to psychological disorder. *Journal of Health and Social Behavior*, 1975, 16, 393–405.

Moos, R. H. Sources of variance in response to questionnaires and in behavior. *Journal of Abnormal Psychology*, 1969, 74, 405–412.

Moos, R. H. *Evaluating treatment environments: A social ecological approach*. New York: Wiley, 1974.

Moos, R. H. *Evaluating correctional and community settings*. New York: Wiley, 1975.

Moos, R. H. *The human context: Environmental determinants of behavior*. New York: Wiley, 1976.

Moos, R. H., & Otto, J. The COPES: A methodology for the facilitation and evaluation of social change. *Community Mental Health Journal*, 1972, 8, 28–37.

Murrell, S. A. *Community psychology and social systems*. New York: Behavioral Publications, 1973.

Pace, C. R. *College and university environment scales: Technical manual* (2nd ed.). Princeton, New Jersey: Educational Testing Service, 1967.

Pervin, L. A. Performance and satisfaction as a function of individual–environment fit. *Psychological Bulletin*, 1968, 69, 56–68.

Politser, Peter E., & Pattison, E. Mansell. The Mental Health Function of Community Groups. Unpublished manuscript, 1976.

Price, R. H. Psychological deficit vs. impression management in schizophrenic word association performance. *Journal of Abnormal Psychology*, 1972, 79, 132–137.

Price, R. H. The taxonomic classification of behaviors and situations and the problem of behavior–environment congruence. *Human Relations*, 1974, 27, 567–585.

Price, R. H. Behavior setting theory and research. In R. H. Moos (Ed.) *The Human Context*. New York: Wiley, 1976.

Price, R. H., & Bouffard, D. L. Behavioral appropriateness and situational constraint as dimensions of social behavior. *Journal of Personality and Social Psychology*, 1974, 30, 579–586.

Price, R. H., & Denner, B. (Eds.). *The making of a mental patient*. New York: Holt, 1973.

Price, R. H., & Moos, R. H. Toward a taxonomy of treatment environments. *Journal of Abnormal Psychology*, 1975, 84, 181–188.

Rappaport, J., Davidson, W., Mitchell, A., & Wilson, M. N. Alternatives to blaming the victim or the environment: Our places to stand have not moved the earth. *American Psychologist*, 1975, 30, 525–528.

Ryan, W. *Blaming the victim*. New York: Random House, 1971.

Sarason, S. B. *The creation of settings and future societies*. San Francisco: Jossey-Bass, 1972.

Sarason, S. B. Community psychology, networks and Mr. Everyman. *American Psychologist*, 1976, 31, 317–328.

Schumacher, E. F. *Small is beautiful: Economics as if people mattered*. New York: Harper & Row, 1973.

Wicker, A. W., Size of church membership and members support of church behavior settings. *Journal of Personality and Social Psychology*, 1969, 13, 278–288.

Wicker, A. W. Undermanning theory and research: Implications for the study of psychological and behavioral effects of excess populations. *Representative Research in Social Psychology,* 1973, *4,* 185–206.

Willems, E. P. Sense of obligation to high school activities as related to school size and marginality of student. *Child Development,* 1967, *38,* 1247–1260.

Willems, E. P. Planning a rationale for naturalistic research. In E. P. Willems & H. L. Aaush (Eds.), *Naturalistic viewpoints in psychological research.* New York: Holt, 1969.

Zimbardo, P., Pilkonis, P., & Norwood, R. The social disease called shyness. *Psychology Today,* 1975, *8,* 68–70.

Zussman, J. Some explanations of the changing appearance of psychotic patients. In R. Price & B. Denner (Eds.), *The making of a mental patient.* New York: Holt, 1973.

IV

PHYSIOLOGICALLY BASED
TRANSFER EFFECTS

11

Drug Instigated Effects

MARIAN L. MacDONALD
T. I. LIDSKY
JEFFREY M. KERN

Twenty-five years ago, the major tranquilizers were introduced as forms of psychiatric treatment (Caldwell, 1970). Evaluated against their treatment alternatives of that time, psychosurgical and electroconvulsive therapies, major tranquilizers seemed both more humane and more effective (Ayd, 1965); they also seemed more reasonable, for they came in the form of medicine and thus were administered following a regimen generally acceptable to professionals and lay people alike. At the time of the treatment's introduction, psychiatric disorders were conceptualized as medical problems; major tranquilizers were viewed, then, as a major medical breakthrough (MacDonald & Tobias, 1976). Like most new psychiatric treatments developed both before and since (Ullmann & Krasner, 1975), drug therapy was shown to be "effective" in its initial clinical trials. Over time, the effectiveness of this form of treatment became accepted as fact (Kinross-Wright, 1967) so that now, at the close of the 1970s, major tranquilizers and other psychopharmacologic therapies

MAXIMIZING TREATMENT GAINS:
Transfer Enhancement in Psychotherapy

(Davis, 1976) constitute the primary form of treatment administered to persons diagnosed as psychotic (Paul, Tobias, & Holly, 1972). Estimates indicate that 87% of all psychiatric inpatients (MacDonald & Tobias, 1976) and 80% of all psychiatric outpatients (Gunderson & Mosher, 1975) are maintained on psychotropic drugs; in the majority of cases, these persons are receiving no other form of therapy.[1]

When the major tranquilizers were introduced, the nature of their effects was not understood (Caldwell, 1970). Like psychosurgical and electroconvulsive therapies before them (Davison & Neale, 1978), their popularity grew because they seemed to make a difference. Theories explaining their effects were developed after, not before, the fact; some investigators, for instance, postulated after the introduction of drugs that schizophrenia arose from specific drug deficiencies (Caldwell, 1970). At present, the biochemical relationship between schizophrenia and major tranquilizers remains unknown; in fact, whether or not such a relationship exists is open to question (Goodman & Gilman, 1970). However, certain other biochemical relationships between drug therapy and central nervous system functioning **are** understood; noting these effects magnifies the importance of replacing prolonged drug therapies with more ameliorative and less inadvertently pernicious forms of treatment (cf. Kolata, 1977).

REVERSIBLE DRUG SIDE EFFECTS

The use of most psychologically-active pharmacological agents has been associated, repeatedly, with some degree of motoric disorder. These drug-induced motoric side effects are varied and differ in severity, time of onset, and reversibility. The most common disturbances arise early during treatment and typically disappear when drug therapy is discontinued. Frequently, when prolonged medication is prescribed, motor side effects can be controlled by using drugs normally employed in treating Parkinson's disease (Stimmel, 1976).

Reports concerning drugs employed to combat certain aspects of depression (tricyclic antidepressants and lithium) have been published only

[1] There is also evidence that drug therapy is the most prevalent and frequently exclusive form of treatment for an increasingly diagnosed childhood disorder. These drugs (Dexedrine and Ritalin) and this disorder (hyperkinesia) will not be included in this chapter, although evidence indicates that many of the statements made herein are equally applicable in the stimulant–hyperkinesia context (K. D. O'Leary, Pelham, Rosenbaum, & Price, 1976; S. G. O'Leary & Pelham, 1978; Sroufe, 1975).

recently: these drugs are relatively new. Moreover, their effects have been researched only over short periods of administration. Even so, gross choreoathetotic movements were observed early during treatment with tricyclic antidepressants (Fann, Sullivan, & Richman, 1976). Other observed side effects include ataxia, or the inability to walk; parasthesia, or tingling sensations in the arms and legs; psysarthia, or difficulty forming speech sounds; visual hallucinations (with high doses); lowering of blood pressure; urinary retention; and tachycardia, or rapid heart beat (Honigfeld & Howard, 1973).

With lithium treatment, side effects involving fine, rapid tremors of bodily extremities are apparently quite common: rates of incidence as high as 80% have been reported (Branchey, Charles, & Simpson, 1976). While these tremors are not responsive to antiparkinsonian agents (Floru, Tegeler, & Wilmsen, 1975), there have been no reports to date of motor abnormalities outlasting lithium treatment. In addition to motor abnormalities, lithium treatment can produce extremely serious, even lethal, side effects if the level of lithium in the blood stream becomes too high; however, continual monitoring of blood levels can prevent lithium intoxification (Honigfeld & Howard, 1973).

In contrast to the relatively recent introduction of tricyclic antidepressants and lithium into clinical practice, major tranquilizers (so-called "antipsychotics" [Dally, 1967]) have been in use for an extensive period of time. As a consequence, the side effects of this latter class of drugs have been described extensively. Many of the major tranquilizers induce a constellation of motor symptoms which appear quite similar to those of ideopathic Parkinson's Disease. These symptoms include resting tremor, muscle rigidity, drooling, and a fixed, masklike facial expression (Stimmel, 1976). As in Parkinson's Disease, these drug-induced movement disorders can be minimized by anticholinergic drug therapy. Unfortunately, there is now evidence that the use of anticholinergics in conjunction with major tranquilizers increases the probability that a qualitatively different, irreversible type of disorder, tardive dyskinesia, will occur (see below). In this context, it is important to note that those types of major tranquilizers which have not been shown to evoke a Parkinsonian syndrome typically incorporate a potent anticholinergic property into their formulae (Sayers, Bürki, Ruch, & Asper, 1976); thus a pseudoparkinsonian syndrome is avoided at the cost of increasing the likelihood of more distressing side effects.

When pseudoparkinsonian movement disorders accompany major tranquilizer use, lessening of symptoms can be accomplished by reducing drug dosage. Discontinuing drug use causes these motor disturbances to gradually disappear, but occasionally, total remission of disturbances can take up to a year (Parkes, 1976). The seemingly long latency between cessation of major tranquilizer use and remission of motor disturbances probably is due to the typically slow excretion rate for this class of drugs (Yates, 1976).

Major tranquilizers induce an additional, more phasic movement disturbance in an estimated 10.1% of treated patients (Swett, 1975). This disorder is termed "dystonia" and is characterized by the sudden onset of a tonic contraction of single muscles or muscle groups. Drug-induced dystonia is most commonly observed in young males; the probability of occurrence is apparently directly proportional to dosage level (Swett, 1975). Since large dosages are most typically associated with dystonia, this movement disorder becomes an important drawback of so-called "megadose therapy" (Donlon, 1976). Reduction of drug intake or treatment with anticholinergic agents seems to be effective in controlling this disorder (cf. Swett, 1975).

An extensive list of less severe but certainly annoying side effects also exists. These include akathisia, or involuntary motor restlessness with constant fidgeting, nausea, diarrhea, constipation, blurred visions, ejaculatory disturbances, abnormal breast growth, dizziness, fainting, and photosensitivity, or an extreme skin sensitivity to sunlight sometimes resulting in a gray to bluish-purple skin discoloration following prolonged drug use (Honigfeld & Howard, 1973). These side effects are typically treated by dosage reduction, drug change, adjunctive medication, or alterations in the individual's lifestyle.

IRREVERSIBLE DRUG SIDE EFFECTS

A qualitatively different type of disorder is also associated with the use of major tranquilizers. This syndrome was first detected several years after the introduction of these drugs into widespread clinical use (e.g., Crane, 1971). The disorder, termed "tardive dyskinesia," is characterized by grotesque, rhythmic mouth movements, lip smacking, and protrusion of the tongue. Less frequently, the distal extremities are also involved and manifest choreoathetotic movements (Simpson & Kline, 1976). "The appearance of these movements is extremely disquieting to patients, who complain of difficulty chewing and swallowing, facial and buccal pain, and extreme embarrassment leading to social isolation [Widroe & Heisler, 1976, p. 162]."

Tardive dyskinesia has only recently been recognized as occurring with sufficient frequency to be considered a clinical problem of major proportions. Rates of incidence range from "conservative," low estimates of

10% (Simpson & Kline, 1976) up to estimates as high as 56% (A. Jus, Pineau, Lachance, Pelchat, K. Jus, Pires, & Villeneuve, 1976). Although the occurrence of tardive dyskinesias has been reported as more frequent among females (e.g., Brandon, McClelland, & Protheroe, 1971), extensive epidemiological studies suggest that the age of the patient is the most important predisposing factor, with greater predispositions in older patients (A. Jus *et al.*, 1976). The disorder usually develops after several years of drug therapy. However, great caution is warranted even with relatively short-term drug treatment since tardive dyskinesia has occasionally been noted after only a few months of low dosage therapy (Simpson & Kline, 1976).

The most disturbing feature of tardive dyskinesia is that it is typically irreversible. Discontinuing major tranquilizer use does **not** lead to the remission of symptoms in the majority of cases (e.g., Klawans, 1976). In fact, the sudden cessation of drug treatment often leads to an exacerbation of such abnormal movements (Degkwitz, 1969). Most pharmacological treatments used to control motor disorders have little effect on tardive dyskinesia. Antiparkinsonian agents lead to an increase of dyskinetic symptoms (Klawans, 1976). Recently, a few reports have suggested that cholinergic precursors may have remedial effects, but, regrettably, these encouraging results are too preliminary to conclude that cholinergic drugs represent a general pharmacological treatment for the disorder.

Tardive dyskinesia has been associated with virtually every major tranquilizer currently in use in the United States (Donlon & Stenson, 1976). Reports that some recently developed drugs in Europe (e.g., Clozapine) do not induce the disorder are, at the present time, premature since, as was noted earlier, tardive dyskinesia usually develops after drug therapy has lasted several years and these newer drugs have not been on the market for a sufficient period of time to allow assessment of long-term side effects.

The onset of tardive dyskinesia is frequently insidious. Parkinsonian side effects usually evoked by drug therapy (see previous section) can effectively mask tardive dyskinetic symptoms (Degkwitz, 1969). Therefore, tardive dyskinesia is often only detected following the withdrawal of the major tranquilizer and, consequently, long after it has developed. Unfortunately, the use of anticholinergic drugs in conjunction with major tranquilizers, a frequent practice designed to minimize Parkinsonian symptoms, only seems to increase the probability of producing tardive dyskinesia (Crane, 1971; Klawans, 1976).

To date, irreversible motor symptoms have been observed repeatedly only with the major tranquilizers. It is important to recall, however, that tardive dyskinesia was recognized as a major problem only many years following the introduction of these drugs. Thus the absence of any observed irreversible side effects from tricyclic antidepressants, lithium, or ritalin must be cautiously evaluated in the context of their relatively recent appearances in clinical practice; there is already some suggestive evidence that some of these drugs, under some conditions, do produce irreversible side effects (W. J. Cohen & N. H. Cohen, 1974).

THE VALUE OF DRUG THERAPY

Few questions in psychiatric treatment have aroused as much controversy as has the question, "Are psychoactive drugs effective?" (cf. Anthony, Buell, Sharratt, & Althoff, 1972; Davis, Gosenfeld, & Tsai, 1976; Davis & Hurt, in press; MacDonald & Tobias, 1976; Marholin & Phillips, 1976, in press; Tobias & MacDonald, 1974). Proponents of drug use argue that drugs provide immediate benefits for persons in acute psychotic episodes (Davis, 1975) and prevent relapses for persons on prolonged maintenance (Davis, 1975; Davis et al., 1976). The evidence is controversial on both issues.

While noting that other investigators had reported beneficial drug effects for patients in acute psychotic episodes, Hamill and Fontana (1975) reported a study in which drugs were not differentially effective. They selected 44 newly admitted patients who met each of the following criteria: (a) fell between the ages of 18 and 55; (b) evidenced no history of childhood schizophrenia, organicity, alcoholism, epilepsy, drug addiction, or mental retardation; and (c) displayed two or more generally accepted symptoms of psychosis including thinking or speech disturbances, catatonic motor behavior, paranoid ideation, hallucinations, delusional thinking other than paranoid, blunted or inappropriate affect, and disturbances of social behavior and interpersonal relations.

Half of Hamill and Fontana's experimental participants were assigned to a placebo treatment, and the other half were administered chlorpromazine; both "medications" looked identical. Patients in either condition who appeared unresponsive to their assigned treatment had the dosage levels of their drugs (placebo **or** chlorpromazine) increased.

Hamill and Fontana (1975) included four dependent variables: a rating scale completed by ward staff, a rating schedule completed by the ward psychiatrist, and two global ratings (of current status and overall improvement) made by a psychiatrist blind to treatment condition. The study extended over a period of 5 days, and Hamill and Fontana (1975) cautioned that the conclusions from their study must be guarded in light of its short duration; each dependent variable was completed on each day of the program.

The investigators concluded that the administration of chlorpromazine had not been demonstrably superior to the administration of placebo. Members of both groups improved similarly over time on staff-rated manifest psychosis and depression and psychiatrist-judged withdrawn retardation, florid thinking, somatic anxiety, psychotic agitation, and hostile depression. Study of those persons who did **not** improve revealed a similar drug–placebo equivalence. In all, 11 participants were dropped from the study due to deterioration. Ten were dropped because of an intensification of behavior potentially dangerous to other persons and/or an intensification of psychotic behavior; half came from each group. The eleventh drop-out came from the drug group and was dropped because of severe drug side effects.

Hamill and Fontana (1975) stated, on the basis of their data, that the widespread belief that chlorpromazine always calms agitated patients was not true; to support their statement, they pointed to the fact that just as many drug as placebo condition patients were dropped due to symptomatic exacerbation. They also demonstrated that hospitalized patients in acute psychotic episodes can improve in the absence of drug therapy; it is important to note, however, that their demonstration occurred in the context of a treatment center with an emphasis on community return and crisis intervention and an active ongoing set of non-physiological, concurrent treatment programs (recreational therapy, occupational therapy, daily group meetings). Other investigators have also noted that persons admitted to psychiatric institutions improve to the degree to which their hospital treatment involves training in coping with extrainstitutional environments (May, 1976), a thesis to which we shall return.

Proponents of drug treatments for chronic psychotics argue that maintenance therapy is effective in preventing relapse (Davis, 1976) and, additionally, that withdrawal of maintenance medication produces psychiatric relapse (Davis et al., 1976). A host of studies have been conducted which have been interpreted as supporting these assertions (cf. Davis et al., 1976; Davis & Hurt, in press). The severity of side effects following long-term maintenance, however, including those reviewed in the previous section, makes it imperative that these studies meet accepted methodological standards if the conclusions based on them are to result in the continued use of maintenance medication. Critical reviews of this literature (MacDonald & Tobias, 1975; Marholin & Phillips, 1976, in press; Tobias & MacDonald, 1974) indicate that the studies, in general, are not definitive: Repeated, serious errors in experimental design and execution characterize the research. Moreover, a review of 1359 studies employing psychotropic drugs revealed an inverse relationship between methodological rigor and demonstrated drug effect (Sulzbacher, 1973). In illustration, Paul et al., (1972) following a rigorously executed, triple-blind design, found no evidence to suggest deleterious effects subsequent to drug withdrawal in the presence of active treatment programming.

It would appear, then, that the case for continued maintenance drug therapy rests more on tradition than it does on fact. As early as 1960, Ellsworth and Clayton reported that persons released from psychiatric hospitals were equally likely to return to such settings whether they were treated with drugs or not. Bockoven and Solomon (1975), following a longitudinal cohort design, reached a similar conclusion by comparing the relapse (return) rates of persons hospitalized before and after the introduction of psychoactive drugs into American psychiatry. Both Ellsworth and Clayton (1960) and Bockoven and Solomon (1975) found a slightly greater tendency for patients to return to the hospital following release if they **had** received medication, a result which the latter authors interpreted to suggest that drug administration, in addition to its physiological side effects, might have the psychological side effect of inducing a sense of dependency and eroding attributions to one's self. Concerned with successful community adjustment as the only veridical measure of treatment success, Bockoven and Solomon (1975) reflected that "the attitudes of personnel toward patients, the socio-environmental setting during treatment, and community helpfulness guided by citizens organizations may be more important in tipping the balance in favor of social recovery than are psychotropic drugs [p. 800]."

That maintenance medication has become dogma perpetuated by tradition rather than fact is illustrated in the following set of citations. The first is the conclusion of a review paper written by Gardos and Cole (1976):

> Our review of drug discontinuance studies in out-patient schizophrenics maintained on antipsychotics suggested that perhaps as many as 50% of such patients might not be worse off if their medications were withdrawn. In view of the long-term complications of antipsychotic drug therapy—primarily tardive dyskinesia—an attempt should be made to determine the feasibility of drug discontinuance in every patient. Close supervision during the postwithdrawal weeks may enable the clinician to differentiate withdrawal emergent dyskinesia from psychotic relapse so that the appropriate therapeutic measures can be instituted [p. 36].

The second, very differently toned, citation is the introduction to the same paper; this introduction was written by the editors of the psychiatric journal in which the paper appeared:

> The serious long-term complications of maintenance antipsychotic therapy led the authors to undertake a critical review of outpatient withdrawal studies. Key findings included the following: (1) for at least 40% of outpatients schizophrenics, drugs seem to be essential for survival in the community; (2) the majority of patients who relapse after drug withdrawal recompensate fairly rapidly upon reinstitution of antipsychotic drug therapy; (3) placebo survivors seem to function as well as drug survivors—thus the benefit of maintenance drug therapy appears to be prevention of relapse; and (4) some cases of early relapse after drug withdrawal may be due to dyskinesia rather than psychotic decompensation. The authors urge clinicians to evaluate each patient on maintenance antipsychotic therapy in terms of feasibility of drug withdrawal and offer practical guidelines for withdrawal and subsequent management [p. 32].

Psychoactive drug treatment, once thought to be the hope for the future, seems to have become the myth of the present. It has mushroomed into a multibillion dollar industry, with well over 5 billion dollars spent annually on direct costs for medication alone (Gunderson & Mosher, 1975). As treatment, it gave a promise unfulfilled (Anthony *et al.*, 1972). At present, there is a tremendous burden to treat those persons currently managed by medication in ways that will foster their successful community reentry. Behavior therapy seems to offer the most strategic set of techniques for this purpose (Nietzel, Winett, MacDonald, & Davidson, 1977). However, there are suggestions that drug therapy—particularly if it is prolonged—may preclude the effectiveness of behavior therapy techniques (see below).

ALTERNATIVES TO DRUG THERAPY

A rather common belief, particularly apparent in advertisements for psychotropic drugs, states that the utilization of drugs will make patients more amenable to adjunctive psychosocial treatments (Hogarty & Goldberg, 1973). Paradoxically, the administration of drugs may very well militate against the effectiveness of learning-based therapies (cf. Marholin, Touchette, & Steward, in press). Short-term administrations of chlorpromazine result in an effect known as state-dependent learning: Responses acquired while in the drug state do not generalize to nondrug conditions (Hartledge, 1965; Otis, 1964; Vestre, 1965, 1966). While the demonstration of this effect has been limited to simple experimental tasks, there is no reason to suspect that more complex tasks involved in programs such as skills training (e.g., Foy, Eisler, & Pinkston, 1975) would be immune to state-dependent effects, for "results of research with chlorpromazine on hospitalized psychiatric patients show, for the most part, generalized decrements on a wide variety of learned behaviors [Hartledge, 1965, p. 329]."

State-dependent learning, which interferes with the maintenance of new responses following drug withdrawal, has been thought to be a physiological phenomenon (Otis, 1964). In accord with the observation of Bockoven and Solomon (1975), it may also be, at least in part, an attributional one. There is evidence suggesting that the conviction that one's own efforts were responsible for producing behavior change leads to an improved maintenance of that change (Davison, Tsujimoto, & Glaros, 1973; Valins & Nisbett, 1971). Individuals receiving drugs, however, may well misperceive the drugs as primarily responsible for any changes that occurred; following drug withdrawal, then, the probability of change maintenance with these individuals would be greatly decreased.

The compatibility of learning-based therapies and short-term drug administration is questionable because of the state-dependent learning phenomenon. Research on the effects of prolonged drug administration indicate an even less likely union with learning-based therapies.

The irreversible nature of tardive dyskinesia indicates that long-term therapy with major tranquilizers induces lasting abnormalities in the central nervous system. If those neural systems which are irreversibly damaged are also crucial for affective or cognitive functioning, it follows that the long-term use of these drugs could render patients incapable of undergoing therapy-induced learning processes necessary for relatively permanent ameliorations of psychotic symptoms. In essence, treatment instituted to temporarily control abnormal behavior could eventually preclude the learning necessary for a more permanent improvement in behavior. It therefore becomes important, in a clinical context, to be able to specify both the brain area damaged by major tranquilizers as well as the behavioral involvement of that neural tissue.

The area of the brain which is most strongly implicated in tardive dyskinesia is the basal ganglia. There are several lines of evidence indicating that major tranquilizers produce damage in this neural system. First, all major tranquilizers share the common pharmacological action of blocking dopamine receptors (Baldessarini & Tarsy, 1976); by far, the highest levels of dopamine in the central nervous system are located within the basal ganglia (Bertler & Rosengren, 1959). Second, experimental evidence from ablation and electrophysiological studies demonstrates that the basal ganglia exert a strong controlling influence over oropharyngeal sensori-motor processes (Levine, Ferguson, Kreinick, Gustafson, & Schwartzbaum, 1971; Lidsky, Robinson, Denaro, & Weinhold, 1977). Third, pathological conditions in humans which primarily affect the basal ganglia (e.g., Huntington's Chorea, Wilson's Disease) are characterized by abnormal mouth and tongue movements similar to those of tardive dyskinesia (Denny-Brown, 1962). Fourth, animal research shows that long-term treatment with major tranquilizers is correlated with both behavioral and pharmacological evidence of long-lasting basal ganglionic abnormalities (Burt, Creese, & Snyder, 1977; Yates, 1976). Finally, a recent postmortem analysis revealed that patients with tardive dyskinesia have abnormally high incidence of degenerative changes in the basal ganglia (Christensen, Moller, & Faurbye, 1970).

The basal ganglia's putative involvement in the mediation of behavior has been the subject of intensive research since the 1800s (reviewed in Laursen, 1963). While this neural area is classifically categorized as a motor system (DeLong, 1971), a great deal of evidence suggests additional important functions in affective and cognitive processes (cf. Buchwald, Hull, Levine, & Villablanca, 1975; Teuber, 1976). Specifically, pathological conditions affecting the basal ganglia in humans (e.g., Huntington's Chorea, Wilson's Disease, Parkinson's Disease, strokes, manganese poisoning) are characterized by affective and cognitive disturbances in addition to the typical motor disorders (Denny-Brown, 1962; Klawans, 1973; Morgan, 1927); moreover, the onset of affective and cognitive disturbances often precedes the emergence of motoric abnormalities by a considerable period of time (Klawans, 1973; Klawans, Goetz, & Westheimer, 1972). In this context, it is interesting to note that many of the basal ganglionic conditions listed above have been frequently misdiagnosed as schizophrenia early in the disease process (Klawans et al., 1972; Morgan, 1927).

Results from the animal literature are also supportive of a basal ganglionic role in affective and cognitive processes. A variety of studies employing a wide array of methodologies implicate the basal ganglia in memory (Stamm, 1969; Wyers, Peeke, Williston, & Herz, 1968), learning (Zis, Fibiger, & Phillips, 1974), reward (German & Bowden, 1974; Phillips, Carter, & Fibiger, 1976), and attention (Buser, Pounderoux, & Mereaux, 1974).

The literature on the effects of long-term drug administration and basal ganglionic involvements, then, suggests the following conclusions. First, long-term maintenance therapy with major tranquilizers results in an irreversible movement disorder in a significant proportion of patients. Second, this irreversible disorder, tardive dyskinesia, probably reflects damage in the basal ganglia. Third, the basal ganglia is important for affective and cognitive behavior. Taken together, these conclusions suggest that prolonged drug maintenance may thwart the effectiveness of concomitant or subsequent learning-based treatments.

In light of the evidence reviewed in this chapter, it appears incumbent on the helping professions to make a transition from drug treatments to less pernicious treatments demonstrably relevant to successful community adjustment. Community adjustment is related to four factors: being employed, participating in social activities, refraining from displaying bizarre behavior, and caring for one's daily needs (Paul, 1969). Each of these factors has been shown to be effectively addressed by learning-based treatments (Nietzel et al., 1977). For those persons who are diagnosed schizophrenic, then, the following guidelines are recommended:

1. Every chronic schizophrenic currently maintained on psychotropic medication should be removed from drugs. If the person is currently maintained on several drugs simultaneously, each should be withdrawn sequentially. If antiparkinsonian drugs have been administered along with psychotropic medication(s), they should be continued for 2 weeks following the last psychotropic drug withdrawal to guard against cholinergic withdrawal symptoms. Drugs should always be withdrawn gradually, rather than abruptly (Sherman, 1967), and efforts should be made to expose persons undergoing withdrawal to whatever therapeutic learning experiences they were receiving (or should have been receiving) while on medication. Furthermore, every effort should be made to encourage individuals to attribute positive behavioral changes to themselves rather than to drugs.

2. Following drug withdrawal for persons formerly maintained on medication, drugs should not be readministered unless there is a clear and present danger that a person's behavior will be damaging to self or others. Once readministered, medication should be continued only as long as there is reason to believe danger is present, and routine maintenance medication should not be considered a treatment alternative.

3. First admission patients should not be given psychotropic medication routinely. They should enter a setting emphasizing community return and crisis intervention, and they should meet with an expectation to improve. When medication appears necessary, in cases of assaultive or self-destructive behavior (but not hallucinations or delusions), drug administration should be clearly temporary and should not be viewed as treatment.

4. Treatment settings housing both acute and chronic schizophrenics should replace their focus on maintenance with a focus on community

return. Learning-based programs (see Nietzel *et al.*, 1977) should be instituted to prepare patients for extrainstitutional environments.

REFERENCES

Anthony, W. A., Buell, G. J., Sharratt, S., & Althoff, M. E. Efficacy of psychiatric rehabilitation. *Psychological Bulletin*, 1972, *78*, 447–456.

Ayd, F. J. Major tranquilizers: The chemical assault on mental illness. *American Journal of Nursing*, 1965, *65*, 70–78.

Baldessarini, R. J., & Tarsy, D. Mechanisms underlying tardive dyskinesia. In M. D. Yahr (Ed.), *The basal ganglia*. New York: Raven Press, 1976.

Bertler, A., & Rosengren, E. Occurrence and distribution of catecholamines in brain. *Acta Physiologica Scandinavia*, 1959, *47*, 350–361.

Bockoven, J. S., & Solomon, H. C. Comparison of two five-year follow-up studies: 1947 to 1952 and 1967 to 1972. *American Journal of Psychiatry*, 1975, *132*, 796–801.

Branchey, M. H., Charles, J., & Simpson, G. M. Extrapyramidal side effects in lithium maintenance therapy. *American Journal of Psychiatry*, 1976, *133*, 444–445.

Brandon, S., McClelland, H. A., & Protheroe, C. A study of facial dyskinesia in a mental hospital population. *British Journal of Psychiatry*, 1971, *118*, 171–184.

Buchwald, N. A., Hull, C. D., Levine, M. S., & Villablanca, J. The basal ganglia and the regulation of response and cognitive sets. In M. A. B. Brazier (Ed.), *Growth and development of the brain*. New York: Raven Press, 1975.

Burt, D. R., Creese, I., & Snyder, S. H. Antischizophrenic drugs: chronic treatment elevates dopamine receptor binding in brain. *Science*, 1977, *196*, 326–327.

Buser, P., Pounderoux, G., & Mereaux, J. Single unit recording in the caudate nucleus during sessions with elaborate movements in the awake monkey. *Brain Research*, 1974, *71*, 337–344.

Caldwell, A. History of psychopharmacology. In W. Clark & J. del Guidice (Eds.), *Principles of psychopharmacology*. New York: Academic Press, 1970.

Christensen, E., Moller, J. E., & Faurbye, A. Neuropathological investigation of 28 brains from patients with dyskinesia. *Acta Psychiatrica Scandinavia*, 1970, *46*, 14–23.

Cohen, W. J., & Cohen, N. H. Lithium carbonate, haloperidol, and irreversible brain damage. *Journal of the American Medical Association*, 1974, *230*, 1283–1287.

Crane, G. E. Persistence of neurological symptoms due to neuroleptic drugs. *American Journal of Psychiatry*, 1971, *127*, 1407–1410.

Dally, P. *Chemotherapy of psychiatric disorders*. London: Logos Press, 1967.

Davis, J. M. Overview: Maintenance therapy in psychiatry: I. Schizophrenia. *American Journal of Psychiatry*, 1975, *132*, 1237–1245.

Davis, J. M. Overview: Maintenance therapy in psychiatry: II. Affective disorders. *American Journal of Psychiatry*, 1976, *133*, 1–13.

Davis, J. M., Gosenfeld, L., & Tsai, C. C. Maintenance antipsychotic drugs do prevent relapse: A reply to Tobias and MacDonald. *Psychological Bulletin*, 1976, *83*, 431–447.

Davis, J. M., & Hurt, S. W. Methodological issues in psychopharmacological research: A reply to Marholin and Phillips. *American Journal of Orthopsychiatry*, 1978, in press.

Davison, G. C., & Neale, J. M. *Abnormal Behavior: An experimental clinical approach* (2nd ed.). New York: Wiley, 1978.

Davison, G. C., Tsujimoto, R. N., & Glaros, A. G. Attribution and maintenance of behavior change in falling asleep. *Journal of Abnormal Psychology*, 1973, *82*, 124–133.

Degkwitz, R. Extrapyramidal motor disorders following long-term treatment with neuroleptic drugs. In G. E. Crane & R. Gardner, Jr. (Eds.), *Psychotropic drugs and dysfunctions of the basal ganglia*. Washington, D.C.: United States Public Health Service, 1969.

DeLong, M. R. Activity of pallidal neurons during movement. *Journal of Neurophysiology*, 1971, *34*, 414–427.

Denny-Brown, D. *The Basal Ganglia and their relation to disorders of movement*. London: Oxford University Press, 1962.

Donlon, P. T. High dosage neuroleptic therapy. *International Pharmacopsychiatry*, 1976, *11*, 235–245.

Donlon, P. T., & Stenson, R. L. Neuroleptic induced extrapyramidal symptoms. *Diseases of the Nervous System*, 1976, *37*, 629–635.

Ellsworth, R. B., & Clayton, W. H. The effects of drug treatment. *Journal of Consulting Psychology*, 1960, *24*, 50–53.

Fann, W. E., Sullivan, J. L., & Richman, B. W. Dyskinesias associated with tricyclic antidepressants. *British Journal of Psychiatry*, 1976, *128*, 490–493.

Floru, L., Tegeler, J., & Wilmsen, H. Untersuchen des lithium begingten tremors mit verschiedene messmethoden. *International Pharmacopsychiatry*, 1975, *10*, 100–110.

Foy, D. W., Eisler, R. M., & Pinkston, S. Modeled assertion in a case of explosive rages. *Journal of Behavior Therapy and Experimental Psychiatry*, 1975, *6*, 135–137.

Gardos, G., & Cole, J. O. Maintenance antipsychotic therapy: Is the cure worse than the disease? *American Journal of Psychiatry*, 1976, *133*, 323–36.

German, D. C., & Bowden, D. M. Catecholamine systems as the neural substrate for intracranial self-stimulation: a hypothesis. *Brain Research*, 1974, *73*, 381–419.

Goodman, L., & Gilman, A. (Eds.). *The pharmacological basis of therapeutics*. New York: Macmillan, 1970.

Gunderson, J. G., & Mosher, L. R. The cost of schizophrenia. *Archives of General Psychiatry*, 1975, *132*, 901–906.

Hamill, W. T., & Fontana, A. F. The immediate effects of chlorpromazine in newly admitted schizophrenic patients. *American Journal of Psychiatry*, 1975, *132*, 1023–1026.

Hartlege, L. C. Effects of chlorpromazine on learning. *Psychological Bulletin*, 1965, *64*, 235–245.

Hogarty, G. E., Goldberg, S. C., & the Collaborative Study Group. Drug and sociotherapy in the aftercare of schizophrenic patients: One year relapse rate. *Archives of General Psychiatry*, 1973, *28*, 54–64.

Honigfeld, G., & Howard, A. *Psychiatric drugs: A desk reference*. New York: Academic Press, 1973.

Jus, A., Pineau, R., Lachance, R., Pelchat, G., Jus, K., Pires, P., & Villeneuve, R. Epidemiology of tardive dyskinesia, Part I. *Diseases of the Nervous System*, 1976, *37*, 210–214.

Kinross-Wright, J. The current status of phenothiazines. *Journal of the American Medical Association*, 1967, *200*, 461–464.

Klawans, H. L. *The pharmacology of extra pyramidal movement disorders.* Basil: Karger, 1973.

Klawans, H. L. Therapeutic approaches to neuroleptic-induced tardive dyskinesias. In M. D. Yahr (Ed.), *The Basal Ganglia.* New York: Raven Press, 1976.

Klawans, H. L., Goetz, C., & Westheimer, R. Pathophysiology of schizophrenia and the striatum. *Diseases of the Nervous System,* 1972, *33,* 711–719.

Kolata, G. B. Drug design: Developing new criteria. *Science,* 1977, *197,* 36–37.

Laursen, A. M. Corpus striatum. *Acta Physiological Scandinavia,* 1963, *59* (Supplement 211), Pp. 1–106.

Levine, M. S., Ferguson, N., Kreinick, C. J., Gustafson, J. W., & Schwartzbaum, J. S. Sensorimotor dysfunctions and aphagia and adipsia following pallidal lesions in rats. *Journal of Comparative and Physiological Psychology,* 1971, *77,* 282–293.

Lidsky, T. I., Robinson, J. H., Denaro, F. J., & Weinhold, P. M. Trigeminal influences on entopeduncular units. *Brain Research,* 1978, *141,* 227–234.

MacDonald, M. L., & Tobias, L. L. Withdrawal causes relapse? Our response. *Psychological Bulletin,* 1976, *83,* 448–451.

Marholin, D., & Phillips, D. Methodological issues in psychopharmacological research: Chlorpromazine—a case in point. *American Journal of Orthopsychiatry,* 1976, *46,* 477–495.

Marholin, D., & Phillips, D. Methodological issues in psychopharmacological research: Our response to Davis and Hurt. *American Journal of Orthopsychiatry,* 1978, in press.

Marholin, D., Touchette, P. E., & Stewart, R. M. Withdrawal of chronic chlorpromazine medication: An experimental analysis. *Journal of Applied Behavior Analysis,* 1978, in press.

May, P. R. A. Rational treatment for an irrational disorder: What does the schizophrenic patient need? *Archives of General Psychiatry,* 1976, *133,* 1008–1012.

Morgan, L. O. The corpus striatum: a study of secondary degenerations following lesions in man and of symptoms and acute degenerations following experimental lesions in cats. *Archives of Neurological Psychiatry,* 1927, *18,* 495–549.

Nietzel, M. T., Winett, R. D., MacDonald, M. L., & Davidson, W. C. *Behavioral Approaches to Community Psychology.* New York: Pergamon, 1977.

O'Leary, K. D., Pelham, W. E., Rosenbaum, A., & Price, G. H. Behavioral treatment of hyperkinetic children. *Clinical Pediatrics,* 1976, *15,* 510–515.

O'Leary, S. G., & Pelham, W. E. Behavior therapy and withdrawal of stimulant medication with hyperactive children. *Pediatrics,* 1978, *61,* 211–217.

Otis, L. Dissociation and recovery of a response learned under the influence of chlorpromazine or saline. *Science,* 1964, *57,* 3–12.

Parkes, J. D. Clinical aspects of tardive dyskinesia. In H. F. Bradford & C. D. Marsden (Eds.), *Biochemistry and neurology.* New York: Academic Press, 1976.

Paul, G. L. The chronic mental patient: Current status—Future directions. *Psychological Bulletin,* 1969, *71,* 81–94.

Paul, G. L., Tobias, L. L., & Holly, B. L. Maintenance psychotropic drugs in the presence of active treatment programs. *Archives of General Psychiatry,* 1972, *27,* 106–115.

Phillips, A. G., Carter, D. A., & Fibiger, H. C. Dopaminergic substrates of intracranial self-stimulation in the caudate-putamen. *Brain Research,* 1976, *104,* 221–232.

Sayers, A. C., Burki, H. R., Ruch, W., & Asper, H. Anticholinergic properties of antipsychotic drugs and their relation to extrapyramidal side-effects. *Psychopharmacology*, 1976, *51*, 15–22.

Sherman, A. R. Therapy of maladaptive fear-motivated behavior in the rat by the systematic gradual withdrawal of a fear-reducing drug. *Behaviour Research and Therapy*, 1967, *5*, 121–129.

Simpson, G. M., & Kline, N. S. Tardive dyskinesia: Manifestations, etiology, and treatment. In M. D. Yahr (Ed.), *The Basal Ganglia*. New York: Raven Press, 1976.

Sroufe, L. A. Drug treatment of children with behavior disorders. In F. Horowitz (Ed.), *Review of Child Development Research* (Vol. 4). New York: Russell Sage Foundation, 1975.

Stamm, J. S. Electrical stimulation of monkeys' prefrontal cortex during delayed response performance. *Journal of Comparative and Physiological Psychology*, 1969, *67*, 535–546.

Stimmel, G. Neuroleptics and the corpus striatum: Clinical implications. *Diseases of the Nervous System*, 1976, *37*, 219–224.

Sulzbacher, S. Psychotropic medication with children: An evaluation of procedural biases in results of reported studies. *Pediatrics*, 1973, *51*, 513–517.

Swett, C., Jr. Drug-induced dystonia. *American Journal of Psychiatry*, 1975, *132*, 532–534.

Teuber, H. L. Complex functions of the basal ganglia. In M. D. Yahr (Ed.), *The Basal Ganglia*. New York: Raven Press, 1976.

Tobias, L. L., & MacDonald, M. L. Withdrawal of maintenance drugs with long-term hospitalized mental patients: A critical review. *Psychological Bulletin*, 1974, *81*, 107–125.

Ullmann, L. P., & Krasner, L. *A Psychological Approach to Abnormal Behavior* (2nd ed.). Englewood Cliffs, New Jersey: Prentice-Hall, 1975.

Vestre, N. Relative effects of phenothiazines and phenobarbital on verbal conditioning of schizophrenics. *Psychological Reports*, 1965, *17*, 289–290.

Vestre, N. The effects of phenothiazine drugs on verbal conditioning of schizophrenics. *Journal of Psychology*, 1966, *64*, 257–264.

Valins, S., & Nisbett, R. E. *Attribution Processes in the Development and Treatment of Emotional Disorders*. New York: General Learning Press, 1971.

Widroe, H. J., & Heisler, S. Treatment of tardive dyskinesia. *Diseases of the Nervous System*, 1976, *37*, 162–164.

Wyers, E. J., Peeke, H. V. S., Williston, J. S., & Herz, M. J. Retroactive impairment of passive avoidance learning by stimulation of the caudate nucleus. *Experimental Neurology*, 1968, *22*, 350–366.

Yates, C. Long-term effects of dyskinesia-inducing drugs. In H. F. Bradford & C. D. Marsden (Eds.), *Biochemistry and neurology*. New York: Academic Press, 1976.

Zis, A. P., Fibiger, H. C., & Phillips, A. G. Reversal of L-DOPA of impaired learning due to destruction of the dopaminergic nigro-neostriated projection. *Science*, 1974, *185*, 960–962.

12

Transfer and Evaluation
of Biofeedback Treatment[1]

STEVEN JAY LYNN
ROBERT R. FREEDMAN

INTRODUCTION AND GENERAL PROBLEMS

In 1973, Birk proposed, "A new 'behavioral medicine,' biofeedback, . . .
may in fact represent a major new developing frontier of clinical medicine and psychiatry [p. 362]." This statement reflected a sense of optimism about a technique that promised to help remedy various disorders
by bringing bodily processes first under the control of external contingencies, and ultimately, under self-control. The term **biofeedback** refers to the use of external monitors to aid one in influencing bodily
processes previously unregulated by voluntary acts or physiological responses for which regulation has been disrupted by trauma or disease
(Blanchard & Epstein, 1978). In all biofeedback paradigms physiological

[1] Research conducted by the authors was supported by NIMH Grant MHO7345–17
and by the State of Michigan, Departments of Public Health and Mental Health.

MAXIMIZING TREATMENT GAINS:
Transfer Enhancement in Psychotherapy

responses undetectable by an untrained subject are electronically augmented and converted to easily discriminable stimuli. Thus a person may listen to a tone whose pitch varies precisely with the amount of tension in one of his muscles or watch a light display which informs him whether his heart rate is above or below a particular level. The subject uses this information presumably through an operant learning process [2], to achieve control of the desired physiological response. Ultimately, the response must be regulated in the natural environment without the use of external feedback.

Birk's optimism was no doubt motivated by early demonstrations that autonomic responses in both animals (e.g., Miller, 1969) and humans (e.g., Shapiro, Crider, & Tursky, 1964) were amenable to modification when response contingent feedback was available. Evidence for learned control of heart rate (Engel & Chism, 1967), peripheral blood flow (Snyder & Noble, 1968), single motor unit activity (Basmajian, 1963), EEG patterns (Beatty, 1971) and muscle tension (Budzynski, Stoyva, & Adler, 1970) in experimental subjects led to the application of biofeedback techniques to a wide range of clinical disorders. For example, tension headaches are presumably caused by sustained contractions of musculature in the face and neck. Patients trained to reduce forehead muscle tension during 16 half-hour EMG biofeedback sessions reported significant reductions in headache activity compared to control patients (Budzynski, Stoyva, Adler, & Mullaney, 1973). Similarly, cardiac arrythmias have been treated with heart rate feedback (Weiss & Engel, 1971), Raynaud's disease (peripheral vasoconstrictions) with blood flow feedback (Shapiro & Schwartz, 1972; Surwit, 1973), epilepsy with EEG feedback (Sterman, 1973) and muscle injuries with EMG feedback (Jacobs & Felton, 1969).

However, the use of biofeedback in the treatment of clinical disorders has not been as successful as might have been predicted from initial studies on laboratory animals and normal humans. In the same year that Birk (1973) proposed the term behavioral medicine, a critical review was published by Blanchard and Young (1973), entitled, "Self-control of cardiac functioning: A promise yet unfulfilled." The authors maintained that although results frequently attained statistical significance, they rarely were of clinical importance. The following year, the same authors published another review in which they concluded,

> Only in the areas of electromyogram feedback for muscle retraining, elimination of subvocal speech while reading, and elimination of tension

---

[2] There has been much debate regarding the mechanisms by which this learning takes place. Since this issue is beyond the scope of the present chapter, the reader is referred to three excellent review articles for further discussion (Black, Cott, & Pavloski, 1977; Brener, 1974; Katkin & Murray, 1968).

headaches does the evidence support strong conclusions of the efficacy of biofeedback training. In the area of cardiac arrhythmias, lowering blood pressure, and reducing seizure frequency, the results are encouraging, but are subject to a variety of methodological flaws. In other areas, no firm conclusions can be drawn from the available evidence [p. 573].

More recently, Shapiro and Surwit (1976) state "there is not one well controlled scientific study of the effectiveness of biofeedback and operant conditioning in treating a physiological disorder [p. 113]." However, these and other reviewers (Blanchard & Miller, 1977; Inglis, Campbell, & Donald, 1976; Miller & Dworkin, 1977; Schwartz, 1973) acknowledge that the accumulated evidence justifies further exploration of biofeedback treatment for certain disorders.

Certainly, much basic research and many clinical trials are needed before the value of biofeedback techniques is conclusively established for the treatment of any problem. A crucial area in which research has been lacking is that of the transfer and maintenance of physiological self-regulation learned in the laboratory to real-life situations. It is clear that if the promise of a behavioral medicine based upon biofeedback techniques is to be realized, effects generated in a laboratory or clinical setting must be shown to result in relatively permanent modification or amelioration of various disorders. Thus, if a hypertensive individual has effectively learned to control his blood pressure in the laboratory or clinic, he should be able to maintain acceptably low levels at home, at work, in stressful situations, and in the presence of different individuals.

The ultimate goal of biofeedback is to assist the individual in gaining enduring self-control of a relevant physiological response. Self-control is evident when, "changes in a physiologic response are observed in the absence of external feedback, but occur after instructions to change the response are presented [Epstein & Blanchard, 1977, p. 204]." Epstein and Blanchard note that the source of the instructions are not important (Brener, 1974). Instructions to decrease blood pressure, for example, may be presented by the clinician to assess self-regulatory ability in the clinic, or by the patient himself in stressful situations. What is critical, however, is the patient's ability to exert control of his physiology without external assistance.

It is generally assumed that after sufficient biofeedback training, regulation of the target response will be as good without feedback as with feedback. Unfortunately, achieving control of a response with the aid of feedback does not guarantee that regulatory ability will be sustained in the absence of external assistance. For example, Epstein and Abel (1977) found that five of six patients treated for tension headaches were able to reduce levels of EMG frontalis activity as a result of the training procedure, but were not able to maintain comparably low EMG levels when simply instructed to relax with the techniques they employed when they received feedback. Since biofeedback per se may not be sufficient to produce sustained cross-situational effects, increased attention should be devoted to procedures specifically intended to enhance and maintain treatment gains.

The focus of this chapter is the question: "How can the researcher or clinical practitioner maximize the long-term transfer of skills learned in biofeedback training to situations outside the laboratory or clinic?" In the course of our discussion we will suggest procedures to facilitate the production of a lasting, clinically significant response. Some of these techniques will be part of the actual biofeedback process, such as fading the feedback signal, while others will be "ancillary" procedures, such as relaxation and self-management approaches. Since little controlled work has been done in this area, much of what we propose will be speculative and will necessitate subsequent empirical testing. However, we will attempt to bring together relevant work from diverse areas to provide suggestions for researchers and clinicians who employ biofeedback techniques. In order to clarify the need for programmatic assessment and utilization of transfer and gain maintenance techniques, we will first discuss the specificity and limitations of biofeedback training.

Specificity of the Biofeedback Approach

Stokes and Baer (1977) write, "it is frequently observed that when a change in behavior has been accomplished through experimental contingencies, then that change is manifest where and when those contingencies operate, and is often seen in only transitory forms in other places and at other times [p. 350]." Unfortunately, certain aspects of the treatment procedure itself tend to diminish the likelihood of ready transfer outside the training situation. The technical orientation and instruments alone create a situation which is markedly different from the array of stimuli usually encountered in everyday life. Typically, the patient is seated in a comfortable chair in a quiet room with a minimum of distractions. The therapist/technician, after attaching one or more transducers, administers instructions to the patient who in turn attempts to produce the appropriate physiological response by observing or listening to a variety of electronic instruments.

While the traditional psychotherapeutic situation is far removed from the real world, the biofeedback environment is even more distant. In addition to the specificity of therapist and temporal factors in psychotherapy, biofeedback confronts the patient with an impressive array of machinery in an atmosphere which encourages relaxation and tuning out the "noise" of everyday life. Thus the contingencies associated with controlling the physiological response in the laboratory may be very different from those operating in the patient's real life situation.

Furthermore, biofeedback training typically ignores the specific physical, situational, and psychological antecedent stressors that may be essential to the production of a symptom (Mitchell & White, 1977). Rather, the paradigm emphasizes the modification of a specific physiological response presumed to be causally related to the target symptom. For example, Raynaud's disease, characterized by peripheral vasospasms, is treated by laboratory conditioning of increased blood flow in the extremities. This ignores the fact that vasoconstrictive attacks are more frequent in cold environments and may also be precipitated by emotional stress (Blain, Coller, & Carver, 1951). Even if the patient has been successfully trained to control blood flow in the treatment room, he may not be able to produce this response in a cold or anxiety-laden situation.

Similarly, even if modification of a particular response is robust in the clinical setting, transfer may be problematic not only because the stimuli which control it differ in varying situations, but because everyday life situations may evoke responses which compete or interfere with the ability to exercise self-regulation. Rosen (1977) reports that biofeedback facilitates penile tumescence in the absence of direct sexual stimulation in the laboratory context. However, he discusses limitations of this approach for treating sexual dysfunctions. He notes that transfer of treatment gains may be a critical issue both because of the rather unique stimulus conditions frequently associated with erectile problems, and the contribution of interpersonal problems associated with cases of erectile dysfunction (Kaplan, 1974; Masters & Johnson, 1970). Although specificity of control can be achieved in laboratory situations, there is little reason to expect that self-control can be maintained where anxiety associated with sexual performance may compete with whatever skills are learned in the laboratory. Shapiro and Surwit (1976) contend that it may be of little value to utilize biofeedback techniques prior to "analyzing and correcting contingencies that may be aggravating the problem [p. 103]."

Another reason why treatment gains may not be observed across various situations is that symptoms may be reinforced by strong rewards or serve "secondary gains" associated with avoiding more aversive consequences than the symptom presents. Individuals with tension or muscle contraction headaches may experience such gains as avoiding unpleasant or undesirable activities and diminished responsibility for certain tasks. Patients we have treated at Lafayette Clinic often report not only that their headaches are associated with stressors at work and at home, but

that individuals in their social arena often are more willing to assume responsibilities for them when they experience severe headaches. In our
experience, headaches have often appeared to allow hard-driving, per-
fectionistic individuals opportunities to take "time-outs" and rationalize
periods of rest and relaxation which in the absence of symptomology
would be consciously unacceptable and incongruent with their self-
image. Thus stimuli which serve to maintain symptoms may vary in
salience across situations and may be of relatively little import in the
relatively constant, nondemanding, nonsocial laboratory or clinical
situation.

The Placebo Effect

Although we have discussed a number of reasons why transfer of
gains outside the biofeedback situation may be problematic, we have not,
as yet, addressed the issue of long-term maintenance of therapeutic
gains. Indeed, some of the novel aspects of the biofeedback situation
may contribute to quick symptomatic changes which initially appear to
be treatment gains, but do not persist over time. Stroebel and Glueck
(1973) argue that biofeedback procedures may act as an "ultimate
placebo." Like a drug placebo, which contains a therapeutically inert
substance such as sugar, biofeedback may have no specific therapeutic
effect on the problem treated. Rather, potent psychological factors associated with the impressiveness of the treatment and the enthusiasm of
the therapist and patient may result in transitory symptom relief which
may diminish as the patient gains distance from the demands of the
training situation.

In a review of the literature on placebo effects in psychotherapy,
Shapiro (1971) cites a number of characteristics for effective placebos:
"expensive, fashionable, elaborate, detailed, time consuming, and dangerous treatments [p. 458]." Legewie (1977) notes that all of these criteria with the exception of dangerousness apply to biofeedback therapy.
If biofeedback functions, in part, like other placebos, it is likely that
treatment gains which result from the placebo effect will be transitory.
Jacobs, Kraemer, and Agras (1977) analyzed the time course of placebo
effects in studies with hypertensive patients who received placebo medication: Maximal pressure decreases which resulted from the placebo were
evident between the fourth week and the fourth month of treatment.
These results are significant in that if biofeedback treatment gains are
merely an artifact of a general placebo effect, the clinician may be misled
about the need for continued treatment and medication by initial, yet
spuriously impressive results (Miller, 1975).

Since biofeedback appears to share many characteristics of an effective placebo, it is important to ascertain whether the effects of biofeedback treatment are specific to the acquisition of physiological self-control. Results from recent studies of EMG biofeedback for tension headaches (Epstein & Abel, 1977; Holroyd, Andrasik, & Westbrook, 1977) suggest that report of symptom relief is not necessarily associated with the ability to decrease frontalis EMG levels, the response presumed to be related to headache activity.

Andrasik (personal communication) recently completed a study which provided a test for the specific effects of biofeedback treatment of tension headaches. Forty tension headache sufferers were placed in one of four groups. The groups were equated for a variety of nonspecific effects and differed only with respect to the type of feedback provided. The subjects in the first group, which served as a control, were instructed to keep a daily record of their headache activity. The second group received classical frontalis EMG biofeedback to reduce muscle tension. Two additional groups served as biofeedback controls. In one group, subjects received biofeedback to decrease their forearm flexor muscle tension. This was done to insure that frontalis muscle tension levels would remain stable. The other group received inverted auditory feedback from their frontalis muscle, such that decreasing tone levels were actually associated with increasing muscle tension. Although all subjects were led to believe that they were reducing their frontalis muscle tension, their actual muscle tension levels varied as intended during biofeedback training periods and self-control periods. The results indicated that subjects in all three biofeedback groups reported significant reductions in headache activity compared with subjects who only recorded their headache activity.

These findings must raise serious questions about the specific role of biofeedback in the treatment of tension headaches. Since other biofeedback treatment paradigms have not closely examined the placebo issue, the extent to which nonspecific effects account for gains reported in the treatment of other disorders cannot be ascertained. Andrasik argues that the active ingredient in the biofeedback treatment of tension headaches is not decreased frontalis muscle tension, but the acquisition of a new strategy for coping with headaches and a concurrent enhancement of belief in the ability to successfully cope with headaches. Andrasik is currently completing a follow-up study of the headache sufferers. It will be interesting to see whether treatment gains are maintained in the biofeedback control groups as well as in the group which received veridical frontalis muscle tension feedback.

Although the Andrasik study underscores the need for the inclusion of adequate placebo control groups in the evaluation of biofeedback treatment for any disorder, it is unlikely that placebo effects can account for the enduring treatment gains which are clearly associated with physiological self-regulation. Both active and placebo effects probably play a role in the acquisition and maintenance of treatment gains.

Stroebel and Glueck (1973) contend that the interaction of expectations and actual physiological learning can affect the persistence of treatment effects outside the laboratory or clinic. They postulate a curvilinear relationship between the patient's expectations and the long term effectiveness of biofeedback therapy. If an individual's expectancies for success and improvement are not mobilized, motivation for practicing techniques learned in the laboratory will not be sufficient to maintain success. On the other hand, if patients are overly enthusiastic during treatment, expectations which may be relevant to continued success at self-regulation may diminish over time as distance is gained from the "demands" of the training situation. Stroebel and Glueck contend that biofeedback treatment effects can be enhanced by maintaining a balance between actual learning of a physiological response demonstrated in a particular context and the patient's expectations.

Although virtually no experimental attention has been given to Stroebel and Glueck's model, a number of recent studies suggest that expectations may at least influence the ability of the patient to acquire an appropriate physiological response. For example, Leeb, Fahrion, and French (1976) directly manipulated expectations of subjects in a study which examined the effect of instructional set on ability to learn peripheral temperature control. They found that subjects with positive expectations regarding the ability to control their temperature demonstrate greater increases in temperature than subjects who received instruction which engendered negative or neutral expectations. Holroyd *et al.* (1977) found that subjects with tension headaches showed little benefit from frontalis muscle EMG biofeedback when they received counterdemand instructions that led them to believe that they could not expect any symptom relief prior to the conclusion of the training sessions.

The magnitude of the placebo effect may also depend on the enthusiasm of the therapist. Taub (1977) notes that a technician having an impersonal attitude toward the subjects as well as skepticism regarding the method was able to successfully train only 2 of 22 subjects in skin temperature control. However, an experimenter with an optimistic attitude towards this task was able to successfully train 19 of 21 subjects.

Since nonspecific factors exert a potent influence on behavior and cognitions, they are deserving of attention in their own right (Miller, 1975; Miller & Dworkin, 1977; Shapiro & Surwit, 1976). The finding that nonspecific factors may result in improvements which are transient suggests that it may be especially important to include adequate follow-ups and control groups for placebo effects in any rigorous evaluation of a biofeedback treatment's effectiveness. In individual therapy, follow-ups are equally necessary to determine the extent to which genuine, specific effects persist.

ASSESSMENT OF THE BIOFEEDBACK PATIENT

Biofeedback treatment has obviously turned out to be a good deal more complex than was originally thought. Since the etiologies of disorders commonly treated with biofeedback (e.g., hypertension and Raynaud's disease) are often multidetermined, a thorough assessment is necessary to develop the treatment plan which is best for the patient's overall welfare. A headache, for example, may be caused by a tumor or aneurysm. For these problems a medical procedure, such as surgery, may be necessary. If the diagnosis is that of tension headache, a course of biofeedback muscle relaxation and/or cognitive stress management may best attack the causes and produce the most enduring symptom relief.

Psychological evaluation is necessary to determine the patient's appropriateness and readiness for biofeedback or other behavioral procedures. A severely disturbed individual may need intensive psychotherapy rather than symptom removal and may be incapable of complying with the demands of behavioral treatment, such as keeping symptom logs and practicing relaxation at home. In general, patient motivation must be high to insure compliance with the evaluation and transfer procedures proposed in the following pages. For example, many of our patients are reluctant, especially in the early phases of treatment, to keep detailed symptom logs. The importance of this task must be impressed upon the patient and his resistance to documenting symptoms must be adequately discussed.

In addition to collecting information which will help the clinician to determine whether the treatment is having its desired effect, the assessment should include an evaluation of the patient's perception of the problem and the prospective treatment. This is important because the patient may harbor doubts regarding participation in treatment and may entertain a variety of notions that may interfere with potential cooperation and involvement in therapy. For example, the person may indulge in fantasies of being shocked by the electrical equipment, entertain hopes for a magical or "quick cure" and immediate symptom relief, or maintain a "helpless, hopeless" attitude that precludes the ability to envision a positive therapeutic outcome.

Thus the evaluation may suggest that certain behaviors or cognitions are important to eliminate or modify prior to the use of biofeedback. Finally, the assessment may suggest possible procedures which can be instituted to promote gain maintenance and transfer. It will be necessary to continue the assessment process throughout treatment and after an appropriate follow-up interval.

Obtaining a Reliable Symptom Baseline

If the clinician and patient agree on biofeedback treatment, it is necessary to obtain an accurate picture of the severity of the symptoms and the conditions under which they occur in order to judge whether the treatment is having the desired effects. While the patient's self-report is the vehicle by which this information is usually obtained, there may be reasons to doubt its accuracy. Insomniacs, for example, typically exaggerate the length of time it takes them to fall asleep by 200–400% (Freedman & Papsdorf, 1976; Rechtshoffen, 1968). While sleep onset time may be objectively measured by all night laboratory recordings, other symptoms, such as headaches, are almost impossible to observe directly due to their relative infrequency of occurrence. Even if the patient's headache did occur in the laboratory, the intensity of muscle contractions measured electromyographically would not necessarily relate to the intensity of pain reported (Cox, Freundlich, & Meyer, 1975). In addition, retrospective data obtained from the patient regarding symptom frequency and severity are subject to distortion by sympathy seeking or denial or may be unreliable due to poor cognitive functioning.

Some of the unreliability of baseline symptom data is inherent in the nature of the diseases themselves. Miller and Dworkin (1977) have observed that a number of disorders that have been treated with biofeedback are chronic conditions marked by fluctuations in symptom severity. Patients are likely to seek treatment during periods of exacerbation of the problem and to terminate treatment when the symptom is less severe or no longer a source of discomfort. Improvements coincident with the termination of treatment may, therefore, reflect a natural amelioration of the problem rather than a real treatment gain due to successful self-regulation.

Variations in symptom baselines may be so great that they obscure therapeutic changes produced during training. In a study of biofeedback treatment with hypertensives, Surwit and Shapiro (1976) obtained baseline measurements of blood pressure on five occasions prior to treatment. Values varied from mean of 139/88 mm Hg to 165/103 mm Hg. Since the pressure decrements produced during training were only a few millimeters Hg in magnitude, it was difficult to assess their significance.

Brady, Luborsky, and Kron (1974) found that variations in blood pressure ranging from 4–33.9 mm Hg during evaluation and baseline periods were greater than changes observed during a 4-week "metronome-conditioning relaxation" treatment.

While little can be done about the waxing and waning of the symptoms themselves, the reliability of the baseline may be improved by collecting symptom report data for at least several weeks prior to treatment, lessening the possibility of error due to chance variation. The length of this period must be balanced, of course, by regard for the continuing discomfort of the patient and possible harm which may result from delaying treatment. Reporting errors due to distortion by the patient may be lessened by the use of symptom logs to be completed at a specified time or whenever symptoms occur. An example of an hourly headache log can be found in Budzynski et al. (1973). The patient should be instructed in the use of the reporting forms to insure that all details are understood and to encourage him to be a sufficiently motivated, reliable, and accurate observer. However, even highly motivated patients may not provide accurate data on symptom frequency and severity. When possible, corroborating information from family members or coworkers may be useful in validating reports from the patient as well as "harder" evidence such as medication dosages, lost work time, or interference with other life events.

The ease of monitoring the symptom or maladaptive physiological response may vary with the nature of the disorder. Disorders associated with pain such as migraine headaches, tension headaches, and Raynaud's disease are easily monitored and pose no assessment problem in that pain is a readily discriminable event. Heart rate and respiration are also easily detected by monitoring the peripheral pulse in the case of heart rate and counting breaths in the case of respiration. However, detecting a response such as blood pressure may be problematic because it does not produce any peripheral sensations (Blanchard & Epstein, 1978). Unfortunately, a noninvasive and portable device for measuring blood pressure is not available at the present time. Patients can be encouraged to monitor their blood pressure in different life situations with portable sphygnomometers, although this approach has the obvious disadvantage of being inconvenient and intrusive.

Importance of a Functional Analysis of the Disorder

Towards the end of developing the most effective treatment and transfer enhancement program for a particular patient, it is necessary to understand the causes and functions of his symptom. One approach to this task is to examine the situational precipitants of the symptom as well as the contingencies which tend to control, maintain, and possibly aggravate it. Meichenbaum (1976) contends that the initial assessment should include a situational analysis of the problem as well as exploration of the cognitions which precede, accompany, and follow the symptom. If the assessment reveals that the patient's tension headaches are repeatedly preceded by similar work or family conflicts it is likely that this symptom is well enmeshed in the dynamics of the patient's life. Even if biofeedback can successfully teach a person to reduce tension in muscles relevant to the headache, it may be unrealistic to expect him to produce this response in the face of potent psychological or situational stressors. In a study of eight male hypertensives Kleinman, Goldman, Snow, and Korol (1976) found that high levels of stress and low levels of motivation were associated with higher initial levels of blood pressure and smaller decreases during feedback training both in and outside the laboratory.

If the patient is able to verbalize symptom precipitants, it may be worthwhile to try an *in vivo* procedure where the patient is asked to imagine the symptom related situation while the maladaptive physiological response is electronically monitored by the clinician. The labile hypertensive patient may be able to specify certain situations which are experienced as stressful. If relatively elevated pressure is evident when the patient is asked to imagine subjectively stressful situations, and lower levels are recorded when imagining nonstressful situations, it may help to confirm the relationship between the subjectively experienced stressor and the maladaptive physiological response. Along the same line, it may be feasible to introduce stressors or classes of stimuli reported to be associated with the problem and monitor the target physiological response. However, such procedures may be time consuming and costly.

The functional analysis of the symptom can also provide suggestions for appropriate criteria for evaluation of therapeutic outcome. For example, if certain situations are reliably associated with the symptom, it will be important to determine whether the symptom is still present in the target situations after treatment.

Evaluating Ability to Control the Response without Feedback

In addition to gathering appropriate outcome data regarding the symptom, it is essential for the clinician to assess the patient's ability to regulate the physiological response associated with the problem both before and after treatment. Although we would not expect the patient to be able to exert significant control of the maladaptive physiological response before biofeedback training, we cannot claim that such training has been successful until the patient is able to control the response in the absence of feedback. Clearly, if the person cannot show some degree of control in the training situation, it is unlikely that any degree of control will be maintained in different, probably more demanding extra laboratory situations.

Unfortunately, with the exception of studies of cardiac regulation (Blanchard & Epstein, 1978; Engel & Bleecker, 1974; Pickering & Gorham, 1975; Weiss & Engel, 1971), few investigators have assessed the ability to control the relevant response before and after training in the absence of feedback. Thus, few studies have documented the subject's ability to exercise self-control of the response at the end of treatment.

It is advisable to continue training until the person is able to reliably alter the trained response when instructed to do so in order to confirm that the treatment gains observed are specific to the training procedure. If the patient can consistently alter his physiology so that the symptom can be "turned on or off, on request," it would argue against interpreting this fine degree of control as merely an artifact of a general placebo effect (Miller & Dworkin, 1977). Pickering and Miller (1977) replicated earlier findings of Engel and Bleecker (1974) which showed that patients who developed control of their PVCs could reliably alter their heart rate to either produce the symptom or abort it at will.

Self-control of a physiological response in the face of relevant stressors or symptom precipitants can be valuable outcome data. If a Raynaud's disease patient can maintain control of peripheral skin temperature in an environment of gradually decreasing temperature, it is an impressive demonstration of transfer of treatment gains (Surwit, Pilon, & Fenton, 1977). Equally impressive would be the ability of a hypertensive patient to maintain decreased blood pressure when stressors previously associated with arousal were introduced into the training situation. In order to assess situational generalization of the response, techniques of biotelemetry may prove useful, along with portable feedback devices, for monitoring physiological functioning in different physical settings.

Differential Treatment Strategies

Having thoroughly evaluated the patient's physical and psychological condition, the practitioner should discuss with him the available treatment alternatives. In the case of painful disorders, biofeedback may be an alternative to medication where concerns about side effects, habituation, or lack of effectiveness are relevant. With other maladies such as

Raynaud's disease, biofeedback may be the initial treatment of choice because it is less risky or costly than other alternatives such as surgery, which have irreversible effects.

In weighing the potential rewards and costs of various alternatives, the clinician may opt to try other behavioral approaches before embarking on a lengthy course of biofeedback sessions. There is some evidence that various cognitive and relaxation approaches are effective in treating certain disorders which have been treated with biofeedback. A variety of relaxation procedures have been used in the treatment of hypertension. Meditation (Benson, Beary, & Carol, 1974), yoga relaxation exercises (Datey, Deshmukh, Dalvi, & Vinekar, 1969), autogenic training (Luthe, 1963), a "metronome conditioned relaxation" procedure (Brady et al., 1974), relaxation and hypnosis (Deabler, Fidel, & Dillenkoffer, 1973), and relaxation (Taylor, Farquhar, & Nelson, 1977) have all been found to be useful for lowering blood pressure.

In the treatment of tension headaches certain studies suggest that relaxation instructions can produce amelioration of headache symptomatology equal to that of EMG biofeedback over follow-ups as long as 7 months (Chesney & Shelton, 1976; Cox, et al., 1975; Haynes, Griffen, Mooney, & Parise, 1975). However, other evidence suggests that EMG biofeedback is superior to progressive relaxation (Hutchings & Reinkung, 1976). Budzynski (1977) remarks that not all tension headache clients show elevated sustained contractions of muscles implicated in tension headaches. He suggests that EMG biofeedback may be maximally effective for tension headache sufferers whose maladaptive physiological responses are closely associated with the symptoms. However, with other individuals in which muscle tension is not particularly elevated, more general, nonfeedback oriented behavioral and relaxation programs may be sufficient to promote long-term transfer of gains.

Behavioral and relaxation techniques have also been effective with migraine sufferers. Mitchell and White (1977) reported successful treatment of migraine patients using a self-management approach which incorporated self-recording and self-monitoring of stressors as well as self-control techniques of physical and mental relaxation and self-desensitization. Blanchard, Theobald, Williamson, Silver, and Brown (1978) recently completed a controlled group outcome study with migraine patients and found that treatment by progressive relaxation was equally as effective as thermal biofeedback training combined with autogenic training.

The clinician may decide to first attempt some of the approaches cited above where elevated levels of muscle tension appear to mediate or exacerbate a particular problem. Clearly, if patients can learn to discriminate sensations linked with relaxation, such cues could be employed to help achieve control in a variety of situations (Budzynski, 1977). Such techniques may be particularly valuable for enhancing transfer of treatment effects with patients suffering from hypertension since elevated blood pressure is not as easy to discriminate as peripheral sensations associated with muscle tension. The hypertensive patient could be trained to more accurately detect elevated muscle tension and to practice relaxation in stressful situations.

It should be kept in mind that indirect behavioral techniques may be effectively combined with "direct" biofeedback approaches to treat disorders where cognitive or muscular relaxation is one component of the overall symptom picture. Using combined hypnosis, relaxation, and temperature biofeedback, Jacobson, Hackett, Surman, and Silverberg (1973) alleviated Raynaud's symptoms in one patient for seven and one half months after termination of treatment. In a controlled study, Surwit *et al.* (1977) produced improvement in response to a cold stress challenge and in Raynaud's symptoms using either autogenic training or autogenic training plus skin temperature biofeedback. Patel (1977) has developed a program for treating hypertensives. The treatment includes training in relaxation, mediatation, GSR and EMG biofeedback, twice daily home practice of these techniques, as well as practicing relaxation in stressful situations.

Although it is clear that relaxation approaches may be viable ancillary procedures as well as treatment approaches in their own right, it is not clear which specific relaxation treatment may be more beneficial. The long-term benefits may vary in terms of the extent, degree, and persistence of self-control and the physiological concomitants of such control (Shapiro & Surwit, 1976). More research is necessary to establish the relative efficacy of biofeedback and other behavioral approaches with different types of individuals suffering from different disorders. Nevertheless, relaxation and behavioral relaxation approaches may provide the clinician and patient with a nontechnical, inexpensive strategy for producing and possibly enhancing treatment effects.

ENHANCING PATIENT MOTIVATION

After a careful assessment it may become clear that certain procedures are necessary to enhance patient motivation and minimize environmental and psychological factors that interfere with the goals of treatment. The Raynaud's disease patient will need to practice vasodilatation at home, in cold weather, and with different persons. She (the disease usually occurs in women) may need psychotherapy to overcome the secondary gains of her symptom or to help her cope more effectively with stress. She will need to reliably and objectively record her symptomology for many months so that the effects of the treatment can be accurately determined. Clearly, this type of treatment requires a well-motivated patient who is involved in all aspects of the plan. This may be particularly problematic in a disorder such as hypertension, where the symptom is not painful and its long term consequences are usually not salient (Shapiro & Schwartz, 1972). Gaarder and Sherman (1977) conclude that when patient involvement is low, behavioral treatments for hypertension are ineffective.

High motivation is important in biofeedback therapy because many hours of repeated practice may be necessary to maintain self-control of a physiological response. A number of studies suggest that if the patient does not consistently practice, adequate self-regulation will not be achieved or will not be sustained. In reviewing the literature on biofeedback treatment of hypertension, Blanchard and Epstein (1978) conclude that maintenance of therapeutic gains seems to be dependent on continued monitoring of blood pressure and consistent practice following biofeedback training. Budzynski et al. (1973) found that two subjects who did not regularly practice relaxation at home were not as successful in reducing the frequency of tension headaches as subjects who consistently practiced. Similarly, in a study with migraine headache sufferers, Blanchard et al. (1978) found that headache symptoms returned in those subjects who did not practice autogenic training or progressive relaxation at home. In disorders such as headaches, where termination of treatment may coincide with naturally occurring symptom reduction, it is particularly important to ensure that individuals are sufficiently involved in treatment to remain in therapy beyond the point of initial symptom reduction.

Engaging the Patient in Treatment

Although clinicians and researchers acknowledge the importance of maintaining appropriate patient motivation (Blanchard & Epstein, 1978; Budzynski et al., 1973; Miller & Dworkin, 1977; Schwartz & Shapiro, 1973), little attention has been devoted to elucidating procedures for enhancing patient cooperation and motivation. One exception worthy of mention is the work of Patel (1977) with hypertensive patients who participated in a biofeedback and behavioral treatment program. Prior to actual biofeedback treatment, patients attended a number of meetings during which they viewed slides and films about high blood pressure.

Individuals were encouraged to discuss their problems and ask questions concerning their disorder and the treatment in groups in which the nature of the treatment, the concept of biofeedback, and the relationship between emotion and physiological processes were elaborated by the therapist. Patel believes that this procedure strengthened the rapport between the patient and the clinician and was important in securing maximum cooperation.

Meichenbaum (1976) outlines an approach for enhancing motivation which emphasizes the role of self-statements and images as covert mediators of involvement in therapy. Procedures intended to foster motivation may be implemented at the earliest "conceptualization" phase of treatment, prior to actual biofeedback training. The therapist, after conducting a careful assessment of the patient, works with the person to arrive at a "common conceptualization" of the problem and the form of treatment. During this process the individual's self-statements and expectations are taken into consideration and the therapist may attempt to modify negative self-statements, unrealistic expectations, and misconceptions regarding the treatment. Evolving a common conceptualization encourages the patient to see himself as an active participant in his own treatment. If the patient is committed to work with the therapist toward mutual goals, more complete participation and diminished resistance may develop.

In addition, the therapist provides the patient with a clear rationale for biofeedback treatment. This may provide a cognitive framework for increased understanding of the potential of the feedback and ancillary procedures to assist him in achieving self-control of the symptom. The ability to envision a positive therapeutic outcome may represent a potent, cognitively based source of motivation (Bandura, 1977).

Dealing with Secondary Gains

When the symptom is strongly reinforced by "secondary gains," and the patient is ambivalent about achieving a positive therapeutic outcome, additional interventions may be necessary. Consider the case where the clinician's initial assessment reveals that the patient's painful muscle contraction headache is used as an excuse for not participating in difficult decisions at work. It may be necessary not only to examine and modify self-statements supporting the tendency to avoid such situations, but to teach the person to cope more effectively in these aversive situations. Surwit (1973) reports on his treatment with a patient suffering from Raynaud's disease who required social skills training during biofeedback therapy because she used her symptoms to rationalize an unsatisfactory social life. In accord with our experience, Shapiro and Surwit (1976) observe that it may be necessary to utilize behavioral treatments "aimed at making up any social deficit left by removal of the symptom [p. 102]." They suggest that when the patient is not aware of the contingencies maintaining the symptom or is not willing to accept the clinician's formulation relating to the benefit derived from the symptom, insight-oriented therapy may be an appropriate strategy. In certain cases it may be necessary to modify the patient's family and social interactions to help the person to derive maximum benefit from biofeedback treatment.

PROBLEMS DURING TRAINING

Shapiro and Surwit (1976) comment on another potential motivational difficulty—the patient may value and engage in behaviors which are incompatable with the goals of therapy. To illustrate this, Shapiro and Surwit (1976) cite an interesting case discussed by Schwartz (1973). During a week of biofeedback training decreases of as much as 20 mm Hg systolic blood pressure were achieved by a patient treated for essential hypertension. However, due to the patient's penchant for gambling at the race track on weekends, his blood pressure rose to pretreatment levels.

Unfortunately, it is not always clear which behaviors will interfere with treatment before biofeedback training; even after therapy is initiated it may be difficult to identify such behaviors where measurement of the physiological response is not available on a continuous basis in extra-training situations (blood pressure, EEG). However, when counter-therapeutic behaviors are identified, the patient may be faced with the decision of whether to "give up" the behavior, or continue to endure the symptom. Factors such as the nature and severity of the disorder, the involvement of the patient in the therapy regimen, as well as the value of the behavior to the individual, will no doubt have bearing on the patient's decision.

Interventions such as systematic desensitization and relaxation techniques may be appropriate adjunct treatments in the case of psychosomatic disorders where the assessment reveals that they are related to identifiable situations or eliciting stimuli (Schwartz & Shapiro, 1973; Shapiro & Surwit, 1976; Sirota, 1976). Relaxation techniques may be particularly useful where it is apparent that anxiety or high levels of muscle tension interferes with the acquisition of biofeedback skills. Practice in active and passive relaxation prior to biofeedback training may enhance biofeedback assisted self-control, although research is certainly needed to confirm this notion.

Psychological problems may also interfere with biofeedback learning. Adler and Adler (1976) utilized psychotherapeutic interventions to enhance biofeedback training. Brief and intensive psychotherapy was provided for patients with psychological problems which included hypomanic defenses, repressed rage, and unresolved grief. Adler and Adler report on 58 patients suffering from migraine, mixed, cluster, and tension headaches treated with EMG and/or temperature feedback. Over three-fourths of the patients required some form of therapeutic intervention. After a 5 year follow-up, success rates ranging from 60% (mixed and cluster headaches) to 88% (tension headaches) were found. Interestingly, Adler and Adler believe that the psychotherapeutic procedures played an important role in the impressive maintenance of gains which were achieved. However, since they failed to include a control group of patients who did not receive psychotherapy, it is impossible to conclude that therapy contributed to the maintenance of gains beyond what would have been found with biofeedback alone.

Motivational Problems during the Biofeedback Session

Motivational difficulties may also arise during the biofeedback session as a result of the patient's reaction to the information indicating success or failure at control of the psychophysiological response. It is important to emphasize that individuals who participate in biofeedback typically do not receive tangible rewards for controlling their physiological response. Task relevant behavior is probably maintained by such factors as the expectancy of symptom relief associated with mastery of physiological control, the clinician's approval at the patient's demonstrations of control, and self-approval generated by success at the task. However, attempts to control a physiological response may prove to be difficult and even frustrating, particularly early in treatment. Bandura (1977) states that: "Successes raise mastery expectations; repeated failures lower them, particularly if the mishaps occur early in the course of events [p. 195]." Stern and Berrenberg (1977) found that successful biofeedback training of frontalis EMG resulted in increased belief in internal personal control. In contrast, early failure at the task may well engender a sense of inability to master the task and create a generalized negative attitude toward treatment. Our experience with clinical biofeedback is consistent with the latter possibility. A patient whom we treated for muscle contraction headaches at Lafayette Clinic commented that he felt "depressed and agitated" after the first session during which he failed to demonstrate an ability to control frontalis EMG. During the next few sessions he reported that he avoided looking at the feedback display in order to "not get the bad news."

Failure to control the target response in a "therapeutic" direction may trigger a kind of vicious circle where self-deprecatory, distracting self-statements give rise to performance decrements which in turn spur a counterproductive internal dialogue. The disruptive effects of such cognitions may be minimized by informing the person that "successful" patients experience a wide range of thoughts and feelings during treatment; if frustration and inability to control the response are experienced, this may be seen as a cue to relax, attend to the feedback, and possibly try a different strategy. Such instructions can be conveyed to the patient either prior to biofeedback training and/or at any time during treatment. Furthermore, if patients are informed that the task may require many sessions to master, initial inability to control the response may more likely be attributed to task difficulty than personal inadequacy.

Although the clinician does not have direct control of the patient's performance-related cognitions, he does have control of the sensitivity of the feedback display. The display can be adjusted so that very small changes in the response in a therapeutic direction may be seen as a change of relatively large magnitude, thereby furthering a sense of task mastery. Alternately, feedback contingencies can be manipulated so that feedback is provided only when the patient is successful. After the individual has achieved some degree of regulatory ability, the feedback criterion can be gradually adjusted so that greater increases in frontalis EMG, for example, are required to produce an equivalent indication of success.

For certain patients attending to the feedback display can prove to be a boring and monotonous task. Surwit (1973), for example, reported that one patient who complained of being bored made no progress. In our own work, we have observed that patients who make similar complaints report that they engage in task irrelevant strategies to maintain their interest such as looking around the room and "playing mental games." To our dismay, several patients have fallen asleep in the quiet, relaxing ambience of the laboratory. Obviously, the feedback display is not always a sufficient stimulus to maintain the patient's concerted attention. Altering the training situation, shortening or providing breaks in the sessions, and/or changing or making the feedback display more interesting may be viable options for the clinician. Providing various reinforcements which differ from the feedback display (i.e., money, social reinforcement, nude slides) may be incorporated into the sessions, although in experimental studies, the evidence for their efficacy in facilitating control is mixed (Blanchard & Epstein, 1978).

PREPARING THE PATIENT FOR TRANSFER

Overlearning the Target Response

One of the goals of the biofeedback therapist is to train the patient in control of the physiological response until it is overlearned so that it can be produced in the absence of feedback. Many training sessions may be required before control of blood pressure, for example, is regular, consistent, and automatic. In the majority of controlled group outcome studies, 6–12 training sessions are used. While the "learning curve" may well have plateaued by this point, sufficient overlearning may not have occurred to train a stable, enduring response. If a response is not overlearned, the ability to control it may be interfered with by competing tasks. For example, the control of peripheral skin temperature may be easily disrupted by attending to stressful stimuli (Boudewyns, 1976).

It is possible that some degree of symptom relief will be reported before the response is overlearned. Since patients are more likely to terminate treatment when their condition improves, it is crucial that treatment continues beyond the point at which initial symptom reduction occurs.

Some evidence suggests a relationship between length of treatment and therapeutic outcome. Blanchard and Epstein (1978) recently reexamined the findings of a study by Weiss and Engel (1971) which reported data on eight patients with premature ventricular contractions. Patients who received 47 or more training sessions made clinical gains, while those who received fewer sessions did not. The same authors reviewed the literature on biofeedback-assisted regulation of blood pressure and concluded that massed practice appears to be more effective than sessions spread over a period of weeks (Benson, Shapiro, Tursky, & Schwartz, 1971; Elder, Ruiz, Deabler, & Dillenkoffer, 1973; Elder & Eustis, 1975; Kristt & Engel, 1975).

However, achieving control of different physiological responses may require unequal amounts of training, and massed practice may not be the most effective training schedule for all disorders and individuals. In a classic study, Basmajian (1972) described how many subjects could develop delicate control of single motor units within short periods of time using auditory and visual feedback. When a person rapidly develops a cognitive or physical strategy for control of a relevant response, additional training may be perceived as a tedious exercise which may diminish patient compliance. For clinical purposes, it is probably sufficient to train the person until control of the response can consistently be manifested without external assistance. However, additional research is needed to determine what effect length of training and massed versus spaced practice has on persistence and transfer of treatment gains with various disorders, response systems, and individuals.

Booster Sessions

Additional biofeedback training may be necessary in cases where therapeutic gains are not maintained. It is crucial for the clinician to know when treatment effects do not endure since certain evidence suggests that booster sessions following treatment may reinstate physiological control. Miller (1972) trained a hypertensive woman in bidirectional blood pressure control to achieve a decrease in diastolic pressure from 97 mm Hg to 76 mm Hg after three months of training. Although she was not able to retain this degree of self-control as a result of emotional stress, Miller (1975) later noted that the woman quickly regained self-regulatory ability with additional laboratory training after a 2½ year training interruption. Schwartz (1972) reported that booster sessions were necessary to maintain treatment gains in a patient suffering from Raynaud's disease who returned for additional treatment after a year and a half. Budzynski (1973) was able to assist a patient in recovering control of tension headaches shortly after the termination of treatment by reinstituting biofeedback training when headaches returned to pretreatment frequency.

It is indeed unfortunate that few studies have included long term follow-ups and assessments in the natural environment. Our understanding of the parameters that mediate gain maintenance may be furthered by carefully examining variables that are associated with both success and failure to maintain therapeutic gains. Although the exact mechanisms that are associated with transfer and gain maintenance have yet to be elucidated, procedures for enhancing self-control by manipulating the feedback the subject receives, do appear promising.

Fading the Feedback

In order to facilitate self-control, it may be necessary first to obtain a robust response, and subsequently, to train individuals under conditions in which feedback is gradually reduced or "faded" (Shapiro & Surwit, 1976). "Fading the feedback" may be one way of furthering the production of the desired response without feedback. After a response has been conditioned under continuous reinforcement, feedback may be progressively reduced to the point where the person is able to demonstrate adequate control both with and without the assistance of feedback. Two studies frequently cited in this context are those by Weiss and Engel (1971) and Hefferline and Bruno (1971). In conditioning discrete EMG responses, Hefferline and Bruno (1971) gradually decreased the audible level of the feedback tone while preserving the desired response. Weiss and Engel (1971) taught patients control of premature ventricular contractions with feedback, which was increasingly interspersed with periods of no feedback. Eight patients initially received bidirectional heart rate feedback which was available at all times. After the patient was able to maintain heart rate control within a specified range, feedback was faded on the following interval schedule: 1 min on, 1 min off; 1 min on, 3 min off; and, finally, 1 min on, and 7 min off. The researchers' objectives and their appraisal of this technique are expressed as follows:

> Our purpose in including this procedure was to wean the patient from the gadget, because the clinical value of the conditioning depended on the subject being able to perform successfully in non-laboratory environments. Apparently, this technique was successful, since the patients report that their ability to perform without feedback is strong evidence to them that they have developed their own intrinsic cues, and that they "know" when their hearts are beating normally and that they "know" how to change the rhythm in either direction [Engel & Bleecker, 1974, p. 472].

It is important to note that five patients who were able to gain laboratory control of their PVCs were also able to sustain treatment gains during follows-ups which varied from 5 to 21 months. In a later report, Engel and Bleecker (1974) note that one patient maintained a low PVC frequency after a 5 year follow-up. Unfortunately, Weiss and Engel (1971) did not include a control group to rule out the possibility of placebo effects. However, it is unlikely that nonspecific factors accounted for their impressive findings since the self-control effects did not dissipate over time. In addition, the ability of patients to control PVCs when monitored on the ward with portable ECG units, and patients' reports of ability to detect and control their arrhythmia at home, suggest the transfer of a specific treatment effect. However, the investigators failed to include a control group in which patients did not receive a fading procedure; therefore it is impossible to determine whether this procedure played a unique role in producing self-control.

The length of time prior to fading the feedback may vary with the nature of the disorder and the ease with which feedback assisted control can be established. Blanchard and Epstein (1978) suggest that for persons who develop a self-control strategy in a short period of time, it may not be necessary to reduce the feedback on a gradual basis. When reliable control can be maintained in the absence of feedback, the feedback can be withdrawn abruptly. A few basic research studies have explored the use of different reinforcement schedules with autonomic responses (Greene, 1966; Shapiro & Crider, 1967; Shapiro & Watanabe, 1971), but additional research is necessary to establish that partial reinforcement increases resistance to extinction in the control of autonomic responses (Shapiro, Mainardi, & Surwit, 1977). It will be important to ascertain under what conditions fading the feedback contributes to gain maintenance above and beyond continuous feedback, what schedules of reinforcement produce optimal effects, and when in the course of the training to initiate fading procedures.

Stimulus Control Procedures

Blanchard, Haynes, Young, & Scott (1977) describe an approach to facilitate transfer of training that is based on a stimulus control paradigm where control initially is associated with biofeedback, but eventually brought under voluntary control by the person. Their approach will be detailed in that it represents an adaptation of stimulus control procedures to physiological self-regulation. The strategy in Blanchard *et al.* involves a three step procedure aimed at producing large magnitude heart rate increases in an extralaboratory situation.

Eight normal subjects were trained to bring heart rate acceleration under stimulus control; this involves the production of the desired response when the appropriate stimulus (SD) is presented. Subjects were asked to increase their heart rates by "purely mental means," when signalled by a light. Another light (SΔ) served as a signal to the subject to rest and not try to change his heart rate. Subjects were assisted by visual heart rate feedback if stimulus control of heart rate acceleration was not achieved.

The goal of the second, self-control phase, was to transfer control of the SD onset and offset from the experimentally manipulated external stimulus to a self-instruction generated by the subject. Subjects were instructed to control the time points at which they attempted to increase their heart rates (SD) or rested (SΔ). They were asked to inform the experimenter, over an intercom, when they were increasing their heart rate by saying "raise" or "rest" when they were not attempting to change their heart rate.

Finally, in the generalization phase of the study, subjects were instructed to attempt to increase their heart rates in a room outside the laboratory with their heart rates monitored via telemetry. Subjects informed the experimenters over a telephone when they were attempting to raise their heart rates or resting. Four of the six subjects who completed the experiment were able to demonstrate increases in heart rate of from 15–35 beats per minute without the assistance of feedback and outside of the laboratory. While conditioned heart rate acceleration is probably of little clinical value, this study represents the beginning of a necessary line of research designed to systematically test methods for promoting generalization of biofeedback training outside the laboratory.

It is important to note that a recent study by Elder, Welsh, Longacre, and McAfee (1977) showed that discriminative control of a clinically relevant response, blood pressure, can be achieved with normotensive subjects. Initially, subjects received feedback for bidirectional control of blood pressure. When room illumination was bright, they were instructed to try and raise their pressure; when room illumination was dim, they were instructed to try to lower their pressure. All subjects in one of the experimental groups which received continuous blood pressure feedback were able to increase and decrease blood pressure by 10–15% of basal value. In addition, during sessions in which feedback was not presented but room illumination was varied, control was maintained even after the external feedback signal was no longer available. Although only 14 of the 24 subjects were available for follow up tests, bidirectional control was maintained 3 weeks after training. Replication of this study with hypertensives is surely warranted; it would be important to see whether self-control can be fostered by procedures suggested by Blanchard et al. (1977) and Elder et al. (1977), and whether such control can be reliably maintained.

Training under Stressful or Stimulating Conditions

Given that many psychosomatic disorders are precipitated by stress, and that the patient's life environment is probably more stressful than and certainly different from the biofeedback laboratory, it would seem logical to attempt to train the patient in self-control procedures under "real-life" or stressful conditions. A number of studies suggest that autonomic responses can indeed, be conditioned in stressful, atypical training conditions. In a study of heart rate control in normals, Goldstein, Ross, and Brady (1977) trained eight experimental subjects to lower their heart rates with beat-to-beat feedback while walking on a treadmill. After five weekly 5-min sessions, these subjects had significantly lower mean heart rates and systolic blood pressures than control subjects who walked on a treadmill but did not receive feedback. These differences were maintained after feedback was withdrawn for 5 more weeks. Shapiro (1977) was able to show that subjects who received bio-feedback training for heart rate (increase and decrease) were able to demonstrate the same changes even when exposed to cold pressor stimu-lation. After training, subjects who learned to reliably increase their heart rates when exposed to cold pressor stimulation, showed average increases in heart rate three times as high as shown during pretraining exposure to the cold-pressor task. Subjects trained to decrease their heart rates also showed lowered heart rates during the cold-pressor posttest, as compared with a habituation control. However, the changes in these sub-jects did not differ significantly from those found in a group given in-structions to lower heart rate without feedback. In summarizing these results Shapiro (1976) states, "In some respects, learned control of visceral activity appears to be of a greater magnitude in situations placing a "demand" on subjects, that is, under conditions of stressful or aversive stimulation, than under mild non-stimulating, non-demanding conditions typically employed in biofeedback research studies [p. 319]."

A number of examples may be drawn from clinical reports. In the treatment of neuromuscular disorders, patients have been trained under a variety of conditions. For example, of 48 spasmodic torticollis patients treated by Brudny, Korein, Grynbaum, Friedman, Weinstein, Sachs-Frankel, and Belandres (1976), 27 showed significant improvement de-termined by direct observation as well as family interviews. Nineteen of these patients maintained their gains at follow-ups ranging from 3 months to 3 years. Patients were given biofeedback training "under conditions of. mental stress, standing, or walking, as well as the usual comfortable sitting position." Taub (1977) was able to train three nor-mal subjects to control the skin temperature of one hand in a 55° F room. One Raynaud's disease patient was able to regulate hand tempera-ture while wearing a 60° F water cooled suit.

Although these studies are certainly of interest, it has not been es-tablished that training in stressful or real-life situations does, in fact, increase resistance to stress or transfer of control beyond training in nondemanding environments. Controlled studies in which training con-ditions are systematically manipulated and transfer and gain maintenance are assessed are necessary to evaluate the efficacy of training the patient in stressful situations. It would also be worthy to explore whether intro-ducing various stressors, distractors, and stimuli to vary the training en-vironment early in treatment is more effective than altering the situation after self-control has been established. Although we have cited several studies that suggest that elements of the situation can be manipulated early in training, when competing stimuli may interfere with response acquisition it may be best to alter the setting after self-control has been achieved.

If the person cannot demonstrate biofeedback assisted regulation of the response in a mildly stimulating environment, it may first be necessary to establish reliable control in a nondemanding situation. One possibility is to introduce stressors on a gradual basis. For example, in our laboratory at the Lafayette Clinic, we are currently training patients with Raynaud's disease to control their skin temperature while wearing thermoelectric modules which are gradually made cooler. The patient must first maintain acceptable control at a criterion temperature before being required to attempt biofeedback assisted control at a lower temperature. This approach is in many ways analogous to systematic desensitization, in which a relaxation response is conditioned during the gradual introduction of a stressful object or fantasy. One measure of therapeutic effectiveness is the lowest temperature at which the patient can maintain control when the feedback is no longer present. The degree of transfer and gain maintenance with patients who undergo this experimental procedure will be compared with a group of Raynaud's patients who participate in conventional, peripheral skin-temperature biofeedback treatment.

Another procedure for increasing the patient's resistance to extinction in the presence of stressors involves fading the feedback when the subject is exposed to stressful stimulation. The patient's relevant physiological response could be continuously monitored; feedback could be faded on a time contingent or a response contingent basis. If control begins to falter in the presence of the stressor, biofeedback could be resumed on a continuous basis and again faded after an acceptable degree of self-regulation is demonstrated. This procedure could be continued until the feedback can be completely withdrawn with no measurable decrease in control of the response.

Other Transfer Strategies

There is considerable evidence that when behavior is learned in the presence of a narrow range of stimuli, it may not transfer (Stokes & Baer, 1977). It may be desirable to employ more than one therapist to increase the range of stimuli to which the patient is exposed in the training situation. The ability of the person to achieve control in the clinic with multiple therapists might increase the likelihood of transfer to the natural environment where control of the response must obviously be maintained in the presence of various individuals. Again, there are empirical questions regarding at what point in the training to introduce the transfer procedure: Would gains be maximized if the second therapist were introduced at the beginning of treatment, after a relationship was established with the first therapist and the patient was engaged in treatment, or after the person is able to show control without external assistance?

Similarly, varying the physical setting of the biofeedback treatment may promote transfer outside the laboratory. The above mentioned experiment of Blanchard et al. (1977) utilized telemetry to monitor self-control of heart rate outside the laboratory. With techniques of bio-telemetry it should be possible to monitor physiological responses in different settings and provide feedback in different physical settings. The Raynaud's disease patient, for example, can be monitored outdoors in cold weather. If peripheral skin temperature fell below a predetermined criterion level, the patient could be signalled to use whatever self-control strategies were successful in the laboratory. Alternately, actual biofeedback could be administered outdoors, assuming, of course, that the person was in close proximity to the laboratory.

An obvious extension of this procedure would be to utilize inexpensive, portable biofeedback devices to train the person at home and in the naturalistic environment. Home training offers advantages of convenience and economy to the patient, who can be sent home with a machine after being thoroughly instructed in its use. He could return to the therapist every few weeks for a laboratory training session, discussion of problems and progress, and technical check of his machine. Surwit et al. (1977) has reported home and laboratory training to be equally effective in the treatment of Raynaud's disease. Sterman (personal communication) reports that portable EEG biofeedback devices specially designed for sensorimotor rhythm are useful, if not necessary, for the lengthy training involved in the treatment of epilepsy. Solbers and Rugh (1972) developed a portable EMG feedback unit that could be used in the treatment of bruxism to signal patients when levels of masseter muscle tension were excessively high.

A simple but useful temperature feedback device that can be worn continuously was described by Surwit et al. (1977). In addition to electronic feedback units, a group of their patients was given temperature sensitive liquid crystal strips to be worn on their hands during waking hours. These strips, which change color with temperature, are inexpensive and provide an unobtrusive method of monitoring skin temperature. Of course the simplest "feedback devices" for monitoring skin temperature is one's own sensorium. We are all familiar with the mottled red appearance of warm hands as well as physical sensations of warmth.

Ultimately, where possible, all biofeedback patients should be trained to develop their own techniques of physiological self-awareness.

Laboratory biofeedback programs can also incorporate practice of various relaxation techniques at home and in different situations. Progressive relaxation, autogenic training, and meditation are examples of some approaches that can be "brought home" with the patient. Surwit *et al.* (1977) instructed subjects with Raynaud's disease to practice warming their hands with autogenic exercises for brief periods 30 times a day using gold stars as reminders. In a study of hypertensive patients conducted by Patel and North (1975), each patient was provided with a red disk to attach to his watch to remind him to relax whenever he looked to see what time it was. In addition, patients were instructed to relax in the following situations: before answering a telephone, before an interview, examination, public speaking engagement, during a flight, when meeting strangers, waiting in a dentist's or doctor's office, and during any other stressful situations. Patients can be instructed to practice relaxation at home at regular times; suggestions for relaxation and autogenic training can also be recorded on cassette tape.

Utilizing a Self-Control Strategy

In order for a person to consistently influence the response associated with his problem or disorder outside the training situation, it is no doubt helpful to learn a strategy of self-control. The strategy may be defined as "what the patient or subject actually is doing to reliably influence the problem response [Blanchard & Epstein, 1978, p. 171]." Budzynski (1973) has stated that one way of helping the person to develop a strategy for controlling the response is by encouraging him to verbalize sensations as well as successful and unsuccessful means of manipulating the feedback. In our own clinical work we have observed patients alternately "try out" and discard various strategies before ultimately adopting one associated with reliable control of the response. Although some patients are able to develop a well articulated strategy which they can report to the therapist, many are not able to specify exactly how they were able to manipulate the response. However, what is important is that the patient learns a strategy that is consistently associated with the production of the desired response. In many biofeedback treatment studies, subjects are instructed to practice at home the techniques which have been learned in the laboratory (Budzynski *et al.*, 1970; Budzynski *et al.*, 1973; Chesney & Shelton, 1976; Hutchings & Reinkung, 1976; Surwit *et al.*, 1977).

Meichenbaum (1976) suggests a number of behavioral procedures to assist the patient in utilizing strategies learned in the laboratory in situations which precipitate the symptom. For example, during biofeedback training, the patient can be instructed not only to imagine situations where the symptom (tension headache) is experienced, but also to visualize noticing the onset of tension and invoking the strategy learned in the laboratory. In addition to imagery rehearsal techniques, the therapist and patient can role-play stressful situations: The therapist can model how to identify the onset of tension and how to employ the strategy the patient has developed. Meichenbaum (1976) contends that the most effective means of teaching coping responses is by means of modeling films. He states, "Imagine being able to show your biofeedback clients a modeling film of other patients who have undergone biofeedback treatment. In the film, a client (i.e., a trained confederate who is role-playing as client) describes to the therapist how he successfully employed the coping procedures in handling various situations: recognizing the onset of symptoms (e.g., headache) and how this was a cue to cope [p. 62]."

A Self-Management Approach

Blanchard and Epstein (1978) have proposed a biofeedback "technology of self-management." Self-management emphasizes the potential of the person to ultimately manipulate the events that influence behavior. Blanchard and Epstein's approach is significant in that it represents an adaptation of self-management techniques to physiological responses. The components of the self-management approach which Blanchard and Epstein emphasize are self-monitoring of the physiological response, or symptom, learning when to implement self-control strategies developed during biofeedback training, and self-reinforcement to maintain the practice of self-control.

Initially, the subject is taught how to observe and monitor the occurrence of the maladaptive response or symptom. Data collected by the patient can be used to evaluate the effects of the procedure. In addition, it is important for the patient to be sensitized to when and where the response occurs so that self-control strategies can be employed at the appropriate times. As we have indicated earlier, detection of the maladaptive response is usually not problematic, particularly with phasic disorders, such as tension headaches. However, with chronic problems such as hypertension, discrimination can pose difficulties. Blanchard and Epstein (1978) note that additional procedures may be necessary to assist patients to discriminate responses such as changes in blood pressure. The authors propose a procedure to train patients to detect variations in their blood pressure. First, it is necessary to obtain accurate measures of blood pressure at several time points during each day for at least a week to establish a reliable baseline for the patient's pressure. The midpoint of the readings could be determined and pressures greater than the mean would be defined as an increase, while pressures less than the mean would be defined as a decrease. The patient's blood pressure could then be monitored and he could be instructed to attempt to ascertain whether pressure levels are higher or lower than the mean. Here, feedback is the accuracy of discriminating variations in pressure. Social praise is suggested as a reinforcer for correct discriminations. Although this procedure has not yet been put to an empirical test, Epstein, Cinciripini, McCoy, and Marshall (1977) used a similar methodology to successfully train subjects to increase their ability to discriminate variations in heart rate. After the person can reliably demonstrate self-control, can detect the response and learns when to implement self-control strategies, the therapist can turn his attention to insuring that the patient continues to practice it in daily life.

In order to maintain regular practice after termination of treatment, it may be essential to not only use some of the procedures to enhance motivation which we have previously discussed, but also to present a reinforcer after the self-control strategy is implemented. Shapiro and Surwit (1976) believe that it may be necessary to insure that the self-control response is controlled, in part, by social contingencies. Family members and other significant people in the patient's life can be involved in the treatment program, they can verbally reward the patient for practicing self-control or conforming to the demands of the therapy regimine. One interesting suggestion is that "groups of hypertensive patients could meet regularly, as do Weight Watchers, publically recording their pressure and exposing themselves to the social consequences [p. 108]." Blanchard and Epstein (1978) believe that ultimately, reinforcers can, for the most part, be self-administered so that the patient is not dependent upon external reinforcers. For example, jogging, watching a movie, reading a novel or some other valued activity can be made contingent upon completing a self-control strategy. Of course, if self-management strategies are not sufficient to promote enduring self-control, biofeedback or other forms of external support could be reinstituted.

CONCLUSION

Thus far, we have emphasized the complexity of the disorders often treated with biofeedback and the necessity for thorough and continuing evaluation procedures. Depending on the patient, it may first be desirable to employ psychotherapy to help him engage in a treatment aimed at removing an overdetermined symptom. Then it will be necessary to teach self-regulation of the desired physiological system to the extent that the learned response is replicable without the use of external machinery and in the conditions of everyday life. We have reviewed a number of procedures which might facilitate the generalization of self-regulation to extralaboratory situations: manipulating reinforcement schedules, varying the trainer and setting, training under stress, and *in vivo* techniques. It is not yet known when to employ these procedures, the sequence in which to use them, with whom they will work best, or the length of time necessary to teach them. Clearly, a great deal of research is needed in which the use of generalization regimens is systematically manipulated with patients and normals and the outcomes carefully assessed over time.

Research thus far suggests that biofeedback is most effective in the treatment of disorders in which the response to be modified is easily observed, such as muscle paralysis, stuttering, or premature ventricular contractions. In 1976, Brudny *et al.* reported on 39 hemiparetics whose impaired upper extremities were treated with EMG biofeedback. Twenty of the patients made significant functional gains which were maintained at follow-ups ranging from 3 months to 3 years. In the only controlled group outcome study of muscle retraining Basmajian, Kukula, Narayan, and Takebe (1975) compared the effects of EMG feedback plus physiotherapy with those of physiotherapy alone in cases of dorsiflexion paralysis following stroke. Increases in muscle strength and range of motion in the biofeedback group were almost twice as great as those of the physiotherapy group. Four of the patients in the biofeedback group were able to achieve a more normal gait pattern by consciously controlling dorsiflexion and three were able to walk without short leg braces. All maintained their gains after a 1–4 month follow-up period.

These studies are important because they demonstrate that clinically significant improvements made during biofeedback treatment can be maintained outside the laboratory and over periods of time. In comparison to work in other areas, such as hypertension and tension headaches, biofeedback treatment of neuromuscular disorders has produced more impressive results. A number of factors inherent in the nature of these disorders may account for some of the differences in treatment outcome. For example, the neuromuscular disorder is generally present 24 hours a day, both inside and outside the laboratory. Its effects are usually readily observable without the use of external instrumentation. As opposed to tension headaches, which may occur with varying frequency and very rarely in the laboratory, the neuromuscular problem is always available "to be worked on." Baseline measurements tend to be relatively easily obtained and the patient can literally see his daily progress. The fact that neuromuscular disorders often have a clear physiological correlate (EMG activity) which is generally under voluntary control in normals, no doubt facilitates treatment with biofeedback. Tension headaches, on the other hand, may not be consistently related to abnormal EMG or other physiological activity (Cox et al., 1975).

Furthermore, regulation of muscle activity may simply be an easier task to learn than control of blood pressure, for example. Sophisticated control of single motor units has been demonstrated, in various muscle groups (Wagman, Pierce, & Burger, 1965), in children (Fruhling, Basmajian, & Simard; 1969), while engaged in other tasks (Simard, 1969; Basmajian & Simard, 1967), across different physical environments (Lloyd & Shurley, 1976) and over time (Lloyd & Leibrecht, 1971). These studies have generally required only a single brief training session to produce the desired response.

Thus certain conditioned EMG responses may be robust enough to be reproducible without the continued use of external monitors and in the face of the stresses and distractions of daily life. This notion is supported by work in the treatment of stuttering, which presumably involves a different type of regulation of EMG activity. Guitar (1975) demonstrated decreases in frequencies of stuttered words associated with conditioned reductions of EMG activity in the chin, lip, and larynx. Lanyon, Barrington, and Newman (1976) found similar results using feedback of masseter muscle activity. Like muscle paralysis, stuttering is a disorder which is generally present, is readily observable, and has a clear physiological indicator.

Similarly, premature ventricular contractions may occur frequently and are physically detectable by patients. Previously cited work in this area (Engel & Bleecker, 1974; Weiss & Engel, 1971) suggests that patients trained in heart rate control have maintained decreased PVC frequencies for periods of up to 5 years.

In contrast to the above research, work on blood pressure biofeedback has been less encouraging. Patients in one study (Benson et al., 1971) show average changes in systolic blood pressure of only 5 mm within each of 12–34 training sessions. In another study (Surwit & Shapiro, 1976), 24 hypertensive patients produced virtually no blood pressure decreases using either blood pressure or EMG biofeedback or a relaxation meditation procedures. However, Patel (1977), using combined training in relaxation and meditation, EMG and GSR biofeedback, and educational talks has demonstrated lasting and significant pressure decreases (28 mm Hg systolic, 16 mm Hg diastolic) with 12 biweekly training sessions. These results suggest that "indirect" procedures may well be more effective in the treatment of hypertension than direct blood pressure biofeedback. This is supported by a recent review of relaxation therapy in the treatment of hypertension which found a mean reduction of 26/16 mm Hg given a baseline pressure of 170/105 mm Hg (Jacob et al., 1977).

Of course the mechanisms by which biofeedback relaxation training, or treatment "packages" such as Patel's affect complex psychosomatic disorders like hypertension are virtually unknown. Shapiro and Surwit (1976) have suggested a few of the numerous possibilities:

> For example, relaxation techniques acting on the muscles could have their main effect on the vasculature, producing a decrease in peripheral resistance. Yogic exercises emphasizing breath control might have their main effect on cardiac output by changing intraventricular pressure.... Verbal instruction acting on the cortex might also ... affect blood pressure [p. 109].

Many of the problems often treated with biofeedback are similarly complex, as is biofeedback treatment itself. It should be clear from the literature we have reviewed that successful biofeedback treatment involves more than training a target physiological response for a given disorder with the hope that it will generalize across time and environment. Work on insomnia (Freedman & Papsdorf, 1976), tension headaches (Cox et al., 1975), and hypertension (Blanchard & Miller, 1977) suggests that continued daily practice of self-regulation will be necessary to maintain whatever benefits are derived from biofeedback training. Patients who lose the ability to self-regulate may profit from returning to the laboratory for booster (retraining) sessions. As in any self-management procedures, some patients will not be willing to expend the time, energy, and money required for a full course of biofeedback treatment. This program would probably include several hours of pretreatment evaluation, a period of home self-monitoring, laboratory training of at least 12 sessions, daily home practice, a posttreatment evaluation and periodic follow-up sessions. The nature and variety of generalization techniques employed could considerably lengthen the process as could the necessity for psychotherapy or other ancillary procedures. Clearly the types of generalization and other procedures employed with each patient will have to be individually tailored to produce optimal clinical results. Disorders having clear environmental or emotional precipitants may be best treated with biofeedback training in the face of these stressors. The addition of "mental" techniques, such as cognitive stress management, may also promote generalization of treatment effects in these cases. Regardless of the plan arrived at, the patient should be fully aware of the entire process before beginning treatment. Therapists might consider the use of therapeutic contracts whereby the patient agrees ahead of time that he will complete the full treatment regimen.

Certainly, some patients will choose alternatives to biofeedback such as medication, surgery, or no treatment. A tension headache patient maintained on a low dose of a muscle relaxant may well choose to continue this course of treatment despite side effects such as drowsiness, or sleep disturbance. In the case of Raynaud's disease, however, self-regulation might be the treatment of choice since procedures such as surgery (sympathectomies), or medication (oral reserpine) are generally ineffective.

As in all other treatments, the efficacy of biofeedback will be evaluated relative to the available alternatives. Much research is needed to determine optimal programs for different types of patients suffering from different disorders. Perhaps lengthy generalization procedures will not be necessary for certain persons. However, it is clear that the biofeedback patient must be actively engaged in his treatment process as opposed to being passively cured by a machine.

REFERENCES

Adler, C. S., & Adler, S. M. The pragmatic application of biofeedback to headaches—a five year clinical follow-up. *Biofeedback and Self-Regulation*, 1976, *1*, 346–347.

Bandura, A. Self-efficacy: Toward a unifying theory of behavioral change. *Psychological Review*, 1977, *84*, 191–215.

Basmajian, J. V. Control and training of individual motor units. *Science*, 1963, *20*, 662–664.

Basmajian, J. V. Electromyography comes of age. *Science*, 1972, *176*, 603–609.

Basmajian, J. V., Kukula, C. G., Narayan, M. G., & Takebe, K. Biofeedback treatment of foot-drop after stroke compared with standard rehabilitation techniques: Effect on voluntary control and strength. *Archives of Physical Medicine and Rehabilitation*, 1975, *56*, 231–236.

Basmajian, J. V., & Simard, T. G. Effects of distracting movements on the control of trained motor units. *American Journal of Physical Medicine*, 1967, *46*, 1427–1449.

Beatty, J. Effects of initial alpha wave abundance and operant training procedures on occipital alpha and beta wave activity. *Psychonomic Science*, 1971, *23*, 197–199.

Benson, H., Beary, J. F., & Carol, M. P. The relaxation response. *Psychiatry*, 1974, *37*, 37–46.

Benson, H., Shapiro, D., Tursky, B., & Schwartz, G. E. Decreased systolic pressure through operant conditioning techniques in patients with essential hypertension. *Science*, 1971, *173*, 740–742.

Birk, L. Biofeedback-furor therapeutics. *Seminars in Psychiatry*, 1973, *5*, 361–364.

Black, A. H., Cott, A., & Pavloski, A. The operant learning theory approach to biofeedback. In G. E. Schwartz & J. Beatty (Eds.), *Biofeedback theory and research*. New York: Academic Press, 1977.

Blaine, A., Coller, F., & Carver, G. Raynaud's disease: A study of criteria for prognosis. *Surgery*, 1951, *29*, 387–396.

Blanchard, E. B., & Epstein, L. H. *A biofeedback primer*. Reading, Massachusetts: Addison-Wesley, 1978.

Blanchard, E. B., Haynes, M. R., Young, L. D., & Scott, R. W. The use of feedback training and a stimulus control procedure to obtain large magnitude increases in heart rate outside of the laboratory. *Biofeedback and Self-Regulation*, 1977, *1*, 81–92.

Blanchard, E. B., & Miller, S. T. Psychological treatment of cardiovascular disease. *Archives of General Psychiatry*, 1977, *34*, 1402–1413.

Blanchard, E. B., & Young, L. D. Self-control of cardiac functioning: A promise as yet unfulfilled. *Psychological Bulletin*, 1973, *79*, 145–163.

Blanchard, E. B., Theobald, D. E., Williamson, D. A., Silver, B. V., & Brown, D. A. Temperature biofeedback in the treatment of migraine headaches. *Archives of General Psychiatry*, 1978, *35*, 581–588.

Boudewyns, P. A. A comparison of the effects of stress vs. relaxation on the finger temperature response. *Behavior Therapy*, 1976, *7*, 54–67.

Brady, J. P., Luborsky, L., & Kron, R. E. Blood pressure reduction in patients with essential hypertension through metronome-conditioned relaxation: A preliminary report. *Behavior Therapy*, 1974, *5*, 203–209.

Brener, J. A general model of voluntary control applied to the phenomena of learned cardiovascular change. In P. A. Obrist (Ed.), *Cardiovascular psychophysiology*. Chicago: Aldine, 1974.

Brudny, J. B. B., Korein, L., Grynbaum, L. W., Friedman, S., Weinstein, G., Sachs-Frankel, G., & Belandres, P. V. EMG feedback therapy: Review of treatment of 114 patients. *Archives of Physical and Medical Rehabilitation*, 1976, *57*, 55–61.

Budzynski, T. H. Biofeedback procedures in the clinic. *Seminars in Psychiatry*, 1973, *5*, 537–547.

Budzynski, T. H. Clinical implications of electromyographic training. In G. E. Schwartz & J. Beatty (Eds.), *Biofeedback theory and research*. New York: Academic Press, 1977.

Budzynski, T., Stoyva, J., & Adler, C. Feedback induced muscle relaxation: application to tension headache. *Journal of Behavior Therapy and Experimental Psychiatry*, 1970, *1*, 205–211.

Budzynski, T. H., Stoyva, J. M., Adler, C., & Mullaney, D. J. EMG biofeedback and tension headache: A controlled outcome study. *Psychosomatic Medicine*, 1973, *35*, 484–496.

Chesney, M. A., & Shelton, J. L. A comparison of muscle relaxation and electromyogram biofeedback treatments for muscle contraction headaches. *Journal of Behavior Therapy and Experimental Psychiatry*, 1976, *7*, 221–225.

Cox, D. J., Freundlich, A., & Meyer, R. G. Differential effectiveness of electromyngraphic feedback, verbal relaxation instructions, and medication placebo with tension headaches. *Journal of Consulting and Clinical Psychology*, 1975, *43*, 892–899.

Datey, K. K., Deshmukh, S. N., Dalvi, C. P., & Vinekar, S. L. "Shavasan": A yogic exercise in the management of hypertension. *Angiology*, 1969, *20*, 325–333.

Deabler, H. L., Fidel, E., & Dillenkoffer, R. L. The use of relaxation and hypnosis in lowering blood pressure. *American Journal of Clinical Hypnosis*, 1973, *16*, 75–83.

Elder, S. T., & Eustis, N. K. Instrumental blood pressure conditioning in out patient hypertensives. *Behavior Research and Therapy*, 1975, *13*, 185–188.

Elder, S. T., Ruiz, H. L., Deabler, R. L., & Dillenkoffer, R. L. Instrumental conditioning of diastolic blood pressure in essential hypertensive patients. *Journal of Applied Behavioral Analysis*, 1973, *6*, 377–382.

Elder, S. T., Welsh, D. M., Longacre, A., & McAfee, R. Acquisition, discriminative stimulus control, and retention of increases/decreases in blood pressure of normotensive human subjects. *Journal of Applied Behavioral Analysis*, 1977, *10*, 381–390.

Engel, B. T., & Bleecker, E. R. Application of operant conditioning techniques to the control of cardiac arrhythmias. In P. Obrist, A. H. Black, & J. Brener (Eds.), *Cardiovascular psychophysiology*. Chicago: Aldine, 1974.

Engel, B. T., & Chism, R. A. Operant conditioning of heart rate speeding. *Psychophysiology*, 1967, *3*, 176–187.

Epstein, L. H., & Abel, G. G. Analysis of biofeedback training effects for tension headache patients. *Behavior Therapy*, 1977, *8*, 37–47.

Epstein, L. H., & Blanchard, E. B. Biofeedback, self-control, and self-management. *Biofeedback and Self-Regulation*, 1977, *2*, 201–212.

Epstein, L. H., Cinciripini, P. N., McCoy, J. F., & Marshall, W. R. Heart rate as a discriminative stimulus. *Psychophysiology*, 1977, *14*, 143–149.

Freedman, R., & Papsdorf, J. D. Biofeedback and progressive relaxation of sleep-onset insomnia: A controlled, all night investigation. *Biofeedback and Self-Regulation*, 1976, *3*, 253–272.

Fruhling, M., Basmajian, J. V., & Simard, T. G. A note on the conscious controls of motor units by children under six. *Journal of Motor Behavior*, 1969, *1*, 65–68.

Gaarder, K., & Sherman, R. *Clinical closure on effective methods of training essential hypertension*. Paper presented at the annual meeting of the Biofeedback Research Society, Orlando, Florida, 1977.

Goldstein, D. S., Ross, R. S., & Brady, J. V. Biofeedback heart rate training during exercise. *Biofeedback and Self-Regulation*, 1977, *2*, 107–126.

Greene, W. A. Operant conditioning of the GSR using partial reinforcement. *Psychological Reports*, 1966, *19*, 571–578.

Guitar, B. Reduction of stuttering frequency using analogue electromyographic feedback. *Journal of Speech and Hearing Research*, 1975, *18*, 672–685.

Haynes, S. N., Griffen, P., Mooney, D., & Parise, M. Electromyographic biofeedback and relaxation instructions in the treatment of muscle contraction headaches. *Behavior Therapy*, 1975, *6*, 672–678.

Hefferline, R. F., & Bruno, L. J. J. The psychophysiology of private events. In A. Jacobs & L. B. Sachs (Eds.), *The psychology of private events*. New York: Academic Press, 1971.

Holroyd, K., Andrasik, F., & Westbrook, T. Cognitive control of tension headache. *Cognitive Therapy and Research*, 1977, *1*, 121–133.

Hutchings, D. F., & Reinkung, R. H. Tension headaches: What form of therapy is most effective? *Biofeedback and Self-Regulation*, 1976, *2*, 183–190.

Inglis, J., Campbell, D., & Donald, M. W. Electromyographic biofeedback and neuromuscular rehabilitation. *Canadian Journal of Behavioral Science*, 1976, *8*, 299–323.

Jacobs, R. G., Kraemer, H. C., & Agras, W. S. Relaxation therapy in the treatment of hypertension. *Archives of General Psychiatry,* 1977, *34,* 1417–1427.

Jacobs, A., & Felton, G. S. Visual feedback of myoelectric output to facilitate muscle relaxation in normal persons and patients with neck injuries. *Archives of Physical Medicine and Rehabilitation,* 1969, *50,* 34–39.

Jacobson, A. M., Hackett, T. P., Surman, O. S., & Silverberg, E. L. Raynaud phenomenon: Treatment with hypnotic and operant techniques. *Journal of the American Medical Association,* 1973, *225,* 739–740.

Kaplan, H. S. *The new sex therapy.* New York: Brunner/Mazel, 1974.

Katkin, E. S., & Murray, E. N. Instrumental conditioning of autonomically mediated behavior: Theoretical and methodological issues. *Psychological Bulletin,* 1968, *70,* 52–68.

Kleinman, K. M., Goldman, H., Snow, M. Y., & Korol, B. *Effects of stress and motivation on effectiveness of biofeedback training in essential hypertensives.* Paper presented at the annual meeting of the Biofeedback Research Society, Colorado Springs, 1976.

Kristt, D. A., & Engel, B. T. Learned control of blood pressure in patients with high blood pressure. *Circulation,* 1975, *51,* 370–378.

Lanyon, R. I., Barrington, C. C., & Newman, A. C. Modification of stuttering through EMG biofeedback: A preliminary study. *Behavior Therapy,* 1976, *7,* 96–103.

Leeb, C., Fahrion, S., & French, D. Instructional set, deep relaxation, and growth enhancement: A pilot study. *Journal of Humanistic Psychology,* 1976, *16,* 71–78.

Legewie, H. Clinical implications of biofeedback. In J. Beatty (Ed.), *Biofeedback and behavior: A NATO symposium.* New York: Plenum, 1977.

Lloyd, A. J., & Liebrecht, B. C. Conditioning of a single motor unit. *Journal of Experimental Psychology,* 1971, *89,* 391–395.

Lloyd, A. J., & Shurley, T. J. The effects of sensory perceptual isolation on single motor unit conditioning. *Psychophysiology,* 1976, *13,* 340–344.

Luthe, W. Autogenic training: Method, research and application in medicine. *American Journal of Psychotherapy,* 1963, *17,* 174–195.

Masters, W. H., & Johnson, V. E. *Human sexual inadequacy.* Boston: Little, Brown, 1970.

Meichenbaum, D. Cognitive factors in biofeedback therapy. *Biofeedback and Self-Regulation,* 1976, *1,* 201–216.

Miller, N. E. Learning of visceral and glandular responses. *Science,* 1969, *163,* 434–445.

Miller, N. E. Postscript. In D. Singh & C. T. Morgan (Eds.), *Current status of physiological psychology: Readings.* Monterey, California: Brooks/Cole, 1972.

Miller, N. E. Applications of learning and biofeedback to psychiatry and medicine. In A. M. Freedman, H. J. Kaplan, & B. J. Sadock (Eds.), *Comprehensive Textbook of Psychiatry II.* Baltimore: Williams & Wilkins, 1975.

Miller, N. E., & Dworkin, B. R. Critical issues in therapeutic applications of biofeedback. In G. E. Schwartz & J. Beatty (Eds.), *Biofeedback theory and research.* New York: Academic Press, 1977.

Mitchell, K. R., & White, R. G. Behavioral self-management: An application to the problem of migraine headaches. *Behavior Therapy,* 1977, *8,* 213–221.

Patel, C. H. Biofeedback-aided relaxation and meditation in the management of hypertension. *Biofeedback and Self-Regulation,* 1977, *2,* 1–42.

Patel, C. H., & North, W. R. S. Randomized controlled trials of yoga and biofeedback in the management of hypertension. *Lancet*, 1975, *2*, 93–95.

Pickering, T., & Gorham, G. Learned heart-rate controlled by a patient with a ventricular parasystolic rhythm. *Lancet*, 1975, *1*, 252–253.

Pickering, T. G., & Miller, N. E. Learned voluntary control of heart rate and rhythm in two subjects with premature ventricular contractions. *British Heart Journal*, 1977, *39*, 152–159.

Rechtshoffen, A. Polygraphic aspects of insomnia. In H. Gasteaut, E. Lugaresi, G. Berti-Ceroni, & C. Coccagna (Eds.), *The abnormalities of sleep in man.* Bologna: Aulo Goggi Editore, 1968.

Rosen, R. C. Operant control of sexual responses in man. In G. E. Schwartz & J. Beatty (Eds.), *Biofeedback theory and research.* New York: Academic Press, 1977.

Schwartz, G. E. Voluntary control of human cardiovascular integration in man through operant conditioning. *Science*, 1972, *175*, 90–93.

Schwartz, G. E. Biofeedback as therapy: Some theoretical and practical issues. *American Psychologist*, 1973, *28*, 666–673.

Schwartz, G. E., & Shapiro, D. Biofeedback and essential hypertension: Current findings and theoretical concerns. *Seminars in Psychiatry*, 1973, *5*, 493–503.

Shapiro, A. K. Placebo effects in medicine, psychotherapy, and psychoanalysis. In A. K. Bergin & S. L. Garfield (Eds.), *Handbook of psychotherapy and behavior change.* New York: Wiley, 1971.

Shapiro, D. Biofeedback and the regulation of complex processes. In J. Beatty (Ed.), *Biofeedback and behavior: A NATO symposium.* New York: Plenum, 1977.

Shapiro, D., & Crider, A. Operant electrodermal conditioning under multiple schedules of reinforcement. *Psychophysiology*, 1967, *4*, 168–175.

Shapiro, D., Crider, A. B., & Tursky, B. Differentiation of an autonomic response through operant reinforcement. *Psychonomic Science*, 1964, *1*, 147–148.

Shapiro, D., Mainardi, J. A., & Surwit, R. S. Biofeedback and self-regulation in essential hypertension. In G. E. Schwartz & J. Beatty (Eds.), *Biofeedback theory and research.* New York: Academic Press, 1977.

Shapiro, D., & Schwartz, G. E. Biofeedback and visceral learning: clinical applications. *Seminars in Psychiatry*, 1972, *4*, 171–184.

Shapiro, D., & Surwit, R. S. Learned control of physiological functions and disease. In H. Leitenberg (Ed.), *Handbook of behavior modification and therapy.* Englewood Cliffs, New Jersey: Prentice-Hall, 1976.

Shapiro, D., & Watanabe, T. Timing characteristics of operant electroderman modification: fixed interval effects. *Japanese Psychological Research*, 1971, *13*, 123–130.

Simard, T. G. Fine sensorimotor control in healthy children: an electromyographic study. *Pediatrics*, 1969, *43*, 1035–1041.

Sirota, A. D. *Heart rate feedback and instrumental effects on subjective reaction to aversive stimuli.* Unpublished doctoral dissertation, The Pennsylvania State University, 1976.

Snyder, C., & Noble, M. Operant conditioning of vasoconstriction. *Journal of Experimental Psychology*, 1968, *77*, 263–268.

Solberg, W. K., & Rugh, J. D. The use of biofeedback devices in the treatment of bruxism. *Journal of the Southern California State Dental Association*, 1972, *40*, 852–853.

Sterman, M. B. Neurophysiological and clinical studies of sensorimotor EEG biofeedback training: some effects on epilepsy. In L. Birk (Ed.), *Biofeedback: be-havorial medicine.* New York: Grune & Stratton, 1973.

Stern, G. S., & Berrenberg, J. L. Biofeedback training in frontalis muscle relaxation and enhancement of belief in personal control. *Biofeedback and Self-Control,* 1977, *2,* 173–182.

Stokes, T. F., & Baer, D. M. An implicit technology of generalization. *Journal of Applied Behavioral Analysis,* 1977, *10,* 349–367.

Stroebel, C. F., & Glueck, B. C. Biofeedback treatment in medicine and psychiatry: An ultimate placebo? *Seminars in Psychiatry,* 1973, *5,* 483–490.

Surwit, R. S. Biofeedback: A possible treatment for Raynaud's disease. In L. Birk (Ed.), *Biofeedback: behavioral medicine.* New York: Grune & Stratton, 1973.

Surwit, R. S., Pilon, R. N., & Fenton, C. H. Behavioral treatment of Raynaud's disease. *Journal of Behavioral Medicine,* in press.

Surwit, R. S., & Shapiro, D. Biofeedback and meditation in the treatment of border-line hypertension. In J. Beatty (Ed.), *Biofeedback and behavior: A NATO symposium.* New York: Plenum, 1977.

Taub, E. Self-regulation of human tissue temperature. In G. E. Schwartz & J. Beatty (Eds.), *Biofeedback theory and research.* New York: Academic Press, 1977.

Taylor, C. B., Farquhar, J. W., & Nelson, E. The effects of relaxation therapy upon high blood pressure. *Archives of General Psychiatry,* 1977, *34,* 339–342.

Wagman, I. H., Pierce, D. S., & Burger, R. E. Proprioceptive influences in volitional control of individual motor units. *Nature,* 1965, *207,* 957–958.

Weiss, T., & Engel, B. T. Operant conditioning of heart rate in patients with pre-mature ventricular contractions. *Psychosomatic Medicine,* 1971, *33,* 301–321.

Subject Index